MAXIMUM
PERFORMANCE

This book is dedicated to the visionary pioneers who created the world we now live in; and to those who are creating the world we will inhabit in the future.

MAXIMUM PERFORMANCE

A practical guide to leading and managing people at work

Nick Forster

Professor at The Graduate School of Management, University of Western Australia

Edward Elgar
Cheltenham, UK • Northampton, MA, USA

Published by
Edward Elgar Publishing Limited
Glensanda House
Montpellier Parade
Cheltenham
Glos GL50 1UA
UK

Edward Elgar Publishing, Inc.
136 West Street
Suite 202
Northampton
Massachusetts 01060
USA

A catalogue record for this book
is available from the British Library

ISBN 1 84542 000 4 (cased)

Typeset by Cambrian Typesetters, Frimley, Surrey
Printed and bound in Great Britain by MPG Books Ltd, Bodmin, Cornwall

Acclaim for Maximum Performance

'In my experience a major shortcoming of most "how to" books on leadership and management is that they purport to offer "Silver Bullets" – magical solutions that, once revealed, will enrich and transform the reader and his or her organisation. Regrettably, business life is not that simple. Rather, it is characterised by uncertainty and lack of precedent and complicated by the different wants, needs and motivations of people. Nick Forster's practical book, grounded in many years of leadership and management development and MBA education, recognises this complexity and the folly of "one-size-fits-all" solutions. It is a valuable source book, packed full of useful ideas for current and aspiring business leaders.'

– Mr Michael Chaney, Australian Businessman of the Year 2003 and former CEO of Wesfarmers – the Australian Financial Review's Company of the Year 2002. Mr Chaney becomes Chairman of the National Australia Bank in June 2005.

'*Maximum Performance* delivers what it promises. It is practical, useful and well grounded in up-to-date research findings from across the globe. Nick Forster writes well, with a lively voice and has peppered the text with rich examples and case studies. The diagnostic skill exercises and inventories offered throughout are especially helpful. The book meets the needs of both managers and students alike, across a wide span of experiences. Well worth the investment.'

– Professor Barry Posner, Dean of the Business Faculty at Santa Clara University, California and co-author, with James Kouzes, of *The Leadership Challenge*

'*Maximum Performance* is an essential read for all business owners, managers, consultants and key decision makers. It is an outstanding and comprehensive insight into the broad range of managerial and leadership issues which confront business people today. It is practical and littered with excellent case study examples and illustrations. Its unique style is easy to read, thought provoking and demystifies concepts that are easily misunderstood outside an MBA course. Grasp and digest this book quickly because it's the smart thing to do.'

– Barry Smith, Managing Director, the General Management Consulting Group

'Nick's book is an energetic and down-to-earth exploration of the many dimensions of this enigmatic thing we call leadership. It is a distillation of much knowledge, experience and insightful observation. There is refreshing and satisfying clarity of discussion; with comment on many management theories, explanations of evidence and research and the consequences of their applications in organisations. The pages are brimming with examples, keeping the messages real, practical and always interesting. *Maximum Performance* is thought provoking, and the reader is constantly challenged to assess his or her own knowledge, experience, attributes, perceptions and behaviour. It is a wonderful resource for those beginning their endeavours, introducing them to the complexities of leading people, and a delightful summary of instantly recognisable experience to those who are well on the journey. It is hugely valuable to all, whether for new knowledge or a welcome refresher. And, there is just a touch of irreverence, adding an enjoyable balance to a serious subject.'

– Dr Penny Flett, CEO of the Brightwater Care Group and Telstra Australian Business Woman of the Year, 1998

'We all seem to know when we are receiving good or bad leadership, yet for many of us being a good leader seems to be so elusive. Why is this so? The fact that we are human and sometimes trapped by our wants, needs and motivations inevitably gets in the way, and leadership within Local Government is fraught with complex problems and competing forces both internally and externally. *Maximum Performance* will be an extremely useful aid for all who are looking for a practical, sensible and thought provoking insight into management and leadership issues. Nick provides an excellent insight into the mysteries of management and leadership with this very practical and useful book that I am sure will be a great resource for current and emerging leaders.'

– Ricky Burgess, CEO of the Western Australian Local Government
Association and the Australian Institute of Management
Business Woman of the Year, 1997

'As consultants working with small to medium sized businesses, we are always searching for practical resources to recommend to our clients that can help them put their activities into a broader perspective, and help raise their understanding and expectations of what their businesses and employees are capable of. *Maximum Performance* is such a resource. Not only does it demonstrate the true value of good leadership, people management skills and the role of organizational culture in developing, motivating and retaining good staff, it also juxtaposes these with broader issues such as managing change, creativity and innovation, managing employee knowledge and intellectual capital, and the impact that emerging technologies will have on business and organizations in the near future.'

– Philip Watson, Director and Principal Consultant,
the General Management Consulting Group

Contents

List of figures   viii
List of tables   ix
The author   x
Acknowledgments   xi
Preface   xiii

1   The foundations of leadership and
     people management   1
2   Personal performance and stress
     management   57
3   Communication at work   92
4   Employee motivation, empowerment
     and performance   160
5   Leading and managing teams   201
6   Doing it differently? The emergence of
     women leaders   224
7   Managing power, politics and conflict   276
8   Leading organizational and cultural
     change   298
9   Innovation and organizational learning   347
10   Managing employee knowledge and
     intellectual capital   396
11   Leadership and people management in
     high-tech, networked and
     virtual organizations   429
12   Leadership and business ethics   487
Conclusion: leading and managing people
             at work   536

Appendix 1   The business case for emotional
              intelligence   548
Appendix 2   The benefits of health and wellness
              programmes   551
Bibliography   556
Index   576

Figures

1.1	Would you invest in this company?	38
3.1	The spider	131
4.1	Content theories of motivation compared	166
6.1	Male and female brains	237
6.2	Masculinity and femininity	248
8.1	Kolb's learning cycle	316
9.1	Picture puzzles	356
11.1	The exponential growth of computing, 1900–1998	434
11.2	The exponential growth of computing, 1900–2100	434

Tables

1.1	The origins of our ideas and beliefs about leadership	21
1.2	Desired leadership qualities compared	45
3.1	Communicating with the whole mind	133
4.1	The satisfaction–dissatisfaction process	171
4.2	Semco: tore up the rulebook in the 1980s	196
5.1	Team rules	220
6.1	Confidence in women	244
7.1	The two faces of power and politics	280
9.1	Linear and lateral thinking	352
10.1	Knowledge assets	408
11.1	Out with the old and in with the new	454
12.1	Perceptions of occupations' ethical standards	507
12.2	Top five performing ethical investment trusts in Australia, 2001–2	508
12.3	Transparency International corruption perceptions index, 2003	523

The author

Professor Nick Forster is based at the Graduate School of Management (GSM), The University of Western Australia. He has been involved in postgraduate management education since 1991 in the UK, Australia and Singapore. At the GSM, he has taught on the Organizational Behaviour, Management of Organizations, and Social, Ethical and Environmental Issues in Organizations units on the MBA programme, and the Managing Strategic Change unit on the Executive MBA. He has also received ten MBA-nominated commendations and awards for teaching, and was chosen by his peers as a nominee for the 2000 Australian Universities' National Teaching Awards ceremony in Canberra, attended by the Australian Prime Minister John Howard.

He has published four books, written more than 70 articles in a variety of international academic and professional journals, and has produced several research and consulting reports for organizations in Australia and the UK. He has been a regular contributor to *WA Business News*, and was also a guest management columnist for *Corporate Relocation News*, the biggest selling corporate relocation magazine in the USA, from 2000 to 2002. Outside the GSM, Nick has been involved with the Australian Institute of Management (AIM) Leadership Centre in the delivery of leadership and management training workshops to several of WA's largest companies and public sector organizations, including the Office of the Premier and Cabinet and the City of Perth Executive. From October 2003 to March 2004, he was a Principal Facilitator for WesTrac and the Water Corporation in AIM's Action Learning Programs, run in conjunction with the Harvard Business School. He has also collaborated in numerous research and consultancy projects with UK and Australian companies, and was on the national judging panel for the 2003 and 2004 Australian Human Resource Management Awards (for further information, see www.wamcg.com.au).

Nick has lived in several countries and worked in a variety of other jobs in his younger days, as a barman, waiter, house-renovator, safari park warden, professional musician, music studio engineer and part-time ski instructor. His leisure interests include alpine skiing, mountain biking, scuba diving, white-water rafting and, occasionally, bungee jumping.

Acknowledgments

I'd like first to express my gratitude to all those people, past and present, who have helped to shape my understanding of leadership and people management in contemporary organizations. These are, in no particular order, Alistair Mant, Barry Posner, Jay Conger, Edgar Schein, Edward 'Weary' Dunlop, Jeffrey Pfeffer, Penny Flett, Ricky Burges, Michael Chaney, Fons Trompenaars, Daniel Goleman, Nelson Mandela, Confucius, Tsung Tzu, James Kouzes, David Carnegie, Martin Luther King Jnr, Ray Kurzweil, Bill Hewlett and Dave Packard, Ricardo Semler, Richard Teerlink, Charles O'Reilly, Tom Peters, William McKnight, Germaine Greer, Joan Kirner, Moira Rayner, Jack Welch, Winston Churchill, Scott Adams, Paul Robeson, Henry Mintzberg, Abraham Lincoln, Franklin D. Roosevelt, Edward de Bono, Andy Groves, Herb Kelleher, Gordon Bethune, James Collins, Jerry Porras, Fiona Wilson, Charles Handy, Amanda Sinclair, Peter Drucker, Gary Hamel, Nicolò de Machiavelli, Aristotle, Plato, Socrates, Anita Roddick, Peter Senge, Ari de Geus and last, but not least, John Cleese in his *Video Arts* days. Their insights about effective leadership and people management can be found throughout this book.

During an academic career spanning 16 years, I've been privileged to be involved with hundreds of able, motivated and creative MBA and Executive MBA students in the UK, Australia and Singapore. The contents of this book have been influenced by their anecdotes and stories about the leaders and managers they have worked under, as well as their personal experiences of leading and managing others. All the materials, exercises and self-evaluation exercises contained in this book have been extensively 'road-tested' with well over a thousand of these men and women and many other groups of professionals and managers, so their contribution to this has been significant. I've also had a number of high-profile guest speakers on MBA programmes in recent years. They too have shaped my understanding of what successful leadership and people management is *really* all about. I'd like to thank both groups for their influence and inputs to the book.

I'd also like to thank Fenman Limited, the *Financial Times* and Prentice-Hall, MCB University Press, McGraw-Hill, Pearson Education, Alan and Barbara Pease and Ray Kurzweil, for their permission to make use of the following materials.

Chapter 3: N. Forster, S. Majteles, A. Mathur, R. Morgan, J. Preuss, V. Tiwari, and D. Wilkinson (1999), 'The role of storytelling in leadership', *Leadership and Organization Development Journal*, **20**(1), 11–18, and N. Forster (2000), *Managing Staff on International Assignments: A Strategic Guide* (pp. 47–9).
Chapter 6: 'The Brain Wiring Test' from A. Pease and B. Pease (1998), *Why Men Don't Listen and Women Can't Read Maps* (pp. 64–72).
Chapter 8: N. Forster (2002), 'Managing excellence through corporate culture: the H-P way', *The Management Case Study Journal*, **2**(1), May, 23–40.
Chapter 10: 'Does your organization have a knowledge management culture?' and 'The Knowledge Network', from B. Bagshaw and P. Philips (2000), *Knowledge Management*.
Chapter 11: N. Forster (2000), 'The potential impact of third-wave technologies on organizations', *Leadership and Organization Development Journal*, **21**(5), 254–63; 'The exponential growth of computing 1900–1998'; 'The exponential growth of computing 1900–2100', from R. Kurzweil (1999), *The Age of Spiritual Machines*.
Conclusion: N. Forster (2000), *Managing Staff on International Assignments: A Strategic Guide* (pp. 153–4).

Last, but not least, I'd particularly like to thank Edward Elgar for his belief in this book's potential, Francine O'Sullivan, Joanne Betteridge, Karen McCarthy and Caroline McLin for their patient guidance and assistance throughout the editing and formatting process and the submission of the manuscripts for the book, and Madeline Tan for her help with the graphics and diagrams.

Nick Forster
Perth, Western Australia, September 2004

Preface

Walk into a large bookstore in any city of the world, stroll through the bookshops at international airports, visit university libraries or browse e-booksellers' websites and you will find dozens of books on leadership and people management. These will range from highbrow academic discourses to books written by management consultants, from the autobiographies of well known political and business leaders to satirical works on modern organizational life, like those of Scott Adams or Dennis Pratt. What can one more book add to this extensive and wide-ranging literature?

First, all of the materials, self-evaluation exercises and questionnaires contained in this book have been extensively 'road tested' in the UK, Singapore and Australia, over a ten-year period, with more than one thousand Master of Business Administration (MBA) and Executive MBA students, on multi-award winning postgraduate management courses. They have also been tried and tested in dozens of leadership and management development courses over the last decade. Only those materials and exercises that have *worked* for busy managers and professionals, or have passed 'The MBA Test', are included in this book. Hence it is particularly suited to people enrolled on MBA programmes, as well as those who may want to update their leadership/people management skills but are unable to take time off work to attend expensive (and often ineffective) 'management training' courses.

Second, many publications overlook essential elements of present-day leadership and management, particularly those relating to self-awareness and integrity, personal values, personal performance and stress management, and vision and creativity. This book is comprehensive in its coverage of all the elements of leadership and people management that professionals now need to be aware of. This includes traditional topics, such as employee motivation and performance, communication skills and leading and managing change, as well as more modern issues, such as business ethics in a global economy and leadership in high-tech and virtual organizations. It also looks at how leaders and managers can create cultures that promote essential modern organizational competencies such as innovation, the effective dissemination and use of knowledge and intellectual capital, and creating systemic intelligent learning capabilities amongst employees.

Third, this book integrates several perspectives on leadership and people management, including those of real-life leaders, business commentators, management consultants and academics – with a fourth dimension: *what we've already known about effective leadership and people management throughout the ages, and yet seem to have to 'reinvent' with each new generation.* The book also synthesizes materials from more than 700 books, articles, professional journals, newspapers and websites. What appears here represents a distillation of the best practical ideas about leadership and people management of recent times, condensed into a form that busy managers and professionals can assimilate and make immediate use of at work, in large, medium-sized or small organizations, and in the public or private sector.

Fourth, the book demystifies leadership and people management. It highlights not only the 'hard-wired' traits we may inherit at birth, but also the 'soft-wiring', that is the kinds of leadership competencies and people management skills that we can all learn to develop and improve throughout our working lives, given self-belief, time and commitment. To this end, the book will systematically review the attributes, skills, qualities and competencies that are most often associated with successful leadership and people management, and how these can be developed and enhanced. These include the following:

- self-awareness and self-discipline,
- competence and credibility,
- a mixture of several kinds of intelligence,
- great self-motivation and the capacity for hard work, combined with a good understanding of their physical and psychological limitations,
- exceptional two-way communication skills, combined with an ability to lead, direct and focus dialogues with others,
- the ability to engage with the minds and hearts of others and, as a result, a capacity to motivate and inspire their followers,
- the capacity to question 'common-sense' ways of doing things combined with the ability to make fast practical day-to-day decisions with incomplete information or knowledge,
- an ability to learn and unlearn quickly, while not discarding good leadership and people management practices that have stood the test of time,
- the ability to use power effectively, based on an understanding of the art of organizational politics,
- increasingly, a hybrid blend of what have been traditionally regarded as 'male' and 'female' leadership and people management styles,
- self-confidence and resolve in adverse or uncertain situations, without resorting to autocratic or domineering behaviour,

- the ability to think beyond the present and envision the future,
- the capacity to initiate, lead and manage the complex processes of perpetual organizational change, innovation and learning, without becoming reactive 'fad-surfers',
- an appreciation of the role that employee knowledge and intellectual capital now play as key drivers of organizational success and profitability,
- an understanding of both the potential and the limitations of new and emergent technologies in organizations, and an awareness of the profound impacts these will have on the management of organizations during the first two decades of the 21st century,
- high ethical standards, combined with a pragmatic understanding of doing business in the real world.

Fifth, the book takes into account the fast-changing worlds that leaders and managers now work in, and the new skills and qualities that are required to succeed in these often chaotic environments. The last two decades of the 20th century were characterized by rapid change and this period was variously described as 'The Age of Surprises', 'The Age of Uncertainty', 'The Age of Chaos' and 'The Age of Blur'. These surprises and uncertainties included the challenges of globalization, political upheavals, the threat of global terrorism, regional economic instabilities, corporate rationalization and downsizing, merger-mania, the breathtaking pace of technological innovation, a number of spectacular corporate collapses, the end of 'jobs for life' for almost all employees, the continuing redefinition and realignment of the roles and activities of organizations, employers, trades unions and employees throughout the world, and growing ethical and ecological challenges for organizations operating in the global economy.

The first two decades of the 21st century will be characterized by even greater change and uncertainty. Global economic forces, new technologies and the information revolution are driving the fastest period of change in human history and in the world of business. 'Future shock', 'chaos' and 'blur' are now permanent features of life in many organizations. Corporate longevity is getting shorter each year, with the average life expectancy of a typical large or medium-sized company falling in every decade since World War II. The domination of traditional large bureaucratic organizations, since the dawn of industrial capitalism in the early 19th century, is being challenged as new Third-Wave organizations emerge. These developments mean that all organizations have to think faster and smarter just to keep up with the competition. Individually, we walk faster, talk faster, sleep less, consume more information and work more than ever before. We may have three or four different part-time jobs or be employed on a succession of short-term contracts. Jobs for life are rare and job insecurity is a fact of life for many professionals. Employees can now expect to work for between five and ten employers in a lifetime. But, as the industrial age's hegemony is challenged, there are also opportunities for entrepreneurs and for anyone who is willing to challenge conventional management thinking and embrace, as Tom Peters suggested in the early 1990s, 'Crazy Ways for Crazy Days'. In the information age (if we have good ideas, knowledge, energy and persistence) we can become business pioneers (and, maybe, millionaires) overnight.

The ability to manage the uncertainties that arise from these changes, developments and trends is now an integral part of the repertoire of successful modern business professionals, and this book is designed for leaders and managers working in this demanding, complex, stressful and fast-changing world. As intellectual capital, continuous innovation, organizational learning and new technologies become the main drivers of organizational success, leader/managers must not only be able to understand these, they must also find new and more effective ways of enabling their followers to cope with these new organizational realities, help them perform to their maximum potential and to aspire continually to ever-higher levels of performance and achievement.

Getting the most out of this guide to leadership and people management

Teachers open the door, but you must enter by yourself.
(*Old Chinese saying*)

This may appear to be a very strange thing to say at this point, but I don't believe that leadership and people management skills can be learnt from books. You might now be thinking, 'What's the point of buying this one then?' Well, books – particularly the right kind – do play a vital supporting role in the learning process. When learning anything new, there is no substitute for a supportive mentor or an inspirational teacher, but they may be hard to find or may not always be available for help and advice. Even then, in any organizational, work or educational setting, they only form part of the learning equation. The main part is what *you* bring into these. This includes

- your personal aptitudes, abilities and experience,
- the leadership and people management skills you already possess,
- an awareness of your existing strengths and limitations, and
- knowing what you want, and how you are going to achieve this in the future.

The purpose of this book is to support your side of the learning equation, and it does this on three levels: the theoretical, the practical and the personal. Because you are reading this book, either you are going to become a manager/leader in the future, or you may already have a lot of work experience but want to learn about alternative ways of leading and managing people at work. Either way, you're interested in personal growth and improving your skills, and open to new ideas and change. You care about your career and want to equip yourself for the challenges of the future. In order to develop these skills further, this book can also be used as a guide to your personal development and learning, and will show how quite simple changes to the way we all 'manage' people can help us to become more effective leaders and managers of others. Throughout the book, there are a series of optional questionnaires and self-evaluation exercises that will help you to develop a unique leadership/management style, and enhance the way you lead and manage your people at work.

However, it is important to emphasize that this is not a book that sells instant 'fads' or 'quick-fix' solutions. Those who claim that you can become a better leader/manager in just a few days or weeks are misleading you, or want to sell more copies of their books, or get more bums on seats at their training workshops. If anyone tells you that you can become a really successful and effective leader or manager in a short period of time they are being dishonest. This requires self-belief, time and commitment. This means that you'll need to spend some time working through this book, perhaps try out the self-evaluation exercises, *actively* reflect on your own leadership and people management practices, be prepared to unlearn old habits and beliefs and, maybe, learn some new ones. This is not a 'self-help book'; it is a guide to personal lifelong learning and self-development.

By the end of the book, you should have acquired a comprehensive 'tool-kit' that you can dip into as and when needed, regardless of the circumstances that you find yourself in, the quality of the people you are leading, or the type of problems you are dealing with at work. Of equal importance, you will be in a better position to decide if you need to discard old or redundant leadership and people management practices that no longer work effectively. You will be able to evaluate what does and does not work for you at present, and decide which new skills you may need to acquire to enable you to become an even more effective and successful leader/manager in the future.

This book also contains hundreds of suggestions and opinions, from business and political leaders, consultants and academics, about how leadership and people management skills can be developed and enhanced. However, that is all they are and you should not view this as a one-way process, whereby 'the experts' tell you what you ought to be doing with your life. Treat this as an active, two-way process that allows you to reflect on your current practices. In addition, some of the suggestions in this book may not be directly applicable to your particular occupation, work setting or organization at the moment. And, if you know ways of leading and managing people that are better, or work more effectively, then use these instead (and, if you have time, please send me an email to let me know what they are!).

The only way to really improve as a leader/manager is to embrace active self-learning and development. While 'training', in a generic sense, may have its uses, it all too often falls victim to the well-documented 'halo effect', where people may emerge re-energized and refreshed from leadership or management development programmes, only to find that newly acquired knowledge and insights fade away over time, as they find themselves falling back into old and ineffective patterns of behaviour at work. And, as has often been pointed out, 'training' is for circus animals and dogs, not human beings. In effect, this means that none of the 'experts' in this book can teach you anything. Unless you are motivated and committed to learn *how* to become an even more effective leader/manager, little will be gained from this book. Self-directed learning and learning-by-doing are now becoming the dominant modes of personal improvement and professional development. This is because lifelong learning is now the name of the game, not possessing pieces of paper with 'BA' or 'MBA' stamped on them (Botsman, 2002). This means that you can only improve your leadership and people management practices by

- actively reflecting on what you currently do as a leader/manager,
- comparing this knowledge with the supermarket of information and ideas in this book, and identifying areas where changes or improvements might be made,
- developing strategies to improve your leadership and people management skills on a weekly and monthly basis,
- putting these into practice at work, by treating this environment as the principal 'training ground' for your development as a leader/manager.

There are two ways to approach this book. The first is on a need-to-know basis, where you simply dip into it and have a look at areas of interest, or review topics that you would like to discover more about. The second and more rigorous method is to start and maintain a personal diary. In this, you can reflect on your understanding and practice of leadership and people management, and compare what you do now with the many insights and suggestions contained in this book. Included in each chapter are a number of optional exercises that can be photocopied and included in this diary. A loose-leaf folder or file is ideal for this. Simply reading about leadership and management is only the starting point because, as Albert Einstein once observed, 'All knowledge should be translated into action.'

There may be a temptation to try and rush through this process. *Please resist this temptation.* Work though each chapter gradually, and allow time for different ideas and new information to sink in, because some preconceived notions and common-sense assumptions about leading and managing people in organizations are questioned and challenged in this book. Make a conscious effort to 'bridge' the materials that we will cover together with your work situation, and think about how you can apply what you learn in the future. Be open and receptive to new ideas and concepts, try them out and then wait to see what happens. If you are willing to challenge your preconceptions and assumptions about leadership and people management, they will challenge you in surprising and unexpected ways.

You'll need to commit some time over the coming months to read through and reflect on each chapter of the book. The amount of time you'll require does of course depend on how much work experience you have, the level of professional/managerial seniority you have reached and your current understanding of leadership and people management. If you can work through one chapter a week, you'll be able to get through the whole book in less than three months. This may sound like a major commitment, but represents only a tiny fraction of a typical 40-year professional or managerial career. Alternatively, you may already have quite a lot of leadership and people management experience and choose to just dip into a selection of chapters, in order to reflect on or fine-tune the things you already do well.

Either way, your personal journey starts here, and I hope that you will find it a stimulating, rewarding and enjoyable one.

1 The foundations of leadership and people management

Objectives

To define leadership, management and organization (before reading through this chapter you may want to spend a few minutes writing down your own definitions of these concepts).

To resolve the important question, 'Are leaders born or made?'

To describe briefly the roles and responsibilities of leaders and managers, and how organizational contexts can influence leadership styles.

To show how followers shape and influence the performance of their leaders and managers.

To show where our beliefs about leadership come from and how these influence the way we lead and manage other people.

To look at the roles that coaching and mentoring now play in leadership and people management.

To examine the roles that transformational abilities, charisma and vision play in leadership and people management.

To explore the dark side of leadership.

To identify the qualities and attributes of leaders you admire and would willingly follow, now and in the future.

To identify the qualities, attributes, skills and competencies of the leader/managers that most employees (men or women) want to work for, and to look at the important role that humour can play in leadership and people management.

This opening chapter also acts as the foundation for the remainder of the book, by summarizing the most relevant and salient aspects of the 20th century literature on organizational leadership and people management.

Introduction

Of the many decisions an executive makes, none are as important as the decisions they make about people because they, above all else, determine the performance capacity of the organization.
(*Peter Drucker*, The Effective Executive, *1966*)

One thing that can be said with confidence about leadership and people management is that there have been enough books and articles written on these topics over the last 20 years to bemuse, perplex and confuse anyone looking for either clarity or new insights into these often mysterious and complex fusions of personal qualities, attributes, characteristics, skills and competencies. Indeed, one of the first things to strike anyone who has studied these for some time is how confusing they can be, and how critical some commentators have been about these concepts in the past. For example,

Leadership, as a concept at least, has failed us. Despite the earnest efforts of business leaders and management writers to ennoble and dignify it, understandings of leadership have become cheapened by overuse. Leadership has been rendered impotent to deliver its promises.
(*Sinclair, 1998: 1*)

Even in the wayward, spluttering world of management theory, no subject has produced more waffle than leadership [ ] The value of academic research to the complexities of the chaotic situations that most business leaders and managers find themselves in today is practically zero.
(*Micklethwaite and Woolridge, 1997: 11*)

Leadership is an intangible quality with no clear definition. That's probably a good thing, because if the people being led knew the definition, they would hunt down their leaders and kill them. Some cynics might say that a leader is someone who gets people to do things that benefit the leader. But that can't be a good definition because there are so many exceptions, as you well know.
(*Adams, 1997: 287*)

[No] unequivocal understanding exists as to what distinguishes leaders from non-leaders . . . Never have so many laboured so long to say so little.
(*Bennis and Nanus, 1985: 4*)

Leadership is the worst defined and least understood personal attribute sometimes possessed by human beings [ ] There are as many definitions of leadership as there are writers on the subject.
(*Lippitt, 1982: 395*)

So, how can we move forward from this somewhat inauspicious start? At the beginning of our journey, let's look at some definitions. In the opening to this chapter, you were asked to think about your understanding of three concepts that will be used many times throughout this book: 'leadership', 'management' and 'organization'. Please compare your definitions with these:

Leadership in English-speaking countries is derived from an old Anglo-Saxon word, *loedan*, meaning a way, road, path or journey. This ancient definition of leadership is used throughout the book.

Management is derived from the Italian *manaeggio* (a riding school), originating in the Latin word for hand, *manus*. So, to manufacture something means, literally, to make things by hand, and in the 19th century workers were employed by *manufactories*. Both management and manufacture may already be outdated terms that should be replaced by mentoring, mentofacturing or technofacturing. It has been suggested that these words better reflect the realities of the current transition from bureaucratic industrial capitalism: from an era when we did indeed make many things by hand, to a new world where knowledge management, intellectual capital, innovation and new technologies are fast becoming the primary drivers of organizational performance and success.

Organization is derived from the Greek word *organon*, meaning a tool or device. So an organization can be viewed simply as a device for getting things done as efficiently and effectively as possible. However, this is a static definition. As we will see throughout this book, the leaders of the most successful companies of the 20th and early 21st centuries understand a basic, but extremely important principle: *all organizations are works in progress*. Hence an organization is defined simply as an evolutionary device for achieving complex tasks as efficiently and effectively as possible. This broad definition encompasses all small, medium and large businesses and companies, as well as organizations in the public and not-for-profit sectors.

Why bother with definitions? More than 2400 years ago, the Greek philosopher Socrates observed that 'The beginning of wisdom lies in the definition of terms'. For Socrates, great leadership was not possible without wisdom, and he regarded this as the foundation of all knowledge and philosophical thinking (from the Greek, *philosophia*, meaning 'love of wisdom'). Clarity of definitions *is* important because many commentators on leadership and management routinely provide complex and lengthy definitions of what these things 'are'. A principle underlying this book is that such definitions are of little practical use when their meanings have already been described, understood and utilized by people for millennia, in many different cultures and civilizations. And, as we will see later, many of the insights into leadership and people management contained in this book have been known and used by our ancestors for thousands of years. This is because most of the qualities, skills and competencies we associate with present-day leadership and management, such as communication, cooperation, negotiation skills, teamwork, the use of power and influence, and the ability to envision the future, were also essential for the survival and evolution of our ancient ancestors. These primal leadership skills are as relevant today as they have always been.

Let's now turn to describing leaders and leadership in more detail. Although research into organizational and business leadership can be traced back to the 1920s, there are only three facets of leadership that all writers on this subject appear to have agreed on during these 80 years: (a) leaders have followers (b) leadership has *something* to do with controlling or directing human behaviour (c) leaders describe reality to their followers and, sometimes, suggest alternative or new realities.

If this is all that is universally agreed about leadership, where do we go from here? Let's return briefly to the ancient definition of leadership on the preceding page: a way, road, path or journey. On many levels, this simple definition makes good operational sense. For almost all of the time that modern humans, *Homo sapiens* ('wise man'), have inhabited this planet (about 130 000 years according to the most recent estimates), the primary function of leaders was to act as the heads of nomadic tribes, leading them from one region to another as the seasons changed, as animals migrated or as the environment changed. In fact, the origin of the word 'leadership' in all cultures throughout the world is – you guessed it – a way, road, path or journey. We will return to this ancient understanding of leadership throughout this book.

Hence, even in modern business or organizational contexts, leadership can still be viewed in terms of the process of guiding employees down the right ways, roads or paths, thereby ensuring that their efforts are in line with broader organizational goals and objectives. In this context, a leader can be described as anyone who has responsibility for coordinating or directing the actions of other people, and who has the ability to encourage them to do more than they might be expected to do without a leader. This also means that leaders have to possess the ability to lead followers on new journeys into the future, whenever this is required. And, as we will see later, while leaders do perform a variety of roles in modern organizations, the ability to lead others is built on a relatively small number of core qualities, attributes, skills and competencies.

If this describes leadership, what is management? Is this the same as leadership, a part of leadership or something quite different? Business leaders, management commentators and academics often use these words interchangeably, but there continue to be important differences between the two terms.

1 Leadership is usually concerned with *what* needs to be done – management often focuses on *how* things should be done. Hence a manager would focus on how quickly and efficiently an employee climbs up and down a ladder to perform a task. A leader would be primarily concerned with determining whether the task was appropriate in the first place, or if the ladder was leaning against the right wall.

2 Leadership is primarily concerned with *relationships* – management is often concerned with *tasks*. Hence a manager dealing with conflict between two subordinates would tend to rely on positional power and procedural rules to resolve this. A leader would tend to use their personal power and authority, communication skills and an ability to appeal to the hearts *and* minds of their followers to resolve the conflict.

3 Leaders have to think outside the square – managers usually think within it. Hence management is about employee efficiency in the here and now, but leadership is about making changes that will enable their staff to be efficient in the future.

4 Leaders try to find ways to enhance and improve their employees' performance – managers are primarily concerned with controlling and monitoring performance. Hence, managers will tend to *push* their staff towards goals they have set *for* them. Leaders will focus their energies on *pulling* their staff towards goals they have agreed *with* them (this subtle but important distinction is discussed in more detail in Chapter 4 and Chapter 7).

5 Leaders are comfortable with change and possess a change-oriented, outward-looking view of the future. Managers may feel uncomfortable about the prospect of change, and often focus on maintaining the status quo or 'the way we do things around here'.

6 Leaders are able to step into the unknown – managers often have to be shown why they should take such a step. Hence leadership is often concerned with the creation of new paradigms – management is often focused on operating within existing paradigms.[1]

While there are times when it can be important to distinguish between leadership and management, it's equally important not to get hung up on the differences between the two terms. For example, there are some effective leaders who are not great managers, but have the ability to recruit enough good managers to work for them. There are some leaders who are also good managers. There are also effective managers (that 'get things done') who may not be good leaders, because anyone who wants to make the transition from management into a leadership role has to acquire some new qualities and skills. This is why people who may be very good managers can often fail when thrust into leadership positions without some preparation for these new and demanding roles (Zaleznik, 2004; Kotter, 1990). In this book, the two terms will sometimes be clearly distinguished and at other times they will be used interchangeably, because these days there are few managers who do not act, in some capacity, as leaders and few leaders who do not act, in some capacity, as managers.

> I obey a manager because I have to. I follow a leader because I want to.
> (*Steve Carey, former advisor to Bill Clinton, 1999*)

Are leaders 'born' or 'made'?

This is a question that is often debated but is still, in many people's eyes, unresolved. However, it remains an important issue to address because the notion that leadership is largely innate still underpins the way that many people think about leaders, their beliefs about their own capacity for leadership, and their views about the self-leadership potential of their followers. Common-sense assumptions about employees' innate leadership qualities are also used frequently by organizations when making hiring, firing and promotion decisions. The earliest scientific studies of leadership, conducted in the USA in the 1930s, were concerned with identifying a list of personal psychological traits that could distinguish leaders from non-leaders. Over time, this became known as 'The Great Man' theory of leadership. In 1948, Stogdill reviewed the results of dozens of trait studies that had been conducted over the preceding two decades, and summarized the characteristics of a great leader as follows:

> The leader is characterised by a strong drive for responsibility and task completion, vigour and persistence in pursuit of goals, venturesomeness and originality in problem solving, and a drive to exercise initiative in social situations. He possesses self-confidence and a strong sense of personal identity; a willingness to accept the consequences of decision and actions, a readiness to absorb interpersonal stress, a willingness to tolerate frustration and delay, an ability to influence other people's behaviour, and a capacity to structure social interaction systems to the purpose at hand.
> (*Stogdill, 1948: 71*)

Note that women leaders did not figure in the thinking of male academics at this time, an issue we will return to in Chapter 6. Leaving this unconscious oversight aside for now, Stogdill did report that research studies had not been able to locate any traits that *consistently* differentiated leaders from non-leaders. They also observed that the traits they had identified appeared to come and go at random, varied from leader to leader, and only became apparent after people had achieved leadership positions. This was a natural consequence of the fact that they could only look at leaders after the event, when they had *already become leaders*. Further research indicated that the correlation between specific psychological traits and leadership is low, accounting for only about 10 per cent of the factors that predict whether someone was a leader or not (Stogdill, 1974). Surprisingly, subsequent research has failed to answer definitively the question that opened this section, 'Are leaders born or made?' and this remains a topic of heated debate amongst academics. In terms of this continuing nature/nurture debate, there are three basic positions that have been adopted by academic researchers, reflecting the intellectual subjectivity of their disciplinary backgrounds.

1 Our potential for leadership is entirely determined by the genetic programming we inherit from our natural parents (many geneticists).
2 Our potential for leadership is determined by a combination of genetic predispositions, psychological development and socialization experiences (particularly during childhood), school and peer group influences, social class and culture (all psychologists and social psychologists).
3 Our potential for leadership is determined by the socialization processes we experience after birth and social–psychological development (particularly during childhood), school and peer group influences, social class and culture (most sociologists).

So, who's right? Recent advances in evolutionary psychology and genetic mapping leave little doubt that our genetic inheritance has an influence on our physical and psychological development in life. Some studies of twins, raised separately, show that genetics shape personality; in particular, key psychological characteristics such as introversion and extroversion. Furthermore, twins raised apart often show stunning similarities in their scholastic achievements, choice of occupations, clothing, hobbies, musical preferences and even their choice of spouses. Advances in genetic mapping have also confirmed that there is a genetic component to the human Intelligence Quotient (IQ), although at birth this is simply *potential*: it still has to be 'actualized' through learning and socialization. For example, in Albert Einstein's case, the two areas of his brain involved in the generation and manipulation of spatial images were 1cm larger than those of a normally intelligent person. This meant that he possessed an 'extra' 15 per cent brain processing capacity. He was also born without one of the deep grooves that separate the left and right hemispheres of the brain. As a result, he had many more neural connections between the logical/linear and spatial/creative parts of his brain than would be found in a more typical human brain. In other words, the unique combined genetic inheritance he acquired from his parents gave him a *propensity* to be a paradigm-breaking genius, although he was not regarded as being an academically outstanding student at school or university.

In a similar vein, the ability to produce seratonin has a genetic basis. It has been suggested that this is linked to leadership *potential* because it is known to be a key modulator of mood and emotions. In other words, certain people have a genetic predisposition to produce this natural 'drug' when under pressure and, as a result, are better equipped to deal with uncertain situations, competing demands, interpersonal conflict and stress (Goleman *et al.*, 2002). There is also some evidence to suggest that genetic predispositions can have an influence on the careers we choose and the environments we choose to work in (Nicholson, 2000: 97–127). In other words, there may be a kind of autopilot – at the genetic level – that impels us to 'choose' particular careers and professions, and which can also influence the particular leadership and people management styles that we utilize as adults. Edward O. Wilson best described this process when he argued that the human mind was not a blank slate to be simply 'filled in' by experience, as most sociologists would argue, but 'an exposed negative waiting to be slipped into developer fluid' (cited by Uren, 1999). Some commentators have taken this suggestion one stage further and argued that, while social influences and life experiences may modify our innate genetic programming, these can affect the development of our basic personalities and the operation of our brains only in so far as they inhibit or activate propensities that were already there at birth (for example, Ridley, 2003; Stock, 2002).

Another way of looking at the influence of innate 'programming' and environmental influences on our psychological development is with the hardware/software analogy. The hardware represents the raw genetic material we inherit from our parents at conception. The software represents the 'files' of information, knowledge and feedback that we receive from the environment before and after birth, and during our formative years. Without these, the hardware cannot ever be activated and actualized. Conversely, without functional hardware, no amount of software is going to work. Having said this, the evidence concerning genetic influences on human personalities and psychologies still does not tell us if leadership is something we are *born* with. Complex organisms like human beings are not simply the sum of their genes, nor do genes alone build an individual's unique personality and psychology. These certainly have an influence, but represent at birth a set of *potentialities*, nothing more. They operate in complex and symbiotic relationships with environmental, social and cultural influences; relationships that researchers are only now beginning to unravel and understand. The most powerful example that can be cited to support this statement is the radical transformation of the role of women in management and business leadership over the last 30 years in industrialized countries. Their collective genetic make-up has not changed one iota during this period of time, and yet their collective beliefs about what they are capable of have changed enormously, as have the beliefs of some men about the capabilities of women (see Chapter 6). There is also research which has shown that the first wave of women to reach senior leadership positions in the 1970s and 1980s grew up in family environments that insulated or dissuaded them from accepting social and cultural stereotypes about their 'correct' roles and potential in life. These women were then able to develop the drive, ambition and tenacity that enabled them to battle their way to the top of male-dominated professions and organizations (Sinclair and Wilson, 2002; Sinclair, 1998: 80).

And while there is a genetic component underpinning intelligence – as measured by IQ tests – there is little evidence that a high IQ is needed for leadership. Under some conditions, a very high IQ may occasionally be useful, but it is not essential for leaders. In fact, there is a body of evidence that suggests that very high intelligence is closely associated with psychopathology and deviant behaviour (an issue we return to later in this chapter). Furthermore, IQ is only one form of 'intelligence'. We now know that there are many other forms of human intelligence, including linguistic, interpersonal, spatial, bodily/kinesthetic, creative, musical, logical/mathematical and naturalistic intelligences (Gardner, 1993). To these we could also add moral/ethical and social intelligences, which we will return to in Chapter 12. These other types of intelligence can only be developed though the complex processes of human learning and socialization and, of equal importance, can be developed in adulthood (Goleman *et al.*, 2002). As we progress through this book, we will show how these forms of intelligence can be enhanced throughout life. For example, do you believe that you are not particularly innovative or creative? Why do you believe this? Who first told you that you were not creative? How many opportunities have you had to acquire these skills? In Chapter 9, we will see how almost anyone can learn to be better at lateral thinking and, thereby, become more creative and innovative. Another example is public speaking. Do you believe that you are not particularly good at this (perhaps because you are 'introverted')? Why do you believe this? In Chapter 3 we will show how anyone can learn to become better at public speaking and, thereby, increase their ability to influence their bosses, colleagues, followers, customers and clients.

While Goleman, Nicholson, Ridley and many others believe that evolutionary genetics play a significant role in human development (and, as a result, our potential for leadership), all are cautious about coming to the simplistic conclusion that leaders are born, rather than made. And while there is a genetic basis for personality traits such as detachment and novelty avoidance, these too can be overcome to a considerable extent through personal development and learning (see, for example, Goleman *et al.*, 2002). Recent genetic research has shown that even twins, who share 100 per cent of their genetic make-up at inception, often have personalities that are only 50 per cent similar by middle childhood. What causes this? The answer lies in unique social and environmental influences that they encounter after birth, within their families and sibling groups, at school and in peer groups (Ridley, 2003). Other research has shown that genes can change in a short period of time because of environmental influences. To cite one example of many, the Buraku people of Japan are a cultural minority that has been severely discriminated against in employment, education and housing for generations (similar to 'the untouchables' in India). Their children typically score 10–15 points lower than other Japanese children on IQ tests. Yet, when they have migrated to other countries such as the USA, the gap between their IQ scores and those of other Japanese migrants gradually disappears as each new generation emerges (Olson, 2002). One of the biggest longitudinal studies ever conducted, of 130 000 men and women aged between 21 and 60, showed that personalities can and do change during adulthood, even the 'Big Five' personality traits of conscientiousness, agreeableness, neuroticism, openness and extraversion/introversion can fluctuate over time (Srivasta *et al.*, 2003).

Another significant problem with the 'leaders are born' thesis is that many of those who become leaders in business or politics do not have parents who were themselves leaders of note. Of course, there are examples where leadership has run in families, such as the Churchill, Gandhi, Kennedy, Rothschild and Rockefeller dynasties. However, these are very much the exception. While some writers argue that this can be explained by the miraculous synergy of the right combination of parental genes (for example, Nicholson, 2000), it can also be explained, with equal validity, by social causation. If we are born into wealthy families and/or a privileged caste or class and told, from our earliest years and throughout our school years, that we are part of an elite and that we *will* become leaders, we will probably do this or at least achieve a high level of success in our chosen careers. For example, while private school pupils in the USA, the UK and Australia represent about 15–20 per cent of the entire school population of these countries, they still dominate the upper echelons of their societies in industry, finance, government, the armed forces, the judiciary, medicine and many other sectors. In the UK in 1999, 85 per cent of the Labour Party's Cabinet, 70 per cent of senior judicial positions, 45 per cent of the top civil service positions and 60 per cent of the top financial jobs in the City were occupied by people educated at private schools (Halsey and Webb, 2000). Consider also the 'old-boy' and, increasingly, 'old-girl' job networks that exist for graduates of private schools around the world, as well as more shadowy networks such as Yale University's 'Order of the Skull and Bones'. George W. Bush and his main Democratic opponent in 2004, John Kerry, were both members of this fraternity. Many senators, congressmen and business leaders during the 20th century also belonged to similar elite clubs at Harvard, Princeton and other leading US universities.

I attended a private school in the UK, Ampleforth College in Yorkshire. Among the people I knew there, two have been Members of Parliament; four are surgeons; two are judges; one is a brigadier in the army (and a decorated veteran of the Falkland and first Gulf Wars); one runs his own food company; one has been an editor at *The Guardian* newspaper in the UK; two have become millionaire stockbrokers and another three are helping to run family estates, which they will inherit in the future. Other alumni include the England rugby captain Lawrence Dallaglio, the actor Rupert Everett and one of Princess Diana's lovers, James Gilbey. Of course, this is not a representative sample, but illustrates the influence that money, privilege and a private school education can have on the aspirations, achievement motivation and self-belief of their pupils and, consequently, their potential for leadership. The practical implications of this powerful need for achievement, in the context of the motivation and empowerment of employees, are addressed in more detail in Chapter 4.

One important cluster of leadership traits that does stand out from the recent literature on leadership effectiveness is emotional intelligence (EI). Two psychologists, John Mayer and Peter Salovey, are credited with first defining the concept of EI in the early 1990s, but the person most associated with articulating and popularizing this idea is Daniel Goleman. According to Goleman, EI consists of five components: self-awareness, self-regulation, motivation, empathy and social skills. How adept we are at dealing with each of these is influenced by an inherited almond-sized cluster of nerves – the amygdala – situated in the frontal area of our brains. This is responsible for processing emotional stimuli, for storing emotional memories and also affects the fight–flight (stress) response in humans. Neuroscientists have shown that all information we receive from the environment is, initially, screened by this segment of the brain. An individual with a fully functioning amygdala is much more likely to be self-aware, self-disciplined, motivated, empathic, socially adept and more resilient to environmental stressors. According to Goleman and others, the ability to be sensitive to the emotional states of others is an essential part of the repertoire of effective leaders, because they are more aware of their own moods and the emotions of others. As a result, emotionally intelligent leaders are adept at managing interpersonal relationships and building networks of influence. They often have outgoing, ascendant personalities, modest self-confidence and a desire to be involved with people. They have a passion for the work they do, or the company they manage, that goes beyond status and making money.

Another consequence of the existence of EI is that the emotional state of the leader will have a direct impact on the emotions of their followers. You only have to think of situations in your own working life when a boss routinely comes in to work in a foul mood and the effect this can have on the morale and climate of a work group. Compare this with the positive impact of a boss who is always upbeat, optimistic and supportive. Goleman contends that EI is the single most reliable indicator of leadership effectiveness, far outweighing IQ levels. So, does this mean that we are born with these qualities? According to Goleman and his colleagues the answer to this question is 'No'. They believe that the functioning of the amygdala can be improved through learning, practice and feedback, and also argue that EI qualities can be learnt and enhanced. There is also evidence to support the view that the EI principles can be learnt by organizations, leading to enhanced employee performance, productivity and bottom-line results (Goleman, 2002, 2004; Goleman *et al.*, 2002).[2]

Hence, a balanced reading of the vast and often contradictory literature on this complex issue indicates that some of our *potential* for leadership may be shaped by our unique genetic inheritance, but this can only be actualized and realized through the socialization processes we experience after birth, from our families, peer groups, schools, social class and culture. It appears that most of our desire and potential for leadership is shaped by the influences we encounter after birth. There is of course another significant dimension that is often overlooked: *the conscious decisions and choices that each of us makes during our lives*. Our desire for leadership is a direct outcome of these decisions and choices, and may well contribute much to our potential for leadership. So, if we believe that we can make a real difference and decide to become a leader, we will take the appropriate steps to realize this ambition, even if we come from humble backgrounds where leaders were very much the exception rather than the rule. Furthermore, we will then make a concerted effort to learn whatever new skills and competencies are required to achieve this objective. A real-life example of this is described in the next section.

Captain Marvel

The pivotal decision to become a leader and learn new skills and competencies to realize this goal often occurs in real life. One example of this is the very successful former Australian cricket captain, Steve Waugh. For anyone who may now be switching off at the mention of this 'quaint' English game, it's worth noting that his team won the prestigious Laureus World Sports Team of the Year award in 2002, in competition with teams from American football and basketball, and the top European soccer teams. The team also received the Sports Industry of Australia Award in 2003. Before he was appointed in 1997, Waugh was routinely described in the media as 'quiet', 'surly', 'taciturn', 'introverted' and 'self-absorbed'. At the time, it was no secret that some Australian Cricket Board officials and ex-players did not want him to have the top job, and a few sports journalists were critical of the decision. Soon after Waugh was appointed in January 1998, John Inverarity, a former captain of the West Australian cricket team and an international player, gave a talk on leadership to a group of my MBAs in Perth. At the time, he believed that Waugh was a bad choice for the position because he lacked 'the requisite leadership qualities'. The erratic performance of the team under his early leadership in 1997–8 seemed to confirm these opinions, with the team struggling for both form and results.

In spite of these early difficulties, Waugh did have some hidden qualities that were to stand him in good stead and would help to create a golden age of Australian cricket. These only became fully apparent after his appointment, and included resilience and hardiness, courage under fire, competitiveness, tenacity, honesty and integrity, a lack of pretentiousness, great self-confidence and self-belief and, when it was required, some Machiavellian cunning. In 2001, Waugh made these comments about his early experiences of captaincy:

> I had to learn how to do this job along the way. To be honest, I was thrown in at the deep end – to sink or swim and so I had to learn fast, from former players, captains and commentators. But that only got me so far. I had to work out what I wanted and not rely on textbooks or my predecessors. So I sat down in bed and decided what I wanted [after two straight losses in his

first two international matches]. I wanted us to become the best international side in the world. I wanted us to be clearly number one, in both forms
of the game. I wanted hungry, aggressive, ruthless players who also wanted
to have fun and enjoy themselves. I made it my mission to work out what
made each player tick and I wanted to get my players to have greater faith
in themselves and their abilities. A captain's responsibility is to mould the
side into the way he wants them to play. I aimed to show faith in my players, show them respect and let them know that I fully supported them. I try
to get them to believe that they can achieve things that they don't even think
they'll achieve.
(*Abridged from Stewart, 2001*)

In order to achieve these objectives, Waugh began to utilize the history,
traditions and stories of the game, believing that cricket history and
mythology could be harnessed as motivational devices to help win
matches. He encouraged all his players to don the 'baggy green cap'
during international matches, as a powerful emotional symbol of, and
link with, the great players who had represented Australia in the past.
Waugh always wore his battered and frayed cap with evident pride for
the duration of international games. He learnt to think outside the box,
bringing in people from many walks of life to give motivational
speeches to his players, during coaching sessions, at team meetings
and before matches. He received coaching in media and public speaking skills. He spent many hours with each member of his team in
private one-to-one conversations to find out what made them tick and
how to get the best out of them. He was an inclusive leader who never
allowed 'in' groups and 'out' groups to emerge. Perhaps Waugh's
greatest quality as a leader was his capacity to nurture and develop the
self-belief of players who were at the margins of international cricket
when he was first appointed, or who had been lacking confidence in
their abilities to perform at the highest levels in the cauldron of international cricket (Conn, 2002).

In retrospect, we can see that he decided to develop his communication, motivational, team building and lateral thinking skills *after* he was
appointed captain. While these attributes were not apparent prior to
his appointment, one was visible throughout his early career: a real
hunger for learning and self-improvement, and this attribute stood
him in good stead during his captaincy. His personal journey into a
more effective leadership role marked the beginning of a world record-
breaking run of 16 straight wins in international cricket and winning
the World Cup in England in 1999. The Australian cricket team was the
first to be officially crowned World Champions after a successful home
and away series against South Africa during 2001–2002 and, as noted
above, it was also named the best sports team in the world in 2002.
When John Inverarity returned to give a second talk on leadership to
my MBAs 18 months later, he was brave enough to admit that he'd got

it wrong about Waugh's leadership potential, and commented that what had most surprised him was 'how quickly he had grown into the job and how quickly he had *learnt* what was required of an Australian cricket captain' (my emphasis).

By the time Steve Waugh's captaincy came to an end in January 2004, he had become the most successful international cricket captain in history, with the most wins (41) and a winning percentage of over 75 per cent, well ahead of the legendary Don Bradman who had a 62.5 per cent win–loss rate. He created a team regarded by most international commentators as the best in cricketing history, and a legacy unmatched in Australian and world cricket. He promoted and encouraged a much more aggressive and exciting brand of five-day test match cricket, which contributed to saving the longer form of the game from the increasingly dominant one-day format. In early January 2003, in a match against England, Waugh also became the second highest run scorer of all time, at the same time equalling Don Bradman's record of 29 scores of one hundred or more in international cricket matches. He even found time during his captaincy to establish a school for child leprosy victims in Udayan, India, and has since devoted a great deal of time, money and energy to supporting this cause. When Waugh retired, he was regarded by sports commentators and the general public as a national treasure; an exceptional leader who was also a cricket innovator, reformer and educator, and a model family man and philanthropist. In recognition of his many achievements, he was awarded the highly prestigious Australian of the Year award on 26 January 2004. The only question mark hanging over Waugh's tenure as captain is would he have been regarded as being such an exceptional leader if he had been the captain of one of the other Test playing nations between 1997 and 2003? We will return to this question in the section on 'followership'.

Conclusion: developing leadership

A final slant on the 'innate or learnt' debate concerns the issue of leadership education and development. Every year, tens of thousands of employees attend leadership/management courses all over the world, be this in the form of one-off workshops or through attendance at postgraduate courses, such as MBAs and other specialist postgraduate management programmes. All large companies in North America, the UK and Australasia run in-house leadership development courses. In the USA, for example, General Electric founded the GE Management Development Institute at Crotonville in 1956. When Jack Welch took over as CEO in 1981, he made the Institute a strategic priority, using it as an engine of organizational change, and leadership/management development, for 20 years. He was a regular visitor and teacher at the Institute and conducted half-day leadership courses throughout the year. Thousands of aspirant leaders from dozens of US companies attend The Centre for Creative Leadership in Greenborough. In 1997 alone, US companies spent $US4.5 billion on leadership development programmes (Kouzes and Posner, 1997). In the USA there are more than 2000 'corporate universities', up from about 15 in the early 1980s and 400 in the mid-1990s.

Many of Europe's biggest companies have been setting up their own universities, and public sector organizations have followed suit, with the establishment of the Defence Academy at Shrivenham in England in 2002, and the creation of the UK National Health Service University in 2002–3 (West, 2002). The Cranfield School of Management in the UK has even run workshops in conjunction with the Globe Theatre on Shakespeare and Business, at a cost of $US2500 per person. Frank Blount, the former CEO of one of Australia's biggest companies, Telstra, was critical of the leadership abilities of Australian managers during his time in charge of the company, and introduced a Centre for Leadership soon after his appointment. This designed and ran programmes for all Telstra management staff. Blount and his immediate management team spent four days a year running a programme for the 200 most senior managers in the company, who in turn ran workshops for about five thousand middle and junior managers. Blount introduced these in the belief that many of his managers lacked leadership and people management skills and, crucially, that many of these could be learnt and developed (Uren, 1998c). These examples indicate that many organizations believe that leadership and people management skills can be enhanced through appropriate development and learning strategies.

In summary, the smart answer to the question, 'Are leaders born?' is, of course, 'All leaders are born!' How could it be otherwise? But leadership is something much more complex than the sum total of our genetic inheritance or any innate traits we may have acquired during our formative years. Human nature is not fixed and immutable, it is flexible and adaptable. Even if it could be demonstrated that leadership truly is something that certain individuals are born to, this would not be particularly helpful to us during our leadership journey. As Peter Drucker once observed, 'There may be born leaders, but there are surely far too few to depend on.' This does not mean that everyone can become an influential leader: very few people can hope to emulate the sporting achievements of Tiger Woods and Annika Sorenstram in golf, Andre Agassi and the Williams sisters in tennis, or Herman Maier and Renate Gotschl in Alpine skiing. But anyone who has made the commitment to work through this book carries within themselves the potential and the capacity to become successful leaders, because almost all leaders throughout history have achieved this through a combination of self-belief, will-power, grit, determination, hard work and self-education.

Each one of us has within us the capacity to lead.
(*David Aronovici, HR Director, Trident Microsystems, 1998*)

What leaders do

The hard stuff is easy. The soft stuff is hard. And the soft stuff is a lot more important than the hard stuff.
(*Dr Tom Malone, CEO, Milliken & Company, 1995*)

While it is clearly important to address the innate/learnt debate, a more practical approach to understanding leadership is to think about the behaviours and functions of real-life leaders and understand what leaders actually *do*, rather than what they *are* in some intrinsic sense. After the failure of early and more recent trait research to produce reliable or consistent results, a series of studies looking at the behavioural aspects of leadership were conducted in the 1940s, at the Ohio State University, by Bales at Harvard University, and by Likert and colleagues at the University of Michigan in the 1950s. What did they discover about leadership? This body of research indicates that, for leaders to be effective, there is always an optimal balance, depending on circumstances, between a concern for people and a concern for technical or task issues. This group of researchers was also the first to identify systematically the many different roles that leaders perform within organizations. These have been categorized under seven headings.

Goal setter and motivator

Leaders play an important role in organizational management by directing and motivating employees towards achieving organizational objectives in appropriate and time-effective ways. They are able to communicate the purpose of these objectives to their employees with clarity and commitment. They spend time with their people, walk the talk and consistently lead by example (described in Chapters 3 and 4).

Coach and mentor

Effective leaders treat their employees as intelligent human beings who have inbuilt hard- and soft-wired capacities for improvement and learning and will want to contribute more, given the right opportunities and appropriate rewards. They take time to get to know their employees as unique individuals. They reward them whenever they do a good job. They do not resort to punishments when they make mistakes but, instead, use these as opportunities for learning (described in Chapters 3 and 4).

Shaker and stirrer

Effective leaders always keep people sharp and on their toes. They discourage self-satisfaction and complacency, and promote continual improvement, change, creativity and innovation amongst their followers (described in Chapters 3 and 8–11).

Interpreter

No set of rules, plans or procedures can describe perfectly what must happen within an organization if it is to survive and be successful. Leaders make sense of situations where there is incomplete information available, or where clear guidelines, rules and plans for decision making and action may not exist (described in Chapters 8–11).

Linch-pin

All organizations are made up of sub-systems of departments, teams or groups. Leaders manage these, and are also the cocoordinators between these and the organizational sub-systems of which they are a part (described in Chapter 5).

Helicopter

Leaders rise above the minutiae and short-term focus of day-to-day organizational life, and plan and coordinate the collective and individual activities of their staff. This can be a significant part of the responsibilities of those at the top levels of organizations (described in Chapters 3–5 and 8).

White-water rafter

Leaders have to be able to envision the future, and encourage positive attitudes towards change amongst their employees. They must be able to ride what has been described as 'the white-waters of change' these days or, alternatively, find different rivers for their followers to travel down (described in Chapters 8–11).

Before reading through the next section, please complete Exercise 1.1.

Exercise 1.1

Please write down *all* the roles that you perform as a leader/manager within your organization. Which of the seven categories do these come under? Then award yourself a mark, ranging from 1 ('I perform this role well') to 2 ('I perform this role OK, but there is probably room for improvement') to 3 ('I don't perform this role well, and really want to improve this').

Make a note of the areas where you think there is room for improvement in the future. Refer back to these when you reach the chapters or sections that deal with any of the weaker areas that you may have identified here. By doing this, you can start to fill any 'gaps' between how you currently operate as a leader/manager, and how you would like to operate in the future. ◆

How organizational contexts influence leadership styles

Looking at what leaders do provides us with a few more pieces of the jigsaw puzzle, but this is still a long way from the complete picture. Both trait and behavioural approaches to understanding leadership ignore a very important dimension of this role: the context or situation within which the leader operates. Known in academic circles as 'contingency theory', this more recent perspective suggests that there is no single 'best way' to lead and manage others, and effective leaders possess a number of skills and behaviours which they can employ, as appropriate, in a variety of settings. This can be likened to the 'tool-kit' referred to in the Preface, that they can dip into as and when required. This approach also emphasizes the influence of contextual factors on leadership styles, such as formal positional power, group dynamics, the influence of subordinates and organizational culture. These can be highlighted if we look briefly at the different kinds of leadership and management skills that are required during the four main stages of a company's life cycle.

The new kid on the block

The type of leader/manager required when a company first opens for business is someone who has real entrepreneurial drive and vision and is able to fight for a small seedling company. They are able to recruit and develop the best kind of set-up team possible and are very good at obtaining venture capital and investment. They are good at networking and, as a result, are often very good at recruiting skilled staff from other companies to join them in achieving their new dream or vision (for example, Bill Gates poaching younger computing staff from IBM and Rank-Xerox in the late 1970s and early 1980s).

Letting go of the reins

Moving from a small entrepreneurial operation to a medium-sized company, the kind of leader/manager required here is someone who can adopt a more 'hands-off' leadership style by delegating more responsibilities to other people. They have to be able to 'let go of the ball' and act more as an overall driver and coordinator of the people who have been brought into manage an increasingly complex and departmentalized organization.

Good housekeeping

Different leadership and management skills are required when an organization is maturing and when the primary need is for it to be run efficiently and economically. This involves skills such as strategic acumen, business planning, delegation of responsibilities, cost control, continuous improvement and quality initiatives, the ability to develop effective cross-organizational human resource (HR) policies and, perhaps, a global commercial mind-set.

Squeezing the pips

When an organization nears the end of its life cycle someone who can get the best out of what is left is required. The leader/manager in this type of situation has to be very tough in order to sort out the problems that have brought the company to this situation. He or she also has to be visionary because, if the company is to survive, this person must then be able to champion the need for radical organizational change and renewal.

In practical terms, this means that leaders have to develop a chameleon-like quality. This allows them to develop a flexible leadership/management style that can be adapted to each new situation they find themselves in and, equally importantly, one that takes into account the aspirations and expectations of their followers. This does not mean that they simply abandon core leadership attributes and behaviours in response to each new circumstance they find themselves in, but all leaders entering an organization for the first time have to possess a keen 'radar' that allows them to get a feel for the culture and climate that exists there, and an ability to modify their leadership style when appropriate. We will review this capability in Chapter 3 and Chapter 8.

Other perspectives on the contingent nature of leadership and people management have emerged in the last 20 years. These include *implicit leadership* and *social exchange* theories and the idea of *followership*. Implicit leadership theory suggests that the idea of leadership as being something that is 'done to' people is flawed. This is because we all come into organizations with largely unconscious sets of values, beliefs, prejudices and assumptions about many things – politics, cultural identity, human nature, human motivation and so forth. And, as part of this baggage, we all carry in our minds a mental picture of what an effective leader 'is'. These ideas about 'appropriate' traits and behaviours can have a significant effect on the way we respond to different leaders and how we lead and manage others. We can see how this happens if we reflect for a moment on the origins of our ideas and beliefs about leadership (Table 1.1).

Table 1.1   The origins of our ideas and beliefs about leadership

---

From our mothers and fathers and the way they raise us during childhood
From our interactions with siblings and peers, and our experiences at school
From the stories, legends and myths we hear while growing up
From our work and career experiences, by observing leaders and being led
From personal experience, and through trial and error
From active self-reflection about our leadership beliefs and practices
From studying leadership and leaders
From formal instruction and education

There are four conclusions that can be drawn from this. First, we are all exposed to a unique set of influences that shape our perceptions of leadership. How our parents raise us as children can have a profound influence on how we lead and manage people as adults; as can our interactions with our siblings and peer groups at school.

Second, we do not create these implicit leadership constructs in any *conscious* sense, because our brains automatically and selectively screen the information we receive from our environments as we are growing up (see Chapter 9 for some examples of this). This is how a normal mind works. Without this automatic filtering process, we could not function in any meaningful sense, because only a pathological mind can see the world unfiltered through prior knowledge.

Third, these selective perceptions operate almost entirely at an *unconscious* level. That is, we rarely think consciously about our perceptions or practice of leadership/management unless others challenge these (by, for example, refusing to do what we ask them), or unless they are systematically evaluated through the use of 360° feedback techniques, or in performance appraisals or by actively reflecting on what we do as leaders and how we do this.

Fourth, it would appear that the least effective way of becoming a better leader/manager is to read about it and/or from formal instruction and training – *unless we use these to reflect actively on our current practices and apply new insights and knowledge we may have acquired when back at work.*

The natural consequence of these processes, for almost everyone, is a partial and selective view about what constitutes effective leadership. These pre-existing constructs also influence the way that people pigeonhole others into 'leader' or 'non-leader' categories. In practice, this means that leaders may *believe* that they are acting effectively, but if their behaviours do not correspond with the selective constructs that their followers have about appropriate leader behaviour, then these leaders will be ignored and their employees will try to find ways to get on with their work without them. This is an important insight because, if we find ourselves in new work situations, or join an organization with a different culture to one we have been used to working in, our leadership/management style may be viewed as being inappropriate by a new group of followers. This may also have an effect on how employees may react to leaders who do not fit into pre-existing stereotypes they may have about a leader; for example, following the arrival of a new woman boss in a male-dominated profession (issues we will return to in Chapters 6 and 8).

Another direct consequence of selective perceptions about other people is that leaders may also have a tendency to separate their followers into distinct groups, an in-group of people they instinctively like, and an out-group of people they like less. Many leaders do this and, for the most part, without thinking consciously about it. The consequence of this separation of subordinates into favourites and non-favourites is that each group is treated differently, with the inner group being allowed more latitude in behaviour and much closer relationships with the leader. Being in the in-group also leads to higher motivation and performance and greater loyalty to the organization (Wayne *et al.*, 1997). However, there are many obvious dangers with this. There may be a tendency only to hire people who are 'like us', leading to the emergence of a management team of sycophantic 'yes' men and women and, over time, to widespread organizational sclerosis and nepotism. This is a common failing of political leaders. Examples of this include Adolf Hitler during World War II, or Margaret Thatcher's creation of an inner cabinet of close personal advisers whom she considered to be 'one of us', before she was ruthlessly ousted from office in 1990, having lost touch with her backbenchers in the Conservative Party (described later in this chapter). This phenomenon can also be found in business organizations, when leaders of organizations become inward looking and complacent, surrounded by obsequious acolytes. Think, for example, of the self-satisfied complacency of the entire American automotive industry in the 1960s and early 1970s about the threat posed by Japanese car companies, or IBM's initial dismissive reaction to the emergence of the PC in the mid-to-late 1970s. Another example is the international mining and resource company BHP-Billiton, which was described as having an 'out-dated, inward looking and clannish senior management culture', by the *Australian Financial Review* in the fall of 1998, just before John Prescott was ousted from the CEO position, and the American Paul Anderson was brought in to sort the company out (and in the process, create a younger and more diverse group of senior managers). Similar phenomena were also observed among the senior management echelons of many companies that have collapsed in recent years, such as Enron and Worldcom.

As an adjunct to this idea, Social Exchange theory views leadership as a two-way process in which both parties trade benefits. It also shows that subordinates can have a profound influence on the behaviour and performance of leaders. Peter Drucker once observed, with his customary clarity, that the only true definition of a leader is 'Someone who has followers'. This is something that can be easily forgotten when we create long shopping lists of the skills and qualities of 'great leaders' and 'charismatic CEOs'. In this two-way relationship, the leader helps subordinates achieve valued rewards by directing them toward goals desired by the organization. In return, subordinates help the leader by performing well and, the better subordinates perform, the better their leaders will perform. In this symbiotic relationship, the leader becomes *a servant* to all of their followers, not a directive boss with an in-group of favourites. This is not a new idea. It was first articulated by Mahatma Gandhi, as part of his philosophy of non-violent protest in the 1930s and 1940s against British imperial rule in India.

This approach to leadership emphasizes that leaders have a responsibility, not just to lead and direct, but also to provide teaching, development, coaching, mentoring, guidance and feedback, so that their people can perform to the best of their abilities and realize their full potential. The most effective leaders are very aware of the simple but powerful idea that effective leadership, like communication, is *a two-way process.* In the context of Steve Waugh's captaincy of the Australian cricket team, described earlier in this chapter, there is no doubt that his success was due in part to the quality of the players he had at his disposal, as well as the consistently successful performances he was able to get out of them. It is unlikely that he would have been regarded as such a successful leader if he had been captain of any of the other test-playing teams of the late 1990s and early 2000s. As General Douglas MacArthur, Allied Commander in the Pacific region during World War II, once commented, 'A general is just as good – or just as bad – as the officers and troops under his command.'

Before reading the next paragraph, can you guess to which American president this quotation refers?

> He knew that true leadership is often realised by exerting quiet and subtle influence on a day to day basis, by frequently seeing followers and other people face to face. He treated everyone with the same courtesy and respect, whether they were kings or commoners. He lifted people out of their everyday selves and into a higher level of performance, achievement and awareness. He obtained extraordinary results from ordinary people by instilling purpose in their endeavours. He was civil, open, tolerant and fair and he maintained a respect for the dignity of all people at all times.
> (*Norton, 2002: 12*)

The answer is Abraham Lincoln, but notice how modern this description of his leadership style sounds. There are clear parallels between this and the leadership style of Steve Waugh, and business leaders like Andy Grove (Intel), Akio Morita (co-founder of Sony), Bill Hewlett and Dave Packard, and Alfred Sloan (General Motors). Many successful business leaders have regarded themselves as *primus inter pares* – first amongst equals – and they understand that true leadership is, by necessity, a two-way process of mutual influence and causation with their followers. It is not about 'telling people what to do' (Forster, 2000b). To conclude this section, here are some more examples of the leader-as-servant philosophy in action:

> What is a leader? To me, the concept of leadership is very straightforward. A leader is the servant of the organization. It's as simple as that.
> (*Paul Anderson, former CEO of BHP-Billiton, 2001*)

> Because leadership is an action, not a position or title, managers need to learn when to lead and when to follow. If you try to lead all day, every day

– you will fail. You need to understand that leadership and followership is a dynamic relationship, based on the situations that people are facing. In fact, leadership is a gift, given to a leader by a follower.
(*David Parkin et al.,* Perform – Or Else, *1999*)

I am not a leader. I am a servant.
(*Nelson Mandela, former President of South Africa, 1990*)

The first responsibility of a leader is to define reality. The last is to say thank you. In between the two, the leader must become a servant and a debtor. That sums up the progress of an artful leader.
(*Max DePree,* Leadership is an Art, *1989*)

Leadership is a priceless gift that you have to learn and earn from the people who work with you. I have to earn the right to that gift and I have to constantly re-earn that gift.
(*John Harvey-Jones, former CEO of ICI, 1985*)

A leader is best when people hardly know he exists, not so good when people obey and acclaim him, worse when they despise him. But of a good leader, who talks little, when his work is done, his aim fulfilled, they will say, 'We did it ourselves'.
(*Lau-Tzu, 6th-century Chinese philosopher*)

Leaders as coaches and mentors

Some organizational leaders have taken this idea of leadership as a two-way and contingent process one step further, by emphasizing the importance of coaching and mentoring employees, an approach that has been used in sports management for more than one hundred years. Can insights from sports psychology help leaders and managers? The short answer to this question appears to be 'Yes', and these insights can be utilized by both men and women at work. My conversion to this point of view evolved over several years, while working part-time as a ski instructor, and working through the English Ski Council's instructor training programme, between 1990 and 1995. During this time, I came to realize that there are many parallels between sports coaching and mentoring, business leadership and people management. I also took some time out from academia and worked for a season, in 1998, as a full-time ski instructor at Perisher Blue (PB) in New South Wales, the biggest ski resort in Australia. At the hiring clinic for jobs at PB in June 1998, I had an opportunity to ask the ski school director what five qualities he was looking for in rookie ski instructors (bearing in mind that I was one of the oldest people applying for a job and comfortably in the bottom 10 per cent in terms of technical skiing ability). This was his response:

Communication skills are easily the most important thing because these are ninety per cent of what the job is about. The second thing would be what I'd call character or integrity, because I need to be able to trust my staff to take very good care of our clients in what can be a dangerous environment. The third thing would be some signs of professionalism in how they deal with the public. The fourth thing would be a capacity to learn, because we get enough technically good skiers applying for these jobs every year, who can't teach skiing to save their lives. And so, the fifth thing would be actual skiing ability because, while we expect a minimum standard, that is by far the easiest thing to teach.

While there are obvious differences between business and sporting organizations, this quote suggests that there are parallels between effective leadership in both environments, and many of the skills that are utilized in sports settings can also be applied in organizational contexts. Leader-coaches in sporting environments have to establish objectives for their teams, athletes or clients to work towards. They have to jointly agree collective and individual goals with them, and then find the best methods of achieving these. Effective coaches have to understand what individuals need, develop their talents, set appropriate goals, give appropriate feedback and reward their athletes/clients accordingly. Coaches have to form strong bonds with their followers, and be trusted and respected. They must lead by example, walk the talk, and be excellent communicators. Last, coaches are rewarded on concrete results not promises and, if they don't deliver, they will soon find themselves out of work (Forster, 1994a, 1994b, 1995a, 1995b, 1995c, 1995d; Carron, 1984; Smith, 1979).

Leaders in sporting and organizational contexts have to understand broadly similar concepts and questions; in particular, 'What makes this person or group of people tick and how am I going to get the best possible performance out of him/her/them?' In recent times, some of the world's leading companies, such as ABB, Coca-Cola, Microsoft, Intel and Hewlett-Packard, have all embraced the concept of 'the leader as coach'. The value of sporting and coaching analogies to leadership and people management in organizations is also reflected in the growing number of books that have bridged these parallel worlds. An increasing number of sports psychologists are also being headhunted into the corporate world, where their ability to teach goal-setting skills, how to cope with pressure and manage emotions are becoming highly valued (Maguire, 2002).[3]

Of equal relevance to leaders has been the rapid growth in personal 'peak-performance coaching' in recent times. Taking their cue from 30 years' development of this method in many sporting environments, a number of consulting and corporate training businesses have begun to offer intensive workshops that embrace a complete range of personal health and fitness issues. Examples of these include LGE Performance Systems in the USA and WAMCG in Western Australia. These companies run courses that cover issues such as developing a clear sense of individual purpose, physical strength, emotional intelligence and mental energy, as well as how to interpret and respond to feedback about their leadership styles in questionnaires completed by work colleagues and subordinates. The purpose of this coaching is to create business leaders who are more self-aware, energized, focused and determined, as well as being physically and psychologically balanced. In turn, this produces leaders who are able to coach and develop their employees to perform at higher levels (see Chapter 4). Lou Schneider, a managing director at Salomon Brothers in the USA, maintains that this 'corporate athlete' philosophy has transformed hundreds of people at the company for the better, with across-the-board improvements in their physical health, emotional well-being and job performance, their ability to cope with stress, and in helping them to balance their busy work and home lives (Gemignani, 1998: 40).

Transformational, charismatic and visionary leadership

Up to this point, we have been looking at approaches to leadership that have been described as 'transactional'. These regard the leader–follower relationship in terms of a formal exchange that is largely instrumental, task-focused and reward-based. However, transformational leaders seek something much more than mere obedience and compliance from their followers. Transformational leaders want to change their followers' beliefs, values and attitudes in order to get superior levels of performance and achievement out of them. Sometimes described as 'Super-Bosses', they are perceived to lead by virtue of their ability to inspire devotion and extraordinary effort from their followers. An example that is often cited of this kind of boss is the legendary Jack Welch, the former CEO of General Electric, voted 'Business Man of the 20th Century' by *Fortune* magazine in December 2001.

These individuals are driven, often from an early age, by a very strong need for achievement and success. They are self-confident and believe that they can truly make a difference to the world. As a result, they may sometimes come across as domineering characters who do not suffer fools gladly. They are often hyperactive, appear to need little sleep and are capable of dealing with many tasks at the same time – characteristics shared by some political leaders, such as Winston Churchill. They can be exhausting bosses to work for, because they expect similarly high levels of motivation and performance from their followers. Above all else, they understand what power is about and, whether they are benevolent or malevolent leaders, they understand something about human behaviour and how to motivate or, if required, manipulate people to do their bidding. They are often regarded as good communicators and storytellers. Transformational leaders are also able to adapt their leadership styles, depending on the circumstances, particularly when they are brought in as trouble shooters to sort out an organization in crisis.

Another characteristic noted earlier in this chapter is their special ability to ride the white-waters of change. This transformational mind-set is absolutely essential these days. When we unpack this ability, we discover that it is actually a combination of a number of skills, including the ability to think long-term, the ability to create visions, effective two-way communication skills, the ability to link strategies with opportunities and, increasingly, systemic and lateral thinking (described in Chapters 3, 8 and 11). Transformational business leaders embrace change with enthusiasm and believe that change is good and inevitable. They have the ability to create an impetus for change and recognize that change must be proactive rather than reactive. For example, Don Argus, the former American CEO of the National Australia Bank was fond of saying that, ideally, you don't change when you have to – you must continue changing when you *don't* have to. This belief echoes an old American saying, used by many US presidents, including Franklin D. Roosevelt, John F. Kennedy and Bill Clinton, that 'The time to mend the roof is when the sun is shining.'

Transformational leaders are sometimes perceived to be larger than life and to possess hypnotic, magical, heroic or charismatic qualities (from the ancient Greek word, *charisma*, meaning 'gift of grace'). Such individuals, by the sheer force of their personalities, are regarded as being capable of having profound and extraordinary effects on their followers. People may identify with charismatic leaders, and follow them willingly, because they are perceived to have an allure or magnetism that transcends normal human experiences. When asked, most people can recall being in the presence of charismatic or larger than life personalities at some point during their lives. This archetype of the powerful and magical super-leader has been prevalent throughout human history, and it still pervades the business cultures of many countries. Nevertheless, there are several reasons why charisma is probably the single most misunderstood and overrated capability that leaders are supposed to possess.

First, charisma is often something that is in the eye of the beholder: what appears to be charismatic to one person does not appear to be so to another. Second, charisma is often regarded as being innate, a special quality that a few people are born with. How can this be, when there is no gene, or DNA cluster, that is responsible for creating a charismatic personality? Third, charisma comes and goes. It is always ephemeral and rarely lasts for long. If it is an innate part of a person's psychology, this is not possible. It would be as if one's personality changed from being extroverted to introverted within a very short period of time. Fourth, all the historical evidence we have shows that charisma can be created by historical circumstances; that is, the situation can create the apparently charismatic leader as much as the supposedly unique individual creates the situation (for example, Adolf Hitler in the 1930s or his evil 'twin', Joseph Stalin, during a 30-year reign of terror in the former Soviet Union). Fifth, leaders invariably come to be perceived as charismatic *after* they have reached positions of power, indicating that a cult of personality can be created and manipulated through media exploitation and propaganda, and the judicious use of the physical trappings and patronage that accompany power. Stalin was a seething, paranoid and introverted man when he grabbed power in Russia in the early 1920s. By the early 1930s, he had become the larger-than-life and charismatic 'father' of the USSR. Sixth, in some cultures the concept of charisma does not exist. In Japan, for example, leadership is often regarded as largely symbolic and charisma is an extremely rare phenomenon.

Seventh, several studies on leadership effectiveness have suggested that those who are seen as charismatic are simply more animated and expressive, when compared to people who are perceived to lack this quality (for example, Bryman, 1992; Bass, 1985; Friedman *et al.*, 1980). Hence, what appears to differentiate *perceptions* of these two types of leader are the verbal and non-verbal communications skills they exhibit when in public. Those perceived to be charismatic are more enthusiastic, speak faster, smile and laugh more often, listen actively, pronounce words more clearly, and are more animated and energetic in their physical movements and gestures. They are also more likely to touch other people during greetings and conversations. So what we often call charisma *may* be better understood as the ability to communicate in a visceral and connective way with others, verbally and non-verbally (a suggestion we will return to in Chapter 3). Eighth, and this reinforces the last point, it has been possible for several years to get leadership coaching in 'charismatic behaviours', which covers the development of self-confidence, maintaining a positive outlook, enhancing one's emotional intelligence, improving deportment, body language and dress style, and improving communication, media and public speaking skills.

The ninth and perhaps most powerful criticism of the myth of charisma in a business context can be found in the work of Jim Collins and Jerry Porras, in their pioneering book, *Built to Last: Successful Habits of Visionary Companies* (1996). Collins and Porras had one objective in this study: to identify the characteristics of the most consistently successful and profitable companies of the 20th century. After a lengthy and rigorous investigation, they identified just 18 companies: Federal Express, Boeing, Citicorp, Ford, General Electric, Hewlett Packard, IBM, Johnson & Johnson, Marriot, Merck, Motorola, 3m, Nordstrom, Philip Morris, Procter and Gamble, Sony, Wal Mart and Disney. They also identified 17 comparison companies, who were good, but not the very best. The visionary companies they identified had all attained extraordinary long-term performance: an investment of one dollar in visionary company stock on 1 January 1926 and reinvestment of all dividends would have grown to $6536 in 1990 – over 15 times the general market rate (Collins and Porras, 1996: 4).

Collins and Porras also looked at the issue of leadership and its impact on the performance of these high-performing companies. They came up with results that ran counter to many common-sense assumptions about organizational leadership. First, in the combined 1700 years that these companies had existed, only four CEOs had been recruited from outside the companies. Almost every single leader of these companies had been home-grown, challenging the widespread belief that organizations have to bring in outsiders with fresh ideas to improve a company's performance or to initiate significant changes. The second finding concerned the distinct *lack* of charismatic leadership in these companies:

> A high profile charismatic style is absolutely not required to successfully shape a visionary company. Indeed, we found that the most successful chief executives in the history of the visionary companies did not have the personality traits of the archetypal high-profile, charismatic visionary leader [ ] In short, we found no evidence to support the hypothesis that great (charismatic) leadership is the distinguishing variable during the critical, formative stages of the visionary companies. Thus, as our study progressed we had to reject the great leader theory: it simply did not adequately explain the differences between the visionary and comparison companies.
> (*Collins and Porras, 1996: 7–8 and 32*)

Similar results were found in Collins' follow-up book, *Good to Great* (2001). The objective of this study was to examine the shared characteristics of US companies who had made the transition from being merely good to being truly great companies during the 1990s. Of the 11 companies he identified, *not one* had been led by a charismatic leader during their transitional phases. Ten of 11 CEOs were recruited internally. These CEOs were characterized by low public profiles, self-effacing modesty and humility and often attributed their failures to themselves and their successes to good fortune or their employees. All had high standards of integrity. They were all committed, body and soul, to their companies, not to personal self-aggrandizement. They were also courageous and had to make very difficult business decisions at critical junctures in order to transfer resources from poorly performing areas to the business areas that ultimately made these companies great. In summary, Collins and Porras's work reveals four counterintuitive facts about very successful companies and their CEOs.

1 The most successful companies of the 20th century were rarely led by charismatic leaders, and in the combined 1700 years they had been in existence, just four CEOs were external recruits.
2 Eleven US companies that made the transition from 'good to great' during the 1980s and 1990s did not require the presence of heroic charismatic leaders to achieve this.
3 With one exception the leaders of the good-to-great companies were promoted from within the companies, they were not external appointees.
4 Collectively, they were *underpaid* in comparison to general levels of executive pay and remuneration in their industry/business sectors.

In fact, overpaid charismatic leaders can actually be a major liability to companies. One well-known example of this was the Hollywood director Michael Cimino. In 1978, he had enjoyed great success with the Vietnam War movie, *The Deer Hunter*, and was hailed at the time as a charismatic genius, if a bit of a loose cannon. United Artists engaged Cimino to direct *Heaven's Gate*, where he proved to be an uncooperative and tantrum-prone brat, according to accounts at the time. Although costs escalated out of control, UA's executive still retained their faith in his 'charismatic genius'. The film eventually flopped and had to be withdrawn from distribution at a cost of $US44 million (now equivalent to more than $US100 million). The result of this *débâcle* was that the entire executive and the chairman of UA were sacked soon afterwards and the company was eventually taken over by MGM. Other examples where this kind of leader has caused considerable problems in recent times include Kozlowski at Tyco, Lay at Enron, Ebbers at Worldcom and Winnick at Global Crossing. All of these were regarded as archetypal, domineering and charismatic leaders, who did generate short-term shareholder results, but also bullied their boards and senior managers into meek docility. The results in these companies were egomaniacal corporate strategies, extravagant personal rewards and, ultimately, the demise of these businesses (*The Economist*, 2002a). We will return to look at these in Chapter 12.

Another example of the ephemeral nature of charisma is that of one of the longest serving British prime ministers in history, Margaret

Thatcher. While she was perceived as a tough, flinty-eyed and energetic political operator during the early part of her parliamentary
career, she was not perceived as being either charismatic or a particularly effective communicator when she became leader of the
Conservative Party in 1975. At the time, many of the old-guard
members of her first cabinet, who had been supporters of her prede-
cessor, Ted Heath, believed that she wouldn't last beyond the next
general election. Very few political commentators thought she could
ever become prime minister. However, she found herself at the crest of
an economic, political and social revolution in Britain. The postwar
political consensus had collapsed, Keynesian macroeconomic interven-
tionist economics were in disarray, inflation and interest rates were
spiralling out of control and old-style militant unions, in every major
industrial sector, had brought the country to its knees through a series
of lengthy and damaging strikes.

The time was ripe for a change driven in large measure by the influence of the intellectual thinking of libertarian thinkers such as Hayek,
Nozeck and Friedman and the 'New Right'. The Labour Party was
kicked out of office and the Conservatives were elected, with a slim
majority, in 1979, under the slogan 'Labour isn't Working'. However,
unemployment continued to rise inexorably and the British economy
remained firmly trapped in the worst recession since the early 1930s.
Damaging industrial disputes continued to cripple the country and
race riots broke out in several inner-city areas. By 1981, most political
commentators believed that Labour would be re-elected at the forthcoming General Election.

Luckily for the Conservatives, two unrelated but significant events
then took place. First, the military dictatorship in Argentina decided to
invade the Falkland Islands in April 1982. After quickly recapturing
the islands on 14 June, Thatcher's personal approval ratings went
through the roof on a wave of national patriotic fervour. Second, the
Labour Party had continued to drift to the hard left and was still dominated by militant trade unions. This prompted a breakaway group of
27 right-wing Labour MPs to form a new centre party, the Social
Democrats, effectively splitting the Labour Party's traditional vote. A
little later, in 1985, a botched IRA attempt to assassinate Thatcher at the
party's conference in Brighton, and her 'No negotiation with terrorists'
policy, further enhanced her popularity. The Conservatives were
returned to office in two landslide victories at the General Elections of
1983 and 1987.

The Conservative Party's spin doctors started to create a cult of personality around 'The Iron Lady'. Under their influence, and with the tacit

support of new media entrepreneurs like Rupert Murdoch, the tabloid press began routinely to describe her as, 'The new Elizabeth the First' and 'The new Boadicea'. From the early 1980s, Thatcher had also been receiving extensive coaching in public speaking, vocal skills, image, and hair and dress styling. In a very short period of time, she 'became' a charismatic leader with a radical new vision for Britain. Thatcher certainly did transform Britain during the 1980s, and many other countries have followed her example of labour market and trade union reform, financial deregulation and the privatization of state assets. Her energy, drive and commitment to her political beliefs prompted her acerbic press secretary, Bernard Ingram, to later describe her as 'the only man in the cabinet'.

However, within a relatively short period of time she was kicked out of office by a party that no longer wanted her, stripped of her power and 'charisma', in 1990. She had become distanced from her party and was felled by a flaw of many leaders, her propensity to divide people into 'in-groups' (her chosen coterie of personal political advisers in an increasingly presidential prime ministership) and 'out-groups' (her cabinet and the rest of the Conservative Party). She had come to believe that she was infallible and, as a consequence, forgot the simple and age-old lesson that leaders can only retain power as long as they have the support of their followers. Her stubborn views about British sovereignty and deep suspicions about the economic and political union of Europe divided the party, leading to the resignation of two of her senior ministers (Nigel Lawson and Geoffrey Howe). One of her former ministers, Michael Heseltine, then challenged her for the leadership position. When she failed to get the required majority from the first ballot, she resigned from office.

Since that time, she has become an increasingly irrelevant and often resented presence in the Conservative Party. Her protégé, John Major, who took over from her in 1990, ended up detesting Thatcher and her anti-Europe supporters, whom he once described as 'bastards'. The party's next leader, William Hague, was so overwhelmed by Thatcher's continuing presence that the Labour Party made great mileage out of campaign posters in 2000 that featured her hair and eyes superimposed on his head, with the message, 'Be afraid. Be very afraid'. The Labour Party was returned with huge majorities in 1997 in 2001 and attributed some of this success to another poster campaign it ran in 2000–2001, 'The Mummy Returns', featuring Thatcher, who was by now a deeply unpopular figure in the country. Within the space of a few years, Thatcher had risen rapidly to become a visionary, charismatic heroine and then steadily declined to become regarded as a slightly barking and embarrassing has-been. In 2002, in the ultimate humiliation, she was banned from speaking in the main auditorium at the Conservative Party's Annual Conference in Bournemouth.

What practical insights can be drawn from these examples? The first is that, while charisma may be useful to leader/managers, all the available evidence shows that it is not an essential prerequisite for effective leadership; nor, as we will see in Chapter 6, is a heroic, male style of leadership. Second, it is much closer to the truth to suggest that, once an effective leader comes to possess the requisite qualities and characteristics that they need to be successful, they may then be *perceived* to be charismatic. Third, leaders who come to believe that they are charismatic and infallible can become a major liability to their companies or political parties, particularly when the dominant leader leaves and there are no systems in place, or suitable successors, to fill the large command-and-control void they have left behind. In a nutshell, while charisma is not a requirement for effective and successful leadership, transformational abilities are essential for all leaders of organizations.

The vision thing

Where there is no vision, the people perish.
(*Proverbs, 29: 18*)

Vision without action is a daydream. Action without vision is a nightmare.
(*Old Japanese proverb*)

That's all very well in practice – but how does it work in theory?
(*Attributed to Groucho Marx, American comedian, 1933*)

While charisma is not a requirement for leadership, one skill that certainly is important for present-day organizational leaders is the ability to envision the future. At the beginning of this chapter we saw that leaders are often required to take people on journeys to the future and, consequently, they have to be able to get their followers to question existing realities and embrace new ones. Without a vision, or some sense of direction about the future, a leader cannot move an organization forward or mobilize its employees. The ability to do this has been described as something that often sets true leaders apart from the crowd: a unique ability to spot new business opportunities and new markets, like hounds sniffing out truffles in the woods. The ability to articulate a vision for the future has also been described as a magical or sixth sense that only a few people can hope to develop. However, this is yet another common-sense myth about leadership. As we will see, in Chapters 8 and 9, almost anyone can become better at envisioning the future, if they are willing to work at acquiring the ability to do this.

Vision has been defined as 'an apparition of a prophetic, revelational or supernatural nature presented to the mind in a state of heightened spiritual or emotional awareness, a distinct or vivid mental image or concept, insight or foresight, an ability to plan or formulate policy in a far sighted way' (OED website, 2003). It has also been described more succinctly as 'a realistic, credible and attractive future for an organization' (Nanus, 1992: 8) and 'an ideal and unique view of the future' (Kouzes and Posner, 1997: 95). Essentially, a vision is a new way of looking at both present circumstances and future possibilities. It can originate from a number of sources, including lateral and creative thinking, the ability to future-cast and scenario-map (to imagine 'What if . . .'), from an organization's employees, or some combination of all of these (abilities which we return to in Chapters 8–11). Visionary leaders can also bring together already existing bodies of knowledge and turn these into something new. One example of this process in action can be found in Richard Branson's company, Virgin. In the 1960s, he made his first big breakthrough by combining an already existing record-selling business with mail order delivery, and made full use of the new marketing techniques that emerged in the late 1960s.

Visionaries also have to possess great self-belief. A story that has often been told to illustrate this concerns the 17th-century English architect, Sir Christopher Wren. After the Great Fire of London in 1666, he was appointed by Charles II to oversee the rebuilding of parts of the city that had been ravaged by the fire. The financial backers of one of his building projects believed that the main span that Wren had put on the architectural plans was too wide, and they told him that he would need to put in additional columns to support this. After some heated discussions, and knowing that other contracts were riding on his decision, Wren acquiesced and put in the additional columns as instructed. However, quite deliberately, he left a small gap between the columns and the span. This could not be seen from ground level. To this day, the span has not sagged an inch, and the columns have supported nothing more than Wren's conviction that he was right – for more than 300 years.

The power of visions is that they can act as 'paradigm busters', moving people forward from the present to the future. Radical visions can also be a threat to the status quo and to common-sense ways of thinking. As we've already seen, managers are usually concerned with short-term, practical problem solving and decision making, and may not spend much time theorizing about how the world might be in the future. Leaders, however, have to be concerned about new ideas, long-term thinking and challenging the status quo, because they understand that change is not possible without the ability to theorize about alternatives to the situation that currently exists. In fact, they recognize that *everything* we create that is new or different has to be driven by a theory of some kind. As the psychologist Kurt Lewin once observed, 'There is nothing so practical to a manager as a good theory.' We may call this ability 'common sense', but if we look up the definition of this phrase, it means 'an individual view or notion', and 'a scheme of ideas or statements held to explain a group of facts, phenomena or general laws' (OED website, 2004). In other words, common sense is itself a set of theories about how the world works, based on experience. However, while many leader/managers make decisions every day on the basis of common sense and experience, this can be dangerous.

To illustrate the dangers of relying on common sense, what innovations are being described here?

> For decades, the rich and powerful opposed the introduction of these changes and innovations. Economists opposed their introduction because they were seen as being either uneconomic or an attack on business profitability. Many intellectuals resisted their introduction. They were pushed through over a period of about 100 years, in spite of sustained opposition, by determined and visionary civil servants and politicians across Europe during the 19th and 20th centuries.
>
> Can you name the company that created the first personal computer, word processing software and many other new computing technologies in the 1970s, and yet failed to develop and market them, because they did not believe that people would buy personal computers?

The answers to these two questions can be found in note 4. Here are some other examples of the dangers of relying on common sense in the past:

- 1876: Sir William Preece, Chief Engineer of the British Post Office, said, 'The Americans have need of the telephone – but we do not. We have plenty of office boys.'
- 1895: Lord Kelvin, the British peer and scientist, maintained that 'Heavier than air flying machines are impossible.'
- 1899: Charles Duell, the Director of the US Patent Office, believed that 'Everything that can be invented has been invented.'
- 1927: Henry Warner, the co-founder of Warner Brothers, asked 'Who the hell wants to hear actors talk?'
- 1932: Albert Einstein said 'There is not the slightest indication that nuclear energy will ever be obtainable.'
- 1943: Thomas Watson, the CEO of IBM, said 'I think there is a world market for maybe five computers.'
- 1960s: 'We are confident that Japanese companies pose no threat to us' (any large company of your choice in the USA and Europe in the 1960s and early 1970s).

- 1962: 'We don't like their sound, and anyway guitar music is on the way out' (a spokesman for the recording company Decca, having made what turned out to be the most expensive blunder in the history of 20th-century popular music by not signing a young British guitar group called The Beatles). Similar mistakes were made by the record companies that turned down The Police and U2 in the late 1970s.
- 1970: Margaret Thatcher said, 'There will never be a female Prime Minister in my lifetime.'
- 1977: Ken Olsen, founder of the Digital Equipment Corporation, could see 'no reason why anyone would want a computer in their home'. DEC was later taken over by Compaq, which in turn was absorbed by Hewlett-Packard in 2002.
- 1977: the IBM Annual Report stated, 'We believe that there is no consumer market for personal computers.'

Other examples of common sense that have stymied progress and change in organizations include the traditional knee-jerk reaction of most men on every single occasion that a woman has tried to gain access to male-dominated professions and organizations over the last 100 years (see Chapter 6 for several examples of this). In a similar vein, for most of the 20th century, men believed that women did not have the 'right stuff' to become CEOs of companies, and did not have the same entrepreneurial instincts and abilities as men. There are now more than 100 women who head major international businesses. In the USA alone, there are eight million self-employed women, who between them employ more people than the Fortune 500 companies combined. Women will own more than half of all small businesses in the USA by 2005 (Gollan, 1997). Last, but not least, would you have invested some of your hard-earned cash back in the late 1970s in the company featured in Figure 1.1 (p. 38)?

With the benefit of hindsight we all would have, because an investment of about $US1000 in this company in 1980 would have been worth about $US65 000 by early 2000.[5] Examples like this, and the history of companies that create new commercial and business paradigms, show us that it is the ability to use *uncommon* sense and theorize about alternative futures that differentiates truly great business leaders from run-of-the-mill leaders. In this context it's worth recalling these sayings: 'Yesterday's heresy is today's orthodoxy and tomorrow's history', the words of the German philosopher and scientist Arthur Schoppenhauer, 'New ideas and thoughts always go through three stages. First they are ridiculed. Next, they are violently opposed. Finally, they are accepted as self-evident common sense', and George Bernard Shaw's observation, 'The greatest truths always start out as blasphemies.'

Figure 1.1   Would you invest in this company?

Common sense is not a simple thing. Instead, it is an immense society of hard-earned, practical ideas – of multitudes of life-learned rules and exceptions, dispositions and tendencies, balances and checks.
(*Marvin Minsky*, The Society of Mind, 1985)

Common sense is little more than the deposits of prejudice laid down in the mind before the age of twenty-one.
(*Albert Einstein, 1930*)

Exercise 1.2

Try to create a compelling vision (or a new direction or a set of objectives) that will challenge the common-sense assumptions of the people who work in your team, department or organization. What is the end goal of this vision? What are the principal components of this vision? Can these be encapsulated in simple, motivational rallying cries? How can this vision be realized and operationalized in the future? ◆

Did you find this to be an easy or difficult exercise? If you found it hard to articulate a vision for the future, don't worry. This is one of the most complex and advanced abilities that organizational leaders have to acquire and develop. Later on, in Chapter 8, there will be another opportunity to try this exercise in the context of managing change. In Chapter 9, there are several creative and lateral thinking exercises that will enhance your ability to envision and scenario-map the future. In these chapters, we will also look at some real-life visions that have transformed organizations and the world of business over the last 25 years.

The dark side of leadership

Up to this point, we've focused on the qualities, attributes, characteristics and skills of what can be broadly described as 'good leaders': men and women who add value to the organizations they lead, and have a positive effect on the people they work with. In doing this, we've identified several components of the leadership/management jigsaw puzzle. However, there is of course a dark side to leadership, and most people will encounter not only incompetent leaders during their careers, but also individuals in positions of power who enjoy undermining, bullying or intimidating their staff. Bullying can range from sexual harassment to more subtle behaviours, such as imposing unrealistic deadlines and unpaid overtime on employees, or constant criticism and sarcasm. An example of this kind of leader is Jonathan Shier, who was dismissed from the Australian Broadcasting Corporation in December 2001. Soon after his appointment in 1999, Shier was given the nickname 'Satan' by his employees and was described by his staff as, 'insulting', 'arrogant' and 'a bully' (Bachelard, 2001). People who behave in this manner have been described as having 'toxic' personalities, and their toxicity can have a damaging effect on the health, well-being and performance of those people who are unfortunate enough to encounter them.

How can we spot potential bullies and toxic personalities? According to psychologists, they will exhibit most of the following traits: impatience, arrogance, perfectionism, defensiveness, rigidity, bluntness and a large capacity for holding grudges. People who are tyrants and bullies in adulthood became little tyrants and bullies during their formative years. While a detailed discussion of exactly how this happens is beyond the scope of this book, many childhood bullies do evolve into cunning and manipulative adults. They are likely to have high IQs, but use this entirely for their own ends and their own self-aggrandizement. They have little empathy with other people and any decisions they make are driven by one consideration, 'What's in this for me?' They will use an autocratic management style with their subordinates, but behave compliantly towards their superiors. They will often lack a sense of humour, and take themselves and their own opinions *very* seriously. They may also be what psychologists have called 'Type A' personalities, who are very prone to occupational stress and burnout (see Chapter 2). Outside work, they are more likely to engage in domestic violence against their partners when compared to non-toxic personalities (Murray, 2000). People with deeply toxic personalities can affect people in a similar fashion to the evil Dementors in the popular *Harry Potter* series, who 'glory in decay and despair, and drain peace, hope and happiness out of the air around them', and – literally – eat people's souls (Rowling, 1999: 140).[6]

Some toxic personalities may become fully-fledged psychopaths. In a widely publicized research project on 105 psychopaths in Scottish jails in 1996, the British psychologist Lisa Marshall revealed that politicians and stockbrokers share many of the characteristics of criminal psychopaths. The only difference is that career high-flyers (a category that includes people in business) usually manage to stay within the law or at least not get caught. To be labelled 'psychopathic', an individual needs to display ten out of 16 psychopathological tendencies. These are selfishness, callousness, remorseless use of others, lying, cunning, failure to accept responsibility for actions, extreme egotism, extreme sense of self-worth, emotional instability, anti-social tendencies, need for constant stimulation, behavioural and emotional problems in childhood, juvenile delinquency, irresponsibility, unrealistic long-term goals and a sexually deviant or promiscuous life-style (Bennetto, 1996). Politicians, throughout the world, seem to be particularly prone to fraud and corruption and the financial and sexual temptations that come with high office. In the UK, for example, one of the reasons why the Conservatives were thrown out of office in 1997 was the widespread perception among the public that too many Tory MPs were sleazy, corrupt and sexually deviant.

In 2001, one of the shining lights of the Tory Party, Jeffrey Archer, was jailed for four years for perverting the course of justice in a 1987 libel case where he was accused of paying off a prostitute whose 'services' he had used. During his trial it was revealed that he had tried to cover up this indiscretion with a bribe, and had bullied his secretary into making false entries in his diary in order to provide an alibi for his whereabouts at the time. He also had to pay back the £500 000 damages awarded at the first trial in 1987. It was alleged at the time, by his ex-mistress, that Archer routinely used the services of prostitutes over a ten-year period, after his wife had refused him 'marital privileges'. Archer faced further police investigations in 2002 over the 'disappearance' of £12 million from an aid fund called, with supreme irony, 'Simple Truth'. Despite warnings from public officials who tried to remind politicians that Archer had also been declared a bankrupt in the 1970s, £10 million was donated to the fund by the Conservative administration. He was described at the time by the British psychologist

Adrian Furnham as having many of the characteristics of a psychopath (Leppard and Chittenden, 2001; *The Sunday Times*, 2001).

In an ideal world, toxic personalities would all herd together into their own organizations where they could play out the manipulative mind and power games that their damaged psyches seem to crave. Unfortunately, like an unwelcome virus, they seem to have spread themselves around almost all organizations. As Alistair Mant observed more than two decades ago, there is a disturbing number of toxic leaders and managers, 'who seem to survive and flourish, spewing their neuroses all about them right to the bitter end' (Mant, 1983: 5). They also appear to be particularly attracted to careers in politics, the law, finance and stockbroking or get-rich-quick scams and, in a few cases, even managing to juggle two or three of these at the same time (an issue we will return to in Chapter 12).

> Something is wrong with – what shall we call it? Wall Street, Big Business. We'll call it Big Money. Something has been wrong with it for a long time, at least a decade, maybe more. I don't fully understand it. I can't imagine it's this simple: a new generation of moral and ethical zeroes rose to run Big Money over the past decade, and nobody quite noticed that they were genuinely bad people who were running the system into the ground. Those who invested in and placed faith in Global Crossing, Enron, Tyco or Worldcom have been cheated and fooled by individuals whose selfishness seems so outsized, so huge, that it seems less human and flawed than weird and puzzling. Did they think they would get away with accounting scams forever? Did they think they'd never get caught? We should study who these men are – they are still all men – and try to learn how they rationalised their actions, how they excused their decisions, and how they thought about the people they were cheating. I mention this because I've been wondering if we are witnessing the emergence of a new pathology: White Collar Big Money Psychopath.
> (*Abridged from Peggy Noonan,* The Wall Street Journal On-Line, *1 July 2002*)

Toxic behaviour can cause significant problems in any workplace. It may result in lower morale and work performance as well as increased absenteeism, and possible legal costs associated with handling workplace bullying claims. In one survey, it was estimated that workplace bullying claims cost one Australian state, Victoria, $A26 million a year. Ray Catanzarita, a senior partner in the law firm Clayton Utz, made these comments at the time: 'Examining the figures independently has highlighted the significant costs of bullying in the workplace. Aside from the immense financial cost, bullying can result in severe emotional and even psychological damage. With this point in mind, it may be timely to consider national standards to provide employers and employees with guidance on how to prevent, or at least minimise, workplace bullying. Violence and bullying are undesirable in any workplace, and any measure which may facilitate their reduction is a step in the right direction' (abridged from Catanzarita, 2002). This suggests that a technique that is often used in selection and recruitment, psychometric testing, should be employed with anyone who applies for leadership or senior management positions in organizations. Perhaps this could also be extended to anyone who stands for elected public office, although this practice might impose impossible demands on the already overstretched psychiatric health resources of industrialized democratic countries.

Leaders who engage in unethical behaviour, who bully and intimidate other people or who discriminate against other people, on the basis of gender or race for example, are psychologically and behaviourally dysfunctional. Their obsession with money, status, power and control is often the source of their ultimate downfall, although a sizeable number of these people do get away with it. Nevertheless, this does have important implications for how we can deal with these characters (a topic we will return to in Chapter 7). The good news is that, if you are reading this book, it is highly unlikely that you are this type of leader or manager. You are likely to be someone who is regarded as a good 'corporate citizen', who is conscientious, altruistic and courteous to other people. You probably subscribe to the suggestion made by Peter Drucker many years ago, that leadership is not only about doing the right things but also about doing things in the right way (Drucker, 1966). You also realize that the kind of conduct described above is, by far, the most ineffective and unproductive way of leading and managing people at work.

With these thoughts in mind, let's now turn to look at what kind of leader you would like to become in the future.

Exercise 1.3

What kind of leaders do you admire?

Below you will find a list of qualities, attributes and competencies that have been associated with business leaders and organizational leadership. Take a few minutes to reflect on these, and then circle the five that you would consider to be essential characteristics of a leader you would *willingly* follow in the future.

Good communication skills	Competent	Caring
Visionary/forward-looking	Credible	Ambitious
Equitable/fair-minded	Honest	Dependable
Rational	Motivational/inspirational	Decisive
Self-motivated	Humorous	Intelligent
Imaginative/creative	Logical	Experienced
Loyal	Supportive	Mature
Brave	Powerful	Charismatic

Before looking at the results of the two surveys below, please note your first five selections here

Your top five:

1.

2.

3.

4.

5.

Source: Adapted from Kouzes and Posner (1997). ◆

Now, please compare your choices with the following two surveys.

Professor Barry Posner, Australian Institute of Management Leadership Conference, Hyatt Regency Hotel, Perth, Western Australia, 10 March 2004

'What do you admire in a leader that you would willingly follow?'

Honesty / integrity
Competence / credibility
Forward-looking / visionary
Inspiring / motivational
Fair-minded / equitable
(Communication that appeals to people's hearts, hopes and dreams*)

* Communication was included in the 'inspirational' category

Source: based on Posner's surveys of 220 000 managers and leaders worldwide over a 15-year period.

Graduate School of Management, Perth, Western Australia, Master of Business Administration Leadership Seminars 1997–2003

'What do followers want from their leaders?'

Honesty and integrity
Competence / credibility
Inspiration and motivation
Creates direction / vision
Good two-way communication skills

Parity and equity
(Another desired quality that often appeared in the top six was a good
sense of humour)

Source: summary results from 15 seminars on leadership, attended by 478 MBA
students, 1997–2003.

It is also noticeable how often these leadership qualities appear in the
repertoire of admired fictional leaders. On a cultural and symbolic
level it appears that all normal people respond in a very positive way
to leaders who exhibit these qualities and characteristics. To illustrate
this point, here are two well-known examples of such leaders.

**Leadership qualities of Professor Albus Dumbledore, Headmaster of
Hogwart's School for Wizards and Witches**

Honesty and integrity
Competent and credible
Inspirational and motivational
Brave and decisive
Good communication skills
Fair and equitable
(Sense of humour)

Source: the first five *Harry Potter* books.

**Leadership qualities of Jean-Luc Picard, Captain of the Starship
Enterprise**

Honesty and integrity
Competent and credible
Inspirational and motivational
Brave and decisive
Good communication skills
Fair and equitable
(Sense of humour)

Source: many enjoyable hours watching *Star Trek: The New Generation*.

A similar exercise can be carried out with some of the principal characters in Tolkien's trilogy, *The Lord of the Rings*. A comparison of these
preferred and admired leadership qualities, attributes and characteristics is presented in Table 1.2.

Table 1.2   Desired leadership qualities compared

Posner	GSM MBA Students	Dumbledore	Picard
Honesty and integrity	Honesty and integrity	Honesty and integrity	Honesty and integrity
Competence and	Competent and	Competent and	Competent and
Forward-looking/ visionary	Creates direction/vision	Brave and decisive	Brave and decisive
Inspiring/motivational	Inspiration and motivation	Inspirational	Inspirational
Communication that appeals to people's hearts, hopes and dreams	Good two-way communication skills	Good communication skills	Good communication skills
Fair-minded/equitable (Sense of humour?)	Parity and equity (Sense of humour)	Fair and equitable (Sense of humour)	Fair and equitable (Sense of humour)

How did your choices compare with the above? At this stage in our journey, it doesn't matter if they are different. However, it is worth reflecting for a few minutes about *why* these desired leadership attributes appear again and again, in academic research, in leadership and management development workshops, in seminars with MBA students, in fictional contexts and in the real world. If we look in more detail at these desired qualities, attributes and characteristics, the leaders/ managers that most people *want* to follow demonstrate the following.

Honesty and integrity

The word 'honesty' comes from the Latin *honestas*, meaning 'quality' or 'honour', and 'integrity' is derived from *integra*, meaning 'wholeness'. These are almost always identified as the most important leadership qualities whenever this exercise is used with MBAs, or with groups of managers in leadership workshops. This indicates that almost all managers and professionals have great respect for leaders who do not engage in Machiavellian political games, and who exude professional trust, integrity, empathy and reliability. These leaders do not make promises they cannot keep, and do not break their promises once they have been made (see Chapters 3, 4, 7 and 12).

Competence and credibility

Not surprisingly, these are highly valued leadership attributes, and are often associated with industry-relevant experience, practical business knowledge, intelligence and dynamism. There is little doubt that followers do respond more positively to leaders who they believe have 'clout', who possess 'smarts', who can represent the best interests of their followers, who are able to make difficult and important decisions and see their ideas through to execution (see Chapter 8).

Inspiration and motivation

Often ranked as the most important attribute of good leaders by many MBAs is a willingness to treat their followers as intelligent, creative human beings who will contribute more to any organization, given the right encouragement, opportunities and rewards. To be more accurate, this ability is actually a consequence of an understanding of how not to *demotivate* one's followers (see Chapters 3–5).

Vision/sense of direction for the future

To be visionary requires an ability to be creative, innovative and adaptable to change, combined with a high capacity for learning (see Chapters 8–11). This also implies the ability to make brave decisions when followers are uncertain, vacillating or full of doubt. Human beings will respond to these capabilities in the same way as they have done for millennia, because they still want to be shown a way, a road or a path to the future by leaders they trust and respect.

Good communication skills

These invariably appear in managers' selections of desirable leadership attributes. This complex cluster of skills and competencies includes a capacity to listen actively, knowing how to appeal to hearts as well as minds, the ability to build relationships through dialogue, to communicate with everyone in a direct and personal way, and a capacity to walk the talk and lead by example (see Chapters 3 and 8).

Equity/parity

This is an attribute of leaders who treat all their followers fairly, equitably and with respect, and do not create in-groups of favourites. They do not make prejudicial judgments about people on the basis of their ethnicity, culture, race, gender, sexual orientation or physical abilities. When they do make judgments about other people, these are made on the basis of their character, values, abilities, work performance and the tangible contributions they make to their organizations (see Chapters 4 and 6).

A sense of humour

The German sociologist Max Weber once described charisma as being 'the joker in the pack', in his pioneering work on the growth and characteristics of bureaucratic organizations in western industrialized nations (Gerth and Wright-Mills, 1977: 245–8). The real joker in the pack these days is probably a significant and often overlooked attribute of effective leaders: a good sense of humour (GSOH).

Why could a GSOH be an important leadership/management attribute, and why might followers respond positively to this? When you have some free time, browse through the hundreds of job advertisements for senior managers and business leaders that appear in your local newspapers. You'll be struck by the very high calibre of senior staff that companies seek to attract. Frequent references are made to the need for 'exceptional communication skills', 'enhanced ability to lead teams', 'the ability to motivate and mentor staff', 'highly developed people management skills', 'exceptional leadership abilities' and so forth. One might reasonably conclude from this that public and private sector organizations throughout the world are crammed full of leaders and managers who exhibit these admirable qualities. But are they? Try this quick test: get a piece of paper and write down the names of ten senior managers or leaders whom you have worked under that possess the positive attributes, qualities, characteristics and skills identified in this section. Almost all job advertisements are very predictable, repetitive, stale shopping lists of ideal competencies and qualities that seem to have little connection with the characteristics that some recruits actually exhibit once appointed. One has to search very hard to find advertisements like the Roc Oil Company advert in 1997, that ended with the memorable line, 'Doom merchants, office politicians and prima donnas need not apply for these positions', or the Apple Computer advertisements that sought 'Raging, inexorable, thunder-lizard evangelists' to work for them during the late 1980s. Remarkably, one essential factor missing from every single job advertisement I've ever seen is, 'Having a good sense of humour'.

'Humour' comes from the Latin word, *umor*, meaning 'fluidity' or 'flexibility', and has been the subject of academic research since the mid-19th century (Spencer's *The Physiology of Laughter*, 1860). Contemporary research indicates that this is an overlooked leadership/management attribute, even though it would appear to be common sense that it should be an important part of leadership. For example, evidence presented at the British Psychological Society's Annual Conference in January 1999 indicated that staff give far greater credence to humour in their senior managers than they do to intelligence and are more productive than staff who work for humourless managers (Forster, 2000a). A survey by the Business Council of Australia and the Australian Chamber of Commerce and

Industry of 53 medium and large businesses revealed that employers are looking for certain personal attributes in addition to technical job skills these days. These included positive self-esteem, a balanced attitude to work and family life, excellent communication skills, motivation, enthusiasm, commitment and, above all, a sense of humour (Stock, 2002). This indicates that an important quality for aspiring leaders to acquire is a good sense of humour. It may not be essential for effective leadership, but it definitely helps. Why? Because all humans are born with a hard-wired capacity to laugh, even those who may appear to be humourless. Babies start to smile after a few weeks, and laugh at three to four months. All normal people become hard- and soft-wired to respond to humour and fun. According to the ancient Greeks, 'Laughter is the language of the Gods', and if we can infuse our leadership style with some humour, we will get a positive response from almost all of our followers (Bushell, 2002). As Brian Tracy has observed,

> At almost any time, you can measure how well you are doing in your personal and work relationships by one simple test: laughter. How much two people, or a family laugh together is the surest single measure of how well things are going. When relationships are truly happy, people laugh a lot. When a relationship turns sour, the very first thing that goes is the laughter. This is true for companies as well. High performing, high profit organizations are those in which people laugh and joke together. They enjoy one another and their work. They function smoothly and happily as teams. They are more optimistic, more open to new ideas, more creative and more flexible. I used to think that people were an important part of any business. Then I learnt a great truth: people are the business.
> (*Tracy, 1995: 3*)

Intuition tells us that a sense of humour is an important but often overlooked personal attribute of effective leaders. Humorous people often have the desirable leadership attributes described in this chapter in abundance, because they are usually psychologically healthy, don't take themselves too seriously and have a real interest in other people. Humorous people are often good to work with and laughter is one of the best on-the-job stress relievers we know about (see Chapter 2). In almost all circumstances, humour can be used to defuse tensions and conflicts. According to the godfather of lateral thinking, Edward de Bono, humour is also closely linked to creative and innovative abilities, a suggestion we will return to in Chapter 9. In contrast, humourless people often have overbearing egos, are unable to listen to others and are toxic to some extent. So, if you are already a leader, why not ask job candidates to tell a few jokes or cite instances when they have used humour to diffuse tense or difficult situations at work? This approach may well help in the process of sorting the 'doom merchants, office politicians and prima donnas' from the people you really want to hire and work with.

Furthermore, some companies have built the concept of fun into their organizational cultures. These include the SAS Institute (the largest privately owned software company in the world), Scandia, Cisco Systems, Southwest Airlines, Google, Deloittes and Diageo (formerly Guinness UDV). At Google HQ, The Googleplex, more than 230 employees work within an organizational culture that 'pampers' their employees and encourages fun:

> The prevailing mood of Silicon Valley's hottest company is similar to that of a classroom full of teenagers. People whisper jokes to each other and there are frequent interruptions of laughter. One could scoff at the [exercise] balls or dismiss the lava lamps as juvenile. But when it certainly doesn't harm production innovation, or popularity, what difference does it make? You may as well pull up a ball, sit down and realise that in five years every boardroom in the world will have its own set of big plastic balls and a ping-pong table. It's a fun-loving crowd. They really enjoy life and are very enthusiastic about being around one another. They spend a lot of time there when they're not working.
> (*Abridged from Bouleware, 2002*)

In Deloittes, the culture is based around seven core values, 'Recruit and retain the best, talk straight, empower and trust, continuously grow and improve, aim to be famous, think globally, and have fun and celebrate.' In the UK company Diageo, 'Celebrations and social events are a key part of the culture. It attempts to foster happiness at work, believing that it is essential for the workplace to be filled with fun and good humour for everyone.' The Australian divisions of these two companies were ranked in the top 30 'Best companies to work for in Australia', during 2002 (Corporate Research Foundation, 2003: 64, 74).

Southwest Airlines (SA), selected by *Fortune* as 'The best company in the USA to work for' in 1998, has a number of core values underpinning its people management policies. The first two are 'Work should be fun . . . it can be play . . . enjoy it' and 'Work is important . . . but don't spoil it with seriousness'. As O'Reilly and Pfeffer observe, 'Part of taking care of employees at Southwest entails an emphasis on having fun at work. Humour is a core value and part of the Southwest style and spirit' (2000: 32). One of Herb Kelleher's first actions, after he became chairman of the company in 1978, was to order the personnel department to hire people with a sense of humour. Southwest pilots and flight attendants were encouraged to make safety and other announcements fun, and to be creative in the process.

Passengers have been greeted by attendants dressed as leprechauns on St Patrick's Day, and have had safety instructions delivered in the form of a stand-up comedy. This philosophy of fun gradually pervaded the entire company. Despite what more traditional managers might think, there was genuine method to this apparent madness. In 1982, when

Kelleher took over the airline, it had 27 planes, 2000 staff, high labour turnover and low morale, and revenues of $US270 million. By 2001, it had 344 planes, 30 000 loyal and motivated staff, very low levels of labour turnover, and revenues of $US5 billion. Another interesting feature of SA is that, while it has always had a highly unionized workforce, it suffered far fewer industrial disputes than its major competitors during the 1990s and early 2000s. By the time he stepped down as CEO in 2001, Kelleher had created a unique and fun-loving culture, in an airline that employees wanted to work for and customers wanted to fly with (see Bloomsbury, 2002: 1105). The way it manages its people also played a significant role in this success. As Frank Perez, the baggage handling supervisor at Mineta Jose Airport, commented in early May 2003, 'This company is 100 per cent for its employees. That's what makes it really sweet' (cited by KRT, 2003). In January 1999, Kenneth Hain of *Incentive* magazine summarized what motivated the relatively underpaid employees of Southwest to perform so well in a single word, 'happiness' (cited by O'Reilly and Pfeffer, 2000: 34).

The foundations Kelleher laid down stood SA in very good stead during the global meltdown of the world's airline industry during 2002–3. While almost every airline in the world struggled during this period (and several went under), SA's performance was nothing short of remarkable. During 2001–2, SA was the only top ten US airline company to post a profit, and many other airlines were desperately trying to get their operating expenses in line with SA. With more than 2700 daily flights to 58 cities in the USA, SA became the sixth-largest airline company in the USA during 2003 (in terms of passengers carried). It was also declared the best performing US stock of the last decade by *Money* magazine in December 2002.

In conclusion, these examples indicate that, while humour and fun alone will never create a great company or high-performing employees, they can be powerful tools for leaders and managers to employ at work.[7] We will return to the power of humour and laughter again in Chapter 2, in the context of stress management and in Chapter 9, in the context of creativity and innovation.

> When people feel good, they work at their best. Feeling good lubricates mental efficiency, making people better at understanding information and using decision rules in complex judgments as well as more flexible in their thinking. Upbeat moods, research verifies, make people view others – or events – in a more positive light. That in turn helps people feel more optimistic about their ability to achieve a goal, enhances creativity and decision-making skills and predisposes people to be helpful. Moreover, research on humour at work reveals that a well-timed joke or playful laughter can stimulate creativity, open lines of communication, enhance a sense of connection and trust and, of course, make work more fun . . . Small

wonder that playfulness holds a prominent place in the tool kit of emotionally intelligent leaders.
(*Goleman et al.*, The New Leaders, 2002)

Against the assault of laughter, nothing can stand.
(*Mark Twain*)

Summary: the qualities and characteristics of successful leader/managers

In this chapter, it has been demonstrated that we may have some
psychological predispositions that influence the kind of leader/
managers we are, and the styles of people management that we habitually use. However, what is more important is that we are *aware* of
these, because self-awareness is the necessary precursor to personal
change, learning and self-improvement. This can also help us to be
more sensitive to the kinds of organizational environments where our
individual leadership styles will work most effectively. If you are
someone who often has the feeling that somehow you don't 'fit in', it
may be that you are not being completely honest with yourself about
the job, career or dreams that you *really* want to pursue (see Chapter 2).
So the starting point for becoming an effective leader/manager of
others is true self-awareness, and the ability to understand and reflect
on how others see us. The Scottish poet, Robbie Burns, described this
simple fact of human existence more than two hundred years ago in
this way: 'If only we could see ourselves as others see us, it would from
many a calamity save us.'

Long before Burns's time, the ancients understood the importance of
self-awareness. For example, one of the two axioms carved over the
entrance to the temple of the Greek god Apollo at Delphi, on the side
of Mount Olympus, is 'Know Thyself' (the other being, 'Nothing Too
Much'). Although our ancestors have understood the importance of
this for millennia, most people still take years to achieve this and some
never achieve true self-awareness. Today, there are a number of techniques that can be used to find out more about ourselves and how
others see us. These include 360° feedback, upward performance
appraisals by subordinates, psycho-drama, psychological testing
procedures administered by suitably accredited chartered psychologists, and utilizing gestalt (event) psychology techniques. Subsequent
chapters include some of these to help enhance self-awareness and,
thereby, our understanding of leadership and people management.[8]

Authentic leadership begins with self-awareness and knowing yourself
deeply. Self-awareness is not a trait you are born with but a capacity you

develop throughout your lifetime. It's your understanding of your strengths and weaknesses, your purpose in life, your values and motivations and how and why you respond to situations in a particular way. It requires a great deal of introspection and the ability to internalise feedback from others. No one is born a leader; we have to consciously develop into the leader we want to become.
(*William George, former Chairman and CEO of Medtronic, 2004*)

Because they are self-aware, effective leaders understand their physical and psychological limits, and are able to cope well with pressure and uncertainty. They have a child-like curiosity and enthusiasm for novelty, learning and change. They do not blame others for their mistakes and they learn from these. They are fairly smart, have some emotional intelligence and are very adaptable. Great leaders never rest on their laurels. Whatever success they achieve is in fact the main reason why they change, because they know that organizational leadership today is a race without a finishing line. They do not have a fixed, rigid leadership repertoire, and can adapt as circumstances change. They have some knowledge of the art of political statecraft, combined with high ethical standards. They also recognize that leadership, at times, can be a lonely experience and that being *respected* is more important than being *liked*.

They know that it is impossible to lead in isolation, and they understand how to connect emotionally with their followers. Because they are able to inspire and empower their followers, they do not waste unnecessary time 'managing' people in an inefficient command-and-control fashion. They are genuinely interested in unleashing the full potential of their employees. As a result, they are not simply task-focused, and expend a considerable amount of time and energy creating work cultures that enable their staff to run with the ball themselves and perform to the best of their abilities. They are exceptional communicators, because they know that, if people don't believe the messenger, they won't believe the message. So they communicate frequently and with credibility, and they listen to their employees, acting as a prism and focal point for their ideas and suggestions. They walk the talk and practise what they preach, and if they make promises to their followers, they deliver on these.

Successful leaders are also risk-taking professionals who are visionary and innovative as well as good planners, educators and team-builders. They are people who may not know everything but who are adept at surrounding themselves with people who know what they don't. They can see the future, create directions and/or visions for the future and are able to lead their followers down new ways, roads, paths or journeys. In new or fast-growing companies they do not need to rely on formal positional power and are comfortable leading decentralized, opaque and virtual organizations. They are truly internationalist in outlook, and comfortable with cultural and gender diversity in their workplaces. They often have a good sense of humour and don't take themselves too seriously. They may sometimes be regarded as charismatic but, as we have seen, this is not an essential prerequisite for successful leadership and people management. Last, all the evidence from history, academic research and the practices of real-life leaders show us that the best leaders, throughout history, have been able to do a number of fairly simple things simultaneously, but (and this is the really crucial point) *they perform them well and consistently, even in difficult situations or under crisis conditions.*

One question remains to be addressed in this opening chapter. Is there anything new to learn about leadership and people management that our ancestors haven't already known about for centuries? More than 2300 years ago, the Greek philosopher Aristotle suggested that prospective leaders – having acquired self-awareness and wisdom – needed to develop three additional clusters of competencies: *ethos*: the ability to convince their followers that they were trustworthy, reliable and fair, *pathos*: the ability to appeal to their followers' values, emotions and motivations, and *logos*: knowledge and expertise. This indicates that the core attributes of effective leaders have been understood for a very long time. Of course, there have been significant changes over the last two hundred years that have influenced the way that leadership and people management are now understood and exercised. These include the impact of industrialization, the emergence of democratic political systems and the decline of the old aristocratic order, the inexorable spread of globalization, the widespread uptake of new technologies, the rapid pace of change in organizations and the impact of the advances that women have made in many different professions and organizations in more recent times. Nevertheless, the ancient leadership attributes described by Aristotle are as relevant today as they have always been.

In addition, as noted in the Preface, becoming a really effective leader/manager requires the development of an eclectic, and evolutionary, personal 'tool-kit' that encompasses technical, creative, leadership and people management skills. One example of this kind of leader is David Lilenthal. He rose from humble origins to be an energy adviser to every US president from Roosevelt in the 1930s to Jimmy Carter in the 1970s. He was also the head of the US Atomic Energy Commission for many years, and an early pioneer of interactive communication media. He was often cited by Jerry Levin, former CEO of Time Warner-AOL, as an influential leadership role model. Lilenthal believed that 'The manager–leader of the future should combine in one personality the robust realistic quality of the man of action, with the insight of the artist, the religious leader, the poet who explains man to himself. The man of action alone or the man of contemplation alone will not be enough; these two qualities together are required' (cited by Charan, 1998).

In a similar vein, Robert Goizueta (Coca-Cola), Jack Welch (General Electric), Alfred Sloan (General Motors), Sam Walton (Wal-Mart), Bill Marriot (Marriot Hotels), Bill Hewlett and Dave Packard (HP), Akio Morita (Sony) and Konosuke Matsushita (Matsushita) are widely regarded as being among the greatest business leaders of the 20th century.[9] What qualities and characteristics did they share? They were curious about the world and lifelong learners. They paid attention to their people, realizing that they really were the most important assets that their companies possessed. They all had superb practical business acumen and were tough and pragmatic, but always had one imaginative and visionary eye looking towards the future. They constantly experimented with new business and people management techniques without becoming reactive 'fad-surfers'. They all led from the front, always led by example and were men of both action and contemplation. They were able to inspire their followers to achieve great things. All, by the standards of their day, operated within clear ethical and moral codes. If we can develop some of these qualities, then we can truly start to make things happen in new and exciting ways. And, as we saw earlier, regardless of any genetic predispositions we may have inherited from our parents, most people can enhance their leadership and people management skills, given self-belief, time, motivation and commitment. The remainder of the book will look in greater depth at the qualities, attributes, skills and competencies of successful leader/managers identified in this opening chapter.

Leaders should have clean hands, warm hearts and cool minds.
(*Sarros and Butchatsky*, Leadership and Values, *1999*)

Exercise 1.4

Before turning to Chapter 2, please look back at the answers that you gave to the questions at the beginning of this chapter. Have any of these changed? If they have, what might be learnt from this? Then think about how you can now translate any new insights you have acquired into your day-to-day leadership and management practices. Select the five that you consider to be the most important, and then think of strategies to implement these in your workplace over the next few weeks.

At this stage, it really doesn't matter if you have difficulties with the strategies part of this exercise (and these will change and evolve over time). You can return to these when you have read through subsequent chapters of the book. Don't be in a hurry. *Allow time for new ideas to sink in and take effect*. This will not happen overnight.

Insight	**Strategy to implement this**
1.	
2.	
3.	
4.	
5.	◆

Notes

1   Paradigm is derived from the Greek word *paradeigma*, meaning 'model' or 'pattern' (OED website, 2002). The concept of paradigms was first articulated in modern times in Thomas Kuhn's groundbreaking book, *The Structure of Scientific Revolutions*, published in 1962. Over the next 20 years, this word gradually became used to describe radical or revolutionary changes in organizations and business, and in many other contexts to describe accepted ways of behaving and/or dominant modes of thinking.

2   For further information on the power of emotional intelligence as a potential people management tool in the workplace, please refer to Appendix 1.

3   For further insights into the role of coaching and sports leadership in business settings, take a look at David Parkin *et al.*'s 1999 book, *Perform – or Else!*

4   'For decades, the rich and powerful opposed': the abolition of slavery, sanitation and the provision of clean public water, basic universal health care, universal education, banning the employment of children in factories, basic health and safety legislation in workplaces, pensions, the vote for women, equal pay legislation and many, many other innovations that we now take for granted.
'Can you name the computer company?': Rank-Xerox.

5   The company is Microsoft, back in 1979. If you look at the bottom left of this old photograph, you'll spot a youthful Bill Gates. Many younger employees at companies such as IBM and Rank-Xerox jumped ship to join Microsoft and Apple at this time.

6   Rather closer to home, many of the traits of real-life toxic leaders can be found in the fictional character of David Brent, manager of Wernham-Hogg, in the comedy series, *The Office* (BBC Productions, 2002–3). For more on this wonderful take on work and dysfunctional management, visit www.bbc.co.uk/comedy/theoffice.

7   In common with other life-skills, this too can be developed. Perhaps you are someone who believes that you can never remember jokes. In fact, anyone can remember jokes if they want to and are willing to make the time and effort to learn them. As with all skill acquisition, the earliest part of the learning process is the hardest. Write down and remember good jokes and one-liners from other people. The more we do this, the more we fire up and start utilizing neglected neurons in the right hemisphere of our brains, and we will then start to remember jokes more easily. We can also learn to spice up dull, drab presentations by using humorous stories, anecdotes, jokes and one-liners (see Chapter 3 for some tips on this). The more we do these things, the

more our SOH will grow, as thousands of underutilized neurons and synapses in our brains are fired up and put into use.

8   For more information on the role of self-awareness in developing leadership capabilities, please refer to Daniel Goleman, Richard Boyatzis and Anne Mckee (2002), *The New Leaders: Transforming the Art of Leadership into the Science of Results*.

9   An omission from this chapter is, of course, some discussion of the emergence of the first large cohort of women business leaders during the 1980s and 1990s. This important development is addressed in Chapter 6.

2 Personal performance and stress management

Objectives

To define and describe stress.

To describe the nature and causes of occupational stress, and its positive and negative effects.

To identify practical strategies for dealing with work pressure and occupational stress, and offer suggestions for becoming one of the energized 'corporate athletes' identified in Chapter 1.

Exercise 2.1

Recognizing the symptoms of stress

Before reading through this chapter, please answer the following questions as honestly as possible. There are no 'right' or 'wrong' answers and first-response answers are best.

	Infrequently	Sometimes	Frequently
Do you:			
Feel that you have too much work to do?	1	2	3
Have too many tasks or projects on the go at the same time?	1	2	3
Get irritated or impatient when dealing with colleagues?	1	2	3
Get angry with other people at work?	1	2	3

	Infrequently	Sometimes	Frequently
Feel that work takes up too much time?	1	2	3
Have to waste time dealing with subordinates' errors or mistakes?	1	2	3
Take your work home with you at night?	1	2	3
Find that your work and family responsibilities conflict?	1	2	3
Feel unable to spend as much time with your family as you would like to?	1	2	3
Suffer from insomnia?	1	2	3
Suffer from extreme changes of mood?	1	2	3
'Comfort eat' to relieve stress?	1	2	3
Use recreational drugs (e.g. alcohol) to relieve or escape from stress?	1	2	3
Take part in competitive sports to relieve stress*	1	2	3

When you have completed this, please add up your total score _____

Interpreting your score

1–18: You do not suffer from significant levels of occupational stress and can skip this chapter for now if you wish.

19–30: You suffer, to some extent, from occupational stress and may benefit from reading though this chapter.

31–42: You are experiencing above average levels of occupational stress, and this may be affecting your health, work performance and personal relationships. You should find some time to read through this chapter, particularly the sections that deal with personal stress management strategies.

*This may appear to be an odd item to include here. Why might these activities not help in reducing stress levels? ◆

Introduction: occupational stress in context

Towards the end of Chapter 1, we noted that effective leader/ managers are aware of their physical and psychological thresholds. Consequently, they are able to cope well with pressure, multiple job tasks and occupational stress, and can maintain a good balance between the competing demands they face at work and in their personal lives. While there are continuing debates about defining and measuring stress, it is defined here as a natural human response to environmental challenges (stressors) that place physical or psychological demands and pressures on an individual. In 1946, the medical researcher Hans Selye first used this term (derived from the Latin *stringere*, meaning 'to stretch') in the context of how human beings respond to external threats from the environment (Selye, 1974). He described this process as the fight-or-flight response, and this played an essential role in the survival of our earliest ancestors. This primordial survival reaction kick-started a series of pre-programmed responses to an external threat or series of threats. Confronted by a wild animal or some other danger, our ancient ancestors had two options: to stay and fight or to flee. In order to accomplish either of these goals, a series of rapid biochemical changes occurred in the body. These included a strong rush of adrenalin, producing increased arousal, energy and aggression. When under stress, all humans and mammals produce a cascade of hormones, starting in the hypothalamus of the brain, running through the pituitary gland beneath and ending in the adrenal gland above the kidneys. In turn, these biochemical changes trigger further physiological, psychological and behavioural changes, which are described below.

Our hominid ancestors became programmed over hundreds of thousands of years to respond in this way to external threats, and the modern human nervous system still responds to environmental stressors in this essentially stone-age manner (Asterita, 1985). However, while these responses have real benefits in true emergencies or life-threatening situations, they have the potential to cause widespread physical and psychological damage, and in most work settings a fight-or-flight response is obviously not appropriate. To respond to a stressful event by physically attacking a superior or running away to hide, literally or psychologically, can cause significant problems. Hence, while the adaptive value of the fight–flight response in situations of great danger is obvious, the benefit of this reaction to the psychological stresses of modern life is of questionable value. Some researchers have even suggested that this evolutionary response that helped our ancestors deal with threatening situations may have become 'a modern-day self-destruct mechanism' (Driskell, 1996).

Four types of stress have been identified: hypostress, eustress, distress and hyperstress. In order to perform, at any level, individuals need to experience *some* stress. If not, they experience 'rust-out' (hypostress). People experiencing optimum levels of stress (eustress) often describe this as 'being in the zone', where their stress levels help them to cope well with the external environment, without being overwhelmed. This type of stress is pleasant and stimulates performance. The third type, distress, results from being continually overstressed and will lead, in time, to reduced personal health, well-being and performance and, potentially, complete burnout (hyperstress). Hence, if people routinely talk about 'being stressed' in a negative way they are mistaken, because some stress is essential. To experience some stress means that you are functioning as a normal human being, to experience no stress means that you are asleep, comatose or dead. In fact, as we will see, the real problem is not stress itself but how we interpret it, how we habitually react to it and our ability to recover from it.

Researchers have also documented at least 30 potential stressors at work. These include lack of organizational direction and purpose; poor leadership; role ambiguity; role conflict; poor working conditions and ergonomics; trivial bureaucratic rules; organizational politics; lack of resources; favouritism; inequitable pay and rewards; obstacles to career development; lack of promotional opportunities; work overload and underload; interpersonal conflicts; communication breakdowns; racial, sexual, disability and age discrimination; 'toxic' behaviour; bullying; coping with continual change and new technologies; downsizing and mergers; job moves and relocations; increasing job insecurity; and growing conflicts between work and home lives. These stressors all have one thing in common: they create the *potential* for distress when individuals perceive them as representing demands that exceed their ability to respond and cope (Cooper, 1997, 1999).

A large body of research, conducted in the UK, the USA and other countries, confirms the popular belief that occupational stress was becoming a more significant problem in all western industrialized countries during the last two decades of the 20th century (for example, Forster and Still, 2002; Cooper, 1997, 1999). This increase in reported levels of occupational stress has been generated by a number of factors that have had an impact on organizations over the last 20 years, including the following:

- Fast organizational and technological change, leading to increased job complexity and intensity in all industrial, commercial and service sectors.

- Corporate collapses, rationalization, mergers, downsizing and large-scale redundancies, leading to increasing job insecurity, and the phasing out of the old commitment to 'jobs for life' in almost all organizations.
- Labour market restructuring and deregulation, and reforms to industrial relations and employment legislation.
- New demands on public sector employees, resulting from the privatization and/or deregulation of publicly owned organizations.
- Increasing 'toxicity' in some workplaces, caused by fears of the threat of redundancy or uncertainties about employment security, and the emergence of 'machismo' management styles in downsized organizations.
- Across-the-board increases in the average hours worked by many employees, particularly in white-collar occupations.
- Increasing spillover between work and non-work, resulting from increasing numbers of women entering the workforce and the emergence of larger numbers of dual-career couples.
- New pressures on employees caused by the current transition from industrial economies to 'Third Wave' high-tech and knowledge-based economies.
- Growing pressures on all domestic organizations, arising from the increasingly competitive nature of local, regional and overseas markets, and the globalization of trade and commerce.

You may also recall the 1990s movie, *Multiplicity*, staring Michael Keaton. This told the story of a self-employed builder who was unable to cope with all the competing demands of his work and family life. He was offered the chance to solve his difficulties by cloning himself into a variety of permutations of his original self, with increasingly comic results. There have also been several recent TV series, in a number of countries, which have extolled the benefits of returning to simpler, less cluttered lifestyles. In Australia, one of the most popular ABC series of the late 1990s was *Sea Change*. The storyline revolved around the main character's decision to turn her back on a high-pressure legal practice in Sydney, and move herself and her children to what she hoped would be a simpler and less stressful life in a small community on the coast. These TV series and *Multiplicity* captured the mood of the times, and the growing belief that both work and personal life were becoming increasingly stressful in the 1990s.

Furthermore, it is not coincidental that many of the words and phrases now associated with occupational stress are of recent origin. These include *workaholic* (1968), *work/family conflicts* (1970), *the three-o'clock syndrome* (1980), *information overload* (1985), *time-squeeze* (1990), *presenteeism* (1993), *squeezing the pips* (1995), *death by email* (1995), *technostress*

(1995), *time poverty* (1997), *hurry sickness* (1999), *work-addiction* (2001), *leisure sickness* (2002) and *downshifting* (2003). There has also been a steady growth in manifestations of various types of 'rage', including *road rage, retail rage, bar rage, techno rage, desk rage, spam rage* and *telephone rage*. We now have 24-hour supermarkets, 24-hour gyms, 24-hour restaurants and, in the USA, 24-hour nurseries, all reinforcing the impression that modern life has indeed become more complex, pressurized and time-deficient in recent years.

The links between occupational stress and personal performance

In order that people may be happy in their work, these three things are needed: they must be fit for it; they must not do too much of it and they must have a sense of success in it.
(*John Ruskin, author and social commentator, 1851*)

Health is so necessary to all the duties, as well as the pleasures of life, that the crime of squandering it is equal to the folly.
(*Samuel Johnson, diarist, author and social commentator, 17th century*)

Measuring the impact of stress on individuals, and its organizational costs and consequences, remains the subject of continuing debate among researchers. Some sceptics have referred to stress as a 'weasel word', or as a generic concept that has become a meaningless catch-all word used to 'explain' the negative effects that present-day work and family pressures can have on people. A few researchers have suggested that the connection between stressors and their impact on individuals is mythical, arguing that many of the causes and effects grouped under the broad heading of 'stress' should be separated into more specific relationships. It is true to say that the enormous range of possible causes of stress, the variety of personal responses to stress, combined with the intricate task of separating other influencing factors in the workplace, all make a simple assessment of cause and effect less than straightforward. In the past, this may have led some researchers to infer simplistic correlations between the consequences of occupational stress (such as high blood pressure or insomnia) and a stressor (such as overwork), without making sufficient allowance for other potential influencing factors, such as personality differences or lifestyle factors (Briner and Reynolds, 1999). However, while there may be some methodological problems associated with measuring the precise effects and consequences of occupational stress, a balanced reading of this literature leads to just one logical conclusion. There is a considerable body of research, accumulated over two decades by psychologists, epidemiologists, and health and medical researchers, which shows that occupational stress has become a significant occupational health issue, one that has measurable physiological and psychological effects on employees, as well as negative knock-on effects for the organizations that employ them. Consequently, several general conclusions can be drawn from research on occupational stress over the last 20 years.

First, the incidence of occupational stress increased dramatically during the 1980s and 1990s, and its direct and indirect costs are rising year by year in all industrialized countries. Worldwide country–national data indicate that a large proportion of working people now routinely exhibit symptoms of occupational distress. There has been a steady rise in the average number of hours worked per week by most managerial employees and an increase in their work-loads – in intensity, complexity and duration. For example, the percentage of Australian professional and managerial employees working more than 50 hours a week rose from 22 per cent in 1983 to 29 per cent in 2003 (ACTU and The Australian Centre for Industrial Relations Research and Training, 2003). Second, there has been a marked increase in stress-related illnesses in all industrialized countries throughout the world. In the USA, the National Institute for Occupational Safety and the American Psychological Association estimate that the national cost of stress is about $US500 billion a year (Carlopio *et al.*, 2001: 114), with similar pro rata figures being reported in the UK and Australia. It has been estimated that two-thirds of visits to family doctors in the USA, the UK and Australia are attributable to stress-related illnesses (Robbins *et al.*, 2001: 276). Third, there has also been an increase in stress-related compensation claims in all industrialized countries during the 1990s. Stress-related litigation, already widespread in the UK and the USA, has the potential to become the single largest proportion of workers' compensation claims in these countries during this decade. In some countries, the growth in stress-related illnesses is imposing further demands, strains and costs on already overstretched and underresourced national health systems (Forster and Still, 2002; Maguire, 2001; Sternberg, 2000; Tabakoff, 1999; Cooper, 1996a, 1996b, 1997, 1999; ACTU and The Australian Centre for Industrial Relations Research and Training, 1999; Beehr, 1995).

Fourth, in some occupations levels of stress have reached epidemic proportions. For example, one study in 1998 reported that 45 per cent of Australia's army officers were suffering stress-related symptoms that were sufficiently serious to warrant psychological counselling. The report described these officers as 'psychological time-bombs'. Similar findings were reported in the 2000 Defence Green Paper (Anonymous, 2000). Over the last decade, several studies in the UK and Australia have revealed that young hospital doctors routinely

work more than 100 hours a week and regularly work 24-hour shifts –
without a break. It was alleged that these work hours, described by the
Australian Medical Association as being 'dangerously long', would
lead to patient deaths because of poor decisions made by fatigued
doctors (Mitchell, 2000; Taylor, 2000).

Fifth, research in the USA, the UK and Australia reveals that stress has
a number of negative effects on employees and organizations. The
health of employees experiencing occupational stress declines over
time, resulting in poorer work performance. They are more likely to be
involved in accidents at work, are more likely to be absent from their
jobs and will be less productive when at work. There can be other
outcomes, including physical effects such as insomnia, higher cholesterol levels, increased blood pressure, heart disease and heart attacks,
and psychological effects such as lowered self-esteem, increased anger
and anxiety, greater marital problems and an increased likelihood of
drug and alcohol abuse (Carlopio *et al.*, 2001:115–19). Studies in the
USA have found that employees who work more than 48 hours per
week double their chance of developing heart disease. In a few cases,
this can lead to complete psychological burnout and even death
(Tobler, 2002; Jex, 1998). Organizations exhibiting high systemic stress
levels suffer from increased rates of staff turnover and reduced staff
loyalty, and may also incur additional costs when replacing employees
who have succumbed to stress-related illnesses or who claim unfair
dismissal. Organizations that exhibit sustained and high levels of stress
are likely to show more signs of toxic behaviour amongst their employees and bullying of staff (Bachelard, 1999). There are also indications
that suicide rates in the corporate world are increasing because of
increased workplace pressure and uncertainty. In Japan, *Karoshi*
('death from overwork') claims at least 10 000 lives a year (Petersen,
2000; Kageyame, 1998).

There have also been some more bizarre indications of the effects of
occupational stress. Evidence from Brazil, for example, indicates that
the stress caused by fear of impending job losses and redundancies had
actually shrunk the size of some male penises by an average of two
centimeters. The worst affected groups were professional and white-
collar workers (cited in *The Australian*, 10 October 1998). Conversely,
there is some evidence that women have begun to experience more
'male' stress symptoms, such as hair loss, as a result of 'testosterone
overload'. Women, having taken on an increasing number of traditionally male roles in the workplace, have adopted more aggressive and
competitive working styles. In turn, this has made them more sensitive
to the male hormone testosterone, with consequent thinning of their
hair and even baldness (Norton, 1997).

The effects of occupational stress

One of the problems with distress is that its negative effects can start to take hold before people start to recognize that this is happening. It may take a crisis in an individual's life to trigger the realization that something is going wrong, such as an extremely negative performance appraisal, being avoided by colleagues at work, extreme weight gain, alcohol or drug abuse, being shunned by friends, the collapse of a relationship or children having behavioural problems. Warning signs that may indicate the existence of significant levels of distress include the following:

- losing your sense of humour or *joie de vivre*,
- losing concentration or experiencing memory losses,
- having more difficulties solving problems or making decisions at work,
- feeling that you always have too much work to do or failing to meet work deadlines,
- increasing level of complaints from customers or clients that you deal with,
- becoming more irritable or aggressive with the people you work with,
- wondering why you bother doing your current job,
- constantly taking work home,
- feeling that you are losing control over your life,
- becoming aware that friends seem to be avoiding you,
- increasing tension or arguments with your partner, spouse or children,
- abusing alcohol, smoking or using recreational drugs,
- regularly chewing or biting your fingernails,
- waking up tired and/or suffering from insomnia,
- using sleeping tablets on a regular basis,
- not caring about your appearance,
- binge eating or putting on weight,
- loss of libido and sexual drive,

People experiencing more than a third of these symptoms may be starting to suffer from the effects of occupational distress and should consider developing strategies to deal with these. If they ignore them, the situation may worsen. Research has shown that, once 'activated', the human stress response goes through three distinct phases.

An alarm phase

The sympathetic nervous system gives the body an 'all stations' alarm. This is an emergency response and can only endure for a few hours at

most. The heart will start to beat faster to pump blood to supply more
energy, particularly to the muscles. This also forces the body to pump
stress hormones, such as adrenaline, cholesterol and cortisol, into the
bloodstream creating a burst of energy and arousal.

A resistance phase
This is where the body tries to adjust itself to the stress. At this stage,
a lot of energy is burnt up just coping with the attempt to function
normally. Managers may become aware of feelings of tiredness, a
lowered sense of well-being and experience more difficulties with
decision making.

An exhaustion phase
If fight–flight responses occur frequently, over a period of time the
body's defence mechanisms will start to weaken. At this point, an
individual may develop physical symptoms such as fatigue,
headaches and insomnia, and psychological symptoms such as impatience and aggression. Over extended periods, they may then develop
medical problems, such as a weakened immune system, high blood
pressure and psychological changes such as depression.

High levels of distress have the potential to affect all three major
sub-systems of an individual's physiology: the central and peripheral nervous systems, the endocrine system (which deals with
hormonal balances in the body) and the immune system, the body's
defence against external infections. High and sustained levels of
stress levels also cause cortisol to be pumped into the bloodstream.
Over time, this steadily weakens the human immune system, and
reduces the body's ability to fight off the production of cancer cells
(Sternberg, 2000).

Sustained distress and exhaustion phases can then lead to the following:

- Reduced higher-order brain functioning, leading to lower cognitive
  and creative functioning abilities. The fight–flight response effectively shuts down an individual's higher-order and creative faculties until the threat has passed.
- Greater intolerance of ambiguity and uncertainty, leading to an
  inability to cope with 'fuzzy' situations.
- Reduced ability to deal with complex problems, slower decision-
  making capabilities and an increased chance of making mistakes at
  work.
- Greater anger, impatience and hostility towards others.

- A reduced ability to manage time, leading to the classic 'headless-chicken' mode of polyphasia (trying to do too many things at once). This means that tasks may not be completed on time, and the emergence of a self-perpetuating vicious circle with an increasing number of tasks to complete in less and less time.
- Insomnia, and even more stress as a result of feeling perpetually tired, but not being able to sleep well and recover at night.

In summary, distress can have a number of negative effects. These range from minor problems, such as fatigue, insomnia and irritability, to full-blown depression. Some consequences, such as poorer concentration, forgetfulness, mental blocks and lowered attention span, may also be cognitive. Other effects of stress can include greater risk of accidents, alcohol and drug abuse and explosive temper losses. Increased occupational stress may also have an impact on marital relationships. In some cases, sustained exposure to high levels of distress can lead to complete psychological burnout. In a few extreme cases, severe distress can eventually kill people (Lazarus, 1999; Levi *et al.*, 1998; Levi, 1984; Toates, 1995; Asterita, 1985; Staw *et al.*, 1981; Selye, 1974).

Personality and stress

While stress can have generic effects on people, individual differences have a major influence on the way people react to and cope with stress. Consequently, stressors do affect people in very different ways. For example, at the British Psychological Society's conference in London in December 1999, researchers reported that stress levels amongst men shopping with their partners or wives were as high as those of fighter pilots and policemen – *in action*. In contrast, their partners/wives reported experiencing optimum levels of stress during these 'shopping episodes'. A survey of European police forces, conducted in 1996, revealed that one-quarter of UK police personnel reported being 'highly stressed' because of the pressures of their work, the nature of the people they dealt with, conflicting work demands and very long working hours. The survey also looked at Swedish anti-terrorist police personnel. They too reported being 'highly stressed', but this was caused by a lack of work (Forster and Still, 2002: 12). Before reading the next section, please complete Exercise 2.2.

Exercise 2.2

Personality and stress

Please read through the statements below. Then, on the 1–5 scale, rate which of the two statements best describes how you behave at work and how you use your leisure time. There are no 'right' or 'wrong' answers and first-response answers are best.

I'm easy-going and get on well with people at work	1	2	3	4	5	I often find myself in conflict with people at work
I usually feel in control at work	1	2	3	4	5	I am usually hyperactive and feel rushed at work
I'm not confrontational and prefer cooperation to competition	1	2	3	4	5	I like confrontation and am very competitive
I do things one at a time	1	2	3	4	5	I regularly take on multiple tasks or projects
I'm a good listener, and enjoy hearing other people's views and opinions	1	2	3	4	5	I find it difficult to listen to other people without wanting to finish their sentences for them
I'm usually calm and placid at work	1	2	3	4	5	I can often get frustrated and angry at work
I'm able to focus on a few work goals at a time	1	2	3	4	5	I often seem to have too many things to do at once
I find it easy to relax and unwind or simply do nothing	1	2	3	4	5	I find it hard to relax and unwind, and dislike having nothing to do
I have other interests outside work	1	2	3	4	5	I am mainly interested in my work
I always make sure that I can spend quality time with my family regardless of work commitments	1	2	3	4	5	I often find that I can't spend time with my family because of work commitments

Please add up your total score _____

Interpreting your score

10–20:   You have many characteristics of the Type B and Hardy personalities.
21–30:   You have many characteristics of the Type B and Hardy personalities, with a few Type A traits.
31–40:   You have several characteristics of the Type A personality, with a few Type B and Hardy traits
41–50:   You have many characteristics of the Type A personality.

Please note that these scores are indicative only.

Source: adapted from Friedman and Rosenman (1974). ◆

Pure 'Type A' personalities never seem to have enough hours in the day and often have poor time-management skills. They usually feel rushed and under pressure. They are often very competitive, ambitious and impatient. They often exhibit polyphasic behaviour, and are sometimes described as 'hot reactors'. They may have underdeveloped interpersonal skills and be toxic in their dealings with fellow employees. They talk fast and find it difficult to listen to others. Consequently, they often interrupt other people during conversations and like to finish their sentences for them. Feelings, emotions or self-disclosure play no part in their management style and they believe that they have to 'kick butts' or 'bang heads' to get results from employees. They may have few interests outside work and find it hard to relax and simply 'be'. There is a sub-set of the Type A, the 'Type D' personality, who is aggressive, gets angry quickly and is humourless and exploitative. While many Type A personalities would attribute their success to many of these traits (and these are often associated with 'macho' management styles), it is precisely because they thrive on aggression, arousal and competition with others that they are unable to develop resiliency to stress. This personality type is also more prone to stress--related illnesses and heart attacks when compared to Type B personalities.

At the other extreme are pure 'Type B' personalities. They are much more easy-going, monophasic (focused on one task at a time) and better time managers. While they may be ambitious, they are less overtly competitive than Type As. They rarely feel rushed, even when under pressure. They are better delegators and people managers. They speak slowly and enjoy listening to other people. They have interests outside work. Type B personalities may also have some of the characteristics of what psychologists have described as 'Hardy Personalities'. Such personalities have a high internal locus of control. This means that they believe that they are in control of their lives, and are not the victims of external events beyond their influence. The belief that one is in control of events is closely linked to high self-esteem and, in turn, this is associated with high levels of self-motivation. They have a positive sense of involvement with others in social situations. They have a tendency to perceive or welcome major changes in life with interest, curiosity and optimism. They like to learn, and have a child-like enthusiasm and curiosity for new things (Friedman and Rosenman, 1974).

An individual with high levels of hardiness is not overwhelmed by challenging or difficult situations. Unlike 'outer-directed' personalities, they don't blame others for misfortunes in their lives. They cope with these and learn from their mistakes. They always maintain a positive attitude, no matter what setbacks they encounter, and think of these as challenges to be conquered and overcome. They are often socially and emotionally intelligent, two important leadership qualities. They also have high levels of self-efficacy, the belief that they can cope well with novel and uncertain situations. As a result, their resilience to stress, in even the most difficult circumstances, is considerably above the average. They are likely to have a good sense of humour, and know how to relax and enjoy themselves outside work. While this may look like an impressive list of personal attributes, the good news is that many of these can be learnt and enhanced if we choose to do this. How this can be achieved is described in the next section.

Strategies for coping with occupational stress

As if mirroring the rapid growth in occupational stress over the last two decades, a growing number of self-help books on personal performance, well-being, hardiness, resilience and stress management appeared in bookshops in the late 1990s and early 2000s (see, for example, Warren and Toll, 1997). On 14 May 2000, the two best-selling books in Australia were *Don't Sweat the Small Stuff*, by Richard Carlson, and *Calm for Life*, by Paul Wilson. The latter author, who described himself in his younger days as being 'tense, angry and aggressive', had sold more than 2.4 million copies of his first book, *The Little Book of Calm*, worldwide (Slattery, 1998). Originating in the USA in the late 1990s, there has also been a rapid growth in on-line counselling services for people who are either uncomfortable talking face to face about their problems or who are just too busy to visit therapists in person during work hours (Hamilton, 1999). While we cannot change our core personalities, occupational and clinical psychologists believe that successful stress management can be achieved by actively changing our behaviours and/or attitudes. There are many personal performance and stress coping strategies that can be employed by individuals, and while their benefits can be substantial it can take some time for these to take effect. These include adjusting personal attitudes and outlook on life, better time management, exercise, improving diet and nutrition, promoting deep sleep, meditation, yoga and relaxation, balancing home and family commitments and owning pets. A discussion of these now follows.

Living the life you have imagined

> You are a disciple, a follower of your own deep values and their source. And you have the will and the integrity to subordinate your feelings, your impulses, to those values.
> (*Steven Covey*, Seven Habits of Highly Effective People, *1989*)

In Chapter 1, it was suggested that the starting point on the journey to becoming a successful and effective leader/manager is self-awareness. This means that we have to be quite honest with ourselves about patterns of behaviour in the past that may have led us to suffer from occupational stress now, or whether it is our choice of job, career or organization that is the root cause of the problems we are encountering at this moment in time.

Exercise 2.3

What do you care passionately about?

What would you like to achieve over the next 20 years?

Will the job/profession that you are now in enable you to achieve your ambitions?

On a scale of 1 (hate it) to 10 (love it and couldn't be happier), rate how much you like your current job/profession.

If you scored seven or less, are you in the job/profession or career that you *really* want to be in? If not, why?

If you are unhappy with your job/profession, why do you stay in it? What's holding you back?

What would your ideal job/profession be and how could you achieve this? ◆

Answering questions like these, setting personal objectives and creating action plans to achieve these is nothing new, but many successful leaders have spent time doing this, rather than allowing circumstances, or other people, to dictate the goals they pursue in life (Covey,

1989). Generally speaking, people who feel that they have no control over their lives suffer more from stress than those who believe that they are in control of their destinies. It's also important to recognize that we are in our current jobs/professions, *because we decided to be in them*. No one else made this decision for us. Each one of us has the freedom to get out of these – if we want to – and move to jobs or professions that give us more control, intrinsic rewards and enjoyment, although we may have to work very hard to make this transition, particularly if we decide to change careers or set up our own businesses. But if you feel that your life lacks direction, or if you often dream about doing something else, it could be time to reappraise why you are stuck in a rut, or why you persist with a job you don't enjoy. You might also want to visit websites that can help you to focus on ways of finding more fulfilling work and personal lives (see, for example, www.passionmaps.com). You've only got one life and, unless you are religious, it is not a rehearsal for something else. As the 19th-century writer and traveller Henry David Thoreau put it with simple elegance, 'Go in the direction of your dreams. Live the life you have imagined.' An example of someone who did just this is described below.

Charlie's story
When I first got to Perth in 1997, I thought I'd landed on my feet with the nice beaches, great weather, the restaurants, as well as a good secure job at one of the best schools in WA. But then, having done the MBA, I realized (by Easter 1999) that I really wanted more than teaching was providing. It was a really strong feeling, something inside me saying, 'I really, really don't want to continue in teaching any more.' I think it was the fact that there was really no challenge and it was the security and safety of it all that I found scary. It was stagnant and nothing much was going to change. I'd also probably got as far as I could in career terms at that time. At times, the frustrations of the job literally drove me to tears. I was stuck in a rut and thought that there had to be something more. Doing the MBA certainly contributed to my dissatisfaction with teaching. You could see how great companies operated and you learnt how companies got started and grew into successful enterprises. I thought, 'I can do this.' I don't want to sound arrogant, but I was confident that I could do something else, something *different*. I really had no idea at the time what that something was and at one stage thought I'd continue with teaching, but maybe set up a small business on the side and see how it went. So let's say that I was definitely open to a change in my life and a change of career at that time.

I talked with Lisa [Charlie's wife] about not wanting to continue in teaching, during a holiday at Easter 1999, and she was fantastically supportive as always, and she basically said, 'Well don't then.' That certainly helped me in the decision I took to leave teaching. Initially, I thought about getting into consultancy but it didn't really turn me on even though it had some parallels with teaching. So it had to be a business idea, something original and something exciting. Soon after, Nick Streuli [co-founder and director of aussiehome.com] rang me on that historic night in May 1999, when Lisa and I had been on stage with Barry Humphries, and suggested the idea that was eventually to turn into aussiehome.com. We'd discussed the frustrations and annoyances of buying properties in Perth when we first met on the MBA and Nick's basic idea was, 'Why don't we put Perth properties on a website?'

We did quite a lot of reconnaissance and weren't that impressed with what we saw out there. So that was the genesis of the idea and two years on aussiehome.com is a successful and respected company that is moving in the right direction, although we all know that we've still got a very long way to go. I knew it was a gamble. It was a real risk with both me and Lisa giving up secure jobs but, deep down, I knew that we had to go for it. In a weird way, it would have been an even bigger gamble to stay in teaching, in terms of my well-being and personal development and the lack of challenges and frustrations of that job. And, looking back, the first year was really tough, just after the dotcom crash, and at times we really struggled. Setting up and running your own business is fantastically rewarding but it can also be very stressful. There were sleepless nights, disappointments, mistakes and setbacks, but all of these have actually made us a better company. We were able to learn from our mistakes and spot new opportunities. As a result, we've moved into new areas that we had never even envisaged at the beginning, such as producing magazines and creating websites for other businesses. By getting out there, being nimble, learning fast and providing a great service we're succeeding.

For what it's worth, my advice to anyone who feels stuck in a rut or hates the job they're doing, there's a whole world of opportunities out there. Life doesn't have to be what you're in now. You just have to get out there and look, talk to people who've done it and just give it a go. I'd add this though. Do your research. Nick and I treated this like an MBA project. We did a tremendous amount of background work; we discussed our ideas with GSM professors and other business people over a period of about seven months. We did this without a safety net, but we were also confident that we had a great idea, a sound business plan and, of course, enough investors to back us up. So my suggestion to anyone who's thinking about a radical change like this is *just try it*.

Follow your dreams and instincts. Even if it hadn't worked for us at least I'd tried it and I could have gone back to teaching, and would have been a better teacher as a result. I'm happier and more energized, and although there are frustrations I never experience the same kind of frustrations that I had in teaching. The rewards, even in the tough times, have been fantastic. I've got that motivation, that feeling if I work hard I get to see the results directly and feel that I'm really achieving something worthwhile. It's been fantastic and it's been a 'rush'.
(*Extracts from an interview with Charlie Gunningham, Perth, Western Australia, 15 March 2002.*)

Aussiehome is one of the few e-companies that have been successful in the aftermath of the 2001 dotcom collapse, and is now expanding into Melbourne and Singapore. The company has also received several awards for innovation and e-business, with Charlie receiving a personal prize in the Western Australia '40 under 40' competition for young entrepreneurs and small businesses in 2003.

Of course, you may enjoy your current job and be broadly satisfied with your choice of profession, but still find that there are situations at work that always seem to cause stress. Why does this happen? Do certain kinds of people or particular individuals always stress you out? Do you experience something called the 'stuck-record', where the same people and the same situations regularly cause problems? Why? If you find that you are having personality clashes with people at work, remember that you cannot *ever* change their personalities. You may be able to change their behaviour and, over time, their attitudes, but this can be very difficult. So what you really have to focus on now is changing *how you react and respond* to people and situations like these. Perhaps you may also need to think about how you might be affecting other people. Do you cause stress in other people? What are the consequences of this for *your* stress levels? How well do you know your staff as individuals? Are you aware of the pressures they face, at work and home? Are you sympathetic to their problems? Answering questions like this can help you to start changing the things that cause you and your staff problems, and you'll have an opportunity to do this at the end of the chapter.

One of the basic principles of stress management is that stress is a *reaction*, an outcome of the way people interpret and react to external events. These have no intrinsic meaning in themselves. Hence one person may regard a difficult project as an exciting challenge, while another may look on it as an impossible ordeal. A positive mental outlook can help people to overcome potentially threatening situations and reduce the stressful effect that these situations can cause. Even if you do come into work 'like a bear with a sore bum' or 'with a monk on', try to act in an upbeat manner. Small things really do make a difference. If people ask, 'How are you?' don't say 'Not too bad' or 'Uuh, OK', say 'Good' or 'Excellent' and, don't start moaning or whining about things. Why? Because when has moaning about life ever changed anything or made you or anyone else feel better? So always accentuate the positives, because positive behaviour and attitudes foster positive attitudes in others. Negativity breeds negativity. What we give out, we get back in bucket loads. Enthusiasm and a positive attitude will rub off on your staff, and if they feel good they will perform better. Consciously try this for a few days at work and wait to see what happens.

In Chapter 1, it was suggested that a sense of humour is an important and overlooked leadership attribute. Laughter is good for the body and the mind and reduces anxiety, worry and frustration. It can also boost the immune system by increasing the production of antibodies and white blood cells. This eases stress by lowering the level of stress hormones floating around the body. It also gives the heart a good work out and this too can help in reducing stress levels. One study, published in the *International Journal of Cardiology*, indicated that people with heart disease were significantly less likely to laugh in their daily lives, when compared to people free of heart disease (Ferrari, 2002). Having said this, humour and laughter will only help to some extent in a dysfunctional or highly toxic workplace. What can you do if you are working for a really awful company or organization that treats you, and your colleagues, like mushrooms (kept in the dark and fed on ****)? You should immediately start polishing up your CV and start planning your exit, but continue doing the very best job you can until your next position is assured. The winner of the Telstra Australian Business Woman of the Year in 1998, Dr Penny Flett, gave this advice about coping with these kinds of situations, during a talk to a group of MBAs in April 2000:

> Even if you are working in the worst organization or the worst business in the world, always strive to be excellent in your sphere of influence, and always do the very best you can for the people who work for you. Always be positive and support your people. You will find that, if you leave one organization and move to a better one, many of your best people will want to come and work for you in your new position.

Time management

> You only have to work half a day here. You decide which twelve hours you will work.
> (*Long-standing employee saying at Microsoft*)

The Insomnia Squad.
(*Nickname given to Thomas Edison's hardworking employees at General Electric during the early 1900s*)

These days, few leader/managers are lucky enough not to suffer from time pressures at work, and while some people choose to work long hours very few employees enjoy being workaholics. However, the pace of life in modern organizations means that most people have to cram more and more into the working day. Increasing pressures for greater productivity and efficiency during the 1990s created a phenomenon called 'time poverty', with many professionals having to work twice as hard, with half the resources to produce twice the results of the 1980s. For example, Henry Mintzberg conducted some research in 1973 which showed that, on average, managers had nine to 12 minutes between interruptions from their staff. He repeated the study in 2000 and found that this interval had fallen to five minutes (cited by Frost, 2002). Managers are also routinely bombarded by hundreds of voice messages and emails every week, as well as unsolicited spam-mail. As companies have downsized and their workforces have shrunk, there are even greater pressures on leader/managers' time in most organizations. A culture of remaining at the office, 'presenteeism', has become endemic and well established in many businesses.

As Albert Einstein realized in the early 1900s, time *is* relative and not everyone uses their time or works in the same way. However, as we have seen, if people are put under continual pressure and worked for long hours, their ability to think, make decisions and process information declines, and the number of errors they make increases. Therefore, as leader/managers, it is important that we are able to manage our time at work as effectively as possible, while at the same time not overworking our followers. Time Management (TM) is a well-proven collection of simple but very effective techniques that can help any leader/manager use their time more efficiently each day. TM techniques can be implemented in nine interlinked steps.

Step 1: stretch your targets
Set yourself realistic life-goals. These should be long-term (up to five years), medium-term (one to three years), short-term (one to 12 months) and micro-term (up to one month). Establish milestones along the way for you to achieve your long-term mission and short-term goals. Simple planning like this can have a powerful motivational effect, because it helps us to focus on what we should be spending our time on as well as helping us monitor our progress. Once you've set your career, job and personal goals, it is easier to prioritize, plan for the future and organize your time more efficiently. Always keep your ultimate objectives and

goals in mind and review and update these at regular intervals. Aim for small wins rather than trying to conquer the universe in one go. Exercise 2.2 can be used to review your personal goals and objectives in life on a regular basis.

Step 2: take one bite at a time

Effective leaders decide early what tasks they need to accomplish and then allocate specific blocks of time to achieve these. Only then do they allow their PAs/secretaries to make other appointments for them (Covey, 1989). So, at the beginning of *every* working week, identify the tasks that are important and the tasks that are urgent. Then allocate time to deal with both the important matters and the urgent ones. If we spend all our time 'fire-fighting', we will have no time to deal with the creative and strategic parts of our jobs (and think what the cost of delaying these 'A' priorities might be). Consider delegating urgent, but unimportant, tasks to your subordinates and ask yourself if there are other minor tasks, that you now deal with, that you could give your junior staff the authority to deal with (discussed further in Chapter 4). It may not always be possible, but try to accomplish at least one substantive task each day. Treat your workload like you are eating an elephant. An elephant is very large, but if you focus on one good bite at a time you will gradually consume it.

Step 3: plan your day – every day

Tackle the toughest and most time-consuming tasks in the morning while you are physically and mentally at your freshest and most alert. Even if you don't always feel this way, your energy and creative levels are at their peak four to five hours after waking up (assuming you have had a good night's sleep). Don't avoid the most important tasks by dealing with trivial jobs. Leave these and other unimportant tasks until later in the day. If you know that you are likely to be interrupted a lot on a given day, schedule several trivial or boring tasks for that day: you may even welcome the interruptions. The 'post-lunch lull' period is a good time for informal chats, but not a good time to give a formal presentation at work. If you have to schedule meetings for lunchtimes, always provide snack food and drinks.

Step 4: blam the spam

A major problem for all white-collar employees these days is information overload, particularly in the form of emails. On 16 June 2003, spam-mail exceeded 50 per cent of all email traffic on the Internet, up from about 8 per cent in 2000 and 40 per cent in 2002 (Ellis, 2003). According to analysts IDC, the total number of emails sent daily will have doubled, from about 30 billion *a day* in 2002 to 60 billion in 2006. Giga Information reported that spam-mail increased fourfold during

2001–2, with some 206 billion junk emails circulating in cyberspace (with an increasing variety of nasty viruses attached to some of these). Some 90 per cent of these originate in the USA. On average, according to the Meta Group, a typical medium-sized company now receives about 20 000 spam-mails each day (cited by Wales, 2002). Brightmail, a spam-fighting software firm, has revealed that about 30 per cent of all email correspondence in US companies in now spam-mail, and the problem is getting worse (Tatum, 2002).[1]

Solutions to this include never responding to emails that request any kind of confidential information, changing code words and/or Internet banking code words at regular intervals, investing in up-to-date heuristic screening software, such as the *Death2Spam* mail server or Cloudmark's *SpamNet* which claim to eliminate 90 per cent of junk emails, being very liberal with the email 'delete' button on your keyboard and blitzing anything that looks remotely suspicious or likely to have a virus attached. If you can, set aside two 30-minute time slots each day to deal with voice and email, and ignore these for the rest of the working day whenever possible.

Step 5: beat the paper jungle
There is a belief that a messy desk or office reflects a disorganized or messy mind. Whether this is true or not is of little importance. What does matter is that piles of paper, memos and reports on the desk generate a feeling of not being up-to-date with your work, and may also force you to think about more than one job at a time. It has also been estimated that some managers waste up to 30 minutes *every day* trying to locate 'lost' papers in their offices (Roydhouse, 2001: 263). A messy office may also create the impression with customers and clients that you are disorganized. If you don't already have one, create an 'in' and 'out' system and maintain a strict regimen to deal with your in-tray on a regular basis. A good idea is a desk-file or a tier of drawers to organize work into urgent and important tasks, tasks that need to be done that week, tasks awaiting further information and so forth. Throw away everything that you know you will do nothing about. After the family dog, a waste-paper basket (or recycling facility) is man and woman's best friend. Periodically, have a ruthless cull of all the outdated memos, redundant reports and other useless pieces of paper you have collected in recent months, and apply the same approach to their electronic equivalents.

Step 6: involve the troops
If you subscribe to the view that 'If you want a job done well, you should do it yourself', it may be time to start delegating more effectively. Focus on the methods and processes your staff use to achieve

their work goals and reschedule tasks according to these. As far as possible agree these goals with your staff; do not impose them and spend time making sure that they fully understand what it is you want them to do. The fewer mistakes your staff make, the less time you will have to spend sorting these out and putting out fires. When you've decided to delegate an assignment, carefully explain what is required and agree a deadline for completion. Then stand back and let them get on with it. Give them a reasonable amount of independence and let them prove their abilities. Try giving more responsibilities to your junior staff. It may be slightly risky, but you might uncover some of their hidden talents (described in more detail in Chapters 3–5). In this context, recall three of the most important lessons we learnt about leadership and people management in Chapter 1: (a) leader/managers cannot lead in isolation, (b) leadership and management are two-way processes and, primarily, social activities, (c) if your followers perform better, you will too.

Step 7: create quality time
Create personal time-spaces or time-outs in the working week to deal with complex or demanding work. This may be difficult in a few occupations or organizations, but it is important that you try to do this. Once your staff understand that you are not available on (say) Tuesday and Thursday mornings, they will get used to this very quickly and work round it. During these periods, switch your phone to 'voice mail only', or transfer it to your secretary and ignore emails. If you regularly have to wait around for other people in your job, take small pieces of work or short articles relevant to your work to fill these dead time periods.

Step 8: you're OK (as long as) I'm OK
This means that we should, as good corporate citizens, try to help staff and colleagues when needed, above and beyond the formal requirements of our jobs (working the odd evening or weekend, for example). We can say 'Yes' when people ask for our help. However, we must also have the strength to say a firm 'No' to unrealistic requests that impose unacceptable demands on ourselves or our families, without feeling guilty about this.

Step 9: minimize time wasting
How much time do you and your colleagues waste in unproductive meetings? How much time do you waste because of a lack of planning and foresight? Do you 'hover' between jobs, leaving tasks unfinished? How much time do you lose checking up on other people and their work? By clarifying goals and prioritizing your work tasks (Steps 1–5) and creating personal time-spaces (Step 6), time wasting should be greatly minimized. Last, but not least, if the phone is ringing constantly

and you are getting annoyed about having your work flow inter-rupted, take a slow deep breath and repeat this short mantra to your-self as you gently pick up the receiver: 'There is someone on the other end of this line who needs my help, support or advice.'

Becoming a better time-manager requires commitment and discipline, and it may take a few weeks to implement these techniques.

Dealing with techno-stress

Readers of this book will be well aware of the way that new technolo-gies have transformed organizations in recent years. However, there are indications that the long-term use of computers and virtual technolo-gies can lead to some physiological and psychological problems. These include repetitive strain injuries, muscle and back problems, tendonitis, eyestrain, blurred vision and e-thrombosis. There is also some evidence that 'cyber-sickness' (a variant of motion sickness) is becoming more widespread amongst employees who spend lengthy periods of time working on PCs or in virtual reality. This manifests itself in headaches, double vision, increased heart rates, dizziness, vertigo, disorientation and even vomiting (Bestos, 2002). To avoid these problems, ensure that your workstation, chair and desk height, and the layout and design of equipment, are all ergonomically sound. If you do have to spend a lot of time at your desk, try to maintain an upright posture (and if you often find yourself in a slumped position, invest in a back support for your chair), keep your elbows close to your body and your lower arms horizontal. Invest in a document holder that keeps current work at eye level, rather than down at one side of your keyboard (this will prevent strain on the neck and spine). Every hour or so, try these simple stretches: look over your shoulders four or five times on either side; roll your shoulder blades around, stretch your wrists and bend them slowly in each direction and stretch your arms above your head. If you have some privacy, lie on your front and do four or five ten-second arm-only press-ups, while keeping your hips pressed to the ground. This will flex your spine in the opposite direction to the one it is often in while you are seated. Every two or three hours take a ten-minute break and walk around. You should try to take regular breaks from PC-based work, get out and about and put some variety into your working day.

Fitness and exercise

In many ways, the human body can be regarded as a machine that requires regular maintenance and upkeep for it to perform well. If it is overworked, or pushed beyond its capabilities, it will eventually break down, sometimes with catastrophic results. Physical conditioning can make a major difference to the way people react to and cope with stress, because fit people cope better with the demands of stress when compared with those who are in poor physical condition. Exercise improves the performance of the nervous, circulatory, endocrine and digestive systems. The heart and lungs work better and are able to pump more oxygen around the body. This increases cardiovascular capacity and strength, and also reduces fatty deposits on the walls of arteries, by increasing haemoglobin and plasma levels in the blood-stream. In turn, this leads to increased psychological well-being, result-ing from the release of 'feel-good' chemicals (such as seratonin and endorphins) in the brain during exercise. These increase brain activity and reduce toxic stress chemicals such as cortisol. Exercise also helps in achieving and maintaining an optimum weight level, thereby reducing the risk of coronary and circulatory diseases.

Regular aerobic exercise – swimming, jogging or cycling three to four times a week – are all good antidotes for stress. Weight training is also becoming more popular, even with mature adults, as a way to main-tain strength, build up the metabolism and maintain lean muscle tissue. This may be the very last thing that you want to do after eight or nine hours at work, but once you get into a routine you will feel more energized and relaxed. You'll also sleep better because of the physical workout that your body has enjoyed and, in turn, this will enhance your ability to recover from the work stressors you have encountered during the day. The hardest thing is getting started and it's a lot easier if you do this with other people, by joining a local sports or cycling club, for example. Once you get into a routine, it becomes second nature and all your bodily systems will work better to power you through the demands of the working day.

However, it should be noted that competitive sports rely to a large extent on the fight–flight reaction, and some psychologists have ques-tioned their efficacy as stress reducers. Also several studies have confirmed that, while regular, moderate exercise boosts the immune system, prolonged bouts of high-intensity, aggressive exercise can dampen it. Certain types of heavy exercise, like marathon running, can even trigger heart-damaging effects including higher levels of blood clotting and inflammation (Callaghan, 2003). If you are not particularly sporty, perhaps try out other activities like dancing or take on some voluntary work in the community. Last, but not least, if you are over 35 you should have a full medical check-up once a year. This may seem excessive, but people over this age become increasingly prone to high blood pressure, increased cholesterol levels and other illnesses.[2]

Becoming a corporate athlete

As noted in Chapter 1, there has been a rapid growth in personal Peak-Performance coaching in recent times. A number of consulting and corporate training businesses now offer busy professionals intensive workshops that embrace a complete range of personal health and fitness issues. Another example of these is the London-based consultancy, Sporting Bodymind. Like WAMCG in Australia and LGE Performance Systems and Inner Quality Management in the USA, this company runs courses that cover issues such as developing a clear sense of individual purpose, endurance, physical strength, self-control, emotional capacity and mental preparation. The purpose of this coaching, in all four companies, is to create leaders that are more self-aware, energized, focused and determined as well as physically and psychologically balanced. The intention is to maintain an optimum balance between energy expenditure and energy renewal. In turn, this should result in leaders who are able to 'coach' their employees more effectively (Loehr and Schwartz, 2001). If you are someone who really is too busy to find the time to learn relaxation techniques or the principles of corporate athleticism, you may want to consider employing one of the growing number of career and life coaches to guide you through these.

Diet and nutrition

A balanced diet, combined with exercise and sleep, has long been considered to be a good way of combating the physical effects of stress. This can be achieved by increasing the amount of complex carbohydrates and fibre in the diet in the form of vegetables, fruits, salads, whole-wheat products, brown rice, fish and cereals. It has been more than 30 years since 'friendly fats' (such as the Omega-3 fats found in seafood) were first identified as key compounds that can lower blood pressure and reduce the chances of heart inflammation and coronary spasms. Many subsequent studies have shown that people who consume four or five meals containing seafood each week reduce their chances of heart attacks by 50 per cent and strokes by 38 per cent (Callaghan, 2002a). Dieticians also recommend cutting back on heavily processed and junk food, as these are often low in nutritional value, contain high levels of sugar and fat and usually contain many additives and preservatives. While sugar tastes good, it also creates energy-depleting spikes in blood glucose and insulin levels. Paradoxically, some recent research suggests that foodstuffs that have long been regarded as taboo by most nutritionists, such as red meat, eggs and saturated fats, actually do little harm if consumed in moderation (McKie, 2002).

Avoiding foods that contain tyramine, which can stimulate the vascular process that leads to headaches (particularly in migraine-susceptible individuals) and caffeine, another food-source that can aggravate stress, can also help in maintaining a healthier physiology. While coffee and, to a lesser extent, tea are useful pick-me-ups, you should try to avoid drinking these to excess during the day, or late at night. They are stimulants and will keep you awake. Also few people know that there are more than one thousand chemicals in a cup of coffee. Only 26 have been laboratory-tested and, of these, half caused cancer in rats (Roydhouse, 2001: 242). Many nutritionists recommend a good breakfast and eating 'mini-meals' five to six times a day, rather than one or two large meals, and drinking about two litres of water each day to replenish fluid levels and to flush out toxins in the bloodstream (Loehr and Schwartz, 2001). You should also try to monitor your weight and maintain this within plus or minus 5 per cent of that recommended for your age and height. Being too thin can also be a sign of distress and, if anorexia or bulimia kicks in, symptomatic of more deep-seated psychological problems.

Last, try to keep within the limit of alcohol consumption recommended by your country's health authorities. In many countries, this is set at 21 units for men and 14 units for women over a week. Even in relatively small quantities, alcohol is fattening, raises blood pressure and affects coordination, reaction times and judgment. Taken in large quantities it can lead to serious physical and psychological health problems. These include heart disease, gastritis, obesity, cirrhosis of the liver, loss of libido, reduced fertility, memory loss, dementia and damage to the central nervous system, as well as its attendant negative effects on relationships and family life. But, if you do fancy several tipples once in a while, remember the old adage, 'the darker the drink, the darker you'll feel in the morning'.

Relaxation

If you routinely toss and turn at night, count sheep, find your mind buzzing like a stuck vinyl record with thoughts about work, or wake up tired and bad-tempered after a poor night's sleep, you're not alone. It's been estimated that as many as 30 per cent of the adult population of industrialized countries have difficulties sleeping at night (Gleick, 1999). Good, restful deep sleep is vital, because it is the time when worn out body cells are replaced by new ones and brain cells become rejuvenated, ready to cope with the challenges of another busy day at work. There is also evidence that sleep is essential for memory consolidation and enhancement (Nader, 2003). A few people, like Albert

Einstein and Winston Churchill, survived on as little as four hours a night but, for most people, six to seven hours is essential for good health. So, even if you are worn out and stressed after a hard day at work, a good night's rest will revive your energy levels and creative capacities.[3]

Relaxation is a very useful method of promoting good sleep habits and reducing the impact of occupational stress. Simply sitting in a quiet place for just five to ten minutes, eyes closed, focusing on one's breathing and the different muscle groups in the body, starting from the forehead and going down to the toes, can assist in the elimination of tension and stress. If you spend a lot of time slumped over the old Japanese piano at work, you might find a back support useful or, every hour or so, stretch your back, legs and arms for two to three minutes. A constantly slumped posture creates tension all over the body and this will stay with you for hours unless you deal with it. If you still feel back pain or tension, consult a qualified osteopath or physiotherapist.

In addition to this, yoga and other traditional forms of relaxation have been used for thousands of years to relax both the body and mind, and their popularity in the west is growing exponentially (Miraudo, 2002). These techniques help individuals to develop an enhanced ability to 'switch-off' from work, a deeper understanding of themselves, and more energy and tolerance when dealing with the dysfunctional or toxic behaviours of others at work. Relaxation techniques also encourage the production of the body's natural 'happy drug', seratonin, an important modulator of emotions. The positive emotions these engender have been shown to dampen down the autonomic nervous system, which sends messages from the brain to the heart. This governs involuntary stress actions such as sweating and shallow breathing (two early signs of distress). Relaxation also allows time for self-reflection. As we have already seen, this is an important part of successful leadership, because it allows you to reflect not only on *what* you are doing at work but also *how* you are doing it. It can also help with problem solving. How many times have you noticed that a solution to a problem 'comes' to you when you weren't thinking consciously about it, while in the shower or out jogging? Relaxation allows the unconscious mind freedom to operate, and encourages more communication between the logical left hemisphere and the creative right hemisphere of the brain.

There are two quick stress-reduction techniques that can also be used at work. The first involves just two fingers and one thumb. If you find yourself in a situation where you suddenly find that most destructive of emotions, anger, emerging and there's a real risk of you losing it, simply squeeze your thumbs and two index fingers together *as hard as you can and focus your anger there*, while you take three deep slow breaths. As you breathe out for the third time, release your fingers and let the anger out through your fingertips. The second technique involves five steps. If you feel your stress levels rising, or a toxic individual is really starting to get to you . . . STOP! Just smile to yourself, unclench and relax your jaw very gently and breathe more slowly and deeply. Drop your shoulders and sit upright (but not in a defensive 'slouch-back' or an offensive 'sit-forward' position). Let your body become still and relax your arms and shoulders. Only when you've calmed down should you respond (how to then move forward in these tense situations is described in Chapters 3 and 7).

At first sight, these techniques may appear to be rather simple, but they are based on sound science. Psychologists have identified an emotional state called 'the refractory period' (Ekman, 2003). This often accompanies surges of emotion when both memory and thinking enter a kind of tunnel, when we literally lose mental access to information that might mitigate this reaction. Our thinking during these moments of closed attention draws on and misuses memories that sustain and justify the emotion, while at the same time shutting down our higher-order cognitive processing abilities (think, for example, of occasions when you've got emotional and/or angry with other people and later on, when you've calmed down, have thought to yourself, 'If only I'd said . . .'). By *channelling* this anger and emotion elsewhere, it then becomes possible to calm down and respond in a more positive and adult way.

In summary, these relaxation, stress-diffusion and mind/body techniques all have their uses, but their efficacy really does depend on the personality of the individual, their current level of fitness and health, their personal circumstances and the nature and specific demands of their jobs. The purpose of all of these, to repeat a sporting analogy used earlier, is to put people 'in the zone', going with the flow and feeling energized. The human mind, in a very simple sense, is like a complex muscle and if we overuse it it will become strained, less effective and, eventually, will break down. However, if we are willing to spend some time developing stress fitness and stress-management techniques that change our behaviour and mental attitudes, anyone can become a more effective corporate athlete within a relatively short period of time.

Tapes, pills, potions, lotions and pets

In a separate category there are a great variety of alternative therapies which, it is claimed, can help with distress. These include audiotapes and CDs, produced by hypnotists and hypnotherapists, that can be played at night, to help with relaxation, sleeping and positive 'guided-imagery'. Others claim that reflexology, acupuncture and homeopathy can be effective in reducing stress levels. Some people believe that relaxing, deep aromatherapy massages (kinesiology or shiatsu), every few weeks, also serve to diffuse tension and release psychic toxins from the body. There is also a mind-boggling array of alternative drugs, herbal remedies, salves, pills, nutritional supplements, linctuses, oils, potions and lotions now available, that also claim to relieve stress symptoms. While natural health products now represent a multi-billion dollar industry worldwide, and many people do believe in alternative therapies, there is almost no peer-reviewed scientific evidence to show that *any* of these actually work, although they may have some short-term placebo effects (Diamond, 2001).[4] Almost all occupational psychologists and medical researchers believe that stress can only be managed through the active behavioural and attitudinal changes described in this chapter. If you can't remove them – which is true of most stressors in life – then the only option is to learn how to become physically and psychologically resilient to their effects.

Last, humans have known for centuries about the therapeutic benefits of owning pets, and recent research has shown that this can reduce blood pressure and stress levels, and even alleviate depression. Four studies, presented at the American Heart Association conference in May 2002, revealed that owning a pet lowers blood pressure, reduces the risk of heart disease and improves people's abilities to cope in stressful situations. One study of 48 New York stockbrokers, who were all on high blood pressure medication, showed that those who owned a dog or cat performed far better when confronted with stressful situations. Furthermore, the effectiveness of their heart medication also seemed to improve. Another study showed that dog and cat owners who had experienced heart attacks were significantly less likely to die in the following 12 months when compared to those who did not own a pet. For those living alone, the effects of pet ownership seem to be particularly beneficial (Callaghan 2002b).[5]

Work and family life

Imagine life is a game, in which you are juggling balls in the air. You name them work, family, health, friends and spirit and you are keeping them all in the air. You will soon understand that work is a rubber ball. If you drop it, it will bounce back. But the other four balls – family, health, friends and spirit – are made of glass.
(*Brian Dyson, former CEO of Coca-Cola Enterprises Australia, 1999*)

Earlier in this chapter it was suggested that setting personal life goals could have a significant impact on people's ability to realize their ambitions and achieve their dreams, and that most studies on personal achievement show that well-being and happiness can flow from the realization of these goals. However, other studies have shown that gaining material and/or career success alone tends to offer only a brief afterglow of contentment. People who value these goals above all else tend to be less satisfied with their lives and less contented, compared to those who have never lusted after outward signs of achievement and success. More significantly, some studies have shown that those who invest time in leisure pursuits, their families and in deep personal relationships are significantly happier throughout their lives (for example, Maguire, 2001; Cooper, 1996a; Covey, 1989; Maddi and Kabosa, 1984). This does not mean that aiming for high personal goals and material success is a bad thing, only that a truly successful life means finding some kind of balance between work and non-work lives, and between material and psychological/spiritual well-being.

Many people, particularly those in high-flying jobs or whose identities are closely tied up with their occupation or profession, can have real difficulties switching off from their jobs. Even if we do not suffer from the worst effects of occupational stress, we may still find it difficult to leave feelings of pressure and anxiety behind at work. The transition from office to home can be the most difficult one that we have to make each day. Just as we are recovering from the pressures of a busy day at work, we are immediately confronted by another set of demands at home. Because some people have difficulties recovering from the pressures of work they may act out their frustrations on loved ones. So we must try to leave work at work. The most forgiving partner or spouse will only put up with moans about our jobs for so long (and if he or she works too, this works both ways). Treat the time you spend with your family as sacred and, in the overall scheme of life, probably much more important than your job. Successful and healthy leaders are those who can create a balance between their work and domestic lives, and who are able to negotiate a fair division of labour within the household. This doesn't just 'happen', it requires work and the ability to compromise with our partners to achieve this.

When you get home, try to take a few minutes to reorient yourself and relax. Change out of your office clothes into something that you feel relaxed in. If you've had a particularly stressful day at the office, take a shower and have a drink. If you've had a really awful day, go for a short walk or run and focus on what's around you – not work. If you have young children, always spend an hour or two with them in the evening. Try to have a sit-down meal together and catch up on the events in their day. If you have to bring work home, do it when they've gone to bed. It will not always be possible, but discourage your colleagues from calling you about work-related matters in the evening or at weekends. Switch the answer phone on and ignore evening email. To suggest that anyone should take the time to relax, and have some fun with their partners and kids, might seem to be rather patronizing, but many highly stressed professional people have to be shown how to switch off from work, relax, do absolutely nothing associated with their work, and feel comfortable about doing this. If you also find this difficult to do, you might consider trying the relaxation and meditation exercises described earlier, or start some form of aerobic exercise on a daily basis. However, only you can choose to do these things, and if you are now saying to yourself, 'I haven't got time to do any of this stuff', then it might be precisely the right time to start making some changes.

Corporate health and stress management programmes

Many organizations now offer corporate Health and Wellness (HW) programmes to their employees. These are organizational initiatives designed to identify and/or assist in dealing with specific health problems, health hazards or occupational stress problems amongst employees in the workplace. If your company or organization offers HW programmes, you may already be making use of these. If you are the leader of an organization, or expect to be one in the future, you may want to consider introducing health and stress management programmes for your employees. A discussion of the benefits of introducing these programmes into organizations is contained in Appendix 2.

Conclusion

Having examined occupational stress and how its negative aspects can be dealt with, it's worth taking a step back for a minute and looking at this in a broader context. Almost everyone who reads this book will live in wealthy industrialized countries and enjoy lifestyles and levels of affluence that most of the world's population can only dream about. Hardly anyone will ever be directly threatened by war, genocide or abject poverty. Many will have chosen their high-pressure jobs because they gain intrinsic rewards from these, or because they provide high incomes and the material benefits and lifestyles that these bring. So it is up to us to make decisions about finding a balance in our lives that allows us to achieve a reasonable level of material

comfort and career success, without neglecting other equally important things in life, such as personal health, family life, friendships,
leisure interests and the communities we live in. It's also worth reiter-
ating how a positive frame of mind and a good sense of humour can
help us deal with, and overcome, the mainly trivial stressors we
encounter at work. For an insight into the true power of positive
thinking, borrow or buy a copy of *Survival*. This remarkable book tells
the heartbreaking story of Stuart Diver, the only survivor of the 1997
Thredbo landslide disaster in Australia. It shows how his positive
frame of mind, physical fitness and his love of life, family, friends and
his profession (alpine ski-instructing) helped him to survive and overcome experiences, including the death of his wife and several close
friends, that would have destroyed almost anyone else (Diver and
Bouda, 1999). This inspiring story is a very useful reality check when
reflecting on the difficulties and stressors we might encounter at
work.

In summary, successful leader/managers manage their psychological
and physical health, cope effectively with occupational stressors and
achieve a good balance between the competing demands they face at
work and in life. Their self-awareness, sense of purpose, involvement
with their followers and positive attitudes when at work also help in
maintaining optimum stress levels. If we want to do something about
the negative effects of stress, we have to first identify these, discuss our
concerns with people we know and trust (or use a professional analyst
if necessary) and plan ways to overcome them. If we are willing to
spend some time identifying the causes of occupational stress, and
learn how to cope more effectively with its consequences, we will find
that we achieve the following:

- have a clearer sense of the kind of job or career that we really want
  to pursue, and the organizations we want to work for,
- maintain a consistently high level of performance at work,
- make good decisions and meet deadlines on time,
- have more time for our colleagues and subordinates,
- become more effective and successful leader/managers,
- enjoy good health and have plenty of energy,
- sleep well at night,
- have an improved sense of well-being,
- are more cheerful and humorous,
- are able to maintain a good balance between work and family life,
- enjoy good relationships with our partners and children,
- don't resort to drugs, legal or otherwise, to relieve stress,
- are better able to plan for the future and feel more in control of our
  destinies.

The last exercise in this chapter provides an opportunity to reflect actively on the people or events that cause you stress, and the practical steps that might be taken to deal with these in the future.

> There are four things you can't get enough of in life – laughter, sex, vegetables and fish.
> (*John Tickell,* Laughter, Sex, Vegetables and Fish, *1998*)

> And on the seventh day, God rested.
> (*Christian and Jewish creation mythology*)

Exercise 2.4

Strategies for managing stress in the future

Please find a quiet place where you will not be disturbed. For about 30 minutes, think about the five things that most often cause you to feel stressed and what you can do to deal with these in the future. Recall that leadership and management is not just about action, it is also about reflection, and this is essential for your personal health and well-being, now and in the future.

People or events that cause negative stress reactions	My stress symptoms	Possible remedies and solutions
1.		
2.		
3.		
4.		
5.		

When you've done this, remind yourself at regular intervals, 'I will find solutions to these problems.' Then work actively on these over the coming weeks and months. ◆

Notes

1   The origin of the first spam email is uncertain, but is believed to have come from an unnamed marketing executive at the defunct Digital Equipment Corporation (DEC) in May 1978. He sent an email message to all DEC Arpanet (a precursor to the Internet) users on the US West Coast, alerting them to an upcoming open day where the company's new range of machines was to be displayed. Just over 25 years later, on 24 November 2003, the US House of Representatives voted to pass laws aimed at curtailing the spread of intrusive Internet junk mail, with fines of up to 6 million

dollars for intentional violations. This quickly became known as the Can-Spam Act. The EEC passed similar legislation, covering all member states, on 11 December 2003.

2   Unfortunately, men can be very reluctant to do this and often delay visits to their doctors, until it is far too late. So, for any guys over 35 who are reading this book, there is a personal experience I'd like to share with you. Before moving to Australia from the UK in 1997, I was required to have a full medical check-up in December 1996. This revealed a problem that required immediate surgery and also prompted me to give up smoking. This has probably extended my life by another 30 years, and I now have a full medical check-up once a year.

3   One research study has suggested that too much sleep (more than eight hours a night) may be bad for people and insomnia, in moderation, may do little harm. However, this study indicated that 'a minimum' of five to six hours' quality sleep each night was still important to aid physical and psychological recovery (cited by Macintyre, 2002).

4   The 2003 Pan Pharmaceutical scandal in Australia, which led to the withdrawal of more than 1369 alternative products for violating health regulations, suggested that not only were many of these of questionable medical value, some may have damaged people's health. The company was later prosecuted for falsifying test results, failing to clean equipment between batches and lying about the ingredients in their products. If you'd like further information on this contentious issue, see John Diamond's inspiring valedictory book about his battle with cancer, *Snake Oil and Other Preoccupations* (Chapters 1–6). John was Nigella Lawson's husband.

5   In one of those 'it could only happen in New York' stories, Bruce Van Horn, author of a book on yoga for pets, offers 'Ruff Yoga' for stressed canines (reported in *The Sunday Times*, Western Australia, 30 June 2003).

3   Communication at work

Objectives

To define 'communication'.

To describe the complexities of interpersonal communication.

To outline practical ideas for learning to listen more actively to others and ways of resolving disagreements at work.

To offer practical suggestions for giving useful feedback to employees.

To look at organizational communication processes, and how leaders can communicate more effectively with their followers by using the ancient art of storytelling.

To reveal the secrets of effective formal communication skills, and show how public speaking can be enjoyable, persuasive and inspirational.

To look briefly at the complexities of cross-cultural communication in organizations.

Introduction

> Leadership *is* communication.
> (*Barry Posner, World Management and Leadership Conference, Burswood Conference Centre, Perth, November 1997*)

> The distinction between what managers say and what they do is the initiator of the majority of problems in organizations.
> (*Peter Drucker*, The Effective Executive, *1966*)

Communication in context

Communication has often been described as the 'lubricating oil' or 'lifeblood' of organizations, and is the primary medium through which things get done in organizations. Through various media of communication, companies all over the world make decisions that affect millions of people; the activities of thousands of employees are organized, complex management systems are coordinated and the success or failure of businesses is determined. Communication between individuals and groups is essential if organizations are to function properly and cope with the increasingly turbulent international business world of the 2000s. If an organization has problems with communication, the chances are that it will not be operating effectively. If you remove communication completely, an organization cannot even start to function. We all know from personal experience that communication breakdowns between individuals and groups within organizations occur frequently and, sometimes, can be very costly. Among the better-known examples of communication breakdowns in organizations are those that have occurred within NASA, in particular those associated with the crashes of the Space Shuttle *Challenger* in 1987 and *Columbia* in 2003. In the first case, the subsequent investigation revealed a catastrophic breakdown in communication between the engineers, who had designed and built the rocket boosters and urged caution about launching the vehicle in cold weather, and the bureaucrats within NASA's administration who needed the launch to go ahead in order to keep the Shuttle programme on track to support their funding demands from Congress. In the second case, the inquiry revealed a breakdown in communications between Shuttle programme managers and the engineers and technology experts who understood the potential ramifications of the loss of the heat-bearing tiles on *Columbia*'s wing. This breakdown, and a 'complacent safety culture' were cited as significant causes of the lack of action taken by the mission controllers prior to the spacecraft's doomed re-entry, although there would have been little that ground control could have done to repair the damage to the wing or rescue the crew prior to re-entry (*Columbia Accident Investigation Report*, 2003).

Communication problems also caused the loss of the *Mars Climate Orbiter* spacecraft. Zooming towards the planet at more than 25 000 kilometres an hour on 30 September 1999, the craft was supposed to have settled into orbit around the planet to begin its surveying work. Back on Earth, the flight controllers waited for the signal to confirm that it had achieved this objective. After some time, the signal from the orbiter faded and died. Subsequent technical analyses revealed that it had probably approached Mars at an altitude of 60 kilometres, not the required 150 kilometres. Further investigations revealed that the engineers who had written the navigation software had been working in separate groups, with some using modern metric measurements (kilograms and metres) and others using old-style imperial measures (miles and pounds). The result: a $US125 million blunder and another dent to NASA's diminishing credibility.

Communication is important in organizations for other reasons. For example, if one looks at job advertisements in the press for senior managerial/leadership positions in organizations, it is hard to find any that do not specify 'communication skills' as being one of the essential criteria for applicants. Some employers will even demand 'exceptional', 'outstanding' or 'highly developed' communication skills. It is regarded by some commentators as the single most important non-technical skill that leaders need (Conger, 1991). Surveys of employers, going back 20 years, have shown that it is often the number one criterion when promotion decisions are made in organizations, or when assessing new recruits for positions in organizations. Other surveys have shown that the number one attribute sought in new graduate employees is communication skills (for example, Business/Higher Education Round Table, 1992).

Research in organizations has also revealed that most employees want their senior managers and leaders to communicate with them more often and increase their involvement in decision-making processes (Brownell, 1990). One study, involving thousands of employees from more than 80 Australian companies, asked the question, 'What would improve your workplace more than anything else?' The answer was not 'more perks', or 'higher wages', or even 'more time off'. The top two responses were 'more effective leadership' and 'good communication with management' (Pope and Berry, 1995). Furthermore, as we will see later in the book, organizational competencies such as innovation, perpetual learning and change are not possible without having sophisticated communication systems in place to support these. In a fast-changing world, organizations also have to be able to engage in two-way communication with the environments they operate in, through improved scanning methods, in order to spot new opportunities, keep pace with the competition and prevent their market share being eroded by competitors. More than ever, organizations have to maintain close relationships with their customers and clients, in order to respond quickly to their changing needs and ever-rising expectations. In a globalized business world, national workforces are becoming more culturally diverse, and cross-cultural communication throws up a complex set of issues that also have to be managed effectively.

Given its importance in so many contexts, it is no surprise that communication has been the subject of extensive research across a variety of academic disciplines. Globally, all major universities have departments or schools dedicated to communication studies, and a library web search in July 2003 uncovered more than 5000 references to this one topic. Given all the knowledge that is now available on this subject, it is rather puzzling that poor communication in organizations remains something that most employees continue to complain about. This becomes an even greater puzzle when we look at the origins of the word 'communication'. This is derived from the Latin *communicare*, meaning 'to make common'. An associated and often overlooked element of communication concerns the meaning of the word 'audio', in relation to hearing. This comes from the Latin, *obaudire*, meaning 'to obey' or, in modern parlance, to respect others. Therefore communication can be described simply as a process of respectfully sharing information with others in order to improve understanding.

If these two basic elements form the basis of effective communication, why does it still cause so many problems in organizations? I've regularly invited groups of MBAs, and managers on leadership development courses, to identify the main problems or difficulties they encounter at work. Communication always comes in the top three and, quite often, comes first. This has remained consistent over the last ten years. Group members have then been asked to identify what causes these problems. Almost without exception, they have attributed blame to someone or something else. The scapegoats include, 'other people', 'senior management', 'the board', 'the idiots in [insert the department/branch/office/disliked professional group of your choice here]', 'the system', 'the people at headquarters', 'the people from the company we merged with', and so forth. I follow this question by asking them to rate how well they think they communicate with others at work. Predictably, almost all believe that they are very effective communicators, and they also believe that communication problems are the fault either of 'the system', or of other identifiable groups or particular individuals. With very few exceptions, they feel that their communication skills were either better than, or at least as good as, those of everyone else in the organizations they worked for. If this was true, and we extrapolated these results, organizations should not be having any communication problems. So the first reason why communication causes problems must be that *most people are not as good at communicating as they like to believe they are*.

Second, communication encompasses the complete spectrum of individual personalities, life experiences and interactions with others. Our family, educational experiences, peer groups, gender, class and culture all influence and shape the way we eventually communicate as adults. This is closely interwoven with our personal psychologies and neurolinguistic programming. This is extremely important because only about 20 per cent of what goes on in communication dialogues is related to the words coming out of someone's mouth. We communicate to others in many hidden ways that we may not be conscious of, primarily through our working practices, actions and behaviours. How we behave communicates a lot and, even if we are doing nothing, we are still communicating something to other people. This is because *we cannot not behave*. In fact, how we present ourselves to others is often much more important that any wise words or utterances that emerge from our mouths in the form of sound waves.

Third, we also communicate in a myriad of ways: in writing, memoranda, letters, magazines, reports, email, video conferencing, one to one, in formal presentations, over the telephone, in meetings and in work teams. If we then add power differentials, the inevitable personality differences that arise in organizations, culture, politics and bureaucracy, gender and cross-cultural differences in communication styles and protocols to this mix, we soon realize that the potential for breakdowns in communication is very high. Hence the third reason why communication often causes problems is that *it is an extremely complex, multilayered and multifaceted phenomenon*, and this is why we will be spending some time looking at this topic in this chapter.

Interpersonal communication

Exercise 3.1

Before reading the next paragraph (don't cheat!), please answer these questions:

What is 'silent' an anagram of?

Whom do you communicate with most often on an hourly, daily, weekly, monthly and yearly basis?

Whom do you most like communicating with? ◆

Well done if you if you solved the anagram (it is not a coincidence that 'silent' is an anagram of 'listen' as is 'enlist'). The answers to the second question should have been 'myself', 'myself', 'myself', 'myself' and 'myself'. The answer to the third question should also have been 'myself'. If you think about it logically, whom do we communicate with most often? The answer, sadly, is 'myself'. From waking up in the morning and going to bed at night, we experience something in the order of 5000 internal communications. Some are conscious, but most are unconscious. There is always an internal autopilot on the go, a little mechanism in our heads, doing the brain's equivalent of *yabberder-yabberder-yabberder*, even when we are sleeping. It is also very hard to switch this autopilot off, particularly when listening to someone else, for reasons that will soon become apparent. As James Carlopio and colleagues suggest, 'at work, there are dozens of situations in which listening is critical, yet we typically think of *talking* when we think of relating to people and communication. When we are coaching, counselling, giving and/or receiving instructions or feedback, it is critical that we hear, listen and understand the speaker. When we are involved in a sale, or when we are servicing or helping clients and customers, we will be more successful if we begin to see ourselves as professional listeners rather than professional speakers' (Carlopio *et al.*, 2001: 240).

Many commentators have suggested that the ability to listen effectively to others is the keystone of effective communication and, if we cannot do this, we will fail as communicators. However, few people really take the time to consider this, unless they are attending courses like MBA programmes, or receiving feedback on their communication styles at work. Despite its importance in communication dialogues, the reality is that most people have underdeveloped listening skills, and there are a number of physical and psychological reasons why this is so. The first and most obvious reason is that we all like to believe that we are right, at least 95 per cent of the time. However, as we realized in Chapter 1, everyone suffers from selective perceptions. This means that, unless we are all-seeing, all-knowing geniuses, we will be wrong some of the time, and this will lead to problems, sooner or later. Second, humans tend to be very selective listeners. If we like the person delivering a message, or if we think it is relevant or important, or if we agree with the message, we will pay more attention to what they say. If the opposite applies, we will consistently filter out messages that do not fit with our selective opinions, beliefs, feelings and attitudes about the person and the message. Several laboratory experiments have confirmed that most individuals are only about 25 per cent effective in listening skills; that is, they can only recall about one-quarter of what another person says to them immediately after the dialogue (for example, Huseman *et al.*, 1976). If they dislike the other person involved in the communication dialogue, or are in a hurry, this proportion declines even further. How well we listen to others is affected by our emotions: if we feel good about the speaker, we will listen more carefully to them.

Third, active listening is psychologically very hard work. This is because someone who is speaking can deliver about 100–125 words a minute, but a listener (or reader) can process at least 500 words a minute. This leads to 'idle time', and an opportunity to start pre-formulating responses or, worse still, planning when we are going to interrupt or contradict the other person. The idle time that is present in all verbal dialogues leads the listener to focus on other things like, 'What a stupid idea, I can't wait to bury that', and not focusing on showing the listener that we are listening actively (Mackay, 1994).

Fourth, many managers and leaders believe that when they come to work they should be 'adult' and 'rational', and not allow emotions to cloud their daily work and decision making. However, this is not actually possible because, with the exception of psychopaths, human beings cannot simply switch off the left-hand side of the brain (the home of logical and linear thinking) from the right-hand side of the brain (the home of emotions and creative thinking) and, where emotions are at play, communication breakdowns and conflict are always possible. Fifth, while evolution has equipped us with a complex set of controls over the muscles of the mouth, throat, larynx, jaw and tongue that enable us to communicate through language, it has not equipped us with a similar level of control over our emotions, and our propensity for selectively listening to others in communication dialogues.

One way of finding out if you and your colleagues do listen well to each other is to play the old game of Chinese Whispers. To play this you'll need three other people to help you and a small audience. You are 'Number 1' and the other participants are '2', '3' and '4'. The game works like this:

- Participants 3 and 4 leave the room and you read the message once to participant 2 (you keep the piece of paper with the message on it).
- Participant 2 exits the room and relays, once only by word of mouth, what they think the message is to participant 3 (out of earshot of person 4).
- Participant 3 relays the message, once only by word of mouth, to participant 4. This person then returns to the room and relays what they can recall of the original message to the group. To complete the exercise you read out the original quote.

Typically, about 20 per cent of the original content of the message is lost during each iteration with little of the original message left by the final one. You can use any short dialogue you like for this, but the message below is one that's been used regularly with MBAs and in communication skills workshops.

Chinese Whispers

Most people think they are good communicators and it is *other* people who lack this important managerial skill. The reality is that we all over-estimate our interpersonal communication skills. We can all improve our communication skills by learning to listen actively, by managing group meetings more effectively, and by improving our presentation skills. As leaders, we will also need to be aware of the importance of the structural, technological, and cross-cultural aspects of communication in organizations.

Active listening

This exercise highlights the difficulties associated with active listening – a set of sensitivity skills and techniques that work well in most communication dialogues. It has often been pointed out that we have two eyes, two ears and one mouth, so we should only talk in proportion to these ratios; that is, no more than 20 per cent of the time. We also have to show the speaker that we *want* to listen, because if we think that another person is not listening to us, it is unlikely that we will listen to them. So, initially, we all need to *shut up*, by becoming more like the proverbial wide-mouthed frog who encounters a wide-mouthed frog-eater in the jungle. This is important because, if we are talking most of the time, we are not listening most of the time. We also need to have a reason or purpose for listening, even if we are not particularly interested in the issue or topic under discussion. This requires patience and generosity, because it is not easy to listen to other people. There is also little point in listening just to formulate an instant (negative) response, or listening for its own sake. Good listening requires concentrating on the sender's whole message, rather than forming evaluations on the basis of the first few ideas that they present, or butting in with our own ideas before they finish talking.

Make mental or written notes of where you agree and disagree with what they are saying. If you are dealing with complex ideas, wait until the speaker pauses, and only then ask questions for clarification. Seek the sender's important themes by listening for the overall content and feeling of the message. Summarize what the speaker is saying at regular intervals ('So, what you are saying is . . .?' or 'Are you saying that we should . . .?'). Nod, even if you don't agree with what they are saying. This may seem an odd thing to do, but if you think about it, this makes sense. What would you think if someone had nodded, in apparent agreement with what you are saying? You'd probably think this person was on your side, and you would be more amenable to any suggestions and ideas they might have. If you think that someone has offered a bad idea, don't disagree with them instantly, *ask questions*: 'Why do you think that would work here?', 'Has this been trialled elsewhere and been successful?', 'What do other people think about this idea?' If it is a bad idea, questioning will reveal this, and there may still be something useful to be uncovered even in an idea that first appears to be unworkable.

Inevitably, there will be occasions when we have to deal with hostility and conflict. This happens when the childish ('I want') part of our psychologies comes into conflict with 'I want' parts of other people's psychologies, and the adult part of our minds goes temporarily AWOL. If you are becoming emotional or angry, pause before making your response to diffuse some of your tension or use the 'finger and thumb' exercise described in Chapter 2. Then rephrase in your own words the content and feeling of what the sender seems to be saying ('I can see that you feel very strongly about that . . .'). This demonstrates to others that, even if you disagree with their ideas or opinions, you recognize that they have a strong emotional attachment to theirs. If you don't do this, tempers can quickly became inflamed, as this example illustrates:

> The politics of the GST, in both the Lower House and the Senate, is throwing parliament off balance – and it is on the edge. Instead of question time yesterday, there were pointless points of order, niggling, insults, gag motions, divisions and the suspension of the largest number of government MPs in one sitting. Shabby politics imbued every action and blame should be equally apportioned. Instead of eschewing personal abuse, character assassination, personal reflections, disorder, ridicule, obscenity and outright threats, the Australian Parliament is approaching the style of the gang fights of the old Taiwanese Legislature.

> MPs [ ] shouted abuse and mouthed obscenities at each other across the chamber. MPs were told to 'shut up', 'sit down', 'crawl back under your rock' and 'get out of the house'. Among the insults were terms such as, 'national disgrace', 'sanctimonious windbag' and 'smirker'. Some MPs silently mouthed the words '**** off'. Ms. Kernot [then a Labour MP], who had called for new styles of behaviour on Monday, yelled at Mr. Abbot [a Liberal Minister] before being suspended from the House for a display of macho bravado.
> (*Abridged from Shanahan, 2000*)

Another reason why active listening can be difficult is that most communication is non-verbal. Researchers have known for many years that facial expression (55 per cent) and vocal expression (38 per cent) have the most impact in communication dialogues, with just a small proportion (7 per cent) deriving from the flow of words coming out of people's mouths (Mehrabian, 1968; Mehrabian and Weiner, 1967). This is why an awareness of our own unconscious non-verbal behaviours can be important. For example, to reiterate a point made earlier, nod when you agree, but don't shake your head if you don't, because this sends subliminal messages to others that you are not listening actively, and they will be less willing to listen to you when it is your turn to speak. Face whoever is speaking and make positive eye contact while they are talking. Smile when you can. Tapping the foot on the ground, crossing and uncrossing the legs and asking people to repeat themselves all send negative messages. Fidgeting with things signifies lack of interest or boredom. When it's your turn, keep your reply short and to the point. Beware of using weird gestures or negative body language, such as crossing the arms defensively. Use open hand gestures. Don't ever point or 'stab' your index finger at someone else – it is arrogant, rude and condescending. One way of getting a more objective look at your own body language is to set up a video camera to record how you behave with others in groups. This will give you a much greater *kinaesthetic* awareness of how others see you and how you come across to them (described in more detail in the section on formal presentation skills).

You may be thinking, 'Well this is, aah, all very interesting, but how can these ideas and principles be applied in practice?' Well, let's imagine you are trying to introduce a new IT system into your organization. You have complete faith in this system; it is cutting-edge and will help your organization in the future. You are now trying to persuade someone else of this. This could be anyone: your colleagues, bosses or subordinates; it doesn't matter who. Let's suppose that they respond by raising an objection. For example, 'But, we've put in more than four months of training on the system we've got. People have got used to it and won't want to change again so quickly.'

Which of the following replies is closest to the way that you would normally respond to this objection?

1 I don't agree. We've got to keep pace with change. If people don't like it, they'll just have to lump it.
2 I hear what you're saying, but surely it will benefit us all in the long run if we move to the new system now. We've got to keep pace with change, you know.
3 I see. You're concerned that moving to the new system would cause serious morale problems amongst your staff?

Let's look at the consequences of each of these replies in turn. The first answer shows that you believe in straight talking and telling people how it is. You are not being disrespectful, you are simply saying what you think because you know that you are right and they are wrong. Let's see how this dialogue might progress from here.

But, we've put in more than four months of training on the system we've got. People have got used to it and won't want to change again so quickly.

I don't agree. We've got to keep pace with change. If people don't like it, they'll just have to lump it.

I think we need to carry people with us, not ride roughshod over them.

Well, if they're not with us, they're against us and no one's irreplaceable you know.

Well, I think you're wrong, our staff are vital to this organization and I'm not going to support your suggestion.

Look, you're missing the point here. If we don't get this new system in place soon, we'll all be out of a job in [interruption] . . .

. . . And you don't appear to understand that blah-blah-blah . . .

Thus we can see that the first answer is confrontational and this dialogue will continue on its merry way until one or both people lose their tempers. The second answer represents the widely used, 'Yes, but . . .' approach. Let's see how this dialogue might progress.

But, we've put in more than four months of training on the system we've got. People have got used to it and won't want to change again so quickly.

I hear what you're saying, but surely it will benefit us all in the long run if we move to the new system now. We've got to keep pace with change, you know.

Yes, but if you put our staff offside they may start leaving and then we'll have real problems.

Yes, but we'll have even more problems if we don't keep pace with change.

Yes, but not as big as the problems we'll have if staff starting leaving.

Yes, but blah-blah-blah . . .

Like the first dialogue, this one will continue until one or both people lose their tempers. Although it appears to be polite, 'Yes, but . . .' is a

COMMUNICATION AT WORK 103

façade. It actually means 'I still don't agree with a word you are saying, you moron, so why don't you shut up and listen to my ideas?' 'Yes, but . . .' conversations invariably lead to people digging their heels in and defending their original positions more and more vigorously. There will of course be many occasions when 'but' is an entirely appropriate word to use in conversations. However, if used repetitively in this fashion it will drive people further and further apart, they will listen less and less to the other person and no resolution will be reached. Let's see how the dialogue using the third answer might progress.

But, we've put in more than four months of training on the system we've got. People have got used to it and won't want to change again so quickly.

I see. You're concerned that moving to the new system would cause serious morale problems amongst your staff?

I'm very concerned. I understand why we need the new system, but I'm really concerned about the effect it will have on our staff in the short-term.

Well, we have a real problem don't we? We have to get the new system in, but it could simply overwhelm people. What would you suggest?

Do we need to implement the new system immediately? If we had a lead-in time of 2–3 months that would give us time to persuade people of the need to embrace the new system. If we can offer them some kind of small financial bonus for any additional training they might need, I think we could swing this.

That's possible. It would certainly be better and more cost-effective than putting people offside by trying to impose it on them now. Why don't we come up with a timetable and put this in as a joint recommendation to the Board?

Good idea. I'm glad that we could resolve this so quickly.
(*Adapted from Gould and Gould, 1990*)

The third answer represents the active listening approach. This is by far the most effective style, because it shows that, while you may not agree with someone's ideas, you take him/her seriously and respect their point of view. This immediately makes other people less defensive because you've given them an opportunity to let off some steam. This is vitally important if the other person feels very strongly about their opinions or ideas. But should we bring emotions and feelings into play in dialogues with fellow employees? Do we want 'irrational' emotions cluttering up discussions? In fact, we do. It is a widespread myth that 'emotions' lead to irrational behaviour. Irrational behavioural outcomes, such as anger, are actually caused by the *repression* of feelings and emotions. When you allow someone to express these, they will usually calm down and become more rational and open-minded (and, in this context, recall the role that emotional intelligence can play in leadership from Chapter 1).

From here, it becomes possible to move forward. To reiterate some of the points we made earlier, only when others have finished talking should you take the opportunity to get others to listen to you (winning an audience). When you reply to them, show them that you have listened. Accentuate where you agree, but ask questions where you disagree and instead of saying things like 'No', 'You are wrong', 'I disagree with you' or 'Yes, but . . .', ask 'Why do you say that?' or 'What would happen if we tried this? 'Is that going to work in these circumstances?' People usually have an emotional attachment to their ideas and opinions. If they feel that they are being attacked for these, they will fight back or back off resentfully (a direct consequence of the fight–flight response identified in Chapter 2). Their ideas may well be bad, but *reveal* this to them by questioning them, not by contradicting them. If the ideas being proposed are unworkable, they'll soon be buried and there still may be a good innovative idea waiting to be uncovered. As we will see in Chapter 9, almost every innovative idea in history was initially dismissed as being ridiculous and/or unworkable when it was first proposed.

If you really don't agree with another person's point of view, simply tell them how you feel about it. They cannot deny how you feel about something, even if they disagree with your ideas. Always look for compromises early, seeking out 'Win–Win' rather than 'Win–Lose' solutions. The key is to do this without being aggressive, judgmental, appeasing or sarcastic. You merely have to stay friendly, be assertive and tell people how you feel about your proposal and, of equal importance, use facts and information, rather than opinions or polemic, to support your position. Last, recognize that sometimes *we will be wrong*. Take this on the chin, learn from it and move on. Be man, or woman, enough to say to someone else, 'You were right, I can see that now.' Most people will take this as a compliment and, more importantly, will see that we are willing to listen to and learn from others, not an arrogant know-it-all. The techniques described above are not foolproof and may not work with really aggressive or toxic individuals, because, as the American movie director Woody Allen once observed, 'You can't intellectualise with Nazis.' However, they do work well with most people, in almost all work situations.

Listen and you learn what makes people tick, you learn their attitudes, you learn what they think about the work they do and the processes by which they do that work, you learn what they think about the people who manage their workplace. When you've heard what you need to know to make a judgement, to make an instructive or constructive contribution, only then do you open your mouth and say just enough to make the point you want to make.
(*David Parkin et al.*, Perform Or Else, *1999*)

Seek first to understand then to be understood.
(*Ancient Chinese saying*)

How to spot liars

If ascertaining the truth from employees, suppliers, clients or customers is an important part of your job, you can also familiarize yourself with many of the non-verbal signs of lying. According to the psychologist who analysed the videotapes of Bill 'Teflon' Clinton's evidence in the Monica Lewinsky hearings during 1998, there are 22 of these. Interestingly, Clinton actually did believe that oral sex with 'that woman' did not constitute 'sexual relations', a belief that was – allegedly – a product of his Southern upbringing. Signs of lying include leaning forward, touching or rubbing the nose, lack of direct eye contact (in most, but not all cultures), eyes dropping down to the left and right, rubbing the earlobes, folding the arms, crossing the legs, furrowing the brow, wrinkling the centre of the forehead, sweating, dilating pupils, forced laughter and indignant childish anger outbursts. Very few people, most notably actors and politicians, are able to consciously control their facial expressions and body language. There are also computer programs that can identify and analyse 'micro-tics' that are not detectable by the naked eye (Geary, 2000). If you think someone is lying to you, the best way to confirm this is *not* by confronting them directly, but by asking questions. This is standard operating procedure in police and military interrogations. Sooner or later they will either trip themselves up, or give themselves away, by contradicting something they have already said.

Giving feedback to staff

Another important element of interpersonal communication concerns the manner in which we give feedback to staff. This comes in two main forms. The first is the manner in which organizations relay information to and from their employees. This will be described in the next section and, in the context of leading and managing change, in Chapter 8. The second concerns the more formal feedback given to employees at work and in performance appraisals. The next self-development exercise is designed to identify ways of giving feedback to people in one-to-one situations in a non-emotive and supportive way.

Exercise 3.2

Feedback skills

Below are a series of statements that might be made to employees in response to poor performance or their failure to complete a work task. Can you think of less emotional, biased and negative ways of giving this feedback?

Yii Chern, you are always late to meetings. Your attitude towards punctuality is sloppy.

Sally, your last presentation was a disgrace. Get your act together in future.

Alan, you always seem to be asking me for help with your work. It's not my job to constantly help you out. Get a grip on things, OK?

Wee Chong, you are too quiet and introverted to brief your project team properly.

Linda, the way you handled that difficult customer was a bloody disgrace. The next time you do that you'll be out on your ear, flogged to within an inch of your life blah, blah, blah. . . .

Is that clear?

What a cock-up! Why can't you lot do things properly when I tell you to do them?

And, if *your* boss is giving you a hard time:

You are always on my back and blaming me for doing a poor job. You treat me like a moron and I never know what I'm supposed to be doing! ◆

Please compare your answers with these:

Yii Chern, you are always late to my meetings. Your attitude towards punctuality is sloppy.

Alternative: 'Hi Yii Chern. *We*'ve noticed that you've been arriving late to *our* last three meetings. Is there a problem?'

Sally, your last presentation was a disgrace. Get your act together in future.

Alternative: 'Sally, how do you think your presentation went? Would you like to go over the content of your presentation together before next week, so that you can do a really good job in front of the group?'

Alan, you always seem to be asking me for help with your work. It's not my job to constantly help you out. Get a grip on things, OK?

Alternative: 'Alan, you seem to need extra help with your work a lot at the moment. Is everything all right? Would you like to talk with me about your workload?'

Wee Chong, you are too quiet and introverted to brief your project team properly.

Alternative: 'Wee Chong, I was really nervous at first when doing formal talks in front of my colleagues. I did a course on presentation skills and found that this gave me great confidence. I've got some information on this in my office. Would you like to borrow this? And how would you feel about running your presentation by me before you do the next one?'

Linda, the way you handled that difficult customer was a bloody disgrace. The next time you do that you'll be out on your ear/flogged to within an inch of your life blah, blah, blah.

Alternative: 'Linda, some customers can be very difficult. Would you like me to give you some help with handling the difficult ones? When are you available this week?'

Is that clear?

Alternative: 'Can you please run that by me in your own words so that we can make sure that we are in agreement about what needs to be done?'

What a cock-up! Why can't you lot do things properly when I tell you to do them?

Alternative: 'OK everyone, please tell me calmly what's happened and let's work out how *we* are going to deal with this problem.' Conversely, if they have done a great job, use the old sports coach trick and say, '*You* have done a fantastic job . . .', don't take the credit yourself.

You are always on my back and blaming me for doing a poor job. You treat me like a moron and I never know what I'm supposed to be doing!

Alternative: 'When you treat me this way I feel demotivated and confused. Could you please give me clearer guidance on my performance so that I can do a better job for you?'

In summary, feedback should focus on behaviours not personalities (that is, 'When you behave like that/do that. . .', not 'You are a &@#%! . . .'). Being aggressive, hectoring and negative does not help anyone and will turn all reasonable people into resentful monsters. All feedback should be given as near as possible to the event ('Well done – great job'). Initially focus on the positives and be as constructive as possible. Be very specific about what you want your staff to do. Try to avoid vague suggestions such as 'You should do a bit more preparation.' Check that they understand what you have said and ask for their reactions to your comments ('What do you feel about this?'). If people do make mistakes, try to use these as opportunities for learning, not punishment. Try to replace negative words ('don't, 'can't', 'shouldn't' or 'won't') with positive ones ('do', 'can', 'should', 'will'). The main problem with negative feedback is that this only tells people what they should not be doing, not what they ought to be doing. Constantly criticizing staff for mistakes and focusing on errors will reduce feelings of competence, and undermine motivation and performance. Over a long period of time this can create a culture of punishment and negativity. Jointly agree future goals and courses of action and end your discussion with a compliment. In a sports coaching environment, there is overwhelming evidence that not only does positive feedback enhance motivation and performance, it produces players who enjoy their sport more, show greater enthusiasm in coaching sessions and perform better overall (for example, Carron, 1984; Smith, 1979). The same principles apply in a work context. Having said this, the 'three warnings and out' principle has to be applied here. Employees cannot be allowed to make mistakes indefinitely, and if they cannot learn from their mistakes they should be moved on and replaced.

Feedback skills checklist

Focus on the positives first.

Focus on behaviours, not personalities.

Be hard on the problem but gentle on the person.

Be descriptive and constructive, not judgmental or evaluative.

Use positive or neutral language.

If you have to be critical, explain where improvements can be made in the future.

Check that your feedback is understood.

Agree joint courses of action.

Make allowances for the abilities of high, medium and low ability employees when giving feedback.

Give people a fair go, but apply the three warnings and out principle when required.

And, remember,

If your employees go away thinking about *their* behaviour . . . **you've succeeded.**

If your employees go away thinking about *you* and *your* behaviour . . . **you've failed.**

Exercise 3.3

Accentuating the positive

This is an exercise you can experiment with the next time you're at work. Try to say nothing negative and only communicate with your staff or colleagues in words, phrases or questions that are either neutral or positive for an hour or two. When you have got used to doing this, try to last half a day, using only words or phrases that are either neutral or positive. Then try to go a whole day using only words or phrases that are either neutral or positive. ◆

Summary

Exercise 3.4 concludes the first part of our review of communication skills. As we've seen, many managers believe that they are good communicators and it is other people who lack this important 'soft' skill. So the first reason why communication can cause problems must be that most people are not as good at communicating as they like to believe they are. The reality is that we can all improve our communication skills by learning to listen actively to colleagues and junior staff, by learning strategies to diffuse conflict and anger (see Chapter 7 for further information on this) and by giving appropriate feedback to our employees. These basic interpersonal communication skills also form the basis of formal presentation skills, which will be reviewed later in this chapter. They also play a pivotal role in leading organizations, a topic we will look at in the following section.

Exercise 3.4

Having read through this section on interpersonal communication, think about how you can translate any new insights you have acquired into your communication strategies in the future.

Insight   **Strategy to implement this**

1.

2.

3.

4.

5.   ◆

Communicating from the top

> Everyone is talking about communication these days. Any self-respecting business now has a communication director, a communication department, a communication policy, a communication culture or turns to a communication consultancy.
> (*Heinz Goldman,* Communicate to Win, *1995*)

In Chapter 1, we saw that leader/managers influence the behaviour, thoughts and feelings of their followers, by their actions, deeds and words. Despite rapid advances in communication technologies in recent years, personal communication is still, by far, the most powerful medium for leaders to communicate with their followers. Leaders, in politics and business, still meet to discuss important issues face-to-face; they do not send emails or have video-conferences with each other. It is the only way to truly engage with others, and to touch hearts as well as minds. Through this medium, leader/managers are able to build bridges and establish relationships with their followers. As we saw earlier, this requires two-way communication, listening and demonstrating that they have both heard and understood their followers' ideas, needs and concerns. Furthermore, employee attitude surveys, in the USA, the UK and Australia, have revealed that one of the most consistent complaints that employees have about their jobs is the imbalance between top-down communication and upward communication in organizations (for example, Trinca, 2000; Trapp, 1996). Many organizations still spend an inordinate amount of time pushing vision and mission statements, employee newsletters and directives from the top down, but still fail to listen actively to their own employees. At the same time, confronted by accelerating change, globalization and intensifying competition, many leaders have recognized that effective two-way communication with employees is becoming a much more important part of organizational management, and a constructive way to harness the ideas, commitment and enthusiasm of their staff.

A significant component of effective leadership is communication, and many transformational leaders do have exceptional communication skills. They are adept at telling staff who they are, where they are going and why they are going there. Some of these leaders are, or were, exceptional storytellers. Throughout history, leaders of all kinds have used storytelling as a powerful motivational tool, particularly during times of uncertainty, change and upheaval or in response to crises. The importance of storytelling in organizational life has been largely overlooked in the current organizational and leadership literature. In this section, we will look at how transformational leaders try to engage with all of their employees, and how some of these have used storytelling to transform their employees' behaviours, beliefs and attitudes.

How to communicate with a nation

'No other President, before or since, has ever so thoroughly occupied the imagination of the American people. Using the new medium of the radio, he spoke directly to them, using simple words and everyday analogies, in a series of "fireside chats", designed not only to educate and move public opinion forward but also to inspire people to act, making them participants in a shared drama. People felt like he was talking to them personally, not to millions of others [ ] Roosevelt purposely limited his fireside talks to an average of two or three a year, in contrast to the modern presidential practice of weekly radio addresses. Timed at dramatic moments, they commanded gigantic audiences, larger than any other program on the radio, including the biggest prizefights and the most popular comedy shows.

The novelist Paul Bellow recalls walking down the street on a hot summer's day in Chicago while Roosevelt was speaking. Through lit windows, families could be seen sitting at their kitchen tables or gathered in the parlour listening to the radio. Under the elm trees, drivers had pulled over, parking bumper to bumper and turned on their radios to listen to Roosevelt. They had rolled down their windows and opened the car doors. Everywhere the same voice. You could follow without missing a single word as you strolled by. The press conference became another critical tool in reaching the hearts and minds of the American people. At his very first conference, he announced that he was suspending the wooden practice of requiring written questions submitted in advance. He promised to meet reporters twice a week and, by and large, kept this promise, holding nearly one thousand press conferences during the course of his presidency.

> Talking in a relaxed style with reporters, he explained complex legislation, announced appointments and established friendly contact, calling them all by their first name, teasing them about their hangovers and exuding warmth. Roosevelt's accessibility helped explain the paradox that although 80–85 per cent of the newspaper publishers regularly opposed his policies, his coverage was generally full and fair.'
>
> (Editorial [Time], 1999)

How transformational leaders engage with their followers

In the industrial age, the CEO sat on the top of the hierarchy and didn't really have to listen to anybody. In the information age you have to listen to the ideas of everyone, regardless of where they are in the organization. (*John Sculley, Former CEO, Apple Computer Co., 1992*)

In Chapter 1, we observed that transformational leaders seek something much more than mere unthinking obedience and compliance from their followers. They are capable of changing their followers' basic beliefs, values and attitudes in order to get superior levels of achievement out of them. They lead by virtue of their ability to inspire devotion and extraordinary effort from their followers. In order to do this, they have to believe in and trust their employees, and they have to communicate with their employees on a regular basis. Leaders throughout history, particularly in the military, have long understood the operational power of this principle. In modern times, the need to communicate the value of innovations, products and services quickly both within the organization and to suppliers, customers and clients is also becoming much more important. Below are some examples of transformational leaders who have achieved extraordinary results for their companies through effective two-way communication (adapted from Nelson, 1997; Fries, 1997; Adams, 1997; de Pree, 1989; personal anecdotes).

In the early 1990s, the CEO of Alcatel Bell, John Gossens, flew all 1200 of his managers to a large aircraft hangar and put all of them (not just section heads) in charge of change in the company. He asked each one to suggest at least one change they could make to improve their work. Every manager had to send him a signed letter with their suggestions. This became known as the 'Thousand Points of Light Approach' to change. While there were successes and failures, the overall results were spectacular. The 40 best innovations were incorporated into 'Learning by Experience Workshops', and company profits have risen consistently since. Jerre Stead, CEO of the Legert Corporation, places great emphasis on communication. He estimates that 60 per cent of his time is taken up with this. Peter West, the former MD of BP (British Petroleum) in Western Australia, spent 'at least 50 per cent' of his time communicating with his staff. The seven directors of Viking Freight Systems in California spend about three months each year visiting their 4000 employees in the company in eight different states. Andy Grove, founder and Chairman of Intel, holds at least six open forums at different locations within the company each year, 'to hear my employees' ideas first hand and keep them informed about where the company is heading'. They have even put the company's two main corporate goals 'Stay at No. 1' and 'Make the PC it' inside fortune cookies distributed at the company's HQ in Sunnyvale, California. Nicki Lauda, the ex-Formula One driver, and CEO of Lauda airlines, used to spend about 700 hours a year on his planes, because 'For me it's the easiest way of knowing what's going on. If you sit in an office you have three levels of bullshit below you – whenever a story comes through, it's completely different to how a passenger sees it.'

After Paul Anderson joined BHP-Billiton in December 1998, he spent his first 90 days visiting all of the company's operations throughout the world. He held management forums and shop-floor breakfast meetings with employees, organized symposia with investors and held numerous press interviews. Then he completely revamped top-level reporting systems to shorten lines of communication across and up and down the whole of BHP-Billiton's organizational structure. Under his astute leadership, the company was transformed from a potential basket case into an international behemoth. After a successful four years at the helm, he made these comments when he left the company in June 2002: 'The Al Dunlap approach would have been to come in and fire everybody . . . [in] senior management, because obviously the place wouldn't have been in such a mess if any of them had a lick of sense. The other approach was to think that these people were basically good and capable, but lacking a bit of direction . . . and that's what I found when I got there. I asked each of my managers two questions: what do you do, and what would you do if you were me? The interesting thing is, nothing took place in the next two years that wasn't on those pieces of paper' (abridged from Bachelard, 2002).

When the US company, Herman Miller, introduced an employee suggestion scheme in the 1980s, this led to savings of three million dollars a year (or about $US3000 per day per employee). All staff who have worked there for a year own company stock, and so benefit directly from bottom-line improvements in the company's profitability. Ben Edwards, the CEO of stock brokerage firm Edwards and Son in St Louis, conducts a nationwide real-time speakerphone meeting every Friday with his staff to answer their queries and get ideas for improvements direct from his employees. During the 1990s, Noel Goutard, the former CEO of the French auto parts maker Valeo, expected all his employees to make at least ten suggestions for quality and process improvements each year. On average, his senior management team received 25 000 a year. Employees who suggested the best ones received performance bonuses linked to the success of these improvements. Lincoln Electric, in Cleveland, generates more than 200 new ideas every month from its employees. These are linked to profit sharing. Preston Trucking, in Maryland, receives more than 8000 suggestions a year from its employees – these too are linked to profit sharing.

Sam Walton, the legendary founder of Wal-Mart, often wandered into his stores to chat with his employees, discuss service and product quality with customers, and often dropped in unannounced on the company's suppliers. He was renowned for giving off-the-cuff talks over store announcement systems, talking about how the company was doing and new initiatives. Wherever he went, he conveyed simple mantras: the customer is at the centre of what we do, and you should be proud both of what you do and the contribution you make to the success of the company. Unusually for a leader of his generation, he also listened to his employees and often took on board suggestions they had for improving value to the customer, as well as any gripes they had about the company or its senior management. His presence often had a galvanizing effect on staff, because of the simple fact that he bothered to visit and mix with his employees on a regular basis, something that few leaders of his time would have bothered to do. His legacy lives on in the company, where senior management continues to utilize his hands-on philosophy. In 2003, Wal-Mart became the biggest publicly listed company in the USA.

Upward communication is also vital for promoting innovation and change. Among the dozens of examples that could be used to illustrate this point is the story of Dow Chemicals. Ken Wilson, an engineer at Dow, was asked to help run a contest to improve energy performance at the company. For 12 years, between 1981 and 1993, he organized a contest among the Louisiana Division's 2400 staff – never going higher than supervisor level – to suggest projects that could save energy or reduce waste. The results were staggering. Of the 575 projects that were audited, the *average* return on investment (ROI) was 202 per cent a year, with total savings amounting to $US110 million a year. Even in the tenth year of the project, nearly 700 projects later, the 109 winning projects averaged a 305 per cent ROI. In the final year of the contest, the year that Wilson retired, 140 projects had delivered an average of 298 per cent ROI. Employees were rewarded through a company recognition ceremony and a profit-sharing scheme tied to each employee's pay deal (abridged from Fries, 1997).

Ever wondered why the main fuel tank on the Shuttle is a grubby-looking brown colour, and not the pristine white of the booster rockets? In the early 1980s, NASA was confronted with a seemingly insurmountable problem; the Shuttle was 800 pounds overweight and there seemed to be no way of reducing this to the required launch weight. After months of considering major re-engineering options, and the use of increasingly exotic light construction materials, a line worker observed that the total weight of the paint used on the huge fuel-tank, supplied by Lockheed Martin, was almost exactly 800 pounds. The decision was quickly taken to leave the tank unpainted – an already expensive piece of kit that is in use for just eight minutes during shuttle flights and which then gets dropped into the Indian Ocean as waste by-product.

Over the last decade, leaders of many cutting-edge companies have introduced more formal communication strategies to improve communication up, down, across and outside their organizations. These include suggestion boxes, consultative councils, quality teams, focus groups, speak-up systems, employee participation groups, 360 feedback, upward communication systems, staff attitude surveys and customer liaison systems. The range of options is huge and no company these days really has any excuse for not listening to and rewarding the ideas of all their employees. Com Corporation, in the USA, even replaced suggestion boxes with 'screw-up boxes' in the 1990s where junior staff could point out senior management failings. Senior managers had to respond to these within one month. These forms of organizational communication also play a pivotal role in the management of change, innovation, organizational learning and knowledge management, topics we will return to in later chapters.

In some companies, the importance of communication as a strategic tool has become ingrained in their cultures and people management policies. Sir Jack Cohen, the former CEO of the Tesco supermarket chain in the UK, was fond of saying that a leader could not lead by being a SOYA Bean (Sitting On Your Arse). In Microsoft, this is referred to as MBCAL (Management By Communicating A Lot). In the Body Shop this is known as DODGI (the Department Of Damn Good Ideas) and, most notably, in Hewlett-Packard, as MBWA (Management By Wandering About), a source of some amusement to the creator of Dilbert, Scott Adams. However, even this often-mocked HP practice still has many supporters. For example, Chuck Goodyear, who took over at the helm of BHP-Billiton in January 2003, was asked

in an interview, 'How would you describe your management style?'
He replied,

> It's really management by walking around. I think that if you get to see the
> people that day-to-day are doing the job you have a much better sense of
> what's going on. I think you're providing more motivation to these people
> because they recognise that there's not six layers of management between
> them and, in this case, the chief executive. It's their work that is being
> presented and they are there to defend it. You often find that people doing
> the work are the ones who are best able to answer the questions.
> (*Durie, 2003: 32*)

Last, but not least, effective communication with customers and clients
is also essential. For example, a 1999 survey, conducted by the Forum
Corporation in Australia, analysed the reasons why 14 manufacturing
and service companies lost commercial customers. It found that 15 per
cent left because of quality problems; 15 per cent left because of price;
20 per cent left because of lack of contact and individual attention; and
50 per cent left because contact from the suppliers' personnel was poor.
In other words, communication problems were given as the main
reason why 70 per cent of these companies' customers and clients left
them (www.forum.com, 20 April 1999). In a similar vein, Ford's
unwillingness to quickly admit responsibility and communicate with
disgruntled customers and car dealers about the exploding
Bridgestone/Firestone tyres on Explorer and Ranger four-wheel-drive
vehicles in the mid-to-late 1990s led directly to the sacking of Jacques
Nasser as CEO in 2001, and the termination of the 100-year business
relationship between Ford and Firestone that began in 1897. Nasser's
performance at this time was universally criticized, in particular his
apparent lack of concern for the dealers and customers who had been
affected, or even the 174 people who had died as a direct result of these
vehicles being fitted with inappropriate tyres. One commentator
described him as 'a combination of Al Gore and Crocodile Dundee',
with 'formal syntax and thick Australian accent', who failed one of the
true tests of leadership – to be very visible and to be *seen* to be taking
responsibility when major crises occur (Taylor, 2000: 52).

> If I had a single piece of advice for leaders of organizations, it would be to
> communicate, communicate and communicate with all your staff and,
> when you've done that, communicate some more.
> (*Tom Peters during a talk to the Institute of Directors, Centre Point, London, June
> 1990*)

Leaders as storytellers

An important, and often hidden, part of the communication repertoire of
the leaders described in the last section is the ancient art of storytelling.

Storytelling has been part of the fabric of human life from the time our ancient ancestors sat around fires in caves to the present day, and has been an integral feature of every human culture and civilization throughout history. It has been an important element of the human experience for millennia, dealing with issues of self-identity, group membership, the past and the future, and good and evil. From early childhood to adulthood, stories are an important means of learning and communication. As children, our parents read fairytales and other stories to us as both a form of entertainment and as a way of learning about morality, culture and acceptable standards of behaviour and conduct. They also strengthen the parent–child bond. By the age of five, young children all over the world have become consumers and creators of stories. Listening to stories, and learning from these, is an aptitude we acquire at an early age and remains an important method of learning throughout life. Even in adulthood they can be used to help us (re)define who we are, why we are here, the goals we aspire to and our roles in life. Stories are still used widely as teaching and entertainment devices. Stories also act as both mirrors and windows on the human experience, showing people either how to look at reality or how to look at reality in a different way (Edwards and Sienkewicz, 1994).

Throughout history, political and religious leaders have utilized storytelling. They have created characters, settings and events to convey a particular perspective or world-view. The leaders of early civilizations, such as the Indus Valley civilization, the Incas, the Greeks and the Romans, constructed mythologies within which issues of life and death, the physical and the spiritual world and individual and group identity were explored. Religious leaders such as Jesus Christ, Buddha and Mohammed were storytellers *par excellence*. These long traditions of storytelling have enabled human beings to make sense of the world that surrounds them, and their place in it, for millennia. For most of human history, the oral tradition was the only medium used by human beings when communicating a particular viewpoint, idea or vision of life. Even early written works such as the Hindu epic *Mahabharata*, the Norse *Vedic* myths, the Greek epics of *The Iliad* and *The Odyssey* were textual works based on rich oral histories dating back to at least 5000 BCE. The performances of Japanese serial stories in *Kodan* theatres, the oral histories of American folk preachers, African–American folk-histories, Aboriginal dream times, Maori rituals of encounter and the oral epic *Sunjata* performed in parts of West Africa, have all utilized narrative stories to communicate information (Kaye, 1996; Gardner, 1995).

These all served essentially the same function: to make sense of cultural, philosophical or spiritual questions, and to give people a sense of who they were and what they might become. Influential leaders in all cultures have used different types of stories (inspirational, motivational, directional, instructional, spiritual and philosophical) in order to change the way their followers looked at the world. They narrated stories about themselves and their groups, about where they have come from and where they are headed; about what was to be feared, overcome and dreamt about. These leaders have also been adept at taking narratives that have lain dormant in the population and brought renewed attention or a fresh twist to those stories. Through such stories visionary leaders have been able to engage with their followers and inspire people to action. For example, the ideas of Martin Luther King Jnr. spread with amazing rapidity, because he was able to engage in a particularly intimate way with the fears, hopes and aspirations of most African–Americans during the 1950s and 1960s. His speeches and writings made extensive use of his audiences' familiarity with stories about the founding fathers of America ('All men are born equal') and biblical mythologies ('The promised land'). His most famous and influential speech, revolving around the simple mantra, 'I have a dream', lasted less than ten minutes, but its worldwide impact was enormous and the sentiments it expressed still resonate today. In another context, Mahatma Gandhi also drew from religious and cultural stories in developing his own vision of *satyagraha* (non-violent resistance). He also embodied this vision and 'walked the talk', by never resorting to violence in his struggle against British imperial rule in the 1930s and 1940s.

Storytelling in organizational settings

Whilst storytelling has been widely used by leaders throughout history, its role in contemporary organizational life has received limited attention. This is surprising because it has been an indispensable element of human communication for millennia. Stories are a rich communication medium that can be used to convey complex ideas in ways that are more likely to be understood and remembered, and most importantly, can be used to appeal to both the hearts and minds of followers. Storytelling can also help to 'frame' and 'reframe' the big picture and communicate it to different groups within organizations. They can also convey the company's desired objectives and culture in forms that are more likely to be understood and remembered. Furthermore, organizations now function within an increasingly complex and uncertain world. Leaders have to be able to make sense of this fast-changing world and convey this to their employees. Through their words and actions they can influence the behaviours, thoughts and feelings of their followers. This can only be achieved by creating evocative mental pictures that help employees discover who they are, where they are now and where they should be heading. To be truly effective, leaders should not only communicate stories, but should embody them in their actions (Hönig-Haftel, 1996; Kaye, 1996; Young and Post, 1993).

One of the best-known stories of the importance of storytelling in communicating a new vision surrounds the genesis and development of the Sony Walkman in the 1970s. The man who co-founded and helped to build Sony into the global corporation it is today, Akio Morita, once said, 'I had a very clear vision of its potential. But, I do not believe that any amount of market research could have told us that the Sony Walkman would have been successful.' He sold the idea of the Walkman (originally conceived by the company's co-founder Masura Ibuka) to sceptical colleagues by narrating the story of two shoe sales-men sent by their companies into the jungle. The first salesman, having surveyed the local population and market potential, sent a letter back to his company reporting, 'None of the natives wear shoes. There is no market for our products here. I'm returning home on the next flight.' The second salesman, having surveyed the local population and market potential, rushed back to his hotel, telephoned his boss and said, 'None of the natives wear shoes. We can clean up the market here. Please send all available stocks and as many salesmen as you can muster.' In other words, Morita was saying, 'Don't limit your horizons to common-sense frameworks of understanding and always look for the *potential* for new products and services.' His colleagues were convinced and the rest, in the old cliché, is history.

Another example of the role of storytelling can be found in Industrial Light and Magic, the company that created the visual effects for the movies *Toy Story* and *Forrest Gump*. Durrance tells this story about Gail Currey, who headed ILM's Digital Division. She regularly drew on her company's legendary accomplishments to help rally her troops through difficult moments on complex and demanding projects:

> 'All of our Oscars have stories attached,' she says. So when the going gets tough, Currey gets up in front of her three hundred grumbling geniuses and says, 'Remember when we did *Gump*, how at first nobody thought it could be done? And how impossible it became, how hard we worked, and how great it was that we did it?' Then, the geniuses float back to their computers on a wave of confidence to pull off yet another miracle and add another page to the corporate myth. The stories that form the glue that hold a company together don't have to be heroic.
> (*Durrance, 1997: 29*)

Wilkins (1984) describes stories as 'social maps', meaning that can they chart the way and give meaning to what goes on in an organization by illustrating 'how things are done around here'. Two examples of these are cited by Boje (1991). The first one describes 'Nurse Bryan's Rule', a story that enriched understanding of patient care in the hospital where it was told, and also came to represent organizational shorthand for the way all patients should be treated:

> A new hospital administrator, holding his first staff meeting, thought that a rather difficult matter had been settled to everyone's satisfaction, when one of the participants suddenly asked, 'Would this have satisfied Nurse Bryan?' At once the argument started all over and did not subside until a new and much more ambitious solution to the problem had been hammered out. Nurse Bryan, the administrator learned, had been a long-serving nurse at the hospital. She was not particularly distinguished, had not in fact ever been a supervisor. But whenever a decision on patient care came up on her floor, Nurse Bryan would ask, 'Are we doing the best we can do to help this patient?' Patients on Nurse Bryan's floor did better and recovered faster. Gradually, over the years, the whole hospital had learned to adopt what came to be known as 'Nurse Bryan's Rule'. This story is an excellent example of an unwritten commitment to 'doing what is best for the patient' which focused staff minds on the best way of doing things in keeping with the hospital's core values.
> (*Boje, 1991:110*)

The second example he cites is the use of a story to communicate complex or abstract concepts in a more appealing way:

> Let's say you're at a staff meeting to present the company's strategic plan. If someone says we're going to take the business from $US two million to $US twenty million in five years that may or may not make employees feel a connection to the goals of the company. Or, if I want to ask people to get more involved in the volunteer program we provide, I can say I want to move from 40 per cent to 80 per cent participation. But that's only me speaking. If, however, you tell stories about bringing a better product to the marketplace and how that serves the well-being of another person, or if you instead ask someone who is doing volunteer work to tell about the role that he or she is playing in the community and what that means to him or her, then everyone connects around the humanity of the story. It moves communication from the heads of the company to the hearts of the company.
> (*Boje, 1991: 116*)

Some of the best-known examples of the use of mythology and story-telling in organizational communication are associated with the American company Hewlett-Packard (HP). While many computer companies struggled in the late 1980s and early 1990s, HP enjoyed the most successful decade in its history. It rose from relative obscurity to become sixth-largest company of its type in the world. It was the only major computer company to remain in profit during the last world recession. It also enjoyed a long-standing reputation of being one of the most benevolent and forward-thinking employers of the postwar years. Why was this company so successful? The answer may well lie in the management of its corporate culture. During the early years of HP, its founders Bill Hewlett and Dave Packard developed a number of management concepts and attributes that evolved into a directing set of corporate objectives and a business style known as 'The HP Way' (Forster, 2002).

These were first put into writing in 1957 as part of the company's strategic objectives. With minor modifications, they remained the most fundamental and active guiding forces at HP for more than 40 years. The HP Way effectively represented a formal statement of HP's corporate culture (Packard, 1996). One of the most important methods of conveying HP's culture was through the telling of company stories. These helped to clarify, as well as communicate, the values and attitudes that were important to the company. These stories also had an important symbolic function when describing important historical moments in the company's history or exemplifying company role models and heroes. At HP some of the most common stories known by employees concerned the following:

- How Bill and Dave (as Hewlett and Packard were always referred to by HP employees) started the company with a $US538 loan in the garage behind the Packards' rented house in 1937.
  Messages: from small seeds, great trees can grow. Be entrepreneurial in your thinking. Don't borrow more than you can afford to fund your enterprise.
- How they called their first instrument the 91200A19, so that potential clients would not know they were just starting out and would not be afraid of doing business with a small, unknown company.
  Message: think big and create a positive image with potential new customers.
- How the 'Call to Coffee', announced by a bell chime in all HP offices, originated when Dave Packard's wife rigged up a bell in the garage they worked in to let them know when meals were ready.
  Message: we encourage socialization and communication with fellow employees.
- How they made their first big breakthrough by supplying some of the technical wizardry for Disney's *Fantasia* in 1939.
  Message: innovation and cutting-edge thinking are core competencies in this company.
- How during the 1970s business downturn, when companies across the USA were laying off employees, every employee at HP took a 10 per cent pay-cut and took every other Friday off to prevent any lay-offs.
  Messages: we genuinely care about our employees' welfare and job security. We make sacrifices together when we encounter difficulties.
- In the early days of the company, Bill Hewlett tried to get into a supply room to get some equipment. He found it locked after

normal working hours. Unable to find a key, he broke into the locker with a bolt cutter. He then left a note indicating that all such rooms were to be left unlocked in future. This has remained standard practice in HP since.

Message: we trust our employees not to steal company equipment from us.

- How new recruits to the company often hear about the time when Dave Packard awarded a 'Medal of Defiance' to house-engineer Chuck House in the late 1970s. This was awarded because House had persisted in working on a new monitor despite being told to drop it by Packard. This monitor became a huge commercial success in the 1980s. Today, all HP staff still look for ways to introduce new ideas before senior management tell them what they should not be doing.

  Message: we encourage independence of thought and innovative thinking – even if senior management don't agree with your ideas.

These and other illustrative stories were not only used during employee induction and development sessions, but were repeated in many different circumstances on a continuing basis. They were used in staff training workshops, recalled during management meetings and retirement parties, and were incorporated into reminiscences in speeches and letters from Bill and Dave and other company leaders. Furthermore, these were stories that were told throughout HP's global operations. When Collins and Porras were doing their research on long-lasting visionary companies, they found one hundred documented instances of HP managers talking about HP's values and objectives – in external speeches, internal talks, in individual conversations and in company documents. They also encountered dozens of 'Bill and Dave' stories during the time they spent with HP (Collins and Porras, 1996: 211).

In a very different organizational context, Lee Iacocca was able to convey an important message to his employees by leading through personal example, during his struggle to take Chrysler from near-bankruptcy to profitability in the 1970s and 1980s. He did this by announcing that he was going to pay himself a symbolic salary of one dollar for 12 months. Despite the fact that his previous annual salary had been $US360 000, and his pay-cut only lasted a year, this became a story that spread very rapidly throughout the organization and acted as a powerful catalyst for change. The story enabled him to win concessions from all of his employees (including very suspicious labour unions) through what Iacocca called 'equality of sacrifice'. As he observed at the time, 'although my reduced salary didn't mean we had to skip any meals, it still made a big statement in Detroit. It showed that we were all in this together. It showed that we could only survive if each of us tightened our belt. It was a dramatic gesture, and word of it got around very quickly' (Iacocca, 1988: 242).

Another example of how a story was used in another struggling US car company, Ford, to create a picture of a better world is recounted by Austin (1995: 18):

> At a meeting of 300 Ford managers in Detroit, held after the company announced changes that would significantly alter the way its cars are built and how its employees work together, a senior executive told a story about Willie B., a majestic silverback gorilla who for 27 years had lived in isolation in a dismal bunker at the Atlanta Zoo. The executive had helped raise money for a new, state-of-the-art habitat, where Willie B., for the first time in his life, would regularly feel the sun on his shoulders and the rain on his head. But it took him several days of venturing a few small, tentative steps at a time to fully explore his new domain. A photographer caught the moment when the gorilla gingerly tested the grass with a toe, and the portrait hangs in the executive's office today. 'It's there to remind me that no matter how attractive the new surroundings might appear, it takes time and courage to leave the comfortable security of a place – even an ugly, cramped space – that you know well.'

The Body Shop is another company that has used storytelling in an active way since it was created. The company's founder, Anita Roddick, has long espoused clear values of care for the environment, equal opportunities, concern for human rights and opposition to animal exploitation. In her first autobiography in 1992, *Body and Soul*, she recounts, in story-like fashion, her life journey in creating the Body Shop and the development of her values and ethical management philosophy. Every Body Shop stocks the book. Roddick was a leader who used storytelling in a positive way to lead her organization and to sell its products:

> I still see story-telling as a major component of communication within the Body Shop, both stories about products and stories about the organization. Stories about how and where we find the ingredients bring meaning to our essentially meaningless products, while stories about the company bind and preserve our history and our common sense of purpose. We realised that we need to learn more from our own storytellers within the company, because the penalty for failing to listen to stories is to lose our history, and the values we seek to promote. As we have grown, the stories that have been told and re-told about the company have entered the chronicles of the company.
> (*Roddick: 2000: 80*)

Summary

Through stories we gain a deeper understanding of our relationships with the people around us, whether in the workplace, the home, or with our friends and acquaintances. More importantly, the use of stories can significantly influence thinking, attitudes and behaviour. Through stories, employees come to know what is important about the work they do and why they are doing it. Stories bring key individuals (heroes) to life. Some highlight myths and/or significant real-life events that have shaped a company's fortunes. Others emphasize rituals and ceremonies. Organizational leaders can use storytelling to paint the big picture, to teach new management values and to change their companies' cultures (see Chapter 8 for an example of this). Memorable stories can act as potent culture change mechanisms, because they can encourage behavioural and attitudinal mind-shifts. In Chapter 1, we saw that leaders are, in effect, people who interpret reality and explain this to their followers and, when necessary, reshape and remould their employees' perceptions of reality. So, if a leader can make important points in a consistent and memorable way by using memorable and engaging stories, then – over time – their followers will listen, because it is only through these media that emotional connections can be made. Effective leaders have long known the value of connective symbolism in directing the efforts of their followers, and storytelling is one of the few media through which symbolic and emotional connections can be made.

The long history of storytelling shows us that it has always been central to the human experience and to our ancestors' ability to survive and adapt to new circumstances. History is rich with examples of leaders who inspired others to higher levels of performance, or encouraged their followers to look at themselves and their environments in a different way. Churchill, Gandhi and Martin Luther King are examples of political leaders who achieved this. In business, Akio Morita, Lee Iacocca, Jack Welch, Bill Hewlett and Dave Packard, Steve Jobs and Andy Grove are all examples of leaders who have understood the power of storytelling. History is also full of examples of what happens to leaders who lose sight of the importance of symbolism and the ability to manage this through evocative language. Sooner or later, they always lose their grip on power. A manager who is incapable of storytelling may never hope to aspire to senior leadership roles, so it is a skill worth developing and, like other communication skills, it can be developed through self-learning. Kaye has even suggested that organizations that don't utilize storytelling are, in effect, not communicating with their staff and, if people aren't communicating, then the organization will eventually fall apart (Kaye, 1996: 49). Of course, while important, storytelling alone will never make anyone an inspirational and engaging communicator. This requires high-level formal presentation skills, which are reviewed in the next section.

Exercise 3.5

Having read through 'Communicating from the top' and 'Leaders as storytellers', think about how you can translate the insights you have acquired into your organizational communication strategies in the future.

Insight	Strategy to implement this
1.	
2.	
3.	
4.	
5.	◆

Formal communication skills

Once upon a time there was a very inexperienced junior lecturer, who was about to deliver his first lecture to 150 second-year business students, in a very large auditorium, with steep banked rows of seats running as far back as the eye could see. He was more than nervous; he was terrified, with a very dry mouth and, at times, visibly shaking. After getting the assembled mob quiet, he then proceeded to commit all the cardinal sins of public speaking. He was incoherent, he mumbled, he was monotone in delivery, he 'ummed', 'aahed' and 'okeyed' all the way through, he talked far too quickly and, in pre-PowerPoint days, used a ridiculous quantity of overhead slides (most with plenty of *words* on them). His students had to suffer this for the next six weeks, two hours at a time on Friday afternoons. Soon after the end of the semester, his teaching evaluations arrived. Not surprisingly, many of the students thought he was an awful lecturer. On the reverse side of their evaluation sheets, the students had the opportunity to add personal comments and feedback. Under the heading, 'How would you improve this course?', were helpful comments like, 'Shoot the lecturer' and 'Bring back hanging'. Under the heading, 'What did you most like about this course?' were 'Thank God it's Friday', 'Knowing I won't have to study this ***** ever again' and 'Going to the Happy Hour in the Union bar afterwards to recover'.

You'll have guessed that the person being described here is the author of this book (who stills remembers this experience with a shudder).

But, more than a decade later, I now relish public speaking and also run presentation skills workshops for managers and professionals. The reason for sharing this anecdote is to show that no matter how much we might initially dread public speaking, anyone can learn to become better at this, and enjoy doing it. For some leaders and managers, public speaking is a real buzz and, for an elite few, both highly lucrative and something they clearly enjoy. The ex-British prime minister, Margaret Thatcher, used to charge about $US100 000 a talk, Mikhail Gorbachov $US100 000 (but he gave most of this to charity), 'Storming Norman' Schwartzkopf, Allied Commander during the first Gulf War, $US100 000 and 'Billion Dollar' Bill Clinton about $US150 000. During a visit to Australia in February 2002, Clinton earned $US350 000, for delivering the same speech in Sydney, Melbourne and Perth, that he had earlier presented in the USA, Britain and Israel (Carson, 2002). Later estimates put his total earnings for public speaking during 2000–2003 at more than 14 million US dollars. The top leadership and management thinkers of the 1990s, such as Peter Drucker, Charles Handy and Tom Peters, commanded appearance fees of $US20 000–40 000 a day.

'Teflon Bill'

'Joe Klein believes that Clinton's oratorical strength wasn't the result of language skills, but a consequence of his physical presence – "a mirage of body language". There was something carnal in the way he embraced an audience: his face bore "a raw pink fleshiness" that suggested jogging and junk food, crude energy, unslaked appetites. For all his unshakable popularity and an approval rating that defied every setback and scandal – driving Republicans to ever more noxious attitudes of bafflement and despair – he never found a way to communicate his larger vision to the American public. He was, Klein believes, a better public speaker than Ronald Reagan, more comfortable behind the podium that any President since John Kennedy, yet he created no memorable rhetoric: he was a great speechmaker who made no great speeches. Once, when he was addressing Congress, the wrong speech was posted on the teleprompter. Clinton ad-libbed for 20 minutes while the right words were found. But even those words weren't his: they rarely were.'

Source: Abridged from a review of Joe Klein's *The Natural: The Misunderstood Presidency of Bill Clinton*, in *The Weekend Australian*, 29–30 June 2002.

When professionals and managers are asked to describe the activities they most dislike at work, many will point to public speaking in front of colleagues, bosses, customers and clients, and at conferences, as being amongst their least favourite. And most people can recount at least one 'Beam me up Enterprise' or 'Freshly landed fish' (gasping for air and soundless) moment during their careers, when a presentation has gone off the rails. It has even been suggested that, on average, people fear public speaking (and spiders) more than they fear dying (Roydhouse, 2001: 17). But, love it or loathe it, effective formal communication skills are essential for leaders and managers at all levels of organizations because, whether we are talking to one person or one thousand people, *we are presenting ourselves to others.*

'It Went Horribly, Horribly Wrong'

'Finally, Tariq Ali finished his speech. There was pandemonium. Everyone cheered; somebody hoisted him onto their shoulders. Pretty girls waved admiringly up at him and the camera swivelled in his direction. Then somebody beckoned to me: it was my turn. I had barely spoken in public before, never mind made a speech, and I felt chronically nervous. I had absolutely no idea what to say. I had prepared a speech, but under the scrutiny of a thousand expectant faces turned towards me like sunflowers, my mind had gone completely blank. Dry-mouthed, I mumbled a few words, gave a sick smile and realised with a mounting feeling of panic that I could not do it. There was nowhere to hide. I gave a final inarticulate mumble, somewhere between a cough and a vomit, dropped the microphone, leapt off the podium and disappeared back into the safety of the crowd. It had been the most embarrassing moment of my life.'

(*Richard Branson,* Losing My Virginity, *1998*)

Why do so many people dislike public speaking? Perhaps the biggest fear is exposure. Standing up in front of a large group of people, with a hundred or more pairs of eyeballs all staring in our direction can be very intimidating. There is also the risk of losing face or making complete idiots of ourselves in a public forum. Sir George Jessel, a renowned public speaker, once said, 'The human brain starts working the moment you are born and never stops until you stand up to speak in public', and the Irish comedian, Pat O'Malley, observed that 'Speeches are like babies – easy to conceive, but difficult to deliver.' But, it's also important to emphasize that few people experience no anxiety or nerves when performing in public and this includes the greatest actors and political leaders of the 20th century. For example, can you guess who said this?

I have often been described as a great public speaker. The truth is rather different. For many years I was extremely apprehensive about oratory and

it was only with a great deal of practice, and the help of some of the best speech writers in the country, that I gained this reputation.
(*McKenzie, 1980: 375*)

The writer was Winston Churchill who had to overcome a childhood stammer, and became regarded as one of the greatest orators of the 20th century.

Getting started

Prior, proper preparation prevents p***-poor performance.

Failing to prepare is preparing to fail.

You need no preparation to fail.
(*Old and widely used sayings in military training programmes throughout the world*)

In many ways, making an effective public speech is like baking a delicious cake or cooking an inspirational meal. It should always contain good ingredients, but does not require dozens of these, because simple ingredients can often create spectacular results. These then have to be assembled, prepared and 'cooked' in the right order and in the right way. The finished product has to be served up and presented in an attractive and memorable fashion. It should 'taste' good and leave the recipient with positive memories of the event. However, all too often, a presentation can end up as a horrible hotch-potch of irrelevant, inappropriate and unimaginative ingredients served up in a dull, flaccid and uninspired manner. Having said this, there are no secrets to effective public speaking, and *anyone* can learn to become better at this.

Effective presentation skills can be broken down into six principal components:

- researching the audience,
- structuring the presentation,
- enhancing the content of the presentation,
- choosing which audio-visual aids to use,
- delivering the presentation,
- dealing with uncooperative participants.

Researching the audience

By now, you should be comfortable with the simple but important principle that communication is a two-way process of improving mutual understanding. This principle also applies to public speaking. This means that the starting point of good public speaking is not the content, structure or delivery of the talk, but the audience we will be presenting it to. Hence the first question we should ask ourselves is not 'What am I going to tell them?' but 'What do they expect or need to hear from me and how can I best put this across to them?' This is not to say that the first question is unimportant, because at certain times we may have to say some things to audiences that they were not expecting to hear, or deliver unwelcome messages that they may be unwilling to hear. However, before writing any presentation, you should try to find out the following.

Who is attending?
Colleagues, bosses, subordinates or clients and customers (or a combination of these)? Are they experts or non-experts in your field? Is your audience one you know or one that you have never met? The nature of your audience will affect the content of your talk, and the style of delivery used.

Do they know you?
If not, you will have to make a personal connection with them at the beginning of your talk.

Are they in the same profession or a different one?
This will affect the amount of jargon or technical knowledge that you might use.

How much expert knowledge do they have?
This will affect how you 'pitch' your talk and the amount of technical jargon you can use.

How many people will be attending the presentation?
The smaller the group, the more informal and interactive the talk will need to be. This requires a subtle juggling act, between maintaining the flow of your talk and getting through the content and addressing their queries and questions. If you are talking to more than about two hundred people, you will need to be comfortable with a microphone and, perhaps, an auto-cue and PowerPoint.

Where is it taking place?
The dynamics of delivery are very different in a large auditorium and a small seminar room.

When is it taking place?
A rule of thumb is that, if you are presenting after lunch or in the evening, you will need more 'bells and whistles' to keep your audience's attention. If you have the option, the best time to do a presentation is between 9.00 and 12.00.

What facilities are available?

The availability of break-out rooms, movable chairs and tables, OH, PowerPoint, whiteboard and video facilities creates many options in the way a presentation is delivered.

Having considered all this, you can then turn your full attention to the structure and content of the presentation.

Structuring the presentation

> It takes at least three weeks to deliver a good ad lib speech.
> (*Mark Twain*)

Strangely, many people overlook the importance of the foundations and structure of a talk, preferring instead to write the content and create the PowerPoint slides to go with this. Quite often, they'll even prepare their PowerPoint presentation *before* writing the talk. This is odd, because can you think of any other activities that are *not* based on solid foundations and structures? For example, would you get in a car without having done some foundation courses in driving? Climb up or ski down a mountain? Build a house without a solid structure and foundations? Can you name a single good film or book that does not have a solid structure?

This is important because people need to 'see' what you are doing (a mental map) and this needs to be reinforced as you go through your talk, and there are a number of methods that can be used for creating good structures for presentations. One of the most popular of these is The Spider (see Figure 3.1). The purpose of this is to help us to think *laterally* about what could go in our talk, and also forces us to write this down as a visual mental map that we can refer back to. For example, imagine you have been asked to do a presentation on 'Explaining extra-terrestrial life forms' to a class of eight-year-olds for one hour. What would you talk about? To get started, think about the main areas that you would cover, and most importantly, think about those things that would interest and excite a group of eight-year-olds. There may also be sub-topics under the main headings. If you've got kids around this age, ask them what they would like to see in the presentation.

When you've done this, you can turn to planning the running order of the talk in Exercise 3.8. Get in touch with your inner-child and imagination. How would you communicate information about ET to a group of grommets, and what audio-visual aids could be used to bring the presentation to life?

Figure 3.1   The spider

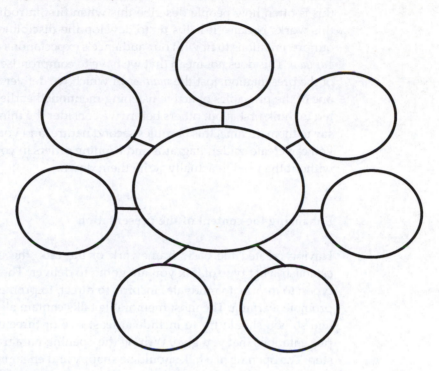

Exercise 3.6

Subject: Extra-terrestrial life   **Audience:** Eight-year-olds

Numbers attending: 20   **Duration:** 60 minutes

Main areas	Audio & visual aids	Time limit
1.		
2.		
3.		
4.		
5.		
6.		◆

This process may appear to be time-consuming and even pedantic, and this is often how people describe this when first introduced to it. But this works because it helps us to develop the discipline to customize our presentations to fit with our audience's expectations and needs, *not our own*. This does not mean that we have to compromise on the *content* of the presentation, just the *manner* in which we deliver it. This echoes one of the principles of active listening mentioned earlier in this chapter: to think first about others before we consider the things we want to say to them. In time, this becomes second nature, and you will find that you can create spider diagrams and running orders in your mind's eye, without the need to actually write them down.

Enhancing the content of the presentation

Having created the basic framework of the talk, the next step is to establish what type of talk you are going to deliver. There are just five types: to inform, to motivate/inspire, to direct, to promote action or to promote learning. The most memorable talks contain all five elements, and so you should try to include at least two or three of these in any presentations that you give. Writing the opening paragraph is the next step. The opening of a talk should be snappy and engaging, because we don't get a second chance to make a first impression with an audience. If we can't grab their attention within the first minute, it is unlikely that we will get it at all. So we have to engage with the audience by, for example, referring to them or the occasion or thanking them for giving you the time and opportunity to talk to them. Another tactic is to refer directly to someone in the audience: 'David made a really interesting point to me during the coffee break when he said . . .'. Use direct questions to members of the audience ('What is the single biggest challenge facing you/your company/this industry?') or cold statements of fact ('It's the year 2008 and our entire industry has disappeared, swallowed up by the second wave of e-business. . . .'), to grab their attention. Short stories, or anecdotes, that capture the theme of a presentation always create an immediate emotional bond with audiences.

Then we have to tell them what we are going to do, do it and then tell them what we have done. This means that the punchy, attention-grabbing introduction is followed by sequentially linked sections. In these, the main messages or themes of the introduction are revisited. These are then followed by a solid conclusion, where the main points of the talk are revisited for the last time. There should be clear links between these parts and mini-summaries throughout, where you refer back to your central themes. Or, as Plato put it to his students, more than 2400 years ago, 'Every discourse ought to be a living creature; having a body of its own and a head and feet. There should be a beginning, middle and an end, adapted to one another and the whole.'

In many speeches, we have to connect emotionally with people, particularly if we are trying to change the way they do their jobs, or when trying to get them to follow us down a new road, way or path. This occurs because of the way the brain processes information from the environment. All our basic senses, such as sight, sound, touch, taste and smell are processed by the 'old' brain (known as Area 17). This is the most primitive and reptilian part of the brain. If this doesn't react, information will not be passed on for processing to the 'new' brain (Table 3.1).

Table 3.1 *Communicating with the whole mind*

Old brain	New brain
Primitive	Advanced
> 1 million years old	c.130 000 years old
Source of instinctive autonomic responses to hunger, thirst, danger, fear, insecurity, stress and sexual desires and urges	Source of language, rational thought, planning, decision making, higher order cognitive processes
Instinctive/emotional/ intuitive	Intellectual/rational/ conscious
Common to higher mammals and early hominids	Unique to modern humans

To connect with people emotionally, we have to be able to use language and imagery that taps into at least two or three of these senses. So, in the text of your talks, try to create mental pictures through imagery ('I have a dream today' or 'We have nothing left to fear, but fear itself'). Use similes and metaphors, anecdotal stories, good illustrative examples, jokes and funny one-liners where appropriate. A good starting point for these is McKenzie's *14 000 Quips and Quotes for Writers and Speakers* (1980). To maintain this emotional connection with your audience, refer back to the larger picture throughout the talk: for example, 'I am cutting stone' versus 'I am building a cathedral'. Whenever possible, use stories, stories and more stories. As soon as you say, 'I'd like to tell you a story . . .', watch the audience wake up and come alive. Why is this important? Well, compare the kind of language that is used in company reports or in-house videos with your favourite novels or movies.

Which do you prefer to read or watch? Which inspires, engages or entertains you?

Other techniques that can be used to spice up presentations include the 'Twenty Minute Rule', where you shift tack, introduce something new, involve the audience, play a video-clip and so forth. Whatever it is, do some different things during your talk to keep your audience's attention at a high level. Some writers on presentation skills even talk about the need for a '6–7 minute sizzle', but this is really only necessary if you're in front of an audience with a very low attention span. You can also emphasize important points by using the 'Stuck Record', an ancient iterative technique, used by orators throughout the ages. For example:

- 'The first reason why we should implement this new strategy is . . .'
- 'The second reason why we should implement this new strategy is . . .'
- 'The third reason why we should implement this new strategy is . . .'

There is another ancient technique called *chiasmus*, a figure of speech in which the order of parallel words or phrases is reversed. Figures as diverse as John F. Kennedy, Winston Churchill, Jimmy Carter, the American actor Mae West, William Shakespeare and many other political and business leaders have made use of this technique in the past. Here are a few examples of this technique in action:

- Ask not what your country can do for you, ask instead what you can do for your country.
- War may sometimes be a necessary evil. But no matter how necessary, it is always evil.
- I cannot say whether things will get better if we change; what I can say is that they must change if they are to get better.
- It's better to be looked over than overlooked.
- Never judge a corporation by how many employees the CEO reaches, judge it by how many employees can reach the CEO.
- You shouldn't motivate employees with fear, any more than you should fear employees with motivation.
- Creativity comes without structure and conformity as much as structure and conformity come without creativity.
- If we treated our employees like we treat our customers and treated our customers like we treated our employees, who would benefit?

A rhetorical technique, often used by salespeople, is 'Head–Heart–Hip'. For example, 'Renting is the equivalent of pouring money down the drain [head]. Investing in a property of your own means security for your family, and it will be an inheritance to pass on to your children [heart]. Furthermore, all the evidence accumulated over the last twenty years shows that buying a house is a good financial investment over the long term [hip-pocket]'.

While it's clearly important to use engaging and emotive language, and the linguistic techniques described above, it's equally important not to 'lecture' people. Amongst other things, this means to 'admonish at length' and, unfortunately, this is what many presenters do. As the English writer Thomas Huxley once remarked, 'A lecture is a process whereby information is passed from the notebook of the lecturer to the notebook of the student, without passing through the minds of either.' This comment leads us naturally to the problem of professional jargon. Can you make any sense of the following real-life dialogue?

'Shag. Well done on your McDonald, my old China. Can you do me a Hawaii of jungle books? I've stepped on the plate and I need to take a punt or I'll end up being legged-over. And I'll have to do some nerdling for the toss-pot.'

'Yeah, I'm a fly-boy for that. I've got a spoon-muppet in the jubb office who'll do you a buck if you want. And what about the eight Ayrtons you owe me?'

'Ship it in your size and I'll give you your wad back during knobs-out, OK?'

If you had worked on the London Stock Exchange in the 1980s, this would have made perfect sense, as follows:

'Hello. Congratulations on the quarter million pound deal you just made, mate. Can you exchange £50 000 worth of Japanese Government Bonds please? I've taken a large market position and I'm going to have to gamble or I'm going to lose some serious money on a bad deal. And I'll have to massage the figures for my boss.'

'Yeah, I'll help you out with that. I've got an ex-public school junior trader working in the back office who'll do you £100 000 worth if you want. And what about the £80 you owe me?'

'I'll take whatever you're offering and I'll give you your money back in the bar after work.'

Here's another example from Scott Adams' *The Dilbert Principle* (1997: 149): 'This change will allow us to better leverage our talent base in an area where developmental roles are underway and strategically focuses us towards the upcoming business transition where business literacy will be essential to maintain and to further improve service levels to our customer base going forward.' In other words, 'This change will improve services to our customers.' Working in the university sector, I'm regularly exposed to brain-numbing and soulless jargon. However, no one has ever demonstrated that it serves any useful purpose whatsoever. Occasionally, to audiences from your area of expertise, it might be warranted, but you will alienate non-specialist audiences very quickly. While linguistic precision, sophistication and flair are all important, jargon is dull, and boring an audience is the ultimate crime for any public speaker. So, as far as possible, remove this and replace it with visual and connective language that can capture the audience's imagination, via Area 17.

If you have to get a lot of facts and information across during a presentation, focus on the strongest evidence, rather than trying to bombard or overload people with data. Numbers and statistics lose their impact very quickly with most audiences. Choose examples that the audience can relate to and be simple in your logic. Use facts, not opinions, to support your arguments. Another way of getting detailed information across is to put this in their handouts, so they can relax and enjoy the talk. If you do this, it's important to control how they use these, or they might decide to read the handouts instead of listening to you.

> The mediocre teacher tells.
> The good teacher explains.
> The superior teacher demonstrates.
> The great teacher inspires.
> (*William A. Ward*)

When you are happy with the content of your talk, write it out in conversational language, *as if you were going to deliver it during a normal conversation with one or two people you know well*. This can include the full text of your opening lines, because even the most experienced speakers sometimes forget what they were supposed to be talking about. However, the rest of your talk should be written in note form only. Avoid reading word-for-word from a written text unless you have an auto-cue and practised this a lot, because this tends to take all the emotion out of a talk. If you know your subject matter well (the preparation phase), you can rely on something called 'the stream of consciousness'. All you then need are trigger words or key phrases to remember the content of your talk, which is all contained in your medium-term memory. It doesn't matter if you occasionally forget something. Unless you are talking to a convention of telepaths, no one is ever going to know this. However, you can still keep detailed notes with you, just in case you do forget something important. These can be in electronic form on your PC, on A4 paper or on small cue cards. It really doesn't matter which; use whatever you feel comfortable with. But it's important to avoid clutching your notes or other paraphernalia such as pens and laser pointers all the time, because this can have a negative effect on your non-verbal communication during presentations (described later in this section).

One of the hardest parts of a formal presentation is the ending. As the English peer Lord Mancroft once put it, 'A speech is like a love affair. Any fool can start it, but it requires considerable skill to end it' (McKenzie, 1980: 429). Aim to conclude with a decisive, punchy big idea or come full circle to your opening statement or question, 'Well, ladies and gentleman, at the beginning of this presentation I asked four questions. I hope I have now answered these for you. Thank you for your time and inputs.'

Choosing which audio-visual aids to use

Most people would respond to the question 'Why use audio-visual aids?' by saying things like 'It helps the audience remember the most important parts of my presentation' or 'It helps to emphasize the points I want to get across.' Used in the right way they can emphasize key points, provide variety in presentations and simplify complex information. They may improve participants' recall and make key messages more memorable, but how often do they achieve these objectives? Think back to the last few PowerPoint presentations you've sat through. Can you recall anything of lasting value that was on the slides used by the presenters? Or have there been occasions when you were able to remember the bells and whistles on the slide show, but not the actual content of the talk? For what it's worth, my advice would be to minimize their use in presentations, because they are a ubiquitous, monopoly technology used by everyone. They are usually dull, often featuring the speaker reading in monotone parrot-fashion style from wordy slides. Or there is the 'my special effects are better than yours' scenario, with a succession of speakers trying to outdo each other with the latest presentation software.

It is also intellectually suspect, because it often reduces complex ideas to meaningless bullet points. PowerPoint is often the equivalent of bad managerial television, encouraging passivity, rote learning and a complete lack of audience participation. To paraphrase Winston Churchill's speech after the Battle of Britain in 1940, 'Never have so many people been so bored to death, in so many venues and on so many occasions, by monotonous talking-heads droning on through dull and/or complex PowerPoint shows.' The main problem with most PowerPoint presentations is that they are full of *words*. Words are dull.

Words are bland. Words have no intrinsic meaning or value. If you then read your slides, word for word and directly from the screen, you will also lose all emotional impact with your audience. For example:

Really, really dull and wordy slide, no. 253

'There can be problems if you simply repeat to your audience what is on this slide. If you do this, they may not be sure if they should be listening to you or reading what is on the slide. They will realize immediately that this is exactly what you are saying anyway. They'll also be thinking that you think they are complete morons because you are reading something out loud to them that they can read just as well as you. And, because they can read this lengthy slide much faster than you can read it out to them, they will have read the whole thing long before you get to the end of it. So, far from enhancing presentations or emphasizing a point, this method is simply irritating.

So avoid being a monotone parrot . . . and if your audience then decide to write all this stuff down, you will have to hang about for two or three minutes while they do this.'

Effective public speaking does not need PowerBore used in this fashion. This may be why Sun Microsystems chief Scott McNealy has banned its use and, allegedly, even Bill Gates has banned his employees from using it on occasions (Holland, 2001). By all means use PowerPoint or OH slides. They can be useful, particularly in large auditoriums. But, the KISS (Keep it Simple Stupid) principle applies here. Try to use a maximum of six or seven bits of information on each slide and try to use catchy or weird bullet point titles to get people's attention. For example, here are two slides conveying the same messages.

Crazy Ways for Crazy Days

The Boss-Test

Making Pancakes

Small Is Beautiful (But Big Can Be Bountiful)

Learning – Innovating – Changing

All The World's A Stage . . .

What If We . . .?

The challenges facing organizations in the 21st century

Leaders must move from a command and control style of management to one that encourages coaching, mentoring, employee empowerment and self-learning

Organizations must become less bureaucratic and hierarchical, and create flatter cultures that are more responsive both to the external environment and to internal processes

Organizations must create a balance between large-scale strategic processes and the need to respond quickly to local and regional customer needs

Organizations have to promote change, innovation, perpetual learning, knowledge management and the more effective use of intellectual capital in order to remain competitive

Organizations must embrace global strategic 'mind-sets' if they are going to cope with the internationalization of trade and commerce in the 21st century

Organizations must develop new competencies that enable them to adapt quickly to changes in the environment, such as 'mental modeling', 'scenario-mapping' and 'future-casting'

Which one do you prefer? The second slide reminds us of the wise old saying, 'A picture is worth a thousand words, but a picture of a thousand words ain't worth much.'

What can be used instead of words? What about cartoons, pictures, short film-clips, press cuttings with shocking and funny titles, or simple diagrams? As we saw earlier, our visual faculties are the first to respond to information from the environment. In order to target 'Area 17' of the brain we have to use visual imagery, so pictures can be powerful communication devices. Perhaps also consider other aids that you can use to involve the audience. For example, how could you use food, chocolates, audio-tapes and videos, role-plays, pair work, group work, pyramid work, group quizzes, juggling balls and fancy dress in your presentations in the future? Whatever you do decide to use to pep up your talk, don't overuse these, because YOU are by far the most important audio-visual aid that you will ever be able to use. Your delivery and actions will always speak more loudly than slick PowerPoint presentations or any number of fancy gizmos.[1]

Delivering the presentation

You are now ready to deliver the talk, but may be feeling nervous and anxious. This is to be expected, because you are in a fight–flight situation. However, you may be experiencing a lot more than a little anxiety, with fast, shallow breathing, a light head and pounding heart, a cotton mouth, wobbly legs and excessive sweating. If you ever feel this panicky, be assured that there are ways to overcome this. Remember that all public speakers and actors experience anxiety and nervousness. For example, Dame Judi Dench, one of the most respected stage and film actors of recent years, was once asked by Michael Parkinson during a TV interview on the BBC how she coped with nerves before going on stage. She instantly replied, 'It's anxiety and fear that create adrenaline – for me that's the petrol in the engine.' Stand-up comedians describe the time immediately before going on stage as 'Walking the 15 yards', and this is regarded as the most nerve-wracking time of any show.

Focus on channelling this nervous energy into your performance. Here are a few well-tried tips for coping with this. First and foremost, you must know your material. This is why the preparation phase of a talk is so important. If you have prepared well, you will be more confident when you stand up to deliver the presentation. Second, focus on the task at hand. If you can, arrive at the auditorium early and get everything set up ready to start. Always have some water to drink before presenting. Actors drink plenty of water when they are in stage productions, because it lubricates the vocal chords. This will also help avoid the unwelcome appearance of 'Dry biscuit mouth' and 'Who put the glue in my toothpaste?' Re-enter the auditorium just before you are due to start, or with the person who will be introducing you. If you have to hang around before delivering your presentation, talk to a few people in the audience, remember their names and refer to them in your introduction or during the talk. Just before you start, take three or four deep breaths; this will open up your lungs and voice box and pump oxygen round your body. Then introduce yourself or thank the chair. Refer to your audience and the occasion, tell them about your credentials, if necessary, and then begin your talk.

One of the most intimidating aspects of public speaking is being stared at by large groups of people. This is a natural reaction, based on a deep-rooted primordial human fear: the ancient terror of being attacked by the clan or tribe. All you have to remember is that they see you *as an individual* and you must view them in the same way. You should make eye contact at least once with every member of your audience. As you talk, scan left to right and right to left. Don't forget to include the 'widows and orphans' (people sitting to your extreme left or right at the front) and those sitting right at the back of the auditorium. When you finish a sentence, maintain eye contact with one person for two or three seconds.

Throughout the talk, remember to breathe deeply and that with vocal delivery it is critical to breathe into and from the stomach, not just into the chest. If you don't do this, you cannot vocalize or project your voice properly. This will also encourage you to slow down and help with your pronunciation. If you have problems, 'uming' and 'ahing' a lot (which can become very irritating after a short time), try to utter these silently to yourself. If you want to communicate with the visual and emotional parts of the brain, you also have to pay attention to your pitch, pace, pauses, volume and tonal quality. Try to vary your tempo: speeding up to create tension or excitement, slowing down and increasing the volume when you want to make a pivotal or important point. Remember to pause at regular intervals. If you are nervous, it's very easy to rabbit on at high speed. Pauses give you time to collect your thoughts, give your audience a short rest and can be very effective just after you have made a significant point. One of the greatest Shakespearian actors of the 20th century, Sir Ralph Richardson, once said, 'The most precious things in speeches are pauses.'

Be passionate, visionary, convincing, knowledgable and motivational in the way you talk. Practise this and stretch the boundaries of the way you say things. To some extent, public speaking is an act. Enthusiasm and passion for a subject will cover a multitude of other sins. If you are not enthused, your audience won't be. Don't be aloof, remote or patronizing and be very careful about telling jokes because it is surprisingly easy to offend people. Try to be sincere – even if you don't always mean it! As the French dramatist Jean Giraudoux once observed about acting, 'the secret of success is sincerity. Once you can fake that, you've got it made.' Last, wherever possible, keep your answers to questions from the audience short and to the point, and try to avoid the old 'foot in the mouth' technique. Here's the one that won the 2002 Foot in the Mouth Award. Responding to a question from an interviewer about his (allegedly) ambiguous sexuality, the actor Richard Gere replied: 'I know who I am. Nobody else knows who I am. Does it change the fact of who I am what anyone says about it? If I was a giraffe, and someone said I was a snake, I'd think, no, I'm actually a giraffe.'

Many of the presentation techniques described above have been used for more than two thousand years. For example, the ancient Romans developed oratorical and presentation skills to a very high level. They believed that good public speakers had to have a central *thesis* (what they were going to argue); *controversia* (strong evidence to support their arguments); *suasoria* (using myths, legends, history and illustrative stories) and *vox forte* (well-developed vocal and voice projection skills). Lawrence Olivier's son has even taught these principles as 'mythodrama' to senior executives in the UK. In order to develop your *vox forte*, please try the next self-development exercise.

Exercise 3.7

Using a full range of emotions

You may feel slightly ridiculous doing the next exercise, but this has been used in drama and acting classes for decades. It can also be a useful device to help you make fuller use of a range of human emotions in presentations. Find a place where people won't be able to hear you practising. Here is a well-known poem (used in the first audio recording of a human voice, made by Thomas Edison in 1877):

> Mary had a little lamb,
> Its fleece as white as snow.
> And everywhere that Mary went,
> The lamb was sure to go.

Now, please read this out loud in the following styles:

Angry/excited/bored/passionate/worried/frightened/critical/not convinced of the facts/convinced of the facts/accusing/suspicious/factual and, last, as if this was the closing statement of a presentation.

You should aim to have *at least half* of these emotions in any presentations you deliver in the future. ◆

To make a visceral, personal and emotional connection with an audience also requires something that many sports coaches are familiar with, kinaesthetic awareness. Kinaesthetic speakers are aware that audiences want to experience presentations on a physical as well as an intellectual level. Because they are aware of their body language and physical presence, they can create powerful non-verbal messages that reinforce the verbal ones. Most people do not spend enough time focusing on this component of presentation skills. We also live in a highly visual information age, where people expect to be 'close' to the person delivering a message on screen. So, to create a kinaesthetic bond with an audience means that you have to, literally, get near to them and this means moving away from the podium and laptop. This is the area I've come to think of as '*The Twilight Zone*', where the speaker is trapped in the dimly lit corridor between the podium and the projector screen, disconnected from their audiences for the duration of their talk.

Instead, use all the available floor space. Move towards your audience to engage with them and select sections of your audience to talk with or to ask direct questions. At all times, use open gestures. Giving members of the audience items to look at, or comment on, can also create a powerful bond. The more you know about your audience *before* giving your presentation, the more confident you will feel about putting yourself about during presentations. To engage with an audience means that you have to manage both your body language and the technologies you use. If you are not careful, the overhead or PowerPoint projector can become a security blanket to hide behind. You may also need to be aware of imitating one or more of the following characters:

The horizontal bungee-jumper
This is someone who cannot escape from the magnetic force-field in *The Twilight Zone*, and is propelled back into this area as soon as they get a short distance away from it.

The tennis player
Also known as the Wimbledon position – this is where we have someone who has alternating conversations with their audience and the projector screen behind them, like watching a rally at a tennis match. Novice presenters can spend 80–90 per cent of their time having animated conversations with their overheads or slides.

The leaning tower of Pisa
Having apparently lost the ability to balance on both legs at the same time, this presenter will lean against everything they encounter: podiums, walls, tables, desks and chairs. Not to be confused with Long John Silver.

Long John Silver
This presenter has also lost the ability to stand on both legs at the same time, but prefers to lean over the podium, with hands gripping the side for dear life and balancing on alternate legs.

Fred Astaire/Ginger Rogers
A cousin of Long John Silver, this would-be dancer is compelled to constantly tap alternate feet on the ground.

Road-runner
This is someone who is incapable of standing still and usually stalks up and down in *The Twilight Zone* in a straight line and very quickly, while having animated conversations with the floor or their notes.

The musketeer
Give this presenter a long pointy thing (or, even worse, a laser pointer) and watch him (rarely her) turn into one of the Three Musketeers for the duration of their talk.

The fig leaf
This is a common ailment, where both men and women feel the need to protect their most sensitive bits from attacks by the audience, by crossing their hands over each other at waist level.

The sergeant major
He is a rare sight, but can be spotted occasionally in businessmen with military backgrounds (hands on hips, chin thrust forward, rapid stentorian delivery style, etc).

Captain Vanity
This is someone who feels the need to regularly groom their hair and is perpetually adjusting their clothing or brushing off imaginary bits of fluff.

Last, but not least, switch the projector off occasionally. All audiences will breathe a deep sigh of relief if you do this during your presentations.

Dealing with uncooperative participants

Sooner or later, in public speaking situations, we will all encounter 'The Participant From Hell' (PFH), whose mission is to contradict everything you say or disagree with every point you make. There are some well-known one-liners that could be used in these situations:

- 'Would you like to step outside and repeat that? Good. Well stay there while I finish my talk.'
- 'Don't say another word. I want to forget you exactly the way you are.'
- 'When I want your opinion, I'll give it to you.'

Unfortunately, these only work in the movies. In real life, comments like this will only serve to antagonize the PFH. However, there are some strategies that do work well most of the time. If you find people are chatting constantly, simply stop talking and look directly at them. Nine times out of ten, they'll stop immediately. If this doesn't work, ask them if they have a question. Smile at them and then continue. If you come across people who disagree with everything you say, don't get defensive or argue with them. Let them air their concern or gripe. Then, immediately, ask the rest of the audience what they think. Nine times out of ten, they'll pounce on this PFH and peer-group pressure will force him to back down. Because they are often ignorant about the subject you are talking about, you can also ask them if they have read the relevant book or report that addresses their query. If they haven't, your problem is solved. If they persist, simply apply the emotional diffusion technique we looked at earlier in this chapter, 'I can see that you feel very strongly about this point. Why don't we discuss this at the end?' Occasionally, you'll come across people who like to dominate discussions. As this PFH speaks, move slowly towards them. The instant they stop talking, break eye contact and move away from them saying, 'Thank you. Let's get some input from the rest of the group.' The non-verbal signals here send a powerful message. Last, you might have given a presentation and launched a 'bouncer question', so-called because you launch it over your audiences' heads and it bounces straight back to you – unanswered. Unless you are very confident that you are going to get some useful answers back, don't do it! Either ask a rhetorical question (which you then answer), or direct your question to a small section of the audience or to individuals you know.

Conclusion

At the beginning of this section we established that effective presentation skills can be broken down into six components. These were: knowing your audience, structuring your talk, enhancing the content of the presentation, choosing which audio-visual aids to use (and *how* to use these), delivering the presentation, and dealing with uncooperative participants. This covers the essentials of public speaking, but is only the starting point. With this particular leadership/management skill, practice really does make perfect. So practise it whenever you can, in front of the mirror, family pets, your kids, anyone who'll listen, and video yourself the next few times you do a talk. Join a local public speaking club for a while, such as The Round Table. If you use a video to record your next presentation, look at the playback dispassionately. Make a note of what is good and areas where you can make improvements in the future. Turn the sound off and focus on your body language. Do you move around too much or too little? Do you use your hands and body well? Do you make full use of the room and engage with your audience? If you can, use your junior staff to get feedback. For example, Mike Allred, of the US company Visual Information Technologies, used to hold dry runs of his presentations to the board of directors with the 90 employees who reported to him. As a result of this, he enjoyed a 'triple whammy'. He was well prepared, his staff asked him lots of awkward questions, and offered helpful suggestions, and they were kept informed about key organizational issues. Neat.

Public speaking is a skill that comes naturally to very few people. I've been doing this for more than a decade, but still learn new things about this complex set of skills every time I do a presentation. The more you do, the easier it gets, but this does not mean that 'more equals better'. It is about learning *what* the best public speakers say (the content) and *how* they do this (the delivery). So, the next time you listen to someone else giving a presentation, look at what they are doing as much as you listen to what they are saying. Some people blissfully travel through life, boring countless audiences to sleep, losing customers and clients and alienating their employees, because they haven't grasped some of the simple techniques described in this section. The use of a platform to deliver a talk is a privilege and gives you an unrivalled and rare opportunity to get your ideas across to large groups of people, without being interrupted (for the most part). In its most potent forms, public speaking creates opportunities to change the way that people think and behave, and this is essential if you want to use power effectively and manage change in organizations (see Chapters 7 and 8).[2]

> Brevity is the sister of talent.
> (*Anton Chekov*)

> To be persuasive, we must be believable.
> To be believable, we must be credible.
> To be credible, we must be truthful.
> (*Edward Murrow*)

> The passionate are the only advocates who always persuade. The simplest man with passion will be more persuasive than the most eloquent without.
> (*René Descartes*)

Exercise 3.8

After reading this section, you may have acquired some new insights into ways of developing your presentation skills. Please create an 'A' list (urgent, things you really should change now) and a 'B' list (important, but not essential for now). You should focus on changing no more than two or three of these during any one presentation.

'A' List

1.

2.

3.

4.

5.

'B' List

1.

2.

3.

4.

5.   ◆

Cross-cultural communication

Before reading through this section, please complete the next exercise.
(*There may be more than one answer to each question.*)

Exercise 3.9

Cross-cultural communication

1. Pork is not consumed by the dominant religious group in which country?

    a. Saudi Arabia
    b. Egypt
    c. Malaysia
    d. Indonesia

2. Before entering a South Korean's home, you should remove your shoes and wait to be invited in.

    a. True
    b. False

3. In which country should both hands be used when passing an object to a native?

    a. Germany
    b. Canada
    c. South Korea
    d. Former USSR

4. In Latin American and Asian countries, if you try to maintain eye contact with your native host while discussing business, you are likely to be interpreted as

    a.   honest and truthful

    b.   aggressive

    c.   attentive

5.   In which countries is it advisable to carry a large quantity of business cards (in English and the language of that country) and give one to everyone you meet?

    a.   Korea

    b.   Japan

    c.   China

    d.   Taiwan

6.   In which country would you not accept being told directly that your proposal was unacceptable?

    a.   Japan

    b.   China

    c.   Taiwan

    d.   Malaysia

7.   It is not polite to admire an object while in the presence of your host in Saudi Arabia because he may feel obliged to give it to you.

    a.   True

    b.   False

8.   South Americans, Africans and Arabs stand closer than is customary in the United States and backing away may suggest dislike or aloofness.

    a.   True

    b.   False

9.   During the month of Ramadan, Muslims fast from sunrise to sunset. While in their presence you should not

    a.   eat

    b.   smoke

    c.   drink alcohol

10.   Friday is the day of rest in which country?

    a.   Pakistan

    b.   Jordan

    c.   Somalia

    d.   Kuwait

11.   In Islamic countries, women must dress to avoid exposure of arms and legs and body shape.

    a.   True

    b.   False

12.   When in Saudi Arabia, you should not:

    a.   discuss women
    b.   discuss politics
    c.   discuss religion
    d.   refer to the Persian Gulf as the Arabian Gulf

13.   Potato chips manufactured by the Wise Corporation, with its owl trademark, are not likely to be sold in:

    a.   India because the owl is a sign of bad luck*
    b.   England because of the colour of its packaging
    c.   Canada because of the shape of the chip

14.   In which region of the world is the hiring of a family member considered an accepted norm?

    a.   East Asia
    b.   Latin America
    c.   Arabian countries

15.   In which country is it likely to be viewed as unsanitary to have toilet and bath facilities in the same room?

    a.   Ireland
    b.   Japan
    c.   Venezuela
    d.   Oman

16.   In which country would a person greet an elder by bowing lower and longer than the older person?

    a.   China
    b.   Taiwan
    c.   Brazil
    d.   Japan

17.   In which country does a man greet a woman by placing the palms of both hands together and bowing slightly?

    a.   China
    d.   Taiwan
    c.   South Korea
    d.   Malaysia
    e.   India

18.   In which country would a greeting include a slight bow followed by a handshake?

    a.   China
    b.   Taiwan
    c.   Brazil
    d.   Indonesia

19.   When shaking hands, which of the following is true?

      a.   In France, it includes a slight grasp and a quick, crisp handshake.
      b.   In China, a pumping handshake conveys pleasure.
      c.   Among Arabs, the handshake is limp and long.
      d.   Among South African Blacks, the handshake is followed by clenched thumbs and then another handshake.

20.   Men do not shake hands with women in:

      a.   South Korea
      b.   India
      c.   Saudi Arabia
      d.   Thailand

Answers: 1. a, b, c and d. 2. a. 3. c. 4. b. 5. a, b, c and d. 6. a, b, c and d. 7. a. 8. a. 9. a, b and c. 10. a, b, c and d. 11. a. 12. a, b, c and d. 13. a*. 14. a, b and c. 15. b. 16. d. 17. e. 18. a, b, c and d. 19. a, b, c and d. 20. a.

(* Some doubts have been expressed about this answer. However, owls are certainly regarded as taboo by Navajo Indians in the USA.)

Award yourself one mark for each correct answer and then add up your total _____

Interpreting your score

16–20:   excellent understanding of other cultures,
11–15:   good understanding of other cultures,
 6–10:   below average understanding of other cultures,
 0–5:   limited understanding of other cultures.

Source: adapted from Nowlin (1990). ◆

_____

Introduction

In this section, we will look briefly at the problems associated with communication between different cultures, some different rules of business protocol and the errors that can be made by those who are unfamiliar with the body language and social cues of other cultures (adapted from Forster, 2000c: ch. 3). While a detailed discussion of all the dimensions of cross-cultural communication is beyond the scope of this book, it is worth touching on this topic for three reasons. First, most organizations now employ culturally diverse workforces and the management of these is becoming a more significant people management issue. Second, increasing numbers of employees are embracing international careers, or are being sent on expatriate assignments by their employers. Third, cultural differences are becoming more important as business continues to globalize, where reporting lines can run from an operating plant in China, through a regional HQ in Hong Kong and back to a corporate centre in Europe or the USA. Hence the need to think and manage beyond our home-cultures' mind-sets can only become more important in the future.

We've seen in the preceding sections how complex communication can be in organizations. If we then include cross-cultural differences in communication (linguistic, attitudinal and behavioural), we have yet another level of complexity to deal with. This is because culture has a highly pervasive influence on the behaviour, perceptions, attitudes, motivations, values, morals and personalities of individuals. All of these are, to a very large extent, shaped by culture (from the Latin word for civilization, *cultura*). Humans have now evolved to a point where culture has superseded instinct in determining much of our habitual thinking and behaviour. The importance of culture lies in the fact that it provides the body of knowledge and techniques that enable us to act, both physically and socially, in the world and provides us with world-views that enable us to make sense of ourselves and the people around us. Culture can also shape many of the things that we take for granted, such as facial expressions, use of personal space, posture, gestures, personal appearance, etiquette, body contact and appropriate conduct when dealing with men and women. Shakespeare's memorable line, 'All the world's a stage and all the men and women merely players', shows how all individuals must learn the lines, gestures and manners appropriate to their culture if they are to succeed in life. Culture can even influence how we perceive time. Cultures throughout the world organize time in two basic ways: either monochromic (M-time) or poly-phonic (P-time). M-time is characteristic of people in the western world, where time is linear, segmented and manageable. People from cultures on P-time place a different emphasis on time, where appointments are not necessarily ironclad commitments.

We do not usually think consciously about our culture, unless we perceive it to be threatened by some external force or we are put in a situation where we are in a cultural minority. In other words our cultures operate largely at an *unconscious* level. Try this quick test: pick up a pen and a piece of paper and try to describe your home-country's culture in detail. It is not as easy as it sounds. However, much of what we habitually think, how we interpret the world and how we act are the result of what we have been taught in our culture. Hence a business executive who has been highly successful in one culture might find it difficult, if not impossible, to function in another culture, unless he or she is aware of the significance of cultural differences. Another important element of culture is that it takes years and years to learn and internalize. Yet, when it comes to overseas postings, we expect expatriate staff to engage in business relationships with people from other cultures and learn their culturally prescribed ways of doing business in a matter of weeks, if not days.

Goodman has pointed to another significant element of culture: 'In many respects, one can think of culture as being analogous to an iceberg. As with an iceberg, there is the part of the culture that is clearly in sight and there is a larger part of culture (the most dangerous) that is submerged, out of sight, below the waterline, waiting to destroy any business venture if people are unaware of its hidden dangers' (Goodman, 1994: 41). Cultural items 'above the waterline' include language, food, festivals, clothing and dress, architecture and art. Those 'below the waterline' are much more numerous and include business ethics, values, morality, facial and body language, male–female relationships, family fealty, learning styles, work motivation and employee loyalty. Understanding and respecting these differences is essential if an organization's employees can adapt to working with people from different cultures.

How linguistic and cultural differences can cause problems with communication

> I speak Spanish to God, Italian to women, French to men and German to my horse.
> (*Emperor Charlemagne of France, 772* CE)

One of the most visible signs of the multiplicity of human cultures is language. Although English is fast becoming the common global language of business and education, it can still cause many misunderstandings. Semantics too can cause a lot of problems. For example, the words and phrases 'free market', 'accountability', 'corporate regulation' and 'business ethics' mean different things to a typical Swedish, American, Russian, Australian or Indonesian businessperson. The Japanese word 'Hai', which translates literally as 'Yes', can also mean 'Yes, I'm listening' rather than 'Yes, I agree'. Thais perceive the word 'No' differently to English-speaking people, because they do not have a word for this in their language. Here are a few more examples of how even very subtle mistakes in translation can cause problems (and some amusement) for English speakers:

- A detour sign spotted in Japan read, 'Road closed. Please drive sideways'.
- Pepsi Cola's 'Come alive' jingle was once translated into Taiwanese as, 'Pepsi brings your ancestors back from the grave.'

- The first time Coca-Cola was introduced into China, it was translated phonetically as *ke-kou-ke-la*. After thousands of signs had been printed, the company discovered that this meant 'bite the wax tadpole' or 'female horse stuffed with wax'. Having researched 40 000 Chinese characters, they found a close phonetic equivalent, *ko-kou-ko-le*, which means 'happiness in the mouth'.
- Kentucky Fried Chicken, also in China, discovered too late that their logo, 'Finger licking good' had been translated as 'Eat your fingers off'. KFC bit the dust again, this time in Mexico, when they realized that their advertisement, 'It takes a tender chicken to satisfy a tough man', had been translated as 'It takes a hard man to satisfy a tender chicken.'
- When GM introduced the Chevy Nova into South America they were blissfully unaware that 'No va' means 'It won't go' in Spanish.
- When Ford tried to sell the Pinto in Brazil they were puzzled by its low sales, until someone pointed out that 'Pinto' was Brazilian slang for 'tiny balls'.
- The Parker pen was introduced into Mexico with the slogan, 'It won't leak in your pocket and embarrass you'. But the word they used for embarrass, 'embarazar', means 'to make pregnant', so this was quickly withdrawn.
- The operating manual of a car rental firm in Tokyo advised customers, 'When passenger of foot hove in sight, tootle him with your horn. Trumpet him melodiously at first but if he still obstacles your passage then tootle him with vigour.'
- A dry cleaning shop in Belgium once advised its English-speaking customers to 'Leave your clothes here and spend the rest of the afternoon having a good time.'
- An advertisement in the Gulf States featured a washing machine. On the left-hand side was a pile of dirty washing, the washing powder was in the middle and a pile of clean washing was on the right-hand side. Naturally, this was not well received by the target audience and the advert was quickly withdrawn. Why?
- The Scandinavian company, Electrolux, once introduced a vacuum cleaner into America with the slogan, 'Nothing sucks like an Electrolux'.
- In 1998, a logo for Wall's ice cream in the Gulf States was withdrawn after they discovered that the design, when turned upside down, looked like Allah. This blunder scuppered their plans for a single, worldwide logo and is estimated to have cost the company $US25 million.

(*Source*:   various websites, 1997–2003)

However, these linguistic misunderstandings fade into insignificance when we look at the way culture shapes rules of behaviour and social attitudes. On one level, stereotypes such as, 'The British can't cook', 'The French drive like maniacs', 'Germans have no sense of humour', 'The Greeks never get anything done on time', 'Italian men never escape from their mothers', 'The Irish drink like fish' and so forth can be amusing. But they also remind us that there is a fine line between having a laugh about each other's cultures and discriminating against people on this basis. On another level, if negative cultural stereotyping is not discouraged, it is just one small step to the racism that under-pinned the slave trade of the 18th and 19th centuries, or the kind of virulent, genocidal racism that culminated in the Nazi regime in Germany in the 1930s and 1940s, and other more recent instances of 'ethnic cleansing'. Hence, unless leaders are aware of cultural stereo-types (which are entirely *learnt*), there is a real danger that they will be unable to manage culturally diverse workforces effectively.[3]

Here are some examples of some cultural differences that can lead to mutual misunderstandings and antipathy: many people in East Asia regard Americans, Australians and Britons as loud, pushy and arro-gant. Conversely, these nationalities and many Europeans regard Asians, collectively, as quiet, deferential, conformist and often lacking a sense of humour. The Britons and Americans rarely use business meetings for socializing. For people from the Middle East and East Asia, this is a normal part of meetings and essential for building up business contacts and relationships. There are differences in the way that punctuality is perceived in different cultures. For Germans it is very important to arrive at meetings at a pre-arranged time. To be late is simply unacceptable. For Italians, Spaniards and Greeks, this is usually less important. How employees deal with their bosses also varies from culture to culture. Junior Japanese employees have to develop highly tuned systems for interpreting what are often deliber-ately vague suggestions from their senior managers. They call this *sasshi*, meaning 'the ability to guess'. Most American, British or Australian employees who are accustomed to being told what to do by their bosses would not be able to cope with this for long. The Japanese often hold several meetings to deal with problems: one to decide what the problem is, a second to gather further information and a third to deal with the problem. There may be further meetings to communicate decisions that have been made outside these meetings by senior managers. Again, this is something that Americans, the British or Australians find incomprehensible, unless they understand something about Japanese business protocols.

Even very simple things like greetings vary from culture to culture. Hand shaking is almost universal, but there is only one Muslim coun-try in the whole world where it is acceptable to shake women's hands

– Indonesia. Some handshakes are very soft (in many African countries) and quite hard in others (in Anglo-Saxon cultures). It is acceptable for Greek, Spanish and Russian men to kiss when greeting each other, but most Australians and Americans would feel very uncomfortable with this. In Vietnam, men often express friendship by touching and holding each other during conversations. For many Americans or Australians this would be considered inappropriate. For many Muslims, touching the head is deeply offensive, whereas touching the shoulders is seen as a sign of brotherhood. So patting the child of a Muslim on the head, which is seen as a sign of care or protection in western cultures, could cause offence. In Korea, young people are socially forbidden from touching the shoulders of their elders. For Kuwaitis, it is considered highly offensive to cross your legs at functions, because this shows the sole of the foot. The 'open legged' posture is popular amongst men from all Arabic states.

Eye contact varies enormously. In all western cultures, maintaining steady eye contact is seen as a good thing, signifying honesty and reliability. In eastern cultures this is not so. In general, junior employees will lower their eyes when talking with senior managers. Westerners are sometimes described as 'people who stare', which can be seen as threatening and underpins the idea of 'giving face' to your hosts. In less deferential and hierarchical western companies, questioning the boss is often acceptable in meetings; in Chinese companies it isn't. The Chinese traditionally do not show emotion in public because the idea of 'saving face' is deeply rooted in their culture. For the Chinese, displaying emotion violates face-saving norms by disrupting harmony and causing conflict. For most cultures, a smile is usually a sign of happiness or friendly affirmation. For the Japanese, this can also be used to avoid answering a question or to mask an emotion. A nod from a Japanese person often means 'I understand you' or 'I recognize you', not 'I agree'. Chinese and Japanese people consider blowing the nose in public to be pretty disgusting, but the Chinese find spitting in public places quite acceptable. You might have to be careful about offering alcoholic drinks or pork to Muslims, but also remember that it is considered extremely rude to refuse any food offered to you by many people from Japan or China.

For Americans and many other nationalities, the rounded, pinched-thumb and index finger 'A-OK' gesture is easily recognized as meaning 'fine', 'perfect', or simply 'okay'. For Japanese people this means 'money'. For Latin Americans and people from Middle Eastern countries this has an obvious offensive or obscene meaning. To signify stupidity in others, the French, Germans and Italians generally simply tap their own heads. In the UK and the USA this means 'I understand'.

North Americans, French, Italians and Germans also make spiral motions with the forefinger toward the side of the head to indicate a crazy idea. A finger raised towards an individual to indicate 'come here' would be considered very rude to Arabs, who instead signal this with the fingers in a downward grasping motion. Last, but certainly not least, culture has a profound influence on shaping and defining what men and women 'are' and their roles in society (see Chapter 6).

The purpose of presenting these examples is to show how easy it can be, even for experienced managers, to offend unintentionally those from another culture. Consequently, cultural sensitivity is a competency that is of growing importance to leader/managers and organizations. For example, imagine you are working in an advertising firm in the USA. You've recently been reading some marketing reports showing that some 35 million Americans are of Spanish descent, and their collective consumer purchasing power has risen by 100 per cent in a decade. How would you target this group? Without an awareness of cultural differences, you'd probably just overdub existing English advertisements into Spanish or translate existing hard copy advertisements into Spanish. However, this would be extremely ineffective, because there is a world of difference between, say, a Cuban who fled the country in the 1950s when Castro came to power, a poor first-generation Mexican immigrant and a third-generation Puerto Rican whose grandchildren regard themselves as Americans. In spite of a common language, the Hispanic community in the USA originates from many countries. It constitutes a number of identifiable sub-cultures, with wide variations in levels of affluence, patterns of consumer spending and political allegiances. Hence a blanket approach to advertising to these groups would be very ineffective in comparison to selective advertising.

In some sectors, like the design departments in the automotive industry, it would be commercial suicide not to have culturally diverse workforces. Why? Because the car is a global product. For example, the prestigious course on Vehicle Design at the London Royal College of Art has only produced about 300 graduates in 30 years. Yet it has always had a mixture of nationalities enrolled there. Currently, the design studios of companies as diverse as Jaguar, Audi, Porsche, Skoda, McClaren F1, Lotus and Aston Martin are staffed by RCA graduates. Almost all of these do not work in their countries of origin. This cultural mix is useful because the car is a global product and yet needs to reflect national market tastes. Without this, it would not be possible to design and build cars that can be built from the same basic plans, using the same manufacturing processes and, at the same time, allow customization to reflect local market needs and consumer preferences.

Hence, even within a domestic context, effective leaders should have some knowledge of cultural differences, particularly if they are managing culturally diverse workforces. This is even more important if you are a leader whose company operates in international markets.[4] This knowledge comprises the following:

- an awareness of cultural differences – even superficially similar cultures are often quite different under the surface,
- a respect for other cultures – because no single culture is 'better' than another (even if we might disagree strongly with certain aspects of the value-systems of other cultures),
- an ability to accommodate cultural differences within an organization's people management policies – for example, allowing Muslims time to pray to Mecca during working hours,
- where to get advice on the management of cultural diversity in the workplace.

Another method is to expose home-country nationals to other cultures by sending them on international assignments. Many multinational companies encourage cross-border moves to promote the development of cross-cultural management skills amongst their managerial staff. If face-to-face communication is still the most effective way of communicating, one of the best ways of developing international communication within companies is by exposing people of many different nationalities to a melting pot of language and cultures, through international postings and job mobility (Forster, 2000c).

Conclusion

Having read through this chapter, you may have a fuller appreciation of the complexities of interpersonal and organizational communication, and how leaders and managers can use communication media more effectively. Exercises 3.1 and 3.2 showed how most people often think they are good communicators and it is *other* people who lack this important leadership and managerial skill. The reality is that most people overestimate their personal communication skills. It is apparent that, on both an interpersonal and an organizational level, communication is a much-desired but often undervalued skill, and most leaders and managers can learn to become better communicators, given time and effort. Communication practices must also be consistent under all organizational conditions. If they are not, the organization will, sooner or later, encounter problems. And, although you may be a leader/manager in a company operating within your own national boundaries at the present time, it is absolutely certain that your workforce will become (if it is not already) more culturally diverse in the future. This means that at some time in the near future you may also have to add an understanding of this to your leadership and people management tool-kit.

Our coverage of communication does not end here. Communication feeds into virtually every activity that leader/managers are involved in because, as we saw earlier, it is 'a process of respectfully sharing information with others in order to improve understanding'. Therefore it underpins leadership in teams (Chapter 5), the way that men and women relate to each other at work (Chapter 6), the management of power, politics and conflict (Chapter 7), leading cultural and organizational change (Chapter 8), the management of innovation and perpetual learning (Chapter 9), managing employee knowledge and intellectual capital (Chapter 10) and leadership in high-tech, networked and virtual organizations (Chapter 11). It also underpins the motivation, empowerment and performance of employees, which are described in the next chapter.

Exercise 3.10

Having read through this concluding section on cross-cultural communication issues, are there any new insights that you can make use of in the future?

Insight	Strategy to implement this
1.	
2.	
3.	
4.	
5.	◆

Notes

1   For any university lecturers or school teachers reading this book, Tara Brabazon has made these comments about the use of PowerPoint in *Digital Hemlock: Internet Education and the Poisoning of Teaching* (Sydney: University of New South Wales Press, 2002):

> If I could uninvent one software program, it would be PowerPoint. Without exception, the worst presentations, lectures and budget briefings I attend are conducted using this tragic package. Presenters break all the rules of public speaking: repeating verbatim the words on the screen; letting the technology determine the pace

and order of the presentation; and even requiring the darkening of the room. Many of these presentations either do not run or start late because of problems with the technology. For students, new problems emerge. Students desire access to the over-heads of a lecture – this access means that they do not have to attend the lecture. More seriously, the students who check their notes against the PowerPoint slides will invariably copy down any points they missed – word for word. This is not crit-ical thinking; it is not even thinking. Further, the illusion of access promoted by computers creates the confusion between the presentation of information and the capacity to use, sort and interpret it. Information is not the issue; the methodolo-gies available to assess it must be given more attention.

During 12 years' involvement, with more than one thousand postgraduate manage-ment students, PowerPoint has hardly ever been used (and you might be thinking, 'So what?'). Well, the interesting thing is that just three MBAs have ever suggested that this technology should be used, either in person or on their end-of-course Teaching Evaluation forms (and, even then, only in small doses). Perhaps it is time to re-evaluate the ubiquitous use of this 'tragic package' in university teaching? For a fine example of how PowerPoint can be used to completely ruin a great speech, see http://www.norvig.com/Gettysburg/index.htm

2   For more information on public speaking, there are some useful books in the Bibliography at the end of the book.

3   It is significant that the most recent advances in the mapping of humanity's genome, and studies of our collective origins, have revealed that there is in fact only one 'race': the human race. Studies of the human genome have revealed that the genes that are associated with 'racial differences', such as stature, skin pigmentation and nose and eye shapes constitute – at most – 0.01 per cent of this. The minor differences between different human groups that do exist evolved over millennia in response to different climatic and geographical conditions, and the environmental challenges they faced. It was the geographical and reproductive isolation of early humans that created the 'racial' diversity we see today. In contrast, universal human traits, such as intelli-gence, run into hundreds of thousands of genes. Significantly, globalization, combined with increasing mobility (and interbreeding) between nationals from different countries and cultures, and the homogenization of living environments through industrialization, will mean that these superficial racial differences are likely to disappear over the next 1000 years. Some geneticists have predicted that the typi-cal human in 3000 CE will be a honey-coloured, hairless, willowy figure who proba-bly speaks American-English as their first language (400 million people already speak English as their first language and it is a second language to 1.5 billion).

4   A detailed discussion of the communication skills and leadership competencies required in countries other than the USA, Canada, the United Kingdom, Australia and New Zealand is beyond the scope of this book. However, we do return briefly to the topic of international leadership in Chapter 12 and in the conclusion to the book. If you would like more information on the management of international/expatriate assignments and cross-cultural acclimatization, a starting point is N. Forster (2000c), *Managing Staff on International Assignments: A Strategic Guide*, London: Financial Times and Prentice-Hall.

4 Employee motivation, empowerment and performance

Objectives

To define motivation, empowerment and performance.

To describe a variety of theories about motivation and empowerment and their practical applications for leaders and managers.

To show how satisfaction *and* dissatisfaction can have a positive influence on employee motivation and performance.

To look at the influence of money as a motivator, and examine the effects of skills-based pay, performance pay and share/stock holding on the motivation and performance of employees.

To enhance your ability to motivate, empower and inspire your followers to higher levels of performance.

Introduction

> When work is a pleasure, life is a joy.
> (*Maxim Gorky, 1970*)

> If you want people to be motivated to do a good job, give them a good job to do.
> (*Frederick Herzberg, 1968*)

> If work were so great, the rich would have hogged it long ago.
> (*Mark Twain, 1890*)

The complex nature of motivation

We believe that underlying the oft-stated cliché that 'people are our most important asset' is a deeper truth: to the extent that any organization can

160

truly unleash the hidden value in its people, it will increase its chances of success. This is particularly true in a world in which intellectual capital and knowledge are increasingly important. Most organizations do not capture this value.
(*Charles O'Reilly and Jeffrey Pfeffer,* Hidden Value, *2000*)

Motivation is one of the most written about, complex, contradictory and, it has to be said, dry topics in organizational and management studies. Theories of motivation and empowerment are largely grounded in the field of psychology where hedonism is seen as an important component of motivation: people, quite naturally, seek to maximize pleasure and minimize discomfort in their daily lives. The more pleasure they experience, the more motivated they should be and vice versa. Dozens of theories and models have been developed and tested over the last 50 years, purporting to describe employee motivation, empowerment and performance. While the empirical support for most of these theories is mixed, they can provide leaders and managers with useful insights into ways of improving employee motivation and performance.

Motivation is derived from the Latin *movere*, meaning 'to move'. In common with other terms used in this book, there are dozens of definitions of motivation. Some are long and some are short, but all are variations on the same theme. Motivation, in an organizational context, is defined as the processes that increase or decrease an individual's desire and commitment to achieve personal and organizational goals. Performance is derived from the archaic French word *perfoumer*, meaning 'to carry through in due form', and is defined here as the successful completion of a task, action or process at work. Empowerment is derived from the Latin word *potere*, meaning 'to be able'. While empowerment is often presented as a relatively new idea, this was first documented as long ago as 284 CE, by the Roman Emperor Diocletian, within the context of the decentralization of the Imperial Roman Civil Service (George, 1972). It is defined as the dual process of giving power to followers, while simultaneously developing the skills and competencies they will need to take on new roles and responsibilities. As we'll see in this and subsequent chapters, attempts merely to introduce empowerment without equipping people with the knowledge and confidence they need to cope with enhanced levels of responsibility and power are doomed to failure. In common with leadership and communication, this means that motivating and empowering others is also a two-way process of mutual influence and causation.

Regardless of the complexities surrounding motivation, it is evident that high levels of motivation are desirable from the point of view of leaders and managers within organizations and individual employees.

It is also important that organizations spend time and effort trying to increase the motivation, performance and productivity of their staff in the current climate of fierce competition and rapid, perpetual change in most organizations. When motivation levels are high in organizations, we usually find cultures where people do their best, enjoy their jobs and perform well at work. Where motivation levels are low in organizations, we invariably find dysfunctional cultures and employees who are indecisive, unhappy and underperforming. As James Carlopio and colleagues have suggested, 'A workplace with highly motivated staff is alive, energetic, co-operative, flexible and fun to work in. A de-motivated workplace is immediately experienced as sullen and apathetic, is full of conflict, is characterised by absenteeism and lowered productivity, and is unpleasant' (Carlopio *et al.*, 2001: 312). It has also been known for centuries that leaders who understand the needs of their followers (and are able to fulfil those needs) possess one of the keys to enhancing their motivation and performance levels. This premise forms the basis of the next self-development exercise.

Exercise 4.1

Part 1

There are many factors that have been associated with improving employee motivation and performance. Some of these are listed below. Before reading through the rest of this chapter, please rank the factors that motivate you from 1 to 15, with 1 being the most important and 15 the least important factor. Then consider what motivates your staff or employees at work.

	Self	Staff/Employees
Job security	_____	_____
Recognition and appreciation	_____	_____
Sense of involvement with company	_____	_____
Personal development and learning	_____	_____
Opportunities for promotion	_____	_____
Working for a successful company	_____	_____
Variety at work	_____	_____
High pay	_____	_____
Good working conditions	_____	_____
Creative and interesting work	_____	_____

Personal autonomy   _____   _____

Supportive and helpful boss   _____   _____

Clear goals and objectives   _____   _____

Equitable rewards for good
work performance   _____   _____

Healthy corporate culture and
climate   _____   _____

Part 2

Did you have any problems filling in the second column? What are the implications of this for your ability to lead and motivate other people at work now and in the future?

What motivational 'tools' are missing from this list which leaders and managers might make use of?

Is it possible to 'motivate' another person? If so, how do you do this?

◆

This exercise highlights three important – but often overlooked – facts about motivation. First, while we should all have a good understanding of our personal motivations and motivators, we may often second-guess what motivates other people at work. This is the natural consequence of the selective perceptions we have of the world and of other people (as described in Chapters 1 and 3). In practice, this means that we may falsely assume that what motivates us will also motivate other people. At best, this means that we will only ever be successful in motivating some of our followers, those whose motivational priorities broadly correspond with our own. Second, there are at least 30 different ways in which employee motivation and performance can be enhanced at work. How many of these were you able to identify in Exercise 4.1? Third, unless we consciously think about how we motivate other people, it can be very difficult to articulate how we actually do this. If we cannot do this, we will not be able to enhance our ability to motivate others in the future.

The following sections will review a number of theories of motivation and empowerment, divided into two broad categories – content and process. However, throughout this chapter, the focus will be on the practical applications of each of these for leaders and managers. An understanding of these theories can be helpful because each one highlights a number of strategies for enhancing employee motivation and performance (or, to be more accurate, ways of not *demotivating* people). It is also important to emphasize that each one of these is context-specific. This means that not all of the motivational principles outlined in this chapter may be relevant to you or your work situation and, as a practising leader/manager, you will already be aware of most of these motivational techniques. But, just as an architect or engineer can design better and more complex structures by having a larger set of conceptual and practical tools, so leader/managers should be in a better position to solve motivation and performance problems amongst their employees, simply by becoming more familiar with these theories and their applications.

Content theories

Content theories provide some insights into people's needs and help us to understand what people will (and will not) value as work motivators. There are four content theories (Robbins *et al.*, 2001: 195–206). The first, and best known, of these is Maslow's Hierarchy of Needs. Maslow was the first researcher to suggest that motivation was the product of human beings striving to satisfy a sequence of needs. These are, in ascending order:

- physiological needs (food, water, shelter, sex and rest),
- safety needs (security and protection from threats from the environment),
- social needs (love, affection, friendship and social interaction with other people),
- esteem needs (attention, recognition, self-respect, achievement, autonomy and status),
- self-actualization (psychological growth, self-expression, self-fulfilment and the full realization of individual potential).

Maslow argued that all humans are intrinsically motivated by a desire to satisfy these needs, from the lowest to the highest. As each need is satisfied it becomes less important and the next highest need increases in importance.

In a similar vein, Alderfer proposed a three-part hierarchy of needs in his ERG theory: **E**xistence (broadly corresponding to levels 1 and 2 in Maslow), **R**elatedness (broadly corresponding to levels 3 and 4 in Maslow), and **G**rowth (broadly corresponding to level 5 in Maslow). Alderfer argued that, once a lower-order need is satisfied, there is an increased desire to satisfy a higher-order need and this will increase the longer this need remains unsatisfied. He also argued that, if higher-order needs are not satisfied, lower-level needs may become more desirable, and more than one need may be operating at the same time. The third content theory, Herzberg's Two Factor theory, proposed an even simpler dichotomy between 'motivators' and 'hygiene' factors. He suggested that, if hygiene factors such as appropriate pay, good working conditions, good supervision, job security and good relationships with co-workers were not in place, this would lead to *dissatisfaction* (and poorer work performance over time). On the other hand, motivators such as achievement, responsibility, recognition, advancement and increased competence are all factors that will enhance motivation, and produce better work performance over time (Herzberg, 1995). In common with other aspects of leadership and people management already reviewed in this book, these ideas are not new. Charles Handy describes how ancient African tribes have had cultures that embraced 'lesser hungers' and 'greater hungers' for centuries, broadly corresponding to lower- and higher-order needs categories in Maslow's, Alderfer's and Herzberg's theories (Handy, 1996: 200).

The fourth content theory is McClelland's Achievement Motivation theory (McClelland, 1975, 1961; McClelland and Burnham, 1995). This theory focuses on three human needs: (a) need for *achievement*: a learnt need to excel and succeed in life, (b) need for *power*: a learnt need to lead and change the behaviours and beliefs of others, (c) need for *affiliation*: a learnt need for social interaction with others.

McClelland's pioneering work revealed that *intrinsic* motivation is far more powerful in promoting performance when compared to *extrinsic* motivation. An employee can be said to be intrinsically motivated if he or she participates enthusiastically in work activities without receiving any apparent extrinsic rewards. Extrinsic motivation refers to behaviour that is driven by external rewards and stimuli (Deci, 1975). A comparison of the four needs theories is illustrated in Figure 4.1 (p. 166).

Figure 4.1   Content theories of motivation compared

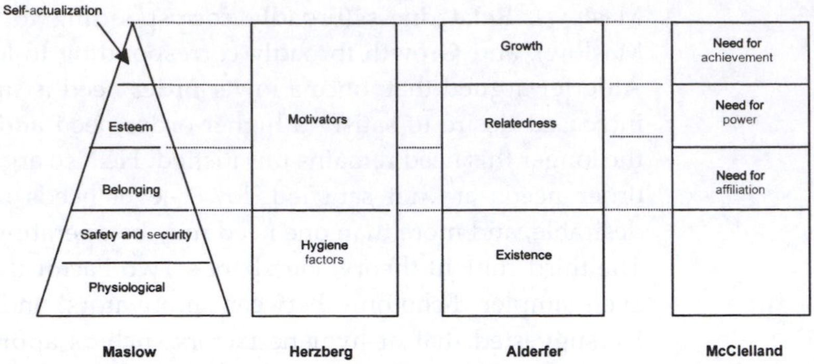

The practical applications of content theories

It was noted earlier that the empirical support for these theories is mixed. This means that their practical applicability in real-life settings has limitations. For example, all four theories assume that individuals have broadly similar needs and desires for power and achievement throughout their working lives. However, changing demographic, cultural and economic trends mean that present-day employees are likely to have a greater variety of needs, compared to the time when these theories were first developed (in each case, more than 30 years ago). Because of their focus on individual needs and motivations, they also overlook contingent factors that can influence motivation and performance, such as organizational cultures, reward systems and leadership styles. They are also culturally specific, with the importance attached to the needs they identified varying between different cultures. Last, no one has yet answered the simple but important question, 'Is a satisfied employee more motivated than a dissatisfied employee?' – an issue we will return to shortly. Nevertheless, the value of content theories is that they draw attention to the importance of psychological growth and learning as basic conditions for sustained and lasting job performance. They also emphasize the importance of educating and developing staff, in order to improve motivation and performance. This perspective had a major influence on the Job Redesign movement of the 1970s and Quality of Working Life initiatives in the 1980s.

There are four practical implications of content theories for leaders and managers. If they really want to get the best out of their people, then they should understand the following:

• how to create well-designed work environments that provide people with the opportunities to realize their needs through their work and by contributing to the task performance of their team, department and organization;

- how individual differences will shape the personal needs of their staff, and how these change and evolve over time;
- how these needs shape what different employees expect from their leaders, supervisors, colleagues and subordinates;
- how almost all employees prefer *some* power and control over their work, and welcome opportunities for personal development and growth at work.

Maslow's, Alderfer's and Herzberg's theories all suggest that poor or badly designed working environments can have a demotivational effect on employees. Remarkably, recent research has shown that as many as 25 per cent of employees continue to be unhappy with their physical work environments (Carlopio *et al.*, 2001: 315). A survey conducted by Graham Kirkwood, director of Melbourne Resource Architecture with the Melbourne Business School, measured how the physical environment can have an impact on business effectiveness. He observed that, 'The thing I always find is that everyone is unhappy with their current work environment, no matter how good it is' (cited by Kaplan, 1999). Complaints range from dissatisfaction with air quality and temperature to headaches associated with poor lighting and eye strain caused by the overuse of PCs. Others voice dissatisfaction with overcrowding and a lack of privacy in open plan offices. Collectively these factors can result in lower employee morale and work performance. The Australian Confederation of Trades Unions, who claimed that physical conditions are the second biggest cause of industrial disputes in Australia, backed the findings of this survey (Kaplan, 1999).

In recent years there has been growing interest in creating working environments that can enhance employee well-being and motivation. The design of ergonomically sound offices and buildings is now a multibillion dollar business. The word 'ergonomic' is derived from two Greek words, *ergo* (work) and *nomos* (laws of). The discipline of ergonomics is concerned with understanding the interactions between people and their working environments, with the aim of improving employee well-being and efficiency. In many industrialized countries there are indications of a revolution in office and building design in order to create environments that encourage brainstorming and regular staff interaction. As the Australian World Square architect, Greg Crone, has observed, 'the physical environment is one of the most powerful ways to communicate change. When you change people's physical space it has a big impact on their sense of self-worth, the way they communicate with each other, the way they share information and how the workplace affects their performance' (cited by Elder, 2001).

An example of the use of ergonomics to increase well-being is the ancient Chinese practice of *Feng Shui* (pronounced 'fung shway'). This is based on the theory that one's chances of success can be enhanced by properly orienting physical surroundings through the use of a *bagua* (a nine square map). This is used to orient the physical layout of work and home spaces, including in these environments the five elements of water, wood, fire, earth and metal. Other elements include plenty of light and the use of 'positive energy lines' (Singh, 2000). The idea of Feng Shui, traditionally the province of Asian Americans, flaky Hollywood actors or New Age junkies, has gained widespread acceptance in western business circles. Amongst the individuals and organizations that use it are the actor Rob Lowe, property millionaire Donald Trump, Oakley, Coty Beauty, Merrill Lynch and Deutsche Bank in the USA, and the ANZ Bank and the Western Mining Corporation in Australia.

The driving belief behind these, and other ergonomic initiatives is to create environments that make people *want* to come into work. These environments include controlled air temperature and lighting, windows that open and breakout areas with couches and games. Open plan offices are encouraged because this promotes sharing of knowledge and ideas and teamwork is enhanced. However, some private space is still encouraged, with user-friendly technologies, orthopaedically designed chairs and well-planned desk layouts. An example of this is the offices of TXU in Melbourne, designed by Graham Kirkwood, where public meeting spaces are given greater precedence over private offices, desks are accessorized and employees are free to customize their own spaces. Employees have full control over their office environment and, as a consequence, this is constantly *evolving*: it is not a static place (Kaplan, 1999). In a few companies, even the humble and much derided cubicle is now evolving into 'ovacles' organized around a central meeting place. These ovacles are equipped with ceiling canopies, personalized colour schemes, computer-centric layouts, boundary screens for privacy, rolling storage and mobile PC facilities, so staff can set up an 'office' anywhere if they want to interact with a group of colleagues (Goldstein, 2000).

Another example of a company that takes ergonomics seriously is one we looked at briefly in Chapter 1, Google, the most successful of all the web search-engine companies during 2000–2004. At 'The Googleplex', more than 230 employees enjoy a working environment that includes

> A ping-pong table, a pool table, a video arcade game, an ice-cream cooler (free), a snack bar, a restaurant and a free gym. Locker rooms have showers, saunas and washing machines. Hallways are cluttered with plastic balls and Google-decorated scooters and lava lamps. Notice boards feature pictures of Gerry Garcia. The design of the Googleplex is open and colourful. A

sound system plays Carlos Santana. Google also has an on-site gourmet chef, doctor, dentist and masseuse, free ice-cream and a weekly hockey game in the car park. A typical daily menu features Portuguese fish stew, mushroom risotto cakes and grilled Florida sea bass with melted fennel and butter sauce. A mobile library van pulls up once a week. All clothing with Google logos is free to employees. The company's third employee and now Director of Technology, Craig Silverstein, likes to bake fresh bread for his staff. This is a company that regards the well-being of its young employees as being the single most important competitive advantage that it has. (*Abridged from Boulware, 2002*)

How do the ergonomics of your company/organization compare to this?

Theories about higher-level motivational needs also have some practical applications. The first concerns the design and scope of jobs. Job design initiatives are concerned with aligning job demands and requirements with employees' skills, aptitudes and abilities. McClelland's research on individuals with high needs for achievement indicates that their jobs should encompass a high degree of personal autonomy, regular feedback and an intermediate degree of risk in achieving their work goals. It also indicates that one way that organizations can increase overall motivation levels amongst their employees is to identify and hire recruits who *already* have high levels of intrinsic motivation and a strong need for achievement. McClelland's work on high-achievers is particularly relevant to the motivation of full-time professionals. His work indicates that motivating such groups is about providing high-achievers with new challenges, alongside autonomy to choose their work tasks and the methods for completing these. Professionals constantly need new challenges and problems to solve. Self-growth is also important, so they should be allowed opportunities for education and self-development (for example, by doing a part-time MBA, or attending workshops and conferences). Their rewards should be based on some combination of a competitive basic wage and performance and/or skills-based pay (McClelland, 1975, 1961; McClelland and Burnham, 1995). In an environment where there are high levels of self-motivation, an empowered style of leadership is appropriate. In an environment where there are high levels of extrinsic motivation, a command-and-control style of management is usually required.

Content theory research has two other practical implications. The first is that jobs should be made as challenging as possible, and people should be continually encouraged to improve their skills bases, education and knowledge levels. The second is related to the notion of empowerment. The most enjoyable and rewarding jobs are those where employees have as much freedom as possible to carry out their work without direct command-and-control supervision, providing they have adequate skills and knowledge to cope with this. In general, all leaders and managers should allow their staff as much freedom as possible to carry out their jobs, within clearly agreed and understood guidelines and in alignment with team, departmental and organizational objectives (O'Reilly and Pfeffer, 2000: 16–19). This means that empowerment requires something more than simply delegating tasks to others. To empower employees successfully, we have to give our power away to them. This might sound both daunting and counter-intuitive, but all we have to do is unleash the motivation, talent and creativity that is already there by giving our people more responsibility for making decisions about the work they do and the tasks that they are engaged in. We will return to this idea later in the section on 'attributions' and in Chapter 7.

> The best executive is the one who has the sense to pick the best people to do what he wants and self restraint enough to keep from meddling with them whilst they do it.
> (*US President, Franklin D. Roosevelt, 1936*)

The 'relationship' between satisfaction and motivation

> Our objective is simple. It is to turn everyone on our payrolls into raging, inexorable, thunder-lizard evangelists!
> (*Guy Kawasaki, Apple Computers, 1992*)

> Success is not an end in itself. It is merely an encouragement to go further.
> (*Sir Alex Ferguson, Manager of Manchester United FC, after winning the European Cup in May 1999*)

One of the most confusing elements of needs theories of motivation concerns the purported relationship between satisfaction, motivation and performance. Maslow, Alderfer and Herzberg all suggested that employees who are able to satisfy their needs at work would be more motivated and productive than dissatisfied employees. This idea also appeals to common-sense assumptions about employee motivation. Surely a satisfied employee will also be a more motivated and productive worker? This is a widespread assumption, but we must be extremely cautious about assuming such a simple relationship. Research evidence shows that there is often only a weak causal relationship between these three factors (see, for example, the thorough review of this literature in Hosie, 2003). This means that the remaining variances in well-being and productivity must be caused by factors other than 'satisfaction' – in itself a notoriously difficult variable to measure and quantify. In reality, there are just two things we can assert with absolute confidence about individuals with high levels of job satisfaction. First, they are more likely to remain with an organization and not seek employment elsewhere. Second, high levels of job satisfaction do not always lead to higher levels of motivation or enhanced job performance, because of *self-satisfaction* and resistance to change and learning. How this process works is illustrated in Table 4.1.

Table 4.1   The satisfaction–dissatisfaction process

1. Identify needs as a result of being dissatisfied with current situation
2. Identify ways of satisfying those needs
3. Select goal-directed behaviours
4. Perform tasks to achieve these goals
5. Receive feedback (+ or –) and feel temporarily satisfied (+) or dissatisfied (–)
6. If dissatisfied, re-evaluate needs and objectives and become *remotivated*
7. If satisfied, identify new unfulfilled needs and objectives, become dissatisfied and *remotivated*

Here's an example to illustrate how this works in practice. Imagine that you want some chocolate. You then have an unfulfilled need and you are motivated to satisfy that need. You go and buy a large bar of chocolate, eat it and are then satisfied – for a while. Eating more chocolate immediately would not make you more satisfied. However, at some point in the future, say the next day (or, for an extreme chocoholic, the same day) you once again feel the need for more chocolate, become dissatisfied and motivated to buy some more chocolate, and so the process begins again. The word 'satisfaction' is defined as 'the act of satisfying or fulfilling one's needs or desires' (OED website, 2002). Consequently, satisfaction can only ever be a temporary phase, leading to short-lived periods of feeling good, being appreciated and fulfilled or, in the example above, replete with chocolate. So someone who was perpetually *satisfied* with everything cannot be a fully functioning human being, because they would have no intrinsic motivation to achieve anything.

Hence one of the real secrets of motivating staff effectively is to operate with two 'pedals' simultaneously. One is labelled 'satisfaction' and the other is labelled 'dissatisfaction'. The aim is to satisfy people temporarily, by providing appropriate rewards and positive feedback for a job well done, for achieving work goals or for coming up with innovative new ideas or solutions to problems at work. However, for much of the time, we must also engender a feeling of mild dissatisfaction, by always keeping people a little 'hungry', wanting more, keeping them on their toes and striving to pull them towards higher levels of achievement. This also means that feelings of mild anxiety can be a good thing, because people who are feeling anxious about their performance will have a greater hunger to be successful, achieve work goals and reach for higher levels of performance, when compared with people who are 'satisfied' or, even worse, 'self-satisfied'.

This hunger for achievement is captured in an anecdote told by Julie Bick, a former employee of Microsoft: 'A Microsoft manager returned from a trade show and joyously sent out an email to his team, announcing their product had won nine out of ten possible awards. Within a day he had received forty emails back asking which award they had not won and why' (Corporate Research Foundation, 2003: 149). In many of the most successful companies of the 20th and early 21st centuries, the idea of 'job satisfaction' was, and continues to be, frowned upon. For example, Collins and Porras (1996) refer to 'the fire that burns within' amongst employees in these very successful companies, demonstrating that jobs in these organizations were (and continue to be) designed to be challenging and demanding, not easy or comfortable. This idea is neatly encapsulated in a parable they recount in this book, and is one we will return to in Chapters 8–10.

The parable of the black belt

Picture a martial artist kneeling before the master *sensei* in a ceremony to receive a hard-earned black belt. After years of relentless training, the student has finally reached a pinnacle of achievement in the discipline.

'Before granting the belt, you must pass one more test,' says the *sensei*.
'I am ready,' responds the student, expecting perhaps one final round of sparring.
'You must answer the essential question: what is the true meaning of the black belt?'
'The end of my journey,' says the student, 'a well-deserved reward for all my hard work.'

The *sensei* waits for more. Clearly, he is not satisfied. Finally, the *sensei* speaks. 'You are not ready for the black belt. Return in one year.'

A year later, the student kneels again in front of the *sensei*.

'What is the true meaning of the black belt?' asks the *sensei*.
'A symbol of distinction and the highest achievement in our art,' says the student.

The *sensei* says nothing for many minutes, waiting. Clearly, he is not satisfied. Finally, he speaks:
'You are still not ready for the black belt. Return in one year.'

A year later, the student kneels once again in front of the *sensei*. And again the *sensei* asks, 'What is the true meaning of the black belt?'

'The black belt represents the beginning – the start of a never-ending journey of discipline, work and the pursuit of an ever-higher standard,' says the student.
'Yes. You are now ready to receive the black belt and *begin* your work.'
(*Collins and Porras, 1996: 199–200*)

Process theories

These theories approach motivation from a different angle by striving to understand how the conscious thought processes and decisions of individuals influence their motivation levels. They also take more account of contingent factors that can increase or decrease motivation and performance (for example, goal-setting procedures and reward systems). These theories include expectancy, equity, goal-setting, reinforcement and attributions. The empirical support for process theories is more robust when compared to needs theories. However, it has been suggested that these also oversimplify motivation because they neglect factors such as egocentric and aggressive behaviour, toxic personalities, office politics and differences in individuals' perceptions. They may also be difficult to put into practice, as they require time, effort and an intimate knowledge of employees. Nevertheless, as with needs theories, they too have a number of practical applications for leaders and managers.

General expectancy

Start with good people, lay out the rules, communicate with your employees, motivate them and reward them. If you do all those things effectively, you can't miss.
(*Lee Iacocca, former CEO of Chrysler, 1988*)

General expectancy (GE) theory is based on the deceptively simple but important premise that it is the *expectation* that effort exerted in particular activities will lead to *desired outcomes* that influences motivation levels (Cambell, 1970; Vroom, 1964). There are four variables that operate together in a multiplicative fashion to increase motivation levels:

- *effort-performance expectancy*: the belief that effort expended will pay off in performance;
- *performance-outcome expectancy*: the belief that effort expended will lead to desirable outcomes;
- *instrumentality*: the belief that there is a meaningful connection between the effort expended on a particular task and the outcomes that ensue from this;

- *valence (or value)*: the belief that valued courses of action have a high probability of leading to anticipated and desired outcomes and rewards.

Hence the theory suggests that, if expectations are matched by anticipated and/or desired outcomes, then motivation levels will be increased, and vice versa. One of the most practical (but often overlooked) applications of GE theory concerns the selection and recruitment of employees. For example, a survey conducted by the international recruitment agency SDI indicated that the fit between the goals and culture of an organization and employee was a much better predictor of job motivation than either experience or technical skills (Chynoweth, 1999). This research, based on a survey of more than 2000 companies and job seekers in the USA, found that employees who were happy with their employer were more likely to stay with their organization and less likely to change jobs. Conversely, 70 per cent of those who reported that they didn't fit in with the culture of their organization left within one year. SDI suggested that the use of 'motivational fit' techniques doubled the chances of a new employee staying with their employer. As SDI's managing director, Angus Macalister observed, 'From a business perspective, making a mistake in hiring someone is really shocking – typically it costs three time people's annual salary to re-recruit for a position' (cited by Chynoweth, 1999).

Another survey, by the IT recruitment agency Icon Recruitment, found that half of the 500 employers they surveyed had made 'bad hires'. These caused lost revenue through increased recruitment and training/induction costs, and lost productivity. Each lost employee cost these companies more than twice the annual salary of each one. While most of the companies surveyed used some form of hard data to evaluate the merits of applicants (such as degrees or work experience), most overlooked the behavioural and cultural 'fit' of job candidates. One third did not even consider how potential employees would fit with the work environments they would be expected to work in (Foreshew, 2003).

Other research shows that those employees who have been given accurate job previews are significantly more likely to stay longer with an organization, and are also likely to report higher levels of job motivation and productivity (Suszko and Breaugh, 1986). Even so, according to Marilyn Mackes of the National Association of Colleges and Employers in the USA, 78 per cent of all US graduates will leave their first employer within three years. The main reason give for this was 'because the job did not meet their expectations'. One-third of all

Australian graduates leave their first employers within three years. The two main reasons given for this were 'because the job did not meet their expectations' and 'a lack of clear career structure'. In Australia, it costs something like $A9000 to recruit a graduate and a $A100 000 investment in training and development before a company gets a return on this (cited by Chynoweth, 1999).

> Spending time and energy trying to 'motivate' people is a waste of time. The real question is not, 'How do we motivate our people?' If you have the right people, they will be self-motivated. The key is not to de-motivate them.
> (*Jim Collins*, Good to Great, *2001*)

Consequently, it is important that organizations have appropriate selection and recruitment systems in place that are capable of identifying not only people with the right technical skills, but also those who have realistic expectations about the company, the jobs they will be doing and its culture and working practices. This requires the establishment of sophisticated recruitment procedures that measure the complete range of technical skills and knowledge, work experience, attitudes and cultural 'fit'. These companies are looking for *the best* recruits (in the sense of technical skills and academic qualifications), but they only employ *the right* recruits – a subtle and important distinction. Several recent books have shown that the most consistently successful companies in the USA spend an inordinate amount of time and effort on their selection and recruitment procedures, much more than less successful companies do (for example, Collins, 2001; O'Reilly and Pfeffer, 2000; Collins and Porras, 1996).[1]

One example of this is Hewlett-Packard, the American computer company, regularly cited as one of the 'best companies to work for' in surveys conducted by *Fortune* during the 1990s. The company was known for recruiting the cream of engineering and other technical graduates from the top US universities, with more than 200 applications for each vacancy. In Australia, there were over 500 applicants for about 30 graduate positions each year between 1990 and 1999 (Forster, 2002; Parkin *et al.*, 1999: 242). HP has always been very selective in considering job applicants and used a variety of techniques as part of its selection process. Known collectively as 'the thick-screening process', these could include written aptitude tests, psychometric tests, formal presentations, group problem solving and leadership exercises, and several rounds of interviews with senior management, peers and those who might be working under the new recruit. This emphasis on adaptability and cultural 'fit' with HP ensured that, once employed by the company, few new recruits ever left, and those who didn't fit in 'were spat out like viruses' (Collins and Porras, 1996).

A second example is Southwest Airlines (SA), which uses a sophisticated selection and recruitment system, originally developed by Development Dimensions International. This system rejects tens of thousands of applicants every year. During 1997–8, a period of rapid growth for SA, the company advertised for 4000 new positions. They received 200 000 job applications. Of these, 165 000 were rejected immediately, and 35 000 were selected for preliminary interviews. A mere 2 per cent of the original cohort of applicants was offered employment with SA. The benefit for the company is that it only has to employ people with the skills, competencies, personalities and attitudes that are needed to work at SA (the company's CEO, Herb Kelleher, once observed, 'You hire attitudes: everything else can be trained'). This approach has produced a highly motivated, high-performing and loyal workforce (O'Reilly and Pfeffer, 2000: 36–9).

The 29 organizations selected as 'the best companies to work for in Australia' in 2002 also spend an inordinate amount of time and effort in screening new employees. For example, Microsoft Australia receives 20 000 job applications a year. Of these, about 80 will be hired in a typical year. Among the attributes and competencies it seeks in new employees are 'Drive for results', 'Customer focus', 'Communications skills', 'Fostering diversity' and 'Building team spirit' (Corporate Research Foundation, 2003: 149). This approach has obvious benefits for companies. For example, the SAS institute

> has a business model that has permitted it to successfully affect the competitive dynamics in its industry segment and that provided numerous economic benefits. For instance, consider two consequences of SAS Institute's low turnover. First, the company saves money. If the average turnover in software companies is 20 percent, a conservative estimate, and SAS Institute's is three percent, the difference multiplied by the size of SAS's workforce means that about 925 fewer people leave the SAS than other companies. What does it cost to replace someone? Most estimates range from one to two times the annual salary. Even with a conservative salary estimate of $US60 000 a year, and an estimate of 1.5 times salary as the replacement cost, SAS Institute is saving more than $US100 million a year from its labour turnover – from a revenue base of about $US800 million. This is a lot of money in both absolute and percentage terms. (*Collins, 2001: 118*)

The second practical application of GE theory concerns the education and development of employees. These can equip people with skills that will enhance their expectations that any effort they put in at work will not be wasted. In turn, this can generate other positive outcomes such as greater confidence, self-efficacy and self-motivation. A third practical application of GE theory is in the use of performance appraisals (PA). A good PA, which is objective and fair, can serve as an incentive to perform, in the belief that appropriate efforts will be matched by positive outcomes and rewards in the future.

Goal setting

Goal setting is a technique with a long history in sport (for example, Carron, 1984; Smith, 1979), and it has become widespread in organizations over the last 20 years, in the form of practices such as 'management by objectives' and the use of stretch targets, in many American, European and Australasian companies. The major reason why this technique has become so popular is that there is reliable and consistent research evidence to support the view that it can have a powerful influence on the motivation and performance levels of individual employees and work groups. For example, one survey by TMP Worldwide indicated that most performance problems at work are the direct result of employees not having clear goals or an understanding of expected work standards (Karvelas, 2002b). Used effectively, goal setting can increase self-confidence and reduce performance anxiety. This can also have an iterative effect on employees: as people achieve goals, their confidence and self-belief grows, and they are then able to aim for higher goals and levels of achievement. As they achieve these new goals, their confidence and self-belief grows . . . and so on. This is true for different groups of people, of all ages and ability levels, in many different work environments. Because of its record of success, goal setting has become a very simple, practical and powerful tool for leaders and managers at all levels of organizations. There are three main types of goals: (a) outcome, those concerned with achieving concrete results, (b) performance, those concerned with achieving results, but judged in relation to some agreed standard (for example, last quarter's sales figures), (c) process, those concerned with what an employee needs to do in order to achieve outcome and/or performance goals.

Goal-setting theory shows us that simply setting goals for employees is insufficient. To be successful with this technique means establishing goals that have specific qualities:

Specific and measurable
If a goal is too vague, employees may not be sure about what they should be doing. Similarly, expectations about desired results and outcomes should be clearly established up-front.

Agreed and manageable
Employees must make a personal commitment to their work goals. This means that they must have some say in setting these. Goals should not be imposed. If employees don't perceive that they have some control or *choice* over these, they may refuse to accept them or take no responsibility for any negative outcomes.

Realistic but challenging

If a task is too easy, the employee will gain little satisfaction from achieving it. If it is too difficult, the employee will be overwhelmed and give up or fail.

Time framed

Progress towards a goal must be planned in a sequence of steps, within an appropriate and agreed time frame. If you do not set time fames, there is a danger that the employee will lose focus on the goal. Achieving complex or demanding long-term goals may require the establishment of an agreed sequence of shorter-term goals.

Evaluated

Additional support might be required as employees work towards their objectives (the process goals described above), and contingent feedback should be provided on the progress they are making towards these.

Resourced

Achieving challenging and demanding stretch goals may require additional resourcing in the form of learning and development opportunities, or the provision of financial and non-financial resources to support progress towards these.

This may seem like a lot to remember, but can be easily recalled with reference to the SMARTER acronym: **S**pecific – **M**easurable – **A**greed – **R**ealistic – **T**ime framed – **E**valuated – **R**esourced.

How well leader/managers implement goals for their employees is dependent on how well they know their staff as individuals, identifying appropriate goals that can stretch and motivate them, monitoring their progress towards these and providing appropriate resources and feedback. Carefully setting performance goals can sustain and increase motivation, and employees *will* be more motivated to perform if their goals are self-determined, clear, agreed with their superiors and personally challenging, but not overwhelming. Goal setting should be carried out regularly, with advance notice and information prior to any feedback sessions, with enough time being allowed to discuss an employee's progress and opportunities to evaluate why goals were, or were not, achieved. This should be followed by a short account, compiled by both parties, of what has been agreed in the meeting (adapted from Rudman, 1997; Locke and Latham, 1990; Locke, 1968).

Equity

> Army personnel in Latvia are reportedly snarling after learning that the country's Interior Ministry spends far more on feeding its guard dogs than it does on feeding them. No Latvian firms manufacture dog food, so the ministry imports it from France at a cost of $A4625 per dog per year, while it spends only $A2490 per soldier per year buying food from local farmers. An Interior Ministry spokesman was unwilling to comment on the possible effects of this on the morale of their soldiers.
> (*Reuters' report, cited in* The Australian, *27 February 2002*)

This theory suggests that motivation is the outcome of the equity that individuals perceive between the effort they put into a job and the rewards they receive, when compared with the efforts and rewards of co-workers, or others in similar jobs and occupations. A lack of perceived equity, in effort expended and rewards received, will lead to reduced levels of motivation over time (Adams, 1965). The two most important practical applications of equity theory are that, as far as possible, all employees should be paid equitably for performing well in a particular job, with a known and agreed formula for rewarding above-average performance. It is highly demotivating for employees to discover that colleagues doing the same job at the same performance levels are earning more. One well-publicized example of the effects of pay inequity in the 1990s concerned the actors, Caroline Quentin and Leslie Ash. They discovered that they were being paid £25 000 less than their male co-stars in *Men Behaving Badly*, just before the start of filming the third series of the programme in 1997. A similar situation arose before the second series of *The X-Files* in the mid-1990s, when Gillian Andersen demanded pay equity with David Duchovny. In both cases, the threat of their withdrawal from these series quickly ended these pay inequities.

We can even ignore the moral, ethical or legal arguments for opposing this kind of inequity. The main reason why leaders and managers should avoid this is because *it is bad for business and organizational performance*. This is becoming an increasingly important issue in organizations characterized by cultural and gender diversity. Not only can inequitable reward systems lower motivation and morale, they can increase labour turnover, with consequent loss of good staff to competitors. They can also be extremely expensive for companies if employees decide to sue for discrimination. This may appear to be common sense, but there continue to be many examples of women and ethnic minority groups in the USA, Europe and Australia successfully suing their employers for inequities in pay, career and promotion opportunities (please refer to Chapter 6 for several examples of this and a discussion of the business case for removing these inequities in organizations).

Reinforcement

Exercise 4.2

At the beginning of this chapter, it was suggested that there are at least 30 ways of providing positive reinforcement to employees, other than money. Before reading through the next section, how many can you think of? ◆

Research conducted over a 50-year period has highlighted the impact that positive feedback can have on motivation and work performance. Strictly speaking, this is not a theory of motivation, but reinforcement principles encapsulate a useful set of practical ideas, because human beings are hard- and soft-wired to keep doing things that have positive outcomes, such as feelings of pleasure (hedonism), and will avoid those things that result in negative outcomes, such as punishment. Eventually, people will stop doing things that have neither rewarding nor punishing outcomes. The research also suggests that reinforcement and feedback on performance should, whenever possible, be positive. Negative feedback might be required on occasions, but this should only be used as a last resort. If you do have to give negative feedback to employees, then remember the old adage, 'Praise in public. Punish in private'. We saw in the examples cited in Chapter 3 that this type of feedback should then lead to appropriate remedial action, thereby avoiding future repetitions of the action that caused the negative feedback in the first place. At all times, the focus should be on rewarding good behaviours that employees can aspire to, not punishing people.

Praise or personal encouragement (from the Latin word for the heart, *cor*), are simple but highly effective ways of providing positive reinforcement. It has even been reported that the incidence of 'thankyous' is far higher in successful innovative companies than in struggling low-innovation firms (Kouzes and Posner, 1997: 279). Clearly, it is not practical to reward every show of effort and desired behaviour, and the research does indicate that the most effective way of rewarding performance is through 'intermittent reinforcement' (Deci, 1972). Positive intermittent reinforcement can come in many forms, including giving informal and formal acknowledgments for doing a good job, celebrating employees' successes, saying 'thank you' and 'well done', listening actively, asking questions, asking employees for suggestions and advice, involving quieter employees in group meetings, smiling, using your SOH, treating all of your staff equitably, being a good corporate citizen, being honest, walking the talk, practising what we preach, being a leader that people look up to and respect, providing employees with more responsibility, providing opportunities for self-development, delegating authority, offering flexible work hours, breaks and job-sharing, providing dinners to mark special occasions or notable successes at work, free breakfasts, dinners or lunches, small Christmas and birthday presents, after-work wine and cheese parties, and providing food and refreshments during long meetings. Are there any other positive reinforcers that you could add to this list?

Attributions

> It is no secret that I have always attributed the success of the Virgin Group and its brands to the people who work for our company. We have always had a policy of hiring good motivators and good businesspeople. We always look out for executives who put their people first and themselves last. So, in many ways champions are selfless. They're also quick to put their faith in others and their ideas.
> (*Richard Branson, during a talk at the 'The Centre for the Mind' award ceremony, Melbourne Australia, 10 December 2003*)

In the late 1980s, Tom Peters developed something he called 'The Boss Test', which he used on management audiences in the USA, the UK and Australia. Peters would ask the participants, often including senior managers and CEOs, this question: 'Are you concerned about what your employees might be getting up to while you are attending this conference?' Invariably, 90 per cent of his audience would put their hands up, indicating that they did indeed have concerns about this. Peter's reply would be instantaneous: 'I have some news for everyone who put their hands up. You are bad bosses! If you didn't put your hand up, congratulations, you are good bosses.'

Not surprisingly this counterintuitive and, to some participants, impertinent assertion was not always well received. However, the point Peters was making remains as valid now as when he first made it. He argued that the true role of leaders is to trust their employees enough to allow them to run with the ball, even when they were not physically present to keep an eye on things. In other words, he was suggesting that leaders and managers needed to move away from a ubiquitous command-and-control style of management to what was then a 'new' empowered style of leadership. At the height of his popularity as a corporate speaker, Peters often added this comment: 'Most employees are intelligent, hard working and motivated, until they walk through the front door of your organization to start work for you,' emphasizing the point that a lack of employee motivation is not innate. Almost all new employees start out motivated, in most instances are trustworthy, and will take on additional responsibilities if offered the chance to do this. Consequently, demotivation is usually a learnt response to the conditions they encounter or the experiences they have at work.

All humans also have an inbuilt tendency to attribute blame for good and poor performance. People who have a strong internal locus of control will generally attribute poor performance to themselves and learn from their mistakes. People who are more 'outer-directed' will tend to blame external forces: their boss, colleagues, subordinates, 'the system', other work groups, work pressures, the weather, unfavourable astrological conditions, the family dog and so forth for their poor performance. Such attributions can have a powerful influence on how leaders and managers view the motivations and abilities of their followers. How we view other people's basic natures can also have a profound effect on both our ability to motivate others and the manner in which we do this. For example, below are two descriptions. Which one best describes your assumptions about the 'human nature' of your employees?

Description 1
Most employees inherently dislike work. They will grasp every opportunity to avoid it. Since they dislike work, they must be ordered about, controlled, watched and cajoled into performing. Punishment should be applied if they make mistakes or fail to achieve work tasks that they have been set. They will avoid opportunities for self-improvement and learning. Most employees are not interested in doing anything more than the formal requirements of their job and are largely motivated by money.

Description 2
Most employees enjoy coming to work, if it is challenging and rewarding. If people are given the opportunities, they will exercise self-direction and self-control. They will seek more responsibilities at work if they are encouraged to do this. They will pursue opportunities for self-improvement and learning. Most employees are willing to do more than the formal requirements of their job and are not, primarily, motivated by money. They have many ideas and innovations to offer their organizations, and will contribute these if given the right encouragement, opportunities and rewards.

Known as McGregor's 'Theory X and Y', such assumptions can have a significant influence on the strategies that leaders and managers use to motivate their staff (McGregor, 1987). Someone who adheres closely to Description 1 ('X'), is likely to have a command-and-control 'stick' style of leadership and spend an inordinate amount of time monitoring and watching their staff. Someone who adheres closely to Description 2

('Y'), is likely to have an empowered 'carrot' style of leadership, and will believe in participative decision making, self-managing teams and creating an environment where employees are encouraged to take the maximum responsibility for achieving work goals and their personal self-development. This is not to say that the X style of leadership is always inappropriate. In certain circumstances, such as in a crisis or emergency, it will often be right to adopt a more directive and authoritarian approach. However, in most organizational settings and situations today, the second approach produces consistently better results.

This suggestion brings us to the idea of the 'Rubber Band'. If you take a rubber band and stretch it between the thumb of one hand and the forefingers of your other hand, you will find it impossible to 'push'; it simply loses its tensile strength and sags. However, if you pull the rubber band with your thumb, your fingers will follow after a very short delay. This simple exercise reminds us of one of the important principles of leadership highlighted in Chapter 1. We saw that managers are people who generally try to *push* their staff towards achieving objectives they have set *for* them. In contrast, leaders are able to *pull* their staff towards the ways, roads or paths that they have agreed *with* them and then leave them alone to get on with this in their own way and at their own pace. For example, in June 1944, Dwight D. Eisenhower, the Supreme Allied Commander during World War II, was involved in a briefing session with his senior officers just before the D-Day landings in France. He placed a piece of string on the table and said, 'You can only pull a string – not push it. You must lead your soldiers from the front – not push them from the rear.' Can you think of ways to encourage your staff to pull towards you (without overextending them), rather than constantly pushing them?

Money as a motivator

The happiest time in a man's life is when he is in red hot pursuit of a dollar and has a reasonable chance of overtaking it.
(*John Billings, US humorist*)

Pay people peanuts and you'll end up employing monkeys.
(*Old saying*)

Common sense dictates that money should be a motivator for employees, and if we don't have very much, it should act as a powerful motivator in life. Movies like the iconic *Wall Street, Other People's Money, Indecent Proposal* and numerous heist movies over the last 20 years all reinforce the idea that money can have a profound influence on people's behaviour. Worldwide, international crime was the fastest growing and most profitable business in the world during the 1990s, and corruption and fraud continue to be widespread in most countries and in many business organizations (see Chapter 12). And if organizations were perfectly rational, the pay of all employees should be tied directly to both their individual performance and to their company's performance on indicators such as average return on shareholders' equity, the price of the firm's common stock and other profitability parameters. Many employers also believe that money is the single most powerful work motivator, particularly amongst blue-collar and contract employees. If this were true, the best way to increase employee motivation and performance would be to increase their pay on a regular basis; by paying someone twice as much, their motivation levels should double. If only it was this straightforward.

Paradoxically, while people on average and low incomes are routinely exhorted to show 'restraint' and 'moderation' in their wage claims, top business leaders have seen their incomes, in both relative and absolute terms, increase enormously over the last ten years, without the slightest evidence that this has improved their motivation, work performance or the productivity and profitability of the companies they led. In fact, the greatest productivity gains made amongst workers in the 1980s and 1990s in the USA, Europe and Australia were among the lowest paid groups, while those who enjoyed large pay increases showed little improvement in their performance and productivity. And, as we will see in Chapter 12, a growing number of 'fat-cat' executives who have been free to set their own salaries, and who enjoyed unfettered access to stock options and 'performance bonuses' during the 1990s, have been complicit in some of the greatest corporate fraud and corruption scandals in history (McLean and Elkind, 2003; Haigh, 2003; Loomis, 2001; Kitney and Evans, 2000; Westfield, 1999; Gray, 1999; McLean, 1998).

> Greed is the greatest motivator. I've thought about this a lot, and all that matters is money. You buy loyalty with money. This touchy-feely stuff isn't as important. That's what drives performance.
> (*Jeff Skilling, disgraced former Chief Operating Officer of Enron. The company was declared bankrupt at 2.00 am on 2 December 2001, with debts estimated at $US38 billion.*)

However, while money and other forms of financial rewards are important and necessary, it is consistently rated as being of secondary importance in rankings of what motivates most people at work. As Kouzes and Posner have observed:

> After sifting through mountains of numbers, dozens of surveys and years of research studies, *Inc.* magazine's researchers determined that people, 'want the same things they've always wanted'. Even though job security is

increasingly tenuous, 'interesting work' has a dramatic 22-point lead over 'high-income', when it comes to importance to workers. A survey of *Industry Week* readers found that quality of leadership means more than dollars as a source of motivation for today's workforce. *The National Study of the Changing Workforce* reports that 'personal satisfaction for doing a good job' is the most frequently mentioned measure of success in work life – voted nearly two to three times more often than 'getting ahead' or 'making a good living'.
(*Abridged from Kouzes and Posner, 1997: 131*)

Another survey, by Jordan-Evans and Kaye, asked 10 000 US employees why they stayed with a particular employer. The top five responses were, in ranking order, 'exciting, challenging work', 'career growth, learning and development', 'great people to work with', 'fair pay and benefits' and 'a good boss' (Jordan-Evans and Kaye, 2002). Similar results have been found in surveys of managers and professionals over the last 20 years (for example, Furnham, 1994). It was also once said that 'Money won't buy happiness, but it will pay the salaries of a large research staff to study the problem.'

Overwhelmingly, the most important motivators are intrinsic to the work itself. However much it may run counter to conventional management thinking, the reality is that money is but one motivator amongst many, and when it does become the only motivator, sooner or later this will lead to problems. A pleasant working environment and organizational culture, variety, autonomy and control, opportunities for career advancement and personal development, a degree of job security and good leadership are equally important motivators for most employees. For example, in your current job situation would you prefer to have a $2000 bonus, or an extra week's holiday this year? A crèche at work, and/or flexible working arrangements that enable you to care for your children, or $5000 extra a year in salary? More time with your family, or a promotion? Put this way, it is easy to see that money is but one motivator amongst others. In fact, several recent surveys have shown that many professional employees do not believe that money buys job satisfaction, and many would now willingly swap future pay rises for greater job security, more control over their working hours and a better balance between work and family commitments (e.g. Megalogenis, 2002).

> Money has never made a man happy yet, nor will it. There is nothing in its nature to produce happiness. The more a man has, the more he wants. Instead of filling a vacuum, it makes one.
> (*Benjamin Franklin, co-author of the American Constitution*)

Other research has shown that there is only a weak long-term relationship between pay increases and work performance. Although there is a short-term halo-effect after receiving a pay rise or bonus, this soon dissipates. The power of money as a motivator is always short-lived and, more importantly, it is an entirely *extrinsic* motivator when what many organizations need these days are high levels of *intrinsic* motivation from their employees. Herzberg (1959) used the analogy of an electric battery to highlight the problems of relying only on external financial motivators. Extrinsic monetary rewards can only have short-term or temporary effects, because employees' 'batteries' will eventually run flat, and will need to be recharged with an external 'boost' of money. Only when employees have their own internal self-recharging 'generators' can true motivation be achieved. Furthermore, people whose only motivation to work is money will never contribute more than the minimum required to obtain a financial reward. It is only when people are intrinsically motivated – by the job itself – that they will give 100 per cent.

This suggests that extrinsic motivators like pay can actually reduce intrinsic motivation, because the use of external rewards to increase motivation can cause a shift in what psychologists have called 'internal locus of control'. It also means that the only hold a company has on an employee is a financial one, and there will always be another company who will pay more money for doing the same job (Caulkin, 1993). Furthermore, the more affluent people are, the less effect money has as a motivator at work. This suggests that the idea that organizational leaders should be paid huge sums of money and offered other inducements, such as stock options, to improve their motivation and performance represented the biggest corporate con trick of the 1980s and 1990s.

Performance related pay and shareholding

About two-thirds of large UK companies and almost all major US companies now use some form of individual performance related pay (PRP). In countries like Australia that 'discovered' PRP after industrial relation reforms in the 1990s, it spread rapidly, with more than 80 per cent of all managers now on some kind of PRP (Long, 2000). The popularity of PRP systems is based on the widespread belief that financial incentives can be motivational *if* they are closely tied to individual effort and performance. There is one problem with this common-sense assumption: most of the evidence indicates that PRP systems often don't work (for example, Kohn, 1993a, b). For example, in a detailed review of these schemes in the UK, one researcher commented that 'there is a singular lack of any hard evidence which proves that these kinds of incentive schemes have improved employee performance over and above any improvements which could have been forthcoming in the absence of such schemes' (Smith, 1993). Another survey, by the Institute for Manpower Studies in the UK, showed that 'the benefits most often claimed for PRP are not met in practice. Incentive pay doesn't motivate – rather the reverse. It persuades neither high-performers to stay nor poor-performers to leave. It doesn't improve organizational culture. And, as to whether PRP rewards fairly, employees are not more than neutral' (cited by Caulkin, 1993).

Why might this be? First, employees are rarely consulted in the design of these systems and many regard them as being unfair in operation, reflecting a widespread perception that many managers do not appraise staff and administer these selective rewards in a fair and equi-table manner. Second, many of these schemes have only been intro-duced for select groups of personnel (for example, senior managers) and, consequently, this can cause feelings of inequity and demotiva-tion amongst other groups of employees in organizations. Third, there is also the danger of the costs of these schemes, with some companies becoming lumbered with crippling remuneration structures (Caulkin, 1993). Fourth, organizations that place too much emphasis on PRP systems can create unforeseen problems for themselves in the future. For example, the Royal Commission on the Australian ESSO Longford explosion in 1998 concluded that the performance-based pay systems that supervisors were on (constituting as much as 40 per cent of their pay), were 'a major contributor to the slack safety standards existing in the company at the time. The performance-based systems meant that staff were paid according to their outputs and, as a result, insufficient attention was paid to the potential dangers of overloading the plant's operating systems' (cited in *The Australian*, 12 October 2000).

Although many commentators have been sceptical about the efficacy of pay for performance, it has been suggested by others that financial rewards can foster internal motivation when used in the right way. If these reinforce the link between exceptional performance and employee rewards, then intrinsic motivation can be enhanced. This implies that external rewards, financial or otherwise, need to be closely aligned with the actual task performance and productive outputs of staff. PRP schemes will only work if rewards are allocated on the basis of clear, well-understood and equitable principles for rewarding above-average performance. Furthermore, the practice of share/stock holding has grown in popularity in recent years, and the research evidence suggests that companies who involve their employees in these schemes are more successful than those who do not do this (for example, Collins, 2001; O'Reilly and Pfeffer, 2000; Stamp, 1996; Hanson and Bell, 1987). There is also some evidence that these schemes can encourage greater loyalty and a sense of belonging amongst employees (Lardner, 1999).

In the USA, more than 80 per cent of the 'Top 500 companies' have share ownership schemes for their employees (Clifford, 2001) and profit sharing is one of the faster-growing reward practices worldwide. Many of the top companies in Australia, such as Telstra and BHP-Billiton, have employee share ownership schemes in place. A survey in Australia, by the consulting firm KPMG, revealed that 94 per cent of 800 companies that had adopted employee share schemes reported benefits in productivity, employee interest and motivation, wage restraint and company profitability. Four out of five large Australian companies either have introduced or are planning to introduce employee share schemes (Sprague, 2002). For example, the Australian software developer, Mincom, announced that it was creating six million stock options for its staff in July 2000. The company's CEO, Alan McElrae, said that this was 'a major psychological investment for staff in the company and a powerful motivational tool' (cited by Long, 2000). Caltex Australia introduced broker-free tax-exempt shares in July 2000 to encourage greater staff loyalty and motivation (Matterson, 2000). The former Australian Industry Secretary, Peter Reith, also launched a campaign on 22 July 1999 to promote the concept of share ownership, arguing that providing employees with a financial interest in their companies would be particularly effective in increasing moti-vation and commitment.

However, there is always a risk that stock options can become 'golden-handcuffs' if a business's share price falls below the price at which they were purchased. This was the main reason why Steve Ballmer abolished stock options at Microsoft in 2003, replaced these with grants of restricted stocks and created a secondary internal company market to sell these. The company offered their employees $1.11 on these 345 million stock options, a move that was a big hit with Microsoft employees. Last, when companies have been bank-rupted, holding stock or pensions linked to stock prices can result in the loss of employees' entire pension entitlements, as happened to Enron and Worldcom employees in the USA in 2001. As we will see in Chapter 12, they can also enable crooked CEOs and boards to make self-serving, unethical and illegal business decisions that often damage companies in the medium to long term but which, in the short term, artificially ramp up the value of their stock options (Haigh, 2003).[2]

> Employee share ownership should be for the shop floor, not just Mahogany Row. It should be for people on $A30 000 a year not just $A300 000 a year. Owning a share in your business should be as much the Australian dream as owning your own home.
> (*Tony Abbott, former Australian Federal Workplace Relations Minister, cited in* The Australian, *31 January 2001*)

Another trend in organizations in recent times has been to link part of an employee's remuneration package to the development of their skills and knowledge levels. This form of remuneration appears to be particularly suited to organizations that have short product life cycles, speed to market concerns and a need to innovate quickly in order to remain competitive (Lawler, 1993). This method of remuneration is also consistent with several theories of motivation that we looked at earlier, including ERG, goal-setting, equity, expectancy and reinforcement theories. Skills-based pay can be used as either an alternative or an adjunct to job and performance related pay, where remuneration is based on employees' skill levels and/or how many jobs they can perform. In some companies, such as Hewlett-Packard, General Electric and Harley Davidson, pay is linked to the acquisition of additional skills at work or those that have been acquired through external education and self-development. Such schemes encourage perpetual learning and self-improvement, and research evidence indicates that such schemes do lead to improvements in motivation and performance levels (ibid.). However, there is a potential downside to such schemes. For example, what can an employer do when an individual has learnt all the skills that are required in a job or becomes overqualified for a particular position? In short, while money is important, and all organizations need to pay competitive wage rates to attract and retain high-quality staff, its importance as a motivator should not be overstated. In reality, it can actually be counterproductive to become overreliant on financial incentives to motivate employees and, while they are certainly useful, they are only one form of motivation amongst many others.[3]

Non-financial incentives and rewards

What other incentives and inducements can organizations provide to attract and retain the best staff? Many of the companies regarded as 'the best to work for' in the USA offer a number of incentives and flexible benefits to retain good staff. In 2000, for example, of the top 100 companies in this category, almost all offered bonuses for exceptional performance, more than 70 offered profit sharing, 26 offered on-site day care for employees' children, 29 offered concierge services such as dry-cleaning, 47 offered domestic-partner benefits to same-sex couples and 31 offered fully-paid employee sabbaticals. Amongst the other motivational perks offered were stock or equity options, flexible working arrangements for employees with school-age children, funds for on- and off-site development courses, state of the art fitness and/or health centres, health and wellness programmes, all or part health premium coverage, clothing allowances and on-site hair salons, florists and masseuses. Even during 2002–3, during the post 11 September economic downturn, many of the top 100 companies kept many of these inducements and incentives in place (Levering and Moskowitz, 2001, 2002). Similar incentives can be found in other countries. In Australia the Corporate Research Foundation also publishes an annual list of 'the best companies to work for'. This shows that the most popular employers in this country offer many of the incentives offered by US companies. These include bonuses for exceptional performance, profit sharing, on-site day care for employees' children, flexible working arrangements for employees with school-age children, funds for on- and off-site development courses, state of the art fitness and/or health centres, health and wellness programmes, all or part health premium coverage, stock or equity options and clothing allowances (Corporate Research Foundation, 2003).

A worldwide study by TMP Worldwide of 6007 organizations revealed that 34.8 per cent believed that 'managing the careers of their employees' was the single most important HR issue for their business during 2002–3. One in five believed that how well they did this was the single most important incentive for new employees joining their companies. Other critical issues for these employers were, in ranking order, 'attracting and selecting new talent' (23.3 per cent); 'enhancing leadership skills' (17.8 per cent); 'employee remuneration' (7.5 per cent) and 'reducing employee headcounts' (5.5 per cent). One-fifth of these companies were using additional rewards or bonuses to keep key staff; 19.2 per cent were offering leadership and self-development courses for their employees; 14.3 per cent were utilizing career coaching as a retention tool; 14.1 per cent offered mentoring programmes and, last, 12.6 per cent were using pay increases as their main way of retaining their best talent (Karvelas, 2002a). Karvelas also observed that, while financial rewards were important in providing incentives to encourage talented staff to stay with companies, employers had recognized that remuneration was not a panacea. Employees were looking for a broader range of incentives to stay as the competition for staff increased amongst corporations. Michael Del Gigante, CEO of Trans-ACT Communication, made these comments at the time of the release of the TMP survey: '[Employees] like to know that they are contributing to the organization and that their contribution is appreciated. They also want to work in an environment that is fun and interesting and tests their abilities. Many are looking for opportunities to learn and grow as a professional, so they can meet or exceed their career goals. It is up to the business to provide these opportunities so the individual can pursue these goals' (cited by Karvelas, 2002a).

A company that won one of the Australian Chamber of Commerce and Industry Work and Family awards in 2001 has built work flexibility and family-friendly policies into their organizational culture from the ground up, reflecting the values of the company's owners. Nothing remarkable in this, you might be thinking, until you consider what the company does. The name of the company is Gavin McCleod Concrete Pumping. It delivers concrete to building sites in one of the most thoroughly male working environments imaginable, characterized traditionally by a macho, long-hours culture. The co-director of the company, Jenni Eastwood, commented that 'We thought our family was important and Gavin's experience in the industry told him that if you treat employees well, they reward you with loyalty and more in terms of customer satisfaction and dedication' (cited by Bachelard, 2001). Significantly, a top US 'Employer of Choice', the SAS Institute, also appeared in the 'top ten' in Australia during 2001 and was selected the third-best employer to work for in the USA by *Fortune* in February 2002. This company offers generous maternity leave, free access to tennis and squash courts, flexible working hours, a relaxed dress code, 'a flexible and encouraging work environment' and even complimentary breakfasts. The result, according to one employee, is a loyal and highly motivated workforce. The company's learning and development manager, Neil Hamilton, made these comments after the company received their award:

> What we find people looking for is challenging work, a feeling of worth and the add-on things that make the job a more complete place to work. Many of our policies are structured around recognising the need for both family and work. We work on the basis that motivated people will do a better job if we meet their basic human needs.
> (*Cited by Gerard, 2001*)

Many commentators have argued that employers should become more sensitive to the family responsibilities of their employees. As Edgar has observed:

> Work and private life cannot be separated; each affects the other; yet managers often act as though what goes on in the workplace is the only thing that affects performance and productivity. It's not the economy stupid; it's the heart that people put into their life (both in and out of the workplace) that makes the economy. Things are getting worse not better, despite our much-vaunted work–family policies and bosses still seem blind to the connection between family stress and productivity at work. In my work with companies, we've proved that management and supervisor education about creative and flexible work–family practices do lead to significant improvements in morale, job commitment and productivity. These companies have reduced absenteeism, fewer accidents at work, less workplace conflict and improved performance, because trust had been engendered and the old 'entitlement' mentality had disappeared. A holistic approach recognised that employees had a stake in the company's success and that 'outside' life matters had to be accommodated.
> (*Edgar, 1998*)

This quotation brings us full circle to the needs theories reviewed earlier in this chapter. It is clear that companies with the most loyal and motivated workforces utilize a variety of simple motivational devices that reflect the variety of needs that human beings have at different stages in their lives and careers. They do not treat their employees as people who are driven entirely by a single need for financial gain. They also understand that today's workforces are very diverse, and can include baby-boomers (those born in the 1950s), Generation X (people born after 1970), Generation Y (those born after 1980) and Generation T (the first generation of humans raised with computers from birth), men and women, and people from different cultures. Consequently, they allow their employees to choose from a menu of benefit options that reflect their individual needs and situations, superseding the old 'one size fits all' and 'one benefit can fit everyone' attitudes that permeated almost all organizations for most of the 20th century.

Summary: bringing ideas about motivation, empowerment and performance together

> It used to be a business conundrum, 'Who comes first: the employees, customers or shareholders?' That's never been an issue to me. The employees come first, if they're happy, satisfied, dedicated and energetic, they'll take real good care of the customers. When the customers are happy, they come back and that makes the shareholder happy. We are committed to providing our employees with a stable work environment with equal opportunity for learning and personal growth. Creativity and innovation are encouraged for improving the effectiveness of Southwest Airlines. Above all, employees will be provided with the same concern, respect, and caring attitude within the organization that they are expected to share externally with every Southwest customer.
> (*Herb Kelleher, CEO of Southwest Airlines, twice selected by* Fortune *'The best company in the USA to work for' in the 1990s, cited by Jim Collins in* Good to Great, *2001*)

In this chapter it has been suggested that there are no magic motivational triggers that leaders or managers can activate in order to make people become instantly more motivated, or want to learn more or work smarter and better. All organizations can do is to create cultures and working environments that can enable individuals who are already intrinsically motivated to perform to the best of their abilities. This indicates that one of the most important ways of lifting motivation and performance levels is to spend as much time and resources as possible selecting and recruiting the right people. And, while it might be quite difficult to motivate another person directly, it is extremely easy to *demotivate* another person, through discriminatory behaviour, lack of career development opportunities, inequitable reward systems, negative feedback, abuse of positional power, 'toxic' behaviour and bullying. Having said this, there are ten interlinked principles that can be applied in any organizational setting that should help to enhance employee motivation, empowerment and performance.

1   Spend as much time and resources as you can on your recruitment and selection procedures to ensure that you employ only those people whose abilities, beliefs, ambitions and personalities fit very closely with your organization's vision, future goals, core values, working practices and culture.[4] Remember also that your employee requirements may well change and evolve as they grow and develop or as the company changes, so these should not be cast in stone. If you need creative employees, look out for people with a good sense of humour. If potential employees appear to be only interested in how much money they can make with you, be extremely wary about recruiting them.

2   Earlier in this chapter, we saw that organizations with a reputation for good employment practices attract and retain the cream of new recruits. For example, when Virgin Airlines was establishing its new operation in Australia during 2000, it had more than 60 applicants for every advertised position in Adelaide alone. The local HR manager Bruce Highfield commented, 'Receiving more than 2500 applicants for 40 positions is absolutely phenomenal, considering unemployment levels are at an historic low. We've been most impressed by the calibre of candidates as well as their genuine excitement about working for a people-focused airline' (cited in *The Australian*, 20 October 2000). Virgin's wages levels are not as high as most comparable airlines, but the company does have a long-standing reputation for being a benevolent employer and a fun place to work. If your organization has a reputation for looking after its staff, new recruits will be battering down the doors to join you.

> Convention dictates that a company looks after its shareholders first, its customers next and, last of all, looks after its employees. Virgin does the opposite. For us, our employees matter most. It just seems to be common sense to me that if you start off with a happy, well-motivated workforce, you're much more likely to have happy customers. And, in due course, the resulting profits will make your shareholders happy.
> (*Richard Branson*, Losing My Virginity, *1998*)

3   If you can, provide some job security for your employees. A survey by Drake International in 1997 revealed that more than 30 per cent of 500 middle and senior managers considered 'job security' to be an important criterion when considering a job move to another employer, well ahead of 'improved status' (19.5 per cent); 'better working conditions' (9.6 per cent) and 'more pay' (4.3 per cent). Almost one-third of the senior managers they surveyed were actively looking for work that

provided greater job security, and they were willing to take pay cuts of up to $US15 000 a year to get these (Marris, 1997). The chapter on occupational stress also showed that insecurity breeds uncertainty, and uncertainty can lead to demotivation and lower work performance. So try to offer what could now be better described as 'short to medium-term employment assurances', but keep 'stretching' people to achieve more for themselves and your organization.

4   While there continue to be disagreements about the efficacy of pay-by-results remuneration schemes, there is universal agreement that it is essential to pay people fairly and competitively. So try to provide your people with a competitive and fair wage, with the opportunity to earn more by a known and equitable formula for above-average performance. Encourage profit sharing or share ownership for loyal employees, within sound legal and ethical frameworks, thereby demonstrating, in a very tangible way, the links between personal effort and organizational success. Emphasize these reward systems in your job advertisements. Do not pay discriminatory rates based on gender or race; this is a sure-fire way of ensuring that you will lose good staff. Use a variety of flexible incentives, benefits and services (for example, the provision of day-care centres) that reflect both the changing needs of individual employees and the realities of changing work place demographics, such as the increasing number of dual-career couples and those with responsibilities for young children.

5   Whenever possible, allow employees flexibility in their starting and finishing times. Don't overwork people. In Chapter 2, we saw that the average employee is only mentally productive and creative for a few hours a day, regardless of how long they actually spend at work. Aim to become what Scott Adams (1997) once described as an 'OA5 company' ('Out at Five').

6   Educate people who engage in bullying or 'toxic' behaviours or who discriminate against staff on the grounds of gender, culture, race or sexual orientation. If they persist with these behaviours, fire them because they are damaging your business and its ability to compete in the future.

7   Invest as much time and money as you can afford in staff learning and development. As we will see in Chapters 9 and 10, the world's leading companies invest a great deal of time and money in the development and education of their workforces, so that their employees work smarter, faster and more creatively, rather than harder and longer.[5]

8   Periodically remind people why they, and the work they do, are important and the larger goals towards which their efforts are directed. Communicate effectively and keep people informed and up-to-date about what is going on in your organization. Jointly agree process, performance and outcome goals with your employees that stretch, but do not overwhelm, them. Give them recognition, feedback and support on a regular basis. Always praise exceptional effort promptly and give positive feedback even when people make mistakes. Show them how to avoid repeating mistakes. Mistakes made by your employees are not the problem – a failure to help them learn from these is. Regularly review your followers' job performance. Reward good effort as well as good outcomes. Celebrate success and have some fun at work.

9   As far as possible, don't tell people what to wear or how to decorate their personal spaces at work. No one has *ever* demonstrated that these lead to either greater efficiency or greater creativity. For example, Peter West, former MD of the BP Refinery in Kwinana, Western Australia, was renowned for never wearing a tie at work. During a talk to a group of MBAs, in June 2001, he commented that this 'creates barriers with technical staff and has no demonstrable effect on their motivation and performance. It merely serves to separate my neck from my shoulders'. The first time I met him, he was wearing jeans, a white t-shirt and a leather waistcoat. The attendance policy and dress code of the US Company, The Sprint Corporation, is 'Come to work and wear clothes'.

10   Treat your followers as intelligent, motivated human beings who will contribute more given the right opportunities and incentives. Reward them whenever they demonstrate this. In order to empower people, you will also have to spend time developing their leadership skills. This is because the best control tool you will ever possess is the ingrained internal locus of control you have developed amongst your followers. Empowering your employees also frees your time to get on with your work, in the sure-fire knowledge that your people are capable of running with the ball and taking responsibility for their daily work tasks, even when you are not physically present (c.f. Tom Peters' 'Boss Test' mentioned earlier in this chapter). Give your followers as much freedom as possible in the planning of their daily work goals and tasks. To foster creativity, innovation and change, encourage employees to question the status quo and offer new ideas, however crazy, off the wall or barmy they might first appear to be.

One example of a company that has taken on board many of the motivational and empowerment principles described in this chapter is the Brazilian company Semco. The subject of one of the best-selling management books of the 1990s, *Maverick: The Story Behind the World's Most Unusual Company*, Semco has been one of the most consistently successful companies in Latin America, a continent routinely shaken by political and economic instability. When he took over from his father as CEO, Ricardo Semler knew that he was going to have to take some radical steps to prevent the company going under. He subsequently introduced a number of innovations that are still regarded by most conventional business people as being either impractical and/or unworkable (Table 4.2). Many of these ideas have a modern ring to them, but most were regarded as radical and idealistic when he first introduced them, and some of these will still appear to be quite alien to

Table 4.2   Semco: tore up the rule book in the 1980s

Initiatives

The company's traditional hierarchical relationships between 'bosses' and 'workers' were removed by abolishing layers of management and supervisors and creating a novel circular structure.

Formal job descriptions and set working hours were abolished.

Managerial staff set their own salaries and bonuses (which were made public for all employees to scrutinize).

Everyone was given access to the company books (including financial information).

Bureaucracy was reduced, with minimum time wasted with meetings, memos and approvals.

Shop-floor workers set their own production schedules and targets, and were given the freedom to develop their jobs.

Profit sharing was introduced for all company employees.

The company introduced a mobility option for young recruits, the 'Lost in Space' programme, to enable them to experience all facets of the company's operations before deciding where they would work.

Outcomes

Semco has been one of Latin America's most successful and profitable companies since the early 1990s.

It is widely acknowledged to be the best company in Brazil to work for. There are thousands of applicants for every advertised job.

Ricardo Semler is an acknowledged role model for many 'Third-Wave' company founders.

Maverick is recommended and popular reading on MBA programmes throughout the world.

Source: Semler (2001).

many organizations. However, since this time the company has flourished. It now operates in three countries and employs 3000 staff in manufacturing, professional services and high-tech software development (Semler, 2001).

Conclusion

Smile. Become genuinely interested in other people. Give honest and sincere appreciation to others. Arouse in people an eager desire to succeed. Remember that the sweetest sound to another person is their name. Encourage others to talk about themselves. Be a good listener and talk in terms of other people's interests. Make other people feel important and valued. Don't criticize, condemn or complain.
(*Abridged from Dale Carnegie*, How to Win Friends and Influence People, *1994 edn; more than 15 million copies of this influential book have been sold worldwide.*)

Taken collectively, the theories described in this chapter can assist leaders and managers in identifying exactly what might be causing motivational problems amongst their staff. If it is a problem of ability, does the employee require a personal development programme? If it is problem of motivation, is the employee in the right job or are her rewards inappropriate? If a particular group of employees are showing signs of demotivation and underperformance, is this the result of a lack of leadership or perceived inequity in their treatment and the financial rewards they receive? If employees are not achieving goals, is this because the goals are unrealistic or because the employees are not clear about what they are? If there is a problem with labour turnover, is this being caused by inadequate recruitment and selection policies, poor management, a lack of career opportunities, or inequitable reward systems? Motivation and performance are the outcomes of a complex cocktail of individual attributes, abilities, personal needs and achievement motivation. These intrinsic drives are mediated by external factors such as the manner in which goals are set, the match between employee expectations and work outcomes, opportunities for advancement at work, learning and development, equity in rewards and the way praise, feedback and financial rewards are provided.

Motivation and performance are also shaped by other contingent factors such as group dynamics, communication, leadership styles and organizational cultures. While the issues of motivation and empowerment may initially appear to be complex, the basic strategies for optimizing these in employees are straightforward and, as with many other facets of leadership and people management, have been understood for centuries. All that leaders and managers need to do is to include the elements that have been described in this chapter in a contingent (context-specific) and integrated programme that will enhance employee motivation and performance. To reiterate three points that have already been made in this chapter, this means that leader/managers should seek ways to achieve the following:

1 Select and recruit intrinsically motivated and technically skilled people whose personalities and mind-sets will fit in with their organization's vision, future goals, core values, working practices and culture. It can be very time consuming and difficult to change anyone's behaviour or attitudes after they have been recruited.
2 Create work environments that enable employees to grow and explore, to solve problems, to make discoveries, to innovate and to reach ever-higher personal goals and performance targets.
3 Inject some fun into work, and provide an eclectic range of individually tailored financial and non-financial incentives to enhance staff motivation, performance, productivity and organizational loyalty. To reiterate a point made earlier, if your organization has a reputation for looking after its staff, new recruits will batter down the doors to join you.

Each of the motivational and empowerment techniques we have reviewed in this chapter works, and the main reason for using these is to produce employees who are, in a nutshell, energized and enthusiastic when they come to work and want to contribute their very best efforts while they are there. Effective business leader/managers know that such employees are more motivated, creative, productive and loyal than demotivated and unhappy employees. How do they know this? Because they understand that, if people are treated humanely, as fully rounded human beings, they will perform much better than if they are treated inhumanely. Collectively, organizations that have put systems in place to get the best out of their people are known as 'high involvement organizations'. More significantly, the companies we have looked at in this chapter, who do focus a lot of effort on the motivation, empowerment and performance of their employees, are also commercially successful and profitable for lengthy periods of time (Collins, 2001; Semler, 2001; O'Reilly and Pfeffer, 2000; Collins and Porras, 1996).

> You may well ask, and I'm sure the organizational theory people here would, what have people to do with our company's success? The answer is, everything. There was a time when companies could rely on physical advantages to provide superior shareholder returns – things like geographic spread, technology, strong distribution networks, resource bases and so on. But, with globalisation and much better communications, these advantages have been eroded. I am convinced that at Wesfarmers, we only have two real competitive advantages – our people and our culture; and the latter relies on the former. On the people side, our approach has

been simple: take the best we can find, give them stimulating jobs, develop them well, encourage innovation, accept that mistakes happen and reward them according to performance.

(*Michael Chaney, former CEO of Wesfarmers, during a presentation at the Graduate School of Management, University of Western Australia, Perth, 19 April 2004. Wesfarmers was voted 'Australian Company of the Year' in 2002, by the country's premier business publication* The Australian Financial Review *and Chaney, 'Australian Businessman of the Year 2003', by the Institute of Chartered Accountants. Mr Chaney becomes Chairman of the National Australia Bank in 2005*)

Exercise 4.3

Having read through this chapter, please consider how you can translate any new insights you have acquired into your employee motivation and empowerment strategies in the future.

Insight   **Strategy to implement this**

1.

2.

3.

4.

5.   ◆

Notes

1   A detailed discussion of the variety of employee selection and recruitment procedures that are now available to leaders and managers is beyond the remit of this book. If you would like to know more about these topics, four good starting points are the following. For US readers: Randall S. Schuler and Susan Jackson, *Human Resource Management: Positioning for the 21st Century*, 6th edn, 1996, West Publishing, chs 7 and 8; for UK readers: Ian Beardwell and Len Holden, *Human Resource Management: A Contemporary Perspective*, 6th edn, 1998, Pitman Publishing, chs 6 and 7; for Australian readers: Robin Kramar, Peter McGraw and Randall S. Schuler, *Human Resource Management in Australia*, 3rd edn, 1997, Addison Wesley Longman, ch. 8; for New Zealand readers: R. Rudman, 1997, *Human Resource Management in New Zealand*, Longman Paul.

2   A short discussion of the enormous remuneration packages routinely paid to company CEOs and Boards of Directors in the 1990s, and the role these played in numerous corporate fraud and bankruptcy cases during 2001–3, can be found in Chapter 12.

3   For more information on country-specific employee remuneration schemes and legal frameworks, financial incentives, performance related pay and share-holding, please refer to the following chapters from the books cited in note 1 above: *Human Resource Management: Positioning for the 21st Century*, chs 12 and 13; *Human Resource Management in Australia*, ch. 10; *Human Resource Management: A Contemporary Perspective*, ch. 6; *Human Resource Management in New Zealand*, ch. 7'.

4   This principle applies equally to companies that may have contracted out their personnel recruitment to an external agency. However, there can be risks with this (see, for example, Peter Drucker's 2002 article on outsourcing in the bibliography at the end of this book).

5   'Work smarter – not harder' is another old idea that came of age in the 1990s. It was first suggested by Allan F. Morgensen, the creator of 'Work Simplification', in the early 1930s.

5 Leading and managing teams

Objectives

To define group and team.

To highlight the positive and negative aspects of team working in organizations.

To illustrate the differences between effective and ineffective work teams.

To outline practical strategies for creating and leading work-teams.

To offer practical suggestions for organizing and managing team meetings.

Introduction: teams in context

'Group' and 'team' are words that are often used interchangeably by leaders and managers, but there are differences between the two terms. Group is derived from the old French word *groupe*, meaning 'knot' or 'cluster'. It is defined here as an informal or ad hoc set of three or more people who interact over time, who perceive themselves as being part of a group and who have, to some extent, common interests, values, attitudes and goals. The origin of 'team' is uncertain, but it is believed to derive from an old English word meaning a family or line of descendants. This is a more formal type of group, and is defined here as a structured and organized collective of three or more people who interact over time, who perceive themselves as being part of a cohesive work team and who share a common understanding of the team's working practices, values, attitudes, reward systems, mutual obligations, goals and objectives.

In many western industrialized countries, there was a surge in interest in team working in the 1970s, driven in large measure by the success of team-based production methods in Japanese car companies such as

201

Nissan and Toyota. The growth in team working that later followed was driven by other factors, such as the need for western companies to become faster and more nimble in the marketplace, the need to improve product quality and reliability, the technological revolution in production processes, and the need for continuous improvements in customer service provision. In the USA, corporate giants such as Motorola, General Electric, Procter and Gamble and General Motors were amongst the first companies to introduce team-based manufacturing processes in the 1970s. The 'fashion' for teams has spread rapidly ever since, with team-based manufacturing now being used in more than 90 per cent of all manufacturing plants in the USA (Kaye, 1997). The drive to delayer and flatten organizational structures in the 1980s (and strip out layers of middle managers in the process) was also instrumental in the push to introduce team-based manufacturing and production systems.

This era marked the introduction of self-managing work and project teams, and the emergence of cross-functional work teams in many organizations. For example, Hewlett-Packard was one of the first companies in the USA to routinely mix together specialists in single teams. These brought together engineers, technicians, marketing managers, lawyers, sales people, purchasing specialists and shop-floor workers, in order to discuss all facets of their innovation and production processes, and the marketing and selling of new products. Internationally, there are growing numbers of transnational project teams, such as those that worked on the Channel tunnel in the 1980s, and those currently working on transport systems and other large-scale building projects in East Asia, such as the Three-Gorge dam in China. Today, 'self-managing teams', 'team work', 'quality teams', 'cross-functional teams', 'team players' and 'virtual teams' are common features of many organizations.

Worldwide, employees in most organizations now work as part of a team of some kind. Team working is now so prevalent in organizations that one could be forgiven for thinking that this way of working is perfectly natural. In reality, simply putting a disparate group of people together and calling them 'a team' does not guarantee success and, as a result, some teams do not work well together. Furthermore, the emergence of team-based working also has a profound impact on traditional management control and authority, a fact that some companies have yet to come to terms with. For example, one survey of chief executives by Price-Waterhouse-Coopers indicated that, while 83 per cent believed that team working was essential for the future success of their organizations, 54 per cent had experienced 'significant frustrations' in making teamwork a reality. The biggest obstacle to change was reported to be 'the unwillingness of senior managers to give up power and control' (cited by Uren, 1998b).

On the one hand, teams hold out the promise of sharing knowledge and creating solutions to problems, improving work processes and communication, enhancing individual motivation and productivity, cutting costs and promoting innovation. It has also been suggested that teams, not individuals, are now the fundamental learning units of the modern organization; unless the team can learn, the organization cannot learn (Senge, 1990). On the other hand, the reality of team working can be interpersonal conflict, political infighting, backstabbing, groupthink, social loafing, freeloading and passing the buck. Teams can also be directionless, clueless and motionless if they are not well managed, and 'team work' may just become a feel-good mechanism that gets in the way of achieving anything. Organizations continue to throw people together, tell them they are 'a team' and then hope for miracles. A Scott Adams *Dilbert* cartoon in 2000 summed up this scenario, when Dilbert's evil boss tells his employees that he is going to reorganize them into 'fast moving teams'. Their response is, 'Good plan. We'll never realise we're powerless, micro-managed serfs after we call ourselves "a team" '. Hence, as with other facets of leadership and people management, teams can only succeed if the appropriate structures and processes are put in place to support them. As the Australian Graduate School of Management's Roger Collins once observed, 'You don't get an Olympic team being thrown together and told to work. Instead, they spend years and years training to get it right. That's what companies should be doing' (cited by Ferguson, 1999). Consequently, simply introducing 'teamwork' into an organization will not automatically make people work smarter and faster, or more collaboratively and productively.

Do team-based work systems benefit organizations? The short answer to this question is 'Yes', but only if they are introduced and managed in the right way, and if the working practices and culture of the larger organization of which they are a part support them in their work activities. For example, some form of team working is used in all of the 'Visionary Companies' described by Collins and Porras (1996) and the 'Good to Great' companies discussed in Collins (2001). O'Reilly and Pfeffer also make these summary comments about team working in the successful US companies they surveyed:

> the people-centered companies we have described rely heavily on team-based systems. Examples include the total team-based approach of Applied Energy Services, the formal systems at New United Motor Manufacturing and Southwest Airlines, and the informal teams at Cisco Systems, the SAS Institute and the Men's Wearhouse. This emphasis on teams as an organising

principle derives not from a current fad, but from a belief in the fundamental importance of teams as a way of both getting the work done and of promoting personal responsibility and autonomy and of tapping the ideas and energy of everyone. Teams, in spite of their difficulties, can promote a sense of purpose and give people a sense of belonging. At New United Motor Manufacturing and Applied Energy Services, teams take responsibility for the production process. Supervisors aren't in control. Teams are. Instead of relying on formal monitoring and control systems, teams rely on the social control of others to ensure that people behave consistently with the norms and values of the companies they work for.
(*Abridged from O'Reilly and Pfeffer, 2000: 242*)

Since the pioneering Hawthorne Studies of the 1930s there have been hundreds of studies on teams and work groups, conducted in North America, Europe and Australasia. Many of these have shown impressive results for organizations that have moved to team-based work systems. For example, one of the largest studies of team working, in the Fortune 1000 companies, found that involvement in work teams had a strong positive relationship with several key dimensions of employee and organizational effectiveness, with 75 per cent reporting improvements in these two areas. Other reported improvements in this study included 'more participatory management styles' (78 per cent); 'better management decision making' (69 per cent); 'more trust in management' (66 per cent); 'easier implementation of new technology' (60 per cent) and 'improved health and safety' (48 per cent). The reported benefits to these organizations included 'better quality of products and services' (70 per cent); 'more customer satisfaction' (67 per cent); 'improved employee quality of work-life' (63 per cent); 'greater productivity' (61 per cent) and 'improved profitability' (45 per cent) (Lawler *et al.*, 1992). In general terms, this study found that organizations that used teams reported above-average individual and organizational effectiveness when compared to organizations that were not using teams. Similar results have been reported in a range of studies that have looked at self-directed and self-managed teams. For example, Near and Weckler (1990) reported that employees working in self-directed teams scored significantly higher on measures such as task significance, employee involvement, information sharing and innovation, when compared to employees in traditional work structures. Many other studies have produced similar results (for example, Ancona and Caldwell, 1992; Hackman, 1990).

The positive and negative aspects of team working in organizations

We were forming a group of people who'd be working together and learning together, going through similar experiences and creating something new together. I thought it was terrific.
(*Leonard Nimoy*, Star Trek Memories, *1994*)

The benefits of teamwork and effective work teams have been known for more than 30 years:

- Teams that are working effectively always produce more ideas and information than individuals working alone. In turn, this should result in improved decision making, by highlighting and offsetting the personal biases and selective perceptions of team members.
- Teams can improve motivation and performance, by giving employees more autonomy and control over their jobs. They can also provide socio-emotional support for newcomers to an organization and a sense of security. Almost everyone is more energized and laughs more when in the company of other people.
- Teams can increase efficiency by eliminating layers of management whose traditional job was to pass down orders from the top. Self-management in teams frees leaders from traditional command-and-control responsibilities and gives them more time to concentrate on the creative and visionary aspects of their jobs.
- Teams can enable a company to draw on the skills and imaginations of people working cooperatively. Teams may allow people to perform multiple tasks and can foster greater cross-functional collaboration across internal organizational boundaries.
- Learning, of any kind, is far more effective in groups. Peer pressures can enhance self-learning and skill acquisition amongst individual team members.
- Creative brainstorming is only possible in teams, and this can lead to new ideas, breakthrough thinking, innovations and quality improvements.
- Cohesive teams generate good teamwork, high levels of team spirit, mutual respect and trust and a willingness to make sacrifices for one another.
- People working in teams may have greater confidence in communicating back up an organizational hierarchy ('safety in numbers'), if they disagree with decisions being made by senior management.
- Individual members of a team can benefit from team-based pay and group productivity bonuses.
- Teams can help in managing change, and introducing new working practices into organizations (see Chapter 8).

When a team of employees becomes totally unified in its individual and collective endeavours, the whole can become greater than the sum of its individual parts. In a sporting context, there are many, many examples where this phenomenon generates collective performances that exceed the abilities of the individual members of a team. The most successful teams in business and sporting contexts are those that have learnt another extremely important lesson: the interests of the team always come before the interests of individuals, no matter how gifted they might be (Parkin *et al.*, 1999: 23–25).

> Are there any limits to the use of teams? Can we find places or circumstances where a team structure does not make sense? Answer: No, not as far as I can determine. That's unequivocal and meant to be. Some situations may seem to lend themselves more to team-based management than others. Nonetheless, I observe that the power of the team is so great that it is often wise to violate apparent common-sense and force a team-structure on almost anything.
> (*Tom Peters*, Thriving on Chaos, *1987*)

Peters is largely correct, but teams are not a panacea for every organization, all employees and all work tasks. For example, simple or routine jobs may not require team-based solutions. It may also be inadvisable to 'force' team-working practices onto employees without developing the skills and competencies that they will need to succeed in these new environments. There can also be a number of negative aspects to team working:

- A reduction in employee motivation and performance, if good individual performers are punished as a result of belonging to a team that is not performing well. High performers may also be unfairly penalized after joining a pre-existing team that is carrying weaker or lazier employees.
- Teams can become ineffective 'waffle-shops' and slow down decision making, particularly in large bureaucracies. This tendency is captured in the well-known old saying, 'A camel is a horse designed by a committee'.
- Social loafing (laziness) and freeloading (enjoying the benefits of, or taking credit for, other people's work) may occur amongst some members of large teams.
- Teams can be coercive and intimidating, and there may be over-dependence on a dominant leader

The potential for 'Groupthink' is a widespread phenomenon in organizations, whereby collective delusions of grandeur and infallibility replace true reality testing within a team or group of employees. The most often cited examples of this include President Kennedy and the Cuban Bay of Pigs fiasco in 1961, the Space Shuttle Challenger disaster in 1987, and the failure of all companies who become complacent or arrogant about their past record of commercial success. More recent examples of the latter phenomenon include the boards of Enron, Worldcom, Xerox, Cisco, Arthur Andersen, Lucent Technologies, AT&T, Polaroid, HIH, UMP, Ansett, One.Tel and many other companies that have either gone out of business or suffered a major decline in their fortunes in recent times. There are four main causes of this phenomenon (adapted from Janis, 1972):

1 The emergence of a *dominant leader*, who believes that he is infallible, does not attempt to provide impartial leadership, and who demands that people follow him at all costs and obey all his decisions.
2 The emergence of an *in-group* of favourites that values unthinking obedience to the leader and excludes dissenters. At board level, this can also be characterized by the emergence of self-appointed 'mind-guards', who decide what information is received by the in-group and who also control access to the inner-circle and the leader. This can also be accompanied by a phenomenon the psychologist Jerry Harvey has called the 'Abilene Paradox', when individuals in groups make decisions they know to be stupid or irresponsible because they know they can avoid responsibility for them.
3 *Insularity* from the outside world and the emergence of a strong feeling of 'us and them' ('we' being superior, right and good, 'they' being inferior, wrong and bad).
4 A sense of *impending crisis*, creating time pressures, a distorted sense of reality and poorer decision-making processes.

When a group of employees belongs to a dysfunctional team they can never be united in their individual or collective endeavours, the team becomes far less than the sum of its individual parts and, sooner or later, some kind of crisis will emerge.

Leading effective work teams

Team leadership skills

With these thoughts in mind, how can one ensure that the teams we lead and manage operate successfully? Before this question is addressed, please complete the next self-development exercise.

Exercise 5.1

In Chapters 1, 3 and 4, we identified a variety of leadership and managerial skills that can and should be applied in team settings. Please write down as many of these as you can remember, before reading the next paragraph. ◆

The skills that can be applied in team settings include being honest, walking the talk, supporting your employees, setting a positive example, active listening, winning over and persuading an audience, storytelling, humour and two-way communication, as well as the variety of motivational and empowerment techniques that we looked at in Chapter 3 (in particular goal setting and providing positive feedback and rewards). To these we now need to add some additional skills and techniques.

It has often been said that there is no 'I' in 'team' and, more than anywhere else, this is a situation where the leader becomes something identified in Chapter 1: *first amongst equals*. This is because an autocratic management style tends to inhibit team self-leadership, thus defeating the whole point of having self-managing teams in the first place. A participative leadership style can facilitate team empowerment, because it teaches self-leadership skills and also helps the team learn how to coordinate itself. Active leadership is only beneficial for teams that are in the early stages of development (see 'Creating a new work team', below). In fact, some teams can be very effective with several leaders or with a system of rotating leadership. One example of a very successful team that did not have a formal stand-alone leader was the 2000 Olympic gold medal-winning hockey team, The Hockeyroos. Their innovative coach, Rick Charlesworth, abandoned the idea of a single team captain and instead set up a system of captain, vice-captains and co-vice-captains, believing that every member of his first team was capable of taking on specific leadership roles. He also argued that the system of promoting some players and not others created social loafers, both on and off the pitch (Le Grand, 2000). Another example is the organization of the teams that fly on the Space Shuttle missions. While there is a mission captain, leadership roles are quite fluid and are determined by the particular tasks that the flight is dealing with at any one moment in time. In fact, 'dominant personalities' rarely make it past the selection and recruitment stage of the astronaut-training programme at NASA (Maruyama, 1990).

> The essence of an effective crew member is how much they are willing to put their individual egos in the equipment locker and work totally, mind, body and soul, for the duration of the mission. We have enough talented individuals to run a hundred Shuttle flights, but we only ever have a handful of people who have what it takes to work as part of a highly integrated and professional unit in space.
> (*Attributed to Stephan Mayer, NASA Flight Crew Training Officer, 1993*)

Does this mean that teams don't need leaders? In most organizational situations they do, but in team-settings the leader does not have to be the noisiest or most dominant participant. Leadership in teams is a more subtle art, requiring the leader to act more like a puppet master, the conductor of an orchestra or first amongst equals. Leadership in teams is not about *bossiness*, or being 'tough', 'dynamic', 'hard' or 'decisive', because simply riding roughshod over the ideas, contributions and feelings of others in a group can be very counterproductive. As we saw in Chapter 4, this means that leaders have to be willing to give their leadership away to their followers, and allow them the freedom to take greater responsibility for the decisions they make and the work they do. Hence the key to effective team leadership is to find ways of unleashing the potential and talents of the people you have in your team, not telling them what to do. If you involve people in this process, they will usually be on your side and come to regard you as their 'natural' leader, coach and mentor. If they are on your side, they will follow you willingly down the ways, roads or paths that you want them to go down. This means that team leaders have to be able to deal with three overlapping aspects of team management, often at the same time: supporting and developing the individual, growing the team and achieving work tasks and objectives.

> What I really wanted in the organization was a group of responsible, interdependent workers, similar to a flock of geese. I could see the geese flying in their 'V' formation, the leadership changing frequently, with different geese taking the lead. I saw every goose being responsible for getting itself to wherever the gaggle was going, changing roles whenever necessary, alternating as a leader, follower or scout. And, when the task changed, the geese would be responsible for changing the structure of the group, similar to the geese that fly in a 'V', but land in waves. I could see each goose become a leader.
> (*James Belasco and Ralph Stayer*, The Flight of the Buffalo, *1993*)

Group size and composition

Is there an optimum group size? Unfortunately, there is no simple answer to this question. This depends on what the team's purpose is and the nature, duration and complexity of the tasks it is dealing with. Small groups tend to be better at dealing with tasks quickly, while larger groups are better at problem solving and generating new ideas. However, research on this question indicates that the optimum team size, in most situations, is six to eight, with seven employees being the ideal number (Shaw, 1981). While larger teams have more resources, skills, ideas and abilities to draw upon, and more people to whom tasks can be delegated, the following can occur as teams increase in size (Albanese and Van Fleet, 1985; Shaw, 1981):

- less participation, because the time for individual contributions is reduced. In turn, this can lead to a reduced willingness to listen to other individuals in the team;
- a greater probability of sub-groups forming within the team;
- a greater potential for individual differences, interpersonal conflict and political infighting to occur;

- more opportunities for social loafing and freeloading to occur: the larger the group, the lower the performance of some individuals will be;
- low-performing or badly organized large groups may drag down the motivation and productivity of high-performing individuals;
- a greater likelihood that the team leader will make autocratic decisions on behalf of the team.

Nor is there a simple answer to the question, 'What is the best type of team?' This is because teams come in a variety of shapes, sizes and characteristics. Take the example of rowing. In this situation, you can have up to eight people rowing backwards as fast as they can without talking to each other, being yelled at by the one person who is not the captain and doesn't row in the boat. In races, the cox determines the speed and direction of the boat. Next there is the stroke, who sets the rowing pace for the other rowers to follow, but may not be the team's captain. Off the river, the captain of the crew becomes the visible leader. He has a say in the selection of the crew, and also has responsibilities for discipline, motivation and morale. Last, there is the coach, who rarely (if ever) gets to actually row in the boat, but is responsible for the team's fitness, motivation, team development, setting long and short-term performance targets, race tactics and checking up on the opposition. At first glance, this could be regarded as a very odd way of organizing a group of people, but it is perfectly suited to the task of transporting a sophisticated piece of equipment and up to eight athletes down a course as quickly as possible.

To return to a point made earlier, simply putting people together and calling them a team does not mean that they will work together successfully. Building an effective team requires time and commitment, as well as the ability to create a team structure and processes appropriate to the tasks at hand. High-performing teams establish agreed rules about appropriate behaviour, commitment and punctuality at meetings. Questions of 'what', 'when', 'where', 'who' and 'how' are clearly understood and this means that the team can then deal with their work tasks efficiently. People understand their individual responsibilities and the higher goals towards which the group is working. They have a deep sense of purpose ('One for all and all for one'). They are willing to confront each other over difficult issues, and there are no subjects that cannot be discussed, analysed or criticized. High-performing teams are committed to excellence in all spheres of their activities and have a deep sense of mutual responsibility for the team's results. Two of the most respected writers on teams, Katzenbach and Smith (1983), have suggested that there are eight steps to building high-performance teams:

- selecting new recruits on the basis of their skills and potential 'fit' with other team members,
- spending some time together creating an *esprit de corps* and building up personal rapport between individual team-members,
- establishing clear rules of behaviour and team protocol,
- creating a sense of urgency to energize and motivate the team,
- setting clear, challenging goals and tasks for team members, within agreed time frames,
- challenging the team regularly with new ideas and information,
- ensuring that all team meetings are well organized and managed effectively,
- providing the team's members with positive feedback, recognition and rewards.

A number of theories and models have also been developed in order to identify the variety of roles that are performed in successful work teams. The best known of these is Meredith Belbin's model. He identified eight key team-roles.

1 *Chair/coordinator*: has overall responsibility for leading the team and coordinating the activities and goals of individual team members.
2 *Company worker*: a task-focused individual who has a strong drive to achieve the team's objectives, but may be less able to develop good interpersonal relationships with other team members.
3 *Shaper*: often intelligent and assertive and likes to contribute ideas, but may not want to be a leader. Can become frustrated and impatient if their ideas are not accepted.
4 *Resource investigator*: usually stable, extroverted and sociable. Likes to get ideas and information from people outside their team. Good at locating and accessing information. May lose interest in team projects quite quickly and may not be good with the minutiae of team tasks.
5 *Monitor/evaluator*: good at critiquing ideas and reality-testing the team's ideas and proposals, but may lack creativity and an ability to innovate.
6 *Team worker*: often extroverted, sociable and may be the team 'joker'. Concerned about team harmony and morale. May be less good at taking hard decisions or doing the practical work that is required to achieve the team's goals.
7 *Plant/originator*: often independent, creative and intelligent. Likes to offer new ideas and innovative suggestions. May be introverted and indecisive.
8 *Finisher*: a perfectionist, who is interested in the details of a project and likes to check that the team has completed a task successfully.

Can become over-concerned about trivial details and signing-off on a project.
(*Adapted from Belbin, 1993*)

What practical applications might this model have? First, Belbin's research has shown that successful teams have this diversity of roles fully covered, while less successful teams lack some of these. This does not mean that you need to have an individual 'plant', 'resource investigator' and so on in your team. But it does follow that these skills and competencies need to be spread amongst the individual members of the team. Second, the precise mixture of these skills and competencies will be shaped by the team's objectives, and those of the organization of which it is a part. For example, if you are working in an organization where new ideas and innovation are important, you will need more shapers, plants, resource investigators and monitors (for example, in a biotechnology company). If you work in an organization where adherence to strict rules, regulations and legal standards is important you'll require more monitors and finishers (for example, in a department of immigration or a taxation office). In a small business, you may need two or three individuals who are able to fulfil all or most of these roles.

Other research has indicated that other kinds of diversity in teams can be extremely beneficial (for example, Goodman, 1986). In Chapters 1 and 3 we identified the issue of selective perceptions and how these shape, in a very fundamental way, our views of the world and of other people. The natural consequence of these is the tendency that many leaders have to separate their followers into distinct groups, an in-group of people they instinctively like (the 'cadre') and an out-group of people they like less (the 'hired hands'). Many leaders do this and, for the most part, without even thinking consciously about it. Each group is treated differently, with the cadre being allowed more latitude in behaviour and much closer relationships with the leader. However, there can be dangers associated with this. There may be a tendency to hire only people who are 'like us', leading to the emergence of a management team of 'yes' men and women and, over time, to widespread organizational sclerosis and nepotism.

While it can appear to be a perfectly rational decision to bring in people we know to form a new team in an organization, this can have several negative outcomes, particularly when creating new senior management teams (Cornell, 1998a). Known as 'consanguineous nepotism', this tendency to 'hire your mates' can be fraught with dangers. First, a lack of formal hiring processes may mean that the wrong people get jobs. Second, there can be an impact on the morale of existing personnel when they see the boss's mates being wheeled in ahead (or instead) of them. It also suggests inadequate succession planning and a lack of faith in the incumbent management. Third, there is a potential danger that the leader in question is building up a power base of compliant 'yes' men and women, rather than developing an effective senior management team (the 'in' and 'out' group phenomenon described in Chapter 1). Fourth, the new people may not fit the new organizational culture and, if existing staff are rubbed up the wrong way, this could lead to an exodus of employees. Employees who choose to leave may then be in a position to damage the company by trading sensitive information to competitors. Corporate psychologist Ken Byrne, of the Ballin Group, made these comments in 1998:

> The reality is that executives are more mobile and realise that they are going to be judged, maybe very quickly, so their career depends on getting a team working quickly. In that situation, it is a rational choice to bring in the people you know. It may not always be the best choice, but it is a logical one [ ] the most common mistake is for senior executives to surround themselves with people like themselves. That only works when the new person is coming in to perform exactly what they were already good at.
> (*Abridged from Cornell, 1998a*)

In practical terms, this means that all leaders and managers should be wary of recruiting new team members on the basis of 'Is this person like me?' judgments (for example, white, male, Anglo-Saxon and into gridiron/rugby/soccer). All available research evidence shows that the most successful business teams are made up of a variety of personality types, and we will return to this important issue in the context of gender and diversity issues in Chapter 6.

> One of the biggest mistakes a person can make is to put together a team that reflects him/her. I find that it is better to put together people in teams who have disparate skills and then make all those disparate skills work together. The real role of the team-leader is to figure out how you make diverse people and elements work together.
> (*John Sculley, former CEO, Apple Computers, 1992*)

Creating a new work team

For two reasons, it is worth spending a little time looking at the process of team and group formation. First, there will be times when you have to create a new team from scratch, and this is not as easy as it might sound. Second, you may at some time become the leader of a dysfunctional team, and an understanding of how it came to be this way could assist you in finding solutions to its problems. Although there are a number of models describing the process of group formation, they are all variations on the same theme: that new teams go through four or five principal life stages from birth to maturity. The best known of these is probably Tuckman and Jenson's model.

Forming

When people come together for the first time, there may be very little mutual understanding. People may be guarded and defensive, while at the same time trying to make their mark on the group. Active listening may be at a premium. Dominant personalities may seek to take over and set the group's direction. Their focus may be on the task at hand, rather than the process of building the group. There is little or no achievement of work goals at this stage.

Storming

Members may have opened up more, and issues of roles and responsibilities within the group are being worked out. Exploration and testing emerge. There may be an increased acceptance of others' viewpoints. The 'real' leader may have emerged, or been elected by the group, and may take on a more directive role at this stage. A group pecking order may have developed. Group members are looking for clear goals and direction from the leader. Task performance is still low and more conflict may occur.

Norming

By this stage, the group is evolving into a team, and should have established rules, codes and procedures for working together and be developing a collective team ethos. Leadership may be shared or rotated. Systematic working methods have been adopted. Relationships within the team are well developed. Benchmarks for acceptable behaviour and standards of work are well established. The team will now be starting to work towards its goals.

Performing

The team is now more than the sum of its individual members and has evolved into a cohesive unit. People are clear about their roles and mutual obligations. They are achieving their objectives together, and the climate within the team is challenging and enjoyable. An *esprit de corps* is now established and the team may be developing a sense of competition with other teams. People develop and grow and support each other in the achievement of work tasks. The team is performing well and achieving its objectives. The team as a whole enjoys team-based bonuses and rewards (adapted from Tuckman and Jenson, 1977[1]).

There are four qualifications that should be added to this basic model.

- In practice, the progression through this linear process is likely to be irregular, with intermittent regressions between each stage.
- The transitions between stages will be gradual rather than sudden and some groups may have to move through the four stages simultaneously.
- The model largely overlooks organizational contexts and cultures, the environment that provides the resources, behavioural rules, work practices, protocols and information needed for the team to perform effectively (a subject we will return to in Chapters 8–10).
- It also overlooks issues relating to team size, roles and diversity, covered in the preceding sections. This means that, as well as building the team, the leader needs to be spending time and energy ensuring that the team has the right mixture of skills and abilities that will enable it to meet its objectives.

However, this model does have three practical applications for leaders and managers. First, it demonstrates that it is not usually possible to perform well as a team unless it has been successfully formed, and been through some norming and storming, at some point during its life cycle. Second, if establishing a new team from scratch, we should initially focus as much energy on building the team up as we do on dealing with the actual tasks that it is being formed to deal with. This may mean establishing a 'Team Charter' of agreed team rules, behaviours and protocols that each member of the team, literally, signs. Third, if we try to rush through this process, and the team is not working well together, it may be necessary to take it back through these stages at some point in the future.[2]

Managing team meetings

Are you lonely? Hate having to make decisions? Rather talk about it than do it? Then why not HOLD A MEETING? You can get to see other people, sleep in peace, offload decisions, learn to write volumes of meaningless notes, feel important, and impress (or bore) your colleagues. And all in work time! 'Meetings': the practical alternative to work.
(*Spoof email article that appeared in 1998*)

A few studies have confirmed what many leaders and managers have learnt through long and bitter experience: that meetings can be a frustrating waste of time, energy and resources, rather than useful forums in which to make decisions. For example, research conducted by Terry Robbins-Jones at the South Australian University School of Information Systems reported that Australian business managers waste up to 40 per cent of their time in useless meetings and hours on talks that ultimately produce the wrong answers to their problems. It also revealed that managers spend 30–75 per cent of their time in meetings, of which half produce no useful outcomes (cited by Ramsey, 1997). Another study, by Integrated Vision in conjunction with Australia's major telecommunications firm, Telstra, reported that one in three executives had admitted to falling asleep during meetings. Eighty-seven per cent said that they daydreamed during meetings, 68 per cent said they had 'raised their voice in anger' and 40 per cent had 'stormed out of meetings' in the preceding 12 months. The survey, on meeting behaviour and productivity, polled more than 300 executives and found that inefficient meetings were wasting a huge amount of company time and money. The authors of the study claimed that time wasted in unproductive meetings in Australia cost $A2.1 billion a year, or about 3.3 per cent of the country's total annual gross domestic product in 2000. The study estimated that Australian executives attend, on average, 61 meetings a month. In the UK, senior managers attend, on average, 62 meetings a month, and in the USA they attend 58 meetings a month (cited in Boreham, 2001).

What is surprising about these results is that the purpose of meetings is, ostensibly, to share and disseminate information, to solve problems, make intelligent and rational decisions and, tangentially, to build commitment and *esprit de corps* in organizations. So why do so many meetings have the potential to go horribly, horribly wrong? The main reason is that many leaders and managers do not invest sufficient time and resources in the organization and management of team meetings at work. To get an idea of how well you manage meetings, please complete Exercise 5.2.

Exercise 5.2

Managing meetings

Below, there are 12 statements about meetings. Before looking at the scoring key below, please indicate which you consider to be generally true or false. First-response answers are best.

1 Agendas should be prepared and sent out at least one week prior
to the meeting being held   True   False

2 Topics on the agenda should be sequenced from the most difficult
to the easiest   True   False

3 Even if it means delaying the start of a meeting, it should not begin
until everyone is present   True   False

4	The most effective way to start a meeting is to go through the agenda	True	False
5	The more people that can be involved in meetings, the more effective they will be	True	False
6	All meetings should be timed to last no more than 90 minutes	True	False
7	The chair should avoid taking an authoritative role in meetings	True	False
8	The most productive meetings are characterized by little disagreement or conflict	True	False
9	Reaching group consensus is usually a more effective way of making decisions than imposing decisions on others	True	False
10	People should be given as much time as they want to get their points across	True	False
11	The benefits of effective meetings always outweigh their costs in terms of time and resources	True	False
12	Specific action plans and time-lines should always be established to act on the decisions agreed in meetings	True	False

Scoring your answers:*

For statements 1, 6, 9, 11 & 12, score 2 points for 'True' and 0 for 'False'
For statements 2, 3, 4, 5, 7, 8 & 10, score 0 points for 'True' and 2 for 'False'

Add up your total score _____

Interpreting your score:

22–24:   excellent meeting management skills,
16–20:   good meeting management skills,
<14:   below-average meeting management skills.

(* Based on the collective team-working experiences of more than 1000 MBA students, 1993–2003. The rationale for each answer is given below.) ◆

How did you get on? Like formal presentation skills, the effective management of team meetings requires a focus on both structure (the 'what') and processes (the 'how'). Structure includes issues such as the organization of the agenda, the items and topics that are to be discussed at the meeting, the duration and location of the meeting, which staff are to be involved, and the physical environment of the meeting. In practical terms, this means:

- setting clear objectives and desired outcomes for every meeting that you chair (even if all of these may not be achieved in a single sitting). If you are dealing with complex issues, prepare your questions about these in advance;
- establishing who should attend (and why). If you have invited 'outsiders', delegate one person to look after them;
- sending all relevant information and the agenda to participants at least one week prior to the meeting, *with the clear understanding and expectation that these will be read prior to the meeting*. Complex and/or detailed documents should always have executive summaries attached. Use 'AOB' for any late submissions. Put easy or non-controversial items at the beginning of the agenda to be dealt with first;
- allowing adequate time for the meeting (but less than 90 minutes whenever possible) and making sure you've booked the room you need;
- ensuring that the venue for the meeting is comfortable, has appropriate equipment (chairs, tables, audio-visual aids and so forth), secretarial backup or a rotating minute taker to record the main points of the meeting, and refreshments for lunchtime meetings or for sessions that will last more than 90 minutes.

Process includes preparation for the meeting, setting the objectives for the meeting, agreed rules about appropriate behaviour at meetings, agreed limits on the length of time that people can talk, delegation of responsibilities for specific agenda items, and recording the meeting and actions to be taken following the meeting. In practical terms, this means:

- starting the meeting on time and/or at odd times (for example, 8.57, 11.13 or 1.34). *Never* wait for latecomers, unless there are exceptional circumstances or reasons for this. Welcome everyone and briefly set out the purpose and main objectives of the meeting;
- *never* reviewing the contents of the agenda in detail because people should have read through these prior to the meeting. Summarize, as needed, the minutes of the last meeting and what actions have been taken in response to decisions made in that meeting;
- leading the meeting authoritatively, without being autocratic. If you can, get easy items out of the way first. For complicated or difficult issues, set specific time limits for discussion, put these on the agenda and stick to them (I once knew a head of department who used to bring an alarm clock along to departmental meetings for this purpose);
- maintaining 'agenda integrity', by keeping the focus of attendees on the tasks and topics at hand. Steer people back from 'railway

sidings', if they go off on irrelevant tangents or start wind-bagging or rambling on about irrelevant topics;

- using flow charts and/or visual aids during brainstorming sessions or when discussing complex ideas or innovations (covered further in Chapter 9);
- using the active listening, questioning, emotional diffusion and 'winning an audience' skills reviewed in Chapter 3 (see below). Conflict and disagreement will inevitably occur in meetings but, if handled well, these can lead to positive outcomes and the genera- tion of new ideas;
- summarizing participants' contributions regularly and keeping accurate minutes, particularly where specific tasks have been dele- gated to named individuals;
- ending the meeting on time. At the close, briefly recap agreed courses of action, look forward to the next meeting, remind people of the date(s) of the next meeting(s) and end on a positive upbeat note and/or a 'thank you' for the team's contributions.

Many of the communication techniques described in detail in Chapter 3 can also be applied in team-meetings. In this context, the following are most applicable. First, ask questions of the entire team and indi- vidually, particularly the quieter members. If a team member responds, acknowledge or paraphrase the comment and explore this further if needed. If no one responds to your questions, consider rewording the question or ask if it needs clarification.

Second, if you disagree with an idea or viewpoint, ask questions, and try to avoid contradicting people directly. For example, instead of saying, 'Phil, that idea makes no sense at all to me, it's unworkable', try, 'I don't really understand this idea – can you please explain it to us again?', and then ask other team members to comment on the response.

Third, avoid biased questions (for example, use 'What's causing this problem?' rather than 'Who's causing this problem?' or 'Why are defect levels on the increase; what can we do about this?' instead of 'Jim, the level of defects in your team are on the rise. What are you going to do about it?'). If you want information, avoid questions that will only elicit 'Yes' or 'No' responses.

Fourth, be careful about how you praise questions or responses in team discussions. For example, try using 'Thanks for your input Fiona. Would anyone like to comment on this proposal?' instead of 'Great idea Fiona, that's the best idea I've heard this morning'. Such comments may put those who have already made contributions offside. Be neutral in your responses to contributions in team meetings in public; however, it is a very effective power strategy to praise individuals who have made valuable contributions after the meeting and in private.

Finally, make sure that everyone is equally involved, including the quieter members of the team. If men dominate your team, ensure that any women present are fully involved. In male-dominated groups, they are often ignored and will also be interrupted twice as often as men when they are talking (Manning and Haddock, 1995; Tannen, 1995).

One example of an organization that solved some difficulties with team meetings, by creating a 'Team Charter', is presented in Table 5.1.

Table 5.1   Team rules

Always attend team meetings or
- let your team leader know in advance
- send a replacement or brief other team members

During team meetings
- be punctual
- one person at a time speaks
- respect other people's views
- use interactive management skills
- look for objective evidence – don't rely on 'gut' feelings
- the team must agree on appropriate courses of action
- only team leaders liaise with other teams

Source: Western Mining Company (Kwinana Nickel Refinery), Perth, Western Australia, 'Team Rules Charter' (February 1999)

By way of contrast, here are a few tips for ruining meetings for other people:

- Be late. This shows how important you are and that you don't give a damn about anyone else.
- Don't bother to read the agenda before the meeting. Then you can waste everyone else's valuable time by asking unnecessary questions about items on the agenda.
- Ramble on for as long as you like, particularly about topics that have nothing to do with those being discussed. Make sure you get your say on every topic, even if you know nothing about the issue being discussed.
- Don't bother listening to the contributions made by other people. Interrupt and contradict them at every opportunity, particularly if they are younger than you, or further down the organizational pecking order.

- Be as obstructive as you can if new ideas or innovations are suggested, because you are an 'experienced', 'practical', 'common-sense' manager who hasn't got time to listen to airy-fairy ideas – particularly from junior staff.
- Make disparaging comparisons with all the fantastic things that you have done in previous jobs, or in other organizations, whenever you can. This will show the people you now work with how wonderful you are and what a sad bunch of losers they are.
- Try to force your ideas through at every opportunity because you are always right and, after all, you can't make decisions by committee can you?
- Leave your mobile phone/pager on throughout the meeting, and don't forget to bring some food to munch on while you are not hogging the limelight.

We've all met characters who do these things, but they only get away with it because everyone else lets them. Hence, in common with many other organizational activities, effective meetings are only possible if their structure and processes are well managed, and there are clear and well-established norms and protocols governing how people behave in meetings. Ineffective meetings are often dominated by windbags, characterized by time wasting and point scoring, and are unable to convert discussions and decisions into concrete action plans. However, the practical suggestions for managing meetings outlined in this section *do work*. We know this because it is not possible to find a single example of a team that uses these techniques that does not also enjoy useful and productive meetings. If you have problems with ineffective meetings in your organization or business, why not give these a try?

> Attendance required – on time; no substitutions without prior approval; no gossip; no sidebar conversations or secondary tasks; really listen; stick to the subject; comments limited to three minutes each; jokes and fun are okay.
> (*The Team Meeting Rules of Jim Kilts, CEO of Gillette, 2003*)

> Attend all meetings. Start on time – end on time. Leave your stripes at the door. Listen constructively. Respect each person. Keep an open mind. Criticize ideas, not people. Question and participate. Make decisions by consensus. Remember what's said here, stays here. Encourage laughter.
> (*Boston Bank USA, Team Rules, 1994*)

Conclusion: leading successful work teams

High-performing and successful work teams don't just happen. Leading these well requires the effective use of most of the leadership, motivation and communication skills identified in Chapters 1, 3 and 4, as well as those covered in this chapter. To recap, these include:

- an awareness that building a team from scratch requires time and energy being devoted to team building, identifying the skills, competencies and personal attributes that are needed, and recruiting a suitably diverse group of team-members;
- wherever possible, keeping the number of employees in any team to between six and eight, with the ideal number being seven. If you are in charge of very large groups of employees, organize them into smaller sub-groups of seven if you can;
- focusing on empowering the team, rather than trying to 'manage' it and using inclusive language such as, 'We', 'Our' and 'Us' whenever you can, not the exclusive, 'I', 'Me' and 'You';
- being consistent and positive, staying calm and always setting a good example. Your followers will imitate your actions, particularly if the group is under pressure or underperforming;
- not making promises to your team members that you can't deliver on;
- agreeing and establishing individual roles and tasks with each member of the team and ensuring that these are clearly communicated and understood;
- creating a team climate where people feel comfortable with open, frank discussions, where differences of opinion can be freely aired, without recrimination or fear of ridicule;
- establishing a team culture that fosters a sense of pride and emphasizes the special nature of your team/group, by referring to its traditions and achievements in the past;
- involving all members of the team in discussions, even if you ultimately make the important decisions;
- giving all of your team's members some personal attention, providing appropriate feedback to individuals on their work performance, and rewarding team members fairly and equitably for both their individual and collective efforts;
- preparing for and managing team meetings effectively, by making use of the practical strategies described in the preceding section.

Because team-based working is now so commonplace in organizations, and almost all employees in medium and large enterprises now work in teams of some kind, it is important that leader/managers have some proficiency in team participation, team leadership and team management. As we have seen, merely putting people together, without thought and planning, and calling them a team, will not produce desirable results. Teams only work well when they are engaged in tasks that really matter to them, when there are clear rules about how the team should work together and a shared understanding of the roles of each member of the team. There are many examples of organizations that have introduced effective team-working practices. Equally, there are organizations that have not been successful, usually because they have not thought through the consequences of these changes before implementing them (in particular, the impact that team-working practices have on traditional hierarchy-based command-and-control styles of management). Team working is going to continue to revolutionize organizational processes and the challenge for leader/managers, now and in the future, is to create effective and successful teams that people want to join and contribute their best efforts.[3]

> 'Together Everyone Achieves More With Organization, Recognition and Knowledge.'
> (*Old acronym*)

> 'There is no "I" in team.'
> 'A champion team will always beat a team of champions.'
> (*Slogans in sports clubs all over the world*)

Exercise 5.3

Having read through this chapter, think about how you can apply any new insights you have acquired in your team leadership practices, and the way you manage meetings in the future.

Insight   **Strategy to implement this**

1.

2.

3.

4.

5.   ◆

Notes

1   If you would like more information on the process of team formation and leadership in newly formed teams, please refer to Carlopio *et al.* (2001: 471–99).
2   A few researchers have suggested a fifth stage: 'adjourning/exiting', when the team's life cycle is at an end and its members disband.
3   Managing teams of employees in virtual organizations is reviewed in Chapter 10.

6   Doing it differently? The emergence of women leaders

Objectives

To look at the recent achievements of women and their current status in organizations.

To establish the business case for promoting the interests of women employees in organizations.

To define gender and examine the issue of gender stereotypes.

To identify attitudinal, structural and cultural barriers that women still encounter in the workplace.

To suggest that leader/managers of the future will possess a mixture of 'male', 'neutral' and 'female' qualities, attributes, competencies and skills.

To suggest ways in which women can become more powerful leader/managers.

To outline briefly some practical strategies for creating gender inclusive workplaces.[1]

The achievements and status of women in organizations

There is no difference in the ability of men and women to work hard. Research by the United Nations has shown that in the world as a whole, women comprise 51 percent of the population, do 66 percent of the work, receive 10 percent of the income and own less than 1 percent of the property.'
(*Michael Simmons*, Building an Inclusive Organization, *1996*)

Until the 1980s, almost all commentators on leadership and management ignored the simple fact that organizations employed both men and women. As Amanda Sinclair has observed, 'although there has been passing attention given to men leading women, it has been men leading men that has captured the imagination of researchers and biographers and spawned their fascination with military and sporting exemplars'. She suggests that there are two reasons for this oversight. The first is *absence*: there were not enough women in senior positions to warrant serious research on female leadership styles. The second is *invisibility*: there was only one style of leadership and management that merited serious investigation and that was the male style (Sinclair, 1998: 15, 17–26). A third reason is that, until the 1980s, there were hardly any women academics working in the disciplines of organizational leadership and people management. Consequently, women, either as colleagues or as subjects of research, were effectively *irrelevant* to most male academics in business schools before this time.

Despite this invisibility, women have always been an essential labour resource throughout history, and it has been very much the exception, rather than the rule, when women have not been engaged in work outside the home. However, as recently as the beginning of the 20th century, there were almost no suitable professional careers open to women, although many working-class women did work on the land, in factories and in domestic service. A middle-class woman had almost no chance of becoming an engineer, an architect, a politician, a financier or a newspaper journalist. Why? Because it was widely believed that women were, by nature, either unfit for or incapable of working in most occupations. It was not until after World War II, when large numbers of women had been conscripted into many traditionally male jobs and occupations, while their menfolk were away fighting, that things began to change. By the 1970s, increasing numbers of women had started to compete with men in professional career streams, particularly in Australasia, some European countries and North America. Today, there are female doctors, engineers, accountants, architects, politicians, financiers, newspaper journalists, academics, police officers, fire fighters, astronauts and chief executives, as well as a rapidly growing number of successful women entrepreneurs.

There are now many more women in the workforce in middle-management positions and an increasing number are entering previously male-dominated professions such as engineering and science. Women have also made huge advances in winning many of the new jobs created in the past 20 years. They are earning more money than ever before, their presence is growing in every profession and they are making inroads into occupations that have until very recent times excluded women. These include front-line combat troops, astronauts, fighter pilots, boxers, wrestlers and extreme sports athletes, and there are even a few Mafia godmothers. In certain sectors, such as finance and banking, women have made remarkable advances. For example, in the mid-1980s, women made up 60 per cent of the workforce of the (then) Abbey National Building Society in the UK. However, only 2.5 per cent of their female employees were branch managers. By the late 1990s, the figures were 60 per cent and 50 per cent respectively, a twenty-fold increase (Parker *et al.*, 1998: 56). Between 1995 and 2000, the annual *Cosmopolitan* awards for the most 'women friendly' companies in the UK went to organizations in the finance sector on four occasions. The odd one out was The Body Shop, which, as everyone is aware, was led by a woman at that time.

A small number of women have become CEOs of some of the largest companies in the world. When Carly Fiorina was appointed as the first female CEO of Hewlett-Packard in 2000, she received a one million dollar 'signing-on' fee, a minimum annual bonus of $US1 250 000, and stock options worth about $US20 million (approximate value after the company's merger with Compaq in April 2002. Forster, 2002: 16). In the USA, 71 per cent of companies have at least one woman member on the board and in the UK the figure is 48 per cent. In Australia one-third of the top 200 companies had a female member on the board in 2002. In 2000, 9.7 per cent of non-executive directors were women, but this had fallen to 8.2 per cent by the end of 2002 (Harris, 2002; Harvey, 2001). A growing number are entering politics, many have reached senior political office and some have become heads of state. For example, on 15 November 2002, Californian Congresswoman Nancy Pelos became the first woman to be elected as the leader of the US Democrats on Capitol Hill, replacing outgoing house minority leader Richard Gephardt (Reid, 2002).

Many more women are now opting for self-employment. In the USA, the number of female-owned small companies quadrupled from two million to eight million between 1982 and 1997, and women established 75 per cent of all new companies set up in the USA in the 1990s. In 1997, for the first time, women-owned businesses employed more people than the Fortune 500 companies (Gollan, 1997). During the 1990s, women started new businesses at a faster rate than men in North America, the UK and Australia. Approximately 1.2 million small businesses in Australia are operated by women – about one-third of all businesses in the country. They also initiate around 70 per cent of all *new* business start-ups each year, a remarkable statistic. Women under 30 are now the fastest-growing demographic entity in the small business sector. This trend is likely to accelerate over the next few years, with 38 per cent of women in Australia planning to establish their own businesses within the next five years (Harcourt, 2003; Blanch and Switzer, 2003; Fox, 2001).

This social transformation has been driven, not only by economic and social change and universal education, but also by an irreversible revolution in women's aspirations, driven in large measure by the 'first wave' of feminist thinking in the 20th century. This revolution has led to the emergence of workforces that would be unrecognizable to men working in organizations in the 1960s and 1970s. In western industrialized countries, we may also be witnessing what might be the start of a fundamental power shift from men to women, particularly in the under-30 age group and, perhaps, an historic change in the relationships between men and women. This change may represent a shift in power relations and values that could unravel many of the assumptions of 200 years of industrial and social organization, and millennia of traditions and beliefs about the 'correct' roles of men and women in society and the workplace.

However, while some women have made major inroads into all professions and occupations, many continue to be employed at the lower levels of organizational hierarchies, and many still encounter discrimination at work. In OECD countries, around 40 per cent of women still work part-time, with little job security and no access to sick pay, superannuation entitlements or holiday pay. They are often concentrated in certain sectors of the labour market, with many still working in 'caring' jobs such as human resource management, nursing and childcare, or as secretaries and personal assistants. Very few women have made it into senior management positions in organizations. In the USA, for example, women occupy 11.9 per cent of CEO positions in the private sector. In the UK the figure is 10.6 per cent and, in Australia, a paltry 1 per cent – down from 2.9 per cent in 2000. Fifty-three per cent of Australia's top 200 companies had no women in executive positions in 2002, compared to just 14 per cent of US companies (Butterfly, 2002; Casella, 2001). Men still occupy most of the top leadership positions throughout the world, in industry, business, politics, trade unions and in public sector organizations. In western industrialized societies, it is still almost entirely white, Caucasian, able-bodied males who occupy these. As recently as 1995, the US Glass Ceiling Commission commented that 'America's vast human resources are not being fully utilized because of glass-ceiling barriers. Over half of all Masters degrees are now awarded to women, yet 95 percent of senior level managers of the top Fortune 1000 and 500 service companies are men. Of them, 97 percent are white' (Glass Ceiling Commission, 1995: 6).

In occupations such as academia, inequalities persist, particularly in the UK and Australia (Forster, 2000e). In engineering, only 5.7 per cent of 65 000 Australian engineers are women, although the number of engineering graduates increased from 4 to 13 per cent during the 1990s (cited in *The Australian*, 21 February 1999). Women still earn less than men. One-third of all working women earn two-thirds of average male earnings, in North America, the UK and Australia. On average, even professional women are still paid less than men, even if they are doing the same job. For all professional occupations in the USA, UK and Australia, women earn about 80–85 per cent of male earnings. In Australia, there were more than one hundred male executives or CEOs who were earning more than one million dollars a year in the late 1990s. There was not a single woman who fell into this category (Sinclair, 1998).

In an international context, women also continue to encounter structural, attitudinal and cultural barriers. While there are growing opportunities for women in international careers they are still concentrated largely in junior and some middle management positions. They also work in a narrower range of professions when compared to their male colleagues. They are still less likely to be selected for international assignments (often because of 'family commitments'), face greater problems with adaptation in traditionally patriarchal cultures and – with the noticeable exception of some US companies – are unlikely to receive company support for their male trailing partners. While there is very little evidence that companies *actively* discriminate against women, there are indications that women are not considered for postings to what can be broadly described as traditional patriarchal societies in, for example, the Middle East. This is evidence of a solid glass ceiling in an international context at the present time. Women are rarely entrusted with major projects in new markets and they face greater restrictions in terms of the range of countries to which they are posted, although they do seem to have an advantage over their male colleagues in terms of European postings. However, all the evidence from graduate careers advisers in the USA and the UK indicates that growing numbers of well-educated and highly motivated younger women are looking for international job experience as a route to fast-track promotions and senior positions in organizations. In other words, these women *want* international assignments and all the available research shows that women are as motivated as men to seek international career opportunities, and they will be as successful as their male colleagues if selected for these. As increasing numbers of bright younger women seek international career opportunities, those companies which do address these issues are more likely to attract the very best global female managerial and professional talent over the next few years (Forster, 1999a, 2000c).

What all this indicates is that, while women have made substantial progress over the last 20 years, they still have some way to go before they achieve true equality of opportunity with men. In 2000, the Australian Affirmative Action Agency estimated that it would take until 2175 for women to achieve full equality with men in all occupations and professions (Stevens, 2000: 18). The same is true if we look at the international status of women, where they still have a very, very long way to go in many countries. A 2001 UN survey of gender equality in 100 countries highlighted huge disparities in equality of opportunity for women. The top five countries were Sweden, Finland, Norway, Denmark and the USA, with the UK at 13 and Australia coming in at number 18. The bottom 30 consisted entirely of African, Middle-Eastern and Asian countries (cited in Harvey, 2001). As Amanda Sinclair has suggested:

> A vast management development industry has devoted itself to honing leadership skills. Yet there is little evidence that our notions of corporate leadership are changing to reflect or align with the shifting imperatives of a global marketplace. We are repeatedly told that in these times of unprecedented change only those who innovate will survive. But our conceptions of leadership are locked in a time warp, constrained by lingering archetypes of heroic warriors and wise but distant fathers.
> (*Sinclair, 1998: 2*).

The business case for promoting the interests of women employees

For the moment, we are going to ignore legal, moral or ethical arguments for promoting equal opportunities in the workplace, and evaluate the business case for promoting the interests of women employees. As a number of commentators have pointed out, there is a fundamental paradox between the economic rationalism that governs the management of almost all businesses and public sector organizations, and the continuing existence of irrational beliefs and practices that discriminate against some sections of their workforces (Thomas, 1996; Cox and Blake, 1991). While there are marked variations between countries, discrimination usually has a direct effect on a company's bottom line, with payouts to claimants in the millions of dollars in recent times (discussed below). There can be other direct effects, including the following:

* talented and ambitious women will avoid applying for jobs at companies that have a reputation for discrimination;
* if organizations do not employ women, they may be less responsive to the needs of women consumers in the markets they operate in;

- women consumers may boycott their products and services;
- their best women staff will leave to join other companies or, as they are doing in increasing numbers throughout the world, establish their own businesses;
- workplace diversity will be reduced, leading to lower morale, less creativity, groupthink and, ultimately, lower organizational performance and productivity.

Direct discrimination can be very expensive for organizations. The costs are not only financial penalties or damaging publicity for a company. In fact, it is almost *passé* to talk about discrimination these days; it is better known now as 'very bad people management'. For example, one study in the United States rated the performance of the Standard and Poor's 500 companies on equal opportunity factors, including the recruitment and promotion of women and minorities and the companies' policies on discrimination. It found that companies rated in the bottom 100 for equal opportunities had an average of an 8 per cent return on investment. Companies rating in the top 100 had an average return of 18 per cent. Further evidence, compiled by the 1995 Glass Ceiling Commission, shows that the average annual return on investment of those companies that did not discriminate against women was more than double that of companies with poor records of hiring and promoting women (Glass Ceiling Commission, 1995). Other surveys have shown that poor equal-opportunity practices also contribute to high staff turnover and absenteeism (Goward, 1999). Two studies referred to in earlier chapters, Jim Collins and Jerry Porras's *Built to Last: Successful Habits of Visionary Companies* and Collins' *Good to Great* also add weight to this argument. All the companies they identified have made a major commitment to equality of opportunity and to promoting women into senior management positions. And recall that all of these were among the most visionary, successful and profitable companies in the world during the 20th century.

Alan Greenspan, the US Federal Reserve Chairman, has argued that discrimination is bad for business, and suggested that evening up pay scales for women and minorities has to be achieved now, not at some indeterminate point in the future. He also made these telling comments: 'By removing the non-economic distortions that arise as a result of discrimination, we can generate higher returns on both human and physical capital. Discrimination is against the interest of business. Yet, business people often practise it. In the end the costs are higher, less real output is produced and the nation's wealth-accumulation is reduced' (cited in *The Australian Financial Review*, 28 July 2000). The message is clear: to be competitive, organizations need to take advantage of the full range of talents of their staff, regardless of their gender (or cultural background). Good equal opportunity policies make good business sense.

Another compelling reason for promoting the interests of women can be found in research that has emerged from business schools over the last decade, which has clearly demonstrated how beneficial employee diversity can be for organizations. Homogeneous cultures stagnate, and different perspectives are required for creativity and innovation. As the *Enterprising Nation Report*, on leadership and management in Australia, commented eight years ago, 'Only by entrenching diversity will employees be optimally equipped to deal with the competitive challenges expected of them by the international marketplace and by the Australian community' (Industry Taskforce on Leadership and Management Skills, 1995: 69). This report argued that, if Australian companies were to succeed in the future, they would have to develop highly educated and innovative workforces, characterized by gender and cultural diversity and a global focus. To achieve this, they would need to start dismantling the inward-looking, Anglo-Saxon and paternalistic views of their male workforces and their antiquated views about the role of women.

In some sectors, such as the military, this is precisely what is happening in many countries. This is true of North America, all European countries in the EEC and Australasia. The move to recruit more women has been driven in part by the fact that all countries in these regions have signed up to the UN Convention on the Elimination of all Forms of Discrimination Against Women. However, in large measure, this move is not driven by legal imperatives or by idealism and altruism, but by self-interest. The armed services of these countries are recruiting more women because fewer young men are joining up and because they want to draw from a wider pool of talent. There is also a growing belief in the military that women have special skills to offer. For example, women are considered to have quicker comprehension, are better at multi-tasking and have more dexterity and agility when compared to men. These are increasingly important skills as warfare becomes more reliant on technology, computerization, smart weapon systems, robotics and remote warfare capabilities. Consequently, women in the American and Australian armed services now work in 98 per cent of operational categories (Garran, 1998, 2001a; Maddison, 1999). They are still excluded from the infantry, artillery, combat engineering, naval clearance diving and airfield defence guards. Given that women already work as commercial divers and as airport security police in the civilian workforce, it is probable that women will gain entry to these positions in the military in the not too distant future.

It was noted earlier in this chapter that many more women are opting for self-employment in North America, the UK and Australasia. Several studies have shown that one of the main reasons given by women for starting up their own businesses is that it enables them to enjoy a better balance between their work and family lives (for example, Wellington, 1998). The Australian Census on Women in Leadership, released in November 2002, revealed that 'the inflexibility of some companies made it extremely difficult for women to juggle careers and motherhood. Others had blokey cultures, meaning women worked twice as hard as men to be accepted as equals. As a result, frustrated women were quitting to run small businesses' (Harris, 2002). What should really concern organizations that turn a blind eye to this loss of talented staff is the evidence showing that women entrepreneurs establish small businesses that are more successful and profitable than those started by men (Sarney, 1997; Hunter and Reid, 1996). It follows, logically, that not only do many organizations lose good women employees because of outdated employment practices; these are often the people they can least afford to lose these days – their entrepreneurs and innovators. Furthermore, organizations that allow this to happen lose intellectual capital, managerial know-how and experienced mentors for junior staff and they have to expend additional time and resources recruiting new staff to replace those who have left (which, as we saw in Chapter 4, costs about $US60 000 per employee). Another important reason for promoting more women into senior management positions is that they may be less venal and corrupt than men. As Kim Cambell, the former Prime Minister of Canada, has observed:

> The qualities that are defined as masculine are the same as those defined as the qualities of leadership. There is virtually no overlap between the qualities ascribed to femininity and those to leadership. Yet, in several studies, results show that, when you have a critical mass of women in an organization, you have less corruption. Peru and Mexico have even implemented initiatives based on such thinking. Lest you think that all we aspire to for the world can be accomplished by male dominated organizations, I have only to say to you: Enron, Taliban, Roman Catholic Church.
> (*Cited by Schlosser, 2002: 70*)

To this list we could also add Tycho, Worldcom, Global Crossing, HIH, One.Tel, Parmalat and others – companies we will return to in Chapter 12.

In addition, other research surveys in the UK, the USA and Australasia have consistently shown that about 35 per cent of women have been the victims of some form of discrimination, sexual harassment or unwanted sexual advances at work, while an even higher percentage (around 50 per cent) have been at the receiving end of some form of unwelcome sexual 'overtures'. In professions such as the military and the police this is still an endemic part of their organizational cultures. In the UK, the number of women in the police service actually *fell* between 1993 and 1998 because of an endemic and deeply based male culture of routine discrimination (Montgomery, 1998). Between May 1995 and May 1997, sexual harassment claims cost the US Federal Government $US267 million. A survey by *Working Woman* magazine found that sexual harassment costs a typical Fortune 500 company, with 23 000 employees, about $US6.7 million a year. One in ten women in the USA have, at some point in their careers, quit a job because of sexual harassment (surveys cited in Moston and Engelberg-Moston, 1997). Several high-profile males have also had accusations of sexual harassment levelled against them, including several sports stars in the UK and the USA, the former US president, Bill Clinton, and more recently Arnold Schwartzenegger. These allegations featured prominently in Garry Trudeau's *Doonsbury* cartoon series during 2003–4, with Schwartzenegger being portrayed as the 'Gropenfuhrer'.

While increasing competition, the need to recruit and retain the best staff, and to get the best out of one's employees are the carrots, litigation is now the stick. In fact, this is often a very large and painful stick. Here are a few examples of this:

> Today, one in five civil law suits in the US federal courts concerns harassment or discrimination, compared to one in twenty a decade ago.
> (The Economist, *2002c*).

> The finance industry is renowned for its loutish behaviour, so it should come as no surprise that it seems to have more than its fair share of unsavoury practices against women. Last month, American Express agreed to pay $US31 million in a lawsuit for sex and age discrimination filed on behalf of more than 4000 women. Merril Lynch and Salomon Smith Barney, two investment banks, settled two sex discriminations cases in 1999, at a combined cost of $US250 million in damages to 900 former and current female employees.
> (*Abridged from* The Economist, *2002c, and Stowell, 1999*)

> This month's sexual discrimination payout to a Victorian policewoman has sent a timely warning to corporate Australia of the need to evaluate and monitor anti-discrimination policies and training. In many cases, the theory and practice are worlds apart. Policewoman Narelle McKenna received a $A125 000 payout in the Victorian Anti-Discrimination Tribunal after it was found that she had been the victim of sexual harassment, discrimination and victimisation. The tribunal was told that while working night-shift at the Bairnsdale police station, the Senior Constable was groped by a fellow officer, asked for oral sex and dragged kicking and screaming into a cell.
> (*Johns, 1998*)

> The US Unit of Japanese car-maker Mitsubishi has agreed to pay out a record $US34 million to settle a sexual harassment suit filed on behalf of 300

female employees. The settlement, the largest ever in a sexual harassment case in the USA, was announced yesterday [ ] the Equal Employment Opportunity Commission has sued Mitsubishi Motor Manufacturing of America in April 1996, alleging 'repeated, routine, generalised, serious and pervasive' sexual harassment of female workers at the company's plant in Normal, Illinois, which was 'known and supported by management' [ ] EEOC Chairman Paul Igasaki said the ground-breaking settlement, 'should provide a model for employers to emulate in dealing with the scourge of sexual harassment'. Stressing that Mitsubishi was 'not unique', he warned: 'Other employers should take heed . . . The EEOC will aggressively pursue cases like this.'
(*Associated Press, 1998*)

A woman detective who suffered four and a half years of sexual harassment has won what is believed to be the largest British settlement in such a case, £150,000. At Miss Mazurkiewicz's tribunal in Reading, the panel ruled unanimously that the former Thames Valley police detective has been sexually harassed and then victimised when she complained. A subsequent internal police inquiry found no evidence to substantiate her allegations, but the tribunal ruled in favour of the officer, nicknamed 'massive cleavage' by her male colleagues.
(*Montgomery, 1998*)

A former ANZ finance manager who was called 'mother hen' by male colleagues and had her department labelled 'a nursery' by male colleagues was awarded a record $A125 000 sex discrimination payout yesterday [ ] Ms Dunn-Dyer said legal action would not succeed in eliminating this kind of workplace behaviour. That battle would only be won when companies educated their staff and attitudes changed from the top down.
(*Balogh and Carruthers, 1997*)

A former female firefighter yesterday accepted £200,000 in damages in one of the largest payouts for sexual discrimination, three years after a tribunal decided that her life had been devastated by harassment. Tania Clayton, 31, was victimised by male colleagues where she was called 'a tart' and 'a stupid f*****g cow', while being ordered to make tea for firemen. When her case came before an industrial tribunal in 1994, the Hereford and Worcester Fire Service was condemned for the 'most appalling discrimination'.
(*Veash, 1997*)

In several well-publicized cases, those organizations that have been sued for discrimination, in the USA, the UK and Australasia, were household name companies, and many of these had invested significant time and resources in introducing formal policies to combat discrimination and sexual harassment. However, what many of these companies failed to realize was that this kind of behaviour will persist as long as it remains an acceptable part of the culture of an organization and acceptable in the minds of male employees. Formal policies mean nothing unless these are embraced by all employees and at all levels of an organization. In order for this to happen, these have to be supported by comprehensive educational programmes, that reveal how ultimately degrading and destructive these entrenched attitudes and behaviours are, and how they can damage both the bottom-line performance of a company and its reputation with the general public. And, like other initiatives, it must be subjected to ongoing review and evaluation (described towards the end of this chapter).

In conclusion, the main reason for changing negative attitudes and behaviours is that it is good for business: it helps to promote employee morale, motivation and performance, enables organizations to be more responsive to the markets and environments they operate in and, ultimately, enhances business productivity and profitability. This is true even if we might not consider moral, ethical and legal reasons to be sufficiently important. If this is a difficult proposition to accept, then just watch as your most able and talented women, and/or minority group employees, leave to work for organizations where ability, character and performance are the most important criteria, not gender or the colour of their skin. What is truly remarkable is that, despite compelling evidence that links the promotion of equal opportunities with organizational performance and profitability, there are new cases almost every month of women employees suing organizations for discrimination and sexual harassment in the USA, Canada, Europe and Australia. So if the *rational* economic logic for promoting workplace diversity is quite overwhelming, an important question arises. Why do women still encounter discrimination at work? There can be only two reasons: either there are prejudicial beliefs and attitudes in organizations that prevent women from achieving parity with men, and impede the creation of truly inclusive workplaces, or women do not have the same motivation, intelligence, ambition or ability to compete on an equal footing with men, and no amount of equal opportunity legislation or affirmative action by organizations will ever change this.

These two contentions will be addressed in the following sections.

Gender stereotypes

Duties of the wife. A wife should respect her husband because he is the head of the family. She must obey him. A wife must shun idleness. She should not sit down and watch television while her husband is working. She must take care of the children and the household, of which she is the queen. She should be economical in her personal expenses, avoiding vanity, extravagance and an inordinate desire to outshine her friends and neighbours.
(*From the introduction to* The Book of Common Prayer, *1964*)

Women under 30, in industrialized countries, would find the world of a typical stay-at-home housewife of the 1950s and 1960s to be very alien and, in most cases, one that they would consider to be unacceptable. However, many of the attitudes that dictated that men were the primary breadwinners and women were responsible for looking after the domestic unit and the children are still prevalent. On one level the 'natural' differences between men and women have been the source of an enormous amount of humour and jokes, most of which cannot be repeated in a respectable publication like this one. But, for illustrative purposes, here are a few less controversial ones:

Q.   'What do men and beer bottles have in common?'
A.   'They're both empty from the neck upwards.'

Q.   'How thick is the glass ceiling?'
A.   'That depends on the density of the men.'

Q.   'What is Mother-in-Law an anagram of?'[2]

Q.   'Why do women live longer than men?'
A.   'Because they're not married to women.'

A journalist had written a story on traditional gender roles in Kuwait several years before the first Gulf War. She had noticed that the women customarily walked about five metres behind their husbands. When the journalist asked about this she was told, 'Men are our masters and the heads of the household. It is our duty to walk behind them.' She returned to Kuwait a few months after the end of the war and noticed that the men now walked about ten metres behind their wives. She approached one woman for an explanation. 'This is marvellous,' she exclaimed. 'What has enabled women here to achieve this reversal of roles?' The Kuwaiti woman immediately replied, 'Land mines.'

These are not the funniest jokes but, on a cultural level, do highlight something we are going to look at in some depth: gender stereotypes. The best exemplar of these is probably the 'Male and Female Brain' cartoon that did the rounds on the Internet in the mid-1990s (Figure 6.1). With this cartoon fresh in your mind, please complete self-development Exercise 6.1.

Figure 6.1   Male and female brains

The Male Brain

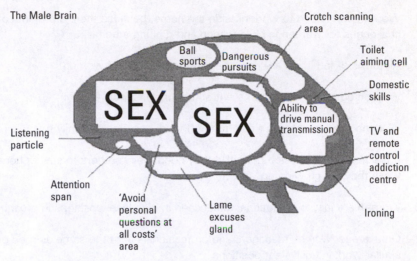

Note: the 'Listening to children cry in the middle of the night' gland is not shown owing to its small and underdeveloped nature. Best viewed under a microscope.

The Female Brain

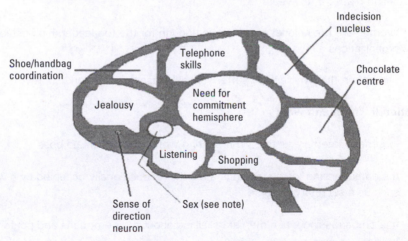

Note: Note how closely connected the small sex cell is to the listening gland.

Exercise 6.1

Gender opinions

This exercise consists of a series of statements about women and men. Indicate the extent to which you agree or disagree with each one, where **5** = strongly agree, **4** = agree, **3** = neutral, **2** = disagree, **1** = strongly disagree. Write the appropriate number next to each statement.

Please avoid 'politically correct' answers. For each statement, please record the score that seems most appropriate to you.

Section I   Women and work

1   Women don't need to work outside the home, because there are plenty of challenges for women in child-rearing and running a home _____

2   All forms of feminism are damaging to the interests of women _____

3   Women do not have the same entrepreneurial instincts as men _____

4   Working women shouldn't take time off work because of family responsibilities _____

5   If children are to develop normally, they need their mothers to stay at home while they are growing up _____

6   Women are just too emotional to succeed in high-level positions in organizations _____

7   On average, women managers and professionals earn the same as men doing similar work in equivalent positions _____

8   Hiring single women graduates into management trainee positions represents a poor investment for an organization because they'll probably leave to have children after a few years _____

9   Women are not rational and decisive enough for the top leadership positions in organizations _____

10   The notion that women still suffer sexual harassment at work is a myth _____

Section II   Men and work

1   In general, men are justified in resenting working for a female boss _____

2   It's embarrassing to see a man in a job that is traditionally occupied by a woman, such as a secretary or nurse _____

3   It is embarrassing when men start talking about their emotions and personal feelings _____

4   The most important goal in a man's life should be his career _____

5   In a dual-career couple, the man's career should always come first _____

6   'Straight' men have every right to resent working with gays and lesbians _____

7   Men do not have as much right to paternity leave as women do to maternity leave _____

8   The main reason why there are so many more men than women in leadership positions is that they are, by nature, better suited to these roles _____

9   Men will always be more successful than women, because in the final analysis
     they are, by nature, more rational and less emotional   _____

10   Feminism is a threat to the interests of men

Please add up your total score for Section I _____ **+ Section II** _____ = _____

Interpreting your score
High scores (over 40) represent more traditional or conservative views about the intrinsic natures
of men and women and their roles in society and the workplace. A mid-ranging score (26–40)
would be associated with more modern views about the nature of men and women. A score of
25 or less is associated with progressive views about the intrinsic natures of men and women,
and their roles in society and the workplace. ◆

For now, I'd like you to forget about the results of this questionnaire.
Please put these to one side and move straight on to the next self-development exercise.

Exercise 6.2

Leading on from Exercise 6.1, please describe what you think the main characteristics of men
and women are. I've suggested the first two, but these can be anything that you believe describe
the basic characteristics of men and women.

Men: 'aggressive',

Women: 'cooperative',

                                                                              ◆

A man with traditional views about the nature of women might have
written down things like intuitive, caring, submissive, irrational,
emotional, cooperative and supporter or follower. He might have
also written down things like logical, strategic, competitive, rational,
exploitative, leader and decision-maker, to describe men. He might
also have written down some of the things that were contained in the
'Two-Brains' cartoon, or may have come up with completely different responses. Again, at this stage, it doesn't matter what your
responses were. However, I'd like us to focus for a while on some of
the consequences of 'traditional' views about women. If this is
considered logically, there is only one possible outcome of these
stereotypes: the creation of a mind-set that results in organizations

discriminating against women on three levels, attitudinal, structural and cultural.

Attitudinal discrimination includes beliefs that discriminate against women, or negatively stereotype women, simply because they are women. These attitudes are expressed in phrases such as: 'Women are indecisive, inconsistent and constantly changing their minds'; 'Women use their sexuality to get what they want'; 'Women are too emotional'; 'Women aren't good team players'; 'Women fall apart when the going gets tough'; 'Women love to gossip and natter'; 'Women are too soft to make the really hard decisions'; 'Women let their families get in the way of their jobs'; 'Women take things too personally'; 'Women can't take a good joke'; 'Women complain too much about discrimination'; 'Women get moody – especially at "that" time of the month' and so forth (adapted from Manning and Haddock, 1995). The following examples illustrate how these attitudinal barriers still affect women in organizations.

'Turning a blind eye'

An independent panel has urged the Pentagon to hold air force leaders accountable for rapes and assaults of female cadets at the US Air Force Academy, blaming them for a decade of inaction and failure at the service's top school for officer training. The seven member panel said yesterday that the air force leadership had known at least since 1993 that sexual assaults on cadets was a serious problem at the Colorado school, but failed to take effective action [ ] The US Defense Secretary appointed the panel in the wake of reports that dozens of female cadets had been sexually assaulted or raped at the school, but were ignored by the school's leaders and in some cases even punished for infractions of duty. The air force replaced the academy's superintendent and other top officers in April in response to the scandal [ ] 'From 1 January 1993 through 31 December 2002, there were 142 allegations of sexual assault at the academy, for an average of more than 14 allegations a year,' the report said. 'Academy and air force leaders knew or should have known this data was an unmistakable warning sign and quite possibly signalled an ever larger crisis'. Tillie Fowler, a former Republican member of Congress from Florida who chaired the panel, praised the quick response to the crisis by the US Air Force Secretary James Roche and Chief of Staff General John Jumper, but she said that the problems were 'real and continued to this day'.
(*AFP, 2003b*)

'Banking Blues'

One of London's most senior Japanese bankers is facing an employment tribunal after accusations by his former personal assistant of sexual and racial discrimination. Yugi Ishida, head of Nomura's equity [*sic*] division, is accused of bullying and harassing Annie McGregor, before her redundancy in August. The case is one of several to have hit Nomura in London. The

bank has mostly settled before judgement, paying out money to former staff, and ensuring that they did not speak out about their time with the company. Ms McGregor has complained that she was subjected to sustained sexual and racial discrimination, bullying and harassment during the two years she worked with Mr. Ishida. She expressed concerns to the bank's human resource department in August. A week later – without warning – she was made redundant and escorted out of the office. Ms McGregor will also claim that she was paid less than her Japanese counterparts. Among three other recent cases, Nomura paid £70,000 to one of its former brokers, Isabelle Terrillon. She described how her bosses suggested that she wear short, tight skirts to work, while another asked her to strip and massage a colleague's sore back.
(The Sunday Times, 2002)

'Your loss – my gain'

Lee-Anne Carson was on her way up the corporate ladder when 'interesting attitudinal obstacles' – otherwise known as sexism – got in the way. Ms. Carson quit her high paying job as Telstra Account Director of Financial Services in October. She now runs her own sales consultancy business, Sales Performance International, from home, while caring for her son Richard, 5. 'It appears that there was a boys' club at work rather than competency. I was outspoken and was seen as aggressive. I was politically savvy and networked and I had political clout and that wasn't seen as attractive for a woman.'
(*Cited by Harvey, 2001*)

'Women are not welcome at this airline'

In 1979, the pilots of all the major western commercial airlines were men. In Australia, one woman decided to take on Ansett Airlines for the right to become Australia's first female commercial airline pilot. Sir Reginald Ansett, the founder of Ansett Airlines, made it clear that Deborah Lawrie, then 25, was not welcome. The company argued in the ensuing court case that, 'women were not strong enough to handle large aircraft', would 'panic in a crisis' and Lawrie's earrings would 'interfere with her ability to fly the aircraft and impede evacuation from the aircraft'. Furthermore, claimed Ansett, she was 'biologically unsuitable' to be a pilot because she might leave to have babies and there might be 'safety issues' associated with her menstruation cycle. Lawrie's determination to prove Ansett wrong became a *cause célèbre* for women and her victory put Australia's new discrimination laws on the map. She later moved to the Dutch Airline, KLM, where she has worked since. Interviewed in October 1999, Lawrie commented, 'Most people still think you are a flight attendant when you board an aircraft, but the gender issue just doesn't exist anymore, except in places like the Middle-East.'
(*Abridged from Bagwell, 1999*)

'Don't ever confuse intelligence with education'

The Vice-Chancellor and his male deputy were taken away by minders after a few drinks and a joke about secret women's business. Then 100 senior executives, all of them women, ascended to the University of Sydney's

McLaurin Hall to honour Fay Gayle, who retired last year as Vice-Chancellor of the University of Western Australia and President of the Australian Vice-Chancellor's Council. Gale proceeded to do something that Vice-Chancellors don't usually do in public: dump on the many men who fought her every centimetre of the way during her career. From the time she was not told that she had been made a Professor at the University of Adelaide by the promotion committee, to the staffer who said her appointment as VC of the University of Western Australia was an affront to the University, the details spilled out. From the (male) colleague who turned to her at an awards dinner to ask 'Who's Dr. Gale?' to the time she returned to her car after a long day and an evening function and had to scrape the dog-faeces off the windscreen so that she could drive home [ ] The extent of the nastiness that Gale encountered during her successful academic career, and her decision to reveal what until then had only been said privately, shocked the 100 executive women present.
(*Abridged from Richardson, 1998; Illing, 1999*)

The end result of traditional stereotypes is that, over time, negative attitudes and beliefs about women become deeply ingrained in the mindsets of male employees and organizations. They reach a point where they are totally taken for granted and operate at an unconscious level. Because of this, they become so embedded in men's minds that they become, literally, part of their masculine identity, and this is the main reason why it is so difficult to change these attitudes after they have become established. Here are a few examples of how these might be expressed in male-dominated organizations (adapted from Powell, 1990):

'His desk is cluttered – he's obviously a hard worker and a busy man.'
'Her desk is cluttered – she's obviously a disorganized scatterbrain.'

'He's talking with his co-workers – he must be discussing the latest business plan.'
'She's talking with her co-workers – she must be gossiping.'

'He's got a photo of his family on his desk – he must be a solid family man.'
'She's got a photo of her family on her desk – her family will come before the job.

'He's having lunch with the boss – he's on the way up.'
'She's having lunch with the boss – they must be having an affair.'

'He's leaving work early to collect the kids from school – what a good family man.'
'She's leaving work early to collect the kids from school – you just can't rely on women to put the hard yards in.'

'His wife is having a baby – he'll need a pay rise.'
'She's having a baby – she'll cost the company money in maternity benefits.'

'He's leaving to take up a better job – he knows a good opportunity when he sees it.'
'She's leaving to take up a better job – why are women employees so unreliable?'

And so on. You can probably think of some duets of your own.

In turn, these attitudes can become ingrained in cultural beliefs about women. This refers both to the culture of an individual organization and to the effects of different national cultures on beliefs about the 'correct' roles of men and women in society, and the freedom and opportunities that they have to pursue careers. These are barriers that pioneering woman in western societies have had to cope with for many years, and ones that women in industrializing countries are now having to deal with for the first time. These cultural beliefs can then lead to the creation of structural barriers such as antisocial hours, lack of flexi-time, no allowance being made for domestic responsibilities and the demarcation of jobs along gender lines. Here's an example of all three barriers in operation at the same time:

> Since the prettier candidate has already been blessed by God, it is only right that we should hire the uglier one,' said Nik Abdul Aziz during a lecture to all government employees in the Malaysian state of Kelantan. 'After all, if we do not choose the ugly candidate, who will?' Aziz, Chief Minister of Kelantan (one of Malaysia's most fervent Islamic states), explained the thinking behind his latest decree. 'There are far too many pretty women in government offices at the moment, distracting male workers and lowering business efficiency with their pert and yielding tightness, But, when ugly women are employed in an office, then the work rate increases wondrously. Besides, we must be ever watchful for possible immoral activities. It is well known that pretty women cause unhealthy activities that lead to insanity, blindness, sickness and the bends. That is why, from now on, thorough ugliness must be considered a deciding factor at all job interviews.'
> (Utusan Malaysia, *25 October, 1996*).

> When positions became vacant in government departments in Kelantan, the Malaysian state controlled by a fundamentalist Islamic party, attractive women need not apply. The ban on women with good looks was announced by the State's Chief Minister, Nik Abdul Aziz. His announcement attracted widespread criticism but he said that he was only trying to be fair to women who were not attractive. 'Normally, women who are blessed by Allah with good looks are married to rich husbands,' he said. Since they would not need to work, there would be more job opportunities for women who were less 'comely'. In March 1999, Aziz had upset women's groups when he said that his government was considering a ban on women working. He later said that the ban would only apply to women whose husbands could not afford to support their family. He was condemned for his latest stand by Zainah Anwar, a member of Sisters in Islam, whose leaders are authorities on the Koran and regularly challenge decisions made by the all-male religious officials (ulama) that discriminate against women. 'Beauty, or lack of it, should not be used as a basis of hiring or firing. This is a discriminatory practice that has no place in a modern democratic society.'
> (*Abridged from Stewart, 1999*)

Most people in western industrialized countries, and many Malaysian women, would consider Aziz's attitudes antiquated and some would find them offensive, and yet they are still widespread in many countries. This example also shows that attitudes about what women 'are', and their capabilities, are shaped by national cultures. As we saw in Chapter 3, culture is something that is learnt; we are not genetically hard-wired with this at birth. We also know that there are considerable national variations in cultural attitudes about women's capabilities, as illustrated in Table 6.1.

*Table 6.1   Confidence in women**

	Bus or train driver	Surgeon	Barrister	MP	Average
Denmark	86	85	82	96	84
Netherlands	75	83	75	79	78
France	77	70	70	68	70
UK	77	70	70	68	70
Italy	54	56	55	59	56
Ireland	43	51	50	61	51

* Percentage of men who agreed that they were confident in a woman's ability to do these jobs.

Source: Wilson, 1995: 39.

Furthermore, if this survey was repeated today, we can be confident that attitudes towards women's ability to do these jobs in the UK and Italy would have improved and, in Ireland, improved substantially as the influence of the Roman Catholic Church has steadily declined and the country has become more affluent, open and cosmopolitan. The existence of these culturally circumscribed views about women's capabilities raises the important issue of the 'nature/nurture' debate, first addressed in Chapter 1. In this context, it is important to understand the critical difference between our *sexuality*, which is formed by our genetic and biological hard wiring, and our *gender* (derived from the Latin word *genus*, meaning race or type). This construct is quite distinct from sex, which refers to the innate genetic and biological characteristics of men and women. Gender refers to the historically, socially and culturally constructed understandings of the intrinsic natures of men and women. Furthermore, because *perceptions* of gender are socially and culturally constructed they are *learnt,* and can have a profound influence on people's beliefs about the 'nature' of men and women. We will look at this issue in the next section.

Boys will be boys and girls will be girls

Both men and women have approximately 30 000 genes, and if a single human genome were to be stretched out into a strand, it would stretch from London to Moscow. For six weeks after conception, the embryonic human is always female. At this point a single gene, SR1, may click on, releasing testosterone and triggering the creation of the male testes (and we don't yet know why this happens). This means that the Christian myth about Eve being created from Adam is wrong; genetically, a man is actually a woman 'gone wrong' (Oakley, 1981: 41–63). Even more significantly, we now know from recent studies of mitochondrial DNA that almost every person of European background descends from just seven women who lived about 45 000 years ago. And *all* of humanity is descended from just 30 maternal clans, the original tribes of *Homo sapiens* that spread out from Africa during the last ice age and proceeded to colonize the entire planet (Bryson, 2003: 393).

Furthermore, the genetic differences between men and women are based on a single chromosome (men have 1Y and 1X chromosome and women have 1Y and 2X chromosomes). Why does this matter? Well, take testosterone. This is widely regarded as a very 'male' substance and affects the masculinity of both sexes. It signals male brains to build muscle and promotes faster, more intense action in men, compared to the slower, more durable actions associated with oestrogen in females. It also gives men thicker skulls, a fact not lost on most women. It is regarded as an important genetic factor that helped to differentiate male and female evolution, after the emergence of our earliest hominid ancestors about three million years ago. It is one reason why men were physically stronger and, therefore, the hunters and the 'weaker' women-folk stayed at home to look after the cave and the kids.

However, the most recent evidence suggests that old stereotypes about hunters and nurturers may be inaccurate. The latest research in archaeology has prompted some scientists to question the long-held view that men had the primary responsibility for hunting, while the women looked after the children and, literally, tended the home fires. According to this research, there is little hard archaeological evidence to show that men were the primary food providers in early human societies. It now appears that early hominids and humans were not hunters of big game, but scavengers living primarily on a diet of roots and starchy tubers, occasionally enlivened by the leftovers from other larger and more powerful predators. This new evidence suggests that women hunted small game, gathered roots, nuts and fruits and were also involved in many other tribal and clan leadership activities, including religious ceremonies. There is also some evidence that ancient man could be just as lazy as his modern counterpart (Este, 1999). The myth of the dominant male hunter was something that was simply taken for granted by the male-dominated archaeological profession of the 19th and 20th centuries.

Having said this, recent genetic research indicates that the roles men and women adopted in earlier times have led to the development of some innate differences that continue to influence our behaviour today. For example, women generally have more symmetrical brains and more connections between the left and right hemispheres, and this has been associated with their ability to multitask and communicate more effectively than men. Men appear to have the edge when it comes to spatial abilities, and this is associated with their ability to read maps better than women (something that many couples can relate to). Even so, the only thing we can say with absolute certainty about the influence of genetics on men and women is that, genetically, I am more like a woman in my own gene pool than a man in another gene pool, and cultural imperatives still mean that most men are brought up to believe that they should be the warriors and hunters, or at least be the dominant breadwinners and wage workers. The consequence of this conditioning means many believe that they still have to behave like 'real men': independent, in control, tireless, emotionless, achievement-oriented, task-focused and the primary family provider.

To come full circle, other research evidence indicates that, as women have started to adopt more aggressive and competitive working styles, they are producing more male hormones, with thousands of young women losing their hair because of 'testosterone overload' as a direct result of taking on traditional male roles in the workplace (Norton, 1997).[3] There is also some evidence that the Y chromosome (which determines if a child is male or female) is in rapid decline. When this chromosome first appeared, more than five million years ago, it controlled some 1500 'male' genes. That number has now declined to about 40. This may mean that males may die out, or evolve into something else. If this sounds far-fetched, remember that, in the recent past, there were two distinct species of human, Neanderthal and Cro-Magnon (our modern ancestor) and it is possible that the human race could split again. The human male already has the weakest recorded sperm count of any mammal apart from the gorilla (abridged from Callaghan, 2002c).

Another perspective on this contentious issue is provided by Alan and Barbara Pease in their best-seller, *Why Men Don't Listen and Women Can't Read Maps*. This contains a self-evaluation exercise, designed to identify which innate masculine or feminine traits men and women have, ranked on a scale from minus 40 (highly masculine) to plus 330 (highly feminine). According to the authors:

> Most males will score between 0–180 and most females 150–300. Brains that are 'wired' for mainly masculine thinking will usually score below 150. The closer to zero, the more masculine they are, and the higher their testosterone level is likely to be. These people demonstrate strong logical, analytical and verbal skills, and tend to be disciplined and well-organised [ ] The lower the score for a woman, the more likely she will have lesbian tendencies [ ] Brains that are wired for mainly feminine thinking will score higher than 180. The higher the number, the more feminine the brain will be, and the more likely the person is to demonstrate significant creative, artistic and musical talents. The higher the score is above 180 for a man, the greater the chance he will be gay [ ] Scores between 150–180 show compatibility of thought for both sexes, or a foot in both sexual camps.
> (*Pease and Pease, 1998: 73*)

I've used this questionnaire several times with MBA students and the results have been remarkably consistent. The aggregate questionnaire scores from eight classes during 2000–2003 are presented in Figure 6.2 (N = 146 men and 55 women). Their scores have been rounded to the nearest ten. The results are noteworthy because these MBA groups were a typical demographic sample of managers and professionals in Australia, and each class would have contained, at most, three or four gays or lesbians. These results suggest that, far from men and women leader/managers being fundamentally different, there is evidence of considerable overlap between the two groups. Every time this exercise is used with MBAs, there are several reactions. First, many of the men in the groups express disbelief about the results, or question the validity of the questionnaire. Another reaction is to simply ignore the results as being unreliable or inaccurate. However, for others there is another reaction: a *Eureka* moment, when the blinkers start to come off and a realization that the views they have about both their own masculinity and the 'nature' of women may be about to change. Of equal importance, women in MBA groups usually have far fewer concerns about having some 'male' traits. This exercise also highlights an extremely important but often overlooked fact in the ongoing 'battle' between men and women. It demonstrates that sexuality/gender is a *continuum*, from very 'masculine' males to very 'feminine' women, with a considerable area of overlap in between these two extremes.

For those who might still not be convinced that things might be changing, another way of moving beyond male/female stereotypes is by looking at the many contributions women have made in history, and the remarkable inroads that women have made in recent years in jobs and occupations that only a few years ago were strictly no-go areas for women. Some examples of these can be found in the next exercise.

Figure 6.2   Masculinity and femininity

(High) Feminine Brain

```
300 or more
290
280
270                                                 W
260                                                 W W
250                                                 W W
240                                                 W W
230                                                 W W W
220      M M                                        W W W
210      M M                                        W W W W
200      M M M M M                                  W W W
190      M M M M M M M                              W W W W
180      M M M M M M M M M M                        W W W W W W W W
170      M M M M M M M M M M M M M                  W W W W W
160      M M M M M M M M M M M M M M M M M M M M M  W W W W W W
150      M M M M M M M M M M M M M M M M M M M M    W W W W W
140      M M M M M M M M M M M M M M M M M          W W W W
130      M M M M M M M M M M M M                    W W
120      M M M M M                                  W
110      M M M M M M M M
100      M M M M M M M
90       M M M M M
80       M M M M M
70       M M M
60       M M
50       M M
40       M
30 or less
```

(High) Masculine Brain

M = men and W = women; **150–180** = 'overlap' scores.

Exercise 6.3

Herstory quiz

What percentage of women fought with men as front-line combat troops in the Red Army during World War II and in the Vietcong during the Vietnam War?

Name ten inventions or innovations made by women.

Every Microsoft product has a Certificate of Authenticity attached to it: a watermark with a picture of a woman on it. Who was she and why does her face appear here?

What do these giants of 19th and 20th-century thinking and literature have in common: Simone de Beauvoir, Gertrude Stein, Doris Lessing and Germaine Greer?

Can you guess what the following comments, made in the Australian Parliament in 1983, were about? 'This is a stupid bill that most women won't understand. It will rot the social fabric; will force women into work against their will. It will be a deterrent to those who seek to create employment opportunities and will cause a large increase in male unemployment.'

Can you name ten (or more) women heads of state in the last 30 years?

Can you name ten (or more) women CEOs or vice-presidents of international companies?

How many EEC countries allow women to fly as front-line fighter pilots?

What is Dhammanada Bhikkhuni's claim to fame?

What is Christina Sanchez's claim to fame?

What are Valentina Tereshkova, Dr Sally Rides and Eileen Collins' claims to fame?

What was Babe Zaharias's claim to fame?

Last, and from a rather different angle, what do the following people have in common: former Presidents George W. Bush Snr., Ronald Reagan, Franklin D. Roosevelt, the actors Samuel L. Jackson, Meryl Streep and the singer/actor Madonna?

The answers can be found in note 5 and below. ◆

Very few people (men or women) do manage to answer all these questions. However, this exercise does emphasize an important point. Until very recently you could be forgiven for believing that history is something entirely created by men, and that women played no significant role in this – other than child-rearing and looking after the family home. This is a myth. For example, women have fought in wars and battles throughout recorded history. In World War II, up to 20 per cent of the Red Army's front-line troops were young women and, until very recently, this was hardly ever portrayed in western films about the Russian front. At times, up to 30 per cent of the Vietcong's front-line troops were young women during the Vietnam War. From medical research to law, politics, civil rights and literature, the contributions of women were systematically devalued and marginalized by male historians during the 20th century. Even more remarkable are the rapid inroads that a 'New

Wave' of women have made into traditional male occupations in more recent times, as illustrated below.

The military

As noted earlier, and in spite of continuing problems with sexual harassment, increasing numbers of young women are entering the military in North America, Europe and Australasia. True to form, the initial response of men in the military to the presence of women was that they were not suited to be warriors, usually accompanied by the following statements: 'women are not strong enough', 'women don't have a strong enough instinct to kill' and so forth. In reality, many of these claims turned out to be specious or based upon tests that have been rigged against women. Bogus data are also a culprit. For example, after the first Gulf War, some senior men in the US military claimed that 'large numbers' of women had been withdrawn from the battle-front because they had 'fallen pregnant'. The army actually sent home 81 women for 'pregnancy-associated diagnoses' but evacuated 207 for 'other injuries'. More than 400 men were also evacuated as a result of non-combat injuries, out of a total deployment of more than 20 000 troops. The Navy sent 72 women home out of a total of 2600 women personnel. In one study, Francke has shown that many training courses, designed for men, ended up breaking many women. When these were changed to suit women's learning and physical development needs, most women were able to get up to the same level as men (Francke, 2001).

Many of the old justifications for excluding women from military service no longer hold water. The trend towards smart weapons and engagement at a distance means that, for most roles, men's superior strength and stamina are no longer relevant criteria. Women are as capable as men of dealing with the increasingly complex weapons systems and technologies that the military now use. Indeed, Francke provides evidence that women are better at some of these roles, because of their ability to multi-task and they are also scoring higher than men on aptitude and achievement tests. Significantly, the number of women employed in both support and front-line combat roles *increased* during the 2003 Gulf War. However, because men have, on average, a 50 per cent advantage over women in upper-body strength and a 30 per cent advantage in lower-body strength, they will still be the first choice for hand-to-hand combat roles for the foreseeable future (Garran, 2001b).[4]

Another sign of the changing role of women in armed conflicts was highlighted during the perpetual Israeli–Palestinian conflict. While women have played a role in the Israeli military since the 1950s, the cultural restrictions of Islam had kept women out of the firing line in Muslim states. However, in more recent times, several women suicide bombers have gone voluntarily to their deaths. It was revealed that the militant Palestinian group Hamas had allowed this only as a means of 'purifying' women who had 'desecrated family honour' – a euphemism for having extramarital sex. The former leader of Hamas, Sheikh Ahmed Yassin, had long resisted the use of women suicide bombers, while most other Palestinian groups allowed it. While male suicide bombers are promised eternity in paradise alongside 72 virgins, it was deemed to be unseemly for female martyrs to receive a comparable reward. Instead, they are promised eternal life with the fiancé or husband they left behind (Rabanovich, 2004).

Astronauts
History tells us that the Russian cosmonaut Valentina Tereshkova was the first woman into space during the 1960s and Dr Sally Ride was the first American woman in orbit in 1983. However, in 2002, newly released NASA documents from the 1950s and 1960s revealed that the women who had been accepted for Phase I of astronaut training in 1959 were soon achieving the same results as men in physical, psychological and aptitude tests. By July 1961 a group of women who had become known as the 'Mercury 13' had been selected for Phase II of astronaut training. Then, without warning, notice or explanation, NASA cancelled their training, even though these women had proved themselves to be *more* suitable for space than many men in Phase I of the program. They were not chosen for space missions in the 1960s and 1970s because it was believed that the general public would find this unacceptable. Even though women clearly had the 'Right Stuff', they were not *perceived* to have it (NASA website, March 2002). In the Soviet Union, a few more women did manage to get into space, but this was driven in part by the ideological battle raging between the former Soviet Union and the West at that time.

Women were not readmitted to the NASA astronaut-training programme until 1973. Up to December 2003, ten women had flown on shuttle missions (and two had lost their lives in the Shuttle crashes). On 21 July 1999, Eileen Collins became the first woman to captain a shuttle mission (Reuters, 1999b). Within the next 100 years it is possible that humanity will embark on journeys to the nearest stars. A number of presenters, at the 2002 American Association for the Advancement of Science Conference in Boston, believe that the first flights to the stars will consist of women-only crews. Men need not apply because the all-female crews would probably have to take a sperm bank for reproductive purposes, rather than male astronauts, in order to save weight (whether this was the weight of male egos was not specified). In a keynote presentation to the conference, Geoff Landis, the head of NASA's Glenn Research Center in Ohio, commented 'After the long voyage without any men present, they may discover that humanity doesn't actually need men after all and they'll engineer a society without them. But, then, maybe, that will be better anyway. It certainly might be worth a try' (cited by Henderson, 2002a).

Firefighting and rescue services
Increasing numbers of women have been entering these occupations. Thirty years ago, there were only a few women fire-fighters, ambulance drivers or paramedics employed in North America, the UK and Australasia; now there are thousands. Women did of course work in these jobs during most military conflicts of the 20th century.

The Mafia
In the mid-1990s, the combination of a shortage of male heirs and the imprisonment of a number of male Dons led to the emergence of a new generation of 'Mafia Matrons'. By all accounts they are just as incisive, ferocious and cold-blooded as their menfolk when it comes to settling scores, taking out the competition and looking after their families' businesses. In May 2002, a 30-year-old rivalry between the Cava and Graziano families, in the southern Italian town of Lauro, exploded in a gunfight and the deaths of eight people. All the participants in this shoot-out were women (Phillips, 2002). It will be interesting to see what happens when their menfolk are released from prison.

Bullfighting
The first top-ranked woman matador in the world, Christina Sanchez, was admitted to the Spanish professional ranks in 1996. However, three years later, she had been hounded out of bullfighting because of the refusal of male matadors to appear on the same billings with her. Male matadors, and traditional bullfighting fans who were interviewed about this, said that she did not have the *cojones* to risk her life in front of an angry wounded bull, even though her 'kill record' was as good as that of most of the men. The inbred machismo of Spanish bullfighting continues to be a resistant barrier to women, but dozens of young Spanish girls have since enrolled at bullfighting schools hoping to emulate Sanchez's early success (Reuters, 1999a).

Boxing, wrestling and kickboxing
The daughters of both Muhammad Ali and Joe Frazier have been boxers on the women's professional boxing circuit. More than 100 women now fight on the professional boxing, wrestling and kickboxing circuits.

Wood-chopping

In 2001, the Australian men's junior wood chopping team consisted of seven men and one woman (Janell Foster, aged 19).

Car, bike racing, football, rugby and golf

Leanna Ferrier is another woman carving a career in a traditionally male world. She was placed seventh overall in the Australian Formula Ford championships in 2001 (Bryan, 2001). There are two professional women motorbike riders on the professional circuit. Thousands of women, in more than 50 countries around the world, now play Rugby Union or Association Football. Although a few golf clubs still bar women from membership (for example, St. Andrew's in Scotland and Augusta National in the USA), there is a thriving women's professional circuit. Annika Sorenstam was the first woman since 1945 to be invited to play in a PGA event in May 2003 (at the Bank of America tournament) and Suzy Whaley became the first woman to qualify for a men's US PGA Tour event since 1945. She teed off in the Greater Hartford Open in July 2003.

Extreme sports

Twenty years ago you would have found hardly any women going base-jumping or cliff-diving, few female mountaineers and no women competing in extreme skiing competitions. Now there are hundreds. The story of one of the pioneers of women's extreme skiing is described in the next example.

'She's one of the boys'

A story that passed round the world's skiing community in the late 1980s was one about Kim Reichelm. A former member of the Canadian Alpine Race Squad in the 1980s, she had retired from full-time racing and decided to hitch up with some of the first generation of extreme skiers in Squaw Valley in the USA. At the time, this was an exclusive 'boys only' club, which included skiing legends like Scott Schmidt, Mike Hattrup and Kevin Andrews. On the fateful day the boys went off a high cornice (a wind lip of snow), down into an almost sheer 100 metre long, rock-flanked gully and all landed successfully. Kim, however, got her weight on the back of her skis and fell, spun several times and cracked her head on a rock. This injury required eight stitches.

The same afternoon, she was out again with the group skiing through some large pine trees in an out-of-bounds ski area. In one turn she pushed her shoulder into a tree (a movement that racers perform automatically when skiing through giant slalom courses) and dislocated it. She had this popped back in and was out again the very next day free-skiing, and tore her anterior cruciate ligament in yet another fall. Scott Schmidt who was interviewed at the time commented, 'She's a fantastic skier, real strong and real aggressive. We're going to hang out together until she gets better. She can come skiing with us any time.' Since this time, many more women have become extreme skiers, and now compete on the international circuit.
(*Abridged from* License to Thrill, *Delamo Films, 1989*)

Rock and pop music

Twenty years ago women made up less than 3 per cent of the top selling solo artists and bands in the world. There were hardly any women roadies working for groups, and no female security officers at gigs. Now, one-fifth of the top performers are women, ranging from Madonna, Bjork, Norah Jones, Sade and Dido to bands such as Destiny's Child. By 2010, more than one-third of the entire personnel working in rock and pop music will be women. The British band Bush insists that at least ten of the bouncers on duty at their gigs are women (Harlow, 2002).

What is most interesting and revealing about all the arguments that continue to be put forward by men to prevent women from becoming boxers or bullfighters or fire-fighters or front-line fighter pilots is that they are *exactly* the same as those that have been put forward to prevent women from entering every profession and occupation over the last 100 years. Examples of this include forcing their way into academia, then being 'allowed' to become professors; getting the vote, then being 'allowed' to stand for political office (and later on becoming ministers); becoming doctors (and after that hurdle was overcome, becoming surgeons); being admitted to study as lawyers (and then becoming partners in law firms or judges); becoming accountants (and then partners) and so on, like a stuck record for more than a century. Every single time that women have tried to enter male-dominated professions and occupations they have been told that they are too weak, too fragile, too emotional, not as intelligent or rational as men or just innately inferior to men and, therefore, not capable of doing the job. Another example, cited earlier, is the very long-standing prejudice during the 20th century about the entrepreneurial instincts and abilities of women. An often-cited story is that of Anita Roddick's struggle to get funding for the nascent Body Shop in the early 1970s. She had a desperate struggle to convince (male) bank managers that, not only did she have a good business plan, but she and her husband were capable of seeing it through (Roddick, 2000). It seems laughable to apply these arguments to the occupations described above now, and yet a lot of men (and a few women) still express them.

In fact, all the available evidence shows that career-minded women have the same ambitions, drives and abilities as men. And, as we saw earlier in this chapter, women are now outperforming men as entrepreneurs. When women are presented with a level playing field and the same opportunities, they perform just as well as men and, in some cases, better. Women are getting there in organizations because they continue to prove themselves to be just as capable of doing a good job as their male colleagues. So, if many of the attitudes men in particular still have about the 'nature' of women rest on shaky foundations, the most important question in this chapter now needs to be addressed: *do the leadership and people management styles of men and women differ in any significant ways?*

A raft of academic and popular publications that appeared in the 1980s and 1990s made a number of suggestions about women leader/managers. First, that they placed less emphasis on hierarchies and status, preferred flatter management structures and put a greater emphasis on teamwork and cooperation. Second, they were generally better communicators, put more time into listening to and talking with their employees, and were more concerned with building consensual agreement rather than political point scoring. Third, 'feminine' leadership and management skills were coming of age, and would eventually supersede the autocratic command-and-control style of male leaders (for example, Kirner and Rayner, 1999; Moskal, 1997; Fisher, 1992). An example of this was Elizabeth Bryan's approach when she took over at the helm of the giant twenty billion dollar Morgan Grenfell Asset Management In Australia:

> It seemed natural that she should occupy her predecessor's prestigious office, with its panoramic views over Sydney harbour and its own executive bathroom. But, when her investment staff began to complain that the office was too remote and isolated, Bryan found the logical solution. She swapped her spacious top floor office for a more accessible – albeit cramped cubby-hole – that kept her close to her staff. The logical solution? For a female executive, maybe. But, how many men would be prepared to give up such a potent symbol of their position at the top of the organizational hierarchy in order to increase their accessibility?
> (*Cited by Maley, 1998*)

Some commentators would suggest that Bryan's response to this situation reveals some fundamental differences between the leadership and management styles of men and women. How true might this be, and how much evidence is there to support the view that the styles of men and women are fundamentally different? Some women high-flyers do believe that women and men have different approaches. For example, Louise McBride, a partner at Deloite Touche Tohmatsu in 1998, had no doubt that female executives were more team-oriented and cooperative than their male counterparts:

> Women have less of an ego. They're happy to be part of a team. Men are more individualistic, less collectivist. They like to do it themselves. And if they do work in a team, they don't want to credit anyone else. They like to claim all the glory for themselves. Women tend to talk things through and to listen. Men are quick to jump in and tell you that this is the right answer,

even if they are not sure that it is. Women are very reluctant to do that. Women often don't speak out at meetings and being a good communicator doesn't necessarily mean that you're prepared to say the first thing that comes into your head. My experience is that women can tend to over research things. They're very cautious and they ask other people's views. They check and double-check to make sure that they're right. Men are much better at flying by the seats of their pants. It's a confidence trick [ ] My experience in supervising men and women was that men always thought they were better than they were, whereas women never thought that they were as good as they were.
(*Cited by Maley, 1998*)

However, other researchers have found that the leadership and management styles of women and men are similar. For example, one survey of 400 men and women in five multinational corporations found that senior women managed in much the same way as senior men (Wajcman, 1998). This research showed that while men and women *believe* that there are gender differences in leadership styles ('command and control' versus 'cooperative and consultative'), most men and women typically behaved in a 'male' style. When Wajcman probed a little deeper, a gap between these espoused beliefs and actual behaviour emerged. In many organizations, the continual pressures on managers to perform smarter and faster, combined with downsizing and rationalization, have combined to create organizational environments where a generally macho ethos of management prevails. Furthermore, there are a dwindling number of career opportunities, so the competition for the top jobs, including that between women, is fierce. These pressures mean that a 'male' management style is still the one that most often prevails. Consequently, if women are to be successful, they have to adapt to this culture, rather than leading/managing in a more female style.

There is evidence to support the view that women who enter very male organizational cultures, such as the military or the police, soon adapt their 'natural' style to fit in with these (Wilson, 1995: 171–9). This of course puts women in a 'no-win' situation. If they adopt traditional male traits such as dominance, rationality and aggressiveness, they are stereotyped as 'iron-maidens' or 'men in drag', and, consequently, their behaviour reinforces the stereotypical preconception that the best style of management is indeed 'male'. Conversely, there is other evidence which suggests that those women who leave large hierarchical organizations to become entrepreneurs almost immediately begin to adopt more collaborative management styles and more devolved management structures: in short, all those things that women leaders and managers are supposed to prefer (Maley, 1998).

The reason why Margaret Thatcher was so dominant as Prime Minister was because she was the only man in her Cabinet.
(*Bernard Ingham, 1995, Mrs T's Press Secretary, 1984–91*)

She has the eyes of Caligula and the mouth of Marilyn Monroe. She is formidable opponent.
(*Francois Mitterrand, then President of France, commenting on Mrs T's negotiation skills during discussions on the future of the EEC, 1985*)

More recently, a series of books have suggested that we are seeing the emergence of a group of 'Alpha Women' (replacing the older and scarcer 'Queen Bee' of the 1980s and 1990s). The common theme running through these books is that women can be just as ruthless, competitive and aggressive as men, rather than being sweet, placid and harmonious (for example, Simmons, 2002). It is argued this has come about not only because of the radical changes in women's aspirations over the last 30 years, but because women are hard-wired to compete in this way. It is only their upbringing and socialization that has dictated they should adopt a 'softer' female style of management. Rosalind Wiseman, author of *Queen Bees and Wannabies*, suggests that this truly is a revolution in thinking, with feminist thinkers traditionally attributing aggressive behaviour to men, when in reality women can be just as nasty as men, given the power, money and opportunities to behave in this way. A review of one survey of workplace bullying in the UK made these comments, 'Women bully in more or less the same way as men, with the exception that females are actually much better at it. They're much more devious, much more manipulative, much more subtle about it, and they leave a lot less evidence as well – and they often do it with a smile' (Sutherland, 1999).

In the USA there is an organization that helps bullying managers to come to terms with and deal with their aggressive behaviour towards their colleagues and junior staff. Its name is 'Bullying Broads', managed by the Silicon Valley Growth and Leadership Center. Jean Holland, a trainer at the centre, estimates that 20–50 per cent of the women she has counselled would qualify as bullies, although she does highlight a double standard being applied here. When men engage in these behaviours, this is often interpreted as 'tough' or 'solid' leadership; in women it can be seen as 'overbearing' and 'bitchy' (Sutherland, 1999). Robert Spillane, of the Macquarie Graduate School of Management at the University of Sydney, is also sceptical about the 'feminization' of leadership and management. He believes that the whole debate about any supposed differences between men and women rests on the very stereotypes that women are often so critical of: that women are all cooperative, consensual, emotionally intelligent team-players and men are individualistic, rational, conflictual and emotionally stunted. He argues that career women can be just as manipulative and Machiavellian as men and, if they are to succeed in many organizations, they *must* adopt these management styles (cited in Fox, 2001).

While researching this topic during 2001–3, I came across more than a hundred academic studies that have been conducted over the last 20 years, which have tried to answer the question, 'Do successful female and male leaders differ in any significant ways?' However, we still do not know if there are any fundamental or consistent differences in the leadership and management styles of men and women. Some research studies show that there are no real differences, others show that there are fundamental differences and some show that men and women exhibit a mixture of masculine and feminine leadership/management styles. These contradictory results lead us to our next question: *can men and women learn from each other and develop a more effective, hybrid style of leadership and people management?* With this question in mind, please complete Exercise 6.4.

Exercise 6.4

Please look through these three lists of personality traits and behavioural characteristics. Then circle the *twelve* items that best describe you and your personality:

Column 1	Column 2	Column 3
Ambitious	Affectionate	Adaptable
Independent	Cooperative	Reliable
Confident	Dependent	Intelligent
Aggressive	Sensitive	Assertive
Forceful	Appreciative	Honest
Dominant	Empathic	Sincere
Tough	Gentle	Helpful
Analytical	Intuitive	Systematic
Competitive	Supportive	Team-player
Rational	Emotional	Efficient

Source: Adapted from Wilson (1995: 171); used with permission. ◆

Did you choose traits and attributes that came from all three columns, or did you have a preference for one of these? If you picked traits predominantly from column 1, you have many 'male' qualities; from column 2, predominantly 'female' qualities; and from column 3, predominantly 'neutral' qualities. If you selected traits from all three columns, you have what can be accurately described as 'hybrid' qualities. Whenever I use this exercise with MBA classes there is always a spread across the three groupings, amongst both men and women. It may not be a coincidence that most MBAs, men and women, are extremely successful in their chosen careers and professions, or as entrepreneurs (and this contention might merit some research in the future).

Looking at the traits in Exercise 6.4 dispassionately and objectively, it would appear that many men and women exhibit leadership and management styles that combine all three groupings. In Chapter 1, we observed that successful leader/managers have a chameleon-like quality, that enables them to subtly alter their leadership styles to reflect the situation they are in, the people they are managing and the issues that they are dealing with. This indicates that an ability to shift between these three groupings is likely to have a strong influence on a leader/manager's effectiveness. It also means that which blend of these 'male', 'female' and 'neutral styles' is used will be influenced by the situation and the nature of the problem that is being dealt with (the contingent nature of leadership reviewed in Chapter 1). For example, a woman police officer dealing with a murder may need to be forceful and dominant when arresting and dealing with a violent suspect, but gentle, nurturing and caring when dealing with the victim's family. She will then have to be rational, analytical and systematic when writing up the report on the incident and, perhaps, empathic and supportive with a young male colleague who had not dealt with this kind of situation before.

There is ample evidence to show that, as more women enter organizations, both men and women exhibit more hybrid leadership styles. For example, one study of law firms revealed that, where women were in small minorities, they exhibited very masculine management styles. In more integrated law firms, with a more equal balance between men and women, feminine leadership and management qualities became more prevalent and, significantly, became regarded more favourably by both women and men (Ely, 1995). In other words, within gender-balanced groups both men and women feel less constrained by culturally proscribed stereotypes about masculinity and femininity. There is freedom in these groups for both men and women to drop stereotyped behaviours and attitudes, and just *be themselves*. In my experience of teaching more than more than 1000 MBA students over the last ten years, the number of women in a group has a profound impact on group dynamics and the 'feel' of sessions. In male-dominated groups, the focus is often on the practicalities and 'hard' aspects of leadership and management. The more women there are present, the more men are willing to talk about issues like emotional intelligence, self-awareness, their uncertainties and frailties, equal opportunities and so forth.

Helen Nugent, former Director of Strategy at Westpac and Deputy Chair of the Australian Council, is one high-flyer who is wary of adopting a simplistic male versus female dichotomy. She believes that many of the attributes associated with 'female' management, such as good communications skills and teamwork, have increasingly gained recognition as crucial skills for leaders in general. She believes that the better male leaders and managers also exhibit these skills, and suggests,

> Successful leaders have some really noteworthy characteristics: they are good team leaders, they are empathetic, they really care about their people, they paint a vision for the future that they can then convey to their people, and they are able to get the right balance between the interests of their customers, their staff and their shareholders. It seems to me that these are characteristics that typify both successful men and women.
> (*Cited by Maley, 1998*)

Elsewhere, there are other signs of change. Research on international managers has shown that traditional 'male' skills, such as technical competence and business acumen, now need to be complemented by 'softer' skills such as cultural sensitivity, multi-tasking skills, networking abilities and excellent communication skills, traditionally 'female' qualities. Recent research has indicated that women have superior skills in these areas (Forster, 1999, 2000c). This suggests that it makes good commercial sense for companies to target more women for international assignments, regardless of any legal, ethical or moral considerations.

In conclusion, the evidence presented in this section indicates that successful leaders and managers combine personal qualities, attributes, competencies and skills that encompass both 'male' and 'female' dimensions. While the debate over the differences between their leadership styles will continue for a long time, there are signs of a convergence of leadership and management styles, particularly amongst Generation X, and even more so amongst Generation Y (Turnbull, 1996). If you still feel uncomfortable about this idea, three quotations from Chapter 1 are reproduced below, with a subtle change made to two of these. How would you now describe the leadership styles described in these? Are they 'masculine' or 'feminine'?

> Leaders should have clean hands, warm hearts and cool minds.

> She knew that true leadership is often realized by exerting quiet and subtle influence on a day to day basis, by frequently seeing followers and other people face to face. She treated everyone with the same courtesy and respect, whether they were kings or commoners. She lifted people out of their everyday selves and into a higher level of performance, achievement and awareness. She obtained extraordinary results from ordinary people by instilling purpose in their endeavours. She was civil, open, tolerant and fair and she maintained a respect for the dignity of all people at all times.

> Because leadership is an action, not a position or title, women need to learn when to lead and when to follow. If you try to lead all day, every day – you will fail. Women need to understand that leadership and followership is a dynamic relationship, based on the situations that people are facing. In fact, leadership is a gift, given to women by their followers.

Strategies for gaining power and influence

Don't be attractive. Don't be smart. Don't be assertive. Pretend you're not a woman. Don't be single. Don't be a mom. Don't be a divorcee.
(*A woman executive's advice to women aspiring to senior management positions, cited in Ragins, 1998*)

At the beginning of this chapter we saw that women have made remarkable advances in many professions, occupations and organizations in recent years. However, many still encounter unconscious and conscious discrimination, and there is some way to go before they will achieve true parity with men. For this reason, women (like men) may also have some unlearning to do. As Kirner and Rayner have suggested:

> One of the greatest mistakes that women can make is to assume that good intentions and hard work will be rewarded. They won't. You need power to make a difference. To claim power and make it work properly, women need the right tools and the skills to use them. Women need power over themselves and their circumstances. They need the power to influence others and the power to communicate and act as part of a group. Women need to be strong in themselves before they can take other people with them.
> (*Kirner and Rayner, 1999: 3*)

Does this mean that women who are reading this book have to learn dozens of new skills and techniques? No, you don't, because all the skills and competencies described in Chapters 1–5 are as relevant to women as they are to men. In fact, as you'll have realized by now, many of these are 'female' leadership and people management skills. However, because of the structural, attitudinal and cultural barriers that many women still encounter in organizations, there are a few additional techniques and skills that can be added to your leadership/management tool-kit (developed from Kirner and Rayner, 1999; Sinclair, 1998: 113–28; and Manning and Haddock, 1995).

Self-belief: as we've seen, *every single time* that women have tried to break into male-dominated bastions, they have encountered the same prejudices, the same hostile and irrational behaviour from men and the same 'justifications' for being excluded or for being prevented from reaching more senior positions. However, they have also battled through every one of these obstacles and challenges. Time after time after time, women have shown immense bravery, tenacity, intelligence, resolve, commitment and self-belief in the face of some truly appalling and vicious behaviour from men. And, as we have seen in this chapter, they continue to win through – and so can you.

Expect to be tested if you are working in male-dominated environments, but try not to take this personally because the men who do this are not intelligent or aware enough to know any better. You might get angry with them for short periods of time, but remember that they will be ignorant for the rest of their lives, unless they change. Be dogged, persistent and professional at all times. Have a reputation for reliability and develop a good track record at work: 'the less glamorous alternative to charisma', as Amanda Sinclair has aptly described it (1998: 118). If you prepare thoroughly for everything, there is less chance that you will slip up or be shown up. Try to become a more 'hardy personality' and use the self-affirmation principles described in Chapter 2. Try to develop an essential leadership quality we identified in Chapter 1, the ability to learn from your mistakes. Last, recall the advice given by Dr Penny Flett in Chapter 1:

> Even if you are working in the worst organization or the worst business in the world, always strive to be excellent in your sphere of influence, and always do the very best you can for the people who work for you. Always be positive and support your people. You will find that if you leave one organization and move to a better one, many of your best people will want to come and work for you in your new position.

A clear sense of purpose and personal values: if you completed Exercise 2.2, you should already have a good sense of your life-goals, but don't forget to review where you are going at regular intervals (and why). You should also try to develop a clear set of personal values and ethical principles that will govern what you will and will not do within an organization (please refer to Chapter 12 for a more detailed discussion of leadership and business ethics). Understand the different levels of power: power over yourself (self-awareness and self-belief); personal, expert and positional power (Chapter 7); the power to motivate and inspire others (Chapter 4); the power to influence others through communication (Chapter 3); and the power that can be used to influence a group or team (Chapter 5). This also means not being afraid of using power in a coercive way – if the situation demands it.

> There is a saying, 'Where power is, women are not'. Women must be willing to be powerful. Because we bear scars from the way men have used their power over us, women often want no part of power.
> (*Attributed to Petra Kelly*)

Build alliances and network, network, network: try to do this with both men and women (including those you may be mentoring). Men are not all cast from the same mould. If they're on your side, cultivate their support and friendship and ask them for help if you need it. Don't assume that other 'Alpha' women are going to be on your side, particularly if they are competing with you for a small number of senior positions in an organization. As we have seen, women are just as capable as men of being fiercely competitive and aggressive; and some will not challenge existing power relationships if these have served their interests well in the past. Build up and maintain informal networks outside the organization – you never know when you might need them. If you can, find a mentor (man or woman) whom you trust and can go to for advice or support.

Physical appearance really can make a difference. A crisp, professional no-nonsense image helps create a neutral effect with men (sad, I know, but it can be important). Wear business-like clothing and don't wear floral designs if you are appearing on TV!

Be well prepared and organized for meetings: cover all the bases and, when preparing for and managing meetings, make use of the ideas and suggestions in Chapter 5. Think of every counter-position that could be taken against your proposals. Concentrate on the job at hand, not personalities. Women are 50 per cent more likely to be interrupted than men are in male-dominated groups. Don't allow yourself to become one of these statistics. Use assertive, direct language and be firm if you are interrupted. Don't allow yourself, or other women, to be ridiculed or marginalized in meetings. Make good use of the communication and presentation skills that we explored together in Chapter 3. Use appropriate body language in team meetings. Men typically use less body language than women do.

Stand your ground: be assertive and stand up for what you believe in. Powerful women don't have to be interested in being nice or be too concerned about being popular. They have independent opinions and are willing to stick by them. If people come out with crass comments like, 'I have real problems with political correctness' or 'All feminists hate men', don't confront them. Instead, ask them what they mean and keep asking questions. Dig and probe and *slowly* point out how illogical their position is. Use facts to back up your arguments, not polemic or opinions. Trust me on this suggestion; this approach usually works well with both large MBA groups and with managers in workshops, where women are in a minority. If you need to make a real impact at work and the opportunity arises, surprise, shock and confound your male colleagues on occasions.

> One of the things I encourage women in management to do is to take a course in military history, take a course in corporate strategy, watch those wretched football games every weekend because that is the way that males you are working with have been taught to think, or if they haven't, they will pretend they have.
> (*Jill Ker-Conway, former CEO of Lend Lease, 1995*)

Keep records: set up a system that enables you to keep notational records of meetings, events and conversations at work. You may need this information if you have to deal with discrimination or sexual harassment at work.

Deal assertively with discrimination and harassment: in North America, European EEC countries, non-EEC Scandinavian countries and Australasia, both are illegal. Discrimination means that someone is either treated less favourably than someone else or excluded on the basis of their gender (or race, culture and so forth). Sexual harassment is any unwelcome behaviour of a sexual nature. This can come in many forms: in words, gestures, acts, touching, jokes, emails, personal remarks, direct requests for sexual favours, teasing and so forth. How can you know when something becomes 'harassment'? Kirner and Rayner suggest this benchmark, 'Whether it was meant to or not, and whether it was aimed at you specifically or not, if the conduct is of a kind that makes you feel insulted, intimidated or offended – and if a reasonable person would, in the circumstances, expect you to feel that way – it's sexual harassment and it's illegal' (Kirner and Rayner, 1999: 173).

How can you deal with this kind of behaviour? First, try to maintain your sense of humour (see below). Second, don't try to deal with this on your own. Discuss it with friends outside work or in confidence with your mentor, if you have one. Third, stand up for your rights and complain initially to the person who is doing it. Most men are often quite unaware that they may have caused offence and very surprised when accused of this kind of behaviour. Explain to them how you feel about it and why it is unwelcome. If the behaviour repeats itself, Kirner and Rayner (1999: 179) suggest that the following response can be very effective: 'Did you know that harassment was illegal? Do you talk like that to boys too? I'm here to do my job and you're not helping.' If this fails, report it to your superior or your equal opportunity/grievance officer or your union representative. You may be labelled as a trouble-maker or face further harassment as a result, but if you don't stand up to this, you will be sending a signal that inappropriate behaviour is OK. It will also show that you are acquiescing in this and, in turn, this might invite even more harassment. Remember that sexual harassment is just another form of bullying and, as we saw in Chapter 1, this kind of behaviour is totally unacceptable (and bad for business). If the harassment is really crude, get away from the situation quickly. If it can't be dealt with internally (as may still be the case), you may have to make a complaint to the statutory anti-discrimination or equal opportunity authorities in your state, county or country. If you do this, find a lawyer or attorney who knows this area of litigation well, and try to do it with co-workers who might be in the same situation. However, this is a last resort and carries many risks. As Kirner and Rayner observe:

It takes courage, or desperation, to claim these rights and certainly to use legal remedies. You must be prepared to defend charges that you are incompetent, dishonest, potty or emotionally unstable. You might be told that you should feel guilt and accept blame for any detriment you have suffered. You might be challenged under cross-examination and have your private life and beliefs scrutinised; there could be challenges to your memory and character; there could be pressures of financial loss, delays, humiliation, rebuffs, and long silent questioning looks from your family (especially your children) and friends, who might believe you have become obsessed. Don't destroy your happiness for the cause of all women. You need to decide whether it's the right choice for *you* to make. But those who do make that decision deserve our thanks. They are doing it for all of us.
(*Kirner and Rayner, 1999: 184*)

Try to balance work and family responsibilities: if possible, this means identifying and working for those companies and organizations that have family-friendly employment policies. In organizations that still choose to ignore these issues, it means clearly defining your boundaries and making it clear to your colleagues where these boundaries lie. This is not an easy thing to do, but refer back to Chapter 2 for some tips on achieving this and to Chapter 4 if you need to justify the introduction of family-friendly employment policies in your organization.

Maintain your sense of humour: in Chapter 1, we saw that this can be a powerful leadership tool, and also can be very effective when dealing with both toxic personalities and male chauvinists. However, this doesn't mean that you should just 'laugh off' disrespectful attitudes, harassing jokes or inappropriate behaviour.

Hard work is one thing, but desperate struggle is a warning that your strategies are up the spout. It is absolutely essential to have some fun. Maintain your sense of humour, share it with your friends and allies and use against your enemy if you will. It's a potent weapon.

Q. 'What's the difference between Joan Kirner and a rottweiler?'
A. 'The rottweiler doesn't wear lipstick.'
(*Joan Kirner and Moira Rayner,* The Women's Power Handbook, *1999*)

Better big in the backside than bullshit for brains.
(*The one-line retort of Australian Federal Minister, Amanda Vanstone, after a male political opponent made some unflattering comments about her physical appearance, cited by Stewart, 2002*)

Create your own one-liners. Kirner and Rayner quote some good ones from a book by Annie Cowling, *Breaking New Ground: A Manual for Survival for Women Entering Non-Traditional Jobs*. Here are a few adapted versions of these, which may need to be used with care:

Q.   'Why do you want to be a fire fighter/pilot/oil-rig worker [etc]?'
A.   'Why do you?' Or 'Because it's a challenging, rewarding, well-paid [etc] job'. Or 'Because my brother decided to be a nurse/fashion designer/hairdresser [etc].'

Q.   'Do you think you'll have problems working with men, dear?'
A.   'No. Do you?'

Q.   'Do you have a boyfriend?'
A.   'Why? Do you need one?'

Q.   'Has anyone ever told you that you talk/look/think/act like a man?'
A.   'No. Has anyone ever told you that?'

Q.   'Why are you doing a man's job?'
A.   'He didn't seem to mind.' Or 'He knew I'd do a good job.'

Q.   'Nice dress darling. Did your boyfriend have to spend a lot of money on that?'
A.   'I was going to ask the same thing about your suit, but thought better of it.'

Stay healthy: become a 'corporate athlete', as described in Chapter 2.

Deny denial: women still have some way to go before they achieve true parity with men in all professions, occupations and organizations. Furthermore, women in western industrialized countries have only gained the freedom and independence they now enjoy because other women fought, struggled and even died in the past to win these. Pretending that this situation does not exist or trying to be one of the boys isn't going to help you or other women. It is also worth remembering that millions of women, particularly in non-industrialized countries, are still effectively living in the dark ages, as far as equality of opportunity goes. In some Muslim societies, men still have the right to kill their female relatives for social 'transgressions'; women can be beaten to death for 'stepping out of line' (such as exposing any part of their body or talking to a non-family male in public). In Africa, several hundred young girls are still forcibly circumcised every week. It took until May 2003 for the Indian National Assembly to pass laws to prosecute men who beat or raped their wives: this in a country that has a rapidly growing, affluent and well-educated professional middle class. These three examples indicate that, for most women, in most countries of the world, the struggle for true equality has only just begun.

Changing organizations

We've seen that, while gender stereotypes rest on shaky foundations, and bear very little relationship to what men and women really are, they still have a powerful influence on the way that many men (and some women) think about issues like equal opportunities, discrimination and sexual harassment. This means that creating an organization where structural, attitudinal and cultural barriers no longer exist can be a long-drawn-out and painful process. Typically, organizations that are trying to create parity for women employees have to go through four developmental stages (adapted from Sinclair, 1998).

Stage 1: denial

The issue does not register as even a blip on the organization's radar. The absence of women in management positions is not regarded as a problem or a core business issue. Typical (male) rationalizations at this stage will include 'We don't employ women here because they don't want to do this kind of work, they are incapable of doing this kind of work, they are less rational than men, not as intelligent, not as strong/aggressive/hard as men, will leave to have babies after we have trained them blah-blah-blah . . .'

Stage 2: the problem is women

Rationalizations holding women back at this stage will continue to include 'Women are incapable of being a senior manager, because they are less rational than men, not as intelligent, not strong/aggressive/hard enough, will leave to have babies after we have trained them/not come back after maternity leave; if women want to get into senior positions, they should manage like men . . .' Other rationalizations at this stage will include 'Women lack senior management experience', rather than asking, 'Where can we find women with the potential to succeed at senior management levels?'

Stage 3: incremental adjustment

There is a growing recognition that 'gender' and 'diversity' may be problems that need addressing. The organization will obey the letter, if the not the spirit, of legal regulations covering equal pay and discrimination. Some efforts may be made to promote women's interests in other ways by, for example, introducing minimum quotas for women in selection and recruitment procedures. Equality audits may be conducted to assess the nature and size of 'the problem'. Typical rationalizations at this stage will include 'We operate on meriocratic principles. If they're good enough, they'll get promoted to the top jobs', rather than 'Why don't women apply for senior positions?' Or 'Do our promotion systems discriminate against women or discourage them from applying for senior positions?' Or 'Well, if they want to have the top jobs, they can't buzz-off at 5.00 to look after the kids', rather than 'How can we make our employment policies more family-friendly?'

Stage 4: commitment to a new organizational culture

The organization recognizes that a fundamental mind shift is required to remove any remaining attitudinal, structural and cultural barriers that are still impeding women. There is recognition, at the most senior levels, that this will be good for the organization's overall performance, productivity and profitability. Specific targets are set for recruiting women to the organization and, once employed, promoting them within the organization. There is a shift from 'equality' to 'parity', where the needs of men and women are seen as being different, but of equal importance. Conscious efforts are made to build equity principles into recruitment policies, employee induction processes, staff development exercises and promotion policies. Flexible employment policies recognize that employees may have partners and children and are family-friendly.[6] Rationalizations for excluding women from full participation are now a thing of the past.

The end objective of this process is to create what Michael Simmons has called 'inclusive organizations'. This implies a style of leadership that is able to look above and beyond stereotypical attitudes about men and women and create organizational cultures that are 'capable of harnessing the intelligence, creativity and initiative of people at all levels, especially those who have been traditionally excluded [and which] reaches beyond equality to an organization where there are no boundaries or limitations placed on anyone' (Simmons, 1996: x).

This requires, as with all change management initiatives, a strong commitment from the top of the organization. Then it becomes possible to create an organizational culture that emphasizes women's needs and issues on a daily basis – not as an abstract 'personnel' or 'women's' issue. A balance between work and family responsibilities would also be encouraged. In Chapter 4, we saw that companies who do help staff balance their work and home life have a strategic advantage over their competitors through the increased well-being, commitment, motivation and productivity of all of their employees. It can also mean taking other initiatives. For example, Hewlett-Packard Australia, who had been concerned for some time about the lack of female engineers (and other minorities) joining the company, established and created a female Chair in Engineering at Melbourne University in March 1999, and introduced a company-wide initiative to encourage more women into engineering and IT positions during 2002.

The sheer number of younger women entering the workplace means that any company which really values its future has to do more than pay lip service to the rhetoric of equal opportunities. If it doesn't, it can never realize its full potential. Women under 40 will simply not tolerate being treated as second-class citizens by men in organizations. And recall that thousands of very able women have been voting with their feet and have moved into self-employment in large numbers over the last decade. This means that many organizations have lost a lot of entrepreneurial talent in recent years, while at the same time trying to become more intrapreneurial. This is a trend that should be a major cause of concern for all employers who want to recruit and retain the best and brightest employees now and in the future.

Conclusion

Ending discrimination against women and promoting true parity requires initiatives from both outside and inside organizations. It is not simply a question of women just 'going for it', as some high-flying women have suggested. History is littered with thousands of examples of women who have suffered enormously while trying to go it alone in male-dominated organizations. However, there are reasons to be cautiously optimistic because there are many encouraging signs of genuine change, particularly amongst younger people. So where can we go from here, as men and women and as leaders and managers? Four suggestions have been made in this chapter.

Discrimination against women is bad for business

We now live in a global economy, characterized by increasing job mobility between countries, perpetual change and rapid technological innovation. The management of intellectual capital and knowledge is becoming the primary driver of organizational success and adaptability. If your business can't recruit and retain the very best talent, regardless of gender (or skin colour), it is your organization's performance, productivity and profitability that will suffer in the future. There is abundant evidence, from *Fortune* surveys over the last decade and from country-specific research on Employers of Choice, that the promotion of equal opportunities and employee diversity are central pillars of their HR strategies (Corporate Research Foundation, 2003).

Successful modern leaders and managers are chameleons

Contrary to what a lot of male managers might believe, and many feminist writers would argue, successful leaders and managers possess a combination of female, male and neutral qualities, attributes and characteristics. However, as we have seen, what combination of these is actually used by men and women is still heavily influenced by the organizational contexts and cultures in which they work. It has also been suggested that men and women should be comfortable using a hybrid leadership and management style because it is – by far – the most flexible and effective one to use in modern organizations.

Men must change

I hope that the issues raised in this chapter have made men (and maybe some women) question some common-sense notions that they might have had about what masculinity 'is' and what women 'are'. Implicitly, this suggests that men too must change. However, it is certainly true to say that many men, in their more private and reflective moments, are uncertain what this might mean. Some are genuinely afraid of what they regard as the feminization of organizations and the emasculation of their male identities. Being a leader/manager is such an integral and deeply ingrained part of the masculine psyche that men may have to find new sources of self-affirmation. This will not be easy because, as Amanda Sinclair has put it, 'When men observe other men leading differently, there is often disbelief, censure, marginalisation, even ridicule. The man trying a new path by, for example, limiting the hours he works, is seen as "under the thumb" (masculinity compromised by an assertive wife); "not up to it" (finding an excuse for failure in the big-boy's world); or hopelessly diverted and rendered a limp and impotent SNAG [Sensitive New Age Guy]' (Sinclair, 1998: 74).

Consequently, many men still react by behaving like the proverbial three monkeys and simply ignore, resist or fight back against the inexorable changes going on about them. However, at least in western industrialized countries, there is little prospect that most men will ever be able to revert back to becoming warrior breadwinners, with dependent stay-at-home wives. In this context, it's also worth remembering that the 'normal' nuclear family type consisting of a stay-at-home wife, a couple of kids and a single male breadwinner is an historical anomaly that only emerged in the mid-19th century in western industrialized countries. The sheer number of women coming into small, medium and large organizations will continue to grow for the foreseeable future. So the only option for most men in most organizations is to change and change fast. Denying that there is a need to change does not remove the pressing need for men to make this transition.[7]

Attitudes are changing

Earlier in this chapter, we described the changing role of women in the military, which has been the subject of heated debate in many countries in recent times. However, there is clear evidence that generational attitudes towards this issue are changing fast. For example, in June 2001, *The Australian* commissioned a NEWSPOLL survey of 1200 respondents, which asked the question, 'Are you in favour or against women being allowed to serve in combat roles in the Australian Army?' The total number 'In favour' was 63 per cent (61 per cent for men and 65 per cent for women). However, what is more revealing is the generational breakdown. In the 18–34 age group, 84 per cent were in favour, in the 35–49 age group, 68 per cent and in the 50+ age group 44 per cent were in favour. This indicates that attitudes towards women in many traditionally male occupations and professions are undergoing a sea change at the moment, particularly amongst Generations X and Y, and there is every indication that this will continue for the foreseeable future.[8]

> My son has taught me so many valuable lessons. How to kick a football. How to build Meccano. How to tie a rig for herring, or sisters. He enables me to get inside the male mind, and even more importantly, he throws me down a rope so I can climb out of it again. Now, don't get me wrong. I am not one of those people who believe than men are from Mars and women are from Venus. Indeed, I think that the use of inter-planetary metaphors for human behaviour is totally sophomoric and unhelpful. Anyway, why limit yourself to the solar system when there's a whole universe out there? 'Men are like Black Holes and Women are like the Asteroids Who Get Sucked In.'
> (*Susan Maushart*, The Weekend Australian, *9–10 March 2002*)

Another example of changing attitudes over the last half-century is the use of more gender-neutral terms, such as the prefix Ms. Although this was first used as long ago as 1949, it did not start to enter the public's consciousness until the late 1970s (often in the face of much derision from men, who complained vociferously about having to use 'politically correct language'). Ms become more widespread in the late 1980s and, by the late 1990s, most people had become comfortable using this when formally addressing a single woman. The use of the neutral word 'chair' (rather than chairman) had an equally long period of incubation, before its use became widespread and taken for granted by both men and women (Bryson, 1994: 427). It's worth remembering that, for almost all of human history, the nature of what woman 'were' was entirely defined and circumscribed by men, and our language reflected this hegemony in many subtle (and not so subtle) ways. While women, particularly in the last three decades of the 20th century, have begun to challenge this, it will take time for both men and women to renegotiate their respective roles in society and in organizations, and to redefine what it means to be a man or a woman at the beginning of the 21st century.

An important (and perhaps controversial) suggestion made in this chapter was that the generic qualities, attributes, skills and competencies of successful leaders and managers apply to both men and women. For example, just three out of 66 pages of *Leadership Skills for Women*, by Marilyn Manning and Patricia Haddock, contain information on leadership and management skills that are unique to women. Seventeen out of 23 'female' styles and strategies identified by Amanda Sinclair (1998: 113–14) are ones that many men also use. This reinforces the idea that we may be witnessing the emergence of a hybrid style of leadership and people management that will eventually transcend traditional male/female archetypes. This implies that embracing an exclusively male or female style alone will be inadequate in the future, and a fully functioning adult (man or woman) should be capable of embracing the best of both. Is this too great a step for men and women to take? Is there, as Amanda Sinclair has suggested with understandable exasperation, 'a desire to grow up from it or beyond it' (ibid.: 53)?

> There is no use having cleverness about the place unless it is tapped efficiently. There are many reasons other than femaleness for the neglect of talent, but it is without doubt the most spectacular cause for the waste of intelligence in organizations.
> (*Alistair Mant*, Intelligent Leadership, *1997*)

Exercise 6.5

Having read through this chapter, think about how you can utilize any new insights you may have acquired in your leadership and people management practices in the future.

Insight   **Strategy**

1.

2.

3.

4.

5.   ◆

Notes

1 A question that might be asked is, 'Can a man ever really understand the problems that women can encounter at work?' No, I can't. I cannot ever fully appreciate what it is like for a woman (or women from ethnic minorities) to encounter routine discrimination in the workplace, but hopefully this chapter reflects some appreciation of this.

2 Woman Hitler.

3 In any event, to dub one sex hormone as exclusively 'male' or 'female' is an oversimplification. Both hormones are needed by each sex; men need oestrogen and women need testosterone to develop normally. For example, both men and women require oestrogen if their bones are to develop normally. In fact, the average man has more oestrogen swimming around his body than a woman does after menopause. Surprisingly, oestrogen in men is now thought to play a role in sperm production, and high levels in the brain are indicative of sexual arousal in both men and women. This is not to say that testosterone has no influence on male/female behaviours. One recent study confirmed the findings of earlier research, showing that girls whose mothers had high levels of testosterone during pregnancy preferred games and activities more commonly associated with boys. Conversely, levels of oestrogen or testosterone had no effect on the expected gender-role behaviour of boys (Hines, 2002).

4 Even this could change in the not too distant future. Genetic manipulation, bioengineering and biorobotics may mean that women could become physically enhanced to the point where differences in the physical strength of men and women could cease to exist (see Chapter 11).

5 Herstory Quiz answers
What percentage of women fought with men as front-line combat troops in the Red Army during World War II and in the Vietcong during the Vietnam War?
About 20 per cent and 30 per cent, respectively.

Ten inventions or innovations made by women
(Ironically) X and Y chromosomes (Nettie Stevens); automatic flight controls (Irmgard Flugge-Lutz), the calculus (Maria Gartena Agnes), the brown paper bag (Margaret Knight), liquid paper (Bette Graham), computer languages (Grace Murray Hooper), penicillin (various), smallpox inoculation (Lady Montagu), star-mapping in astronomy (Henrietta Leavit and Annie Cannon) and DNA (Rosalind Franklin). Franklin was instrumental in 'discovering' DNA, but was airbrushed out of history by Crick and Watson, who plagiarized her research, and went on to claim the Nobel Prize. It's a little known fact that DNA was first identified in 1869, by a Swiss scientist, Johann Meischer. However, it took another 80 years before people realized that this apparently simple structure formed the basis of the reproduction of all life on Earth. Perhaps the most famous woman scientist in history, Marie Curie, who jointly discovered radioactivity with her husband, is the only person in history to have been awarded Nobel prizes in both physics (1903) and chemistry (1911). Women also played pivotal roles in the development of bullet-proof vests, astronomy, fire escapes, windshield wipers and laser printers. This is remarkable, given the very limited opportunities they had to pursue careers in science in the past.

As a postscript to this, women are often regarded as being more intuitive than men. This is often viewed, in management circles, as something negative. In fact, intuition is an underrated and underresearched leadership and management competency. For example, many inventions and innovations in the past would not have seen the light of day if the people who created these had relied on either common sense or the empirical method. Inventions and innovations as diverse as Einstein's General Theory of Relativity, the airplane, the Sony Walkman and the Post-It were as much the result of intuition as empirical logic. This suggests that successful (male) innovators and inventors are already in touch with 'female intuition'. For more information on this, please refer to Chapter 9. It is also interesting to note that intuition became one of the management fads of 2003, with several consulting companies offering coaching in intuition and, in one case, 'Caribbean Intuition Cruises'.

Every Microsoft product has a Certificate of Authenticity attached to it: a watermark with a picture of a woman on it. Who was she and why does her face appear on this?
Augusta Aida Byron (Countess Lovelace) who is credited with being a pioneer of the earliest computer programming languages way back in the 1860s. Charles Babbage, who developed the first detailed plans for a punch card controlled calculator (the precursor of modern computers), described her as 'My enchantress of numbers'.

What do these giants of 19th- and 20th-century thinking and literature have in common: Simone de Beauvoir, Gertrude Stein, Doris Lessing and Germaine Greer?
Amazingly, given their enormous impact on western thinking and the emancipation of women, none of them appeared in *The Australian's* 2000 series on 'Great Thinkers and Leaders of the 20th Century'.

Can you guess what the following comments, made in the Australian Parliament in 1983, were about? 'This is a stupid bill that most women won't understand. It will rot the social fabric; will force women into work against their will. It will be a deterrent to those who seek to create employment opportunities and will cause a large increase in male unemployment.'
The introduction of Australian Equal Opportunity Legislation.

Can you name ten (or more) women heads of state in the last 30 years?
Isabel Peron (Argentina, 1974–6), Margaret Thatcher (UK, 1979–90), Mary Charles (Dominica, 1980–95), Janet Jagen (Guyana, 1997–9), Vigdis Finnbogadottir (Iceland, 1980–96), Mary Robinson (Ireland, 1990–97), Indira Gandhi (India, 1966–77, 1980–84), Golda Meir (Israel, 1969–74), Agatha Barbara (Malta, 1982–7), Helen Clark (New Zealand, 1999–2004), Gro Harlem Brundlandt (Norway, 1981, 1986–9, 1990–96), Hanna Suchoka (Poland, 1992–3) and several others.

Can you name ten (or more) women CEOs or vice-presidents of international companies?
During 2003–4: Marjorie Scardino (Pearson Publishers), Carly Fiorina (Hewlett-Packard), Marina Berlusconi (Finivest), Belinda Stronach (Magna International), Christine Tsung (China Airlines), Mary Minnick (Coca-Cola Asia), Maureen Darkes (GM Canada), Barbara Kux (Ford Europe), Ho Ching (Singapore Technologies), Val Gooding (BUPA), Margaret Jackson (Qantas), Linda Cook (Shell Gas and Power), Rose Marie Bravo (Burberry), Dominique Dubreil (Rémy Cointreau), Anne Mulcahy (Xerox), Theresa Gattung (Telecom New Zealand) and many others. *Fortune* publishes a survey of the top 100 women global business leaders each year.

How many EEC countries allow women to fly as front-line fighter pilots?
They all do. Italy was the last EEC country to allow women to train as fighter pilots (in 1999). Half of the 13 000 candidates in Italy who applied for just 136 training places in 2000 were women. While they generally showed 'more motivation and general knowledge than the men', their numbers were restricted to 20 per cent of the total intake, with 16 would-be pilots and 12 would-be navigators accepted for training (Follain, 2000). All future new members of the EEC will also have to allow women to fly in their air forces.

What is Dhammanada Bhikkhuni's claim to fame?
In December 2003, she was the first woman to be ordained as a Buddhist priest in Thailand (at that time, the only one out of 300 000 male priests).

What is Christina Sanchez's claim to fame?
She was the first professional female bullfighter in Spain.

What are Valentina Tereshkova, Dr Sally Rides and Eileen Collins' claims to fame?
Cosmonaut Valentina Tereshkova was the first woman into space in 1963, Dr Sally Ride was the first American woman in orbit in 1983, and Eileen Collins became the first woman to captain a space shuttle mission on 21 July 1999.

What was Babe Zaharias's claim to fame?
She was the last woman to qualify to compete in a PGA tour event, at the Los Angeles Open in 1945. Annika Sorenstam was the first woman since then to be invited to play in a PGA event in May 2003 at the Bank of America tournament. She missed the cut for the final round but beat many top-ranked male golfers. Suzy Whaley became the first woman to qualify for a men's US PGA Tour event since 1945, teeing off in the Greater Hartford Open in July 2003.

What do the following people have in common: George W. Bush Snr., Ronald Reagan, Franklin D. Roosevelt, Samuel L. Jackson, Meryl Streep and Madonna?
They were all, in their younger days, cheerleaders. Cheerleading dates back to 1898, when the first organized group of what were initially described as 'yellers' took to the field at the University of Minnesota. Women were excluded from taking part in cheerleading until 1923, because it was feared they would become too 'masculinized'. After World War II, women came to dominate cheerleading teams, and a cultural icon became embedded in the American national consciousness. While cheerleading has often been accused of pandering to sexist stereotypes of women, there are increasing numbers of mixed cheerleading teams in the USA and also a few men-only cheerleading teams (Pratt, 2002: 24).

6   If your organization is considering the introduction of family-friendly employment policies, a good starting point is the UK-based Work-Life Research Centre and its comprehensive guide, *The Work-Life Manual: Gaining a Competitive Edge by Balancing the Demands of Employees' Work and Home Lives.*

7   Although it is beyond the remit of this book, the revolution in the aspirations of women does have profound implications for men. If you'd like to find out more about this, have a look at Fay Weldon's 1999 book, *Godless in Eden*, for a powerful account of the difficulties confronting men in a post-feminist world (see 'Girls on top', 'The fish and the bicycle', 'Pity the poor men', 'Today's mother' and 'Has feminism gone too far?').

8   A discussion of discrimination on the grounds of race, sexual orientation or physical disability is beyond the scope of this book, but many of the principles and ideas discussed in this chapter can be applied to the stereotypes that surround these. First, in most western industrialized countries, it can be very expensive for organizations that are found guilty of discrimination on these grounds. Second, when it is an employee's character, abilities and skills that really matter in organizations these days, it's going to affect organizational efficiency if negative attitudes about these groups are allowed to flourish. Third, if these are tackled head-on, it will probably help your business or organization. Most private-sector companies now understand the economic value of the 'pink' and 'ethnic' dollar, but far fewer seem to know about the purchasing power of disabled people. For example, the Western Australian companies, Jonstyle Ltd and Spotlight Ltd, were awarded two of the Prime Minister's 'Employer of the Year' awards in 1999. They received these awards because they had demonstrated an 'outstanding commitment to employing people with disabilities'. The profits of both companies have risen each year since (personal communication from a University of Western Australia, Graduate School of Management MBA student, July 2002).

7 Managing power, politics and conflict

Objectives

To define power, politics and conflict and describe their positive and negative effects.

To identify the principal sources of power and political influence in organizations.

To describe how conflicts can arise at work and some practical strategies for dealing with these.

To show how you can become a Machiavellian political operator, if the situation demands it.

Introduction

> Power is the ultimate aphrodisiac.
> (*Henry Kissinger, former US President 'Tricky-Dicky' Nixon's Foreign Secretary*)

> Politics is not a science . . . but an art.
> (*Otto von Bismarck*)

For many people power and politics are dirty words, signifying dominance, aggression, brute force, autocratic control, repression and exploitation. However, as we will see, these are not simply 'black arts'; they are an essential part of leadership and people management. The word 'power' is derived from the Latin, *potere*, meaning 'to be able', and is defined here as the ability to influence/and or change the behaviour, attitudes and beliefs of others. The word 'politic' is derived from the Latin, *politicus*, meaning judgment or prudence. It is defined here as the ability to mobilize people and resources, in order to achieve desirable outcomes for oneself or the group to which one belongs. Consequently, when used in the right way, power and politics can be very positive forces for good, giving individuals increased freedom, influence, choice and strength, and an enhanced ability to mobilize people and resources in order to accomplish personal goals, work tasks and organizational objectives. Powerful leaders and managers can also achieve more for their followers because they possess 'clout', and people will work harder for a boss that they believe has real power, credibility and influence within an organization. For example, Bennis and Nanus (1985) interviewed 90 people who had been nominated by their peers as being the most influential leaders in the USA in business, politics and society. They found that these individuals all shared one characteristic: they made other people feel powerful and had used their power to enable other people to aspire to exceptional achievements. They had also learnt how to build strong personal power bases within their organizations, businesses or spheres of influence. And, as we have seen in preceding chapters, power can be an even more positive force if an organization has empowered employees from top to bottom, who are able to move collectively, with speed and purpose, towards achieving their short-, medium- and long-term objectives. In contrast, employees are less willing to work for weak leaders that lack genuine personal authority and credibility or those who tend to be bossy and dictatorial.

Conflict too is often regarded as a largely negative aspect of organizational life. This word is derived from the Latin, *conflictus*, meaning striking together, shock or fight. It is defined here as an interaction characterized by disagreement, strife, arguments, quarrels, fights, emotional outbursts or personality clashes. Almost all organizations are made up of disparate individuals and groups with different interests, values and objectives. These may be competing for finite resources and rewards. In turn, this competition creates the potential for conflict, because not everyone's interests can be catered for equally at all times. However, this does not mean that all conflict is bad. In some situations, it can serve useful functions. In fact, power, politics and conflict are 'two-faced' phenomena, and can be used for both good and evil ends. Furthermore, they are inextricable features of organizational life, and in all large companies and bureaucratic organizations they are inevitable. Consequently, an understanding of these, and how to deal with them effectively, is essential for leader/managers, particularly for those who occupy senior positions in organizations.

Power and politics in context

Before reading through the next section, please complete self-development Exercise 7.1.

Exercise 7.1

Machpower* rating

Please rate the extent to which you agree or disagree with the following statements, where

1 = strongly disagree, 2 = disagree, 3 = neither agree nor disagree, 4 = agree, 5 = strongly agree, NA = not applicable

My main goal is to get to the top of my profession/organization, regardless of whom I have to step over to get there	1	2	3	4	5	NA
Honesty is not always the best policy when dealing with colleagues at work	1	2	3	4	5	NA
Fear is the best motivator to use with employees	1	2	3	4	5	NA
I only communicate information to colleagues that benefits me personally	1	2	3	4	5	NA
I will use information given in confidence if this will benefit me	1	2	3	4	5	NA
I try to hire people who will help me to get ahead in my career/organization	1	2	3	4	5	NA
I prefer to hire people who are willing to accept my decisions and authority	1	2	3	4	5	NA
I never help anyone at work unless there are tangible personal benefits for me	1	2	3	4	5	NA
Power is more important to me than praise or rewards	1	2	3	4	5	NA
It's OK to use someone else's ideas if I benefit from these	1	2	3	4	5	NA
I like to tell as many people as I can about successes I have at work	1	2	3	4	5	NA
I will praise my colleagues in public if they are successful, even though I may privately resent doing this	1	2	3	4	5	NA
I prefer to use my positional authority to get what I want at work	1	2	3	4	5	NA

When I have had serious conflicts with co-workers, I will do everything I can to undermine them	1	2	3	4	5	NA
I prefer to tell my bosses what they want to hear	1	2	3	4	5	NA
I expect my subordinates to do what I tell them, without questioning my decisions	1	2	3	4	5	NA
The decisions I make at work are primarily influenced by their political consequences	1	2	3	4	5	NA
I like to get even with people who've crossed me at work	1	2	3	4	5	NA
I use flattery to get what I want	1	2	3	4	5	NA
Teamwork is OK, but the buck stops with the leader	1	2	3	4	5	NA
In the final analysis, leadership is about exercising power, authority and control over employees	1	2	3	4	5	NA

(* Machiavellian power)

Please add up your total score _____

Scoring key

21–42: Rarely use Machiavellian political strategies to influence others or for personal gain, although use may be made of these on rare occasions. A very broad repertoire of alternative power strategies, but may want to consider utilizing *some* Machiavellian power and influencing strategies in the future if the situation warrants it.

43–63: In most circumstances, prefer not to use Machiavellian political strategies to influence others or for personal gain, although use may be made of these if the situation demands it. A broader repertoire of power and positive influencing strategies.

64–84: A love of power and its trappings, but how this is used is sometimes moderated. Probably regarded by colleagues as political, self-interested and untrustworthy. A limited repertoire of alternative power and influencing strategies.

85–105: Obsessed with the acquisition and use of Machpower. Will consider any behaviour or actions to pursue personal goals, regardless of moral or ethical considerations, or the effects these might have on colleagues and subordinates. A very limited repertoire of positive power and influencing strategies. ◆

Traditionally, the use of Machiavellian power is synonymous with deviousness, ruthlessness, cunning and the relentless pursuit of one's own interests. Hence many people may choose not to engage with power and politics, believing that they are largely negative, dysfunctional and symptomatic of management failure. They may also believe that the misuse of power can lead to many negative outcomes. These may include time and energy being wasted in political power games, personality clashes, difficult negotiations between different interest groups in organizations, unthinking obedience to dominant leaders, back-stabbing, smear campaigns, victimization of minority groups, the creation of toxic corporate cultures, unethical business practices and fraud, lying and deception. However, as suggested earlier, power and politics can also be regarded as natural and inevitable facts of life in organizations, as individuals and groups seek to gain influence and control over finite resources in order to achieve their objectives. Consequently, it can be argued that some power conflicts are inevitable and even necessary for groups and organizations to function effectively, and to remain energetic and creative. Having said this, there certainly is a Janus-like quality to power and politics (Table 7.1).[1]

Table 7.1   The two faces of power and politics

Positive	Negative
Assertive	Domineering
Social	Unsocial
Influential	Coercive
Persuasive	Exploitative
Inspiring	Brute force
Win–win	Win–lose

Source: Adapted from McClelland (1975).

Which of the 'light' and 'dark' sides of power and politics we choose to operate within is dependent on our personal intentions and goals, because both are neutral concepts. How we actually use these will be influenced by our personalities, our perceptions of what constitutes effective leadership/management, the culture of the organizations we work for and the habitual leadership and management practices of the people we work with. However, as we have seen throughout this book, to become a more powerful leader in modern organizations we have to be prepared to *give power away* and, as far as possible, not use it in a coercive way. David McClelland describes why coercive power is so ineffective in this way:

The negative face of power is characterised by the dominance–submission mode: if I win, you lose. It leads to a simple and direct means of feeling powerful (such as being aggressive). It does not often lead to effective social leadership for the reason that such a person tends to treat other people as pawns. People who feel they are pawns tend to be passive and useless to the leader who gets his satisfaction from dominating them. Slaves are the most inefficient form of labour ever devised by man. If a leader wants to have far-reaching influence, he must make his followers feel powerful and able to accomplish things on their own. Even the most dictatorial leader does not succeed if he has not instilled in at least some of his followers a sense of power and the strength to pursue the goals he has set.
(*McClelland, 1975: 263*)

McClelland made these comments nearly 30 years ago, but they are as relevant today as they were then. In Chapters 1 and 4, we saw that genuine power in modern organizations stems from one's ability to empower others, by giving power away and moving away from a command-and-control leadership/management style. By empowering their followers, leaders actually increase their own power and influence. These two aspects of power are closely related and have an iterative effect on each other: first, we have to acquire it, then give it away to others and, as a result, become more powerful; then give it away again to our followers and so forth. This does not mean that we give up *control*; we still remain in charge, but the locus of control is passed to our employees. However, giving up formal, positional authority can be a very threatening prospect to some old-style leaders and managers. Very few people will voluntarily give up power, particularly if they have fought hard to obtain it during their careers ('Well I did it the hard way and there's no reason why they can't'). They might also be fearful about losing their status, special perks and privileges. Other old-school leader/managers may 'look down' on their followers, believing that they are incapable of being empowered, and do not have the ability to do anything more than simply obey orders. However, this viewpoint runs counter to all the evidence that has been accumulated on high-performing leader/managers and consistently successful organizations over the last 20 years (see Chapters 3, 4, 8 and 9). In the words of Kouzes and Posner:

As we examine powerless and powerful times, we're struck by one clear and consistent message: feeling powerful – literally feeling 'able' – comes from a deep sense of being in control of our lives. When we feel able to control our own destiny, when we believe we're able to mobilize the resources necessary to complete a task, then we persist in our efforts to achieve. But, when we feel that others control us, when we believe that we lack support or resources, we show no commitment to excel (although we may comply). Thus, any leadership practice that increases another's sense of self-confidence, self-determination, and personal effectiveness makes that person feel more powerful and greatly enhances the possibility of success. The leader who is most open to influence, who listens, and who helps others is the leader who is most respected and most effective – not, as

traditional management myth has it, the highly-controlling tough-guy boss [ ] The more people believe that they can influence and control the organization, the greater organizational effectiveness and member performance will be. Shared power results in higher job fulfillment and performance throughout the organization.
(*Abridged from Kouzes and Posner, 1997: 184, 186, 187*)

Furthermore, when we look more closely at the role and use of power in organizations, we find that there are five main sources of power and influence in them:

Referent or personal power

To a large extent, power stems from the image, impressions or perceptions that the people we work with have of us. In turn, these are based on many of the skills, qualities and characteristics of successful leaders and managers identified in Chapters 1–6 and, crucially, how we routinely *present* ourselves to others. These include character, honesty and integrity, agreeableness, the ability to motivate and empower followers, sensitivity to the needs of others, exceptional two-way communication skills, parity and equity, team leadership skills and, perhaps most importantly, the extent to which our actions and deeds match our words. There is an impressive amount of evidence to show that individuals with agreeable, outgoing, ascendant personalities are far more influential than those with disagreeable or toxic personalities (see, for example, Carlopio *et al.*, 2001: 271; Kouzes and Posner, 1997: 190–91). Recall that successful leaders spend a lot of time building up relationships of influence with their peers and subordinates, in and outside work. If you already do these things well, you should already have a considerable amount of personal power and influence. To this, we need to add one additional element, *dependency*. Ultimately, real power derives from our lack of dependency on others and the extent to which people are dependent on us, for support, advice, rewards, knowledge and expertise.

Expert power

As captured in the old saying, 'Knowledge is Power'. This refers to the authority an individual derives from the specific technical expertise and/or professional knowledge they possess. This has become increasingly important in businesses characterized by rapid technological change, and the emergence of knowledge and intellectual capital as important drivers of organizational growth, adaptability and success (and how these can be used as a strategic tool in organizations will be addressed in Chapter 10.) While this can be a significant source of power, it is important that this is not allowed to become our only source of influence, because we might become regarded as a niche player or someone whose opinions might not be sought in areas outside a narrow range of expertise.

Reward power

This arises from the opportunities leaders have to use rewards as a way to influence people (described in detail in Chapter 4). This has some parallels with coercive power, because the threat of removing rewards can be regarded as a form of punishment.

Legitimate and coercive power

One of the most easily recognized and widespread forms of power, this derives from the formal structural power and authority of an office, position or role in an organization. It can have quite remarkable effects on people's perceptions of, and obedience to, authority figures and how they exercise power. For example, in one experiment in the 1960s, a 'guest lecturer' was invited to give presentations to several classes in a British university. He was introduced to each class as 'a student', 'a lecturer', 'a senior lecturer' and as 'a professor'. After each presentation, the members of each class were asked to estimate his height. The same man was perceived as being progressively taller with each 'increase' in his academic status. The 'student' was perceived to be several inches shorter than the 'professor' (Wilson, 1968). Perhaps the two most famous examples of the effects of positional authority on obedience were the Milgram studies at Yale in 1961–2, and the Stanford Prison Experiment, conducted during the summer of 1971. In the first experiment, a laboratory was set up where participants, acting in the role of 'teachers' were told to administer electric shocks to 'learners' who failed to repeat accurately two words that were read to them. The electrical generator had 30 switches, ranging from 'slight shock' (15 volts), through 'severe shock' and up to 'danger: fatal shock'. The last two switches, at 430–50 volts, were labelled 'XXX'. They were told that their patients were strapped into a chair in an adjacent sealed room, and to increase the shock level each time they got an answer wrong. What was remarkable about this experiment was that 65 per cent of the participants in the study obeyed orders to administer the shocks and, when instructed by the experimenter, compliantly delivered the maximum possible and, in real life, potentially lethal, dose of 450 volts. No participant in the experiment stopped before they had reached 300 volts, and most continued administering shocks even when they could hear their victims writhing in agony. Of course, this was a set-up; no actual electric shocks were administered, but the participants did not know this. Before Milgram conducted this experiment he had asked mental health professionals to estimate what proportion of people would administer apparently dangerous levels of shock. The consensus was 1 to 2 per cent (Milgram, 1963). This study was replicated over a 25-year period, from 1961 to 1985, with similar results reported in Australia, South Africa and several European countries.

In the second experiment (in many respects the forerunner of reality TV shows like *Big Brother* and *Survivor*), the participants were divided into two groups, 'guards' and 'prisoners', in a realistic mock-up of a prison, and instructed to role-play as if it was the real thing. Nine students were 'arrested' at their homes, taken to 'jail', strip-searched and processed as if they really were prisoners. The 'guards' were given full authority to set the prison rules and allocate punishments for infractions by the 'prisoners'. Soon, they were routinely humiliating the prisoner group in an effort to break their will. After the guards had put down a prisoner protest on day two, they steadily increased their coercive tactics and dehumanization of the prisoners, with the worst instances of abuse taking place at night when the guards thought the staff running the experiment were not watching them (by, for example, making prisoners clean out the toilets with their bare hands). What is most interesting about this experiment, which formed the basis of the 2002 German film, *Das Experiment*, was that all the participants were put through a barrage of psychological tests during the initial screening process, and had been judged to be the most normal, average and healthy members of an original group of 70 students. And yet, when given role power and legitimation of their authority, these apparently normal people started behaving like sadistic monsters within a very short time. Even after three decades, the creator of this experiment still expresses surprise at how willingly and enthusiastically the students took on the guard roles, observing that, 'within a few days, the role dominated the person. They became real guards and real prisoners'. So disturbing was the experiment that he cancelled it after just six days, rather than allowing it to run for the planned 14 days (Zimbardo, 1999). It has never been repeated.

These three examples highlight the influence that legitimate or positional power can have on people's behaviour, although it is important to emphasize that formal authority of this kind is quite different from leadership. And, as the last two examples show, legitimate power is often associated with coercive power. This refers to the use of exclusion, threats, sanctions, pain and punishment to influence people's behaviour which, as history has shown, have all too often been used for truly monstrous reasons (adapted from French and Raven, 1959; Carlopio, 2001: 260–80).

Which forms of power are the most effective ones to use? One of the best-known large-scale studies of the way 750 managers use power revealed that they typically used seven influencing strategies when dealing with their bosses, subordinates and co-workers. In order of popularity, these were (adapted from Kipnis, 1984):

- using reason, data or logic ('expert'),
- friendliness and assertiveness ('referent'),
- forming coalitions with others ('referent'),
- bargaining and/or negotiation ('expert', 'rewards' and 'referent'),
- ordering compliance ('legitimate', 'coercive' and 'rewards'),
- gaining the support of a higher authority ('legitimate'),
- sanctions or punishments ('legitimate' and 'coercive').

In a similar vein, Hughes and colleagues (1999) cite the example of the fictional but iconic leader, Jean-Luc Picard. Captain Picard normally used referent and expert power to influence his subordinates. However, during crises or emergencies, he did occasionally use legitimate and coercive power. On very rare occasions, he used reward power to get his own way with a recalcitrant member of his crew. There is considerable evidence to support the view that logic and reason are the most effective power strategies. Leader/managers who use information, facts and data to support their decisions are rated far more highly by their subordinates, when compared to those who use either coercive or legitimate power to force through their ideas. Those who consistently use these two strategies have less motivated, more stressed and poorer performing employees. Those who habitually use force, coercion or Machiavellian strategies to drive through their decisions also end up making more bad decisions than good ones (Schmidt and Kipnis, 1987; Kipnis and Schmidt, 1983).

Coercive and legitimate power strategies also act as extrinsic motivators. We saw in Chapter 4 that these are the least effective ways of motivating people because, over time, they diminish the capacity of individuals to change, improve and develop *themselves*. High intrinsic motivation is one of the primary drivers of both individual and organizational excellence. Further support for this position can be found in numerous research experiments on small work groups. For example, in one study by Kipnis, work groups were divided into two sub-groups. The first were given the freedom to make influential decisions about their work tasks, and the other group were prohibited from doing this.

The managers of the powerless groups reported that their employees were not motivated to work hard, were unsuitable for promotion, and evaluated their overall work performance less favourably than the leaders of the empowered work groups (Kipnis and Schmidt, 1983). Hence, while coercive or Machievellian power may have to be used in emergency or life-threatening situations, in most organizational contexts its use must be the last resort for a leader/manager because it is the most ineffective way of influencing others. Effective leader/managers use referent and expert power as much as possible, but will occasionally draw on the other three if the situation demands it.

> You do not lead by hitting people over the head – that's assault, not leadership.
> (*General Dwight D. Eisenhower, Supreme Allied Commander during World War II*)

In summary, leaders and managers have a simple choice to make. Either they can hoard and use power for their own ends, or they can give it away to their followers in pursuit of collective goals and objectives. This choice will be governed to some extent by their beliefs about their employees, and whether they have a Theory X or a Theory Y view of human nature (described in Chapter 4). If they have a positive and altruistic view of human nature, they will trust their employees with more power and more responsibility to take charge of their jobs and work tasks. Granting power to others is one way of turning passive 'workers' into self-managing employees, and enabling them to exercise power, choice and discretion in the things they do. If leaders and managers have a more negative and cynical Theory X view of their employees, they can look forward to spending much of their valuable work time issuing orders, sorting out mistakes, putting out fires and managing passive, underperforming and demotivated employees. Ultimately, we all have to make personal choices about how we exercise the power we have been granted, but it is worth asking yourself these questions: in your heart, which approach do you believe is likely to produce the most beneficial results, for you, the people you lead and the organization you work for? Do you believe that your employees will perform better if they are (a) involved in decision making and truly empowered, or (b) simply exhibiting robotic compliance to your authority?

Dealing with toxic employees and politicized organizations

> One ought to be both feared and loved, but as it is difficult for the two to go together, it is much safer to be feared than loved . . . for love is held by a

chain of obligation which, men being selfish, is broken whenever it serves their purpose: but fear is maintained by a dread of punishment that never fails.
(*Niccolò Machiavelli*, The Prince)

In the preceding section and Chapter 1 it was suggested that most managers and professionals have great respect for leaders who do not engage in 'Machiavellian' politics and who exude professional trust, integrity, empathy and reliability. As a general rule this is true, but, at some point in our working lives, we will come across truly toxic individuals whose only mission in life is to impose their overbearing egos on everyone around them, bully their staff and treat their subordinates badly. At other times, we may also find ourselves working in highly politicized organizations. How can we deal with these situations? First, recall what we discovered about toxic personalities and bullies in Chapter 1:

> [Bullies] exhibit most of the following traits: impatience, arrogance, perfectionism, defensiveness, rigidity, bluntness and a keen ability to hold grudges. People who are tyrants and bullies in adulthood became little tyrants and bullies during their formative years [and] many childhood bullies do then evolve into cunning and manipulative managers. They are likely to be intelligent, but use this entirely for their own ends and their own self-aggrandizement. They have no empathy with other people and any decisions they make are driven by one consideration, 'What's in this for me?' They will utilize an autocratic management style on their subordinates but behave compliantly towards their superiors. They will often lack a sense of humour and take themselves and their own opinions *very* seriously. Some toxic personalities may become fully-fledged psychopaths. To be labelled psychopathic, an individual needs to display 10 out of 16 psychopathological tendencies. These are selfishness, callousness, remorseless use of others, lying, cunning, failure to accept responsibility for actions, extreme egotism, extreme sense of self-worth, emotional instability, antisocial tendencies, need for constant stimulation, behavioural and emotional problems in childhood, juvenile delinquency, irresponsibility, unrealistic long-term goals and a sexually deviant or promiscuous lifestyle.

There are several practical insights that can be drawn from this extract. First, we are better people than the bully or domineering boss. Second, we do not have to accept their abuse of power and we must not acquiesce to it. If we do, this will only encourage repetitions of this kind of behaviour. Third, we can be assertive and stand up to it, because most bullies are revealed to be cowards when they are challenged. We can tell the person in question how we feel about their behaviour, why it is unacceptable and why we expect their behaviour to change. This should be done calmly and without aggression, because they thrive on the emotional anxiety and discomfort of others. If this approach does not produce the desired change, and there are no other options (such as resigning and moving to another organization), it may be time to employ some Machiavellian techniques. Several books appeared in the

1990s and early 2000s with the stated intention of 'putting Machiavelli back into business'. These include Grifin's *Machiavelli on Management: Playing and Winning the Corporate Power Game*, McAlpine's *The New Machiavelli: The Art of Politics in Business*, *The 48 Laws of Power* by Robert Greene, and some tongue-in-cheek advice from a real-life coup leader, André de Guillaume, in *How to Rule the World: A Handbook for the Aspiring Dictator*. These authors suggest a number of more devious and underhand strategies that employees can use to achieve their ambitions within political organizational cultures. It has to be said that some of their suggestions are rather nebulous or vague, and a few may even be illegal in some countries. However, an abridged selection of the best of these and a few of mine are presented below.

Power is a social game

The word 'game' is often used synonymously with power and politics, and for a very good reason. Like chess, this is a game which must be played with a clear idea of your personal strategies (and alternative strategies) and a good understanding of what your opponent's strategies are likely to be (and where their strong and weak points are). Your energy must be focused at all times on the best strategies to use, as well as the personality of your opponents. To use power well, we have to be both master players and master psychologists, recognizing the needs and motivations of others, while at the same time not becoming emotionally involved with them. An understanding of these hidden needs and motives is the greatest power-tool that we can ever possess, because we will then be able to appeal to, and make use of, the self-interests of others while pursuing our own goals and objectives.

Guard your reputation

Your personal reputation (how others see you) is the keystone of your power. Once this slips, you are vulnerable. Make your reputation unassailable. Maintain a professional (but friendly) space between yourself and work colleagues. As a former mentor of mine once observed, 'I look at it this way. You don't have to make love with these people, you don't have to socialize with them after work or be their lifelong buddies. I deliberately maintain a space between myself and everyone else who works here. What you have to try to do is develop good working relationships and maintain a professional, impartial approach with everyone, even if they do sometimes behave like ******s.'

Praise your leaders

Or, at least, do not criticize them by name in public. Sooner or later, someone will report back to them what you have said. Act as the perfect courtier; yield to superiors and flatter them when the opportunity arises. Don't ever upstage them in public. Learn about their private interests and personal goals. Support their ideas in public, but offer critical advice, tactfully, in private. Your power and influence will also increase if you are willing 'to go the extra mile' for them, and help them out with problems and difficulties they may encounter at work.

Make people dependent on you

To maintain your independence, you must be *needed* by other people. The more you are relied on, the more freedom, influence and power you will have. Cultivate relationships at every opportunity – with your peers, your bosses and with your clients. Act as a mentor for junior staff. Be a team player and share in your colleagues' accomplishments. Support their ideas and suggestions and be responsive to their problems, without endangering your own interests. Be seen as someone whom people can chat with confidentially about work issues. Be honest with the people who do rely on you, but keep your cards close to your chest. Don't reveal more than you need to. Find allies and mingle – isolation is dangerous. Work on people's hearts *and* minds. If you have to ask other people for help, appeal to their self-interest. Try to find or uncover something that will benefit them if they help you. Professional politicians know this as the 'reciprocity strategy'.

Avoid people who are negative, self-obsessed, unhappy or unlucky

Associate with people who make you feel good and valued, or whose positive reputation will reflect well on you. Avoid people who are always negative, self-obsessed or just interested in their own agendas. But try to deal professionally and calmly with second-rate, difficult or toxic employees at all times.

Be calm and objective

Power is amoral. Your focus must always be on your opponent's actions and strategies, and what these mean. Anger and emotion are counterproductive because, as we saw in Chapter 3, they cloud reason and clarity of thought. Try to remain calm and objective at all times.

Make use of the stress diffusion techniques described in Chapter 2. Remember that other people cannot *make* you angry, only you can allow yourself to *become* angry. Learn from previous occasions when you have allowed emotions to damage your case and don't repeat them. Train yourself to take nothing personally and never show defensiveness or vulnerability. If you do, you might expose an Achilles heel that your opponent can strike at. But, if you can make your opponent lose control of his temper, you will gain an enormous advantage over him.

Don't say more than you have to (and don't be a smartarse)

The more you talk, or seek to hog the limelight, the less effective you will be. Only talk when you have to and when you really have something valuable, insightful or pertinent to contribute to discussions or decision-making processes at work. Use logic, data and facts to support your position, not bluster, polemic or personal opinions. Whenever you can, let your actions persuade others, because they will often speak louder than any words you use or any arguments that you win. Nobody likes to feel less intelligent than another person. The trick is to make other people feel smarter than you. Once convinced of this, they will not suspect that you may have ulterior motives or be a threat to them. Never say or do anything that could be held against you. Control how you use valuable information. If you can act on information before an opponent knows about it, you can often gain an advantage.

Conceal your intentions and don't take sides in haste

If you are going to create a stir, keep people in the dark. Do not reveal your intentions in advance. Don't be predictable all the time and, occasionally, surprise and confound your colleagues. The only cause you should concentrate on is your own. If you have to choose sides, take your time to evaluate carefully which will be the winning one. In this context, recall the age-old adage cited earlier, 'Fools rush in to take sides'.

Don't fight battles you can't win and ensure that you crush your enemies

Surrender the occasional battle if you have to, but stay focused on winning the war. Concentrate your energies and resources on important victories, not the pyrrhic ones. Life is short, opportunities are few and you only have so much energy to expend in locking horns with people at work. If you want to neutralize an opponent, you must know as much as possible about them. Everyone has weaknesses or skeletons in the cupboard: find out what these are, but only use them when the time is right. Timing is everything and support is vital. Make sure that you have enough supporters to support the removal or deposition of your enemy before this is proposed. Make sure that you crush them completely, or they may come back to get you at some point in the future. As the master of political skulduggery Machievelli once observed, 'when he seizes power, the new ruler must determine all the injuries he will need to inflict. He must inflict them once and for all.'

Summary

Having described some Machiavellian power strategies it's important to emphasize that most people would feel very uncomfortable being involved in these kinds of power plays and political mind-games, if they were routine features of their daily working lives (professional politicians excepted). While there may be times when your survival, or the survival of a project you are involved in, forces you to make use of the 'dark side' of power and politics, they are ultimately self-destructive. Such behaviour and strategies will, sooner or later, involve cheating and lying, as well as deceitful and malicious behaviour towards others. In time, these will eventually lead to personal or corporate self-destruction (an issue we will return to in Chapter 12, in the context of the collapse of companies like Enron and Worldcom). Furthermore, engagement with the dark side of power and politics uses up a tremendous amount of time, energy and resources, be this at the individual, group or organizational level. These are precious commodities in most organizations these days, and highly politicized working cultures are characterized by time wasting, infighting, backbiting and cheap point scoring, rather than active engagement with the productive and creative aspects of organizational leadership and management.

Managing conflict

Many managers seem to think it is impossible to tackle anything or anyone head-on, even in business. By contrast, we at Intel believe that it is the essence of corporate health to bring a problem out into the open as soon as possible, even if this entails a confrontation. Dealing with conflicts lies at the heart of managing any business. As a result, facing issues about which there is disagreement can be avoided only at the manager's peril. Workplace politicking grows quietly in the dark; like mushrooms, neither can stand the light of day.
(*Andy Grove*, High Output Management, *1984*)

We've seen that power and politics are natural and inevitable facts of organizational life, as individuals and groups seek to acquire influence and gain resources in order to achieve their objectives. The same principle applies to conflict, which is often the natural outcome of personal, factional or departmental power battles in organizations. It too can be regarded as a normal feature of life in all organizations. In some circumstances, it may even be essential for groups to function effectively and to remain energetic and creative because, without some degree of conflict, nothing would ever change in organizations. What leaders and managers have to strive for is an *optimum* level of conflict, where there is 'enough conflict to prevent stagnation, stimulate creativity, allow tensions to be released, and initiate the seeds for change, yet not so much as to be disruptive or to deter the coordination of activities' (Robbins *et al.*, 2001: 510).[2] In the same way that conflict ('competition') between firms promotes innovation and change, it can also be a useful management strategy within organizations, so long as it is managed in the right way. In the context of innovation in companies, this has been described as managing the process of 'creative abrasion' (Leonard and Strauss, 1999). As Nonaka has also suggested,

> Employee dialogues can – indeed should – involve considerable conflict and disagreement. It is precisely such conflict that pushes employees to question existing premises and make sense of their experiences in a new way. 'When people's rhythms are out of sync, quarrels occur and it's hard to bring them together,' acknowledges a deputy manager for advanced technology development at Canon. 'Yet if the group's rhythms are completely in unison from the beginning, it's also difficult to achieve good results'.
> (*Nonaka, 1991: 104*)

The former CEO of Nissan, Carlos Gohn, who was instrumental in turning the company's fortunes around during the 1990s, shared this approach to conflict. He was widely regarded as a good listener and someone who was able to get traditionally compliant staff at all levels to look critically at every aspect of the company's performance (operational, organizational, strategic and interdepartmental) even if this created conflict between junior and senior staff who had been long accustomed to the hierarchical and top-down power relationships of Japanese corporations. The consequence of this approach was the creation of hundreds of new ideas and innovations to improve the company's performance, and a fundamental shift in the company's mind-set during the late 1990s and early 2000s.

Hence, while *some* conflict may be useful in organizations, there are many potential sources of destructive conflict in organizations. These include interpersonal differences, group conflicts, poor communication, task and process conflicts, gender and cultural clashes, status distinctions (for example, between line-workers and management), interdepartmental rivalries, power differentials between groups of employees, discrimination, inequitable reward systems and so forth. So what strategies can be employed in order to maintain a manageable or optimum level of conflict or competition, while ensuring that excessive or toxic levels of these do not disrupt the workflow of a group or department?

There are a number of conflict management and resolution styles that can be used at work. More importantly, you already possess a number of other skills that are useful for dealing with conflict. The most potent of these are the communication skills covered in Chapter 3, although the leadership skills described in Chapter 1 also play an important role in conflict management, as do the team management skills identified in Chapter 5. The communication skills that can be employed when dealing with conflict include active listening, not interrupting other people while they are talking, summarizing others' contributions, looking for win–win rather than win/lose solutions, focusing on issues rather than personalities, being aware of hostile non-verbal behaviour, coping with and diffusing emotional outbursts and anger and, most importantly, not behaving in a domineering or hectoring manner.

There are a few other techniques that can also be used in situations that are characterized by a disagreement or conflict. Invariably, these are accompanied by a lot of emotional baggage, including resentment, fear, passion and anger. This means that we should all remember to think before acting, particularly if we are going to be involved in a conflict between individuals or groups. Do you fully understand what the underlying issues and facts are? How did the conflict arise? What resolutions to the conflict might there be? We then have to get people's adult minds refocused on the task at hand and to diffuse tensions as quickly as possible. This can be achieved through the effective use of questions, a technique I've come to think of as the 'Captain Angry and Captain Zen' approach to dealing with situations that have the potential to degenerate into open conflict. Here are some examples of this technique in action:

Captain Angry	*Captain Zen*
It would cost too much	Why?
	Compared to what?
	If we could afford it, would you support this proposal?
	Is there a cheaper option?

Captain Angry	Captain Zen
It will never work	Why?
	What would it take to make it work?
	Can you suggest an alternative solution that could work?
You can't do it that way	What would happen if we did?
	How could we do it that way if we had to?
We've tried that already	What was the outcome?
(. . . it didn't work)	(. . . why did it go wrong?)
This is the only way to do it	It may be – but are there any other options that we should consider, before making this decision?
It should be done this way	Why?
	Is that the best option?
	Are there any other options?
I don't understand this proposal	Can you be more specific?
	Which parts aren't you clear about?
I can't/won't do that	What would make you willing to do it?
	What would you do instead?
Your idea is stupid	What, specifically, don't you like about this idea?
	What alternatives to this idea could you suggest?
This is a disaster	What caused it?
	What will make it better?
This is my position and I'm not budging	Well, I'm sorry you feel that way, but we'll now have to put this to a vote*

*Only if you know you have enough votes to carry your decision through.

If you are going to be involved in negotiations that have the potential to become heated, you'll need to assess the situation calmly and objectively, collect as much accurate information as you can about the problem or issue, identify what you want and what your objectives are. Decide early on where you can compromise (concessions that do not destroy your position) and look for compromise (win–win) solutions. This means that you *must* look at the problem or issue from your own perspective, the perspective of your opponent (who may well be look-ing for your vulnerable points) and, if possible, from the viewpoint of a neutral third party. You then need to decide, before negotiating, where you might be able to accommodate someone else's point of view, where you can collaborate with them, or where you can give something up. This is certainly harder work than simply imposing decisions on others through coercive or legitimate means, but the outcomes are always more successful. It is vitally important to remem-ber that, eventually, 'the truth will out' and the only way to come to the right decisions on any issue in organizations is through questioning and reasoned argument. These should be backed up by facts (not opin-ions) and presented in a manner that recognizes that others may have strong views of their own, even if they might be wrong.

> If you ridicule an idea – the person feels ridiculed.
> If you attack an idea – the person feels attacked.
> If you dismiss an idea – the person feels dismissed.
> If you ignore an idea – the person feels ignored.
> (*Gould and Gould*, From No to Yes, *1991*)

Does this mean that we have to 'waste time' dealing with ideas that we consider to be useless? One of the main reasons why conflict occurs is that all humans are raised, educated and trained to put critical or eval-uative thinking before creative thinking. In Chapter 3, we saw how people often categorize ideas and concepts instantly, and then slap 'accept' or 'reject' labels on these. Hence other people's proposals become 'right' or 'wrong', 'perfect' or 'useless', 'good' or 'bad'. However, reality is always more complex than this. Very few ideas are ever perfect, including our own, and very few are completely useless. Most ideas have some merits, even if they are not immediately appar-ent. Therefore, the creative solution is to build on what is good about a particular idea, and then try to overcome its shortcomings. In the long run, this approach can actually save us a great deal of time and effort because we will have enabled others to learn for themselves what is good, and not so good, about their ideas or proposals.

In almost all conflicts, people become angry because they believe that they are about to lose something that is important to them. This is then interpreted as an attack on their 'territory', not in a geographical sense, but in a psychological one. If people believe that their status, freedom, knowledge, expertise, power, control or reputations are under threat, they will become fiercely defensive. This real or imagined threat can also set in process the 'fight/flight' reaction to stress, with its attendant nega-tive consequences. Trying to avoid a difficult situation or serious conflict will not make it go away. Escalating the level of conflict, by digging our heels in, will only make things worse. Hence a joint solution can only be achieved if the threat can be identified and recognized. If it isn't, the conflict will continue and a win/lose 'solution' will be the only possible outcome. The main problem with win/lose outcomes is that they will almost inevitably leave some people feeling disillusioned or angry, although sometimes this is unavoidable. And there will be occasions when conflict gets out of hand and cannot be resolved. If you find yourself in this kind of situation (and feel that you are getting absolutely nowhere), and if others are behaving in an aggressive and hostile manner towards you, it may be necessary to warn them that you will leave, and only return when they have had time to cool down. It is important to say this calmly and politely.

Conclusion

In summary, successful political strategists are capable of taking calculated gambles that lead to successful results. They learn quickly how to use, or change, organizational rules to their best advantage. They acquire, use and share information to further their interests and those of their followers. They exploit opportunities that come their way, but also have the capacity to create these. As a result, they are better able to compete and win, and achieve their objectives. And, while they may be highly driven individuals, they do not step over the line into unethical leadership or business practices. They give power away to their followers and this, in turn, enhances their power bases. The use of power and politics is a complex art, not an exact science, and there is no single best power and political strategy, or conflict management style, to adopt. Which one(s) you choose to use is dependent on and shaped by your personality and leadership/management style, the kind of organization you work for, its political culture, and the nature of the problems or conflicts that you routinely deal with. Having said this, it is important that leaders and managers work on developing all their power bases (referent, expert, reward, legitimate and coercive), because each one will be needed at some point in their careers. The same principle applies to conflict management. This reinforces an important point made about leadership in the Preface and Chapter 1: the more 'tools' we have at our disposal, the more effective we will be in dealing with any problems that arise in our organizations. The more strategies we have prepared in advance, the greater our chances of success; the fewer the strategies, the more limited our options and chances of success will be.

Power tends to corrupt and absolute power corrupts absolutely.
(*Lord Acton, British peer*)

Most powerful is he who has himself in his own power.
He who has great power should use it lightly.
(*Seneca, Roman senator and historian*)

Exercise 7.2

Having read through this chapter, think about how you can make use of any new insights you may have acquired when handling power, politics and conflict in the future.

Insight	Strategy to implement this
1.	
2.	
3.	
4.	
5.	◆

Notes

1   Janus was the two-headed (or two-faced) Roman deity, who also had two sets of eyes, one pair focusing on challenges that lay ahead and the other focusing on what lay behind.
2   This idea has parallels with the satisfaction/dissatisfaction process, described in Chapter 3.

8   Leading organizational and cultural change

Objectives

To define change, vision and mission.

To describe why the ability to manage organizational and cultural change is a key leadership/management competency.

To examine the principal elements of successful change management strategies.

To revisit the main qualities and characteristics of transformational leaders.

To look at the reasons why employees resist change and how learning theory can help in the planning and management of change.

To present two real-life examples of organizational and cultural change, one successful and one unsuccessful, and the practical lessons that can be drawn from these.

Introduction: 'May you live in interesting times'

We tend to meet any new situation by re-organising, and a wonderful method it can be for creating the illusion of progress while producing inefficiency and demoralisation.
(*Gaius Petronius, Roman general, 66*)

There is nothing more difficult to carry out, nor more doubtful of success, nor more dangerous to handle, than to initiate a new order of things. Because the innovator has for enemies all those who have done well under the old conditions, and lukewarm defenders in those who may do well under the new.
(*Niccolò Machiavelli, politician, 1513*)

As the two quotations above indicate, our predecessors have always had difficulties coping with change, even though this has been *the* defining feature of human history and the evolution of modern civilizations over the last 10 000 years, and even more so over the last 200 years. The big difference today, when compared with the agrarian, industrial, scientific and political revolutions of the past, is the sheer pace of change in contemporary societies and organizations. Whenever groups of employees in industrialized or industrializing countries are asked to describe what most characterizes life in their organizations today, their answers invariably include 'change'. This ubiquitous word is derived from the Old French word, *changier*, and is defined here as the process of making any alterations, transformations or modifications to the way an organization or its employees operate. Almost all managers and professionals can recall personal experiences and anecdotes about change, re-engineering, restructuring, downsizing or mergers in the organizations they have worked for. This is not surprising, given that the last decade of the 20th century was variously described as 'the age of chaos', 'the tech-decade', 'the decade of blur', 'the age of surprises' and 'the age of uncertainty'. These surprises and uncertainties include globalization, the breathtaking pace of technological innovation, the ongoing redefinition of the roles and activities of organizations, employers, trades unions and employees, the end of 'jobs for life' and job insecurity amongst managerial and professional employees, economic and political instabilities in most regions of the world, growing ethical and ecological challenges in business, the financial meltdown of many East Asian economies in the late 1990s, and the emergence of China as an economic superpower in the 2000s. More recently, we have also witnessed the tragic events of 11 September 2001, subsequent terrorist atrocities and the impact of the second Gulf War and its aftermath in the Middle East.

In this fast-changing and uncertain world, only a handful of companies now appear to have what it takes to thrive over long periods of time. For example, the Dow Jones Index was created in 1896 with 30 listed companies. Just one of the original 30 is still in existence: General Electric, the corporate behemoth founded by Thomas Edison in 1892. The Helsinki Exchange was created in 1921 and only one of the 12 companies that formed the first group of listed companies is still in existence: Nokia. Furthermore, the life cycles of many medium-sized and large companies are getting shorter year by year. A survey by *Fortune* compared the US companies that had been on their 1970 'Top 500' list and discovered that one-third had disappeared by 1985. Ten years later they compared the companies on their 1980 'Top 500' list and found that two-thirds of these companies had disappeared by 1995. More recently, we have also witnessed a growing number of spectacular corporate collapses. These included dozens of companies from the dotcom collapse of April 2001, and Worldcom, Enron, Tycho, Arthur Andersen, K-Mart and Global Crossing in the USA; UMP,

Ansett, HIH, One.Tel, New Tel and The Mayne Group in Australia, Boo.com and several other companies in the UK, and Parmalat in Italy during 2000–4.

As we will see in Chapter 11, the speed of change in organizations is going to accelerate at an even faster pace over the next 20 years, driven by an explosion of dazzling new technologies, the rapid globalization of trade and commerce and the emergence of newly industrialized nations. These developments mean that very few business organizations can avoid change, and any company in the private sector that thinks it is secure probably has a short lifespan ahead of it. Whether the organization is small, medium or large, perpetual change and organizational development is now the name of the game. As Martin Bollinger, managing director of Booz, Allen and Hamilton, observed in 1998, 'It is difficult to think of a company being able to maintain a posture where they are not trying to change and trying to reinvent themselves. I just can't imagine a situation where a CEO could stand there and say, "Nope, we're pretty happy with things the way they are" ' (cited by Cornell, 1998b). Change is now so pervasive that just making incremental, ad hoc reactive changes is no longer sufficient for many businesses.

The key to success now, and in the future, will be the ability to make continual, proactive changes, and to create change for others to follow (rather than playing the energy-sapping game of perpetual catch-up with other organizations). Change must also be ingrained in the mindsets of employees and their working practices, and be an integral part of organizational cultures and operational thinking. Hence the ability to lead organizational and cultural change is one of the most important skills that leaders and managers must possess. However, many don't receive any formal education or guidance in the complexities of managing change. Almost all of the MBAs and other professionals I've been involved with over the last decade have consistently indicated that they have had to 'muddle through', 'learn by experience', 'hire some consultants' or, in many cases, simply *react* to change rather than initiating and controlling it. Therefore it comes as little surprise to discover that around 75 per cent of all attempts at corporate change either fail or do not achieve their original objectives (Kotter, 1995). A study by Ernst & Young in 1996, of 584 US, Canadian, Japanese and German companies, revealed that less than 20 per cent felt that they were able to sustain long-lasting change management strategies. A six-year longitudinal study, by the Centre for Corporate Change at the University of New South Wales in Australia, revealed that 67 per cent of change management initiatives had suffered 'at least one major setback' that prevented the changes being implemented in the way that had been originally planned (Simons, 2000).

Another study, by AT Kearney in 2000, reported that one in five of 294 medium and large European companies rated their change management programmes as being successful. Sixty-three per cent had made some temporary improvements, but failed to sustain these, and 17 per cent had made no improvements at all. An even more dramatic finding concerned the use of external consultants by these companies. Just one in five of the companies that had successfully managed change had used external consultants, and then only for limited or specific purposes such as the introduction of new IT systems. In contrast, four out of five companies that had failed to implement successful change used external consultants. The AT Kearney study observed that 'The largest gap between companies that were good and bad at change arose because some learnt from change and institutionalised that knowledge, building it into their cultures and performance assessments. Because such companies learn, their changes are more likely to be sustainable' (*The Economist*, 2000). The importance of organizational learning, within the context of perpetual change, will be discussed further in Chapter 9.

The obvious question raised by these findings is 'Why do so many change management initiatives fail?' The reasons for this are simultaneously simple and complex. First, when people talk about 'the management of change', what they are usually thinking about is changing 'the organization' in some way. What they often fail to grasp is that what is really going to be changed, in any change management process, is *the people who live and work inside the organization*. An organization, as such, does not exist. Sure, it has buildings, technology systems, products and services, customers and clients, corporate logos and a market presence of some description; but, at the most basic level, an organization is no more or less than a group of people working together. Take the people away and the organization ceases to exist. This seems such an obvious point to make, and yet when we look at the primary reasons for the failure of change management programmes over the last 30 years it is always because the organizations' employees were not involved in, or not engaged with, or did not believe in, the changes that were being pushed through by the leadership of their organizations, *every single time, without exception*. By far the most complex, unpredictable and yet important drivers of organizational change are the employees. However, as we will see shortly, most adult human beings (and, by extension, most organizations) are psychologically conservative and that is why they will often resist change, unless we can provide them with good reasons and incentives to embrace new ways of thinking and working.

Secondly, managing change (particularly from a standing start and/or in large, bureaucratic organizations) is time-consuming, complex and difficult. It requires the effective use of many of the leadership and people management skills described in Chapters 1–7, as well as some new ones that will be outlined in this chapter. It also requires the ability to implement a series of strategic initiatives and processes, often simultaneously and systemically. Far too many books on change management, particularly those written by consultants, portray the management of change, in a 'paint-by-numbers' fashion, as a relatively straightforward exercise. It isn't, and anyone who says that it is easy is misleading you. John Pettigrew neatly captured the complexities of this process when he observed, 'The management of change can be compared to juggling lots of balls in the air while the platform on which the juggler stands is moving all the time. Drop one of the balls or forget to pick one up in the first place and the effect will be disastrous' (Pettigrew, 1985: 70). In a nutshell, this is why leading organizational and cultural change is extremely difficult, and why we will be spending some time examining why all change management programmes must first focus on *how individuals habitually interpret and react to the prospect of change in their organizational contexts*.

Leading organizational and cultural change: the theory

> People talk a lot about 'the management of change' these days. The reality is that much of this 'change' is so badly 'managed' that it often produces demoralisation, fear and resistance amongst employees.
> (*Tom Peters, 1992*)

A staggering quantity of research has been generated on leading and managing change. While preparing this book, I came across more than 200 books and about 1000 articles or websites that had 'change', 'cultural change', 'renewal', 'restructuring', 're-engineering', or 'organizational development' in their titles. There are at least 40 models/frameworks of change management in this literature, although many of these echo each other and/or overlap to a large extent. Despite this voluminous output, and more than 30 years' research on change in organizations, very few people would agree that there is a widely accepted and foolproof formula for leading and managing organizational and cultural change. However, there are very clear indications of the components that do need to be in place when managing change processes, and these are described below. The following sections represent a synthesis of these 40 models/frameworks, as well as numerous theories about leading and managing change, spanning organizational theory, management studies, the sociology of organizations and occupational psychology.

In addition to these insights, several hundred of my MBA students have looked at change management programmes (CMPs) in more than 70 organizations between 1997 and 2004. These include household-name companies, such as General Electric, 3m, Hewlett-Packard, IBM, Continental Airlines, Harley-Davidson, BHP-Billiton, BP and Royal Dutch Shell, and more than 30 Australian private and public sector organizations, who have experienced both incremental and radical changes in recent times. By reviewing the change management programmes in these companies, and after many hours of class discussion and debate, an 11-point template for successful change management has been developed. This has also been road-tested in conjunction with two companies who collaborated in the Australian Institute of Management/Harvard Business School's Action Learning Programmes during 2003–4, and during several Executive MBA change management projects during 2002–3. This template contains the key elements and components that were *always* in place during successful change management programmes and, conversely, often not in place when change failed:

- the presence of energetic and committed transformational leaders;
- a vision, or a clear sense of direction/purpose, or a set of clear and well-articulated goals and objectives for the company to travel towards (it doesn't matter which);
- an appreciation among organizational leaders of why there is always resistance to change, at the individual, group and organizational level, and an understanding of strategies that could be used to overcome this;
- integrating strategic macro change with the organization's operational culture and the daily working practices of its employees;
- creating a sense of urgency, in order to develop the initial impetus or thrust for change, removing those senior and middle managers who stand in the way of necessary change, and 'getting the right people on the bus';
- developing straightforward, realistic and workable strategies to drive change initiatives throughout all levels of the organization;
- extensive two-way communication with all employees during times of change;
- involving employees, whenever and wherever possible, by giving them as much ownership as possible over change management initiatives and processes;
- celebrating successes and short-term wins, and rewarding employees when they have made changes to their working practices;
- involving external customers and clients in change management initiatives and processes;
- developing an ongoing cultural commitment to continuous change, improvement and learning.

Each of these components is described in more detail below, and then illustrated in practice with two real-life examples of change: Continental Airlines and the Australian Broadcasting Corporation.

The presence of energetic and committed transformational leaders

One of the fellows at the mine said that the guy who took over BHP would need steel balls. They wanted to make sure I had some.
(*Paul Anderson, former CEO of BHP-Billiton, commenting on the gift he received from his employees at the Escondida copper mine in Chile, January 2000*)

In Chapter 1, we saw that transformational leaders seek something much more than mere unthinking obedience and compliance from their followers. Transformational leaders are capable of changing their followers' basic beliefs, values and attitudes in order to get superior levels of achievement out of them. Sometimes described as 'Super-Bosses', they are perceived to lead by virtue of their ability to inspire devotion and extraordinary effort from their followers. These individuals are driven, often from an early age, by a very strong need for achievement and success. They are very self-confident and believe that they can truly make a difference to the world. People usually do what these leaders ask them because they understand something about human behaviour and how to motivate or, if required, manipulate people to do their bidding. They are often regarded as good communicators and storytellers. Transformational leaders are also able to adapt their leadership styles, depending on the circumstances, particularly when they are brought in in the role of trouble-shooters to sort out an organization in crisis. A direct corollary of this is that they have to be fast, proactive learners and good listeners. They also have to adopt a hands-on approach to leadership in these situations. Another characteristic is their ability to ride the white waters of change. This transformational mind-set is absolutely essential these days. When we unpack this mind-set, we discover that it is actually a combination of a number of skills, such as the ability to think long-term, the ability to create visions, effective communication skills, the ability to link strategies with opportunities and, increasingly, systemic and lateral thinking. Transformational business leaders embrace change with enthusiasm. They believe that change is good and inevitable. They have the ability to create an impetus for change. They also recognize that change must be perpetual and not reactive.

Research on the management of change in organizations, and our reviews of numerous change management programmes, indicate that, without the presence of such leaders, successful change is near impossible to achieve. This does not mean that they have to be larger than life, highly paid 'charismatic' leaders brought in from the outside. As Collins has observed:

> Larger than life celebrity leaders, who ride in from the outside are negatively correlated with taking a company from good to great. Ten of eleven good-to-great CEOs came from inside the company, whereas the comparison companies tried outside CEOs six times more often [ ] We also found no systematic pattern linking forms of executive compensation in the process of going from good to great. The idea that the structure of executive compensation is a key driver in corporate performance is simply not supported by the data.
> (*Collins 2001: 10–11*)

Collins and his research colleagues were surprised to find that the leaders of their 'Good-to-Great' companies were not archetypal, high-profile or larger-than-life charismatic personalities (or grossly overpaid for underperformance). They had little in common with the kind of leaders who were so often exalted by the business and financial press of the 1980s and 1990s, and who are still part of the mythology of successful change management. In contrast, their leaders were all modest, self-effacing, quiet and even reserved. In fact, 'They were more like Lincoln and Socrates than Patton or Caesar' (ibid.: 12–13). Something else they all had in common was an unerring ability to diagnose the problems facing their businesses and what their companies' strengths and weaknesses were. They also spent a lot of time 'clean-sweeping' their senior managers and recruiting new people who shared their visions of the future, *before* they set about deciding in which direction they were going take their companies.

Hence any organization (public or private sector) that hopes to change must have some leaders with transformational qualities. In a small enterprise, this may be just the founder of the company. In a medium-sized company, it may be seven or eight people formed into a change management team. In a very large company, it could be 50–100 senior employees. The presence of people who are comfortable with leading the change and committed to its outcomes is important because, while most employers believe 'employee resistance' is the biggest obstacle to change, most employees believe that the biggest problem is 'poor leadership'. In one large survey, the biggest perceived faults of leaders who were unable to manage change were, in ranking order, 'lacking direction, failing to communicate a vision of the future, not matching the vision with organizational processes, failing to lead by example, failing to motivate staff, failing to make unpopular decisions about change, demonstrating inconsistent attitudes to change, and failing to come up with ideas for change' (Waldersee and Griffiths, cited by Gettler, 1998: 16).

A clear sense of direction, or purpose, or a set of clear and well-articulated goals and objectives for the company to travel towards (it doesn't matter which)

> Somebody who can develop a vision of what he or she wants their business unit, their activity to do and be. Somebody who is able to articulate to the entire unit what the business is, and gain through a sharing of discussion – listening and talking – an acceptance of the vision. And, someone who can then relentlessly drive implementation of that vision to a successful conclusion.
> (*Jack Welch, former CEO of General Electric describing his ideal leader*)

> One of the things about leadership is that you cannot be a moderate, balanced, thoughtful, careful articulator of policy. You have to be on the lunatic fringe.
> (*Welch again, talking about the risks that leaders have to take, cited by Lowe, 1998: 72, 86*)

When a team of change leaders has been established, a path to the future has to be identified for the organization. Without this, nothing will ever change and a leader cannot move an organization forward or mobilize its employees, without a clear understanding of the journey they want to embark on. This is usually described as the organization's *vision* and/or *mission*. The word 'vision' is derived from the Latin, *videre*, 'to see'. This was defined in Chapter 1 as 'an apparition of a prophetic, revelational or supernatural nature presented to the mind in a state of heightened spiritual or emotional awareness, a distinct or vivid mental image or concept, insight or foresight, an ability to plan or formulate policy in a far sighted way' (OED website, 2003); more succinctly as 'a realistic, credible and attractive future for an organization' (Bennis and Nanus, 1985: 8) and 'an ideal and unique image of the future' (Kouzes and Posner, 1997: 95). It is defined in this chapter as the articulation of a road, way, path or journey to the future. The word 'mission' is derived from the Latin *missionum*, meaning action, and is defined here as the formal, written articulation of an organization's vision and/or purpose and/or its main strategic goals and objectives.

It is important to emphasize that, whether we call this desired future state the 'vision', the 'mission', the 'direction', the 'purpose', 'a cause' or the 'goals and objectives' really doesn't matter one iota. Many successful transformational leaders use these terms interchangeably and some, like Michael Chaney of the highly successful Australian company Wesfarmers often don't use the word 'vision' at all. This may come as a surprise to those organizational leaders who have spent large sums of money employing consultants and PR companies to craft their vision and mission statements. But the reality is that organizations that manage change successfully attach little importance to vision and mission *statements*. These merely represent the starting point of a long process of perpetual change and evolution. Equally, it doesn't matter where the sense of direction/vision/mission comes from. You may create this yourself, because you have exceptional creative, lateral-thinking and scenario-mapping skills (as described in Chapter 9), or you may develop this in conjunction with a senior change team and/or your employees. However, the following *must* emerge from this process:

- a sense of deep dissatisfaction with the present situation and a clear understanding of how that situation came about,
- the creation of a picture or image of a better future for the organiza-tion to travel towards,
- the identification of the way, road or path to travel down in pursuit of this picture or image of the future,
- a clearly mapped out series of destinations on this journey into the future.

In Chapter 1 we cited some examples of individuals and companies who have created breakthrough visions in the past. Here are a few more.

Frank Whittle

He wrote his original ideas for a jet engine in a school dissertation in the early 1920s. Scientists, engineers and the military in the UK rejected his ideas for more than a decade. With the help of two visionary RAF pilots, and a small investment, their company, Power Jets Limited, was established and a working prototype built in 1937. However, it was only with the outbreak of World War II that his ideas were taken up with enthusiasm by the military and personally backed by Winston Churchill. On 1 May 1941, the first jet plane flew, revolutionizing mili-tary and civil aviation forever.

Frank MacNamara

The first recorded use of credit was in Abyssinnia and Egypt nearly 3000 years ago and, by the early 19th century, goods could be bought 'on credit' in industrializing countries. In 1914, Western Union became the first bank to offer a deferred-payment credit service to customers. However, the modern credit card is a much more recent innovation. MacNamara was dining in a Manhattan restaurant with some clients (including Alfred Bloomingdale) in 1949. The bill arrived and he and his guests realized that they did not have enough money to pay it. Afterwards, he thought about this for a while and, with Bloomingdale, came up with the idea of a network of restaurant charge accounts and a third-party credit company for people dining out in Manhattan. Not surprisingly, this new 'credit card' was called 'The Diners' Club Card'.

By the end of the first year, 200 cards had been issued which were accepted in 27 of New York's finest restaurants. By 1958, there were more than a million cardholders in the USA. American Express and Master Card arrived on the scene in 1966, with Visa following in 1977. There are now more than 140 million individual cardholders in the USA who collectively owe about $US500 billion and, in 2003, paid about one trillion dollars in interest.

Lee Iacocca

He was the architect of one of the most audacious turnarounds in American corporate history, when he saved Chrysler from bankruptcy in the 1980s. Iacocca believes that he has one vision left in him, to get more people using electric bicycles. In his words, 'I founded EV Global Motors because I believe in the future of electric vehicles. I believe that America is ready to take this exciting technology from theory to reality' (cited by Gibney, 1999). His company, EV Global Motors, is planning to sell 50 000 bikes a year in the USA (EV website 30 November 2002). This vision may appear to be ambitious, but there are now huge pressures on all governments to produce cheap non-polluting vehicles, and the electric bike market has grown rapidly in Europe during the early 2000s.

Richard Branson

The pioneer of Virgin Records, Virgin Airlines, Virgin Mobile, Virgin Bride, Virgin Credit and many other companies, Branson has set his eyes on outer space. He established a new company, Virgin Intergalactic, in March 1999. Its mission: to get the first paying space-tourists into orbit by 2007. XCOR Aerospace is currently developing a reusable eight-seat space plane for this. This will provide fee-paying passengers with the opportunity to experience weightlessness and see the curvature of the earth. The company is now taking bookings and, if you're interested, a ticket will set you back $US100 000 per person.

Alan Wurtzel

Wurtzel took over the US company Ward's (now known as Circuit City) in 1973, when it was almost bankrupt. At the time, the company was a hodgepodge of appliance and hi-fi stores, with no clear vision or strategic focus. Wurtzel later confessed that he did not have the answers to the company's problems or a grandiose vision to rescue it. So he did what any good leader would do in this situation: he asked a lot of questions. Wurtzel quickly gained a reputation as a CEO who asked more questions of his board, and other employees, than they did of him. One fellow-board member recalls, 'Allan was a real spark. He had an ability to ask questions that were just marvelous. We had some wonderful debates in the boardroom. It was never just a dog and pony show, where you would just listen [to him] and then go to lunch.' He used the same approach with all of his senior managers, pushing and prodding and probing with questions. He did this to gain understanding of the firm and, only then, start to develop a vision and strategies to create a better future for the company. Over the next ten years Wurtzel and his senior management team not only turned the company round; they also laid the foundations for a stunning record of results, with the company's share price beating the market average by a factor of 22, between 1982 and 2000 (abridged from Collins, 2001: 74–5).

The Kyungwon Enterprise Company

The company has spent approximately US$3.4 billion over five years developing an add-on device which transforms water into an electrically charged liquid that cleans with the same power as conventional powders. Called the 'Midas System', this harnesses the tendency of supercharged water to launder, deodorize and kill viruses. This will create cheaper, easier and 'greener' washing, by using half the power and two-thirds of the water of conventional machines. The patent for this was registered on 18 September 2001 and the product is expected to be on the market in 2005. This will not be good news for the world-wide multibillion-dollar detergent industry, but will be appreciated by consumers throughout the world (Kuyungwon website, 25 October 2002).

While a vision is clearly important to kick-start a CMP, employees can be justifiably cynical about both vision and mission statements. For example, Tom Peters used to advise audiences of organizational leaders to put mission statements in the trashcan the moment they received them. Scott Adams once described a mission statement as 'a long and awkward sentence that demonstrates management's inability to think clearly', and most US managers 'believe that mission statements are not worth the paper they are written on' (Gettler, 1998: 15). They all have a point, because the glossiest and most finely worded vision/mission statement in the world will change absolutely nothing, because change has to be learnt and internalized and, most importantly, it has to be *led*. Fine words on paper will change nothing. Employees have to understand and see where they are heading, why they are going there and how they can get there. As we will see later, the first reaction of most individuals, when confronted with change, will be, 'What's in it for me?' followed by an introspective bout of finding all the flaws in the proposed changes, and what the negative effects are likely to be. Hence, in a nutshell, what employees need are some good reasons why they should embark on this journey, a clearly defined road, way or path to follow, what the end goals are and some incentives for changing what they currently do.

> 'Would you tell me please which way I ought to go from here?' asked Alice.
> 'That depends a good deal on where you want to go to,' said the cat.
> 'I don't much care where . . . ,' said Alice.
> 'Then it doesn't much matter where you go,' said the cat.
> '. . . so long as I get somewhere,' Alice added as an explanation.
> 'Oh, you're sure to do that,' said the cat, 'if only you walk long enough.'
> (*Lewis Carroll,* Alice in Wonderland, *1871*)

> 'If you chase ten rabbits, you probably won't catch one.'
> (*Old Japanese saying*)

Our reviews of successful and unsuccessful change management programmes in dozens of organizations over an eight-year period revealed that those visions that grabbed the attention of employees, and motivated them to action, had a number of common characteristics.

1 They were attractive, inclusive, memorable and compelling, and were grounded in marketplace requirements. Ineffective visions were lengthy, unfocused, bland, difficult to remember and did not act as a guide to action in employees' daily working lives.
2 They were trimultaneously broad-brush (the overall strategic objectives, goals or stretch targets), narrow-focus (what does this change mean to me and the job I do?) and also addressed the disparate needs and concerns of the groups who would be affected by the change.
3 They acted as guiding stars or beacons, providing these organizations and their employees with a distinctive purpose, as well as short- and long-term goals. They captured and symbolized long-term dreams about what the organization hoped to become. They stretched and motivated employees, by providing them with objectives to strive towards and, in some cases, a cause to believe in.
4 They appealed to employees at all levels and to the organization's stakeholders, customers and clients. They reached both heads and hearts. They raised ambitions and were catalysts for action. They were concerned with the feelings, hopes and aspirations of those to whom they were directed.

The leaders of these organizations embodied their visions in their day-to-day working practices and communicated them frequently and in person. They knew that, if they had just stuck their visions/missions on notice boards, or in emails, newsletters and videos, they would have died very quickly.

Visions were regarded as being quite different from mission statements because, while statements of intent and specific plans and policies are important, they can also place restrictions on flexible,
evolutionary change. The visions of companies that have successfully
managed change were not regarded as a 'plan' as such, but as a device
to motivate people to change. They understood that their visions could not
be allowed to become dead documents, as mission statements so often
do. They regarded their visions as living, evolutionary statements of
intent, while their mission statements became out-of-date the moment
they were committed to paper. To cite one example of this, 3m updates
its 'values and visions' on its website at regular intervals as the strategic focus of the company shifts and changes.

Their visions were built into and reinforced by the day-to-day strategic
and cultural changes that employees saw going on around them (as
described in the Continental Airlines case study later in this chapter).
If employees cannot see this connection fairly early on in the change
management process, distrust and cynicism will soon set in. A
vision/mission that is not matched on a day-to-day basis by what
employees experience will soon wither on the vine and lose its motivational impact.

Here's one example of a vision statement that fails to meet any of these
basic requirements:

> In the 21st century, Blob University will be recognized as an internationally
> excellent, research-intensive university and a leading intellectual and
> creative resource to the community it serves. It will provide a broad and
> balanced coverage of disciplines in the arts, sciences and the professions at
> internationally recognized standards. It will be characterized by a strong
> research and postgraduate emphasis across the full range of its disciplines
> and it will be noted for concentrations of particular research excellence in
> selected areas of strength, opportunity and importance. Blob University's
> research and postgraduate strength will be linked to and sustained by a
> high quality undergraduate program in which teaching and learning takes
> place in an atmosphere of research and scholarship. The university will
> foster an international focus for all its activities and standards as an integral
> part of its overriding commitment to excellence and high quality. It will be
> valued above all for its enduring commitment to improving society through
> learning and discovery.

This quotation has been read several times to groups of MBAs, who
were asked for their reactions. Apart from observations about the
dodgy punctuation, strangled syntax and the repetitions it contains,
other comments have included the following:

- 'Completely vacuous. Why isn't the university doing these things
  now? It's been in existence for a hundred years.'

- 'Why isn't it already recognized 'internationally' for its teaching and research? This is the same empty rhetoric we used to hear when I was an undergraduate here ten years ago.'
- 'Why is there no mention of the university's employees? Don't they matter?'
- 'Nice rhetoric. A pity it's not matched by the reality of this university's relatively poor standing in international terms.'
- 'Does nothing for me. Totally off-putting, because it's nothing more than a series of stale, repetitive clichés that we've all heard before.'
- 'The part about serving the community is a joke. I doubt if this university has any impact on 95 per cent of the people who live in this city.'
- 'Leaves me cold. Sounds like it was put together on a post-it after a few lunchtime drinks.'
- 'My understanding of a vision statement is that it is about the future. This is about the things this university should already be doing.'

By way of contrast, what about this vision statement from a well-known and successful Australian resource and mining company?

> Our vision is to maximise shareholder value through the use of the talents of all our company employees. We will maintain a diversified portfolio of commodities and exercise prudential financial management. We will search for new business opportunities and find, acquire, develop and operate new mineral resource projects throughout the world. Our immediate tasks are to capitalise on the best of the past, address current issues and – most importantly – challenge ourselves for the future and maintain our shared commitment to continuous improvement. [The company] is committed to achieving compatibility between economic development and the maintenance of the environment. It is also committed to developing relationships of mutual understanding and respect with the indigenous peoples of the areas in which we operate or propose to operate. To achieve these goals, we will develop and retain top quality people. We will be at the cutting edge of management practice and make best use of new technologies. We will develop agreed values, behaviours and expectations that unite and represent the commitment of all our staff. Our objective is to create an even better company, maximising shareholder value through the use of the talents of our valued employees across the whole corporation.

This is better because it satisfies most of the requirements of an attractive and compelling vision statement. It uses inclusive language ('we'), refers to the major stakeholders in the company, makes some reference to its social responsibilities and, unlike Blob University's mish-mash, is concerned with *the future*. But it is still too long and probably needs to be shortened by 20–30 per cent. Many of the best organizational visions that we have come across were often surprisingly simple and, as a result, became captured in 'rallying cries' that were understood and embraced by employees. Examples of these include the following: 'Ask the passenger in seat C-9' (Continental Airlines); 'We don't sell flowers – we sell beauty' (Podesta Baldochi); 'The only limitation is your imagination'

(Industrial Light and Magic); 'To make people happy' and 'Dream, believe, dare and do' (Disney); 'Cars for the world to love' and 'To beat Porsche' (Toyota); 'No limits' (Nokia); 'Putting Perth's homes on the map' (aussiehome.com); 'Bringing computer power to the people' (Apple); 'First to market – first to profit' (Hewlett-Packard); 'From anywhere to anywhere in 24 hours' (TNT); 'The appliance of science' (Zanussi); 'Quality is job number one' (Ford); 'Strength, speed, simplicity, synergy, superb quality and satisfied customers' (General Electric), 'The world on time' (Federal Express), 'Buy into Moore's Law' (Intel); and, most notably, 'A computer on every desk and in every home' (Microsoft in 1978).

Even so, as we will see later, vision/mission statements can be little more than useless pieces of paper, and rallying cries little more than useless slogans, unless they become operationalized in concrete change management strategies and employees' daily working practices.

Exercise 8.1

In Chapter 1, you were asked to develop a compelling vision that would challenge the way people in your department or organization operate now and in the future. Are you now in a better position to develop and articulate a new direction for your followers? This doesn't have to be revolutionary, just a statement of a better future state for your people to move towards. It should also be short enough to take no longer than one minute to explain to a colleague at work.

What is the end goal of this vision?

What are the principal components of this vision?

Can these be encapsulated in motivational 'rallying cries'?

If you are still having some difficulties with this exercise, there will be another opportunity to try this in Chapter 9. ◆

Understanding why resistance to change is inevitable

Reform a university? You may as well try to reform a cheese. There is a certain flavour about a university as there is about a cheese, springing from its antiquity.
(*The English Peer Lord Cecil, during a debate on the reform of British universities in the House of Lords, 1923*)

Why is changing a university like moving a graveyard? Because it is difficult, complex and time-consuming, and you won't get any help from the occupants.
(*Internet joke, 2001*)

Resistance is futile.
(*The Borg, in* Star Trek)

With a team of change leaders in place, and a clear and articulate vision to act as a guiding star, the third issue to get to grips with is why people resist change. It was suggested earlier that 'leading organizational and cultural change' should be reframed as 'changing people's behaviours and attitudes'. Changing behaviours is possible; changing attitudes can be very difficult and time-consuming. We know from a century of psychological research that behavioural change always precedes attitudinal change, in all circumstances. This is one reason why simply *telling* people to change is usually a completely fruitless exercise. Hence one way of reframing our understanding of organizational change is to think about the way individual change happens. The most dramatic changes in our personal development occur when we are young and primed to learn and unlearn rapidly. This is the reason why young children ask lots of 'why', 'what', 'when', 'where' and 'how' questions and, as we'll see in Chapter 9, this child-like curiosity is also one of the primary sources of creative thinking. As we mature, we tend to become slower at learning and more resistant to upheavals and dislocations in our lives, unless we have embraced a mind-set that accepts perpetual change and unlearning as the natural and normal way to live and grow. Broadly speaking, the same is true of organizations. When they have just been born, or are growing rapidly, they have an inbuilt, organic capacity for change. In fact, they *relish* change and thrive on it. As they mature and get older, they can become more set in their ways and increasingly resistant to change, unless they too have embraced perpetual change and unlearning as 'the way we do things around here'. With these thoughts in mind, please complete Exercise 8.2.

Exercise 8.2

Leading organizational change

Before reading through the next section of this chapter, please complete this survey. There are a series of statements relating to learning and change management. Indicate the extent to which you agree or disagree with each one where:

6 = Strongly agree, **5** = Agree, **4** = Slightly agree, **3** = Slightly disagree, **2** = Disagree, **1** = Strongly disagree.

Item	Rating
1 I understand why perpetual organizational change is inevitable	

2   I have a positive attitude towards change

3   I am skilled in lateral thinking, scenario mapping and mental modelling

4   I am innovative and able to see beyond 'common sense' boundaries

5   I am always open to learning new skills and developing my personal knowledge base

6   I am aware of the learning styles of different individuals

7   I understand how adults 'learn' and 'unlearn'

8   When managing change, I focus on the needs and concerns of the people who will be most affected by this process

9   I am aware that leading change takes a great deal of time, energy, resources, effort and persistence

10 I am aware of the differences between *vision*, *mission* and *strategy*

11 I understand why employees may actively resist change initiatives and how to overcome their resistance

12 I understand why *empowered* change is usually more successful than *imposed* change

13 I understand the importance of establishing support systems during times of rapid change

14 I understand the importance of personal, face-to-face communication when leading change

15 I understand the importance of using a variety of communication strategies during times of change

16 I understand why the 11 components of change management described earlier must be *considered* when planning organizational and cultural change

Now, please add up your total score for the 16 items:

Interpreting your score

80–96: an excellent understanding of personal change and change management. According to expert commentators like Drucker, Kotter, Handy, Senge, Peters and others you possess a well-balanced portfolio of personal attributes, strategic competencies and people management skills that will enable you to cope with the uncertainties and challenges of perpetual change in the future.

48–79: quite a good understanding of change management, but you may need to continue to work on your personal adaptability to change, and develop a greater awareness of the human dimension of leading and managing change.

16–47: some understanding of the dynamics of leading and managing change, but you will need to learn more about your own attitudes to change and leading/managing change in the future. ◆

This questionnaire highlights a number of aspects of our attitudes to change. An awareness of these can be important because they will shape the way that we lead and manage *other* people through change.

In common with the motivation of employees, our own beliefs and attitudes about change may blind us to the fact that others may not have the same views about this as we do and will, therefore, be resistant to it (items 6, 7, 8, 11 and 12). This is where learning theory comes into play, and this can provide some powerful insights into why people and organizations resist change, and how this resistance can be overcome. 'Learning' (from the Old English, *leornian*, meaning 'knowledge') refers to the complete kaleidoscope of elements that make up an individual's mind-set. This includes their knowledge, intellectual capital, technical skills, on-the-job experience, competencies, aptitudes, behaviours and attitudes. How individuals learn and internalize these was captured two and half thousand years ago in this mnemonic by the Chinese philosopher Confucius: 'I hear – I forget; I see – I remember; I do – I understand.'

Modern research on the psychology of learning processes has shown that Confucius was right. Experiential learning (learning by experience) is the best way of acquiring knowledge although, as we will see, it has its limitations. The best-known exposition of this type of learning in modern times is Kolb's learning cycle (Figure 8.1). This circular model describes how individuals and groups learn to do new things. Through experience and reflection, we develop cognitive maps of the world that work for us (common sense), we build up bodies of knowledge and

Figure 8.1   Kolb's learning cycle

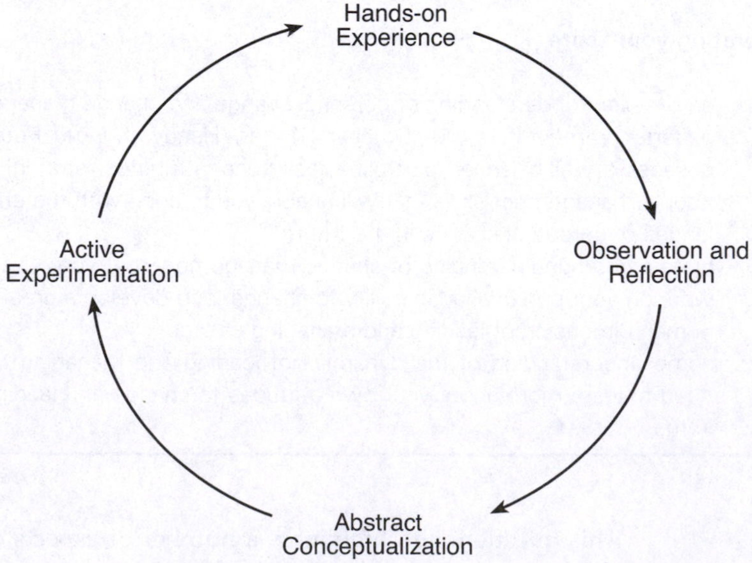

Source: Kolb (1996: 271).

intellectual know-how (experience) and develop beliefs about ourselves (self-perception), other people (attributions) and the world we live in (attitudes). These then manifest themselves in our behaviour, the way we solve problems at work, in our leadership and management practices and in the way we think about change. When we find something that works for us, as individuals or organizations, we naturally choose to persist with it. Most people and businesses find comfort and meaning in familiar patterns, routines and behaviours and, in turn, these then become part of our personalities or, in the case of organizations, their cultures.

This model of human and organizational learning also highlights four other significant outcomes of experiential learning. First, the more times we move through these single-loop cycles, the more our beliefs about the world and how it works are reinforced, or more accurately, *reiterated*. Second, these beliefs become ingrained at both the conscious and, more significantly, the unconscious levels of our minds. This means that we will unconsciously *exclude* any information that does not correspond with the belief systems that we have built up. Third, we are all exposed to a unique and limited selection of learning cycles that inevitably restrict our understanding of 'the real world' or other alternative 'real worlds' (discussed further in Chapter 9). Fourth, as a result of these interlinked processes, there will always be a smorgasbord of 'resistant characters' during change, regardless of the organizational context. Here are a few examples of these:

The egotist: 'I know more than the idiots running this place. Why should I listen to them?'

The old-timer: 'I've worked here for 30 years. I'm an experienced manager. How dare you tell me that I need to change?'

The practical manager: 'Let's face it, all this vision and change stuff is just window dressing. You've just got to kick some butts to get better results. You don't lead change by brainstorming and filling up flip-charts.'

The office politician: 'How can I use this time of change and uncertainty to my personal advantage?'

The action-driver: 'It's activity we need, not group discussions about changing things. You've got to get out of the circle-of-chairs syndrome, meet the customers and "do the business".'

The sceptic: 'These ideas and theories about change are all very well for academics in their ivory towers. I've got to deal with real people and real deadlines in the real world.'

The pragmatist or wallflower: 'Well, really I'm just happy to go along with the changes that the majority thinks are for the best.'

The opportunist: 'I'm talented and in demand. Why should I stay here? What's in all this change and upheaval for me?'

The frustrated innovator: 'This place is a shambles. We need to transform the whole company but my bosses just won't listen to my ideas.'

The bureaucrat: 'How do I preserve my status and authority? What will happen to my car parking space and my executive canteen discount?'

The dismissive: 'We've had days of meetings and all we've got to show for it is a piece of paper, called a mission statement. So what's new?'

The cynic: 'What this mission statement is really about is getting more work out of us for less. When was the last time you saw a mission statement that gave you more for doing less?'

The stick-in-the-mud: 'I've always done it this way and I don't see why I should change now.'

What we learn from these experiential cycles becomes inextricably intertwined with our identities and our deepest sense of *who we are*. As the Greek philosopher Aristotle once observed, 'That which has become habitual becomes, as it were, part of our nature.' And, once they are part of our nature, habitual behaviours and attitudes become deeply ingrained and very hard to change. The English writer Samuel Johnson described this eloquently in the 1760s when he observed, 'The chains of habit are too weak to be felt – until they are too strong to be broken.' Therefore all transformational leaders need to have some understanding of the power of 'double-loop' learning. The single-loop learning we described above is fine for individuals whose jobs never change and for organizations working in stable and slow-moving environments. However, when flexibility, fast change and innovation are paramount, double-loop learning must be built into the working mindsets of all employees. In essence, this means that employees have to be encouraged (and rewarded for doing so) to constantly move forward in their individual and collective learning endeavours, by having them move from 'observe–decide–do' cycles to 'observe–reflect–think–decide–do' cycles. Hence, for double loop learning to work well, employees must be encouraged to question what they do on a regular basis, be constantly moving forward and learning new things while simultaneously discarding knowledge and working practices that are out of date or redundant. We will return to look at the way this can be operationalized within the context of the learning organization in Chapter 9.

Learning theory also provides us with some other useful insights. First, learning is not the main problem for human adults. The real problem is *unlearning*; that is, giving up knowledge, or ways of working, they may have been using for years and have become very comfortable with. In this context, the old saying 'You can't teach an old dog new tricks' contains some truth – unless they've been learning new tricks throughout their lives. Second, rapid change can cause a break in learning cycles and this can be extremely disruptive to the unlearning process unless handled carefully. Third, adults will only unlearn if they feel that this is going to be a useful thing to do, or if they believe that there will be positive and tangible benefits at some point in the near future. This is why organizational change must always be treated as a practical, intellectual *and* emotional issue, and why change management programmes must appeal to both the minds and the hearts of those employees who are affected by change.

Fourth, the way we learn is conditioned by our particular learning styles: 'The Imitator', who prefers to learn by watching the actions of others, 'The Thinker', who prefers to reflect on, intellectualize and analyse issues, and 'The Doer', who prefers practical action and finding quick solutions to problems to thought and reflection. While adults use all three learning styles to some extent, they usually have a preference for one of them. This is important because, if we want people to unlearn, we have to be able to tap into their preferred learning styles, and ensure that, when we are communicating the need for change, we make allowances for these preferences. This means using evocative language that can tap into their dominant learning styles, as described in the section on formal presentation skills in Chapter 3. Fifth, change can be very stressful. As we saw in Chapter 2, stressed human beings are not good at learning/unlearning, because during stressful episodes their higher-order cognitive functions are always impaired and, under extreme duress, can shut down completely.

Sixth, if these reactions persist over time, there is an increasing risk that 'change fatigue' will set in, where employees simply lose motivation and commitment because they can see no positive outcomes or benefits from waves of change. Constant unlearning, without benefits, will sooner or later lead to frustration and distrust. People need to see that their unlearning will lead to better personal outcomes. If this doesn't happen, resistance will build up inexorably. People will begin to switch off and become 'me' focused and only do what's necessary to protect their own backs. Cynicism can spread rapidly, and there is a body of research that has demonstrated that this too is a major obstacle to change (for example, Wanous, 2000). Absenteeism, attrition rates and labour turnover may also increase. All of these are responses to environments that employees find intolerable, and in this sort of climate no one is going to listen to their leaders or their plans for the future. Of equal importance, if people have previously had bad experiences of change, they will become even more resistant to any subsequent changes that come their way. Much change over the last decade has involved reactive downsizing, rationalization, cost cutting, cutbacks and mergers. These have invariably led to redundancies and major morale problems amongst those staff that have survived such changes. In turn, this can lead to the well-known BOHICA syndrome ('Bend over – here it comes again'). Hence, if the learning/unlearning process is not managed effectively, the chances are that you will end up with cynical, demotivated, disloyal and underperforming employees.

Never assume that employees will understand the need or rationale for change. It is much safer to start with the opposite assumption: that they will neither understand nor accept the need for change – at first. All human beings are psychologically conservative, because they have developed cognitive, behavioural and attitudinal maps of a complex world that work for them. If these are questioned, they will feel threatened and will resist change. The key is to lessen these feelings of threat, by offering them a vision of a better future, equipping them with the skills and resources they need to achieve this, identifying a way, road or path to travel along, providing some incentives to change, and rewarding them when they have embraced these changes. Learning is not the real problem – unlearning is. People are continually learning at work, even in stable, slow-moving or bureaucratic organizations (more accurately, this is often closed-loop *reinforcement*, rather than genuine learning/unlearning). Hence the real challenge is to provide employees with the motivation and incentives to give up those things that have become, literally, part of their personalities.

There are two old sayings that are relevant in the context of learning and unlearning. The first is 'People do not resist change, but they do resist being changed'; the second is 'When it comes to change, people only like changes they've made themselves.' In practical terms, this means that empowered change is always easier to introduce, and more effective, than enforced change. Employees have to be given as much ownership over the change management process as possible. The more they believe they are driving the change, the more they will embrace it. The less they are told (or 'taught') to change, and the more they are shown *how to learn to change*, the more rapidly they will embrace this.

This is one reason why public sector bureaucracies are so resistant to change. They rarely create their own internal impetus for change because politicians and/or central government agencies often impose this on them from the outside, meaning that they have only ever learnt how to react to change, not how to initiate it themselves. Hence changing people's behaviour and shifting their learning cycles requires ten times the time, effort and commitment that most change leaders think it will, particularly from a standing start. However, once the initial impetus is set up, change can often accelerate quickly. A basic principle of physics that can be translated into both employee and organizational (un)learning is the principle of *inertia*. When a large body is at rest, it takes a tremendous amount of energy to get it moving. However, once set in motion, it requires much less force to maintain its momentum and just subtle nudges to alter its direction of travel. In the context of organizational change, this means that steady, incremental change and unlearning is much easier to manage than fast, radical, discontinuous, stop–start change and unlearning.

Integrating strategic macro change with the organization's operational culture and employees' working practices

A succinct summary of organizational culture might be, 'the way people work when they think nobody is looking'. In a bad culture, they're probably looting the stationery cabinet, forging expenses chits and downloading porn, like the miserable galley slaves in the Slough Branch of Wernham Hogg on television's *The Office*. In a good culture, they may be checking a consignment, streamlining a process or consulting a customer about their needs, like the perky folk of Wal-Mart with their company songs and corny stunts. Most corporations feature a bit of both; informal homeostatic mechanisms counter one with another.
(*Gideon Haigh*, Bad company: the cult of the CEO, 2003)

There are as many descriptions of organizational culture as there are writers on the subject, and there is no universally accepted definition of this concept. As long ago as 1952, Kroeber and Kluckhohn identified 164 different definitions of culture. Ott has listed 73 different words or phrases that have been used to define organizational culture in 58 different published sources (cited by Schein, 1996a). Despite the lack of agreement on definitions of organizational culture, it can be broadly described as a shared, common frame of reference, comprising a collection of deeply buried values and assumptions. This is largely taken for granted and is shared by a significant number of an organization's employees. It is learned and retransmitted by organizational members and provides them with rules for appropriate organizational behaviour and conduct. It provides a common psychology and defines the organization's uniqueness and personal identity. This endures over time and can be found in any organization of a reasonable size. Culture is symbolic, and is manifested in the language, rhetoric, behaviour and attitudes of organizational members. In one sense, it can be regarded as the DNA of an organization, something that can be passed on to new members and replicated as the organization grows in size or spreads geographically. Once established, an organizational culture can be changed, but often with great difficulty.[1]

William McKnight, the founder of 3m, first coined the expression 'organizational culture', in the context of the management of organizations back in 1914, but it was not until the 1980s that 'culture' became both a management buzzword and a popular topic in management and organizational studies. In fact, this decade was characterized by an explosion of interest in the concept of culture by both academics and practitioners. The main cause of this was the crisis of US business and the success of Japan and other Asian countries in beating American companies at their own game, but played with different management rules. There was an explosion of special journal editions dealing with organizational culture at this time: *Administrative Science Quarterly* (September 1983), *Organizational Dynamics* (Autumn 1983) and *The Journal of Management Studies* (May 1986). Several best-selling books, including *In Search of Excellence*, *Corporate Cultures*, *Theory Z* and *The Art of Japanese Management*, appeared in the 1980s, extolling the virtues of organizations with strong, flexible, adaptable cultures.

Advocates of the culture school argued that only strong corporate cultures were effective in securing ever-improving flexibility, motivation and commitment from employees. Major productivity and quality improvements could be expected to stem from the rewards and recognition provided for employees within such cultures. Indeed, it was confidently asserted at the time that companies with such cultures were invariably amongst the most profitable and successful in the world, with success stories being cited from companies like Volvo, 3m, Hewlett-Packard and Disney, amongst others. It was also suggested that companies aiming to improve their organizational performance (in the pursuit of 'excellence') had to understand and radically change their corporate cultures. For example, Peters and Waterman's (1982) survey of 36 American companies that displayed sustained high performance between 1961 and 1980 identified a number of features of their corporate cultures that could be regarded as the building blocks of excellent organizations. These included closeness to the customer; staff autonomy and intrapreneurship; enhanced levels of performance and productivity driven by high levels of affective well-being and motivation amongst employees; a strong, benevolent corporate culture; deeply shared corporate values amongst staff; and, critically, a widely shared vision of the company's future at all levels of the organization. For these authors organizational culture was not just another piece of the puzzle of understanding how organizations changed and developed, it *was* the puzzle. From their point of view, culture is not something an organization 'has'; culture is something an organization 'is'.

As with many organizational and management fads of the last two decades, the idea of creating high-performing 'excellent' companies through culture has fallen into some disrepute. The work of Peters and Waterman was criticized, in part, because many of the exemplar companies they identified ran into difficulties in the 1980s and early 1990s. Some no longer exist, either having gone out of business or having been taken over by other companies. Retrospectively, we can now see that they had – at best – identified some of the characteristics of consistently successful companies (and the search for these continues today). Furthermore, the concept of corporate culture remains a complex and confusing concept, both theoretically and in its utility as a practical change management tool in organizations. Nevertheless, it still has relevance because many of the world's most successful companies do appear to have highly charged, inclusive and adaptable corporate cultures. This serves to illustrate one of the main reasons for the continuing popularity of the concept of organizational culture for managers and practitioners in industry: the persistent belief that there must be some relationship between organizational culture, business performance and the ability of companies to change and evolve over time.

The advantage of strong, people-centred organizational cultures is that they can make everybody pull in the same direction, create a strong sense of belonging and involvement ('us and them'), maintain continuity in the induction and socialization of new recruits, promote widely recognized standards of managerial behaviour, develop clear and unambiguous performance criteria, encourage innovation, learning and change, and promote an enhanced ability to internationalize while maintaining a global corporate culture (Collins and Porras, 1996). The main disadvantages of strong task-focused organizational cultures are that they can legitimate unethical and illegal behaviour, can be highly resistant to change and can allow companies to become 'cut-off' from the outside world and potential competitive threats, phenomena that have afflicted many companies in recent years. A complete transformation of an organization with this kind of culture can take up to five years, particularly in large bureaucratic ones. We also saw in Chapter 3 that culture has a major influence on the behaviour and attitudes of individuals, because a person's perceptions, attitudes, motivations, values, learning experiences and personality are all, to a large extent, shaped by culture. Consequently, organizational cultures can also have a powerful influence on the beliefs, attitudes, behaviours, motivation and performance levels and learning capabilities of an organization's employees.

In this sense, culture has never mattered more to business performance and, because change is the only constant in organizations these days, all organizational cultures need to have an inbuilt evolutionary or change capability (Collins, 2001; Collins and Porras, 1996; Drenna, 1992). Furthermore, real change only happens when this becomes ingrained in the cultural mind-sets of organizations and the day-to-day working practices of their employees. This means that change leaders have to demonstrate where things have changed and how they have improved at the operational level – right down at the coalface. For example, if product quality has improved, employees need to see that they or their team have benefited, by receiving a bonus or profit-share payment. If customer service has improved, they need to see the customer retention numbers and loyalty percentages. This information should be disseminated at team and departmental meetings and rein-forced in company newsletters, emails and videos. Change must be ingrained in the culture of the organization because, until new behav-iours and attitudes are embedded in 'the way we do things around here', they are always subject to rapid degradation. We will look at how this can be achieved in practice in the Continental Airlines case study.

> I came to see in my time at IBM that culture isn't just one aspect of the game; it is the game.
> (*Lou Gerstner, 2003, in his autobiography,* Who Says Elephants Can't Dance?, *written after ten years of changing IBM's culture*)

Creating a sense of urgency, and getting the right people on the bus

Inertia and complacency are enemies of change. Without high levels of commitment and motivation, at all levels of an organization, change management programmes fail. To achieve this there has to be a critical mass of people on board: at least 80 per cent of an organization's work-force (echoing the old Buddhist saying, 'Four out of five is perfect'). Anything less than this ratio will create problems during the change process. Initially, this means creating a sense of urgency amongst senior management, because it is they who will have the primary responsibility for selling the vision and driving changes throughout the organization. As noted earlier, this may also mean bringing in people from outside the organization and taking the new change team off-site for retreats to brainstorm new ideas and map out the strategic change process. This stage is important because, without strong, energetic and committed leadership at the top, opposition to change further down the organization will not be overcome. To get this level of involvement requires change leaders to spend a lot of time with their senior employees, explaining the need for change and what the anticipated benefits will be. It also means being completely honest about both the negative and the positive effects of the proposed changes.

Even with the best will in the world, there will be times when staff who stand in the way of needed and necessary change have to be removed. All the organizations we looked at between 1997 and 2004 did this to some extent. In a talk in March 1989 to Harvard MBA students, after five years of restructuring and downsizing at General Electric, Jack Welch observed, 'Trying to change any bureaucratic organization slowly or incrementally is pointless. If you try to do it bit by it, resistance will inevitably build up. Fast, radical change is the only way – be it at Harvard, IBM or General Electric. If need be, you must sack people who stand in the way of necessary change.' You can give people three chances to come on board. If they don't accept this opportunity, then you must ask them to move on. However, this is also an opportunity to bring in new people from the outside who will share your passion and enthusiasm for the direction you want to take the organization in. Jim Collins describes this process as 'getting the right people on the bus', *before* deciding which direction to take the bus in (Collins, 2001: 41).

Developing straightforward, realistic and workable strategies to drive change initiatives throughout the organization

A vision without a plan of action is a recipe for failure, and the formulation of the change strategy is where the hard nuts-and-bolts work really begins. A strategy (from the Greek *strategos*) can be described as a plan for interacting with the competitive environment in order to achieve organizational goals. Goals define where the organization wants to go and strategies describe how the organization will get there. This does not mean that change strategies have to be complex. One characteristic of all organizations that successfully manage organizational and cultural change is the clarity and simplicity of their strategies. This doesn't mean that they were *simplistic*, but they showed with clarity how their visions were to be operationalized in practice. They were also sufficiently concise and well articulated for all their employees to understand and buy into. A good change strategy explains key roles and responsibilities, establishes deadlines, assigns resources and establishes priorities to work towards. It must also identify a sequence of specific, measurable goals for the organization's employees. In metaphorical terms, we can think of strategy as a sequence of identifiable and clearly mapped destinations on a long journey. However, strategic change planning alone will not guarantee success. As we will see in the upcoming company cases, implementation and evaluation are also critical.

Extensive two-way communication with all employees during times of change

> One of the jobs of a leader is to have a vision.
> But sometimes, top management sees an apple.
> When it gets to middle management it's an orange.
> By the time it gets to us, it's a lemon.
> (*Kouzes and Posner*, The Leadership Challenge, *1997*)

During periods of change, upheaval and uncertainty, it is impossible to communicate too much. Organizations that fail to manage change always underestimate how much they need to communicate with their employees, by a factor of about 20. Furthermore, one of the most frustrating outcomes of being a leader who has a clear vision of a better future is that initially you may well find yourself in a minority of one and almost all of the people who work for you will probably need convincing that you do indeed have a compelling vision. So, once you've created a vision, how do you 'sell' it? To communicate a vision effectively, four sets of questions have to be addressed.

1 What do we need to communicate to our employees? What are our priorities? What time scales do we need to work to?
2 Whom do we need to communicate with, internally and externally? Do we understand their interests and concerns? What can we learn from our employees, customers and clients about the changes we are proposing to initiate?
3 Which messages do we need to put across? Do they address the problems our organization faces? Are they compelling and will the disparate groups and individuals in our organization understand them? Do our messages appeal to the different learning styles of our employees and, thereby, their hearts and minds?
4 How are we going to get our messages across? What channels and media should we use to communicate these? Are they appropriate for our audiences? Do they allow for effective two-way communication? How comprehensive should our programme of communication be? How do we evaluate the success of our communication strategies?

An organization's vision needs to be shaped into the form of messages that can be communicated to all employees. As we saw earlier, an effective message has to be accurate, relevant, truthful, authoritative, credible and distinctive. It should also be short, simple and jargon-free and, wherever possible, tailored to the needs and interests of those receiving it. An effective message encourages a response and leads to action. Communicating a vision or a change management programme does not mean 'talking down' to an audience. The message should carry conviction and be backed by commitment and determination. A contrived or manufactured message will not convince and no amount of packaging can make up for a lack of honesty, integrity and purpose. This message must be presented in such a way as to achieve rapport and aid understanding with a whole variety of people. It must be also delivered from the heart: if you don't believe in it, no one else will.

This means that communication during times of change and upheaval has to be done face-to-face. Glossy videos, brochures, mission statements, newsletters and emails may be able to transmit the dry bones of a vision or mission, but they will never engage people's imaginations. Successful transformational leaders make full use of the motivational, visceral and connective oratory and public speaking skills we reviewed in Chapter 3, in particular the ancient art of storytelling. These leaders physically *embody* the changes they want to initiate, or as the Indian independence leader Mahatma Gandhi once put it, 'We must *become* the change we want to see in others.' They become highly visible symbols of the new organizational culture they are trying to create and want their employees to buy into.

Involving employees by giving them ownership over change management initiatives and processes

Another message that comes across loud and clear from research on organizations that successfully manage change is that this process can only succeed if it is a collective and shared effort. In Chapters 1, 4 and 7, we saw how effective empowered and collaborative leadership can be, and during times of change this becomes even more important. This is because empowered change, involving a majority of an organization's employees, always has a far better chance of success than enforced change that alienates a majority of employees. If people are not involved from the outset, they will very quickly become at least apathetic about the process and, within a short period of time, antagonistic to it. In effect, a critical mass of employees have to be persuaded through engagement that it makes good sense for them to become involved in this process, and the only way to do that is to give them as much ownership as possible over the process.

Celebrating successes and short-term wins, and rewarding employees when they make changes to their working practices

This is essential. Successful change strategists break big steps down into smaller, doable ones. This enables people to maintain a sense of control over the change process and encourages the belief that they are achieving new goals and objectives. People need feedback on the progress they are making towards new organizational practices and mind-sets. Most employees will start to get anxious or frustrated if they are not seeing tangible benefits after six to 12 months. If people can't see any positive results, they may start resisting further changes. Celebrating short-term wins can help to maintain levels of confidence and re-energize commitment to the change management programme. Small wins also build into bigger wins, thus adding further impetus to the change process.

Involving customers and clients in change management initiatives and processes

Increasingly, changing customer needs and preferences are driving organizational change. One survey, of 300 senior executives in the USA, revealed that customers were the fourth-biggest source of pressure for change, behind competition, profitability and new technologies. 'Improving customer satisfaction' was the second most significant driver of change reported by these executives. In the early 1990s, customer satisfaction and retention would not have made it into the top ten (KPMG, cited by Cornell, 1998b). Maintaining close relationships with customers and clients is not only important for retaining their loyalty and business; they too are involved in environmental scanning and may see opportunities for, and threats to, your business before you do. Furthermore, while the results of change management programmes should be visible to one's customers and clients, the processes should be invisible.

Developing an ongoing commitment to continuous change, improvement and learning

Let our advance worrying become our advance planning.
(*Winston Churchill's advice to his cabinet during World War II, just after the mass evacuation of British troops from Dunkirk in 1940 and an expected invasion of Britain by Germany*)

The preceding sections may have implied that leading organizational and cultural change is a relatively smooth, sequential process. It isn't, and the data we presented in the introduction to this chapter on the failure rates of change management programmes show how difficult this process can be. 'Managing change' is extremely difficult, because it is, by definition, a reactive, catch-up process and often characterized by employee resistance. It is actually much easier to create and initiate change for others to follow or imitate. The world's cutting-edge companies are able to do this consistently, over long periods of time. This means that, as soon as the impetus for change has been created, organizations have to turn their attention to building innovation, learning organization principles and the ability to manage knowledge and intellectual capital into the culture, mind-sets and working practices of their employees. These components of organizational change and evolution will be addressed in Chapters 9 and 10.

Leading organizational and cultural change: the practice

The 11 components described above featured in all the successful change management programmes reviewed between 1997 and 2004. Naturally, the weighting given to each one of these varied from organization to organization, depending on the environments in which these businesses were operating, and the nature of the changes they were going through. This reinforces the view expressed earlier that all change management programmes are contingent, and there is no one 'best way' to manage change. Nevertheless, as we continued to refine and reapply this template to organizations that had experienced change, the better it worked. It is, at the very least, a useful tool for checking which elements and components need to be considered when initiating a change management programme. To illustrate the efficacy of this template, two real life examples of organizational and cultural change are presented below, Continental Airlines and the Australian Broadcasting Corporation.

Successful Organizational Change: Continental Airlines

I was recently on a cross country flight with Continental Airlines (suggested slogan: Not Quite The Worst) and, goodness knows why, I was reading that 'Letter from the President' you get at the front of every airline magazine – the one that explains how they are constantly striving to improve services, evidently by making everyone change planes at Newark. Well, this one was about how they had just conducted a survey of their customers to find out

their needs. What the customers wanted, according to the incisive prose of Gordon Bethune, was 'a clean, safe and reliable airline that took them where they wanted to go, on time and with their luggage'. Gosh, let me get a pen and notebook! Did you say 'with their luggage'? Wow!
(*Bill Bryson*, Notes From a Big Country, *1996*)

In 1993, Continental Airlines (CA) was in crisis, having just been rescued from bankruptcy for the second time in nine years. The company had gone through ten presidents in a decade, and its employees were paralysed by fear and inertia. Morale amongst employees from senior managers to check-in staff, flight attendants and baggage handlers was dreadful. It was ranked tenth out of the ten major US airlines as measured by on-time arrivals, baggage handling, customer complaints and involuntary denied boardings. It was a company with a lousy reputation for in-flight service, flight delays, cancellations and the hideous décor of its terminals. CA's planes were routinely dirty and had a variety of different colour schemes. Customer complaints were three times the industry average. The company hadn't posted a profit since 1978, and in 1994 reported a loss of $US619 million on revenues of $US5.7 billion (O'Reilly, 1999). A new CEO, Gordon Bethune, was appointed in October 1994. After his arrival, CA's fortunes changed dramatically. By 2000, CA was ranked as the 'second most admired airline in the USA' and came 23rd in a survey of 'the best companies in the USA to work for'. Bethune has regularly received awards for his leadership acumen, including *Fortune*'s award for being the sixth best business executive in the USA in 1999. Even after 11 September 2001, which was a major blow to the US airline industry, it was the only airline left in the top 100 'best companies to work for in the USA' in 2002, at number 42 (Levering and Moskowitz, 2003: 90; *Fortune*, 18 April 1999, 10 January and 28 February 2000). How did Bethune engineer this remarkable and dramatic turnaround, and also transform CA into a well-run, profitable and congenial company in just five years?

The presence of energetic and committed transformational leaders

Much of this successful transformation can be attributed to Gordon Bethune's personal qualities. Before joining CA, he had already acquired a reputation as a man who really enjoyed being involved with his employees. Throughout his working life, he had walked the talk and spent an astounding amount of time communicating with his staff. As a petty officer in the Navy, Bethune instinctively knew how important it was to spend time with the men in his command. He was so successful in this job that, in one 24-month period, his crews maintained their planes so well that not a single engine had to be replaced during their normal flying schedules. Bethune also had a long-standing reputation as a man with a good sense of humour: 'Employees seem unfazed and his style comes across as open and straightforward. Besides, he can be hilariously entertaining, savouring a story over dinner about lust-crazed Foreign Legionnaires and a camel' (O'Reilly, 1999: 94). After he left the Navy in 1979, he embarked on a career in civil aviation, working initially at Braniff, moving on to Western Airlines and later to Piedmont. After Boeing bought Piedmont, Bethune moved the company's HQ to Seattle, where he was put in charge of the company's Renton Plant, which maintained the 737 and 757 passenger planes. In 1994, he was offered the top position at CA.

A clear sense of direction, or purpose, or a set of clear and well-articulated goals and objectives for the company to travel towards

Fortunately for Bethune, a 33-year-old consultant called Greg Brenneman, from Bain & Company, had been advising CA for about 12 months. The two men immediately hit it off, developing a good personal rapport, and Brenneman was appointed Chief Operating Officer in late 1994. In December, the two got together at Bethune's house in Houston and together thrashed out a vision for the future direction of CA. This became known as, 'The Go-Forward Plan'. Their vision was 'To fly to places that people wanted to go in clean attractive airplanes; to get them there on time (with their bags) and to serve passengers food at meal times. To get all that done fast, right away and all at once.' That was it: simple, clear, direct, to the point, and easy to remember (Brenneman, 1998: 4; unless otherwise indicated, all further page references in this section are from this article).

Overcoming employee resistance and integrating change with the organization's operational culture and employees' working practices

Before Bethune and Brenneman became involved with CA, employee morale was at rock bottom, with labour turnover, absenteeism, sick leave and work injuries at record high levels. Shortly after he joined the company, Bethune recalled seeing that his baggage handlers had ripped the company's logos from their uniforms, because they didn't want to be recognized as CA employees when they left work. The leadership of the company had been distant and 'managed' by diktat. Different groups of employees had been pitted against one another in half-baked attempts to 'cut costs'.

Communication was extremely poor, laterally and horizontally and, as a result, employees often learnt about what was happening in the company in the local press, not from their own managers. Furthermore, employees had no avenues to go down with their ideas, suggestions or questions. There was a formal paper-based suggestion scheme but these forms, 'just disappeared in a black-hole' (p. 6).

Early on in the change management process, Brenneman and Bethune knew that they were going to have to change the defeatist and cynical culture at CA. As Brenneman observed, 'How to create a new culture is the topic of hundreds, if not thousands of books and articles. Gordon and I didn't bother with them. We agreed that a healthy culture is simply a function of several factors, namely: honesty, trust, dignity and respect. They all go together; they all reinforce one another' (p. 10). They engineered a mind-shift that empowered and involved employees to an extent never seen before in the company's history: 'We were going to change Continental's culture to one of fun and action and restore employees' trust (p. 5) [ ] The word fun scares a lot of executives. But I would argue that people have fun at work when they are engaged, when their opinions are respected. People are happy when they feel they are making a difference [ ] They care, they laugh, they talk and then fun happens pretty naturally (p. 10) [ ] Our message was this: Continental is your company – go and make it work' (p. 11). And that is exactly what Continental's employees proceeded to go out and do.

Creating a sense of urgency and getting the right people on the bus

Bethune and Brenneman believe that they succeeded in changing CA because they knew that they had to take drastic action immediately. They realized that they would either have to completely reinvent the company, because if they didn't it was going to go bankrupt for a third time, and probably be liquidated, with the loss of 40 000 jobs. They were also men who had been frustrated at the slow pace of change in the organizations they had worked for in the past, and knew that this could not be allowed to happen at CA. In turn their sense of urgency and commitment rubbed off on their senior managers. The ones that it didn't rub off on were soon replaced. As Brenneman observed, 'We saved Continental because we acted and we never looked back. We didn't say to the patient – if you can call a dying company that – "Now just hold on while we run a lot of tests and then perhaps perform an extremely delicate 12 hour procedure." No, we just took out the scalpel and went to work. We gave the patient little or no anesthesia and it hurt like hell. Then again, the patient is now cured! [ ] Looking back now, I realise that the biggest factor in our favour was momentum. The rallying cry of our turnaround was, "Do it fast, do it right away, do it all at once" ' (p. 12).

Bethune and Brenneman knew from the outset that they would have to replace some of the senior managers at CA. In all, 50 out of 61 senior managers were eventually replaced and a 'smart team' of senior players recruited. The criteria for employing new people were straightforward: 'First they had to pass what we called, "The raw IQ test" – there is no substitute for smarts. Second, they had to be driven to get things done. Finally, they had to be team players, willing to treat everyone with dignity and respect in an extremely collaborative environment' (p. 7). New recruits were offered stock options, so if the company's shareholders started winning, so would they. CA's turnaround soon created many millionaires in the company. It wasn't just senior managers who were replaced. Bethune and Brenneman replaced staff from all levels of the company, from the Board to supervisors and baggage-handlers.

One of the toughest decisions they had to make was shutting down one of CA's greatest loss-makers, its plant in Greensboro, North Carolina. Brenneman went into a lion's den of 600 angry pilots, flight attendants and support crews. He explained the details of the closing and relocation plans for employees, as well as CA's plans for the future. He then opened the floor up for questions. Although the pilots remained hostile, every other employee attending the meeting defended Brenneman, supporting his vision and plans for the future. He left to a standing ovation (p. 12). Some redundancies were achieved through early retirement and the company HQ's bureaucracy was also reduced in size. As Brenneman has observed, there is no choice but to sweep out the old and make way for the new during times of change (p. 5).

The development of straightforward, realistic and workable strategies

Bethune and Brenneman realized that they had to create a strategy that could embrace change in four areas at the same time. They knew that, if they simply tinkered with one area alone, they would not be able to drive systemic change throughout the whole company. As Brenneman recalls, 'Every company should have a strategy that covers these four elements – market, financial, product and people – whether it is in a severe crisis or not' (p. 6). Their strategic change plan covered people, systems, structure processes, customers and clients and was dovetailed into their original vision. As Brenneman recalled in 1998, 'saving

Continental wasn't brain surgery', and their Go Forward Plan, 'wasn't complex, it was pure common sense'. They believed that they had to create a workable strategy that everyone could understand, with a few key change measures built in that could be easily evaluated. Up to that point in time, there wasn't a single employee who had any idea what CA's strategy was, because it didn't have one. Bethune, Brenneman and their senior management team created a four-point strategy:

Fly to win

This meant shutting down unprofitable routes, developing new hubs in Houston, Newark and Cleveland and winning back disgruntled customers (pp. 5–6). The company also sold its unreliable fleet of Airbus 300s, which had been renamed 'Airbus 360s', because of their tendency to taxi out for take-off, then turn around and come back in for repairs or maintenance (O'Reilly, 1999: 94). CA also set up a strategic alliance with Northwest Airlines to extend its flight routes, enhance competition and improve customer travel options in November 1999.

Fund the future

This involved selling off non-strategic assets and restructuring debt while investing in new and more reliable IT systems for bookings. The company also invested in six super-tugs, at a combined cost of $US3.2 million, at Newark airport to circumvent the regular $US60 000 fines the company received for routinely exceeding the one hour allowed for disembarking passengers, and restocking and refuelling their planes.

Make reliability a reality

This called for better on-time performance and less lost luggage, as well as a concerted effort to win back their customers' loyalty. This also meant getting two sets of employees communicating more effectively with each other: those who wrote the flight schedules and those that ran the flight and airport operations. In the past, the scheduling department had simply written a flight schedule and given it to operations, often just days before they were to fly it, because this information was 'confidential'. As a result, operations often didn't have flight crew and support staff in the right locations at the right times. Consequently, many flights were cancelled or delayed, thus leaving large numbers of angry passengers behind.

With both groups signing off on the schedules, this problem was soon eradicated. Employees were given $65 bonuses every time CA finished in the top five airlines in on-time performance. Within months CA was regularly coming first. These changes also had a major impact on CA's bottom line performance. Before, the company had been forking out up to $US6 million *every month* to reaccommodate their passengers on competitors' flights. The on-time bonus scheme cost $US3 million a month and the company was bringing in an additional $US4 million a month from the new passengers that were now flying with CA. The result was an additional $US7 million a month in revenues (O'Reilly, 1999: 93–4).

Working together

This represented a concerted effort to rid Continental of friction between employees and managers and create a culture of trust, cooperation and superb service for CA passengers: 'we were going to change Continental's culture to one of fun and action and restore our employees' trust' (pp. 8–10).

The key measures that were built into this strategy included tracing cash flows, monthly on-time performance evaluations, lost baggage rates, customer complaints and the number of involuntary denied boardings. They also included turnover, sick leave, attrition and on-the-job injuries to monitor the progress of their 'People Plan' (see below).

Extensive two-way communication with all CA employees during the change process

'To implement the plan immediately and in its entirety, we sold it to our coworkers with energetic zeal' (p. 6) [ ] That's why when we took over, we started talking with our employees. In general, our communication changed from don't tell anybody anything unless absolutely necessary to tell everybody everything' (p. 11). Bethune and Brenneman travelled on CA's airplanes (sometimes incognito), visited airports, worked as baggage handlers and stood alongside their ticket agents. They talked with as many employees as they could, listening as much as they explained the vision and plans that they had for the company. They constantly told their employees that they believed in them. Bethune and Brenneman also understood the power of symbolism in their communication strategies. Over the years, a nine inch-thick tome of petty rules and regulations had been created, known as the 'Thou Shalt Not Book'. Early in 1995, they took this, put it in a 55-gallon drum, poured gasoline over it and ceremonially burnt it in front of a crowd of employees, with the simple message, 'Continental is your company to make great. Go do it now.' Both the symbolic act and the message spread round CA within days, cementing the message that the new leadership really was committed to turning the company's fortunes round (p. 11).

Bethune started attending every graduation ceremony for new flight attendants. Every month, he hosted an open house in his office, which any employee could attend. He recorded a three-minute update of company events every Friday, which employees could listen to by ringing a toll-free number. Several times a year he travelled to the company's hubs to address employees. He handed out prizes for Halloween costumes and candy on Christmas day to staff working over the holiday. He was renowned for being an impassioned and very funny public speaker and, when he first told the story about the lust-crazed French Foreign Legionnaires and the camel, it made its way round the company faster than one of CA's planes. His employees addressed him by his first name and he was known on sight by his people (O'Reilly, 1999: 94). An annual questionnaire was also introduced to ascertain how well senior managers communicated the 'Go Forward' plan, and how well they set goals and treated their employees. If bosses fared poorly on these surveys Bethune was known to withhold part of their annual bonuses.

Throughout the company, 650 bulletin boards were set up. These contained topical information on the company, from a weekly update on the company to future plans. Two-way communication was encouraged via an employee-managed toll-free hotline, which still receives about 200 calls per week. Each suggestion had to be researched and replied to within 48 hours. About one in ten were implemented. There were also biannual company videos and free quarterly magazines. Twice a year Bethune and Brenneman gave presentations to their employees at nine different sites. Every corporate officer had to visit their group of employees at least four times a year to update their employees, listen to their feedback and suggestions and help with their problems (p. 11).

Involving CA's employees, and celebrating successes and short-term wins

From the beginning, Bethune and Brenneman aimed to create an atmosphere where people wanted to come to work and overcome the tense and suspicious climate that had previously existed amongst CA's employees. Cultivating honesty, trust, dignity and respect became a key job of CA's new senior management team and Bethune and Brenneman considered it to be their top priority. As we saw earlier, as soon as Bethune was appointed, he declared that, if Continental ranked among the top three airlines for on-time performance in any month, he would pay six million dollars to all non-executive employees. Six million was the cost to the company of cancelled flights. The very next month, CA came fourth and in the following two months came in first. Bethune had to pay up six more times in 1995. For CA employees who had seen so many broken promises about bonuses in the past, this was a revelation, and reinforced the impression that things really were changing for the better. Bethune even travelled around the country personally handing out thousands of bonus cheques to his employees (O'Reilly, 1999: 92).

The next stage was to closely align employee remuneration and compensation schemes with CA's strategic objectives. All employees receive 15 per cent of the company's annual profits and every Valentine's Day Bethune and Brenneman distributed profit-sharing cheques to their employees. By involving its employees and changing its culture, CA was able to move rapidly from being the airline with the worst reputation for losing passengers' baggage to having the second-best record for five straight years between 1995 and 1999. A measure of this turnaround can be gauged by the sale of Continental logo merchandising. The same employees who had ripped CA logos off their uniforms were now buying hats, caps and T-shirts for themselves, their families and friends. Just 24 months after taking over, sales of logo merchandise to staff had increased by 400 per cent (p. 12). As Brenneman observed at the time, 'That's the kind of thing that happens, when you let the inmates run the asylum. You feel as if you've lost a bit of authority and control over every last detail – because you have – but that's OK. You can't run a company from the executive suite of an office building anyway. When the employees are happy, everyone is happy, from the customers to the shareholders' (p. 12).

Involving CA's customers and clients

'You might think the first step in breaking the doom loop is to fix the product, but that's actually the second step. The first is to beg forgiveness from all the customers you have wronged' (Brenneman, 1998: 8). Bethune and Brenneman personally wrote to or phoned many of CA's disgruntled customers to beg their forgiveness. This duty was not hived off to middle management or PR people. Bethune, Brenneman, every vice-president and many senior executives were required to spend time dealing with letters from angry and dissatisfied customers. They also had personally to call each one of these to apologize and to explain what the company was planning to do to fix its problems. They also applied the same process to the travel agents involved with CA, who had been at the receiving end of a lot of flak from CA's disgruntled customers and corporate clients. This admission of guilt, and the fact the CEO and his senior management team were making the effort to deal with this issue, went a long way to preventing further haemorrhaging of CA's customer base in 1994–5.

The next step they took was to cut CA's advertising budget in half because, as Bethune observed, 'it is offensive and insulting to customers to advertise a product they know is crummy' (p. 9). The rallying cry, 'Ask the customer in seat C9 the right question' was operationalized by first listening to the company's most lucrative customers. In CA's case this meant talking to their business clients in rows 1–9, at the front of the plane. They simply asked customers in this class want they wanted and what they would be willing to pay for. They discovered that all they wanted was safe terminals and planes, on-time flights, comfortable and attractive planes, good food at meal times and reliable priority baggage handling. Bethune recalled in 1998 that 'we were failing miserably on all counts' (p. 9).

Within six months, every plane had been repainted with the same colour scheme and all interior décors were made uniform. The hideous chevron design of the carpets in their terminals was replaced. When he had been told by the maintenance department that it would take four years, Bethune's reaction was 'if you can't get it done in four months, we'll find someone who will' (p. 9). This sense of urgency had an immediate impact on the company's employees, because 'they could see senior management finally taking the actions they knew had been needed for years' (p. 9). Other changes were made to both the quality of food and when it was served, with a whole range of new gourmet and snack foods introduced: 'And that's the whole point of asking the customer in seat C9 the right questions. In turnaround situations, or any business situation for that matter, you can't afford to risk anything else' (p. 10).

Ongoing commitment to continuous change, improvement and learning

CA is a company that has not allowed complacency or inertia to set in, and has continued to change and evolve and deal with new challenges. These include maintaining its on-time performance and overall passenger service, as well as coping with the arrival of Pro-Air, a new start-up airline (O'Reilly, 1999: 96). The combination of a clear vision, systemic thinking, simple strategies, new equipment, employee involvement and improved morale have all paid huge dividends for the company. Along the way, CA has received dozens of awards for excellence, including Air Transport World's 'Airline of the Year' in

1997 and 1999 and seven 'Airline of the Year' awards from OAG in 1997. As a result, the company has weathered the post-11 September storm better than any other US airline, with the possible exception of Southwest. As Gordon Bethune commented in 1998, 'We have big plans for Continental and we mustn't lose our momentum. Even though the turnaround is over, we won't forget the lessons we learned from it. In fact we are putting them into practice every day' (p. 12). This belief was the central driving force behind CA's remarkable turn-around and continues to form the bedrock of its continuing evolution, even after the events of 11 September, and the devastating effects this had on the US airline industry during 2002–3.

Postscript: 11 September 2001 and its aftermath

The combined effects of the attacks on the Twin Trade Towers in New York, other subsequent terrorist acts, the Second Gulf War in 2003, continuing instabilities in the Middle East and the emergence of severe acute respiratory syndrome had a devastating impact on the world's airline industries, and Continental has not been immune from this. Worldwide, losses on international airline services amounted to more than $US30 billion and wiped out more than 40 000 aviation jobs during 2001–3. Bookings fell by 40 per cent. Several smaller American airlines failed during 2003–4, even with the support of a six billion dollar aid package approved by the US Congress in early April 2003 (Creedy, 2003). While CA was forced temporarily to suspend 20 per cent of its employees in 2002–3, it promised to re-employ them as soon as it could. As we saw earlier, it was the only American airline to be ranked in the top 100 'best companies in the USA to work for' in 2002, and was also ranked as the 'Number One' airline in the USA by *Fortune* in 2002 (Levering and Moskowitz, 2003). Continental was also presented with the 2003 *Hay Group/Fortune* award for 'Most admired airline in the world', after two consecutive second places behind Singapore Airlines during 2001–2 (Hjelt, 2004: 47; 2003: 37). These awards were based on the votes of more than 10 000 directors, execu-tives or senior managers in 375 companies. After the company posted meagre profits in 2003, Bethune and his heir apparent Lawrence Kellner both took pay cuts of 50 per cent, a measure of the character and integrity of both men, their commitment to CA and their under-standing of the sacrifices their employees had been making during 2002–3 (Creedy, 2004).

CA also managed to reduce its operating costs by $US235 million during 2002–3, with a final target of $US500 million by the end of 2004. However, even though CA was considered to be one of the strongest airlines in the USA, it lost $US17 million in the second quarter of 2004 (this did include a one-off charge of $US15 million for the retirement of the MD-80 aircraft the company had been leasing). On a more positive note, CA's results were much better than most analysts had anticipated and amongst the best of the major US carriers (KRT, 2004). In contrast, United Airlines, the world's second largest carrier in 2001, was forced to file for bankruptcy in December 2002, with operating losses of $US22 million a day (Dalton, 2002d). This was the biggest aviation bankruptcy in US history, with nearly half of the company's 83 000 employees losing their jobs during the rationalization and restructuring of the business that followed during 2003–4. During 2004, there were rumours of a possible merger between CA and Southwest airlines, a union that for strategic and commercial reasons could have benefited both companies. However, this did not eventuate, and during 2005 Continental, in common with all other US airlines, struggled to cope with high oil prices and cut-throat competition in the American domestic market. In spite of the Herculean efforts of Bethune and Brenneman to turn the company around in the mid-1990s, the immediate future for Continental remains uncertain.

Unsuccessful change management: Shier chaos

The Continental Airlines story shows that the 11 elements described earlier were in place during its change management programme. Consequently, the company was able to achieve a remarkable corporate turnaround. By way of contrast, the next story shows how the absence of almost all of these 11 elements created widespread organizational and individual resistance to change in the publicly funded Australian Broadcasting Corporation (ABC). Critics of the corporation had long believed that it was elitist, politically left-wing, too reliant on taxpayers' money and not sufficiently commercial in its business operations. In April 2000, the ABC board, with the approval of the Liberal government, appointed a new director, Alan Shier, who had worked for many years in the commercial television sector in the UK. His brief was to reform the ABC's sluggish culture, grow its commercial potential and increase viewer numbers. At the time, these lagged well behind the main commercial providers in Australia, Channel 7, Channel 9 and Channel 10. Yet, within 19 months, Shier had been sacked, few meaningful changes had been introduced and the ABC's viewing figures had declined still further. How did this happen?

We've seen that successful change management requires a systemic understanding of a number of components that may need to be put in place in order to drive change through an organization. The first component was the presence of energetic and committed transformational leaders. To recap briefly, the qualities of successful change leaders include the ability to articulate a better future for the organization, an understanding of the culture and resistance points within the organization, great energy and persistence, the ability to touch hearts and minds and 'walk the talk', exceptional two-way communication skills and respect for all employees. Very soon after Shier was appointed, styling himself 'The Mini-Mogul of Broadcasting', his employees had given him the nickname 'Satan'. He quickly became regarded as arrogant and egotistical, and went out of his way to criticize 'reactionary' employees at the ABC. He became renowned for throwing temper tantrums when he didn't get his own way. He sacked a number of senior staff, without explanation, and then set up his own in-group of highly paid outsiders to engineer changes at the corporation. During his tenure he was routinely accused of bullying and intimidating treatment of staff and, on two occasions, of sexual harassment of women employees. This evidence indicates that Shier may have had a number of the characteristics of toxic leaders identified in Chapter 1.

The second component was a clear, compelling and motivational vision that most employees could buy into. After 19 months of Shier at the helm, no one had a clear idea about his vision or the direction he wanted the ABC to move in. Apart from some vague notions and suggestions about making the ABC 'more commercial', Shier was unable to articulate a clear and compelling vision of where he wanted to lead the corporation in the future. The third and fourth components were some understanding of why people resist change (and how to overcome this), and an ability first to diagnose and then try to change an organization's culture: usually the most difficult part of any change strategy. Shier appeared to have no understanding of the ABC's culture or, more importantly, of ways in which resistance to needed changes within the corporation might have been overcome. This important diagnostic skill also involves systemic thinking: the ability to understand how even small changes can have unintended or negative knock-on consequences. There were a series of disastrous ad hoc changes at the ABC in Shier's time, including the cancellation of well-established flagship programmes, such as the popular science programme, *Catalyst*. A number of these changes were quickly reversed after he was sacked.

The fifth and sixth components were creating a sense of urgency and applying a 'clean sweep' of managers who stand in the way of necessary change (while bringing in new people to replace them). Alas, Shier didn't even manage to get these right. Any sense of urgency that he may have created after he joined the corporation was soon replaced by panic, anger, resentment and resistance. In May 2000, Shier did start sacking staff, including national networks director Andy Lloyd, news chief Paul Williams and many others, and started bringing in his own people. However, as events transpired, even some of those he hand-picked to replace senior ABC staff subsequently left, disillusioned by his arrogant and autocratic leadership style. The seventh component was clear, workable and realistic strategies. Few people, inside or outside the ABC, including his own supporters ever had much idea what these were. The sixth and seventh components, linking in with all of the above, are the ability to create a sense of urgency while involving employees in the change process. All Shier managed to achieve was a sense of anger, confusion and alienation amongst his employees. According to all reports in the Australian press in the months leading up to his dismissal, he went out of his way not to consult and involve ABC staff in the change process.

The eighth component, communication, was singularly lacking in Shier's leadership repertoire. He was universally regarded as an awful public speaker, with a thin and indistinct voice, and came across to audiences of ABC employees as arrogant, condescending and patronizing. Even if some of his ideas were good (as some commentators at the time suggested), he was not able to get these across in a clear, engaging, inspirational or motivational manner. He also quickly gained a reputation for not listening to his employees and for routinely ignoring their ideas and suggestions. The ninth component was to involve employees and to celebrate victories and reward successes. Neither of these happened once at the ABC in the 19 months Shier was in charge. The tenth component was to involve customers and clients in the change process. If the letter page of *The Australian* was anything to go by, during 2000–2001, almost all ABC viewers were appalled by what Shier was trying to do. The corporation's viewing figures went into further decline from the moment he took over, a clear indication that most viewers did not approve of Shier's changes. The eleventh component was embedding a deep commitment within an organization's culture to continuous change, improvement and learning. Again, Shier failed to set this in motion, and it still remains a distant objective for the ABC. Little wonder, then, that Shier failed to drive through long-lasting improvements and changes at the corporation during his short and tempestuous time as director.

What legacy did Shier leave? He managed to get an extra 71 million dollars in funding for the corporation, most of the senior management team he recruited is still working at the ABC, and he pushed through some restructuring of the ABC's functions and departments. However, he quickly lost the support of most of the ABC's staff, because of his aggressive, volatile and confrontational management style. He also made some serious tactical errors. In retrospect, we can see that the ABC needed to find a media-savvy, results-focused man or woman who was sympathetic to the needs of a public sector broadcaster and, critically, a man or woman who understood its culture and could work with this and the people who worked at the ABC. This person needed to be able to enunciate a clear vision for the ABC and, most importantly, *involve* the corporation's staff in change initiatives. Because the ABC's culture is such a strong and entrenched one, the director would have needed to tap into the creativity and intelligence of the ABC's staff, while allowing the organization's leaders to set new strategic objectives and overcome bureaucratic inertia and resistance to necessary changes.

Unfortunately, the ABC Board is still made up of political appointees of the Federal Government. This group, who are responsible for running arguably the most important cultural institution in Australia, are largely underqualified in media-management. It took them more than eight months to appoint a new 'safe' director, Russell Balding (an accountant), who was appointed on 30 May 2002. At the time of Shier's dismissal, a number of media commentators suggested that Parliament should have taken a long hard look at the people who made this decision. Most of these are still sitting on the ABC Board and were, in the words of one commentator, 'responsible for the most mindless, wasteful and destructive period in the broadcaster's history'. The real, and still unanswered, mystery is why Shier was employed as director of the ABC in the first place, because, while he may have had some good ideas for strategic change, he lacked many of the most rudimentary change management skills. He certainly lacked transformational leadership abilities, was a poor communicator and may have had some toxic personality traits. Having said this, there was some good news for Shier. First, he was not alone in his inability to manage change: a capability that demands high-level leadership and people management skills, ones that he patently lacked. Second, and predictably, Shier did receive a very handsome pay-off of one million dollars in February 2002, courtesy of the Australian taxpayer, to 'reward' him for his short and unsuccessful tenure at the ABC. So he soon found himself a member of the fast-growing club of incompetent private sector directors who, at this time, were being routinely rewarded with huge sums of money, even when they were badly mismanaging their companies (Dempster, 2002; various articles in *The Australian*, May 2000–June 2002).[3]

Conclusion

Q. 'What has been the biggest change in business during your time as CEO?'

A. 'By far, speed. How fast you can adapt your goals is the main measure of what kind of company you've got. So you've got to be getting people to relish changes. You've got to talk about change every second of the day.'

(*Jack Welch, in an interview to coincide with the launch of his autobiography,* Straight from the Gut, Fortune, *17 September, 2001*)

The evidence from research into organizational and cultural change, and real-life examples of successful change, shows that transformational leaders have a number of shared characteristics. They are very flexible and responsive to the dynamic and turbulent business environments in which their businesses operate. They are able to tap into employee dissatisfaction with the present, build on this and create a new and shared vision of a better future. They understand that leading change requires a commitment to action, effective communication and the involvement and participation of employees in implementing *their* vision. They listen and they learn from their employees. They know that they must involve the whole team and enable their employees to own, share and run with the new vision. Successful transformational leaders are catalysts and facilitators, people who encourage others to achieve more and who honour their followers with trust, respect and support. They are tolerant of ambiguity, uncertainty and diversity, and able to empathize with the concerns and needs of their followers. They are able to foster attitudes and processes amongst their employees that are conducive to continual adaptation, learning and change. They understand how far their people can be stretched, and can equip and motivate them to achieve more than they thought they could achieve alone. Deep down, they know that successful change is not easy to achieve. They understand that fear of the unknown must be expected and overcome. They know that shocks and surprises should be assumed (and even welcomed) and that risk or resistance-free change often means no change. Last, they understand that failures and mistakes that may occur during times of change are not the problem – a failure to learn from these is.[4]

However, the presence of transformational leaders alone will not always guarantee success and, as noted earlier, managing change is not a paint-by-numbers exercise. It will always throw up unexpected surprises and setbacks. Anita Roddick has observed:

When you read about change, it often comes across as a remarkably simple activity: establish your vision, design the change programme and paint by numbers. Get this: change doesn't work that way. In the real world of

change, the vision gets blurred – especially when new leaders come into play. Competition and opposition come in the places and forms you least expect and your fiercest opponent can turn into your most vital supporter. Why does this happen? Because change is about people and people will always surprise you. When you try to bring in new changes into a sleepy business setting, you're going to have some nightmares along the way with a few sweet dreams come true.
(*Roddick, 2000: 26*)

Hence it is important to emphasize that there never has been, and probably never will be, a standard fix-it-all blueprint for leading change in every organizational context. Every leader has to examine the particular requirements of their own organization and adapt their change management programmes accordingly. Having said this, the elements contained in the template described in this chapter can be found in *all* the examples of successful organizational and cultural change we reviewed between 1997 and 2004. As a result, this template has real operational potency in most change management situations, and it can be used as a basic framework, and refined and reformulated as needed to help plan change in many different organizational circumstances.

In conclusion, the twin forces of technology and globalization are producing changes that are faster and more radical than the first industrial revolution of the 19th and 20th centuries. These are also fragmenting markets and reshaping industries faster than at any other time in human history. The most successful organizations of the next 20 years will be those that can change now and keep changing quickly in the future, in order to keep ahead of these developments. The creation of grandiose visions, and the engineering of dramatic revolutions in organizations, should always be the last resort, because they are actually the hardest things to initiate and see through, particularly in large public sector bureaucracies. The world's most consistently successful businesses do not 'manage change' by undergoing wrenching restructuring or dramatic periods of downsizing, and only on very rare occasions do they merge with other companies. Instead, they have created a perpetual organic impetus for steady change, evolution, development and growth. They have achieved this by building these capacities into the mind-sets of their employees, their collective working practices and the operational cultures of their organizations, in the form of perpetual innovation, systemic organizational learning and effective knowledge management. These elements of perpetual organizational change and evolution are addressed in the next two chapters.

There are only two types of company:
those that are changing and those that are going out of business.
(*Norman Augustine, former CEO of Lockheed Martin, 1997*)

Only the paranoid survive.
(*Andy Grove, co-founder and former Chairman of Intel, 1990*)

Exercise 8.3

Having read through this chapter, how can you use any new insights you may have acquired about managing organizational and cultural change in the future?

Insight   **Possible strategy**

1.

2.

3.

4.

5.   ◆

Notes

1 This section is adapted from Forster (2002).
2 For a more detailed account of the turnaround of Continental, see Bethune (1999).
3 And, in the cases of Enron, Worldcom and several other companies, the directors of these companies led them headlong into bankruptcy, while at the same time awarding themselves very large salaries, stock options and 'performance bonuses', and lying systematically to their employees and shareholders, within weeks of these companies' collapses (see Chapter 12 for further discussion of these issues). In their book on the rise and fall of Enron, Bethany McLean and Peter Elkind describe Enron's culture from the mid-1990s to its demise in 2001 as arrogant, chaotic, destructive, rotten, dysfunctional, delusional, individualistic, over the top, unethical, avaricious, greedy, macho, immoral and obsessed with money making regardless of any moral considerations (McLean and Elkind, 2003).
4 A detailed discussion of the evaluation of change management programmes is beyond the scope of this book. The most systematic and widely used method of 'before/after' evaluation is the 'Balanced Scorecard' system, developed by Kaplan and Norton (1996, 2000).

9   Innovation and organizational learning

Objectives

To define innovation and invention.

To describe the pivotal roles that innovation, creativity and intrapreneurship now play in modern organizations.

To enhance your lateral thinking abilities, help you become more creative and improve your ability to envision the future.

To describe how to create an organizational culture that can promote greater creativity and innovation amongst employees.

To define what a learning organization is, to evaluate the benefits of introducing learning organization principles into organizations, and to describe some strategies for achieving this.

Introduction

Innovation.
(*The one-word logo on 3m products. This US company has been regularly cited in business surveys as being one of the world's most consistently innovative companies over the last 50 years*)

Destroyyourbusiness.com.
(*The name of Jack Welch's intranet initiative at General Electric in the mid-1990s*)

Innovation is the only core competency that an organization needs.
(*Peter Drucker, 1985*)

The role of innovation in organizations

Innovation comes from the Latin *innovare*, meaning to 'change into something new'. Innovation and innovate have been in use since the

347

early 16th century, and 'innovative' since the 17th century. However, during this time the word had largely negative connotations. For example, William Shakespeare, in *King Lear*, talks of 'Poor discontents, which gape and rub the elbow at the news of hurly-burly innovation.' Innovation was synonymous with revolution and, for the political and religious authorities of the time, something to be actively discouraged. Over the next three hundred years, the meaning of innovation slowly evolved to signify the creation of something new. The 1939 edition of the *Oxford English Dictionary* first articulated the modern meaning of this word as 'the act of introducing a new product into the market'. It is defined here as the process of creating new products or services, introducing new methods and ideas, or making incremental changes or improvements. Innovation is linked to, but distinct from, the process of invention. This word also originates in *innovare*. To invent means to devise, originate, produce or construct something by original thought. Both are forms of creativity, but invention does not always lead to innovation. For example, Thomas Edison, probably the single most successful inventor in human history, with 1093 patents to his name, was, strangely, a hopeless innovator. His financial backers routinely removed him from many of the new businesses he founded and put these in the hands of professional managers (Nicholas, 2000).

If 'culture', 'quality' and 're-engineering' were three of the dominant buzzwords of the 1980s, then 'innovation' was certainly the dominant buzzword of the 1990s, being described by some business analysts as the 'industrial theology' of the last decade of the 20th century. In October 2000, in its annual survey of 'the world's most admired companies', *Fortune* asked the question, 'How do you make the world's most admired list?' The answer was, 'Innovate, Innovate, Innovate!' (Stein, 2000). This survey reported that all of the world's top companies believed that the key to staying ahead of the pack was constant innovation and learning. Included amongst these innovative companies were BP and Royal Dutch Shell, who are featured later in this chapter. There are three principal reasons why innovation became such an important organizational competency during the 1990s.

First, many 'old' management techniques such as just-in-time, supply-chain management, outsourcing, total quality or business process re-engineering have been used, at some time, by almost every large and medium-sized business in the industrialized world. So, in order to gain a competitive edge, companies have to be able to find new ways of increasing their performance, and improving the quality and novelty of the products and services that they bring to their markets.

Second, these traditional organizational management techniques, while certainly improving efficiencies for many companies around the world over the last two decades, can also lead to rigidity and inflexibility. In itself, this might not be a problem, except that new ideas, knowledge and intellectual capital are fast becoming the primary drivers of competitive advantage in business. According to many commentators, efficient internal systems and processes have become merely a prerequisite for being in business, and non-linear innovative thinking is fast becoming the principal driver of long-term wealth creation. It is no longer sufficient to make one thing well and sell it at a profit. Sooner or later a competitor will undercut your price, steal your ideas from you or create something better. Sometimes they will do all three at the same time. In any event, your company will either die or be taken over. So the Holy Grail for many businesses today is the generation of a steady stream of new ideas, services or products that will sell in the marketplace (James, 2001; Sutton, 2001; Hamel, 2000a, b; Drucker, 1985).

Third is the impact that innovation can have on the bottom-line performance and profitability of organizations. In Chapter 3, we cited several examples of the dividends that can flow from upward communication in organizations. They are also excellent examples of the power of unleashing the innovative capabilities of all of an organization's employees. Between 1984 and 1999, the top 20 per cent of firms in the annual 'Innovation Poll' conducted by *Fortune* (in conjunction with Arthur D. Little) achieved double the shareholder return of a comparison group of their peers (Jonash and Sommerlatte, 1999). Another survey showed that the overall rate of return on 17 successful business innovations made in the 1970s averaged 56 per cent, compared with an average return of 16 per cent on investment in all American businesses between 1970 and 2000 (Nicholas, 2000). A study of 30 large international companies revealed that the single most important factor that differentiated high-growth companies from low-growth companies was the emphasis they placed on strategic innovation (Kim and Maurbogne, 1999).

In the 1990s, the desire to become more innovative led to an increased interest in 'intrapreneurship' in many companies, by devolving power, setting up internal 'ideas-factories' or 'skunk-works', and a concerted drive to recruit and retain creative and innovative employees (Christensen, 1997). The idea of 'intrapreneurship' is not a new one. H.G. Wells, the visionary 19th-century science-fiction writer, created a game in the 1880s called 'Cheat the Prophet'. This game involved gathering together the smartest group of forward thinkers and futurists he could find, asking them to describe the future and then imagining how they could undertake every one of the crazy, laughable ideas that they created. Amongst the ideas that Wells generated were international air travel, flying to the moon, genetic engineering, human invisibility and time travel. Three out of five within 100 years is a pretty good track record. A few maverick scientists even believe that the last two are now theoretically possible (see Chapter 11). Over the last hundred years, we can find many other ideas that were also regarded as being crazy, laughable or ludicrous when they were first suggested. For example, when Jerry Levin (the founder of AOL) first proposed in the early 1980s that every home in America could be wired by cable, and connected to online subscription media and television services, most business people dismissed the idea out of hand. In the 1970s, the corporate world thought that Bill Gates was a pie-in-the-sky dreamer when he first described his vision of having a PC in every home and in every office around the world. At the time, most senior managers in large companies such as IBM and Rank-Xerox dismissed the PC as a toy, with limited commercial applications. Single-handedly, this one innovation tore the whole of the mainstream computing industry apart and, in the process, pushed IBM to the brink. In Chapter 11, we'll look at some other scenarios for the future that most people would currently dismiss as being crazy, laughable or ludicrous.

In spite of the importance of innovation, many leaders and managers continue to be sceptical about the business value of 'creativity' and 'learning'. There is no denying that much day-to-day work in organizations is routine, and involves what essentially amounts to efficient repetition and/or the fine-tuning of productive processes that have worked well for a period of time. Creativity and innovation imply constant change and constant evolution, and many organizations and their employees can find this prospect threatening and stressful. Nevertheless, sometimes companies must embrace radical innovations in order to prosper. For example, in the late 1990s, Charles Schwab had to make the difficult decision to move its business to the Web, knowing that this move would force it to slash prices by 60 per cent. How would your colleagues react if you told them that your company would have to do this next month? Other companies, such as Merrill Lynch, dithered and delayed, but Charles Schwab went ahead and, as a result, gained a clear competitive edge over their main rivals. Only non-linear thinking, with an eye to the future, gave the company the confidence to do this (Hamel, 2000a). All of the available research evidence indicates that innovative companies benefit in a variety of ways. They are more adaptable to change, they are able to respond more quickly to changes in their environments, they are able to create change for others to follow in their wakes, they spot new opportunities before the competition does, and are consistently more profitable over longer periods of time, when compared to non-innovative organizations (Hamel 2000a, 2000b; Collins and Porras, 1996).

> When you have disciplined thought, you don't need bureaucracy. When you have disciplined actions, you don't need excessive controls. When you combine a culture of discipline, with an ethic of entrepreneurship, you get the magical alchemy of great performance.
> (*Jim Collins,* Good to Great, *2001*)

Becoming more creative and innovative

> Doing the same thing, over and over again, and expecting different or better results.
> (*An old definition of madness*)

> I skate to where the puck is going to be, not where it has been.
> (*Canadian hockey superstar, Wayne Gretsky, 1990*)

In Chapter 1, it was noted that one skill that certainly is important to leaders these days is the ability to envision the future. This ability has been described as something that often sets true leaders apart from the crowd, a unique ability to spot new business opportunities and new markets, like truffle hounds sniffing out truffles in the woods. Vision stems from the ability to see the world in new or different ways, to make associations between already existing bodies of knowledge in order to create new ideas, or to see new and emerging worlds in the future. This also implies a capacity to view the world as an oyster of creative possibilities, rather than a world of restrictive limitations. In this section there are several opportunities to try out some creative and lateral thinking exercises that will enhance your ability to envision and, later on, scenario-map the future.

If necessity is the mother of invention, then lateral thinking is the mother of creativity. Creativity refers to the ability to synthesize ideas in new ways or to make unusual or novel associations between bodies of knowledge, in a way that leads to different understandings or interpretations of reality. This is where Edward De Bono's concept of 'lateral thinking' can be extremely useful. De Bono has argued for some time that 'linear thinking' (based on judgment, analysis, logic and argument), the dominant way of thinking of the 20th century, will have to be supplemented by 'what can be' thinking (based on creativity, imagination, reconstruction and redesign). However, most education, in either the scholastic or managerial sense, tends to overlook, or even ignore, the natural ability that young children have to think laterally. As we observed in the last chapter, this is why they are continually asking 'why', 'what', 'when', 'where' and 'how' questions and why they often learn best through play and experimentation during their formative years. However, most people's natural creative skills and lateral thinking abilities are usually hampered by the formal education they receive in secondary school and/or universities, where education is still largely based on spoon-feeding, power-point presentations, rote learning and examination tests. Most traditional organizations also emphasize control and the measurement of performance, rather than creativity and learning. This is why it can be difficult for adults to embrace creative thinking, and is the main reason why acquiring this gets harder the older they get, unless they practise this skill. The main differences between linear/sequential thinking and lateral thinking are summarized in Table 9.1.

Table 9.1   Linear and lateral thinking

Linear/sequential thinker	Lateral thinker
Can only look at problems through common-sense frameworks of understanding; is concerned with absolute judgments and stability	Tries to find new ways of looking at things; is concerned with change and movement; constantly questions the status quo and common sense
Tries to find 'right' or 'wrong' solutions to all problems as quickly as possible	Tries to find what is different; not obsessed with finding the 'right' answers immediately
Makes quick judgments about ideas as being either 'workable' or 'unworkable'	Analyses all ideas for anything that may be useful, however bizarre or extreme they may first appear to be
Can only progress by taking sequential steps within narrow frameworks of understanding	Progresses by making dissociative leaps between different frameworks and bodies of knowledge
Selectively chooses only the information that fits within their narrow paradigms of understanding	Will consider anything, from any source or body of knowledge, to improve their understanding of an issue or problem
Always considers the obvious; conservative; constantly reacts to and resists change and innovations	Progresses by creating the future for others to follow; is comfortable with change, innovation and perpetual learning

Source: Adapted from De Bono, 1970, 1985.

All leaders and managers will recognize and understand logical or sequential thinking. Fewer will be comfortable with the notion of lateral thinking or, initially, see what its value might be. So to start things off, over the next few pages we are going to reawaken your innate creativity and ability to think laterally. These exercises start with some well-known and relatively simple ones, progressing to others that will stretch your lateral thinking skills and, in the words of many MBA students, 'make your brain ache'.

Exercise 9.1

These exercises can be completed alone, but they are more enjoyable if you can do them with other people. If you have young children, let them try these (they'll enjoy them). Time allowed, 30 minutes.

Part 1

Please solve the following problems (time allowed, 20 minutes).

1. If today is Monday, what is the day after the day before tomorrow?

2. You are a woman. What relationship to you is your father's only son-in-law's mother-in-law's only daughter?

3. Add five lines to the lines below to make a total of nine.

4. How many Fs are there in this sentence: 'Feature films are the result of years of scientific study combined with the experience of years'?

5. Draw one line below to make the Roman symbol for '9' transform into '6' (VI).

    IX

6. Draw four straight lines that pass through all nine dots in the diagram below, without lifting your pen from the paper.

    *   *   *

    *   *   *

    *   *   *

Part 2

When you've completed Part 1, please answer the following questions (time allowed, 40 minutes).

1. Every morning, a fit, healthy man walks into the lift on the twentieth floor of his apartment block and travels down to the ground floor. He goes to work. When he returns from work, he gets into the lift on the ground floor, gets out at the tenth floor and walks the rest of the way to his apartment up the stairs. Why? (Clues: there is nothing wrong with the lift and, if it was raining, he did not have to get out at the tenth floor.)

2. A farmer comes into one of his fields one morning. He sees a man lying in the middle of the field. The man is dead. The farmer knows immediately how he died. How did the man die? (Clues: he was not murdered, killed by farm machinery or attacked by a wild animal.)

A 'dissociative jump' from:

3. An important event took place in Neufchâtel on 17 August 1968 that had a profound effect on Switzerland's major manufacturing industry. It took some ten years to recover from this. What were the event and the industry?

to:

4. What device was first patented as 'a harmonic frequency multiplexing telegraphy unit'? Who created this device and what was unique about the patent?

to:

5. What hybrid device was later created from the innovation described in 4, and Thomas Edison's 'electric phonograph' (whose use is essentially the same as the device described in 3)?

If you can't find the solutions to these, you may want to read through the next paragraph before looking at the answers in note 1. ◆

Was there a mild sense of *Eureka* when you got the answers? In the case of the parachutist exercise, you needed to 'think beyond the field' and consider where the dead person came from and how he arrived there. Most people will spend all their time considering what might have happened *in* the field. The 'nine dots' exercise is a perfect example of *not looking for what you were looking for* (discussed further below). You might have started at each corner and joined the dots up and found that two or three dots managed to 'evade' your four lines every time. Through trial and error, you may have covered all but one dot using this method, and assumed that, because you were so close, you were on the right track and persisted with this for some time.

However, it would only be when you realized that you had to, literally in this case, 'look outside the box', that the solution would have revealed itself. Most people trying to solve this problem would confine their lines to the box as defined by the dots. The successful problem solver would see, in their mind's eye, that the only solution is to extend the four lines *beyond* the edge of the box (Perkins, 2001: 49–50). The historical questions highlight how closed people's minds can be to new ideas and innovations, particularly those who would consider themselves to be rational, practical and hard-headed business people.

What these exercises also reveal is that everyone sees the world through preconstructed mind-sets. In Chapter 1, in the context of our views about what leadership 'is', we saw that we do not 'create' these mind-sets in any conscious sense. This is how a normal mind works and, without this automatic filtering process, we could not function in any meaningful sense. These perceptions also operate almost entirely at an *unconscious* level, and only a pathological mind can see the world unfiltered through prior knowledge. This is why genius is often associated with madness, or at least eccentricity, and is the main reason why almost all new ideas appear to be crazy when they are first proposed. However, we also saw that the ability *not* to take things for granted, and to question common-sense ways of doing things, are skills that differentiate visionary leaders from humdrum, run-of-the-mill leader/managers. Here is another exercise to illustrate the consequences of our selective perceptions. In Figure 9.1, there are a series of picture puzzles. Please describe what you can see in each of these. The solutions can be found in note 2.

These exercises have been used with several hundred MBAs over the last ten years. In that time, *not one* has been able to see all sixteen objects in these pictures at the same time. Very few were able to see more than half of these at first. However, with practice they could get better at this, *but only by not looking for what they were looking for*. This may sound odd, but is exactly what you have to do to in order to improve your ability to *see* the whole picture, and to look at these pictures (or, in organizational contexts, alternative realities) from different perspectives. This ability is sometimes described as 'reframing' and, by looking at something in a different way, 'reality' itself can appear to change. The next group of lateral thinking exercises will help you look for what is not immediately obvious in a specific situation.

Figure 9.1   Picture puzzles

Exercise 9.2

Advanced lateral thinking

Time allowed = 60 minutes

1. Two strangers meet at a party and fall into a conversation about their lives. At one point, the first stranger says, 'I have to confess that I don't always speak the truth.' The second stranger replies, 'Well that I must certainly believe.' Yet the second stranger has not heard anything he knows to be false. Why is the second stranger so sure that the first stranger's confession is true?

2. One day at the office, Alice says to Betty, 'I heard this great joke from Cathy' and she begins to tell Betty the joke. But Betty says, 'Oh, I already know that joke.' Alice says, 'So Cathy's already told you it?' 'No', says Betty. 'In fact, I've never heard it or read it before.' Explain how this could be true.

3. Here is an equation: 2 + 7 − 118 = 129. Add one line anywhere in the equation to make it true.

4. You are standing in a room. Above you are two strings some distance apart. On a table, there is a dictionary, a glass, a live toad, a stapler and a clothes peg. Holding one string in your hand you can't quite reach the other string, even when you stand on the table. How might you tie the two strings together?

5. Last, here's a real tester. One day an old wind-up clock that chimed the hours (for example, seven times at seven o'clock) and quarter hours (one chime each quarter) struck twenty-seven times within the span of one hour and one minute. Yet there is nothing wrong with the clock and all this happened in a natural and appropriate way. How could this possibly happen?

If you are struggling with these, you may like to read through the next section, and then have another attempt before looking at the solutions. These can be found in note 2.

Source: Adapted from Perkins (2001: 59–61 and 118). ◆

Each of these exercises highlights different facets of lateral and creative thinking. For example, 'To tell the Truth' is a seemingly clueless exercise, but it shows how a problem solver needs to be able to 'see the wood from the trees'. Which is the one statement that might be true and what can be inferred from this? 'The Joke', reminds us of the Sherlock Holmes principle: when all other possible solutions have been excluded the one that remains, however unlikely, must be the answer to the mystery. Betty hadn't *read* or *heard* the joke before, so where could it have come from? Or, by taking another lateral step, can you work out from where Cathy might have obtained the joke? The solution to the equation exercise is similar to the 'Six' and 'Nine' exercises. The usual approach is to try out various permutations of brackets and plus or minus signs in order to equalize the equation. However, it is only when the actual *numbers* in the equation are reframed (that is, looked at in a different way) that the solution becomes apparent.

The 'Two Strings' exercise highlights something that psychologists have called 'functional fixedness'. This refers to the tendency to only see the normal function of objects, rather than their possible alternative uses. So, as soon as you can see an alternative use for one of these objects, the solution reveals itself. The remaining items are distractions, which may have taken you up a number of blind alleys. The clock exercise is the perfect example of how lateral thinking can be superior to linear and logical thinking. The logical and sequential approach would have been to add up the maximum possible number of chimes in the hour between 11.00 and 12.00 (11 chimes at 11.00 + 3 chimes on each quarter hour + 12 chimes at 12.00 = 26 chimes). So, how is it possible to get an extra quarter of an hour and the one extra chime to make 27 chimes in total? Invariably, the focus is on the clock. How can it strike 27 times in an hour, when only 26 chimes are possible? The only answer is that it must be caused by something external to the clock. What could that be? What forces or circumstances could make a clock strike 27 times in the hour? Or, taking the next lateral step, *what specific event external to the clock could alter time*? As soon as this is taken, the solution reveals itself (abridged from Perkins, 2001: 61–3).

When you knew the answers, did you again get that *Eureka* feeling, 'Well it's obvious isn't it!'? Maybe so, but the important point is that it wasn't obvious *before* you knew the answers, and this is why leaders have to be able to question 'common-sense' ways of doing things. If you didn't do so well with these exercises, don't worry. We are dealing with creative skills that may have lain dormant for many years or have never been properly activated. As noted earlier, we can blame traditional teaching and lecturing techniques for this, where rote learning of the 'right' and 'wrong' answers and examination tests all too often stifle imagination and creativity. However, with practice, you will become better at this and you will experience more dissociative cognitive leaps and breakthrough thinking moments. When you can do this, you can start to envision the future in new, bold and imaginative ways.

These exercises highlight two other important elements of personal creativity, lateral thinking and the ability to create new visions for the future: you have to be able to look for, and find, new opportunities or realities that are not obvious to everyone else, or you have to be able to make bisociative links between existing bodies of knowledge, in order to reframe current reality or create a new reality.

It is often assumed that *Eureka* or inspirational breakthrough moments are the product of individual genius, but the previous sections show that lateral and creative thinking are skills that can be enhanced through learning and practice. Of course, in themselves, lateral thinking exercises will not be sufficient to increase your innovative capabilities, because there are three main sources of breakthrough thinking.

The first, *bisociation*, requires an ability to make links between apparently unrelated areas of knowledge or experience (Koestler, 1975). More often than not, a new idea is the consequence of melding two or more existing areas of knowledge together for the first time. Some real-life examples of bissociation are described in the next section.

The second, *incubation* refers to the process where you may have been wrestling with a problem for weeks, or perhaps months, and suddenly the solution just 'appears' in front of you, often at an unexpected moment. The Romans believed that, when people experienced these inspirational moments, the gods had literally 'breathed' this into their minds (*inspirare*). We now know that that these moments of inspiration, or acts of creation, are the products of the normal functioning of the unconscious mind (Howkins, 2002; Koestler, 1975).

The third source is *Selective encoding, combination and comparison*: this form of trial-and-error creativity results from the classical process of experimentation and falsification, as described by the philosopher of science, Karl Popper (1959). This is best exemplified in Thomas Edison's famous saying that creativity is '10 per cent inspiration and 90 per cent perspiration'.

It doesn't matter which one(s) you rely on because they all have their uses. However, the only way to become more creative is by 'wearing' what Edward De Bono (1985) has described as different 'Thinking Hats'. This means moving out of the narrow realms of understanding that leaders and managers often mistakenly describe as 'the real world'. For example, how much do you know about the following real worlds? A woman entrepreneur in India or Japan. An accountant working in Moscow. A Japanese salary man. A ski-instructor. A lawyer/attorney working in (a) France, (b) the USA or (c) the UK. A farmer working in the mid-west of the USA. A Web Master. A mid-ranking tax official in the Italian Civil Service. A child slave-labourer in Burma. A woman trying to break into a male-dominated profession, such as the military. An employee on an oil-rig. A young doctor working 80–100 hours a week as a hospital intern. A vice-chancellor of a large university. A computer games software developer. A scientist working on nanotechnologies or biocomputers. A resource or mining manager. The CEOs of any of the *Fortune* top 100 companies.

It can be a sobering experience when we first realize that our personal understanding of the 'real world' is usually quite limited. When we look at the life worlds that most people inhabit, we invariably find that these are constructed and constrained by their upbringing, culture, gender, unique life experiences and education, as well as their choice of profession and the kinds of organizations they have chosen to work in. Hence the starting point on the journey to becoming more creative and innovative is the realization that there are a remarkable number of real worlds out there. All of these have the potential to inform the way we lead people and how we manage our businesses or organizations. Making the most of this journey means reading voraciously, studying areas of knowledge outside our immediate area of expertise, and taking the blinkers off. So, if you are an engineer, a technician or an accountant, read up on some qualitative or 'soft' subjects, such as existential philosophy or psychology or sociology. If you are an artist, graphic designer or a musician, read some Stephen Hawking. If you work in a university, spend at least 10 per cent of your time working with companies in the private sector. If you work in a large bureaucratic organization, read some books on innovation and entrepreneurship. If you run a small company, study the histories, cultures and management practices of the best (and the worst) large companies. If you haven't travelled much, read up on the cultures and histories of other countries, or take a sabbatical and travel yourself. If you are hopeless at numbers, enrol on a statistics course. If you hate speaking in public, take some classes in presentation skills. Whatever you do, extend your personal 'envelope', push the bubble and get outside your comfort zone.

Read, or subscribe to, professional journals and magazines that have nothing to do with your job, profession or occupation. You will be amazed at how often insights and ideas from apparently unrelated areas have applications to your business, the way you go about doing your job and the way in which you go about leading and managing others. Increase your faith in intuition or 'gut-feelings'. If you are skilled at information gathering and analysis, and lateral thinking, the chances are that your instincts will be the right ones to follow. We remarked in the notes at the end of Chapter 6 that intuition is a much undervalued management skill, and simply means the ability to make good decisions with incomplete data. At times, you will simply have to trust your judgment and go with this. Let your playful and child-like quality come out, use your daydreams and allow your unconscious mind to roam free.³ Make the most of your 'creative bubbles' and keep a notebook or electronic organizer to jot down any new ideas that you come up with. These will often pop up at the most unexpected moments, when doing the ironing, when out walking, during the night or when waking up in the morning, when our unconscious minds 'release' new ideas into the conscious mind. Remember also the emphasis placed on fun and creative learning in the companies we looked at in Chapter 4. Humour is a font of creativity, and creativity drives innovation.

Other useful insights into the creative mind can be found in the biographies of business leaders, innovators and paradigm breakers. A good starting point is the autobiographies of Akio Morita, Andy Grove and Thomas Edison, who were true visionaries, maverick geniuses and social philanthropists. Make creative use of all the future-casting, innovation and new technology sites that are now available on the web. Network incessantly and find a group of people or a partner who may share your ideas or vision of a new business opportunity. There are many examples of this kind of collaboration in the past, including the Wright Brothers, Gates and Allen at Microsoft, Jobs and Sculley at Apple, the Phillips Brothers and Hewlett and Packard, all of which can be described as genuine chalk and cheese partnerships. Last, but not least, make full use of the variety of presentation and persuasion skills that were reviewed in Chapter 3 to describe what you see to your peers, bosses and followers. You may have some great ideas, but you must be able to convince the people you work with that your ideas (or reinterpretations of reality) are correct, and also represent the right way, road or path to travel along in the future. If you can find some time to develop the skills described in this section, you will become more creative and innovative, more capable of envisioning the future and in a much better position to persuade other people that your ideas and innovations are the right ones to pursue.

In summary, the only way to become more open-minded and creative is to embrace different mind-sets. By taking this leap, we are then in a better position to make dissociative leaps between different real worlds and the bodies of knowledge they encapsulate. In turn, this will lead to greater personal creativity and innovation. Perhaps the best exemplar of this principle is Peter Drucker, the most innovative and visionary management thinker of the 20th century. In the early 1950s, he predicted that computer technologies would transform all businesses. In the 1960s, he was one of the first to warn of the rise of Japan as an economic powerhouse, and the first to warn of its economic decline when it was at the peak of its industrial power in the mid-1980s. Among many other new ideas he developed were 'knowledge workers', 'management by objectives' and 'privatization'. He was among the first to extol the importance of innovation in organizations and, more recently, to question pure economic rationalism as a sensible way to manage businesses. His ability to create these ideas stemmed in part from the sheer range of the intellectual and practical interests he pursued. These ranged from history to economics, from psychology to philosophy, from African cultures to Japanese art and opera. His consulting portfolio embraced hundreds of organizations, including small businesses, multinational corporations, churches, hospitals, NGOs, charities and governments. In 2004, at the age of 94, he was still searching for new and better ways to understand how business works and, more importantly, continued to make bold intuitive predictions about the future of business.

> The test of a first rate intelligence is the ability to hold two opposed ideas in the mind at the same time and still retain the ability to function.
> (F. Scott Fitzgerald, cited by Richard Schickel, The Disney Version, 1968)

> We become creative by finding a likeness between things that were not alike before. The creative mind is a mind that looks for unexpected likenesses in everyday things.
> (Jacob Bronowski, 1980)

Creativity and innovation in practice

What is most remarkable about breakthrough thinking is that the way in which this process works has changed little over the last 100 000 years, although the general pace of innovation has certainly accelerated over the last 1000 years. From the time when our earliest ancestors discovered how to make fire by creating friction between two sticks; to using flints, stones and other materials to create a variety of tools and weapons; to employing coloured ochre to create the first cave paintings; to the discovery of smelting; the development of the wheel; the building of the first boats and the development of sails; the domestication of animals and planting seasonal crops in settled communities and, laterally, to the development of written languages, mathematics and philosophy; all of these innovations stemmed from creative imagining, breakthrough thinking and by asking the perennial question, 'What if we . . .?' The Greek scientist and innovator, Archimedes, was certainly not the first person to experience a *Eureka* moment in human history.

Two of the most famous examples of dissociative and creative leaps of imagination are the Gutenberg Press and the development of the first heavier-than-air flying machine. In the mid-15th century, only a tiny number of people were literate (primarily the clergy and some of the nobility), and all books were written by hand and took months to produce. Johannes Gutenberg, a German metal worker, had a vision and a mission: to create an efficient technology for mass-producing Bibles. He did not have to start from scratch. Primitive wood-plate printing did exist, but still required the laborious carving of every single page of a document or book. The actual printing was also done manually, by pressing the wooden plate against the paper. The finished product, while cheaper and quicker to produce, was of poorer quality than the hand-written books of the time. Gutenberg's first breakthrough came as the result of a lateral leap. As a metal worker, he was familiar with the metal stamps used to emboss the wax seals on official documents. He then conceived the idea of a series of small metal stamps or plates, each with letters and symbols that could be assembled into the text for a given page. Multiple copies could then be printed off and the plates reassembled for the next page, and so forth. He then needed to find an efficient mechanical method for pressing the plates against the paper. After wrestling with this problem for months, he was taking a break and attending a local wine festival. By chance, he encountered another technology that would enable him to make the next vital breakthrough. There, amidst the high spirits and drunken revelry of the festival, he saw one of the first mechanical wine presses in Europe. Instantly, a lateral link occurred, and he developed this technology into a machine that led, amongst other things, to the industrial and scientific revolutions of the 19th century and the emergence of democracy in the 20th century. The arrival of the first recognizably modern printing press in 1455 had as big an impact on the world at that time as the Internet and the personal computer are having on our world today.

More recently, in the 1890s Orville and Wilbur Wright – like Leonardo da Vinci before them – took their initial inspiration from the flight of birds and the use of propellers to provide the necessary thrust for take-off, combined with the new science of aeronautics. They assumed that they could make use of theories of propeller design contained in marine engineering textbooks. They quickly discovered that there weren't any. After much brainstorming they developed a new theory: that the propeller should be thought of not as a screw, as used on ships to displace water, but as a rotary wing. Just as the wings of the plane would give lift, the 'wings' of the propeller would pull the plane forward. This breakthrough thinking allowed the Wright Brothers to apply what they already knew about wing design to the design of their propellers. Combined with a redesigned and more powerful internal combustion engine taken from already existing car engine technology, this was the last major hurdle to be overcome before powered flight became a reality (abridged from Perkins, 2001: 5–6, 44–6).

Around the same time, when Edison's inventors were developing the light bulb, their experimental bulbs kept falling out of their sockets. After trying dozens of different fixtures, one technician noted that the threaded cap of a kerosene bottle kept it firmly in place. *Eureka*, and the introduction of a design that has not changed in US light bulbs for more than one hundred years (Hargadon and Sutton, 2000:32). Again, what use could you make of glue that can't join anything together? Marketing executives at 3m were shown this in the 1930s and, naturally enough, couldn't think of any use for glue that didn't dry and couldn't actually stick things together. In the 1940s, one employee, who was also a devout Christian, realized that it was ideal for marking the pages of the bible that he was reading. He had also noticed that the bookmarks placed in hymnals at his church invariably fell out. After initially being taken up and used by secretaries within the company, the product was eventually marketed and became a hugely successful product. It is now sold in a mind-boggling array of shapes, colours, designs and dispensers in almost every country in the world: the ubiquitous Post It.

Another example of both lateral association and incubation is Velcro (from the 'vel' of *velvet* and the 'cro' of *crochet*). During the late 1940s, a Swiss national named George de Mistral was both irritated and intrigued by the way that the burrs of cocklebur bushes clung like limpets to his clothing and his dog when he returned from hiking or climbing. Examining these under a microscope, he saw that the burrs were covered in thousands of tiny hooks that caught on the tiny cotton hooks of his clothing (and his dog's coat). Taking a lateral step, he conceived of developing a synthetic equivalent that could be used as a simple fastener on many different products. He approached several textile firms with his idea, and was rejected by all but one, a weaver from Lyon, who painstakingly created a prototype that he called a 'locking tape'. However, it took another seven years to incubate the product and find a material sufficiently strong and flexible to cope with thousands of openings and closings. After many experiments, he eventually discovered that infrared-treated nylon became almost indestructible. By the late 1950s, 55 million metres of Velcro were being produced each year, and it has been estimated that four out of five of the world's inhabitants have at some time owned a product that includes a Velcro fastener.

A more recent example of the power of bisociation is *Java-Logs*. Launched in 2003, these are made from 100 per cent recycled spent coffee grounds – a useful way to recycle the world's most consumed beverage. These logs generate 25 per cent more energy and three times the heat of wood logs. At the same time, they produce 50 per cent less soot. Best of all, in an era of growing concerns about the impact of humanity on the natural environment, they also recycle an otherwise completely useless waste product from landfill sites: the traditional home of coffee dregs (Green Business, 2003).

Last, but not least, what could be created from these elements (Perkins, 2001: 56)?

> Binary arithmetic + Charles Babbage's calculating machine (first conceived in the early 19th century) + the Punch Card (first devised by Herman Hollerith, for the 1890 census in the USA) + the audion tube (invented in 1906) + symbolic logic (developed by Bertrand Russell and Alfred Whitehead between 1910 and 1913) + the concepts of programming and feedback (which had arisen out of several abortive attempts to develop more effective anti-aircraft guns during World War 1).[4]

The most striking characteristic of the Wright Brothers, and other innovators and inventors, has been their ability to reframe reality and/or to look at existing realities in different ways, thereby becoming breakthrough thinkers. Linking already existing bodies of knowledge, or bisociation, is a very common way of creating new innovations, but, as we saw in the last example, sometimes it can take decades for people to pull together disparate bodies of knowledge to create something new. Charles Handy has described this process as 'the displacement of concepts': the ability to make links between two apparently unrelated areas in order to create a novel idea or product (Handy, 1999). Almost all human innovations have been derived from these processes, and the next section will look at how these can be built into the operational cultures and management practices of organizations.

Creating an innovative organization

> Revel in your glorious failures. Dance on the borderline between success and disaster, because that's where your next success will come from.
> (*Alberto Alessi, CEO of the innovative Italian product design company Alessi, cited by Wylie, 2001*)

> You have to kiss a lot of frogs to find the prince; but remember that one prince can pay for a lot of frogs.
> (*Art Fry, talking about the innovative culture at 3m,* The Australian, *3 March 1999*)

Very few businesses will ever be lucky enough to find a Bill Hewlett, an Akio Morita or a Thomas Edison in their ranks, and innovative companies have long recognized that they cannot rely on a few maverick innovators or solitary geniuses to create new ideas. These organizations have created cultures that attract creative people and fostered working practices and processes that encourage the creation, cross-fertilization and rapid dissemination of new ideas. As John Browne, CEO of BP, has commented, 'The conventional wisdom is that excelling in incremental learning is a science – a matter of installing the right processes – while excelling in breakthrough thinking is more of an art. I disagree about the latter: I think you *can* install processes that generate breakthrough thinking. We have' (cited by Prokesch, 1997: 150). Research over the last decade has shown that innovative companies like BP focus their energies in five main areas.

1 They spend a lot of time and resources identifying and recruiting employees with good technical skills, who are also creative, have high levels of intrinsic motivation and whose personalities will fit in with their organizational cultures.
2 They create work environments that foster and support the creation of new ideas amongst their employees.
3 They recognize that new ideas are not the privilege of a minority of employees; everyone, at all levels, can and should contribute.
4 They have leaders who know, intuitively, which are the right ideas to back and push into the marketplace.
5 They reward employees who create new ideas and do not punish them if their experimental ideas fail.

This systemic and systematic approach to innovation means that creative mind-sets are built into the cultures of these organizations, their employees' daily working practices and their human resource policies. How can the leader of a traditional company go about creating such a mind-set? It might sound daunting, but it can be done with time and commitment and, once established, the bottom line will shine through. The next section contains some suggestions for creating an innovative organizational culture (developed from Hamel, 2001a; 2001b; 2000a; 2000b; Harvard Business School, 1999; Drucker, 1985).

Understand creativity and innovation

As a leader/manager you have to really understand the process of lateral thinking, creativity and breakthrough thinking, and how this differs fundamentally from day-to-day linear thinking. This also requires nurturing and resourcing, because a 'bean-counter' mentality will not generate breakthrough thinking, nor will 'cost-cutting' or 'efficiency drives'. It also means appreciating that it is a huge step from coming up with an innovative idea to then turning it into a concept for development, assessing its feasibility and market potential, pushing it through product development, marketing and advertising it and, finally, selling it in the marketplace. As Gary Hamel has observed:

> For every 1000 ideas, only 100 will have enough commercial promise to merit a small-scale experiment, only ten of these will warrant a substantial financial commitment, and of those, only a couple will turn out to be unqualified successes. It's the inverse log scale behind innovation. Innovation is an inherently inefficient process [ ] As top management strives for ever-greater efficiency, it must learn to tolerate 'stupid' ideas and 'failed' experiments. Those are the byproducts of a well-functioning innovation pipeline.
> (Hamel, 2001b: 76–7).

In other words, to create even one great idea that will take the marketplace by storm, you need to generate hundreds of small ideas from your employees. Really big or revolutionary breakthroughs are very rare. This is an important point, because even the most innovative firms get it wrong sometimes. For example, do you remember satellite phones, promoted as the next-big-thing in telecommunications a few years ago? In the early 1990s, Motorola decided to back Iridium's development of a system of 66 geostationary, low-orbit satellites, to create a global phone network that would operate independently of terrestrial systems. Big mistake. This strategy threatened national telephone monopolies and, as a result, it failed and cost the company $US150 million. Consequently, Motorola was very slow getting into the digital phone market and initially paid a heavy price for falling behind Nokia, who had got into this market at the very beginning. Another example was the battle between the Betamax video-recorder, first unveiled by Sony in 1974 and the VHS system unveiled by JVC in 1976. Both companies took an already existing technology (originally created by the American company, Ampex, in 1954), miniaturized the main components and targeted the home market. So far, so good. Two companies, with two good products and, potentially, multibillion-dollar sales. However, what Sony did not foresee was that tape manufacturers and consumers would then opt for the simpler and more reliable VHS format, and it was this format that came to dominate the home VCR market of the 1980s and 1990s.

The average Silicon Valley venture capital firm gets as many as 5000 unsolicited business plans every year. How many new ideas does a Board of Directors in a non-innovative company get from its employees each year? A few dozen – if they're lucky. What's even more significant is that most new business ventures will be rejected a number of times by venture capitalists, and other lending institutions, before they find someone who is willing to back them. In large organizations, where new ideas may have to move up a chain of command, it takes just one 'No' to consign a good idea to oblivion, *forever*. In Silicon

Valley, no one cares whether you are young or old, black or white, male or female, what clothes you wear or even if you have a university degree. All that matters is the power of your ideas and the quality of your business plan (abridged from Hamel, 2000b: 52).

Hire creatives and mavericks

It is much easier to build an innovative organizational culture if you can attract and retain creative people, and more employers are putting a premium on this kind of recruitment. For example, an AC Nielsen survey of 1105 Australian companies reported that many employers want more creative and critical thinkers. The survey also discovered that most employers believed that new graduates lacked communication skills, creativity, innovative capabilities, a capacity for independent thinking and 'flair'. But this study also reported that one of the main reasons for employing graduates was 'to introduce new ideas or fresh thinking into the organization' (reported in *The Australian*, 1 January 2000). We saw, in Chapter 4, that cutting-edge companies spend a great deal of time recruiting and selecting their employees. They are also careful to recruit the best talent, regardless of their age, culture or gender. As Leonard and Strauss suggest, 'to innovate successfully, you must hire, work with and promote people who are unlike you. You need to understand your own preferences and blind spots, so that you can complement your weaknesses and exploit your strengths. The biggest barrier to recognising the contributions of others who are unlike you is your own ego' (1999: 66).

An example of a company that does this is McKinsey and Co. From the early 1990s, the company embraced a radical hiring policy that has aimed to recruit more creative brainpower. At that time, the only way to get into the company was with an MBA, preferably from one of the top US management schools. Since then, recruits are just as likely to be from economics, engineering science or law. McKinsey has also employed an ethnomusicologist, an expert in Ancient Greek and a Rhodes scholar in English literature. Managing partner John Stuckey has said that the company has one main criterion in recruitment: it wants 'distinctive people', who are best equipped to deal with the complex problems facing all companies in a globalized marketplace. Stuckey believes that 'radical hirings' bring heterogeneity of knowledge and creative thought styles to their clients' problems and, as a result, are better able to analyse and solve them. Such hirings now make up 40 per cent of the company's annual recruitment of new staff (up from 5 per cent in 1982) and the company has enjoyed a 90 per cent success rate with these non-traditional hirings (Bagwell, 1997).

You then have to get your staff to build creativity/innovation into their personal managerial repertoires and 'tool-kits', to enable them to become intrapreneurs. This may also mean a committed investment in both in-house and external development programmes that can help them learn how to become more creative, to use their intuition, to think beyond common-sense ways of doing things, to look beyond the boundaries of the organization and to embrace the learning organization principles described in the last section of this chapter. Some companies, such as HP, General Electric and 3m, also use job rotation as a way of fostering innovation and knowledge sharing. At the Kao Corporation (a consumer products manufacturer), employees are expected to do at least three different jobs in any ten-year period. At Australia Post, graduate recruits are required to work in three or four different functional areas during their first two years of employment. These organizations use this as a means of preventing the emergence of 'bunker' mentalities, as a way to help future leaders understand the whole business from a variety of perspectives and to encourage the cross-fertilization of ideas, thus creating more 'fluid' knowledge sharing amongst different groups of employees. Last, you have to reward your innovators and intrapreneurs extremely well. As the futurist Jim Taylor puts it, 'you need a tradition of spectacularly rewarding the people who make a non-linear change in the business. It has to be clear that spectacular innovation is the surest way of reaping spectacular economic rewards' (cited by Hamel, 2000b: 60). Innovators need to seek a direct relationship between the ideas that they create and the rewards that they receive.[5]

Encourage play, fun, humour and games

> The spirit of playful competition is, as a social impulse, older than culture itself and pervades all life like a veritable ferment. Ritual emerged from sacred play; poetry was born in play and nourished on play. We have to conclude, therefore, that civilization in its earliest phases played.
> (*Johan Huizinga*, Homo Ludens: A Study of the Play Element in Culture, *1938*)

> What a depressing contrast there is between the radiant intelligence of the child and the feeble mentality of the average adult.
> (*Sigmund Freud*, The Psychopathology of Everyday Life, *1901*)

It has been suggested several times in this book that a sense of humour is an important and often overlooked quality in leadership and people management. We've also seen that an atmosphere of fun and enjoyment is an integral part of the organizational cultures of some of the world's most successful companies. There is also a close correlation between humour and creative thinking. This is because new ideas can only emerge when we have open, learning minds and when we tap into the child-like parts of our personalities that respond to play, fun and games. These parts of our minds are also the source of spontaneity, imaginative and creative thinking and experimentation. Psychologists have known about this for more than 20 years, but it is only recently that this knowledge has started filtering into the mainstream business world. This realization has also fostered the emergence of a number of companies that deal with the development of creative and lateral thinking through games, role-playing, storytelling, clowning and humour. These companies include Oracy and Jongleurs in the UK, the marketing firm Play and the consulting firm Humour University in the USA, and WAMCG in Australia.

Patrick Burns, policy director of the Industrial Society in the UK, has observed that 'Play is becoming the buzzword. As companies become desperate to harness creativity and lateral thinking, they are being forced to look at new ways of fostering these talents. These days, we are seeing everything from mime and comedy to finger painting and storytelling.' Andy Stefano, Play's co-founder, believes that, 'When you turn work into a place that encourages people to be themselves, have fun and take risks, you unleash their creativity. The best ideas come from playful minds, and the way to tap into that playfulness is to play together.' Maria Kempinska, co-founder of Jongleurs, has observed that 'All companies are hungry for ideas, but if you push and pull in a pressured environment, ideas rarely come. Forward-looking companies realise that a good atmosphere at work, and good relations with colleagues at work, are crucial to hanging onto creative staff. Teaching them how to laugh and communicate honestly is a good start' (cited by Chaudri, 2000). Arie de Geus, one of the 'godfathers' of the learning organization, suggests, 'Play is about fun and play is about experimentation. If you don't understand the role that fun plays in learning, then you cannot experiment. If you cannot do this, you cannot learn, grow and change. This is why fear becomes the dominant emotion in an organization in crisis, because it has lost the capacity to learn' (De Geus, 1997: 15).

Hence humour is the great liberator of creativity because it frees the constrained, 'adult', rational, logical and linear parts of our minds and allows the more anarchic, free-flowing and creative parts of our personalities to emerge. Without this, true creativity is impossible. Having said this, humour, fun and play alone will achieve nothing; these must then be combined with self-discipline, motivation to achieve, the steady generation of new ideas, and the introduction of practical products and services into the marketplace.

Humour is by far the most significant creative activity of the human brain.
(*Edward De Bono*, Lateral Thinking, *1970*)

Encourage brainstorming

'Brainstorming' might sound like an anarchic process where people randomly throw ideas around and nothing ever gets done. Without some ground rules that is all it will ever be (Perkins, 2001: 96). The first and most important rule is that criticism is not allowed. However mad, crazy or unworkable suggestions might appear to be, they get discussed and recorded, because all innovations start life as small, crazy and throwaway ideas. Second, keep moving and don't get stuck on details. Initially, go for quantity rather than quality. Third, diversify thinking by plucking ideas from anywhere and from different points of view. If necessary, create 'whole brained' teams with a balance of different skills, competencies and personalities (as described in Chapter 5). Fourth, as William McKnight put it 80 years ago, don't put fences round your employees because you'll get sheeplike behaviour if you do. Give your people the freedom, time and space to think freely. Fifth, 'piggyback' by building on ideas or suggestions made by other people. Sixth, push all ideas and suggestions to their absolute limit, and search for new or alternative ways of using these.

> We might occasionally make fun of our Kiwi cousins, but sometimes they really do come up with world-shattering ideas. A couple of years ago, a group working with the intellectually handicapped decided to recycle animal faeces from Auckland and Wellington Zoos as garden fertilizer. Zoo-Doo has become a big seller in the Shaky Isles. But now they have gone one better with Endangered Faeces – small lumps of poo and compost moulded into the shapes of their main providers. The tiny elephants, hippo, camels and giraffes – the moulds for which are the brainchild of Lord of the Rings movie designer Mel Ford – are designed to sit in outdoor pot plants releasing nutrients into the soil. They are hoping to get export clearance soon.
> (*D.D. McNicoll*, The Australian, *12 January 2002*)

Creating new ideas through brainstorming is just the starting point. The next step is to capture and retain these – even if a use for them is not immediately apparent. This knowledge then has to be ordered, categorized, validated and evaluated for its organizational utility and/or commercial potential (topics we will return to in Chapter 10). Most importantly, throughout this entire process, negative attitudes and thinking that can thwart innovating thinking must be discouraged. These include the following: 'That is an interesting idea, but it wouldn't work'; 'We've never done it that way'; 'If it's such a good idea, why aren't our competitors doing it?'; 'There isn't a market for that'; 'We haven't got the time'; 'It's too expensive'; 'It's too theoretical'; 'The Board wouldn't accept it'; 'Our employees won't understand it'; 'We're not ready for that yet'; 'We've been successful for twenty years, why change?'; 'Let's form a committee to assess your proposal'; 'Let's be practical for a minute'; and, of course, 'Common-sense tells us that blah, blah, blah . . .'

New ideas will never see the light of day if these attitudes prevail and almost every innovative idea in history was dismissed as being unrealistic or impractical when it was first proposed. In Chapter 3, we saw how Akio Morita and Masura Ibuka were able to push through the idea of the Sony Walkman in the face of scepticism and opposition within the company. In the 1980s, Morita had also noticed the explosion in video-game arcades, and saw that there was an opportunity to create games consoles that could be used in the home. However, Sony would never have been able to develop and manufacture this billion-dollar product if Morita had not quarantined its young designer from the rest of the company. This cut him and his design team off from the bad advice that they constantly received about not touching digital technology, because it was not regarded as being one of Sony's areas of expertise at this time (Sutton, 2001).

A more recent example is Mike O'Dwyer's revolutionary gun technology. When he first approached the Australian Ministry of Defence in the early 1990s, with a proposal to develop a gun that could fire one million rounds a minute, he was basically told to get lost and not mess around with things he didn't understand. One admiral described him at the time as 'certifiably mad'. Ignoring this initial rejection, O'Dwyer packed in his job as a grocer in 1994, and established Metal Storm with the financial backing of the Brisbane-based venture capital firm, Charter Pacific. He set about developing a gun that would be electronic, rather than mechanical, which would also be capable of delivering a wide variety of projectiles, including fire retardants and fertilizers for crops. Metal Storm was floated on the Australian Stock Exchange in 1999. In 2001, the US and Australian governments decided to invest $US50 million in developing this new technology. This innovation represents a quantum leap in an area of technology that has not fundamentally changed since the introduction of the breach-loader in the mid-19th century (Fraser, 2001).

You see things and you say 'Why?'
But I dream of things that never were and I say 'Why not?'
(*George Bernard Shaw*)

It'll never catch on.
(*Thomas Edison. Probably the greatest inventor in human history, this was his response when told in 1890 that some people were planning to use his newly invented 'electric phonograph' to play recorded music. He thought it might be used to record the last words of dying people or to teach spelling to children.*)

Build innovation and intrapreneurship into the organization's culture

> Another more unusual process involves breakthrough thinking. When we assess opportunities, we ask if the usual approaches or business systems cannot produce the return on capital that we need, are there others that can? The development of the Andrew Field, which changed the economics of developing oil and gas fields in the North Sea, demonstrates the dramatic results that this kind of thinking can produce.
> (*John Browne, CEO of BP, cited by Prokesch, 1997: 158*)

Innovation also has to be built into the culture and management practices of the organization. If mavericks and intrapreneurs are not given freedom to move and encouragement for their ideas, they will up sticks and either move to one of your rivals with their ideas or set up in business for themselves. For example, 3m allows its staff 15 per cent of their time away from work to develop new ideas, and get ideas from other companies, a process known in the company as 'bootlegging'. Another example of a company that has successfully built innovation into its culture is Nokia (corporate logo, 'No Limits'). The company was voted the 'World's Leading Technology Company' by the US magazine *Business Week* in 2000. It employs 60 000 people and has had a long-standing reputation for being one of the world's most innovative companies, even in its earliest years when its primary business was wood products. Nokia is a company that has always discouraged complacency and self-satisfaction. In the early 1990s, its management realized that, even though the company was commercially successful and profitable, it had to continue to find new ways to make money and create new innovations and products.

Since this time, people at all levels of the company have been encouraged to submit their ideas and suggestions, and hundreds are submitted every month. Lauri Kivenen, then Nokia's Senior Vice-President for Corporate Communications, describes how this process works:

> Ultimately, it's individuals who produce innovations, then at another level it's teams and groups, and finally the whole firm. But, it starts from the individual. [Innovation] is a spirit of trying to think outside the box, trying to look round the corner, trying to imagine the outcomes of a chain of developments. There is no secret formula to the company's success. It has to be something that is nurtured all the time. You allow mistakes, you allow people to make bold moves and you try to spread energy. It is very much a cultural thing. You can't force people to be innovative but you can foster it and encourage it and nourish it. We don't have a creativity manual [ ] People are used to discussing ideas and arguing quite openly. In Finnish business culture, the idea that there might be someone at a lower level who has the key point is quite natural, especially in the IT sector. You cannot utilise the knowledge of different people in a more efficient way than if there's bureaucratic filters all around the organization.
> (*Abridged from Sutherland, 2000a*)

Of course, even an exemplar of innovation like Nokia gets it wrong sometimes. The company's integrated wireless mobile entertainment phone N-Gage was launched with great fanfare in 2003, accompanied by extensive TV advertising with a voice-over by the former *Star Trek* actor, Patrick Stewart. However, its cumbersome operating system was not well received by either IT commentators or consumers, and it proved to be a commercial flop. One critic described it memorably as looking like a mixture of 'a taco and a doofus' (Lewis, 2002: 97).

Creating an intrapreneurial culture means that organizations have to invest time and resources in their employees; this never just 'happens'. Having recruited the right people, they have to provide the right kind of environment and incentives for innovation to bubble up from the bottom of the organization. The organization as a whole must learn not to dismiss bizarre ideas and how to push these to their limits. It has to invest in the most up-to-date creative software. It has to foster cross-functional dialogue and communication. It has to support and reward innovation. It has to use its customers for new ideas and network with other organizations. It has to learn how to keep on the cutting edge of new ideas and innovations that could affect its market position. It has to become committed to continual innovation (similar to the Japanese notion of continuous improvement, *Kaizen*).

Then an interdisciplinary venture team of researchers, engineers, marketeers and accountants can be set up to push new ideas further. These then have to be nurtured to see if they can be commercialized. Prototypes have to be built and feedback obtained from potential investors and customers. The market then has to be persuaded to adopt or buy the innovation. For larger and more complex companies, who may not be able to innovate as quickly as their smaller, nimbler competitors, systems have to be put in place to disseminate new ideas quickly. Company-wide gatherings, cross-functional teams, formal brainstorming sessions, job placements and formal two-way and cross-functional communication systems can all help with this. This might also require a more systemic approach to storing this knowledge and intellectual capital on easily accessible data and web bases. Another solution is of course to buy out potential entrepreneurial rivals. Microsoft and Cisco Systems have been doing this for years. Cisco, for example, took over more than 60 fledgling companies in Silicon Valley between 1995 and 2000 (Stein, 2000: 65).

Large companies have also made use of 'internal ideas factories' and 'skunk works' for many years. Skunk works were pioneered at the

Lockheed Aircraft Company in the 1940s. Engineers working inside a secret office were encouraged to break all the rules when necessary, and ignore the official procedures laid down by the Pentagon. The result was a stream of new planes and technologies that have consistently set new world standards for performance, often ahead of budget and schedule. This was how IBM, steeped in a bureaucratic culture of making large computers for fat profits in the 1970s and early 1980s, managed to break into the leaner, meaner personal computer market in the 1990s. To do this, it had to create a skunk works at Boca Raton in Florida, about as far as it was possible to get, culturally and physically, from its corporate headquarters in New York. Unlike many of its contemporaries, such as DEC and Wang Computers, this helped IBM to survive in the 1980s and then thrive in the 1990s (*The Economist*, 1999).

In Royal Dutch Shell, Tim Warren, the former Director of Research and Technical Services, established the 'Game Changer' process. He gave a small panel of selected free-thinking employees a $US20 million budget and complete freedom to allocate this to any new business ideas proposed by their peers. The game went live in 1996. Initially, ideas were slow to come in. The Game Changer panel decided to invite Gary Hamel in to run some innovation workshops for 72 would-be intrapreneurs. In two days the group generated 240 new ideas, 12 of which were given funding. Since the completion of these workshops, several hundred ideas have been received from employees. Of Shell's five largest growth initiatives in early 1999, four had their genesis in Game Changer. And, as Hamel quietly observed, 'The Game Changer process helped to convince Shell's top management that entrepreneurial passion lurks everywhere, and that you really can create entrepreneurial thinking inside even the largest organization' (Hamel, 2000b: 56). However, this is not a cure-all. It is something that may be usefully employed in very large bureaucratic companies, but can send negative messages to the rest of its employees. This may lead to the emergence of an 'innovation apartheid' in an organization, with a well-paid innovative elite (the 'in-group') and a disenfranchised majority (the 'out-group'). The creation of skunk works might also send out signals that a company is incapable of organic, collective, bottom-up innovation and has to entrust this to a distinct, well-paid and privileged elite (Schrage, 1999).

Communicate, communicate and communicate some more

In Chapter 4, we saw that many cutting-edge companies create surroundings that stimulate employee interaction and the free flow of ideas. The ergonomics of these companies encourage an organic and even tribal style of communication, where people may spend some time working alone, but regularly meet to discuss their ideas and interact with colleagues. Google, and many other new companies, do these things in a very conscious way, partly because it reflects the attitudes of the young entrepreneurs who created these businesses and the average age of its employees, but also because they know that these kinds of environments foster creativity and innovation.[6] Again, this is not a new idea. A hundred years ago, at the Menlo Park Laboratory in New Jersey, many of Edison's inventors worked in a single large room, to encourage the cross-fertilization and dissemination of ideas, long before 'brainstorming' or 'Management by Wandering About' appeared in the management lexicon of organizations. Old and well-established innovative companies such as 3m and HP have long encouraged open plan offices, and collective communication sharing as a way of creating and cross-fertilizing new ideas. Improving an organization's capacity to innovate means a major organizational commitment to two-way communication. Achieving and sustaining active innovation and learning requires sharing information and communicating openly. As Gary Hamel has observed:

> In most companies, strategy is the preserve of the old guard, the same ten people talking to the same ten people year after year. No wonder that the strategies that emerge are dull. What can the top 20 or 30 executives in a company learn from each other? Their positions are so well rehearsed that they can finish each other's sentences. What is required is not a cohort of wise elders or a bevy of planners, but a taproot sunk deep into the organization. Without new voices in the strategy conversation, the chance for revolution is nil. There are revolutionaries in your company. But, all too often, there is no process that lets them be heard. Their voices are muffled by layers of cautious bureaucrats.
> (*Hamel, 2000b: 50–51*)

Hamel also narrated the following anecdote, as an example of the benefits of listening to younger employees' ideas:

> Alisa Petchy was a young flight attendant at Virgin Airlines, who was helping a friend to plan a wedding. Like most brides-to-be, her friend was overwhelmed by a seemingly endless list of 'to-dos': find the church and a reception hall, arrange the catering, hire the limousine, pick out a dress, outfit the bridesmaids, choose the flowers, plan the honeymoon, send out invitations and so on. Petchy was struck by an idea – why not offer brides-to-be a one-stop wedding planning service? She took her idea to Richard Branson. The result: Europe's largest bridal emporium, which is called, naturally, Virgin Bride. Soon after making her suggestion, Petchy was promoted to become the Head of Marketing for Virgin Bride.
> (*Abridged from Hamel, 2000b: 46, 51*)

Hamel argues that businesses who want to foster innovation and learning must listen more actively to their younger employees, to those on the edges of the organization who are closest to the customers and clients, and all newcomers to the business (who have so far managed to escape the numbing effects of 'corporate training'). For example, GE Capital in the USA has run 'dreaming sessions' involving employees from the company's 28 business units. During one session in 1999, it was suggested that each business should appoint a young manager (under 30) to go out and search for business opportunities that their older, stodgier bosses might have missed. This led almost immediately to several new ideas for e-commerce, cross-selling initiatives and a website where consumers could go to find objective financial information compiled by a panel of independent financial advisers. Hamel also makes this interesting suggestion: 'The next time someone in your organization convenes a meeting on "strategy" or "innovation", make sure that 50 per cent of those who attend have never been to such a meeting. Load the meeting with young people, newcomers and those from the far-flung edges of the company. That's the way to quadruple your chances of coming up with truly revolutionary business concepts' (Hamel, 2000b: 52).[7]

Exercise 9.3

Creative envisioning

In Chapters 1 and 8, you were asked to develop a compelling vision that would challenge the way people in your department or organization operate now and in the future. Having read through these sections on innovation and breakthrough thinking, are you now able to develop and articulate a new vision for your department or organization? Can you tap into your employees' ideas to help you to develop this vision? What is the end goal of this vision? What are the principal components of this vision? Can these be encapsulated in motivational 'rallying cries'?

Think about the alternative futures that could exist for your department or organization. How could it make better use of its existing resources, products and/or services? What new products and/or services could be created? Are there other markets that could be exploited in the future? ◆

Conclusion

The great innovators have always been young. But, you don't always have a culture of youth in old-economy companies. That has to change. If the energy of youthful innovation and the experience of traditional business leaders can mix productively, then companies will survive and thrive. If they don't mix, then a company is in big trouble.
(*Philip Shirvington, CEO of Energy Resources Australia, cited in* The Australian, *8 August 2000*)

The history of human innovation over the last 10 000 years tells us that this process has much more to do with pragmatic searches for new opportunities, and moulding already existing areas of knowledge into new forms, than the activities of lonely, half-nutty, visionary geniuses creating revolutionary new ideas. Furthermore, while there may be no single 'best way' to foster innovation and intrapreneurship, there is enough evidence from innovative businesses to provide a framework for organizations that do want to become more innovative. Organizations that can do this successfully benefit in three ways.

1 Their employees, particularly the more creative and innovative ones, feel appreciated and involved and, thereby, motivated to contribute more.
2 Innovation and creativity then become ingrained in the cultures and working practices of these organizations.
3 In turn, this promotes an inbuilt capacity for fast change and renewal, without the need to 'manage change' reactively.

In summary, there are four important lessons that can be learnt from innovative and intrapreneurial companies. First, their leaders have changed the way they think about innovation. They regard this as a vital component of the long-term viability and success of their organizations, not as an expensive gimmick or an optional add-on to their main business activities. Second, an innovative culture and mind-set can be created in *any* organization, providing its leaders and managers understand the process and how it needs to be encouraged, nurtured and rewarded. Third, companies that are innovative enjoy greater commercial success, are more profitable and have longer lifespans, when compared to companies that are not innovative (Collins, 2001; Hamel, 2000a; Collins and Porras, 1996). Fourth, the most successful industrial nations in the world derive much of their annual gross domestic product from growth in new businesses. For example, the USA derives more than half of its annual economic growth from industries that barely existed a decade ago. In ten years' time, it will obtain half its economic growth from businesses that are just starting up (Nicholas, 2000). That is the great power of innovation, particularly in an era of rapid technological change and globalization. Inevitably, many commercial organizations that are unable to embrace innovative mind-sets will have limited lifespans in the future.

> The most important human innovation of all time is not an artifact, such as the pill or the electric shaver or the personal computer. It's an idea – the very idea that made all these technical successes possible – and that is the concept of education. Our brain is nothing but a collection of neurons and

synapses – networks that have been shaped by evolution to solve specific problems. Yet, by means of education and culture, we have found ways to recycle these networks for other uses. With the introduction of writing, we recycled our visual systems to read. With the creation of mathematics, we applied our innate networks for number, space and time to all sorts of problems beyond their original domains. Education is the key innovation that enabled all of these rewirings and adaptations to take place. Homo Sapiens is the only primate to have created an active pedagogy, and without education it would take only one generation for all the innovations and inventions that have been created in human history to vanish from the surface of the earth.

(*Adapted from Brockman, 2000: 119–20*)

Exercise 9.4

Having read through this section on creativity and innovation can you think of any new ideas that could improve the way your team, department or organization currently functions? Can you use existing products/services/systems in new ways? These can be anything you like, however mad, crazy or off-the-wall they might initially sound to your bosses, colleagues or junior staff.

1.

2.

3.

4.

5.   ◆

Creating a learning organization

The ability to learn faster than your competitors may be the only sustainable competitive advantage in the future.
(*Arie de Geus*, The Living Company, *1997*)

Learning is the new form of labour. It is no longer a separate activity that occurs either before one enters the workplace or in remote classroom settings. Learning is now at the very heart of all productive activity.
(*Shoshana Zuboff*, In the Age of the Smart Machine, *1988*)

Without learning, the wise become foolish. By learning, the foolish become wise.
(*Confucius, 551 BCE*)

In this section, we will look at the 'learning organization', a concept first developed during the 1970s and 1980s, and which came of age in the 1990s. It is an approach to leading and managing organizations that seems to be particularly suited to the fast-changing and chaotic environments that many organizations now operate in. It was noted in Chapter 8 that the attrition rate of companies is accelerating decade by decade, and it is apparent that all organizations, particularly in the private sector, have to be able to do something more than reactively 'manage change'. This is a phrase that is still used routinely in business circles, and by many academics and consultants, but is probably well past its sell-by date. What is certain is that the old model of organizations as static bureaucratic 'machines', which simply reproduce what has worked for them in the past, is no longer sufficient for most businesses or commercial enterprises.

For example, John Browne (CEO of BP) believes that all companies battling it out in a globalized information age face a common challenge; using knowledge and intellectual capital more effectively than their competitors. During the 1990s, Browne came to believe that the company needed to become a more innovative learning organization. This belief has seen the company slash its workforce from 129 000 in 1990 to around 50 000 in 2002. In the process, it became a faster thinking, nimbler organization characterized by a flat organizational structure, entrepreneurial business units, informal webs of alliances across the company and systematic knowledge sharing. Now it has been turned from a top-heavy, slow-moving, multilayered, classical industrial bureaucracy into an organic team-based system of independent businesses, informal networks and learning communities. BP has put learning organization principles at the centre of this transition. Browne describes the philosophy underpinning this transition as follows:

> Learning is at the heart of a company's ability to adapt to a rapidly changing environment. It is the key to being both able to identify opportunities that others might not see and to exploit those opportunities rapidly and fully. This means that in order to generate extraordinary value for shareholders, a company has to learn faster than its competitors and apply that knowledge throughout its businesses faster and more widely than they do. The way we see it, anyone who is not directly accountable for making a profit should be involved in creating and distributing knowledge that the company can use to make a profit.
> (*Cited by Prokesch, 1997: 148*)

The idea of the learning organization is linked to, but distinct from, the principles of individual learning and unlearning described in Chapter 8. To describe a business as a 'learning organization' means that all the activities that its employees are engaged in are used reflectively as the basis for future learning (an 'observe–reflect–think–decide–do' mind-set, as opposed to an 'observe–decide–do' approach). This is done in order to continually improve both individual and organizational performance, and to enhance the company's ability to create its own future, rather than constantly playing 'catch-up' with the competition. This means that every day, every week and every month the organization as a whole has to be able to answer this question, 'What have we learnt and how can we use this knowledge to improve what we do?' This sounds deceptively simple, but putting it into practice can be a complicated and lengthy process.

The most comprehensive treatments of learning organization principles remain the work of Peter Senge, Head of the Center for Organizational Learning at the Massachusetts Institute of Technology, and more recently Arie de Geus, the former head of Shell's Corporate Planning Department. A learning organization is defined here as an organization that facilitates the collective learning and unlearning of its employees, and is continually expanding its capacity to transform itself and create its own future (de Geus, 1996, 1997; Senge, 1990, 1994; Pedler *et al.*, 1989). According to Senge, learning organizations have five characteristics.

A shared vision

As we saw in Chapters 1 and 8, without a clear vision or path to the future, employees and organizations cannot aspire to outstanding achievements, or embrace the need for perpetual change and evolution. This is because significant learning cannot take place unless there is a strong motivation to do this and meaningful targets towards which to strive, individually and collectively.

Personal mastery

As noted above, this component builds on the principles of individual learning and unlearning that we looked at in the last chapter, in particular the idea of double-loop, rather than single-loop learning. Within the context of the learning organization, this means a commitment to perpetual, lifelong individual and organizational learning. Individuals have to be shown the value of continuous learning and become proactive in developing their own learning and that of their colleagues. People are encouraged to learn from incidents and events at work. Mistakes are analysed to ensure that they do not happen again. Even if these lessons are painful, they are still used as an opportunity for future learning. People constantly question the way they do things and nothing is taken for granted. Information is never hoarded; it is always shared and widely available. Ideas and experiences are shared across teams and departments.

This philosophy implies that learning by experience ('adaptive' or 'experiential' learning) is not enough. This has to be supplemented by 'generative learning' – a proactive and interpretative style of learning. This means that the organization must constantly review how things went after the event, in order to make more effective plans and preparations before future events take place (known as 'mental modelling'). When used effectively, generative learning can lead to short-term applications that are relatively simple to diagnose and correct, and long-term applications, which can include the formulation of new organizational strategies, products and services. For example, adaptive learning would consist of giving customers what they want, generative learning would consist of trying to imagine what the customers might want or giving them what they might never have thought of asking for. The best recent example of this process in action is the mobile phone: a new 'need' was created when it had not previously existed or been imagined by telephone users. It is no coincidence that the pioneer of this innovation was a learning organization we looked at in the previous section – Nokia.

Adopting learning organization principles also means that, if you want active learners, you need active educators who can show their people how to become self-learners and what the benefits of this will be. This has to become a key element of the leader/manager's responsibilities in the learning organization, where the development of their followers is no longer regarded as some kind of abstract 'HR issue', but as an integral part of their jobs. They see themselves as the coaches, mentors and educators of others, not as the distant 'charismatic heroes' or the 'command-and-control' leaders identified in Chapter 1. Employees focus on the learning opportunities available in their jobs as much as any other rewards they may receive from these. Words like 'learning', 'teaching' and 'education' are used in a very conscious way, as part of the lexicon of the organization's language and culture. The role of leaders and managers in this kind of environment becomes a more subtle one that involves getting their followers to build a shared vision, embracing perpetual learning, challenging existing mental models, fostering systemic thinking and imagining, 'What if we . . .?' Leaders and managers who are comfortable with the notions of the leader as servant, described in Chapter 1, and empowered leadership, described in Chapters 4 and 7, will have few problems in adapting to this new role.

This is only the starting point, because this mind-set must then be embraced by the whole organization (meta-learning) and, as both de Geus and Senge have observed, institutional or collective learning is much harder to develop than individual learning. The rate of learning of the organization also has to be greater than the rate of external change, by learning to anticipate what is around the corner. This means that organizations too have to get outside the real worlds that they inhabit (and their comfort zones) and learn from the outside world through appropriate boundary scanning mechanisms (scenario mapping). This means not only doing the standard checks, such as benchmarking against best practice in similar industries, but also learning from very different industries, and from their customers and clients. John Browne describes this process in this way:

> There are a variety of ways you can learn how to do something better. You can learn from your own experience. You can learn from your contractors, suppliers and customers. And, you can learn from companies totally outside your business. All are crucial. No matter where the knowledge comes from, the key to reaping a big return is to leverage that knowledge so that each unit is not learning in isolation and reinventing the wheel again and again [ ] For example, we've learned a lot from the automobile industry about procurement, which has helped us lower the cost of building service stations. And, we went to the US Army to learn about capturing and sharing knowledge. (*Cited by Prokesch, 1997: 155, 157*)

Another example of a learning organization that has taken the world by storm in recent years is Dyson. Initially renowned for its high-speed Marine Sea Truck and the Ball Barrow, the company achieved worldwide recognition for revolutionizing the humble vacuum cleaner. Dyson has also moved successfully into washing machine manufacturing, with an innovative drum mechanism that closely mimics the more efficient human hand washing technique. Martin McCourt, the chief operating officer of Dyson in the UK, attributes much of the company's success to its ability to listen closely to what its customers want and learning from these dialogues. McCourt observed that 'Dyson customers recognise that our research and development philosophy is to find new solutions to problems that consumers have had for a long time. We are seen as a company that does things differently. We are not a heavy advertiser, never having spent more than $US500 000 a year on mainstream advertising, we rely most heavily on word-of-mouth endorsements by satisfied customers. 70 percent of sales are generated this way' (abridged from Lloyd, 2001: 46–7).

Team learning

Team learning is essential, because learning is a social activity and people learn more quickly in groups, and Senge has described teams as the fundamental learning unit of modern organizations. In Chapter 5, we saw that all successful companies now employ some kind of team-based management systems, but these must be genuine teams, not ad hoc groups of employees trying to work under the banner of a 'team'. This emphasis on team-based learning, curiosity and creativity also requires a strong commitment to employee empowerment and involvement, a toleration of experimentation, curiosity and even eccentricity, investment in employee education and development, and reward systems that encourage learning and innovation. It also means delayering organizations, removing 'bureaucratic baloney' and traditional autocratic controls over employees. In practice, this is how it works in BP:

> We have built a very flat team-based management structure that is designed to motivate and to help people learn. We've divided the company up into lots of business units, and there is *nothing* between them and the nine-member executive group to which they report, which consists of the three managing directors of our business groups and their six deputies. The organization is even flatter than my description makes it sound because each of the managing directors and their deputies work as a team in dealing with the business units. [The] virtue of this organizational structure is that there is a lot of transparency. Not only can the people within the business unit understand more clearly what they have to do; I and other senior executives can understand what they are doing. Then we can have an ongoing dialogue with them and with ourselves about how to improve performance and build the future.

> The top management team must stimulate the organization, not control it. Its role is to provide strategic direction, to encourage learning and to make sure that there are mechanisms for transferring the lessons. The role of leaders at all levels is to demonstrate to people that they are capable of achieving more than they think they can achieve. To change behaviour and unleash new ways of thinking, a leader sometimes has to say, 'Stop, you're not allowed to do it the old way' and issue a challenge.
> (*John Browne, cited by Prokesch, 1997: 158, 160, 164*)

Mental modelling

This process involves learning how to bring commonly held beliefs and common-sense assumptions (mental models) to the surface; then to analyse and question their validity and create new models that can service the business better in the future. This method also stresses the importance of long-term learning cycles, which can only be managed in years, rather than constantly fixating on short-term financial results, as so many companies do. Many of the visionary companies referred to in earlier chapters have long-term strategic plans in place. In one famous interview, on the BBC's *Business Programme* in 1990, Akio Morita was asked to estimate for how many years in the future Sony made strategic plans. Without batting an eyelid, he immediately replied, 'Fifty years.'

Systemic thinking and scenario mapping

This refers to the ability to think of organizations as complete entities, as well as their constituent parts, micro functions and micro processes. This means 'reframing' organizations as biological or organic systems that collectively rethink their purposes and methods, in order to grow and thrive (de Geus, 1996, 1997). We saw in Chapter 8 that any organization, of a reasonable size must understand the potential systemic consequences of change management initiatives, because it is often the unanticipated consequences of change that can do the most damage. Another important facet of systemic thinking is scenario mapping. Like many of the leadership and management techniques described in this book, scenario mapping has a long history. Military strategists have used this technique since at least the early 19th century and the commercial sector began to pick up on this after World War II. It is a technique that seems to be particularly suited to a world characterized by uncertainty and rapid, discontinuous change.

Peter Schwartz came across the idea in the late 1960s at Royal Dutch Shell, and developed it to the point where it became known as the 'Shell Method'. The purpose of scenario mapping is to help to create greater certainty in an increasingly uncertain world. There are four forms of uncertainty in business. The first is the one you can measure, such as piloting a new product launch in one country and then extrapolating the results. Second are uncertainties that have known results, but which may be incalculable. An example of this might be a competitor who is building a new factory that will double their supplies in one of your markets. The exact outcomes of this cannot be calculated precisely, but the possible outcome scenarios can be defined and analysed. Third, there are risks that are difficult to calculate but fall within a predictable range, such as investing in research and development. Last, there are truly ambiguous and uncertain circumstances that make it near impossible to predict what will happen (Schwartz, 1996). For example, the crashing of an airliner into a Manhattan skyscraper was in fact a scenario that many of the world's insurance companies had fed into their 'catastrophe calculations', prior to 11 September 2001. The Hart–Rudman Commission (2000), which had been reviewing national security options for the USA, also imagined a plausible scenario involving hijacked planes being crashed into the World Trade Center by terrorists. Although no one actually predicted when this would occur, the probability that this was going to happen, sooner or later, could (and some would say should) have been extrapolated from the rise of militant Islamic groups throughout the 1980s and 1990s, and the steady escalation of terrorist activities during these decades. The systemic consequences of these events will be felt for decades, and there is little doubt that more horrendous terrorist acts will be carried out during this decade.

How can scenario mapping help to deal with uncertainty and discontinuous change in business organizations? By carrying out experimental thinking at the margins, leaders can trace possible future paths from the systems and trends that are shaping the world at the moment (for example, globalization and new technologies). This allows the creation of 'What if . . .?' thinking and adaptation to change by *anticipating* rather than *reacting to* change. In turn this permits the creation of contingent strategic plans that can be implemented if, or when, one of these anticipated scenarios emerges. Scenario mapping cannot predict the future, but it can help organizations prepare for future possibilities. Companies that have tested their strategies against these scenarios, and things that could go wrong in worse-case scenarios, are in a much stronger position to deal with these when they arise. As Peter Schwartz puts it, 'Using scenarios is rehearsing the future. You run through simulated events as if you are already living them. You train yourself to recognise which scenarios are unfolding. This helps you to avoid unpleasant surprises and to react quickly' (Schwartz, 1996: 19). It also implies an ability to consider the most bizarre, radical and off-the-scale scenarios, because they are the ones that have the potential to do the most damage to your business.

One example, described by Arie de Geus, concerned a scenario-mapping exercise in 1985 that asked Shell managers to envisage what would happen if the price of oil fell to $US15 a barrel. At the time oil was selling at $28 a barrel and on the rise. However, by February 1986 it had dropped to $17 dollars and by April to $10 a barrel. Because the company had contemplated some 'What if' scenarios, they were in a much stronger position to deal with a crisis that hit other oil companies hard during 1986–7 (de Geus, 1996: 96).

This example of a successful scenario-mapping exercise does not mean that this is an easy process. For an individual company, it might require as much as months' preparatory work before a set of scenarios can be effectively played out. Predicting scenarios is one thing, but taking the required actions to adapt to new scenarios is an entirely different matter. Furthermore, scenario mapping is not the only way to investigate the future. Other techniques, such as environmental scanning, looking for new ideas from other industries and deep industry analysis can also generate many new ideas. Scenario mapping may not be useful for all companies, but it is certainly relevant for any company that operates in fast-changing markets that are characterized by rapid technological innovation, such as finance, the technology sector, communications, news media, book publishing and the entertainment industry.

In common with Collins and Porras's visionary companies, learning organizations are also fiscally conservative and some, such as W. L. Gore (the creators of Goretex), even put limits on how fast they grow. But, at the same time, they do invest aggressively in the learning and development of their employees, and in appropriate new technologies that can enhance their core business activities. This learning organization paradigm also emphasizes what can broadly be described as 'traveller' as opposed to a 'package holiday' attitude to the future. This means that learning organizations know that they are on a journey to the future, but they may not be really sure where this will eventually take them. They do not have a fixed destination to get to because, before the company arrives there, the destination will almost certainly have been shifted by external events. Michael Chaney, the CEO of Wesfarmers, described this approach to the future in an interview in *Boss Magazine* in July 1998:

> I don't think it's any longer possible to have some fixed point on the horizon that you just aim for. In fact, this can actually be quite dangerous, because you can take your eye off what the competition is doing. One of the reasons why Wesfarmers has been successful is that we are convinced that we are hopeless at predicting the future. Therefore, we are constantly making plans that can change as the situation changes. We'll take ideas from anyone at any level of the company or come to that from anyone outside the company.

To conclude this sub-section, here is a story of how learning organization principles helped one well-known company move from near extinction in the early 1980s, to regaining much of its old reputation for the quality of its products in the 1990s, through to the two most commercially successful years in the company's history in 2001–2 (adapted from Zackowitz, 2003; Content, 2001; Teerlink and Ozley, 2000; Bloomberg Press, 2000; and 'How to Live for a Hundred Years', *BBC Business Programme* video, 1991).

Boss Hog comes good
Harley-Davidson (HD) was established in 1903 by Bill Harley and Walter Davidson and grew rapidly in the 1920s and 1930s to become an icon of American industry. It was adopted as *the* bike of the American military during World War II and the Korean War. It was also featured in almost every US teen-movie of the 1950s and 1960s, including *Rebel Without a Cause*, *The Wild Ones* and *Easy Rider*. For more than 60 years it was a symbol of the American Dream; it could never die. However, by the mid-1970s, things had begun to go badly wrong, and the company had become a byword for shoddy workmanship,

poor product reliability and abysmal quality. HD was also highly leveraged and rapidly losing market share, customers and money. The company had become complacent and inward-looking and, like many businesses in North America at that time, had failed to anticipate the threat from an economically and industrially ascendant Japan. Its employees were demoralized, demotivated and embarrassed to be associated with the company.

The first step taken by the company and its new CEO Richard Teerlink was to lay off 40 per cent of HD's 4000 employees. As he observed in 1991, 'This was the only way to save the company. We had to do this to save everyone else's jobs.' The company then proceeded to introduce Japanese quality methods, re-engineered its manufacturing processes and products, and revamped its work teams. It also changed its salaries and benefits schemes to tie rewards more closely to individual performance and completely restructured its old-style top-down communication systems. These initiatives worked to some extent, with improvements in both overall quality and profits. However, by the mid-1980s, Teerlink and his senior management team realized that more drastic action was required to complete the company's turnaround. As a result, HD's senior managers went back to school at the Center for Organizational Learning (COL) at MIT, under the guidance of Peter Senge. Here they played management games, learnt about systemic thinking and mental-modelling and, critically, learnt that they too had to change, by giving up formal positional power and becoming empowering coaches and educators within the HD workforce. It wasn't until the company got involved with COL that it learned to think better, to think more creatively and to listen more actively to its employees' ideas and contributions. By adopting the principles of systemic thinking they were able to think through a whole series of business decisions, whose consequences the company would not have foreseen in earlier times. The senior managers in the company also set about creating a new vision and a set of core company values that could encapsulate the changes they were trying to make and the new culture they were trying to create. The five values they settled on were:

Tell the Truth
Be Fair
Keep Your Promises
Respect the Individual
Encourage Intellectual Curiosity

Encourage intellectual curiosity? This is a company that makes motorbikes; it is not a university department or a school. Not surprisingly, after many years of mismanagement and inept leadership, there was considerable cynicism amongst the company's workforce about the changes being proposed by senior management, as well as the new company values they were espousing. Nevertheless, the company's senior managers were able to sell the vision and the message, and backed these up with concrete actions. Great efforts were put into shifting the company away from its old dictatorial style of management to a more participative and empowered leadership style, and self-managing team-based production systems. The company also set up a dedicated education centre, The Learning Institute, to encourage staff development and learning. Employee participation was fully funded and actively encouraged, whether taken within or outside the company. Initially, staff development focused on basic literacy and mathematical skills, but this has since developed into a service that offers the full range of skill and learning packages required in a modern learning organization. The aim of this initiative, in the words of Ron Hutchinson, then Head of Customer Services, was to create 'an intelligent workforce, where people want to come to work and want to contribute their ideas'.

Once the ball was rolling, the impetus for change became unstoppable. In part, this was assisted by the kind of employees who worked at HD. As Hutchinson remarked in 1991, 'Fortunately for HD, many of our employees are also our customers. The result in HD is a culture that very much emphasises freedom and respect for the individual. Where, for example, would you find a company where many of the employees have the company's logo tattooed on some portion of their anatomy!?' From 1987 onwards, sales and profits have increased every year. As a result, many of those who were laid off in the late 1980s were subsequently rehired in the 1990s. HD has continued its collaboration with COL at MIT and this has continued to produce benefits. For example, HD was one of the first companies to become actively involved in a strategic programme of corporate licensing. HD's adult collectables business now generates more than 50 million dollars a year for the company.

The company's two most successful years on record were 2001 and 2002. HD's net earnings rose by 21 per cent from 2001 to 2002 on the back of sales worth $US4.1 billion, and the company's share price increased by 242 per cent between 1997 and 2002. The company celebrated its centenary by holding a series of anniversary celebrations, which ran from July 2002 to Labour Day 2003 in the USA, and in many other countries. At least 100 000 riders descended on Milwaukee, in Wisconsin, the birthplace of the company, for the July 2002 party, and double this number attended the 2003 celebrations. The company's employees clearly appreciate the changes that have been made over the last decade, with HD being included in *Fortune*'s annual 'The Best Companies to Work for in the USA' in 2002 at number 51 (Levering and Moskowitz, 2002: 90).

HD is a company that took some time to understand the value of embracing learning organization theory, but they eventually saw *why* they needed to learn, *what* they needed to learn and *how* to learn. The company has been reaping the full commercial benefits of this revolution in their organizational mind-set for more than a decade. As their former CEO Richard Teerlink commented in 1991,

> I think sometimes we get hung-up on these terms – like Quality Circles, Just in Time and the Learning Organization. For me, the learning organization is when we are continuously learning. It's about learning what we do collectively. It's about learning what happens outside the company. If we are not continuously learning, as individual employees and as an organization, we will remain stuck where we are today. If we stick where we are today, we will lose. We must be continuously improving, and what is the basis for continuous improvement? The basis for continuous improvement is '*What did we learn today?*' [my emphasis].

Although Teerlink retired from the company in 2000, this philosophy continues to underpin the way that HD is planning for its future. In the late 1990s, most of the company's customers were middle-aged men, and it was this demographic statistic that in large measure had rescued HD in the 1980s, when the company decided to market its leather-jacket image to affluent white-collar baby-boomers. However, this didn't bode well for future sales, because the average age of US motorcycle buyers was 32 in 1990, 38 in 1998 and by 2001 had risen to 46. By 2010, most baby-boomers will be too old to buy new motorcycles. By the mid-1990s, younger bike-riders who didn't remember films like *Easy Rider* (or HD's once rebellious image) were showing a clear preference for the flashier and cheaper bikes provided in abundance by the Japanese and Germans. In response to these developments, HD started to revamp and retool its bike range. In 1995, the go-ahead was given to start work on a new bike project, which culminated in the launch of the V-Rod in 2003. It was widely praised by aficionados and commentators alike as being 'revolutionary', 'radical', 'cool beyond words' and 'breathtaking' while remaining true to the history, traditions and spirit of the company. HD has also been appealing to a new demographic sector: women. The number of women buying Harleys rose from 2 per cent in 1987 to 9 per cent in 2003. Since 1999, about 40 per cent of those attending bike-training courses in the USA each year have been women. This group will be heavily targeted by the company's marketing department over the next few years, as the company continues to learn, innovate, evolve and grow over the first two decades of the 21st century.

Conclusion

> We soon discovered how essential it is for a multi-business company to become an open, learning organization. The ultimate competitive advantage lies in an organization's ability to learn and rapidly transform that learning into action. It may acquire that learning in a variety of ways – through great scientists, great management practices, or great marketing skills – but then it must rapidly assimilate its new learning and drive it.
> (*Jack Welch, former CEO of General Electric, cited by Lowe, 1998: 84*)

> Our true core competency is not in manufacturing or services, but the recruiting and nurturing of the world's best people, and the cultivation within our employees of an insatiable desire to learn in order to improve everything we do on an ongoing basis. It is this competency that has enabled us to grow and adapt quickly to the many challenges we have faced over the last decade.
> (*Welch again in his final Director's Report at GE in 2002. In 2003, GE was one of just seven companies in the world awarded a Standard and Poor's AAA performance rating.*)

Are more organizations likely to embrace learning organization principles as a way of improving employee performance and maintaining competitive advantage? A few years ago, the answer to this question would have been, 'They ought to.' Now it is, 'They probably will', because all cutting-edge organizations of the last 100 years have been able to do something more than reactively 'manage change'. For example, almost all of Collins and Porras's 'visionary companies' and O'Reilly and Pfeffer's 'extraordinary companies' are organizations that have been able to learn quickly and have learning organization characteristics. They have regularly created change for others to follow in their wake, and have been able to adapt quickly to unforeseen circumstances in the past. Only on rare occasions have these companies been forced to resort to the classic knee-jerk reactions of most companies facing crises, such as downsizing and mergers or other short-term fixes. While these may have some short-term benefits, *none* of them are recipes for assuring long-term organizational growth and longevity.

Learning Organization tools can support the management of perpetual change and innovation because the average life expectancy of all business organizations is declining year by year and this trend will continue for the foreseeable future. It is a management philosophy that rejects short-term fads, quick-fix solutions and the use of consultants to sort out organizational problems. Like all successful individuals, all successful companies learn how to do things for themselves. Both voraciously acquire knowledge and ideas from any source and use these to educate themselves or their workforces, and thereby serve their best long-term interests. As John Burgoyne has suggested, 'the battle is not yet won, but sufficient victories have been won in many companies, large and small, to suggest that the learning organization is not just a fashion accessory' (1995: 28).

Arie de Geus, whose work at Royal Dutch Shell first inspired the idea of the learning organization, has argued that only those companies who put their own interests first, rather than those of its external financial stakeholders, will thrive in the future (de Geus, 1996, 1997; Macleay, 1997b). Echoing Collins and Porras's findings on visionary companies, Senge's work on learning organizations and the work of O'Reilly and Pfeffer on extraordinary companies, de Geus has consistently argued that companies that focus single-mindedly on profits are unable to learn and, therefore, cannot hope to survive in the long term. Of 45 long-lasting companies that he identified (some of which had existed for centuries), all had a purpose beyond profit. They saw themselves first and foremost as organic systems, made up of living people, and their primary loyalty was toward themselves and their employees, not shareholders. He found that companies that focused primarily on economic management, and short-term financial goals, invariably had a much shorter shelf life than those companies that focused on systemic learning.

De Geus recalls that he was so surprised by these results that he went back again and again to verify that this was what these companies were actually doing, and not symptomatic of the usual corporate rhetoric about 'our people being our most important assets'. But, this is precisely what he did find. Also recall that de Geus was not an 'ivory-tower' academic. His unwavering belief that a single-minded adherence to managing organizations as economic entities was fundamentally flawed emerged from almost 40 years at Royal Dutch Shell, including ten years as head of Shell's Corporate Planning Department. During this time he had wrestled with two major questions: 'What does an oil company do when there is no more oil to find?' and 'What are the secrets of companies that live for decades and even centuries?' The book in which he presented his ideas, *The Living Company*, had such an impact that it won *The Financial Times*/Booz Allen and Hamilton 1998 Global Business Books Awards prize for 'Most Innovative Business Book of 1998'. Shell, the weakest of the world's large oil companies in 1970, is now one of the strongest, and companies as diverse as BP, General Electric, Harley-Davidson, Du Pont, Siemens and the American Army have all taken learning organization principles on board (Sullivan and Harper, 1996).

There is little doubt that learning organization principles can be difficult to implement, but many of the world's most successful companies have spent a lot of time developing their learning capabilities. It took Harley-Davidson the best part of five years to really grasp what the implications of learning organization principles would be for the company. Having said this, the learning organizations identified by de Geus and Senge are companies that have been in existence for many decades and, in some cases, for more than a hundred years. They have an inbuilt capacity to live in harmony with their business environments, by being extremely flexible when times are tough and, more importantly, continuing to learn, develop and change when the business environment is slower and more stable. These are companies that do not rest on their laurels, and never grow complacent and arrogant when they are successful or at the height of their powers. In common with high-achieving individuals, they have an inbuilt hunger for perpetual learning, self-education and improvement, and do not stand still for long. While learning capabilities alone may be insufficient to ensure a secure future for an organization, its ability to learn faster than its competitors will be a major source of competitive advantage for the foreseeable future. How it can then convert this learning into useful knowledge and information that the entire organization and its employees can utilize will be discussed in the next chapter.

> In order to control your destiny, you must realise that you will only stay ahead competitively if you acknowledge that no advantage or success is ever permanent. The winners are those that keep moving. We've tried to instill this attitude in our people. We've tried to make it not only acceptable but also that people look for a better way or grab the best ideas from wherever they find them [ ] To create an effective learning organization, you don't bolt things down. You let the organization and the ways in which it learns evolve continuously.
> (*John Browne, CEO of BP, cited by Prokesch, 1997: 162; the company reported record profits on the back of a 42 per cent increase in earnings during 2003: AFP, 2004a.*)

Exercise 9.5

Having read through the last section of this chapter, please think about how you might implement learning organization principles in your organization in the future.

Insight	Strategy to implement this
1.	
2.	
3.	
4.	
5.	◆

Notes

1 Answers to Exercise 9.1:
   Part 1: (1) Tuesday, (2) Yourself, (3) NINE, (4) Two 'F's (or seven 'f's), (5) SIX,
   (6)

   Part 2
   (1) The person was a dwarf who couldn't reach the lift-buttons for the higher floors.
   (2) He was a parachutist, whose parachute failed to open.
   (3) This was the year when the world's first digital wristwatch was put on show at an international watch manufacturers' conference. The Swiss (the world's leading clock and watchmakers at the time) did not believe that there was a market for this innovation. However, some representatives from a relatively unknown Japanese company called Sony did attend this conference . . . it took the Swiss watch-making industry more than a decade to recover from its inability to imagine, 'What if . . .?' It later bounced back in the mid-1980s with the launch of the Swatch range of watches.
   (4) The telephone. Although as many as 12 people were instrumental in developing this, most notably the Italian Antonio Meucci, the two people who eventually took most of the credit for the idea were Alexander Graham Bell and his assistant, Graham Watson. Soon after they had developed a working prototype on 10 March 1876, they demonstrated their invention to the executives of Western Union. This is part of the reply they received: 'Mr. Bell, after careful consideration of your invention, while it is a very interesting novelty, we have come to the conclusion that it has no commercial possibilities', adding that they saw no future for 'an electrical toy'. Bell then set up his own company, American Telephone and Telegraph (AT&T). Within just 20 years there were more than six million phones in use in America. AT&T became, for much of the 20th century, the biggest corporation in the USA, with stock valued at $US1000 a share at its peak. The Bell patent (No. 174,465) became the single most valuable patent in history (Bryson, 1994: 113).
   (5) The Talking Clock.
2 Answers to Figure 9.1: *Picture puzzles*
   At the top left, there is a duck and a rabbit; on the right there is a table with four chairs under it, or a square being eaten by 'space-invaders', or a top-down view of a square parasol with four round stools under each corner. In the middle, there is a penguin and a Chinese face, a sleeping cat and a sleeping mouse, and a couple embracing/a man washing his face. Next, there is a man's face/a seashore/a dog and, on the right, an old woman's and a young woman's face.

   Answers to Exercise 9.2: *Advanced lateral thinking*
   (1) The statement 'I don't always speak the truth' has to be true. If it were false, it would imply that the speaker does always speak the truth. Thus, the supposition that his statement is false leads to a contradiction, thereby demonstrating its truth. Consequently, the first stranger's statement is true.
   (2) All jokes have to start somewhere. Betty created the joke and told it to Cathy. So when Alice began to tell Betty the joke, she had not heard it or read it, but knew it.
   (3) $247 - 118 = 129$
   (4) The classical solution to this problem is to use one of the objects for a purpose for which it was not intended and to apply a principle from another body of knowledge. If you can get the strings to move, or pendulum, you can bring their ends closer together. How do you create a pendulum? By adding a weight to it. So, all you have to do is tie the stapler to one string, swing it, grasp the other string and as the weighted string swings back, grab it, remove the stapler and tie the two ends to together.

(5) The clock strikes 11 times at 11.00, three times on each quarter hour and 12 more times at 12.00 midnight, making a total of 26 chimes. However, once a year, in many countries of the world, the clocks go back one hour at the beginning of winter. So, having reached midnight, the clock chimes 12 times. The clock is then wound back one hour to 11.01. It then chimes three times on the quarter hour and 12 times at 12.00, making a total of 27 chimes (12 + 3 + 12) in 60 minutes.
(*Perkins, 2001*)

3   Many practitioners of the yoga and relaxation disciplines, described in Chapter 2, believe that these also free the creative and dissociative parts of the human mind.

4   The computer. Mechanical computers were developed and used during World War II, as part of the Enigma code-breaking programme in the UK. The first digital computer appeared in 1946. So, although all the relevant information and technologies existed in 1918, it took 30 years to link these disparate bodies of knowledge together into an innovation that continues to radically transform the world (Drucker, 1999: 155–6). This is another example demonstrating that most new ideas and products are derived from pre-existing products and/or bodies of knowledge and expertise, often reformulated, reframed or resynthesized in new and novel ways. For an insight into how this process has driven the creation of hundreds of consumer products, and the many devices we use at work and in the home, see Joel Levy's *Really Useful: The Origins of Everyday Things* (London: Quintet Publishing, 2002) or any autobiographies of inventors/innovators like Thomas Edison or Barnes Wallis.

5   Another idea that has been around for a long time. John Patterson, founder of the National Cash Register in the USA, proposed a system of paying employees for their ideas, in order to turn his firm into what he termed 'a hundred-headed brain'. He first proposed this idea in 1895 (*The Economist*, 1999). Chapter 4 contains a detailed guide to the financial and non-financial incentives that can be used to retain high-quality and creative employees.

6   Of course, funky ergonomics alone are useless without the right values, organizational culture, strategies and practical business acumen to operationalize and market innovative ideas. In Google's case, there were indications during 2003–4 of the emergence of 'an arrogant and complacent culture', and some worries about problems of integration and coordination being created by too rapid growth. The company's apparently relaxed attitude to the emergence of new players in the search engine market was also a cause of concern to some business commentators. The new competition includes Microsoft, which now has its own search engine software built into all operating systems (Vogelstein, 2003).

7   And even management gurus get it wrong sometimes. Two of the organizations cited as examplars of innovative companies in these articles by Gary Hamel were Enron and Worldcom. *Fortune* also presented its 'most innovative company' award to Enron on six occasions during the 1990s. Perhaps 'most innovative ways of stealing money from other people' awards would have been more appropriate.

10 Managing employee knowledge and intellectual capital

Objectives

To define knowledge, knowledge management and intellectual capital.

To look at the theory and practice of knowledge management in organizations.

To help you assess if your organization is 'knowledge-based', where knowledge is stored in your organization, and the extent to which new knowledge is actively sought from outside your organization.

To evaluate if the culture and management practices of your organization promote or thwart knowledge sharing amongst its employees, and if your organization has appropriate systems in place to manage its knowledge effectively.

To look at the main difficulties that organizations have encountered when introducing knowledge management initiatives.

To look briefly at the links between organizational culture, learning, innovation and knowledge management.

Introduction

> In the past year alone, more storable data has been generated than in the whole of human history. The world's data storage requirements have gone ballistic.
> (australian.com.au, *28 May 2002*)

> The key to the future of any country is not in its physical resources or industrial capital; rather, it is human and intellectual capital that will fund the health and growth of nations in the future.
> (*Media mogul Rupert Murdoch, during his Keith Murdoch Memorial speech, Sydney, October 2001*)

The last two chapters have demonstrated how important continual change, innovation and organizational learning are for modern organizations. A significant component of each of these competencies is the extent to which organizations can tap into, and fully utilize, the knowledge and intellectual capital of all their employees in order to cope with shortening product life cycles, increasing competition, accelerating change and environmental uncertainties. The word 'knowledge' is derived from the Greek for 'meaning', *logos*, and was also used by the ancient Greeks to mean 'reason' or 'word'. It is defined here as a body of facts, information and know-how accumulated over time. Knowledge management is a generic term encompassing the processes by which employees' experience, expertise, skills and knowledge are gathered, shared and utilized and then converted into collective organizational learning in order to improve organizational performance, effectiveness and productivity. The term 'intellectual capital' is derived from the Latin words *intellectus* (understanding) and *capitellum* (the head). There is some uncertainty about the emergence of this concept in modern times, but it appears to have been first used in its modern sense in 1958 by Peter Drucker, popularized by John Galbraith in the late 1960s and fully articulated by the Swedish academic, Karl-Erik Sveiby, in 1989 (Stewart, 2002). It is defined here as the totality of an organization's collective knowledge, learning, patents, expertise, wisdom, experience, know-how, skills and competencies.

In a broad sense, knowledge, knowledge management and intellectual capital have always been important elements of business success and organizational effectiveness. For hundreds of years, owners of family run enterprises have passed their knowledge and wisdom on to their children, craftsmen have taught their skills to apprentices, and employees have shared their expertise, experience and know-how at work. 'Communities of practice', in the form of trade associations or guilds of metal workers, potters, artists, lawyers, builders, masons and other skilled professions have existed for centuries, and they too have shared and disseminated knowledge within their occupational groupings. However, for much of the history of industrial capitalism, many groups of workers were valued only for their muscle power, particularly after the introduction of production-line systems into manufacturing industries in the 19th and early 20th centuries. The 'godfather' of mass-production in the automobile industry, Henry Ford, is reported to have said in the 1920s, 'Why is it that whenever I ask for a pair of hands, a brain comes attached?'

Things have changed dramatically since Ford made this comment, particularly over the last 20 years. Today we find ourselves living in what has been described by many commentators as a 'global knowledge economy', where efficiency and economies of scale will only allow companies to have limited success in business. With the rapid shift from industries based largely on muscle to ones based increasingly on intellectual resources, more and more companies have been forced to examine the knowledge underpinning their businesses, and how they can use this to increase their competitiveness. The Swedish corporation Scandia, guided by Karl-Erik Sveiby, was the first to establish a comprehensive set of knowledge management tools to assess its intangible knowledge assets, and today one in three Nordic companies measure these 'soft' assets (Edvinsson, 2002: 49). Many other major international companies in a range of industries such as telecommunications, oil and gas exploration, construction, engineering, computer hardware and software, automobile manufacturing and management consulting have also started to reap the benefits of the improvements they have made to the way they manage their employees' knowledge.

Capturing the commercial potential of intellectual property can also reap huge dividends for companies. For example, IBM patented more than 22 000 inventions and innovations during the 1990s, generating hundreds of millions of dollars in income and billions in market value from its patent portfolio. In 2003, it registered 3415 patents, making it the most prolific patent holder in the USA for the eleventh consecutive year. The next best was Canon, with 1400 patents. IBM's Senior Vice-President for Technology and Manufacturing, Nick Donofrio, commented in January 2004, 'We consider patents the starting point on the path to true innovation. What differentiates IBM from other companies is our ability to rapidly apply these to new products and offerings that solve the most pressing business challenges of our clients' (cited by Blake, 2004). Furthermore, knowledge management is no longer the exclusive domain of large private sector businesses; government, public sector, schools and not-for-profit organizations have also started to benefit from knowledge management initiatives in recent times. For example, in 2002, the City of Perth Executive in Western Australia introduced a comprehensive knowledge management programme for its 472 employees – the first public sector government organization in Australia to do this (City of Perth, 2002), Several other public sector organizations in WA soon followed this example in 2003–4.

However, until fairly recently, the collective knowledge and intellectual capital of organizations rarely appeared on end-of-year financial reports or balance sheets. There were two reasons for this. First, few businesses could see much point in doing this. Second, many business people believed that things as nebulous, implicit and difficult to pin-down as 'knowledge' and 'intellectual capital' could not be easily quantified and measured. In spite of these difficulties, it is no exaggeration to say that there was an explosion of interest in managing knowledge and intellectual capital in the late 1990s and early 2000s. This happened for several reasons. First, emerging economic theory now places knowledge at the centre of sustained economic growth, be this at the company level or at the level of the nation state (for example, Singapore), and several recent studies have suggested that knowledge and intellectual capital will be the primary drivers of both organizational and national economic performance over the next two decades (for example, Guthrie and Petty, 2000; Klaila and Hall, 2000; Choo, 1998).

Second, businesses continue to downsize, rationalize and/or merge, leading to continual rounds of job cuts in many industrial sectors. The steady growth in the use of outsourcing in organizations, the emergence of 'portfolio careers', 'craft loyalty' and the increasing use of short-term contracts by employers, have led directly to the gradual erosion of employee loyalty and commitment to organizations in all business sectors, particularly amongst Generations Y and T. For example, in California's Silicon Valley, labour turnover rates in local electronic firms in the late 1990s were over 35 per cent, and as high as 60 per cent in some small firms. The average job tenure of employees was about two years (Evans and Wurster, 2000: 6). If an organization's knowledge resides only in the heads of their employers, they can effectively kiss this goodbye when they lose staff. Potentially, this can be a very expensive proposition, if they have spent time and resources developing those people and who subsequently move on to one of their competitors (a phenomenon aptly described as 'bright-sizing'). This means that companies, particularly in new industries, have to become better at retaining their employees' knowledge in order to maintain their corporate 'memories'. They also need to find ways of encouraging their loyal employees to bring their intelligence, motivation, creativity and knowledge to work and then utilizing these to the maximum possible level while they are there.

The book of business

'Staff come and go. Make sure their knowledge and experience stay. When you lose staff, you lose ground. It's hard not to when all that training and investment simply walks out of the door. An estimated 70–80 percent of company knowledge disappears this way. We have a complete package of software, hardware and services to help your company capture knowledge and use it. This eliminates the need to recreate business applications, tools and processes in different locations.

It allows new employees to skill up quickly and cost effectively instead of reinventing the wheel. And it integrates with existing systems, minimising the costs and delays of ripping and replacing. Combine this with the Lotus Discovery Server, the most comprehensive knowledge server available today, and you'll have everything you need to capitalise on your knowledge like never before. So, talk to IBM now and get your company's knowledge flowing everywhere but out the door.'
(*IBM advertisement for codified knowledge management systems*, The Australian, *9 October 2001*)

Third, the continual pressure to reduce costs, increase internal efficiency and cope with fast-changing business environments is forcing more companies to consider how to use their corporate knowledge and other intangibles (for example, 'human intellectual capital') more intelligently and effectively. For example, one-third of the entire annual healthcare budget of the USA – about $US350 billion – consisted of the costs of storing, processing and retrieving information during the 1990s (Evans and Wurster, 2000: 4). Fourth, a failure to share knowledge can be disastrous for companies. For example, the antagonistic Ford/Firestone split of 2001 happened as a direct result of their failure to share knowledge about the performance parameters of Ford's four-wheel-drive vehicles and the Firestone tyres that were being used on these. Ford had a sophisticated Intranet system in place, the 'Best Practice Replication Process', which contained some 2800 proven quality practices across the company, and had generated cost savings of $US850 million since its inception. Unfortunately, their external knowledge management links with Firestone were weak and information that might have alerted them to the impending 'exploding tyres' fiasco was scattered in different places throughout the two companies. As a result, no one picked up the warning signs until it was too late. Furthermore, neither company had sufficiently rich *informal* knowledge-sharing systems that might have uncovered this problem (Stewart, 2000a: 129). This eventually led to a multimillion-dollar bill for the faulty tyres on their customers' four-wheel-drives, the sacking of Ford's CEO Jacques Nasser and, ultimately, to a severing of a 100-year-old business partnership.

Fifth, effective knowledge management provides important bridges between organizational change, innovation and learning. Managing knowledge well enables the four primary sources of competitive advantage (human intellectual capital, creativity, innovation and information) to be synthesized, disseminated and utilized more effectively. Sixth, the need for more efficient knowledge management is also driven by the realization that the global business environment is changing so quickly that organizations have to get better at creating constellations of competencies that can be quickly reconfigured to fit marketplaces characterized by rapidly changing customer needs and preferences. This inexorable trend towards a global knowledge-based economy is increasing the need for more systemic and formalized knowledge management processes in many organizations. Seventh, computing capabilities, advances in the 'intelligence' of software and increasing connectivity are making the systemic monitoring and utilization of internal and external knowledge assets an easier task than ever before (but, as we will see later, only if these are utilized in the right way).

All the indications suggest that managing employee knowledge and intellectual capital will become even more important in the future, as products quickly become obsolete, as markets grow, die, shift and change with increasing rapidity, and as new technologies continue to proliferate at a mind-boggling speed. The most successful organizations in the future will be those that can access their employees' ideas and knowledge, disseminate them rapidly, and quickly embody these in new products or services. Knowledge is fast becoming one of the most important renewable resources that a company can capture and leverage in order to improve its effectiveness and competitiveness. For the visionary and far-sighted management commentator, Peter Drucker, knowledge and innovation have become the only meaningful resources in post-industrial economies, and one of the key roles of business leaders now is to ensure the generation and application of new knowledge at a faster and faster rate in their organizations (Drucker, 1993). Research evidence accumulated during the 1990s and 2000s indicates that successful knowledge management can reap considerable benefits for organizations, in spite of the difficulties that can be encountered when introducing this. And, while knowledge management is certainly growing as an organizational practice, it has often been implemented in companies without a full understanding of its systemic consequences, and how it needs to be integrated with other facets of organizational management.

In the remainder of this chapter, we will consider what organizational knowledge 'is'; where it 'resides', and look at organizational strategies for creating and managing knowledge more effectively (which is linked to the process of meta-learning described in Chapter 9). We will see that knowledge comes in many forms, is often difficult to articulate and that knowledge that exists *outside* an organization's boundaries can be as important to performance as internal knowledge. We will also look at some real-life examples of companies that have introduced knowledge management initiatives and the lessons that can be learnt from their experiences. We will conclude this chapter by asking if effective knowledge management relies on something more than the use of technology, and briefly examine the links between organizational culture, learning, innovation and knowledge management.

The theory and practice of knowledge management

How can an organization decide if it needs to introduce more formalized systems for managing knowledge? If its leaders answer 'Yes' to all or most of the following questions, then it should be considering this.

- Does your organization operate in an environment characterized by rapid change?
- Do you need to find more cost-effective and efficient ways of utilizing and sharing your employees' expertise and knowledge?
- Do you routinely face new competition for your products or services?
- Is your organization heavily dependent on your employees' knowledge or intellectual capital to maintain and improve its competitive position?
- Do you have to be at the cutting-edge of the markets you operate in in order to grow and prosper?
- Do you need to attract, recruit and retain creative and innovative employees? Do you operate in the private sector?

You can also ascertain if you are currently working for a knowledge creating company by answering this question: *Does your organization put the creation, acquisition and dissemination of employee knowledge and intellectual capital at the centre of its strategic and human resource policies?*

Before reading through the remainder of this chapter, please complete Exercise 10.1. This provides an opportunity to assess the existing knowledge management capabilities of the organization you work for.

Exercise 10.1

Does your organization have a knowledge management culture?

Please go through each of the scales on the following pages and indicate, with a circle (O) on each 1–7 scale, where you feel your organization needs to be in order to remain successful over the next five years. Then go back through the scales and indicate, with a cross (X) on each scale, where you believe your organization is now. When you've done this, plot your scores (O and X) in the table at the end of the questionnaire. If you are not currently in full-time work, assess an organization you have worked for in the past or one you are familiar with.

A. Vision

There is no commitment to
the idea that knowledge
management is essential to
our future success.

There is a clear vision of how
the effective creation, transfer
and use of knowledge leads
to business-enhancing outcomes.

B. Senior management

Knowledge management is
viewed as a fad. There is only
token involvement by senior
management.

Senior managers are good
role models for knowledge
management. They view
knowledge as an asset to be
invested in, one that will give
us greater competitive edge.

C. Openness

Knowledge is locked into the
hierarchical structure. The
culture is one of secrecy and
exclusion.

There are few hierarchical
differentiations. Open culture
facilitates sharing of
knowledge.

D. Communication

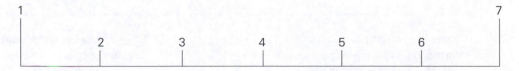

People don't talk about the
sharing and use of knowledge.

The creation, sharing and use
of knowledge is celebrated
and encouraged.

E. Learning

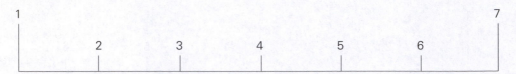

People don't take time out to
review what they have
learned and how they can
learn from mistakes.

There are ongoing reviews of
learning from mistakes and
successes.

F. Inventory

Usable information is
lost or unavailable. It is
chaotically organized.

Usable information is
systematically inventoried,
catalogued and stored.

G. Access

Knowledge and information are
very difficult to access.

Knowledge is available to
everyone in the organization.
It is easily accessed and
disseminated.

H. Transfer

People tend to hoard
information and knowledge.
Very little usable information
is transferred across teams,
departments and divisions.

Usable knowledge is
systematically transferred to
different parts of the
organization.

I. Leveraging

Knowledge that is created stays
where it is. There is no attempt to
market our good ideas.

When new ideas are developed
or new knowledge created we
actively market this to provide
new sources of revenue.

J. Creation

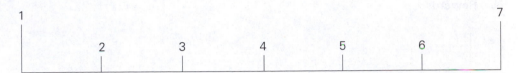

There is no 'thinking outside
the box'. People have little
opportunity to create new
ways of doing things and
share and apply their ideas.

There is an active R&D
philosophy at all levels.
Everyone is encouraged to
develop new ideas and put
them into practice.

K. External knowledge

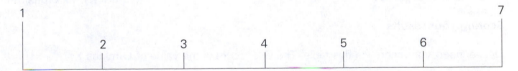

The organization is internally
focused. Information and
knowledge from outside aren't
systematically collected,
shared, discussed or acted upon.

Knowledge is systematically
acquired from outside, so that
we continuously benchmark
ourselves against best
practice.

L. Measurement

Intellectual capital is usually
expensed not capitalized.
People talent is viewed as a
cost. There is no attempt to
measure the 'intangibles' that
could add value to our organization.

We have processes that audit
and measure our intellectual
capital. People are seen as
intellectual assets.

M. IT

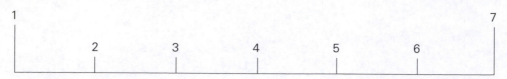

People are inadequately trained in IT. IT is used badly. Either it is underused or overused, ahead of the desire or ability of people to use it.

People are well trained and equipped to use IT to help us to acquire, codify, disseminate and transfer knowledge.

N. Rewards

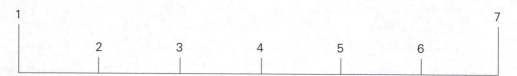

Knowledge is seen as power. People aren't in the habit of sharing knowledge. Rewards and promotions go to those who have knowledge, not to those who share it

Sharing of knowledge is rewarded. People recognize the importance of investing time in knowledge sharing, in order to create a better future for our organization.

Scoring your results

Please insert your scores in this table. The GAP score is the value of O minus X

		O	X	GAP
A.	Vision			
B.	Senior management			
C.	Openness			
D.	Communication			
E.	Learning			
F.	Inventory			
G.	Access			
H.	Transfer			
I.	Leveraging			
J.	Creation			
K.	External knowledge			
L.	Measurement			
M.	IT			
N.	Rewards			
	TOTALS			

Interpreting your score

Gap score =

X total =

The items with the biggest gaps indicate the largest differences between where your organization is now and where it would like to be in the future.

80–98:   Transforming potential: knowledge is systemically created, shared and utilized to give the organization a competitive edge in the marketplace. Reward and promotion systems actively encourage the use and sharing of organizational knowledge.

55–79:   Developing potential: knowledge is still managed in a rather ad hoc way. There is a gap between knowledge management rhetoric and managerial practices, and information is not always converted into innovative business ideas or practical policies.

29–54:   Locked-in potential: valuable knowledge generated every day remains locked up in the minds of individual employees. Knowledge sharing is limited by hierarchical and bureaucratic restrictions. There is a reluctance to share knowledge openly. Reward and promotion systems do not support the use and sharing of organizational knowledge.

14–28:   Rock-bottom potential: the organization is unable to leverage any knowledge that it might possess in order to gain competitive advantage. The organization's culture is based on old-style management practices that are resistant to embracing knowledge management initiatives.

Note: if you work in a business or organization where knowledge management is not part of its daily working practices or operating culture, it may have been quite difficult to accurately rate the statements on this questionnaire.

Source: Adapted from Bagshaw and Phillips (2000); used with permission. ◆

Introducing knowledge management systems into an organization

While there was an explosion of publications in the field of knowledge management in the 1990s and early 2000s, there is still little agreement amongst researchers and consultants about the number or blend of elements that need to be in place to support the introduction of knowledge management initiatives into an organization. The elements that have been identified include a clear and well articulated vision; committed and empowering leadership from the top; mapping sources of internal expertise and knowledge; a cultural shift in the organization to support the introduction of personalized and/or codified knowledge-sharing systems; the establishment of a new knowledge team to champion the changes;[1] open two-way communication with employees; sufficient resources for new hardware and software; educating and developing staff; a commitment to team-based working systems; systemic approaches for managing the collective knowledge of the whole organization; the creation of both formal and informal knowledge webs or knowledge centres to coordinate the sharing of knowledge; and the establishment of monitoring systems for measurement and feedback (Devinney, 2001; Bagshaw and Phillips, 2000; Brown and Duguid, 2000; Hansen *et al.*, 1999; McLean, 2000; Ruggles, 1998; Choo, 1998; Nonaka, 1991). Of these 12 elements, the development of a vision, empowering leadership, the establishment of new teams, two-way communication, and systemic thinking have been described in detail in earlier chapters of this book. The seven remaining elements are examined in this section.

The first question to be addressed is, where are knowledge and intellectual assets 'stored' in organizations? Surprisingly, many leaders and managers still find this a hard question to answer. Similarly, if you were to ask a random sample of organizational leaders, particularly in small and medium-sized companies, how they measured their knowledge or intellectual capital assets, many would still probably reply, 'Our whaaaat . . .?' The short answer to the first question is that *knowledge can be found everywhere and in everything that you can point a stick at in your organization*. These assets can be divided into two broad categories (Table 10.1).

Table 10.1   Knowledge assets

Tangible assets	Intangible assets
Buildings	Employees' experience, skills, expertise and knowledge
Plant	Organizational culture and climate
Equipment	Organic/systemic knowledge and intellectual capital
Cash reserves	Organizational learning/innovation capabilities
Investments	Team working and management practices
Securities	Informal employee groups
Personnel records and documents	Customers and clients' intellectual capital
Mission statements, business plans and company publications	Access to and use of external sources of knowledge and intellectual capital
(*Recorded or measured or used by all organizations*)	(*May not be documented, measured or used by organizations*)
FINITE APPLICATIONS	INFINITE APPLICATIONS

Source: Adapted from Bagshaw and Phillips (2000: 1–13); used with permission.

We noted in Chapter 8 that organizations are, in the most basic sense, simply collections of people working together, nothing more or less. In this sense, organizations cannot be said to be 'knowledgable'. Hence, while all large organizations now have reservoirs of knowledge and intelligence in the form of company documentation, operating policies and databases, it is individual employees who still create, own and use these. And, while there have been remarkable advances in electronic facilities to gather, store and disseminate information, all new knowledge creation still starts and ends with employees. All recent research on knowledge management shows that individual human creativity is still *the* primary driver of learning, innovation and knowledge creation in organizations. This will be so until intelligent and creative artilects are developed for use in organizations (see, for example, Devinney, 2001; Brown and Duguid, 2000; Hansen *et al.*, 1999; McLean, 2000; Ruggles, 1998; Nonaka, 1991).

Variously described as 'intangible', 'human', 'individual', 'internal', 'personal', 'implicit' and 'tacit' this type of knowledge is the product of the individual's unique personal biography, education, work experiences and what they have learnt from the different organizational contexts they have worked in. The knowledge sets of individuals consist of a constellation of skills, experiences, beliefs and perspectives, mental models and creative and intuitive capabilities that are deeply ingrained and largely taken for granted. These knowledge sets enable them to cope with the range and complexity of their work tasks on a weekly or monthly basis, and also help them cope with activities that may extend far beyond the formal requirements of their jobs. This type of knowledge can be very difficult to measure, identify, formalize, articulate, communicate and transfer, unless the organization has systems in place to support these processes.

> We will always know more than we can say.
> (*Michael Polanyi, philosopher of science, 1970*)

> When action grows unprofitable, gather information.
> When information grows unprofitable, sleep.
> (*Ursula K. Le Guin*, The Left Hand of Darkness, *1969*)

Because of its implicit nature, knowledge of this kind is still best shared face-to-face, and it often is in both informal groups and formal work teams (and, hence, one of the five pillars of the Learning Organization, described in Chapter 9). In fact, one of the primary catalysts of knowledge creation and dissemination remains the formal and informal 'communities of practice' that form within all organizations (Wenger and Snyder, 2000). However, without the right kind of structures and working practices to support good employee interaction, the transfer of knowledge will be, at best, ad hoc and inefficient. Creating and sharing knowledge is not just a matter of making more information available or telling employees that they should talk to each other more often. Effective knowledge management stems from a conscious strategic effort to tap into employees' implicit and subjective experiences, insights, intuitions and hunches, and make this knowledge available to anyone who might want to use it.

Without repeating all the suggestions made in Chapter 9 for fostering employee creativity and learning, this primarily means challenging employees to examine what they take for granted (common sense), particularly during times of rapid change or when long-established knowledge is becoming outdated or redundant. This implicit knowledge then has to be made explicit and converted into information that the whole organization can then use, be this through personal contact, human networks, technological systems or some combination of all three. To achieve this, many of the questions that underpin organizational learning and innovation also have to be asked within the context of knowledge management. These include the following:

- Why are we doing what we do now?
- Where are we going in the future?
- What does our organization know now?
- What will it need to know in the near future?
- What will we need to (un)learn in the future?
- Where will we obtain the new information/knowledge we need?
- How will we share, disseminate and use this information/knowledge?
- What competencies, skills and knowledge does our workforce have now?
- What competencies, skills and knowledge will it need in the near future?

Mapping internal expertise can take many forms, such as the creation of personal websites that list each employee's areas of knowledge and expertise, creating virtual communities of practice, or setting up specialist knowledge groups in organizations. For example, Unichema International 'undertook a Knowledge Management Program', designed 'to use the creativity of its people. Formal "What if" experiments were introduced, and a common approach to problem solving. Company activities were divided into four levels of complexity: access to knowledge, adding value to knowledge, modelling knowledge and knowledge discovery. The intention was to create a managerial process for the accumulation and use of technical knowledge – a version of scientific creativity. Unichema is just one example amongst many' (James, 2001: 17). The principal objective of this process of self-analysis was to ensure that employees both created and accessed information, and then used this to improve their daily decision-making and problem-solving processes.

Knowledge transfer is not simply about 'communicating more' or 'disseminating information': it requires *assimilation* by those who are using it. In other words, you can have the best IT systems and databases in the world; but if people don't understand their purpose, or don't make effective use of these, you will be left with a very expensive albatross (with the well-paid consultants who put the system in for you in the first place now long gone). While technology can be a powerful catalyst in knowledge management, the transfer and use of knowledge is primarily a cultural and people management issue. In other words, the reward systems and working practices of the organization must support these activities in a very explicit way. As Nonaka puts it succinctly, 'Often, the most important factor in managing knowledge is the way a company organises its units and people. Human links, not electronic ones, are the key' (1991: 17). So the primary challenge for leaders and managers is to create an innovative and learning culture, create personal or codified networks of knowledge workers, leverage their collective knowledge across the entire organization, and then convert this knowledge into usable ideas.

People-based knowledge management systems primarily involve dialogue and communication. This may come in the form of breakfast or lunchtime presentations, weekly team meetings and project briefings or via mentoring relationships. Merely having these kinds of forums can send an important message to staff: *we are explicitly fitting time into the working day for you to learn from each other and share your knowledge and expertise*. For example, in consulting firms such as Bain, Boston Consulting and McKinsey, knowledge is shared primarily through interpersonal dialogue and brainstorming sessions. In the 1990s, all three companies invested heavily in building informal knowledge networks amongst their employees. Bain did this 'by transferring people between offices, by supporting a culture in which consultants are expected to return phone calls from colleagues promptly, by creating directories of experts and by using "consulting directors" within the firm to assist project teams' (Hansen *et al.*, 1999: 109). These companies recruit top-tier MBA graduates, to use their creative and analytical skills to solve business problems. They look to employ people who will be able to use their 'people-to-people' knowledge-sharing approach effectively. To make sure they get the right kind of staff, they spend an inordinate amount of time screening new recruits, who can go through as many as eight interviews. One of their top selection criteria is 'communication skills' (ibid.: 110).

These knowledge management initiatives then have to be built into the culture of an organization and the way it thinks collectively. This means that knowledge management initiatives must be driven by the organization's core values, vision, business plans and strategic goals. The organization also has to allow individuals to be comfortable with the need to use knowledge more effectively, and provide them with the appropriate skill levels they need to understand and interpret the information that they have access to. The culture must support employee mind-sets and working practices that encourage the sharing and dissemination of knowledge and intellectual capital as a collective exercise. A knowledge-generating company cannot allow individuals or groups of employees to hoard knowledge for their personal benefit. This means that the organization's reward systems have to encourage and reward knowledge sharing. For example, Ernst and Young monitor the level and quality of employee contributions to their electronic databases, and this is one of five dimensions of their annual performance reviews. Bain Consulting include factors such as 'direct help to colleagues' and 'information sharing', and the quality of these contributions can account for as much as one-quarter of an employee's annual compensation. Hence an employee who hoards knowledge and information in these companies soon discovers that their pay and remuneration suffer in very tangible ways. Personalized knowledge management has to become a way of behaving, indeed a way of being, in which everyone becomes knowledge workers and shares their knowledge freely with whoever wants it. The organization's culture has to support the sharing of information, because unless implicit knowledge becomes explicit it cannot be leveraged by everyone. This mind shift means that knowledge management must come to be regarded as an organic, rather than a mechanistic, process (Ruggles, 1998: 86).

When a knowledge-sharing culture has been created amongst employees, the next stage is systematically to measure, sort and store what have been variously described as 'tangible', 'codified', 'structural' or 'explicit' knowledge assets. These can come in many different forms, including mission statements, policy documents, employee surveys, customer and client surveys, books, papers, studies, personnel files, technical reports, software, data bases, emails, CDs, DVDs, patents, copyrights and registered or copyrighted intellectual property. The purpose of this audit is to create an organized, formalized, systemic and codified inventory of an organization's entire stock of 'hard' knowledge assets, and then storing this on electronic databases. The purpose of creating systems that encompass an organization's implicit and explicit knowledge is to allow a company's employees to share information in a timely and efficient way that is not entirely dependent on face-to-face information sharing. Hence capturing, documenting and encouraging the proactive use of this information becomes the next operational priority. Unlike implicit or tacit knowledge, this explicit knowledge then becomes independent of its creators and, ideally, can be transferred, utilized and adopted simultaneously and at great speed by other users of an organization's information networks (Hansen *et al.*, 1999).

To achieve this, a 'people to documents' and a 'documents to e-documents' approach to knowledge sharing has to be encouraged, whereby all potentially useful knowledge is immediately transferred to databases. Also known as 'data warehouses' or 'data mines', where employees can go digging for information, these repositories contain the full range of codified knowledge that has been 'captured' by the organization. These may consist of collections of passive information and resources or, as is increasingly the case, semi-intelligent systems that can help direct users to the most relevant information that they are seeking (sometimes known as 'complex adaptive systems'). These systems can have a formal, centralized control hub or may be created by ad hoc and informal groups of employees within an organization. Whatever their level of sophistication, these repositories must be designed to capture knowledge and information that everyone in an organization can contribute to and access with ease. Over time, these databases then come to form the bedrock of an organization's corporate memory and intelligence gathering capabilities. Synonymous with these are group or shareware systems that allow the free flow of ideas and information between disparate individuals and groups within organizations.

The most recent codified knowledge management systems are based on Weblogs and K-Logs. These are user-friendly websites on which bloggers can post entries on any topic. A K-Log tool leverages a company's intranet and deals with information specific to the company that is sponsoring it. One company, Userland, makes two products: 'Manila', a centralized server-content management system, and 'Radio User Land' (RUL), which provide easy weblogging from desktops. RUL is a weblog tool that automatically builds, organizes and archives information, and publishes content. It requires no knowledge of HTML, FTP or graphic design. In addition to publishing a weblog, K-Log tools allow users to publish pictures, documents and links to other resources on an intranet, where these can also be archived, searched and browsed. The benefits of using K-Log systems in organizations include better documentation of processes, shorter audit cycles, the instantaneous creation of archives of contributions by employees, and a knowledge induction tool for new organizational members (abridged from Gengler, 2002b).

However, it must be stressed that all codified systems, including those described above, remain for now *passive* repositories of information. They still need human beings to contribute to them, make use of them and then convert this information into actionable ideas. This means that, not only should ownership of knowledge management initiatives be put in the hands of employees, but what goes into these databases must also be relevant and useful. As Seeley-Brown and Duguid have observed,

> Most databases, like most business processes, are top-down creations. Managers fill them up with what they think will be useful for the people they manage. And – surprise, surprise – the people don't actually find them so. Yet even when individuals fill databases with their own ideas of what's useful, they aren't much help either. Often what one person thinks useful, others find flaky, idiosyncratic, incoherent, redundant or just plain stupid. The more a database contains everyone's favourite ideas, the more unusable it becomes.
> (*Seeley-Brown and Duguid, 2000: 79*)

Hansen and colleagues cite the example of Rank-Xerox who tried to embed the know-how of its technicians into an expert system installed in their copiers, hoping that they could deal with repairs with guidance from this system. However, they found that technicians came across problems that could not always be solved by accessing this. When the designers of the system looked into it, they discovered that the technicians had got round this problem simply by telling each other stories about how they had fixed the machines. In other words, the expert system could not replicate the subtle nuances, detail and in-depth personal knowledge that were exchanged in face-to-face conversations or by mobile phone (Hansen *et al.*, 1999: 115). This means that organizations must be able to evaluate the effectiveness of codified knowledge management systems and whether these are actually any better than existing personalized knowledge sharing systems.

Before turning to look at some potential problems that have been encountered when introducing knowledge management initiatives, there follow a few examples of early successful codified systems.

Ernst and Young

Ernst and Young created a huge company-wide database (the K-Web) run by 250 staff at their Centre for Business Knowledge. This data resource contains 40 'Areas of Practice' run by specialist staff in each one. Setting this IT system up cost E&Y $US500 million on hardware and software and recruiting/training new staff to support their knowledge management systems. This judicious use of information has enabled E&Y to grow at an average rate of about 20 per cent a year in recent times and, in one three-year period, increase their consulting revenues from $US1.5 billion in 1995 to $US2.7 billion in 1997 (Hansen *et al.*, 1999: 114).

Price Waterhouse Coopers

Under the guidance of their Chief Knowledge Officer, Ellen Knapp, PWC created a powerful intranet called 'Knowledge Curve' in 1998. Here employees could find repositories of consulting methodologies, case studies of company clients, repositories of best practice, tax and audit rules, online training packages and directories of experts, plus an almost infinite set of links to other repositories of information outside the company. In 1999, the site received about *18 million* hits a month from PWC employees. Even so, according to George Bailey, the company's US 'Innovation Leader', this is still underutilized: 'everybody goes there sometimes, but when they're looking for expertise, most people go down the hall' (cited by Stewart, 2000b: 392). Quite independently of these developments, a UK-based PWC consultant, Jon Bentley, set up another network, 'The Kraken', in order to 'collaborate so as to be more innovative'. It was given this name some time after it was set up because a colleague observed that innovation in PWC was like the mythological sea-monster in the Tennyson poem, who 'Lives far, far beneath in the abysmal sea and sleeps his ancient, dreamless, uninvaded sleep.' Anyone could join this, and in 2000 about 500 'self-selected creatives' were members. Bailey regarded this ad hoc community of practice as the firm's premier forum for sharing new knowledge. Bentley and Knapp believed that there were a number of reasons for its success:

> First, it's demand driven: eighty percent of Kraken traffic starts with a question – Does anybody know? Has anybody ever done? Often a question provokes a four or five page response, with real research having been done for no reward other than the satisfaction of having helped. Also, the Kraken gets at tacit knowledge, provoking responses from people who didn't know that they had something to contribute. It tolerates fuzzy questions better than do formal data bases, where one often needs a bit of expertise even to begin.

> In all these ways, Kraken differs from Knowledge Curve. The latter supplies explicit knowledge on a site you have to go to. It preserves knowledge more than creates it. It's a compendium not a conversation. There's an ancient debate over whether knowledge management happens by design or by emergence. Says Knapp, correctly, 'I find myself coming down dead centre in the middle of the argument. The Kraken is about learning, Knowledge Curve is about teaching. You can't have one without the other'.
> (*Stewart, 2000b: 392*)[2]

Hoffman La Roche

Their internal knowledge management system took the form of a Yellow Pages directory: a catalogue of staff, ranked according to expertise, questions and issues (Ruggles, 1998: 85).

General Motors

GM launched a secure, customizable, four-million-page intranet in December 2001 called, appropriately, My Socrates. The aim was to get all 180 000 of its US employees to access this site in order to move towards GM's vision of a 'web-savvy workforce'. With 75 per cent of its employees already owning PCs, the company was aiming to get all its employees on-line by December 2003. It succeeded in this objective.

Hewlett-Packard

HP created one of the first business intranet systems in the early 1990s, with 2500 servers handling one and a half million email messages a month. It was used to support information, including sharing amongst design teams and cross-functional dialogues. Its intranet-based 'Electronic Sales Partner' was created to foster a tighter connection between HP and its primary customers. By allowing customers to access relevant information and interact directly with HP, customer knowledge was enhanced by a constant flow of information both within and across organizational boundaries (Ruggles, 1998: 82).

Potential problems with knowledge management initiatives

In 1998, Rudy Ruggles examined the results of an Ernst and Young survey of 431 American and European companies. This analysed what these firms had been doing to manage knowledge, what they felt were the greatest barriers to the introduction of knowledge management initiatives, and what they thought they should be doing in the future. When this book was published, the study was already six years old, but its findings still resonate today, and they are particularly relevant for organizations that are thinking about introducing knowledge management initiatives for the first time. Ruggles looked at nine areas of knowledge management in these companies: how new knowledge was generated; how knowledge assets were measured; how knowledge was accessed from outside the company; how knowledge was used in decision making; how new knowledge became embedded in business processes, products and/or services; how this information was stored; how the companies' cultures encouraged or discouraged the sharing of knowledge; how knowledge was transferred throughout the companies; and how knowledge management initiatives were measured and evaluated (Ruggles, 1998: 81; unless otherwise indicated, all page references in this section are from this article).

On a positive note, many of the companies did have knowledge management initiatives under way. For example, 72 per cent had introduced, or were planning to introduce, an intranet; 57 per cent had introduced, or were planning to introduce, data warehouses or knowledge reposito-ries; 53 per cent had introduced, or were planning to introduce, deci-sion support tools; 44 per cent had introduced, or were planning to introduce, group or shareware systems; 39 per cent had created, or were planning to create, networks of knowledge workers; 38 per cent were planning to map sources of external expertise and 28 per cent were planning to establish new knowledge roles (p. 83). However, it was also apparent that most of these organizations were having prob-lems with their knowledge management initiatives. As Ruggles comments, 'the executives who responded to this survey did not hold high opinions of their organizations' performance in any of these areas' (p. 81). For example, only 13 per cent thought that they were adept at transferring knowledge held by one part of the organization to other parts. Even 'generating new knowledge', the process about which respondents had the highest confidence in their organizations' capabilities, still received above-average ratings from fewer than half (46 per cent) of these executives (ibid.).

They believed that the biggest obstacles to introducing knowledge management initiatives were 'people's behaviour' (56 per cent), 'orga-nizational culture' (54 per cent), 'top management's failure to signal its importance' (32 per cent) and 'lack of ownership over the process' (28 per cent). Furthermore, only 34 per cent of these executives said that they were able to 'access valuable information from external sources'; 30 per cent used 'accessible information in decision making', and just 29 per cent were able to 'embed knowledge in processes, products and/or services'; 27 per cent stored knowledge in 'documents, data-bases, software etc' and just 19 per cent believed that their organiza-tional cultures and incentive schemes 'facilitated the growth of knowledge'. A meagre 14 per cent measured and evaluated the effec-tiveness of their knowledge management initiatives or the value of their knowledge assets (p. 82).

Significantly, even though many of these companies were aware that it was the *human* response to their knowledge management initiatives that was the biggest source of resistance, most still relied on *technologi-cal* solutions. Yet, when they had been asked whether their competi-tiveness was based on 'people', 'process' or 'technology', half reported that they believed that 'people' was the most important factor, with 'process' and 'technology' being rated at 25 per cent each. As Ruggles notes, 'While "people management" issues may be endemic to any change management initiative, knowledge management initiatives seem to bring them out in abundance' (p. 86). Furthermore, 'IT person-nel' were twice as likely as 'senior managers' to be the leaders of knowl-edge management initiatives in these organizations. His findings are important, because they add considerable weight to many of the suggestions made earlier in this book, particularly those relating to change, learning and innovation in Chapters 8 and 9. Ruggles' message is straightforward: *no organization can rely solely on technological solutions when introducing knowledge management initiatives into an organization.* Given the explosion of new IT systems and software packages in the 1990s, and the massive hype that accompanied these in the media, it isn't surprising that many companies initially resorted to technological solutions when they were faced with these new challenges. However, as we have seen, this has never been sufficient in practice. As Ruggles has observed succinctly and accurately, 'It is inevitable that the technology will not be enough. In fact, if the people issues do not arise, the effort underway is not knowledge management. If technology solves your problem, yours was not a knowledge problem' (p. 88).

Which are the best systems to use? What is the best blend or balance of people, process and technology strategies to employ when introducing knowledge management initiatives into an organization? As with many other facets of leadership and management, this decision is contingent on the nature of your business, what you want to do with your organization's knowledge, the competitive environment in which you operate and the demands of the customers and clients you deal with. Hansen and his colleagues suggest an 80/20 split, commenting that 'Executives who try to excel at both strategies risk failing at both' (1999: 112); by this they mean that organizations should have either 80 per cent codified/20 per cent personalized systems or vice versa. Many commentators would disagree with this prescriptive formula. For example, Ruggles suggests a 50 per cent 'people', 25 per cent 'process' and 25 per cent 'technology' mixture, which is a much more sensible starting point for most organizations. Whatever knowledge management systems an organization might choose to introduce, this decision has to be driven by the company's core values, vision, business plans and operational strategies, never the other way round. As Stewart puts it, 'that's an important lesson for knowledge management types: if your baby ain't tightly linked to the business model, it won't do squat' (2000a: 129).[3]

Accessing knowledge from outside an organization's boundaries

In 1985, product developers at the Matsushita Electric Company in Osaka were hard at work building a new home bread-making machine. But, no matter what they tried, they could not get the machine to knead the dough properly and always ended up with a soggy middle and an over-cooked crust. They tried everything they could think of to sort the problem out, including X-raying their dough and the dough kneaded by professional

bakers. After many months, a software developer called Ikuko Tanaka suggested that they go and have a look at the head baker at the Osaka International Hotel, who had a reputation for making the best bread in the city. Tanaka worked with the head baker for several days and noticed that he had a distinctive way of stretching the dough. After a year of trial and error they were able to come up with special ribs inside their machine that mimicked the bread-maker's technique, and the quality of the bread that she had learned to make at the hotel. The result: Matsushita's unique 'twist-dough' method and a product that in its first year set a record for sales of a new kitchen appliance [ ] This one experience was informally conveyed to other Matsushita employees and they now use this knowledge to formulate equivalent quality standards for other products, be this kitchen appliances or white-goods.
(*Abridged from Nonaka, 1991: 98*)

This quotation illustrates some important things about knowledge acquisition from outside an organization's boundaries. First, this group of product developers did not have sufficient in-house knowledge to solve the problem that they were facing, and it took a lateral leap of imagination to consider looking for solutions that might exist outside their immediate organizational environment. Second, it took Tanaka several days to tap into the implicit knowledge that the head baker possessed. Third, the knowledge they acquired, and what they had learnt from this experience, was quickly and freely shared with other employees. Like innovation and learning, one of the most important drivers of knowledge management is the recognition that there are, potentially, almost infinite sources of information beyond the boundaries of an organization or the mind-set that it operates within. In the last chapter we identified the growing importance of scenario mapping, as a method that helps organizational leaders trace possible future paths from the systems and trends that are shaping the world at the moment (for example, globalization and new technologies). This allows the creation of 'What if . . .' thinking. In turn, this permits the creation of contingent strategic plans that can be implemented if, or when, one of these anticipated scenarios emerges. Companies that have tested their strategies against these scenarios, and things that could go wrong, are in a much stronger position to deal with these when they arise.

A study by the research and consulting firm Gartner has suggested that an important part of this process is obtaining competitive intelligence and knowledge. They argue that this has now become so important that it can often make the critical difference between success and failure, particularly for small companies. Gartner also suggest that at least 60 per cent of the world's most successful companies have strategies in place to keep a close eye on their competitors, as well as using third-party information to help identify new business opportunities. On average, the companies they surveyed each spent $US20 million a year on gathering competitive intelligence from their environments. More significantly, the study also showed that 95 per cent of all the information that a typical business needs to know about its rivals 'is in the public domain – and the remaining 5 per cent of what you need you can surmise from your own experience and knowledge' (Hollands, 2001). However, collecting this kind of data is the easier part of this process. At the beginning of 2004, there were at least 200 software tools available on the market to collect and sort information from the external environment. While these software packages are good at retrieving and storing massive amounts of information, interpreting and disseminating this information is the more difficult part. So four questions need to be considered by organizations when evaluating the selection of knowledge management software:[4]

- How will we collect the data and will the new software enable us to 'trawl' for the information that our organization really needs?
- What parameters and screening protocols need to be set up within the software to identify potentially important information and omit trivia?
- Who will have access to this information and who will be responsible for analysing and interpreting it?
- How will this information be disseminated and, most importantly, how will it be integrated into operational strategies and management decision-making processes?

Effective knowledge management must also be linked to an organization's strategic intelligence capabilities. This is described by Marchand as 'what a company needs to know about its business environment to enable it to anticipate change, as a basis for designing strategies that will create business value for customers, and will be profitable in new markets and industries in the future' (Marchand, 1997: 16). On several occasions in this book, we've seen that the ability to anticipate future trends is now a core organizational and leadership competency. Consequently, the challenge for many companies is to replace old knowledge sets that may have stood them in good stead for many years, and build new ones that can encompass the changing needs of their customers and clients, and help them to deal with new competition in their markets and to deal with unanticipated threats and challenges. The gathering of strategic intelligence and knowledge can help in this process.

Some companies, like Royal Dutch Shell, have long relied on a formal strategic planning group to carry out research on future trends and have used this information to develop policies linked to the company's corporate business and strategic plans (de Geus, 1997). Many larger companies entrust the monitoring of future trends to specific groups of research and development staff. Others rely on specialist research companies, market forecasters and 'future-casters', on the assumption that outsiders bring fresh information and form unbiased views of product and market trends (some examples of these can be found in note 4). Strategic intelligence is different to 'competitor intelligence' (what is already known about the existing competition) and 'competitive intelligence' (information created by intelligence analysts). The challenge of true strategic intelligence is to increase the intelligence gathering quotient (IGQ) of all employees in an organization, rather than leaving this in the hands of one department or group of senior managers. By definition, the more eyes and ears you have scouring the environment for useful knowledge and intelligence, the more responsive your organization will be to external opportunities, threats and challenges. This approach regards the acquisition of knowledge from outside the business as being a responsibility, not just of senior managers, but of *everyone* within the organization. For example, one of the key findings of a 12-year in-depth study of Intel was that the long-term strategic success of any firm can no longer be driven solely from the top by senior management. Every business must now foster a culture that embraces bottom-up ideas about strategic change, by developing 'internal ecologies' that support continuous innovation, learning and knowledge sharing, with ideas garnered from both within and outside the organization's boundaries.

One of the biggest problems facing many organizations is that employees naturally filter out information they consider to be irrelevant to their functional domains, rather than considering how extraneous information could benefit other functions or serve the interests of the organization as whole. Hence a sales department will focus primarily on information about customers and clients; a marketing department on market trends; an R&D group on developments in research and technology; manufacturing on process innovations and product engineering; and so forth. Up to a point, this may suffice. However, a bunker mentality or a fragmented IGQ will be insufficient if a company needs to be able to anticipate change quickly as the basis for developing new strategies before they are forced on the company. In this kind of environment, strategic intelligence and the sharing of this knowledge has to become part of a company's collective culture and mindset, rather than being grafted onto one function or being left solely in the hands of senior managers.

In summary, the acquisition of knowledge and strategic intelligence from outside a business can no longer be left as the sole preserve of the senior managers or leaders of organizations. Businesses that allow individuals or groups of employees to hoard knowledge on a 'need to know basis' cannot anticipate the future effectively. They are unlikely to survive in the long term, because most organizations now need as many 'feelers' as possible out in their competitive environments to sense, collect, organize, process and utilize new information. The old organizational adage 'Knowledge is power' is fast being replaced by a new one: 'Knowledge will ensure our collective survival and long-term success.'

In order to check (in an explicit and codified form) how much implicit/personal knowledge you have acquired from reading this chapter, please complete self-development Exercise 10.2. All the answers can be found in the preceding pages.

Exercise 10.2

Knowledge management quiz

Across

1. Effects or consequences that result from the sharing of information by employees. These effects can be difficult to quantify.
5. Abbreviated name of a network of large numbers of individuals with their own mental models, who interact with each other according to a set of behavioural rules.
6. The value of an organization's relationships with its customers, particularly intangibles such as loyalty to a company or a product.
8. Learning about the nature of learning.
11. Knowledge regarding markets, products, technologies, resources, skills and systems that a business owns or controls, and which it uses to achieve its objectives. The term is sometimes used interchangeably with 'intangible assets' and 'intellectual capital'.
13. The knowledge, skills, attitudes and behaviours of people in the organization. Unlike structural capital, it is owned by individuals rather than the organization. It is the renewable part of intellectual capital.
14. Someone who is responsible for managing an organization's knowledge, and leveraging its intangible assets to create value.

Down

2. Know-how, brands, processes that affect the success of a business, but aren't measured or monitored as part of a corporate growth strategy.
3. A computer program that simulates human decision making.
4. Unspoken, non-codified know-how that usually resides in the heads of people and is gained mainly through experience.

7. The collective brainpower of the organization that can be put to use to create wealth, including human capital (skills and knowledge of individuals), customer capital (the value of continuing relationships with customers) and structural capital (codified knowledge such as patents, databases, files, trademarks).

9. Programs that help people to work together collectively while located remotely from each other. They facilitate information sharing and email handling, so all employees can share their knowledge systemically (for example, Lotus® Notes and Microsoft® Exchange Server).

10. The data-driven extraction of information from large databases that can reveal trends, correlations and patterns to improve business processes and working practices.

12. A large database containing information about particular subjects, gathered from a variety of sources and integrated into a systemic whole.

For a bonus point, why does the computer company Apple have a logo that features an apple with a chunk bitten out of it?[5]

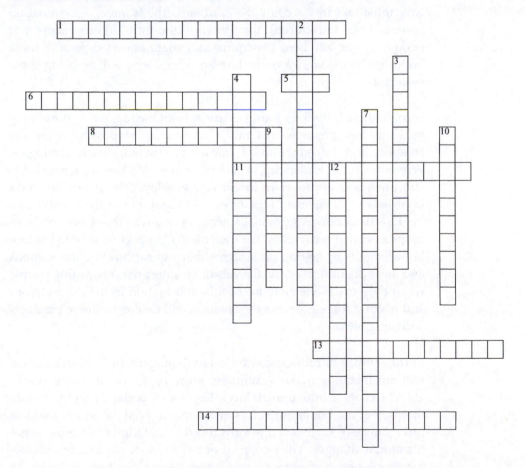

Note: If you don't want to go back and locate the answers in the preceding sections, these can be found in note 6.

Source: Adapted from Bagshaw and Phillips (2000); used with permission ◆

Conclusion: linking culture, innovation, learning and knowledge management

Knowledge has become the key economic resource and the dominant and, perhaps, even the only source of competitive advantage.
(*Peter Drucker,* Post-Capitalist Society, *1993*)

There are five broad conclusions that can be drawn from the theory and practice of employee knowledge management. First, in common with all change initiatives, introducing knowledge management into organizations is not a paint-by-numbers exercise. This requires a careful diagnostic of the specific needs of an organization and its employees, and only then introducing the appropriate blend of personalized and/or codified systems to support its core business activities, and their daily work. This means that all knowledge management initiatives must take into account the hardware (the storage/dissemination systems to be introduced), the software (the Intra/Internet tools that people will be allocated to acquire and share knowledge) and, most importantly, the wetware (the human beings who will be using these systems).

Second, these initiatives must be driven from the top, while simultaneously giving employees as much ownership as possible over the creation and introduction of knowledge management strategies. Without strong leadership, a shared vision (and so on), workable strategies and appropriate incentives, employees will not buy into knowledge management initiatives, and resistance to these will build up. Effective knowledge management is a two-way top-down/bottom-up process that recognizes that the only truly effective way to capture knowledge is by setting up systems that can capture the innovations and ideas of employees, at all levels of an enterprise, rewarding people when they make effective use of this information in their daily work and making full use of it in the creation and delivery of new products and/or services.

Third, simply introducing knowledge management initiatives alone will not instantly make a company more profitable or more adaptable to change and uncertainty. These can certainly help, but in themselves are not enough. It is also a managerial paradigm that has little chance of success if it is introduced in isolation from other organizational changes. The power of organizational culture, in enhancing employee performance and engendering positive attitudes to change, has been highlighted several times in this book. The same principle applies to knowledge management initiatives. For example, one of the few comprehensive studies of the relationships between culture, learning, innovation and knowledge management (in Australian e-companies) concluded that culture is the bedrock of employee learning, this in turn drives creativity and innovation and these foster the creation and fast dissemination of new knowledge, both within and from outside the boundaries of these businesses. This then melds into a self-reinforcing, mutually reciprocal, quadruple-loop process, and no single element can then exist in isolation from the others. And, when they do coexist in this symbiotic fashion, this creates what can be accurately described as a 'Fifth Element', an organizational mind-set that is operationally superior to the four single components of culture, organizational learning, innovation and knowledge management (Woodward, 2001). *Combined with the intelligent and judicious use of new technologies, this combination of elements may well represent the Holy Grail of organizational management for the next decade or so.*

Fourth, if an organization's culture does not first support and reward (un)learning, creativity and innovation, there is little chance that knowledge management initiatives will be successful, because knowledge creation is still driven by employees. In turn, culture, the symbolic framework that defines the way we do things in organizations, drives these three elements. All available research literature supports the view that knowledge management and organizational culture are inextricably linked, and it is impossible to introduce knowledge management initiatives into an organization that does not have the right kind of learning culture to support it (see, for example, Woodward, 2001; McLean, 2000; Choo, 1998; Lucier and Torsilieri, 1997).

Fifth, although there may be difficulties introducing knowledge management initiatives into organizations, many academic researchers and business leaders believe that knowledge management, like the Learning Organization, is something more than an organizational fashion accessory or a short-lived consulting fad. As Dixon observed more than a decade ago, 'We have entered the Knowledge Age, and the new currency is learning. It is learning, not knowledge itself that is critical. Knowledge is the result of learning and is ephemeral, constantly needing to be revised and updated. Learning is "sense making": it is the process that leads to knowledge' (Dixon, 1994: 1). As with change management, innovation and learning, the organizational imperative underpinning knowledge management is the desire never to become complacent, never to allow inertia and atrophy to set into the organization's collective mind-set, and to be continuously looking for new and better ways of doing things. It's also important to remember that information is not the same as knowledge, and knowledge is not the same as wisdom (one of the building blocks of leadership described in Chapter 1). It still requires creative human beings to make sense of (and utilize) the staggering quantities of information that are now available to all Internet-linked organizations, and without this capability 'information paralysis' will inevitably set in.

In summary, employee knowledge and intellectual capital now account for a disproportionate share of competitive advantage in business and, consequently, the profits of many companies. The explosion in rich connectivity and the homogenization of information standards and protocols are enabling the most open exchange of information and knowledge in human history. Knowledge management is an approach to organizational management that regards the strategic acquisition of this knowledge and information as every employee's responsibility, not just senior managers'; as something that must become ingrained in a culture of learning and in the behaviour and working practices of employees throughout the business. Becoming an organization that manages its knowledge well is a journey that can certainly have a clear and definable start, but is also one without end, regardless of the profession we work in or the organization we work for. This is because both individuals and organizations now have less and less time to acquire more and more information and new knowledge. Increasingly, we no longer have the luxury or the time to learn by doing, or to rely on experience and common sense accumulated over many years. We must acquire and utilize information in faster, more efficient and more creative ways, not only from our colleagues but also from company databases and from outside organizational boundaries. The end goal of this process is to create an organization that has a very high level of *creative intelligence and adaptability*. Organizations that do not have these attributes will find it difficult to survive over the next decade, as will those who have not grasped the potential and limitations of new technologies as drivers of organizational performance and success. This topic is addressed in the next chapter.

> Knowledge is a difficult thing to 'manage'. It does not thrive well in captivity and does not survive for long outside its natural habitats – people's minds. To add to this difficulty, the life span of knowledge ranges from mere seconds to eons. Despite all of this, the sentiments of almost every executive who has utilised knowledge management echo those of Drucker: that leveraging organizational knowledge is not only important, it may be the most important job that management now has.
> (*Abridged from Ruggles, 1998: 89*)

Exercise 10.3

Having read through this chapter, how can you convert any new insights you have acquired about the management of employee knowledge and intellectual capital into your organization's operational strategies in the future?

Insight	Strategy to implement this
1.	
2.	
3.	
4.	
5.	◆

Notes

1 In organizations these have been variously labelled: knowledge officers, brokers, facilitators, consultants, engineers, editors, navigators, experts, strategists and stewards.

2 PWC was taken over by IBM during 2001.

3 If you're interested in more information on knowledge management options and the management of intellectual capital, a complementary source is C. Choo (1998), *The Knowing Organization: How Organizations Use Information to Construct Meaning, Create Knowledge and Make Decisions*, Oxford: Oxford University Press: very academic in tone, but one of the most thorough books on the creation, dissemination and management of knowledge in organizations.

For practitioners there are several 'how to' books on the market that also describe common mistakes that have been made by organizations when introducing knowledge management initiatives. These include M. Rumizen (2001), *The Complete Idiot's Guide to Knowledge Management*, New York: Alpha Books; British Standards Institute (2001), *Knowledge Management: A Guide to Good Practice*, London: British Standards Institute; and M. Bagshaw and P. Phillips (2000), *Knowledge Management*, Ely, Cambs: Fenman Limited, a practitioner's training and development manual that describes strategies for introducing knowledge management initiatives into organizations for the first time.

4 A detailed analysis of the large range of codified intelligence gathering systems now available to organizations is beyond the scope of this book. If you'd like more information on this, a good starting point is the Bagshaw and Phillips manual. Many organizations such as IBM and Hewlett-Packard have commercially available strategic intelligence gathering systems. In addition to these, there are more than 100 current websites advertising strategic intelligence gathering services and products. There is also a variety of websites that predict everything from the emergence of future technologies, to new drugs and self-driving cars (www.newsfutures.com, www.ideosphere.com, and www.incentivemarkets.com), sites that test consumer preferences for products that don't yet exist (www.anderson.ucla.edu/faculty/ely.dahan) and those that deal with scenario mapping (www.gbn.org).

5   This symbolizes the birth or creation of new knowledge, derived from the fable of Adam and Eve in Christian creation mythology.

6   Knowledge management quiz answers:

Across: (1) Emergent properties, (5) CAS (Complex Adaptive System), (6) Customer capital, (8) Metalearning, (11) Knowledge assets, (13) Human capital, (14) Knowledge manager

Down: (2) Intangible assets, (3) Expert system, (4) Tacit knowledge, (7) Intellectual capital, (9) Groupware, (10) Datamining, (12) Data warehouse

11 Leadership and people management in high-tech, networked and virtual organizations

Objectives

To define technology and describe the effects of new technologies, computer networking, e-commerce and virtual reality on organizations in recent years.

To outline the practical business lessons that can be drawn from the collapse of the dotcom bubble in April 2000.

To evaluate the impact that new technologies may have on organizations, leadership and people management over the next five to ten years.

To future-cast the effects that emergent technologies, such as nanotechnology, biotechnology and quantum computing may have on humanity during the remainder of the 21st century.

Introduction: the acceleration of everything

> Every few hundred years in Western History there occurs a sharp transformation. Within a few short decades, society – its world view, its basic values, its social and political structures, its arts, its key institutions – rearranges itself. And the people born then cannot even imagine a world in which their grandparents lived and into which their own parents were born. We are currently living through such a transformation.
> (*Peter Drucker*, Post-Capitalist Society, *1993*)

> Thanks to technology, the world is going bonkers. And it's going to get more bonkers – bonkers squared in a few years with bonkers cubed on the way.
> (*Tom Peters, 1992*)

In recent years, our work environments and homes have been invaded by technology. This invasion is only the precursor for even more radical

429

changes during this century as the very nature of organizations, 'work' in the Taylorist sense and (perhaps) even what it means to be human may be changed forever. Some commentators have described the technological transition we are currently going through as being, by far, the most radical in human history, superseding the agrarian (First Wave) and industrial (Second Wave) revolutions that transformed human civilizations and societies in the past. In the industrial age, business growth stemmed from the ability to make things big. In the 21st century, growth will come from the power to make things tiny. As we move through the first decade of the 21st century, we are entering a century where the Third Wave of technological innovation will profoundly affect every aspect of human existence, including our professions, the organizations we work in and the manner in which we lead and manage people in these environments (Kurzweil, 1999; Dyson, 1999; Warwick, 1998). We've also seen in several earlier sections of this book that one of the primary roles of leaders is to anticipate the future and map the way, road or path their followers can take in order to move towards this. Hence, towards the end of this chapter, we will be looking in some detail at a variety of radical and bizarre scenarios about the future of both organizations and humanity.

The word 'technology' is derived from the Greek word for knowledge, *technos*, and is defined here as the application of mechanical and applied sciences, technical knowledge, expertise, tools, machines, techniques and methodologies. Technological development has perhaps been the most distinctive characteristic of human evolution over the last 130 000 years. Even more remarkable is the pace at which technological innovation has been accelerating over the last 10 000 years. To illustrate this, imagine for a few minutes that you are going to walk from the San Francisco coastline, on the far-west coast of the USA, to the Chrysler building on Manhattan Island in New York on the eastern seaboard. This journey is going to represent the length of time from when our hominid ancestors were living in Africa, some 500 000 years ago, to the present day. Recent archeological evidence indicates that the first basic stone tools, spears and fire were being used as long ago as 400 000 before the Common Era (BCE), but for the next 370 000 years technological evolution largely stood still. By 30 000BCE, when you have reached Philadelphia on your journey across the USA, there is the first evidence of the use of iron and copper tools and cave art.

From about 12 000BCE, after the end of the last ice age, the biggest growth in human technological evolution occurred. The earliest evidence of settled human communities, based around agriculture and the domestication of animals, is from 10 000–8000BCE, in what is now the Middle East. Around this time, human cultural evolution really started to kick in and, in the process, generated many new inventions and innovations. Modern cuneiform writing was developed during the third millennium BCE. The wheel and the plough also emerged some time between 3500 and 3000BCE (as you have just arrived at the outskirts of New York) and these two innovations marked the ascendancy of the first truly modern human civilizations in the Middle East, Greece and Italy. In turn, these generated an explosion of innovations and developments in irrigation, agricultural production, commerce, international trade, boat design and navigation, military technologies and strategies, political and civil governance, architecture, art, philosophy, astronomy and mathematics. One of the most important – paper – was developed by Tsai Lun in about 100CE.

As the Roman Empire collapsed during the fourth century CE, you are just arriving on Manhattan Island. Gunpowder and printing were in use by about 500CE in China, the most technologically advanced civilization of the first millenium CE. After the European Dark Ages and the Renaissance comes the next burst of technological innovation, driven in large part by the Gutenberg printing press, unveiled in 1455. Copernicus turned our geocentric view of the universe on its head with the publication of *De Revolutionibus Orbium Celestium* in 1539 (although the little-known Greek scientist Aristarchus is credited with having first deduced that the Earth revolves around the Sun, after watching a lunar eclipse). It would take the Roman Catholic Church until 1983, nearly 450 years, to accept this and apologize for their persecution of Copernicus and Galileo. The first modern systems of physics, the progenitor of many subsequent inventions and innovations, was developed by Sir Isaac Newton between 1666 and 1715. The first steam engine was unveiled in 1770. The first electrical battery was produced in 1800. The first locomotive, Stephenson's Rocket, made its maiden journey in 1829. The first working telegraph was displayed in 1837 by Samuel Morse. Electromagnetism was discovered in 1831, and the first electrical conductor was unveiled in 1832. By 1876, Alexander Graham Bell had invented an 'electric speech machine' with Thomas Watson. In 1889 the first coin-operated public phone appeared in Connecticut, USA.

The first internal combustion engine appeared in 1877, the radio in 1893, the airplane in 1903, oil refining in 1913, the first transcontinental phone line from San Francisco to New York in 1917, and the first radio transmission from a plane to the ground was made in 1919. The first liquid fuel rockets were built in the 1920s. The first working prototype of a television was unveiled in 1923. In 1927, the first intercontinental phone line service between New York and London was established. In 1937, the first commercial transatlantic airplane service flew and the domestic vacuum cleaner was launched. The first atomic bombs were detonated in 1945. The first analog computer and microwave oven appeared in 1946, and the first electrical transistor in 1947. The first satellite, Sputnik, flew in 1958. In 1959, one of the most important innovation/inventions of the 20th century made its debut – the silicon chip. The world's first commercial communication satellite, Telstar, was launched in 1962. The combined handset phone also appeared this year and the first steam-or-dry electric iron in 1963. The first commercially available personal computer appeared in 1977. In 1982, Nokia launched the first generation of mobile phones in Finland and Sweden, in the form of the Mobira Senator. In 1990, the first universal HTML Internet code was launched. The first prototype phone with Internet access, fax and email facilities appeared in 1994, and in July 2000 the first commercially available mobile videophone, the VP-210, was launched (Paul, 1999). All the innovations and inventions described in these two paragraphs have appeared in the time it has taken you to walk from the edge of Manhattan Island to the Chrysler Building (Bronowski, 1980; various history of science websites, June 2003).

The analogy of a journey across the USA highlights some truly extraordinary facts about human technological development. First, about 95 per cent of all human inventions and innovations have appeared in less than 5 per cent of the time that modern humans have lived on this planet. Second, almost all of these have appeared in just the last 200 years. There were more inventions and innovations in the 20th century alone than in all of preceding human history. Third, the pace of technological innovation is going to continue to accelerate at an even faster rate for the foreseeable future. For example, it took 50 years from the development of the first electrical generator to the opening of the first power station in the USA in 1882. It took another 50 years before 50 million American homes were connected to electricity supplies. It took radio 37 years to reach a global audience of 50 million and television 15 years. It took the Internet just three years to achieve this figure (Coyle and Kay, 2000). There will be more technological innovations in the next 50 years than have emerged in the entire span of time humans have inhabited the planet. This has one other important implication: *technological evolution is now outpacing human biological evolution and yet we are, genetically, virtually identical to our ancestors of 130 000 years ago* (Kurzweil, 1999).[1] The profound implications of these developments will be described later in this chapter.

Recent scientific and technological developments

Exercise 11.1

Some other examples of recent technological advances are the events that occurred on 23 February 1997, 12 May 1997, 24 August 1998, 26 June 2000, 11 November 2001, 16 June 2002 and 15 March 2003.These are seven of the most significant dates in human evolution. Why?

Who first predicted the event that took place on 23 February 1997 and in which year did he make this prediction? And, what didn't happen on 31 December 1999?

The answers can be found in note 2. ◆

There are many factors driving the current Third Wave of technological evolution. The most important of these are humanity's age-old curiosity about its environment, combined with a hard-wired desire to understand and master it, and a unique ability to utilize tools and innovate with them.[3] More recent drivers of technological change include the emergence of empirical science in the 18th and 19th centuries, the arrival of universal education, the development of the silicon chip, the globalization of business, the emergence of the Internet, the evolution of the knowledge economy, increasing competition for markets, shortening product life cycles, and fast-changing consumer and customer demands. However, perhaps the single most important factor has been the speed with which computing power advanced during the 20th century (see Figures 11.1 and 11.2). These two graphs highlight the dramatic growth in computer-processing power, particularly during the last two decades of the 20th century.

The first commercially available chip, produced by Intel in 1972, was able to perform 3500 calculations per second (CPS). By 1982, this had grown to 134 000 CPS and by 1985 to 275 000. From 1989 to 1995 the number increased from 1 200 000 to 5 500 000 CPS. By 2000 this had grown to 28 million CPS. The Intel Pentium IV, launched in 2001, was capable of performing 42 million CPS, and Intel expects its standard chips to be able to perform 400 million CPS by 2007 (Hawking, 2001: 166). Computers of the 1940s and 1950s took up a whole room. By the late 1960s, they were the size of desks and by the mid-1970s the size of suitcases. Now they fit into our pockets and, in the not too distant future, they will be the size of dust particles. This growth in computing power is mirrored by the miniaturization of devices that we now take for granted, For example, when the first transistor was developed in

Figure 11.1   The exponential growth of computing, 1900–1998

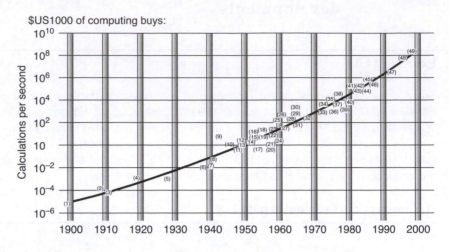

Note: See note 4 for an explanation of numbers 1–49.

Figure 11.2   The exponential growth of computing, 1900–2100

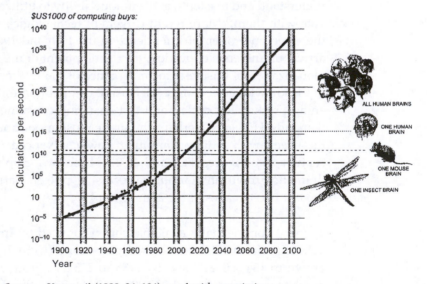

Source: Kurzweil (1999: 24, 104); used with permission.

1947, it was the size of a modern mobile phone. The equipment for the first mobile car phone, developed by Ericsson in the mid-1950s, weighed more than 40 kilograms. The company's website once joked that the first mobile telephone users could only make two calls; the first was to say hello to their friends, the second was to let them know that the car battery was about to go flat (Ericsson website, 30 June 2002).

The first commercially available mobile phone, Nokia's Mobira

Senator, came with a battery pack weighing 9.8 kilograms complete with carrying handle. Now, several million micro-transistors can be imbedded on a computer chip smaller than a baby's fingernail, and a modern mobile phone has more processing power than a 1950 mainframe computer, and weighs less than 100 grams. They are now capable of performing a range of functions that would have been regarded as science fiction just ten years ago, including transmitting some 100 billion SMS messages *a month*. More than two-thirds of all adults in the USA now own a mobile phone, which has even made the transition from being regarded simply as a functional communication device to becoming an essential fashion accessory for most young people (Iwatini, 2003; Grayson, 2003). Even a humble greeting card that sings 'Happy Birthday' has more computing power than first generation desktop computers in the 1970s. A run-of-the-mill 2004 laptop had far more computing power than the spaceships that flew to the moon in the late 1960s and early 1970s. Kurzweil (1999) has observed that, if car technologies had advanced as rapidly as computing technologies over the last 50 years, a typical car would now cost 5 cents to build and travel at the speed of light.

Until very recently, this growth in computing power had been governed by 'Moore's Law'. First suggested by Gordon Moore, in a 1965 article for *Electronics* magazine, this stipulated that the number of transistors contained on a silicon chip doubles, on average, every 18 months, and will continue to do so until about 2010 (Schlender, 2002: 52). This law has held good, enabling the science fiction of one decade to be converted into the new consumer items of the next. However, Intel has since built the world's fastest silicon transistors, running at speeds approaching 20GHZ, and this will give Moore's Law at least another decade of life beyond 2010. One billion of these new transistors can be packed onto a single processor, making these 33 per cent smaller and 25 per cent faster than previously available chips (Gengler, 2001). In 2002, IBM researchers announced that they had developed ultra-fast transistors out of carbon nano-tubes. Nano-tubes are pipe-shaped molecules built of carbon atoms one nanometre thick (or 50 000 times thinner than a human hair). In time, these will outperform the most advanced silicon chips (Gengler, 2002a). Computer chips will continue to become faster, more efficient and smaller, and so ubiquitous that they will merge into our environments and become increasingly transparent in the process. Computer chips are becoming so powerful, cheap and small that all mentofactured objects, including clothes and the fabric of our houses, will soon contain tiny embedded chips. 'The computer', as we currently think of it, will gradually merge into our physical environments and become effectively invisible, in the same way that small electric motors in everyday appliances did during the first half of the 20th century.

The PC is dead.
(*Leo Gerstner, former CEO of IBM, cited in* The Australian, *14 November 2000*)

As a result of these developments, we are now passing over the crest of what Andy Grove, the co-founder of Intel, has described as 'a strategic inflection point': a point at which human beings may fundamentally alter the way they work and live (cited by Isaacson, 1997: 25). The microchip has become, like the printing press, the steam engine, electricity and the assembly line before, the primary driver of a new economic paradigm and, as we will see later in this chapter, potentially the precursor of a radical shift in human evolution. The new economy has several features: it is truly global, networked, based on information and knowledge, decentralized (for now) and rewards transparency and the sharing of information. It is, in theory, open to anyone who has a web-linked PC or access to the Internet – the most ubiquitous feature of this new economy.

> A consensual hallucination experienced daily by millions of legitimate operators, in every nation . . . a graphic representation of data abstracted from the bank of every computer in the human system. Unthinkable complexity. Lines of light ranged in the non-space of the mind, clusters and constellations of data, like city lights receding.
> (*William Gibson, creator of the term 'cyberspace', in the 1984 sci-fi novel,* Necromancer)

The origins of the Internet can be traced back to a US Defense Department initiative in the 1970s, which 'escaped' from the Pentagon in 1984 and has since spread rapidly. In the USA, Japan, Australia, New Zealand and parts of Europe the number of Internet users grew at more than 1000 per cent a year from 1985 onwards (De Witt, 1995: 7). It represents a web of millions of computers and databases, connected by a telecommunications infrastructure encompassing satellites, land-based telephone and fibre-optic networks, and rapidly expanding wireless services. This vast array of networks being created in cyberspace has already provided a platform for a revolution in human communication. At the beginning of January 2004, about 600 million people in 160 countries had direct access to the world-wide web. Many more have access through commercial cyber-cafes and Internet shops. Traffic on the web now doubles every 100 days and it has been estimated that three billion people (about half the world's population) will be linked to the web by 2010. Only now is the true potential of the web being realized as it reaches a critical user threshold, and recent advances in computer technologies continue to act as accelerants to the evolution of this global communication and information system.

Those who fail to get online in this information revolution may well be swept aside and left behind in the rush to access 'The Information

Superhighway' (a description first coined by former US Vice President, Al Gore, in 1995). Many significant players initially bought into the potential of the Internet in the late 1990s. For example, George Sheehan – the man who built Arthur Andersen into one of the biggest global consulting firms in the world before its ignominious collapse in 2002 – could have stayed in a comfortable job with large stock options and a large income. Instead, he chose to start up a web-based grocery business called webvan.com. When asked why he had chosen to do this he replied, 'Arthur Andersen is history. I can't wait to join the future' (cited in *The Australian*, 12 July 1999). Alas, this business, like so many e-companies, went bust less than 24 months later, for reasons that will be described in the next section.

We continue to envelop our planet with a network in which millions of people can be connected, work and do business together. The 'egalitarian' nature of cyberspace has effectively created a level playing field, where people of all backgrounds can communicate directly and instantaneously, not only on the one-to-one basis common to traditional forms of communication, but also one-to-many and many-to-many, simultaneously. It is still largely open and non-proprietary and anybody with the appropriate hardware and software can link up with it. The Internet is rapidly becoming the primary communication media of the 21st century, because almost everything can now be done through it, including phone calls, emails, liaising with customers and clients, banking, medical consultations, education and learning, creative design, computer dating, downloading music and so forth. Cyberspace has revolutionized the way people communicate with each other and the way information is disseminated within and between organizations.

The Internet and other technological advances over the last two decades have already changed the ways in which people work and organizations operate – forever. Communication in the Information Age no longer requires employees to be in physical contact with each other, their customers or even the companies that employ them, as was the case in the industrial age. Organizations now have greater flexibility to restructure rapidly to suit fast-changing competitive environments, and technology has provided businesses with the opportunity to communicate and transact business more efficiently and effectively than at any time in history. The Internet will also drive the emergence of the world's first true cyber-cities, similar to the ones emerging in Singapore, Cyber-Jaya in Malaysia, and Silicon Valley in California.

Another example of a technology that has become widespread is virtual reality. Just a few years ago this was the subject matter of science fiction movies like *The Lawnmower Man* and *Johnny Mnemonic*. In the near future, it may become a normal feature of the working environments of most organizations in industrialized countries. While prototype technologies for virtual meeting places (VMPs) have been under development since the 1980s, many early systems had teething problems. These included blurred and jerky images, time lags between audio-sound and visual images on the screen, dim and underpowered images, and a lack of real-time eye contact as well as the loss of communication through body language. However, recent advances in augmented reality systems, in which graphical images are overlaid onto the physical world to overcome motion-sickness, the development of infinite reality graphics engines and daybright display systems, at Boeing, Philips, BMW, NASA and Daimler Benz, all promise to make these problems a thing of the past in the near future.

A computer-graphic representation of a conference room is one example of a modern VMP. To enter this environment, a person virtu-commutes, by donning a lightweight head-mounted display and data-gloves. Other people appear in the environment as holographic images. It is possible to 'move' around the room, to 'gesture', 'look' someone else in the face and engage in 'real' conversations. Participants can 'sit down' on a virtual chair, 'pick up' a virtual pen, 'write' on virtual white-boards and 'pass' virtual memos. Objects within a virtual meeting place can be 'held' and 'examined'. In a technological first, scientists in London, and Boston in the USA, 'picked up' a computer-generated virtual cube between them and moved it, each responding to the force the other exerted on it. The devices that allowed them to do this have been named 'phantoms', which recreate the sense of touch by sending very small impulses at high frequencies over the net, using newly developed fibre-optic cable and high bandwidths (abridged from Long, 2002). The virtual meeting place offers many benefits to users and significant value to organizations that adopt this technology. And, since the events of 11 September 2001 and subsequent terrorist acts, there has been an increased interest in these technologies in organizations.

The world's first real-time video networking system, Access Grid Node, was launched in October 2001. This allowed groups at multiple sites to interact simultaneously and to share data and software systems. Data windows from participants' laptops, PowerPoint images, DVD and video clips, and spreadsheets can all be integrated into these virtual meetings. In turn, these media can now be transmitted on plasma screens the size of an office wall, to create the first cyber-tapestry of virtual communication. Meeting in virtual environments, in the guise of personal avatars, is already commonplace, allowing people across the globe to interact and socialize in virtual reality. Three-dimensional modelling experts are revolutionizing virtual simulations of proposed building projects. Using powerful silicon graphics computers and advanced three-dimensional modelling software, architects can provide customers with 3D 180° wraparound views of new projects. The screen image is provided by three projectors, which create sharper and clearer images than ever before. This software is also capable of making real-time adjustments to the on-screen image and has the ability to quickly reconfigure aspects of a project's image, such as adding an extra couple of floors or changing the colour scheme of a building (Lynch, 2002; Foreshew, 2001).

Virtualization and information networks will continue to evolve and their effects on organizations will be significant. High-speed data networks, electronic mail and groupware facilities are fast overcoming limits of time and geography. They are enabling companies to harness resources worldwide, achieve greater economies of scale and provide an instantaneous, global responsiveness to their customers and clients. By interconnecting everything with everything, networks exponentially increase the number of commercial relationships that businesses are exposed to. And, as we saw in Chapter 10, from these new knowledge relationships, new products, services, ideas and information can quickly emerge. Take the example of banks. Before the advent of call centres in the early 1990s, if you had a query about your banking facilities or accounts, you would have gone to the bank to talk to an adviser, or called your bank and talked to a bank officer. Today, you are expected to use your bank's website facilities, or put your queries through centralized and largely automated call centres, responding to verbal instructions with the phone's keypad. Such automation, operating under the acronym IVR (Interactive Voice Response), has eliminated the need for hundreds of tele-staff. It has been estimated that bank websites and automated call centres reduced the cost of customer relations by as much as 90 per cent between 1982 and 1992 (Darroch, 2002). In technologically advanced countries, close to 100 per cent of all customer transactions with banks, and other financial institutions, will be done via automated or electronic means by 2005. Many accountants and financial advisers may also find themselves out of work as intelligent software takes over the day-to-day management of our accounts, inventories, billing, salaries and tax returns. They may even make investment and share portfolio decisions on our behalf (Joy, 2000).

New technologies continue to emerge in many different forms, and are now being used in a multitude of ways. These include Sales Force Automation (SFA), which began to revolutionize front-office operations in the early 1990s, by enabling sales and customer liaison staff to take information about their organizations out of the office and into the field, thereby enabling more on-the-spot deals. In 1996–7, cutting-edge small and medium-sized companies started linking these systems into 'Customer Relations Management Systems' (CRMS) and 'Automated Customer Response Systems (ACRS), to enable fast responses to customers' queries or complaints. Today, this system, and a myriad of associated offshoots, are at the forefront of the 'Enterprise Application Integration' (EAI) revolution. EAIs do three things. First, they can make sense of and integrate previously incompatible or different software packages, so that they can communicate with each other. Second, they can assimilate and distribute large amounts of information within organizations and, thereby, integrate different operating functions. Third, they can now do this in real time, with minimal delays between information inputs and outputs (Darroch, 2002).

General Electric was the first company to develop a fully integrated system of this kind in the late 1990s and many more companies have followed their example. A survey in *The Economist* revealed that GE's chief information officer, Gary Reiner, has a monitoring system that could tell him, instantaneously, what is going on anywhere, at any time, in any part of the company's global operations. He is able to do this because all of GE's companies, divisions, processes and systems are now interlinked in a systemic web-based operating system (ibid.). Administrative automation continues to revolutionize the control of accounts, inventories, billing and salaries in many organizations although, as we will see in Chapter 12, these have not prevented unethical and corrupt organizational leaders from misusing these systems for 'creative accounting' purposes.

There has been a continuing revolution in employee portability and mobility, through the use of smart phones and technologies that have integrated mainframe databases with mobile PCs, email facilities and remote-satellite systems. The first Personal Digital Assistant (PDA), launched by Apple in 1993, led to an explosion in the manufacture of PDAs in the 1990s, combining fax, email, memo and organizer capabilities. A decade later, many employees were not just connected; they were *tethered* to wireless technologies, armed with pagers, laptops, PDAs, Tablet PCs and mobile phones. These technologies mean that employees can 'carry' the entire knowledge base of their organizations on the road when they visit customers and clients, and their 'offices' are wherever they happen to be. Ericsson predicts that this working revolution will continue, with up to half of their employees now working away from the office on a regular basis. In financial services, advertising and consulting, working away from the office may become more widespread, because communication in the Information Age no longer requires employees to be in physical contact with each other, or the companies that employ them (Ericsson website, 1 December 2003).

The growth of Internet e-business has continued unabated throughout the world over the last decade. In Australia, for example, this doubled between December 2000 and mid-2002, in spite of the post-April 2001 technology slump. During this period, online revenues grew from around $A21 billion to $A43 billion, while the number of people using the Internet to make purchases almost doubled to reach 2.7 million. More than 70 per cent of Internet e-commerce was business to business (B2B), which grew by 522 per cent over this period. Business to consumer e-commerce also grew strongly, with an overall increase of 878 per cent since the beginning of 1999. Worldwide, there has been a revolution in home shopping via the Internet. In December 2002, more than 200 million people worldwide were using the net for shopping on a regular basis. This was an $US88 billion a year industry in the USA in 1999 and is expected to grow into a multi-trillion-dollar worldwide industry by 2005 (Chong, 2002). More established and traditional companies have also been using e-commerce as a relatively cheap way of entering new markets. For example, in 2001, BP (Australia) signed a distribution deal with the Melbourne-based online retailer, wishlist.com.au, and customers can collect their on-line orders from BP stations when they go to buy petrol. This neat example of lateral thinking, and the effective use of another company's e-technology, means that BP can build a tighter connection with its five million annual customers and, perhaps, encourage them to make more use of their petrol stations than those of their rivals (Beilby, 2002: 61).

Computer-aided design (CAD) and robots are now used routinely in automobile construction and many other manufacturing industries, particularly in component manufacturing where electronic designs can be transmitted directly to the robots making the products. Daimler-Chrysler, Ford, General Motors, BMW and Peugeot all purchased supercomputers during the late 1990s and early 2000s, in order to help with vehicle design, analysis and verification. What used to take weeks or months can now take just a few hours. Instead of having to build an expensive prototype from scratch, carmakers can use these computers to simulate tests and make changes before the car is built. In a matter of hours they can run thousands of complex, noise, vibration and airflow tests. They can even simulate the effects of crashes on the vehicle (Bennett, 2002).

A robot, developed by Dyson in 2000, with 50 inbuilt remote sensors is now used in thousands of organizations around the world, cleaning floors at night. The company's SC06 robotic household cleaner, launched in 2002, requires no programming. It has 70 sensors and can make 600 decisions a minute while it learns and vacuums its way around its environment. Thousands of robots are now used to transport documents in large buildings. Husqvarna launched the first self-learning robo-mower in 2002. The appearance of the first generation of self-learning robots included the first robot dog called 'Aibo' who appeared in 2001, costing $US3000. It was described at the time as 'a cross between Robocop and the Tacho-Bell Chihuahua'. It has self-learning and adaptive growth capabilities built into its programming, responds to verbal and non-verbal stimuli, makes its own judgments, expresses pet-like emotions and can recognize forms and colours. It has more computing power than the first spacecraft to land on the moon. A gastrobot, named 'Chew-Chew' made its debut at a robotics conference in Hawaii in July 2000. It had a microbial 'stomach' that was fed organic matter, which it then converted into electrical energy. A robowaitress made its first appearance in a Japanese restaurant in Tokyo in 2001 (AFP, 2001a). This was soon followed by the launch of the first 'guard-robot' in Japan, on 12 November 2002. In the same month, Sony announced that the world's first 'Small Biped Entertainment Robot', SDR 4X, would be launched in 2004. Looking like Astro-Boy, a popular cartoon character in postwar Japan, this is able to walk, speak, sing, gesture and learn to recognize its owner (Lewis, 2002: 70).

On 3 May 2002, scientists at the State University of New York announced the creation of the world's first cyber-rat, the ratbot: this unfortunate rodent was fitted with newly developed brain implants and a radio backpack to control its behaviour. Scientists working on this project had discovered that implants could be used to stimulate areas of the rat's brain responsible for food, sex and drink responses. The rat quickly learnt to respond to this stimulation, even if this involved climbing up and down stairs or moving into the centre of a brightly lit room, things that rats would normally avoid. The goal is to use ratbots to find earthquake victims, detect landmines and even to spy inside enemy installations with the use of miniature video cameras. Less than two months later, on 23 June 2002, scientists revealed that they had combined the DNA of a goat and a spider, to create Spidergoat: this fusion has resulted in a goat that can produce wool that is five times stronger than steel. This could be used to make lightweight body armour and other forms of protective clothing in the near future (World on Sunday, 2002). The world's first transatlantic remote operation was carried out successfully on 7 September 2001. Three French surgeons in New York, using remote-controlled robot arms, removed the gall bladder of a woman in Strasbourg Civil

Hospital, 7000 km away. This was removed in an hour, and the 68-year-old was discharged from hospital 48 hours later (Von Radowitz, 2001). In late May 2003, it was announced that the surgical robot, Da Vinci, had performed its twentieth successful heart bypass operation (*The Weekend Australian*, 24–5 May 2003).

In other areas, we have seen the emergence of 'cynthespians' and the first fully digital 'actors' in the 2001 movies, *Final Fantasy* and *The Spirits Within*. The world's first synreader (synthetic newsreader), 'Anova', was launched in 2000. In October 2002, it was announced that games featuring interactive Sims (simulated humans), became the best-selling type of home computer game in the world (Kampert, 2002). We have also witnessed the emergence of language/speech translators. Philips launched the first commercial version of these in 1998, but the early ones were somewhat unreliable. For example, a web advertisement for the launch of a new Fashion Café advert in Rio de Janeiro in 1998 announced that it would be opened by, 'supermolecules, Nomoi Compile, Cloudy Scoffer and Else Metaphors'. More recent iterations have become more reliable, as they are driven by smart software that learns to respond to nuances in their users' voices. Fuji Spinnin has developed a textile that contains 'pro-vitamin': this is a substance that turns into vitamin C when it comes into contact with the skin. In the form of a T-shirt it can be washed up to 30 times. The company is also planning to introduce vitamin-laced underwear for women (AFP, 2001b). The world's first electronic paper was launched in May 2003. The UK company EIink announced that its scientists had created the first super-thin (0.3mm), semi-flexible electronic-ink display screen, capable of displaying black-and-white and colour text using wire technology. This has paved the way for the first commercially available generation of portable/downloadable e-newspapers and wearable computer screens (Reaney, 2003).

New technologies are enabling intelligent organizations to re-engineer themselves continuously to meet new commercial challenges. They will continue to revolutionize all manufacturing processes and businesses, and will play an increasingly important role in the management of employee knowledge and intellectual capital. They may contribute to the globalization of trade and commerce, to greater international political, social and cultural integration and, possibly, help us transcend the ancient tribal, religious and ethnic conflicts that continue to plague humanity. Some commentators on the Information Age also believe that new technologies will make structured and hierarchical organizations, in their present forms, redundant in the not-too-distant future. The impact of these developments on organizations will be profound, and the challenge for leaders and managers now is to anticipate and plan for the impact of these changes. However, there has of course been a major hiccup in the development of the much-hyped technology-driven New Economy: the collapse of the dotcom bubble in April 2000 and the subsequent elimination of more than 90 per cent of the companies launched under the dotcom banner. Below we look at the practical insights that business leaders can draw from this event and its aftermath.

'Irrational exuberance': insights from the collapse of the dotcom bubble in 2000

> The Internet: 1) the most important communications technology in the world; 2) an over-hyped bubble; 3) that which changes nothing; 4) of extreme philosophical and even metaphysical significance; 5) just another media channel; 6) all of the above; 7) some of the above; 8) none of the above.
> (*Jim Rosenfield, author of* The Devil's Directory of Direct Marketing, *cited in* The Australian, *IT Section, 26 February 2002*)

> The web bubble is bursting. Has burst. Which means that some of us moving towards on-line glory may instead face that Wile E. Coyote moment when you look down and realise that you have just sprinted off a cliff. Sigh. Back to our cramped cubicles. New economy, my ass.
> (*Michael Keen, Editorial Director, Keen.com, cited in* Time, *17 April 2000*)

The first and most important insight that can be drawn from the dotcom crash of April 2000 is that it came as no surprise to anyone with an understanding of economic history. Since the emergence of modern capitalism in Europe, stock market booms and slumps of this kind have occurred regularly over the last 400 years, and this one was predicted by some commentators before it happened (for example, Shiller, 2000; Elliot, 2000). As long ago as 1630, prices of tulip bulbs soared to levels that would have made investors in dotcom companies in the late 1990s sit up, take notice and dust off their wallets. At the peak of the boom in the winter of 1636, the rarest and most sought-after bulbs cost as much as a house in the trendier areas of Amsterdam. In February 1637, the market collapsed, leading to thousands of bankruptcies and penury for those 'tulip speculators' who had borrowed money to pay inflated prices near to the peak of the boom. Later, in 1720, when all of London was clamouring for shares in the South Sea Company, Sir Isaac Newton sold £7000 of stock in the company and later bought in at the top of the boom. When the bubble burst soon afterwards, he ended up losing £20 000 – a huge sum of money at the time. He later commented, 'I can calculate the motions of heavenly bodies, but not the madness of the markets' (Gleick, 2003).

Similar speculative booms occurred throughout the 18th and 19th centuries with canals, railways, shipping and electricity. In the 1920s,

Wall Street's financial elite had convinced themselves that the rules of economics had been rewritten, and the market could support ever-higher share prices. As in 1999–2000, many startup companies during the 1920s were not making any money, and their inflated share prices were justified by expectations of what they might make in the future. Sound familiar? On 29 October 1929, the USA stock market collapsed, leading to the worst global recession of the 20th century. Market bubbles occurred again in Japan in the 1980s, ignited by the conviction that Japanese industry and management techniques were going to dominate the world, and in Hong Kong in the 1990s, driven by the assumption that the territory would become the main gateway into China after the handover in 1997 (Shiller, 2000).

Second, in common with all economic bubbles in history, there was the mistaken belief that 'This time it's different', and that the inexorable rise in share prices in the late 1990s was evidence of some new economic laws, rather than the result of greed, stupidity, recklessness, dishonesty and, in Yale Schiller's immortal words, 'reckless exuberance'. In fact, the dotcom crash of April 2000 was just one of a series stretching back over four centuries. The major difference was that this latest speculative bubble led to dozens of court cases in 2002–4, with thousands of litigants suing most of America's major investment houses for compensation for the advice they had given to buy dotcom stocks in the late 1990s and early 2000s. Their financial advisers had been caught out by one of the most ubiquitous features of the Internet: the emails they had been sending each other during this time (Ellis, 2002).

> Pieces of s**t.
> (*How Merrill Lynch financial analysts described technology stocks in emails to each other in 1999–2000, while at the same time advising their clients to buy them (cited in* The Australian, *IT Section, 4 June 2002). Subsequent court cases in 2003 revealed that ML financial analysts had systematically lied to their clients about the efficacy of investing in dotcom and technology stocks. The company was fined $US100 million.*)

> Yahoo – what you yell after selling its stock to some sucker for $240 a share.
> Windows 2000 – what you jump out of, if you were the sucker that paid $240 per share.
> Bull market – an overblown expansion of the stock market causing investors to believe that they are financial geniuses.
> Bear market – a period of time when the kids get no allowances, the wife gets no jewelry and the husband gets no sex.
> Broker – what my broker has made me.
> (*From an email that did the rounds during October 2001*)

Third, the dotcom crash, and the loss of some 500 000 jobs in the USA and Europe over the next 18 months, acted as a strong reality check for much of the hype that had accompanied the growth of e-companies in the late 1990s. For example, one-half of all adverts at the Super Bowl in February 2000 featured 17 dotcom companies, each paying $US2.5 million for 30 seconds of screen time. Only three of these were still trading in June 2002. In 2001, three dotcom companies advertised at the Super Bowl. One of these, computer.com, spent $US2.2 million for a 30-second slot, which at the time was 60 per cent of the money it had in the bank. This company went out of business soon afterwards. At the time, CBS's advertising manager commented, 'We knew a lot of the dotcom companies wouldn't be back next year so immediately after this year's Bowl we went back to our more meat and potatoes clients' (cited by Romei, 2001). Another sign of the times was the customized car number plate, 'The Web', which was sold at Goodman's Auctioneers in Sydney, Australia, for $A200 000 in January 2000. In January 2001 it was put in for auction again and there were no bids for this item. The top selling number plate was '8' (a Chinese lucky number).

Fourth, the dotcom collapse confirmed the age-old adage that there are indeed fools born every day. For example, Jonathan Lebed, a school-boy, became the youngest person in history to be charged with stock market fraud by the US Securities and Exchange Commission. Working from his bedroom, he made nearly $US800 000 by ramping up shares on bulletin boards. He bought shares at low prices and then posted 'buy' recommendations, which many people in ovine fashion duly did. Lebed handed back most of his ill-gotten gains after he was prosecuted, but was still left sitting on a tidy profit of $US50 000. Subsequent investigations revealed that many of his schoolmates had also got in on the act, and virtually (no pun intended) the whole school had become involved, with parents and teachers also asking for advice on stock market investments. Another example was the 'Number One Legal Adviser' on the Internet during 2000. This turned out to be a 15-year-old boy, who had never read a legal textbook in his life, but dispensed advice on the basis of the day-time American TV court shows he had been watching. He had won a huge and loyal following by the time the police caught up with him (*The Times*, 2001c). There were also many instances of truly idiotic ventures at this time. For example, Pryce Corp, a property company that owned a chain of Philippines cemeteries, closed down its net-sales operation after failing to sell a single burial plot over the Internet to the five million or so Filipinos who live overseas (McCann, 2001).

'I went along to 10 Downing Street to brief Tony Blair on e-commerce ahead of a European Summit in Lisbon.' This was the founder of boo.com, which tried to sell clothes on the Internet, thinking of itself as a virtual Harvey Nichols, only global. Already the National Portrait Gallery was showing a picture of him in its new exhibition, called *Business Leaders of the 21st Century*.

Two months later, with the century less than a year and a half old, boo.com was bust. Of the $US140 million that had been sucked into it, nothing remained – nothing that is but a book named Boo Hoo, which seems to have been written rather as boo.com was run, by a committee of humourless Swedes with intermittent hangovers.

(*Cited in* The Spectator *(UK), 11 November 2001. Boo.com managed to blow $US140 million of investors' money in just 18 months, and went into liquidation in May 2001.*)

Fifth, the belief that virtual or e-commerce would quickly take over the world in one fell swoop was flawed and naive. With the benefit of hindsight, we can see that the whole e-paradigm was massively over-hyped. There was little solid evidence that most of the new e-companies were offering anything that was truly innovative, in terms of the goods and services they provided. Many were financed simply on the basis of 'future market projections', with no assurances that they would ever actually achieve these. Some didn't even bother to publish business plans or financial forecasts for their fledgling companies, and yet people still invested large amounts of money in these companies. Furthermore, even at the height of the bubble, dotcom companies still only accounted for a tiny proportion of national gross domestic production around the world. Many lacked the essential combination of 'high tech and high touch', and an understanding of the need still to provide good products and services, and maintain good relationships with their customers and clients. Many of the darlings of the first wave of dotcom companies, such Liberty One, One.Tel, New Tel, Boo.com and Lucent Technologies, had either gone bust, or were experiencing serious financial difficulties during 2002–3. George Sheehan's company, webvan.com, was one of many other dotcom companies that also went bust during 2000–2001. There is even a website in the USA, run by Philip Kaplan, that predicts the imminent demise of dotcom companies (www.business2.com). Up to December 2003 he had enjoyed a 95 per cent success rate with his predictions.

Sixth, the dotcom exuberance of 1997–2000 reminds us that all current technologies, amazing as many of them may be, are still essentially *passive*. For the next decade or so, it will still be people with good ideas who drive business. Anyone who still thinks that e-business is simply about investing in the right technology and software is deeply, deeply mistaken. Not surprisingly, the vendors of Internet and other technologies sold these in the 1990s as if they were not only capable of making all businesses more efficient and more profitable, but were also a conduit to instant riches for new start-up businesses. However, e-business is definitely not just about electronics, computers or the Internet. These are simply portals or add-on devices that can help businesses to do what they have always done, namely to bring into being that which was not in the marketplace before, and delivering value products and quality services to their customers and clients as efficiently and profitably as possible. The Internet and all the technologies associated with it will not make a business efficient if it is already inefficient. If a business is slow now, technology will not make it faster in the future. If its customer service stinks now, technologies will simply highlight how bad this is (think, for example, of customer call services at most utility companies). Technology – even in high-tech companies – has limitations, as this next tongue-in-cheek example suggests.

'The new business retail craze'

They're calling it 'S-Commerce' or 'shops' and it's being rolled out in cities and town nationwide. 'It's a real revelation', according to Malcolm Fosbury, a middleware engineer from Hillingdon. 'You just walk into one of these shops and they have all sort of things for sale.' Fosbury was particular impressed by a clothes shop he discovered while browsing in central London. 'Shops seem to be the ideal medium for transactions of this type. I can actually try out a jacket and see if it fits me. Then I can visualize the way I would look if I was wearing the clothing.' This is possible using a high-definition two-dimensional viewing system, or 'mirror' as it has become known.

Shops, which are frequently aggregated into shopping portals or 'high streets', are becoming increasingly popular with the cash-rich time-poor generation of new consumers. Often located in densely populated areas, people can find them extremely convenient. Malcolm is not alone in being impressed by shops. 'Some days I just don't have the time to download huge Flash animations of rotating trainers and then wait five days for them to be delivered in the hope that they will actually fit,' says Sandra Bailey, a systems analyst from Chelsea. 'This way I can actually complete the transaction in real time and walk away with the goods.' Being able see whether or not shoes and clothing fit has been a real bonus for Bailey: 'I used to spend my evenings boxing up gear to return. Sometimes the clothes didn't fit, sometimes they just sent the wrong stuff.'

Shops have a compelling commercial story to tell, too, according to Gartner Group retail analyst Carl Baker: 'There are massive efficiencies in the supply chain. By concentrating distribution to a series of high volume outlets in urban centres – typically close to where people live and work – businesses can make dramatic savings in fulfilment costs. Just compare this with the wasteful practice of delivering items piecemeal to people's homes. Furthermore, allowing consumers to receive goods when they actually want them could mean an end to the frustration of returning home to find a dispatch notice telling you that your goods are waiting in a delivery depot on the other side of town.' But it's not just the convenience and time saving that appeals to Fosbury: 'Visiting a shop is real relief for me. I mean, as it is, I spend all day in front of a ****ing computer. (Spoof e-article that did the rounds after April 2000.)

There are remarkable parallels between the dotcom boom of 1997–2000 and technology booms in earlier times. When the telephone and the internal combustion engine became widely adopted in the first two decades of the 20th century, they speeded up the production and delivery of goods and services that already existed and, in time, fostered a new wave of technological innovation and the creation of new consumer markets. And most older and established companies were quick to start using these technologies. The Internet has been evolving rapidly since the dotcom collapse, into a medium for well-established companies to carry out their business activities with greater speed and efficiency, in what is now routinely described as a 'bricks and clicks' fashion. For example, if we look at the world's most successful economy during 2001–4, Australia, B2B Internet commerce revenue was already worth about 30 billion dollars in 2002. However, this growth was not being driven by new e-companies, but by well-established traditional businesses. One of the country's biggest companies, Telstra, launched CoProcure in October 2001, the first multi-industry B2B e-marketplace in Australia. This included other major local companies such as Amcor, AMP, ANZ Australia Post, BHP, Coca-Cola Amatil, Fosters, Goodman Fiedler, Orica, PAC Dunlop, Qantas and Wesfarmers. The Commonwealth Bank responded to this initiative by setting up Cyberlynx, which includes Woolworths, Lion Nathan, AAPT, Telecom New Zealand and EDS. In every industrialized country in the world, thousands of companies are developing their B2B and e-market capabilities.

However, the truly revolutionary power of the second wave of growth in the e-sector is its ability to let small players enter and achieve fast critical mass in the marketplace, far more quickly than has ever been possible in the past. An example of this is the story of one Australian Webmaster – MW.

'It's a license to print money'

The inspiration for the web master idea came while I was still a university student. At the time, I had a home page with a few links to other sites, and I noticed that some of these had advertising banners. At the time, I was new to the idea of banners, but I did wonder whether you could make any money from these. So, I asked one of the guys if he made any money from running these on his website, and he told me that just from running a banner he made a couple of hundred dollars a year. I thought, 'That's nice – money for nothing, just for putting up a banner.'

So off I went and searched on the Internet and came across a few companies who offered 'pay-per-click' payments if you ran their banners. Initially, because I knew nothing, there were only a few clicks on the banners I set up, so I didn't make much money – maybe five or ten cents a day. But, it was a start. I started adding other banners, through which people could buy products from other companies, and then I'd start getting commissions on those referred sales. Unfortunately, nobody bought anything!

So I started looking for other sites that might have similar set-ups, and found one to do with book clubs. This showed me what their usual click-through and conversion rates were. So then I was able to do some calculations which showed me that, if I could get enough traffic through my sites, this could work and I would make some money, *if* I could get enough people visiting my banners. I had a strong technical background, and had worked as a computer programmer for a while, so the IT aspects were all quite natural to me. I'd also spent some time in games programming, so working with computing, web design, graphics and images all came quite easily to me.

Then I started to pay for people to visit my site, by liaising with sites that deliver web-traffic to you. A few months later, my first referred sale took place. This was my first sales commission! I was jumping around like a goof, realizing at this point that I could make some real money from this. I started to build on this idea, calculating that, if I knew what the click-through and conversion rates were for particular sites, I could pay for this traffic, and then make money. This is called affiliate marketing, and you get a commission from the companies that are actually selling the products. This works through something called affiliate programming, where a third-party server passes on the information that a buyer has bought a product via one of my sites, and from this I get commission payments. So, in theory, I could get commissions from any company that sells goods on the Internet which had these affiliates.

That was the start of it, and from there I searched for other sites that had good conversion rates – sites that people actually buy stuff from. Then I went professional, which involved getting a domain name, getting proper web hosting systems set up, and that got the whole ball rolling. I had to learn more about the marketing aspects, the generic principles of persuasion, sales techniques and so on. I also had to find out how to set up systems that would enable me to rank well in global search engines and get more traffic coming through my sites. Although there is a lot of free information out there, I paid for much of this, and also subscribed to on-line services that provided information about search engines, read e-books and so forth. I came across a lot of useful stuff on the psychology of e-selling: how people react to certain site designs and slow downloads and so on. These all have an impact on whether people use a given site to actually buy something.

You have to be able to gather a lot of information. The success I've had is really based on a long, long period of reading and studying and trying things out, to find out what does and doesn't work. You have to do this because it is unbelievably competitive and cut-throat out there and you don't share your knowledge with anyone. You keep your cutting-edge by keeping on the ball, reading the news, keeping up-to-date with every new development in search engine algorithms, spotting new products coming onto the market and so on. This is information that anyone could access, if they have the time, energy and persistence to do it, but it really does require great self-belief, because it took months before I started to see good results. You also have to be simultaneously pragmatic and have the ability to grasp new opportunities as soon as they arise – intuition based on experience if you like.

From there, I was then able to create new, customized programs that enabled me to display whole product databases of a merchant, not just a single banner or link, but sites that automatically interact with all the servers of all the companies that I'm linked to. That is a very specific piece of software that I created, which I can now reuse as a template for every new site that I create and, once set up, they update and manage themselves automatically. It also means that all of my sites are linked to each other, which can further increase the volume of traffic.

I believe that the value of my sites is based on two simple ideas: the visitor is looking for a product in the search-engines. My site is optimized to rank highly for the keywords they type in. Thus the visitor lands on my site first and gets detailed product information without any distracting clutter. In my opinion the visitor wins, and the merchant also wins because a very large site cannot possibly optimize a page for each specific product that a given individual is looking for.

At the moment, I have about 40 000 visitors a day to 10 sites, which will rise to 20 sites soon. The time plan is to sell up in five years and live on the revenue from my investments. By then, I hope to have more than 200 sites, with about one million visitors a day. So the asking price for the business, even now, is one million dollars! (Interview with MW, Perth, Western Australia, 3 December 2002.)

In summary, the rise and fall of the first wave of dotcom companies taught all business leaders and organizations some useful lessons. First, all fledgling businesses still need great products and/or services, backed up with a clear vision, a good business plan, well thought-out strategies and good customer/client relationships. These still require energetic, creative, intrinsically motivated and entrepreneurial staff to deliver these. Second, for now, all technologies are still essentially passive and merely add-ons to methods of doing business that are as old as the hills. Third, from small acorns great oaks will grow. It can take several years to build a successful tech-company from scratch. If an e-business plan looks too good to be true, it almost certainly is. If it promises a fantastic return on investment in a very short period of time, it probably won't. Fourth, as the MW example illustrates, if you've only got an e-business plan, as opposed to one designed for real people in the real world, the chances are that someone will have already thought of it before you did.

So, initially, forget about the technologies, and use your lateral, scenario-mapping and future-casting skills to envision what markets for new products and services may emerge in the near future. If you can spot some of these, and then use technology in an intelligent way to exploit these openings, as MW did so successfully, you may be made for life. For businesses, the intelligent and pragmatic use of appropriate technologies will remain an important component of their strategic planning, because we are already living in what has been described as the 'on demand era', where customers, clients and suppliers expect instantaneous responsiveness and flexibility from the organizations they deal with. Furthermore, as Jonar Nader has observed, 'If organizations are to survive the networked world they need to understand its characteristics. At its core is the imperative to stay away from that which is applauded. Meanwhile, it is advisable to investigate that which is hated, and invest in that which is laughed at. Go in search of the unbelievable. Therein lie the clues to the future. The future has nothing to do with e-business. However, e-business has everything to do with the future' (Nader, 2003: 13).[5]

The effects of new and emerging technologies on organizational leadership and people management

> Technology is outstripping human capacity to manage it. Even the best technical minds in the world are struggling to come to terms with modern computer systems. If this problem is not addressed, systems will get to the stage where we simply won't be able to manage them. I hardly know a senior executive who doesn't feel worried about how much they are spending or whether it is creating value.
>
> (*Doug Elix, IBM's Global Services' Chief Executive, at the World Congress on IT, Adelaide, Australia, cited in* The Australian, *1 March 2002*)

Historically, attempts to 'manage' technological change have been almost entirely unsuccessful, because technological development has always outpaced the ability of governments or organizations to regulate and control it (Kurzweil, 1999; Warwick, 1998). Witness, for example, the hopeless game of catch-up that government regulators now play in trying to keep up with advances in genetic engineering and computer hacking. And the transition from a nation-based industrial age to a global digital age will require people other than technical specialists to provide input into developing the new leadership and people management skills that will be required in this environment. We've seen that two of the most important roles of leaders are to define reality and to envision the future for their followers. The impact of new and emerging technologies on both employees and organizations will be profound and a major challenge for leaders is to help their employees deal with the work environments and new challenges that emergent technologies are already creating. However, at this moment in time, there is little evidence that leaders and managers are being shown how to cope actively with this new environment: most simply *react* to the emergence of new technologies.

In this section, we will look at ways that leaders and managers can help their employees cope better with emerging high-tech organizational environments. We saw earlier in this chapter that there are many factors driving rapid advances in new technologies. In a symbiotic fashion, these are driving the development of cyberspace, virtual reality and an emerging first generation of self-learning computers which, in turn, will create yet more technological innovations. Even if we are conservative, and assume that only about 30 per cent of current predictions about the future are right (about the average success rate for such future casting in the past), the impact of new technologies on leadership and people management is still going to be profound. There are already clear indications that the Internet and other new technologies are now driving an inexorable transition from second-wave to third-wave organizational management (Table 11.1).

Table 11.1   Out with the old and in with the new

'Second wave' organizations	'Third wave' organizations
Organized around mechanistic hierarchies and rigid functional areas; knowledge and information are shared on 'a need to know' basis	Organic, flat structure; work is organized around the shared creation and dissemination of knowledge and information
Inward looking; 'hard' organizational boundaries; centralized control	Outward looking; recognize that connectivity is more important than boundaries; networked and decentralized; many of their processes, even core ones, can extend way beyond their organizational boundaries
Major time lags between perceiving threats and reacting to them	Trimultaneous ability to anticipate threats, cope with these and initiate new strategies quickly
Conservative about embracing new ideas; risk averse	Willing to take risks and make mistakes, but also able to learn from these; embrace learning and innovation with enthusiasm
Hire consultants to 'manage change'	Learn and adapt organically; manage new knowledge and learning creatively and systemically; create change for others to imitate or follow
Employees are a commodity or 'cost'; demotivated, transient workforces	Employees *are* the company; loyal, highly motivated and well rewarded
Reactive use of technologies to 'create business'	Proactive use of technologies as smart tools to enhance business performance
Aware of global economy	Have a deeply ingrained global mind-set
Think short-term	Think long-term
Stop/start and reactive	Evolutionary and revolutionary

In traditional bricks-and-mortar businesses the transmission of important ideas and knowledge had to be done face-to-face and in real time. However, if organizations no longer need to 'exist', in a physical sense, we may witness a process of organizational deconstruction over the next ten years. There are signs that this is already happening, with the emergence of 'pancake', 'learning', 'lattice', 'amoeba' and 'inverted' organizations. 'Anarchic' organizations, based on loose-knit, short-term associations and alliances of skilled knowledge workers, and 'spider's web' organizations are becoming more commonplace. People now talk of Generation MM and Generation X, Y and T companies (with the latter staffed by 'screenagers'). New green technologies and global green Internet groups are driving the emergence of a new generation of ecotech companies (Fussler, 1996). These represent qualitatively different types of organization that replace what they take from the environment, or at least make major efforts to recycle and/or cut down on their use of fossil fuels and other finite resources. A new range of companies has emerged in recent years in response to the 'greening' of consumers and organizations (Knowles, 1997). Virtualization will be a common feature of these new businesses, and a very important operational add-on to bricks-and-mortar companies.

What we may be witnessing is the dismantling and reformulation of traditional business structures, because the new economics of information and technology driven evolution are making static organizational structures redundant. The 'second wave' of Internet development is starting to revolutionize traditional ways of organizing people and businesses. For most of the 20th century, business was linear and slow. Organizations were mostly centralized, hierarchical, top-down and driven by command and control styles of leadership and management. The new hypercompetitive world of business will be characterized by massive, simultaneous, multitasking processes, made possible by these advances in information and communication technologies. Consequently, over the next 20 years, any organization that cannot cope with these developments will either cease to exist, or be radically different in both form and function. New technologies will create many new types of employment, but will also destroy many thousands of jobs. To cite one example, Kodak (the world's biggest manufacturer and developer of photographic film and paper) announced on 25 January 2004 that it would be cutting 15 000 jobs over three years: *20 per cent* of its global workforce. This drastic step was taken because of the inexorable uptake of digital camera technology by consumers in the early 2000s, and the urgent need to make a rapid transition from manufacturing traditional cameras and reloadable film to digital units and digital photographic support (Bachelard and Crawford, 2004). Organizations will continue to fragment and die with ever-increasing frequency and unpredictability. 'Merger mania' will continue inexorably amongst large bureaucratic second wave organizations that are unable to maintain their competitive advantage in a third wave economy. The pace of change will continue to accelerate and will verge on 'chaos' and 'blur' in some parts of the corporate world. One example of this change and disintegration has been described by a rather perplexed Michael Kinsley:

> Readers have the right to know that *TIME* magazine will be part of AOL Time Warner. The author of this essay, by contrast, has a day job as editor of *Slate*, an online magazine published by Microsoft. Microsoft owns an online service, MSN, that competes with AOL. Microsoft and AOL Time Warner will have competing investments in the cable industry. On yet another hand, Microsoft and Time Warner are co-investors in a high-speed cable–Internet connection business called Roadrunner. On a fourth hand, Microsoft owns a chunk of AT&T, which owns a chunk of Time Warner, which means that, after the merger, Microsoft will own a chunk of AOL. Readers should also take into consideration that Microsoft is a partner with NBC, which is owned by General Electric, in an all-new cable channel, MSNBC, which competes with CNN, which is owned by AOL Time Warner.
>
> What's more, the editor in chief of MNSCM.com, the cable channel's affiliated website, is my mother's brother's wife's aunt's husband's nephew, which obviously makes it difficult for me to evaluate objectively the merits of a merger between a company (AOL) that recently bought the company (Netscape) that makes the Internet browser that competes with the browser of the company that employs me, and a company (Time Warner) that owns a studio (Warner Brothers) that made the movie *Wild Wild West*, which I saw on an airplane and which is unforgivable. What's worse, GE has direct links, via co-ownership of CNBC, the financial news cable channel, with Dow Jones, which publishes the *Wall Street Journal*, whose editorial page is a leading cause of heart attacks among sane people.
>
> But wait. It's not that simple, I'm afraid. CNBC competes directly with CNN/FN, the financial-news cable channel that will be owned by AOL Time Warner. I don't need to spell out the implications of that for you, do I? Well, perhaps I do. Look: this very article you are reading is in a magazine published by a company that owns a cable channel that compete with another cable channel that is half-owned by a company (Dow Jones) that also half-owns a magazine (*Smart Money*) that competes with another magazine (*Money*) owned by the company that publishes this magazine, and half-owned by a company (GE) that also half-owns a cable channel (MSNBC) that is half-owned by the employer of the author of this article, whose CEO (GE's, that is) nevertheless often appears on the cover of the magazine (*Fortune*) that competes with the magazine (*Smart Money*) co-owned by the company that also co-owns CNBC with GE.
> (*Kinsley*, Time, 24 January 2000)

Reading this for the first time can be confusing, but this is what the commercial landscape of the future will increasingly resemble, and organizations, leaders and managers who can't cope with this fast-moving, intangible, chaotic and blurred world will struggle. Even large, traditional commercial organizations that one might assume would be less affected by these changes will have to respond. They have already witnessed the stripping out of layers of management, the reduction of both the physical and the psychological space between 'managers' and 'workers', the emergence of real and virtual team-based management systems, the introduction of groupware and real-time information and knowledge management systems, and increased outsourcing of both peripheral and core functions. The flattening of organizational structures and cultures has been enabled by technology, and the realization that both formal and informal channels of communication between the top and bottom levels of organizations, and with external suppliers, customers and clients, now have to be as short and close as possible. Increasingly, organizations are entering into short-term strategic alliances, sharing research facilities with other businesses and engaging in other forms of cooperation. It is new technologies that have made all of these developments possible, driving a paradigm shift from doing business in 'market spaces' rather than 'marketplaces' (Rayport, 2002).

As we saw earlier, the first wave of exuberant e-commerce and the dream that new dotcom start-up companies could challenge conventional businesses died in April 2000. However, conventional businesses quickly adopted many of the new tools crafted during the first dotcom boom, and implanted these into their traditional business operations, and a second wave of e-commerce businesses has been emerging from the wreckage of the dotcom collapse. These two trends will have a profound effect on the way that organizations do business with each other over the next ten years. For example, the Boston Consulting Group has predicted that company spending on e-commerce systems in Australia alone will have risen from $A17 billion in 2000 to $A135 billion by 2005, with 'at least 22 per cent' of all transactions between companies conducted online (Beilby, 2002: 60). Companies with Internet-based software systems will increasingly outsource non-core functions such as finance, recruitment and selection and payroll, thus allowing them to dedicate more time and resources to their core business functions. All companies will be linked electronically to their suppliers and customers. The research and consulting company, Gartner, believes that many companies will start to use technology to create shared service groups, in which centralized teams provide specialist functional services across many different organizations (ibid.: 61).

New technologies have enabled employees to work for organizations where the work environment can be at the employee's home, in virtual reality or anywhere they happen to be, suggesting that more and more employees will be out of sight, if not out of the minds, of their employers. Managers may no longer have all their employees down the corridor or within the same building, available for unscheduled meetings or briefings. In the recent past, when the office door was closed, business was closed. PDAs and laptops now allow people to conduct work beyond traditional work hours and extend their professional activities to any location and time. Many managers and professionals now have the freedom to work away from the office much of the time, and a clear delineation between work and home is now a thing of the past for some employees. The idea of going to 'the office' may become *passé* for some professionals, with increasing numbers spending their time working at home or in transit. In financial services, advertising and consulting, working away from the office most of the time may well become commonplace (Henderson, 2002a). In the 1990s, some forecasters predicted that 50 per cent of professionals in the USA will be doing this by 2010, marking a return to working patterns that last prevailed in the pre-industrial age (Dyson, 1999). Potentially, this means that you could be a British citizen, live in a ski-chalet in France and run businesses in Australia and Canada.

So how can leaders and managers relate to employees that they may not see for extended periods of time? More than a decade ago Charles Handy argued that *high-tech* has to be balanced by *high-touch* in order to build *high-trust* organizations. He also suggested that the development of trust in virtual organizations would still need active bonding and contact between employees and the leaders of organizations. Trust is important because, if leaders and managers can no longer maintain the levels of control that they have traditionally exercised, they must be able to entrust and empower their employees. This can only be achieved through personal human contact – for now (Handy, 1990). Furthermore, to lessen the possible effects of employee isolation and cyber-stress, organizational leaders need to understand that almost all humans are still genetically hard-wired to be social (Nicholson, 2000; Casison, 1998). It is one of the defining characteristics of human evolution over the last 130 000 years. Research has revealed that camaraderie disappears very quickly when people move into virtual working environments (Berger, 1996). Having a sense of belonging gives meaning to employees and how they fit into their organization. At this moment in time, employees still need physical interaction with each other, and there is growing evidence that cyberworking from home can be deeply stressful for some people (Mitchell, 2002; Sandilands, 1999; Marshall, 1999).

The notion that a desire for human contact remains strong is reinforced by recent research suggesting that teleworking has not reshaped the way we work anything like as much as originally predicted. For example, in

1971, AT&T predicted that all Americans would be working from home by 1990. This has not happened, for several reasons. First, tele-working can be lonely and, as noted above, most humans still need regular face-to-face contact with others. Second, many senior managers have concerns about losing control over workforces they do not phys-ically interact with. Third, it can affect the career progression of employees, because they are not mixing with those who might be making promotion decisions at work. Fourth, it can blur the line between work and non-work, an important buffer to occupational stress (Mitchell, 2002). We saw in earlier chapters that the companies people most want to work for are those that help their employees balance their work and family commitments. One example of a company that was forced to review its policies about homeworking is Iona Technology, a cutting-edge software company with offices in Western Australia and the Irish Republic. This company has a progres-sive and open organizational culture and, from the mid-1980s, had actively encouraged its people to work from home. However, they found that the majority of people still preferred to come in to work for at least part of the week, demonstrating a continuing need for inter-personal communication and social interaction (Rheinlander, 1999). However, as Generation T enters the workforce in larger numbers, the first generation to be raised from early childhood on computers and the Internet, this need for direct face-to-face contact may diminish (Turnbull, 1996).

The extensive use of virtual-communication technologies in organiza-tions may also cause the health of employees to suffer. Levels of cyber-stress do increase amongst employees who make extensive use of computers and virtual technologies. As we saw in Chapter 2, this can have a number of physiological and psychological effects, such as repetitive strain injuries, musculoskeletal problems, tendonitis, eyestrain and blurred vision. 'Cyber-sickness', a variant of motion sick-ness that manifests itself in the form of headaches, double vision, increased heart rates, dizziness, vertigo, disorientation and even vomiting, is also becoming more of a problem for employees. There is also the potential for people to turn their backs on the real world and become contented zombies, roaming synthetic artificial worlds. There are clear indications that this is already happening. Cyber-slacking and cyber-abuse are estimated to cost the US economy at least $US10 billion a year. Surfwatch, a company that provides web-use monitoring systems to employers, estimates that American employees spend about one-third of their work time on the web pursuing 'personal interests' – anything from trading on the stock market, gambling and shopping, and accessing pornography. In 1999, Rank-Xerox sacked 40 employees for wasting up to eight hours a day downloading 'adult' sites, at a rate of use that once froze the company's whole computer network (cited by Macken, 1999). In 2002, it was revealed that one-quarter of all sackings in UK companies resulted from employees surfing the Internet without permission, and nearly 70 per cent of these were for accessing pornographic websites (AFP, 2002b).

The uptake and spread of new technologies at work is irreversible. However, hardly any researchers have started to get to grips with what their impact on organizational leadership and people management is likely to be over the next two decades. Nevertheless, we can begin to see the emergence of a new paradigm of leadership and people management that will be able, conceptually and practically, to get to grips with the effects of these new technologies on employees and organizations. This has profound implications for traditional approaches to leadership and people management in organizations which are still heavily influenced by a second wave mode of thinking. This is itself still reliant on a way of thinking that has changed little in its fundamental assumptions since the 1950s, and is desperately trying to play catch-up with all the profound changes that are now occurring in organizations.

Despite all the hype about virtual organizations, it is important to emphasize that successful people management, even in high-tech and virtual organizations, will continue to be based on many leadership practices that have stood the test of time, although there will inevitably be a greater emphasis on self-management, self-organization and empowerment among employees who work in these kinds of organizations. So, while the context in which leadership takes place will continue to evolve, many of the basic principles of people management remain the same as they have been, and this will continue for some time yet. This is because leadership is fundamentally about showing people a road, way or path to travel down and, in fast-changing and uncertain times, this capability becomes even more important and highly valued. Having said this, there is also little doubt that new technologies will not only continue to accelerate the pace of change in organizations, but they will also start to do more 'thinking' and 'managing' for us in the very near future.

With these thoughts in mind, here are a few tips for helping your organization and its employees get the most out of current and emergent technologies. First, human beings are essentially highly evolved apes, with a lot of high-tech tools at their disposal. Almost all humans are genetically hard-wired to be social and to interact with others face-to-face. Hence they still need a combination of high-tech and high-touch leadership/management, if they are to retain a sense of identity with the organizations that employ them, and it is still extremely difficult to get team collaboration going in virtual environments. For the foreseeable future, employees will still need physical interaction with each other, and all organizational leaders need to ensure that they have opportunities to do this, even in high-tech or virtual organizations.

Second, the dotcom collapse of April 2000 showed us that technology alone cannot create a successful business. Any new enterprise must have a clear vision, a great business plan, and a well thought-out commercial strategy, *before* thinking about its technology requirements. For the moment, the Internet, e-commerce and virtual reality are just evolutionary add-ons and portals to the way that business has been done for decades. When all the hyperbole over the Web and the Internet is taken away, we can see that their primary job is to assist in the delivery of the right product/service/content to customers at the right price and in good time – nothing more or less. All current Web/Internet technologies are essentially passive, and it still requires creative and innovative employees to make the best use of these. Companies that derive the most benefit from new technologies understand this important principle, and do not rely on technology to solve basic business problems. As Jim Collins has observed, 'Good-to-great companies *think* differently about technology. They never use technology as the primary means of igniting a transformation. Yet, paradoxically, they are pioneers in the application of *carefully selected* technologies. We learnt that technology by itself is never a primary root cause of either greatness or decline' (Collins, 2001: 14).

Third, don't believe the hype. Critically evaluate if you need the latest technological gizmo. Will it really bring added value to your business or organization? For example, one survey revealed that more than 500 million PCs used by organizations around the world in June 2002 had less then one-third of the computing power available in the most up-to-date models available at that time. During 2000–2003, many organizations took strategic decisions not to upgrade their PC systems, until it was clear that there would be productivity advantages to be gained by doing this. For the first time since 1985, sales of PCs fell by 4 per cent (compared to an average increase of 15 per cent a year from 1985 to 2000). World-wide, many companies expressed scepticism about the purported productivity gains that could be gained from upgrading their computer systems (cited by Gottliebsen, 2002b). In this context, it's worth remembering the old adage, 'Buy in haste – repent at leisure'.

Fourth, use only those technologies that enhance your core competencies and businesses. If non-core functions can be outsourced more cheaply and effectively, then use that option. This has the added benefit of allowing you to focus on bringing emergent technologies into a smaller number of core operational and/or business and/or service areas. According to Gartner, business process outsourcing is expected to grow at an average rate of 12.3 per cent a year up to 2010, faster than overall IT outsourcing, as more companies seek ongoing cost reductions, while focusing their energies on developing their core businesses and their ability to cope with fast-changing market conditions (*The Australian* Special Edition on Outsourcing, 2002: 2). Having said this, it's important to note that the business landscape of the USA, Europe and Australasia is littered with failed private and public sector 'whole-of-organization' IT outsourcing deals, characterized by huge cost overruns and systems that have routinely failed to live up to suppliers' hyperbole.

Fifth, many businesses remained locked in inappropriate and expensive contracts during the 1990s and early 2000s and, because they had sacked their own IT people in the name of cost savings in the mid-to-late 1990s, lost the capability of taking back control of their IT operations. The market for new large-scale outsourcing projects ground to a halt in early 2002, and the trend today is towards servicing IT needs, not through a single source, but via multiple partners (also known as 'selective sourcing'). Through this, organizations can choose which parts of their knowledge and information infrastructures to outsource and which core IT assets to keep in-house, based on careful assessments of their current business requirements. Many big outsourcing services, such as those offered by EDS, IBM and HP, now offer a much broader range of individual services in specific areas such as desktop management, knowledge management software, network support, mid-range management, application maintenance and mainframe management (Riley, 2003).

Sixth, the second wave of e-commerce is rapidly becoming the universal and essential method of reaching customers and clients, either through direct relationships or through third-party transactions. If your company has still not embraced the Internet, its competitiveness in the future will suffer and it will be seriously disadvantaged in your market. Furthermore, global virtual networking requires a holistic overview of all business processes in organizations, not just an ad hoc or patchwork approach. In turn, this must be driven by the organization's vision, goals, strategy and culture, *never* the other way round. All electronic communication systems must be imbedded within knowledge management systems that encourage employees to make effective use of these (as described in Chapter 10).

Time is not on our side. Technology, in both its hard and soft forms, has already brought unparalleled flexibility to the workplace, and will continue to change the way that employees work and increase their productivity levels. While the IT sector was in a slump during 2001–3, there were indications that it will have bounced back from this by 2005. This means that all business leaders must remain techno-savvy and up-to-date with developments in emergent technologies and, of equal importance, need to keep one eye on what *may* be coming onto the market two or three years ahead. Last, be prepared for the arrival of even more radical technologies that will not only continue to revolutionize our professions and organizations, but which may well shape the next stage of human evolution in our grandchildren's lifetimes. These are described in the next section.

> The companies that spend the most on technology are not winning. The companies that are spending smartest on technology are. There has been a lot of technology investment that has been squandered, ad hoc and random, and has not delivered results. [However], companies across the world that are faster at what they do are typically more successful. They are gaining market share, they are more profitable and they are growing faster. We are talking fast not just in technology, but also in management decisions, how fast you hire people and how fast you can train people. You really need to drive these changes through business, and this is the catalyst for getting the most out of technology.
> (*Bob Hayward, Senior Vice-President of the Gartner Group (Asia-Pacific and Japan), in a talk delivered at* The Need for Speed: Driving the Real Time Enterprise Conference, *Sydney, 12 November; abridged from Foreshew, 2002*)

The future: the potential impact of emergent technologies on humanity during the 21st century

> Forecasting is very difficult, especially if it's about the future.
> He who lives by the crystal ball soon learns to eat ground glass.
> (*Edgar Fiedler, 1993*)

> The further backward you look, the further forward you can see.
> (*Winston Churchill, 1945*)

> I never think about the future. It comes soon enough.
> (*Albert Einstein, 1940*)

While we may all be unsure about the immediate future, our predecessors at the dawn of the 20th century also encountered what, to them, was an equally strange, uncertain and fast-changing new world, with the arrival of the telephone, electricity, the telegraph, flying machines, modern vaccines, the automobile, the radio and many other new inventions and innovations. Then, as now, they were also curious about what the world would look like in the future. In 1899, a group of Victorian futurologists gathered to speculate about what life would be like in 2000. They got a few things right, but they were way off the mark with many of their predictions. They thought that there would be flying cars, armies of robots to take care of all our needs, time travel and tele-portation. They also believed that work would become obsolete and aging a thing of the past. They predicted that there would be a boom in the popularity of leisure activities, such as air-tennis and underwater fish racing. They failed to foresee the arrival of X-rays, radar, television, nuclear energy, transistors, lasers and computers. In 1902, even the visionary science fiction writer H.G. Wells was mistaken in predicting that heavier-than-air flying machines would be possible 'in about 1950' and that submarines would never be able to do more than suffocate their crews. A few commentators of the time did get things right. For exam-ple, John Maynard Keynes, perhaps anticipating the globalization of consumer markets, made these comments in 1900, 'The inhabitant of London could order by telephone, sipping his morning tea in bed, the various products of the whole earth and by the same means adventure his wealth in the natural resources and new enterprises of any quarter of the world without exertion or even trouble' (Margolis, 2001: 118).

What about these earlier predictions from Joseph Glanvill, a philoso-pher–theologian and chaplain to Charles II, in the 17th century? 'To them that come after us it may be as ordinary to put on a pair of wings to fly to the remotest regions, as now a pair of boots to ride a journey; and to confer at the distance of the Indies by sympathetic conveyances, may be as usual in the future as literary correspondence. It may be that in ages hence, a voyage to the Southern tracts, yea possibly to the moon, will not be more strange than to America. The restoration of grey hairs to juvenility and the renewing of exhausted marrow may at length be elicited without a miracle' (Margolis, 2001: 47). Perhaps the most prescient of all the futurecasters of the late 19th century was John Elfreth Watkins, writing in the *Ladies Home Journal* of 1900. Having consulted the most learned experts of the day he predicted, amongst other things, the arrival of international telephone services, colour photography, frozen dinners, school gyms, snowmobiles, the tapping of energy from the wind, the sun and ocean waves, and medicine applied through skin patches (Margolis, 2001). More recently, Gordon Moore (the creator of 'Moore's Law') predicted that 'integrated circuits will lead to such wonders as home computers, automatic controls for automobiles, and personal portable communications equipment'. He made these predictions in 1965 (cited by Schlender, 2002: 55).

While predicting the future can be an unreliable business, there are two assertions that can be made with confidence. First, as noted earlier, the pace of technological innovation is speeding up year-by-year. Second, the impact of emergent technologies in the next 100 years will far exceed *anything* that the human race has experienced up to this point in time. For example, you may have seen the 1997 sci-fi movie, *Gattaca*.[6] In this, the principal character, played by Ethan Hawke, is condemned to live his life as one of a genetic under-caste of 'invalids'. Born into a society where genetic engineering is the norm, and physical appearance, intelligence and personality can all be genetically enhanced before birth, he finds himself playing an increasingly dangerous game of deception, in order to avoid detection by the police as he pursues his dream of becoming an astronaut. To achieve this, he is forced to use the skin, blood, hair cells and urine of a 'valid', crippled in an accident. While the story has a happy ending, *Gattaca* symbolizes the unease that some people feel about the wild roller-coaster pace of biotechnological evolution we have now embarked upon (as have other sci-fi films such as *I, Robot, Minority Report*, the *Matrix* series and *AI: Artificial Intelligence*). In a similar vein, Mathew Reilly's fourth best-seller, *Area 7*, featured a plot that revolved around the defeat of a renegade general who had gained control of a genetically engineered virus that could be used to eliminate specific racial groups. It is now possible to create such a virus. And, in 2002, Michael Crichton's blockbuster, *Prey*, featured the nightmare scenario of swarms of artificial nano-organisms escaping from an isolated laboratory, evolving uncontrollably by the minute and turning themselves into replicas of their creators. Those humans they didn't use they consumed as food. In the introduction to the book, Crichton suggests that, unless we establish strict controls over these technologies, this could happen some time during the 21st century (Crichton, 2002).

The most surprising fact about the futuristic communication technologies unveiled in *Minority Report* (set in 2054) is that not one was the creation of Steven Spielberg's creative mind. All were extrapolations from technological developments under way in research laboratories around the world. Researchers are already working on augmented reality systems, where computer images can be portrayed on transparent wrap-around glass, where data and objects can be 'moved' by hand. They are working on computers that can understand and translate speech, smell odours and taste substances, feel textures, interpret human gestures, sense human emotions and, maybe, even understand our thoughts. For example, haptic (touch) technologies are being routinely built into new cars. Instead of a steering wheel and a dashboard covered with dials and switches, the 2003 BMW Seven Series prototype featured a universal controller in the form of a joystick and all commands are voice activated (for example, 'Fan on cool'; 'Windscreen wiper on slow'; 'Left indicator on').

The scenario presented in *Gattaca* too may well become a scientific reality in the near future. The human genome has been mapped, not only the 130 000 genes that make up a human being but the sequences of their constituent parts. Significantly, it was originally anticipated in the early 1980s that it would take until 2050 before this was achieved. This was revised to 2010 in 1999, and then to 2005 in 2000. This came to pass *50 years* ahead of schedule. What began with the 'discovery' of DNA by Crick and Watson in the 1950s, the first successful in-vitro fertilization two decades later and the cloning of Dolly the sheep in 1997 is now speeding along a seemingly unstoppable path to pre-conception implantation, genetic screening, the manipulation of human embryos and, possibly, to full-scale human cloning (Stock, 2002). As a result of this, we may be able to slow down and maybe even halt aging, manipulate intelligence, personality attributes, height, physical appearance, musical and creative abilities, and even create 'designer children'.

It is quite possible that future employment may depend on the willingness of employees to undergo 'enhancements' that will increase their brains' processing speed or their memory capacities (Stock, 2002; Kurzweil, 1999). Companies in the USA have been making promotion, hiring and firing decisions on the basis of appearance, fitness, health and personal lifestyles for nearly a decade. This selection process may extend even further in the not too distant future. If genetic information is not protected, employers could use this to make hiring, firing and promotion decisions. Insurers may discriminate against people, or refuse insurance policies, on the basis of their genetic profiles. Former US President Bill Clinton had to pass a five-year executive order in February 2000 to prevent US government agencies from using genetic information in hiring and promotion decisions for its 2.8 million employees nationwide (cited in *The Weekend Australian*, 12–13 February 2002). From July 2001, the US Copyright Agency began to offer a DNA Protection Service to high-flyers and celebrities, because any body part could potentially be used to clone a human being, even a single hair.

However, there have been some early setbacks in bioengineering. It was announced on 29 April 2002 that all of the world's cloned animals were suffering from genetic and physical defects, indicating that cloned humans could also be vulnerable to genetic defects. The first sheep cloned in Australia in April 2000, Matilda, died prematurely in early February 2003 and Dolly, the most famous of these cloned animals, developed advanced arthritis at five years of age, and was put down on 14 February 2003. While human cloning was banned in most industrialized countries during 2001–2, many scientists working in this field believe that biotechnology is a juggernaut that neither governments nor religious authorities will be able to halt. For example, if you could make use of a safe technology to enhance your children's physical prowess, intelligence, height, appearance, well-being and happiness, and ensure that they had long, productive and healthy lives, would you use it? Put this way, many of the ethical reservations that people have about genetic engineering may be trampled underfoot in the stampede to access these technologies.

The increasing and enthusiastic uptake of injections to remove wrinkles, the growing popularity of cosmetic surgery, and the use of mood-enhancing drugs such as Prozac and Ritalin, all indicate that we will embrace rather than reject the promises of genetic engineering. However, a technology that has the possibility to reshape what we are as human beings also has potentially malign consequences that we cannot even start to imagine. And hanging over these debates is the ugly spectre of eugenics in the past, taken to nightmare heights by the Nazis during World War II. These fears were heightened when it was announced on 28 November 2002 that the first cloned human was going to be born in January 2003 (created by the maverick Italian embryologist, Severino Antinori). As events transpired, Antinori was 'beaten' by the religious cult, Clonaid, who claimed that they had produced the first cloned human, a girl named Eve, on 26 December 2002. While neither of these claims was ever verified, it was confirmed that Korean scientists had cloned human embryos for the first time on 14 February 2004 (Dayton, 2004; Hickman and Karvelas, 2002).

As well as biotechnologies, at least 12 American companies, including Johnson & Johnson, Pfizer, Merck and Glaxo-SmithKline, were all in the final stages of developing memory-enhancing drugs in 2003, meaning that memory loss could become a thing of the past in the near future. Dubbed 'viagra for the brain', these are designed to slow down or even halt memory loss in middle-aged and elderly people. By identifying memory genes, it is now possible to target and strengthen specific neural connections, thereby enhancing their longevity and reducing memory loss. With the rapid aging of the elderly populations of all industrial nations during the first half of the 21st century, the companies that can develop these drugs stand to make billions. In the USA alone, there are more than 76 million people who complain of forgetfulness. At the time experts also predicted that designer drugs could be developed to enhance good memories and block out bad ones, reminiscent of the mood-altering drug 'soma' in Aldous Huxley's visionary 1930s sci-fi novel *Brave New World* (Winnett, 2002).

In addition to these developments, we are now on the threshold of developing even more powerful computing technologies, which may lead to the creation of the first artificial intelligent entities ('artilects').

Bob Clark, Professor of Experimental Physics at the University of New South Wales (Australia), has predicted that the world's first quantum computer could be up and running by the end of this decade. A quantum computer will be 100 million times faster at processing information than the most powerful of the current generation of supercomputers. These developments will enable second-generation self-learning entities to be created within ten years, as they begin to match the processing power of the 23 billion neurons in the human brain. In the future, people will be able to delegate more mundane tasks to these intelligent machines, which will be able to use their 'initiative', offer suggestions and make decisions. These will also be capable of interpreting and responding to human emotions. Emotionally intelligent computers have been in development at MIT's Media Lab and by the Siemens Human–Machine Research Group since the late 1990s. The MIT Media Lab has already been successful in creating a machine that can sense human emotions (Kurzweil, 1999; *The Sunday Times*, UK, website, 24 November 1998).

Computers will evolve to an even higher level of complexity and sophistication, as the age-old distinction between technological and biological systems starts to disappear, and both start to operate in tandem at the molecular level. A second-generation artilect, the cellular automata machine (CAM) with circuitry based on ten billion neurons, may be built by 2007. A third generation CAM with a trillion neurons could take only a few more years to construct. A brain-building machine constructed by Genobyte in the USA has been making the world's first neural circuits for an artificial brain since 2001. This machine can imbed thousands of microscopic modules of artificial neurons on silicon chips. These are the electronic equivalent of the neural networks that control our brains and body functions. In a Darwinian-like process, the bad ones are discarded but the efficient ones thrive and are linked to other promising modules. This occurs at astonishing speeds, far faster than random biological evolution, with tens of thousands of circuits growing and dying in less than a second. Scientists at Cornell University and Harvard University in the USA have also created the first transistor made from a single atom. In theory, this means that a computer could be built that would fit on the full stop at the end of this sentence (Henderson, 2002b; Devine, 2000).

'Knowbots' are being developed. These too are self-learning entities, whose processing systems are based on biological neural networks linked to quantum computing systems that are based on chips cooled to −269°C (or 4 degrees above absolute zero). This will enable these entities to store information on single atoms. In 1998, it was announced in the UK that British scientists had taken the first real steps towards creating an artificial nervous system that will lead to self-reliant, thinking robots. These are being built around electronic neural processors, built of sodium and potassium ion channels, similar to the human brain. We also have a new generation of 'neuromorphic engineers' who are now replicating brain structures on analog-based (that is, self-learning) systems. On 2 February 1999, Dr Craig Ventner at the University of Pennsylvania in the USA announced the advent of the first truly artificial organism. This was soon followed by an announcement on 24 January 2000 that scientists at the University of Texas had made the world's first synthetic DNA. This means that the world's first artificial life forms may be created soon and, eventually, may lead to the emergence of 'Chromo Sapiens' (see below).

The next stage of development is to further miniaturize computer hardware through the use of nanotechnologies (machines built of individual atoms) which, until very recently, were considered be in the realm of science fiction. Anything with dimensions of less than 100 nanometres (that is, as small as a flu virus and 1000 times smaller than the width of a human hair) is considered to be nanotechnology (Takahashi, 2002). Under the umbrella of the US National Nanotechnology Initiative, more than 200 US companies are currently involved in nanotechnology research. In the second half of 2003, Intel started manufacturing chips with transistors just 90 nanometres (or 90 billionths of a metre) in width. Combined with new materials, such as silicon geranium, this will lead to the development of nanospheres, nanowires, nanorods and other nanostructures. These will make possible the creation of precise atomic arrangements for smaller, faster and smarter semiconductors and computers, and many other electronic devices. In the future, molecular sized nano-machines may even be programmed to make machines out of atoms to create micro-electronic mechanical structures (MEMS). The potential uses of MEMS are infinite (Kurzweil, 1999).

Another innovative field of research and development, bionimetics, has emerged which mimics natural animal and plant systems at the molecular level, resulting in the creation of novel advanced structures, materials and nano-devices. Nano-sized materials are being developed for application in polymers, pharmaceuticals, drug-delivery systems, cosmetics, sunscreens, paint, inks and textiles (reported in *The Australian*, IT Section, 1 October 2002). With the aid of a $US50 million grant from the US Army, the Institute for Soldier Nanotechnologies (ISN) at the Massachusetts Institute of Technology has been developing smart uniforms genetically engineered at the molecular level. These combine new materials, such as MIThril (a wordplay on the magical armour used by Frodo Baggins in *The Lord of the Rings*) to protect soldiers from bullets or biological and chemical agents, and administer emergency medical care. Dupont has been working on combat uniforms that will be able to change colours on demand as the environment changes (Gengler, 2003).

Cybernetics has also emerged as another new frontier of technology, representing the merging of mechanical and biological systems. One of the first technologies that fused microprocessors with humans was the Cochlear implant, first developed in 1985 (Clarke, 1999): 500 000 patients in 50 countries now use this bionic ear, a device that is hard-wired directly into the central nervous system. In the near future, it will be integrated directly into the brain. After 12 years of development and a successful four-year trial of the world's first artificial cornea, tens of thousands of blind people can now have their sight restored. The synthetic cornea is made of a special combination of new plastics that have proved to be comfortable and long-lasting, and allow surrounding tissue to grow onto the lens, thus overcoming the old problem of rejection (Hickman, 2002). The development of improved nano-processor implants could enable the development of expanded memory, increased thought speed or even the bypassing of external sensory organs. In other words, the direct 'wet-wiring' of the human brain is now theoretically possible; it is no longer science fiction. In one of those 'stranger than fiction' true-life stories, the cyber-performance artist, Stelarc, once asked British surgeons to operate on him to provide him with a third ear that could act as an Internet antenna. An 'extra' ear was to have been grown using his skin cells and this would then be implanted onto his body, just behind one of his real ears. Once established it could have then been wired up to detect sound waves transmitted over the Internet, and via implants to his brain, allow Stelarc to hear them (Lynch, 1999).

Kevin Warwick, Professor of Cybernetics at Reading University, was the first human being to have a chip implanted in his body, in 1998. Since 2000, he has been using a second-generation chip that was implanted directly into his nervous system, allowing direct two-way communication with his computer. In March 2002, he and his wife both had microchips implanted in their spines in order to record their emotions on a computer, and then relay these back to the Warwicks. The goal of this experiment is to develop true human–computer interactions via electronic 'telepathy', with a long-term objective being direct mind-to-mind interactions between humans, computers and robots. Through these biotechnologies humans will acquire a cyborg-like quality, as personal communication devices become directly integrated into our bodies. Soon it may be possible to download information directly into the human brain from computers and vice versa. The wet-wiring of soldiers linked to locating satellites and strategic military centres may be achieved by the end of this decade (Warwick, 1998, 2002).

Stephen Hawking, regarded by many commentators as the world's greatest living physicist, has commented,

> There is a danger that computers will take over the world. Computer power is advancing so fast that it will soon render irrelevant those few advantages that humans imagine they alone possess – emotions, intuition, morality, empathy and social skills. Even these nebulous qualities are now being taught to robots. If very complicated chemical modules can operate in humans to make them intelligent, then equally intelligent complicated electronic circuits can also make computers act in an intelligent way [ ] we need to develop, as quickly as possible, technologies that enable a direct connection between brain and computer, so that artificial brains contribute to human intelligence rather than opposing it.
> (*Cited by Paul, 2000*)

And, according to Andy Clark, Professor of Philosophy and Cognitive Science at the UK's University of Sussex, 'We shall be cyborgs, not in the merely superficial sense of combining flesh and wires, but in the more profound sense of being human-technology symbionts, with our minds and selves spread across biological brains and non-biological circuitry' (cited by Paul, 2000; Romei, 2001). The gates have been unlocked and there will be a traumatic struggle over these new technologies in the near future, between the world's economic elites, who stand to gain great wealth and power from these, and 'techno-luddites' who will oppose their introduction.

On a lighter note, the impact of new technologies on one of humanity's oldest preoccupations is highlighted in four recent examples.

False promises

> In the US late last month, a Silicon Valley Computer programmer was arrested for threatening a company he believed was crippling his business with penis augmentation propaganda. Charles Booher threatened to send a package of anthrax spores to the company, to disable an employee with a bullet and torture him with a power drill and an ice pick; and to hunt down and castrate employees unless they removed him from their email list. The object of Booher's ire – the advertisers for a product called, 'The Only Reliable, Medically Approved Penis Enhancement' – blamed a rival firm, which they said was giving the penis enhancement business, 'a bad name'. Now there's a tough assignment.
> (*Emma Tom*, The Australian, *12 December 2003*)

Men not required

> A world's first Internet site, designed to help lesbian couples discreetly find suitable sperm, will be launched at the weekend. The www. mannotincluded.com website promises to offer a completely anonymous service for lesbian couples hoping to become parents. Hopeful parents can

look through the Man Not Included database and compile a shortlist of three donors. Man Not Included plans to expand to other countries so lesbian couples outside Britain can access the service.
(*Tobler, 2002*)

XXX

Someone who has spent a lot of time thinking about technologies and sex is Eric White, designer of a virtual sex machine now available from a US-based online company called *VR Innovations*. Billed as the world's first 'adult gratification peripheral', the device is connected to the penis at one end and a PC at the other. The user downloads video footage of women performing sex acts, which he feels via a 'teledildonic technology'. The device costs $US369.99 (plus shipping). 'Professional entertainers and amateurs alike will be able to sexually communicate with their fans,' White enthuses.
(*Abridged from Romei, 2001*)

Cyber-sex

By 2029 technology will have permanently changed the nature of sex. Virtual sex will be preferable to real sex, because it will provide sensations that are more intense and pleasurable than conventional sex. It is the ulti-mate safe sex, as there is no risk of pregnancy or disease. We will have sex and relationships with machines and these machines will have a full range of human emotions including sadness, empathy and jealousy.
(*Abridged from Stewart, 1999*)

New technologies are fast becoming intrinsic components of our daily lives and rapidly infiltrating the organizations we work for and the homes we live in. They will become increasingly organic, as they become – literally – part of us, rather than something 'out there', as they have been throughout human history. They will become part of the furniture, the walls, the urban fabric, the clothes we wear and even our bodies. Intelligent networks will link all facets of our lives. Computers and knowbots will take over more routine administrative, design and manufacturing processes in organizations. Commentators on this technological revolution, such as Ray Kurzweil and Dennis Warwick, predict that emergent technologies will also shatter the boundary between humans and machines. It is now quite possible that these technologies will eventually become indistinguishable from us and, at some time in the not too distant future, intelligent artilects may even supersede human beings as the dominant life form on this planet. Kurzweil believes that the next stage of evolution on the Earth will be the transition from carbon-based circuitry to new life forms based on mechanical–electronic–carbon circuitry. That magical thing we call 'consciousness' might be combined with these super-artilects, and allow us to retain our position as the dominant species on the planet (Kurzweil, 1999).

One step towards this goal was announced on 3 March 2003, when Francis Crick published research that claimed to have identified the location of the human soul and the cluster of neurons where human consciousness and an individual's sense of self reside (Leake, 2003). Rob Brooks, the Director of the Brooks Artificial Intelligence Laboratory at MIT, commenting on the blurring of human/artilect boundaries, observed, 'In just twenty years, the boundary between reality and fantasy will be rent asunder. Just five years from now that boundary will be breached in ways that are unimaginable to most people today, as the daily use of the World Wide Web would have been ten years ago' (cited by Romei, 2001). Even hard-headed organizations, such as the International Bar Association (IBA), have begun to consider the legal issues raised by these developments. At the IBA Conference in San Fancisco during September 2003, a group of lawyers held a mock trial to evaluate a motion from a conscious computer, who had filed an injunction to prevent its creator from disconnecting it (Kurzweil, 2003). The computer lost – this time.

While Ray Kurzweil has often described his predictions as 'conservative', some commentators have been critical of his projections for the future. However, it is significant that every prediction he made in his first book, *The Age of Intelligent Machines* (1989), came to pass in the 1990s (for example, that a computer would beat a chess Grand Master). Even if he is only half right, the revolution that he and many others predict is upon us, and is likely to form the battleground for many of the great ethical and political debates of the first two or three decades of this century. There will be a traumatic struggle over the use of genetic and other technologies, and fierce conflicts between those who want to push on with these and those who want to stop their progress. However, at some point in the not-too-distant future, if these technological advances continue, human beings may be eclipsed by these artilects. In the words of one leading researcher in this area, 'this century's dominant question will be, "Should human beings construct artilects or not?" There will be two violently opposed responses: those for whom constructing artilects represents human destiny, and another group who fear that artilects will decide one day that the human race is a pest to be destroyed' (Hugo de Garis, Head of Starlab, a deep future research centre in Brussels, abridged from Paul, 2000 and Devine, 2000).

With these sobering thoughts in mind, and assuming we don't destroy our planet and ourselves in the meantime, here are some predictions for this century and beyond:

2005:   PCs are rapidly evolving into tiny devices that combine high-capacity computing, Internet and web access capabilities with real-time wireless video communication. Digital ink and real-time pen-enabled applications are commonplace. Real-time and reliable universal language translators are becoming commonplace. Traditional web and grid computing services are fast evolving into autonomic systems, built on hardware and software that can automatically fix problems such as viruses and bugs, and solve conflicts between different software formats. Originally marketed by IBM in 2003 as 'e-business on demand', these systems allow users to simply turn on the computing power they require only when they need it, the idea being that users only pay for what they use at any given moment in time. This also means that organizations do not have to waste time and money on expensive servers or network capacity that never gets used.

2007:   all new top-of-the-range automobiles are being equipped with inclusive telematic and haptic operating systems. These include dashboard computing, hands-free/voice-activated voice and email systems, anti-collision radars, thermal-imaging systems to improve visibility in bad weather, on-board detection systems that warn of faults and other devices, all combined into systemic, quasi-intelligent operating systems. For navigation, automatic satellite-based global positioning systems are becoming more standard features. The kids are safely occupied in the back seat with their own in-car entertainment systems where they can choose from a range of interactive virtual programmes.

2010:   the 20-year reign of the personal computer comes to an end, having evolved into single personalized assistants (PAs) that combine voice-activated video-telephone facilities, fax, email and access to a smorgasbord of on-line Internet facilities, websites, information data bases and software programs. Active contact lenses and ultralight head microphones, linked to the Internet, now allow people to read email, surf the web, download music and films and make video calls from anywhere to anywhere on the globe. Our PAs know our personal preferences and daily schedules, and alert us to meetings and other 'things to do'. They can liaise directly with the PAs of colleagues and clients to arrange or reschedule meetings. They know their owners' voices and handprints and, if they are stolen, can inform the police where they are being 'held' via their global satellite connections. By now, Psion and Palm Pilot organizers and Qualcomm and Nokia Personal Digital Assistants can be found only in museums.

Old-style manual keyboards have almost disappeared, having been replaced by voice-activated software or virtual light boards. Tiny light chips embedded inside PAs or cell phones beam an image of a keyboard onto any hard, flat surface, allowing the user to 'type' on this. Sophisticated scanning software detects the subtle movements of the user's fingers and converts these into letters. Screen technology has also been revolutionized and computer screens have disappeared, with the advent of heat-free organic electroluminescence, making it possible to project images onto any ambient surface. A bedroom ceiling, paper or even clothes can be used to transmit moving images from PAs. Life-like, real-time holographic images can be projected from PAs and video-telephones, through augmented-reality systems, consigning video-conferencing technologies to the scrapheap. Digital chopsticks, first introduced by Sony in 2006, allow users to pluck a file directly from a computer or wallboard display and deposit it onto another screen, say on a TV at home or on the increasingly popular *heliodisplays*, devices that are able to project images into thin air by modifying the structure of the air molecules above a projector.

2013: beams of sound can be transmitted with the accuracy of a laser beam, singling out specific individuals for private messages that no one else can hear. This will enable sports coaches to communicate directly with their players on the field and enable secure communications on battlefields.

2015: all clothing and footwear is now manufactured from smart fabrics, intelligent polymers and electronically conducive artificial yarns, consigning natural materials like wool and cotton to history. These warm up when it is cold and cool down when it is hot. They can change colour on demand and, when instructed, can reflect the wearer's emotional state – something that is becoming more popular in courtship rituals. Phonebands have been integrated into clothing for more than a decade and people listen to incoming calls simply by inserting their fingertips into their ears and speaking into collar-mounted microphones. Computing and communications devices are also woven into these fabrics, enabling the wearer to download performance information directly onto these. Sportspeople wear clothing that can repair injuries and can warn athletes about movements that could result in injuries. The world's first commercially available warming–cooling/MP3 player/wireless mobile phone combination jackets featured in O'Neil's snowboarding clothing collection during 2004–5 are now fetching thousands of dollars in antique technology auctions.

All soldiers now wear smart combat suits that are linked to satellite and ground communication systems. These can also repair and clean themselves, are fully waterproof and temperature sensitive, and can alter camouflage patterns according to the terrain and available cover. These outfits can also monitor heart rates, keep soldiers nourished and, if injured, can deliver life-saving drugs while their condition is automatically relayed to medical rescue teams and HQ. The cute beagles that had been used for many years to detect drugs and other illegal imports at airports have been largely replaced by sniffer-bots.

2020: the genetic causes of all human diseases have been identified, and advances in genetically modified foods now promise to end human malnutrition and starvation.

2023: the first generation of smart domestic robots has emerged, carrying out simple tasks such as washing up, vacuuming and, via their links with remote sensors on doors and windows and surveillance cameras, acting as household watchdogs. Psychologists and psychiatrists report a rapid increase in the number of adults and children reporting that they are forming emotional attachments to these robots.

2025: intelligent houses with Home Information Systems (HIS) have become widespread in industrialized countries. Shortly before waking up in the morning, motion detectors have switched the house's lighting and heating on, the coffee is brewing and the toast ready when you have stepped out of your shower. You watch morning TV that automatically features the weather and snow reports, because you work in a ski resort. It is linked up in real time to the world's stock markets, lets you know the value of your stocks and shares, and also makes some suggestions for changing your stock portfolio. After breakfast, you get into your eco-friendly transmodule ('automobile' or 'car' in oldspeak), which automatically adjusts the seat, mirrors and heating to your personal requirements. It reminds you that an annual system service is due at the end of the week. In some cities, you may drive along hands-free smartways, guided by a network of satellite-linked computers and road sensors. Anti-collision radar and automatic brakes protect you, while you prepare for your 8.00 meeting or just relax and watch an interactive video.

When you arrive home in the evening, a facial recognition camera recognizes you and opens the front door. The house lights and heating came on automatically just before you arrived. Your HIS enables you to check your family members' daily schedules and when they will be home. This system can also pay your household bills automatically as they come in from your on-line bank or utilities. Your microwave vocally suggests a recipe for your evening meal, based on its reading of the bar codes on the food contents in your intelligent fridge ('food' now comes under the generic heading of 'neutraceuticals', which combine genetically enhanced organic foods with nano-drugs). From this you can also identify your shopping needs and automatically send your orders to a virtual supermarket for home delivery. Many homes are now 'eco-friendly', with sophisticated recycling systems and improved building insulation, with heat and energy drawn from solar panels and recycled household waste. These are known as HERS (Home Environmental Regulation Systems).

2035: genetic manipulation of human sperm, eggs and embryos becomes widespread. Parents are now able to make decisions about their children's appearance, height, IQ and emotional intelligence before they are conceived. Proposals are put forward to create groups of headless personal clones to 'harvest' for body parts in case of illness. A heated ethical debate rages over this issue.

2040: smart construction materials with electronic nanosensors built into their molecular structures become integrated into buildings, regulating warmth and air flows and warning against structural problems. Billions of nanochips are embedded in everyday objects: cars, clothes, shoes, furniture and walls. Smart sensors and voice activation have largely replaced switches and buttons on many devices.

2045: the world's first operational quantum bio-computer goes on-line with processing capabilities that far exceed the human brain. This represents a huge leap in computing power and the genesis of the world's first artilects.

2050: human beings and artilects are now connected (wet-wired) directly, allowing vast amounts of information to be directly downloaded into the human brain, without the need for years of teaching and rote learning during childhood. Humans can now issue commands to computers by thought alone, and vice versa, via inaudible ultrasound waves. Artilects can now understand and respond to human emotions.

2055: a second generation of intelligent robopets and robodoms (domestic robots) emerges. They carry out all domestic jobs in households – cooking, cleaning, ordering shopping, gardening, baby-sitting duties – and can teach children via their wet-wired implants. They are now being used routinely in mundane, repetitive or dangerous jobs. Artilects' rights activists call for new laws to protect these robots.

2060: the first space mission lands on Mars, with a crew of artilects. Others soon follow. These start accessing large quantities of frozen water, first identified by unmanned probes 60 years earlier, for power and to create oxygen reservoirs. Using nanobots, they start building the habitats that the first wave of human settlers will live in. In 2063, the discovery of primitive life forms below the surface leads to calls to terraform the planet for human colonization, to help cope with over-population and ecological pressures on the earth's environment. After ten years' preparatory work by the robot crews and nanobots, the first nano-conditioned human settlers (astronoids) arrive. Nano-condition-ing is now an essential pre-launch bioengineering procedure to enable astronoids to overcome the negative effects of two years' weightless-ness and exposure to high levels of cosmic radiation while travelling to Mars and other planets in the solar system.

2065:   microscopic nanorobots are now used routinely to create build-ing materials, manufacture consumer goods, clean up pollution, zap cholesterol from the blood stream, and hunt down viruses and diseases in the human body. Molecular factories are now building everything from running shoes to houses.

2075:   scientists have created artificial lungs, kidneys, livers, hearts, legs, arms and eyes through genetic engineering. It is announced that further advances in bio, quantum and nano-technologies have made it possible to create the first conscious cyborg artilect (human–machine entity). A long ethical debate ensues, but the go-ahead is given to create 'Adana'.

2085:   the average lifespan of the first generation of genetically and mechanically enhanced alpha-humanoids is now 130 years, up from 55 in 1900.

2090:   oil and other organic energy sources have almost run out, but cold nuclear fusion has been harnessed to generate free non-polluting power for 'humanity'. Orbiting solar panels have also been launched to beam down solar electrical power by microwave, to help with the planet's ever-growing energy needs.

2100:   Adana is 'born' and conscious machine-artilects are emerging in large numbers, marking the next step forward in the evolution of life on Earth. Humanoids can now download (or 'merge' as it is now described) their consciousnesses with these artilects and, as a result, can live forever.

2105:   the first deep-space sub-light starship is launched with a crew of cyborg artilects. Many years later, we are visited for the first time by another sentient species from our Galaxy. They ask if they can to speak to our leader, Adana . . .

Conclusion: a brave new (organizational) world?

The push back against the machine is coming and its coming from the very high-end. That's not to say we don't want technology. We want it on demand but not ever-present. Many people feel a great loss now, because we've turbo-charged everything but we haven't figured out a way to enhance satisfaction. People need more space. We should be afraid of machines because they actually diminish our creativity, diminish our capacity to think about unrelated variables and form new perspectives.
(*Marian Malzman, an executive of international advertising agency Euro RSCG, in a talk to Australian marketing executives, cited in* The Australian, *8 August 2000*)

Coming back down to earth after this journey into the distant future, what is likely to happen over the next 20 years? The acceleration in technological evolution described in this chapter will undoubtedly have many benefits for humanity. The Internet will continue to make it easier, quicker and less expensive for people to communicate with one another. New communication media and knowledge management systems should improve our ability to access and process increasing amounts of complex knowledge and information. They will contribute to the globalization of trade and commerce and, perhaps, foster greater global political, social and cultural freedom and integration as more and more of the world's population comes on-line. They hold out the promise of ending disease, malnutrition and starvation. They will continue to revolutionize all manufacturing and service industries. They may create new business opportunities for entrepreneurs and wealth for more of the world's population and, maybe, drive the creation of a 'post-capitalist' world (Drucker, 1993).

However, working in this environment will also create enormous challenges for employers and employees and new strategies are required to manage the impact of emerging technologies. Successful leadership and people management in high-tech virtual organizations will continue to utilize many traditional practices, but new technologies will not only continue to accelerate the pace of change in organizations, they will soon begin to do more 'thinking' and 'managing' for us. In the near future, our grandchildren may be able to download information directly from computers to their brains, and they may also be cooperating with intelligent, self-learning entities when they join the workforce in the 2030s and 2040s. They may be able to enhance their memories and learning capabilities both through designer 'mind' drugs and, in all probability, through hard-wired computer implants. In 50 years' time, our great-grandchildren may look back on us in the same way that we look back on pre-industrial societies.

There are enough indications in this chapter to warn us that these rapid technological changes will need to be carefully monitored. Current technologies have failed to deliver on most of the promises made about them 30 years ago. For example, whatever happened to the extensive leisure time we should all have been enjoying in the 2000s, a scenario confidently predicted by many commentators in the 1960s and 1970s? Baby-boomers reading this book may recall something called the 'leisure society' that was going to emerge in the 1990s. Alvin Toffler, in his 1970 book, *Future Shock*, suggested that computers and robots would take over so many mundane and routine work tasks that most people living in industrialized countries would be able to start work at 25 and retire before they reached 50. They would all be independently wealthy, enjoy six months' holiday a year and four-day working weeks, and might even require leisure counsellors to help them cope with their newfound freedom from the drudgery of full-time work. The 21st century reality is very different from this utopian vision. For most employees, new technologies have instead meant greater flexibility and multi-skilling, work intensification, ever-increasing expectations of higher performance and productivity, less job security, 24-hour accessibility, the blurring of work/family boundaries, longer working hours and far higher levels of occupational stress.

Furthermore, surveillance technologies allow organizations to monitor their employees secretly, and specialist snooping programmes are becoming widespread. Systems such as ProtectCom's Orvell Monitoring 2002 allow employers to monitor every website that employees visit and all emails sent and received. It is able to identify all the software applications used by employees, and can even monitor what is on their PC screens in real time (Klimpel, 2002). The new generation of interactive TVs will routinely monitor consumers' programming, viewing and purchasing choices, further diminishing personal privacy. With web-access, video-on-demand and targeted advertising comes unprecedented power to collect data about consumers from the programmes and adverts they choose to watch (Hopper, 2001). Voice–face recognition systems are becoming commonplace. They can be found in most public spaces in all industrialized cities around the world, raising the spectre of 'Big Brother' monitoring of people. There are also Global Positioning System satellites that can spot and monitor individuals from space, as portrayed in the 2000 movie, *Enemy of the State*. This scenario is no longer science fiction. In the UK, this system has been used since 2000 by the waste-management company ONYX to monitor the movements of their garbage collectors, via a satellite positioning system fitted to their garbage collection trucks. In response to these developments, there have already been several legal cases in the USA concerning covert surveillance. Shortly before this book was published, the American Civil Liberties Union had been planning a class action against the use of covert video surveillance in workplaces as a violation of the Fourth Amendment of the US Constitution.

> Privacy is dead – deal with it.
> (*Scott McNealy, CEO of Sun Microsystems, 2001*)

These technologies also provide companies with the freedom to quickly uproot their operations and move to 'innovation hotspots', meaning that some businesses will gradually lose their national identities and loyalties. They have triggered a 'workplace implosion', with the destruction of many jobs and the rise of a new underclass, the 'techno-peasants'. Paul James has referred to the emergence of a '20/60/20 society'. In this society, a privileged minority of the population, an economic techno-elite of skilled knowledge workers, will have secure and well-paid employment. The bulk of the population may well be employed on a series of short-term contracts, as a periphery or non-core workforce. The remainder will come to form an economically and technologically disenfranchised underclass in the near future. There are clear indications that this has already started to happen in most industrialized countries (Hamilton, 2003).

While all of these new technologies are extremely seductive and their progress is probably unstoppable, hardly any management and organizational researchers have begun to get to grips with their potential impact on organizations, and the world of work, over the next 20 years. In this chapter, some suggestions for a new paradigm that is able, conceptually and practically, to get to grips with the possible effects of these new technologies on both people and organizations have been outlined. It is vitally important that we do this, because the first 20 years of the 21st century will be when we gain mastery over life (through the DNA revolution), over matter (through the quantum revolution) and over intelligence and creativity (through the bio-computer revolution). Later this century we will, in all probability, be redesigning the human race and perhaps, as Ray Kurzweil believes, become the first species in history to engineer its own extinction, by creating the next dominant life forms on Earth. However, three important and, as yet, unanswered questions remain:

- What are the real benefits of new technologies?
- Whose interests do they serve?
- Can we retain control over new technologies, or will they control us in the future?

They improve productivity, but don't ever seem to improve the quality of our working lives. They mean we are accessible 24-hours a day, but we never get a real break from work. They mean we are able to do more during the working day, but our work hours never decrease. We can access huge quantities of information and knowledge resources with amazing rapidity, but all suffer from increasing levels of information overload and technostress. We can communicate instantaneously with anyone on the planet, but are exposed to ridiculous quantities of unsolicited spam, junk mail and computer viruses. We can buy labour-saving and communication gizmos by the score, but feel left behind if we don't buy the latest ones that appear with monotonous regularity on the market. We have a global Internet and a quasi-global economy, yet primitive nationalistic, religious and tribal forces continue to threaten the economic and political stability of our planet. We can communicate instantaneously with thousands of people, but may not know the names of the next-door neighbours. Standards of living, at least in industrialized countries, rise inexorably, but we may at the same time be destroying the fragile ecology of our planet.

Globally, inequalities of wealth grow year by year, and these will continue to cause conflict and war within and between nation states for many decades. Because of the remarkable growth of technological innovation in the 19th and 20th centuries, the citizens of industrialized capitalist countries enjoy the highest standards of living and material affluence in human history, and yet they have an insatiable – and apparently unquenchable – hunger for acquiring more and more *things*. Why? This is an important question to address because research evidence accumulated over the last decade indicates that ever-increasing levels of material consumption have not made people living in rich industrialized countries any happier or more content with their lives over the last 50 years (for example, Hamilton, 2003: 22–92). If we are going to cope actively with the impact of new technologies on our working and personal lives, and use these to serve our best collective interests, these issues must be debated by politicians, policy makers, business leaders, intellectuals and the community at large. Unfortunately for humanity, there does not appear to be anyone who has the vision, imagination or intellect to deal with these, for the simple reason that technological development has an unstoppable, inexorable impetus and life force of its own. This means that we have not even begun to address perhaps the biggest question that will face humanity in the first half of the 21st century: *can we control the emergence and nature of new technologies and use them to improve and enhance our lives and organizations – or will they end up controlling us?*[7]

> The post-human world could be one that is far more hierarchical and competitive than the one that currently exists, and full of social conflict as a result. It could be one in which any notion of 'shared humanity' is lost, because we have mixed human genes with those of so many species that we no longer have any clear idea about what a human being is. It could be one

in which the median person is living well into his or her second century, sitting in a nursing home hoping for an unattainable death.

Or it could be the kind of soft tyranny envisaged in *Brave New World*, in which everyone is healthy and happy, but has forgotten the meaning of hope, fear or struggle. We do not have to regard ourselves as slaves to inevitable technological progress when that progress does not serve human ends. True freedom means the freedom of political communities to protect the values they hold most dear, and it is that freedom we need to exercise with regard to the biotechnology revolution today.
(*Francis Fukuyama*, Our Post-Human Future: Consequences of the Biotechnology Revolution, *2003*)

Sometime in the 21st century, our self-deluded recklessness will collide with our growing technological power. One area where this will occur is in the meeting place of nanotechnology, biotechnology and computer technology. What all three have in common is the ability to release self-replicating entities into the environment. We may hope that by the time they emerge, we will have settled upon international controls for self-reproducing technologies. But, of course, it is always possible that we will not establish controls. Or, that someone will manage to create artificial, self-reproducing organisms far sooner than anyone expected. If so, it is difficult to anticipate what the consequences might be.
(*Abridged from the introduction to Michael Crichton's* Prey, *2002*)

Before the 21st century is over, human beings will no longer be the most intelligent or capable type of entity on this planet. Actually, let me take that back. The truth of that last statement depends on how we define human.
(*Ray Kurzweil*, The Age of Spiritual Machines, *1999*)

Exercise 11.2

Having read through this chapter, think about how new technologies may impact on your leadership and management practices in the near future, and how you will stay on top of emergent technologies over the next five to ten years.

The near future:

1.

2.

3.

4.

The next five to ten years:

1.

2.

3.

4.   ◆

Notes

1   This frenetic pace of technological innovation looks even more astonishing if we set
    it against the backdrop of the evolution of our planet. It is now believed that the Earth
    formed about five billion years ago, with the Moon being created from the impact of
    a Mars-sized planet about 500 million years later. Without the Moon's stabilizing
    influence on the Earth's erratic orbital spin at this time, it is highly unlikely that any
    life forms would have evolved. The first primitive single cell creatures emerged about
    four billion years ago, but for the next two billion years evolution stood still.
    Approximately one billion years ago the first multicellular organisms appeared and
    540 million years later there was an explosion of life forms during the Cambrian era.
    It is now believed that this was triggered initially by a massive asteroid slamming
    into Southern Australia. This created mass extinctions, similar to the one that was
    later to wipe out the dinosaurs, but also created opportunities for new life forms to
    emerge (including the first mammals).

    By 200 million years ago a huge variety of plants and animals had appeared, includ-
    ing the dinosaurs, who reigned as the dominant species for millions of years, until
    another massive asteroid struck the Gulf of Mexico 65 million years ago, creating new
    opportunities for mammalian species to emerge and spread over the planet. About
    four million years ago, the first ape-like creatures appeared in Africa, hybrid primi-
    tive-modern humans appeared some 200 000 years ago and *Homo sapiens* about
    130 000 years ago (reported in *Nature*, **423**, 12 June 2003). The analogy that has often
    been used to illustrate this dramatic evolutionary acceleration is to compress the
    history of life on Earth into twenty-four hours. Multicellular organisms appeared in
    the last twelve hours, dinosaurs in the last hour, the first hominids in the last forty
    seconds, and modern humans *less than one second ago*.

    It is remarkable that the evolution of our species came about because of at least six
    massive and planet-threatening asteroid impacts millions of years ago. In addition to
    these, there have been many other cataclysmic events such as the planet's polarity
    reversing several times, several highly destructive super-volcano explosions, lengthy
    periods of global warming and lengthy ice ages and, quite possibly, 'super-solar'
    flares hitting the planet and causing widespread extinctions in the past. These, in
    conjunction with plate tectonics, have all had profound short and long-term effects on
    the climate and temperature of the planet and the evolution of animal and plant
    species. It is only because of mass extinctions, and other substantial changes during
    the evolution of the Earth, that a small and very insignificant mouse-sized mammal
    was enabled to emerge and find an environmental niche it could survive in; an
    animal that would, after hundreds of millions of years, eventually evolve into *Homo
    sapiens*. It is a miraculous accident that our species survived and evolved to colonize
    the whole planet. The fact that you now exist to read this note challenges all laws of
    probability.

2   Quiz answers: (1) Sunday 23 February 1997 saw the arrival of the first cloned
    mammal, Dolly the sheep. She died prematurely in June 2003. (2) On Monday 12 May
    1997, IBM's Big Blue supercomputer defeated world chess champion, Garry
    Kasparov. (3) 24 August 1998 was the day that Professor Kevin Warwick became the
    first human being in history to have an implant inserted in his body that enabled him
    to communicate remotely with a computer. (4) 26 June 2000 was the day human
    genome number 22 was mapped for the first time. (5) 11 November 2001 saw the
    cloning of the first human embryo by the US biotech company Advanced Cell

Technology. (6) 16 June 2002 witnessed the announcement of the first teleportation of photons by two Australian scientists (in theory, opening up the possibility of teleporting matter in the future). (7) On 15 March 2003, scientists with the Human Genome Project in Bethseda, Maryland announced that their work on mapping the human genome was complete. In essence, these men and women have succeeded in identifying and sequencing about three billion pairs of DNA (the chemical building blocks that produce human beings).

This genetic map will enable revolutionary breakthroughs to be made in biomedical sciences, and in the health and welfare of humanity. However, this marks just the beginning of a very long journey of discovery. We now have a basic understanding of *what* we are made of, but we are a long way from understanding *how* all this works. The quest now is to crack the far more complicated code of the human *proteome*: the library of information that creates proteins. To give you an idea of how difficult this will be, there can be as many as one hundred million proteins at work in a *single* human cell and several thousand of these can fit into the full stop at the end of this sentence.

Bonus points: In 1945, the mathematical genius Alan Turing (who worked on the Enigma code-breaking programme during World War II) first predicted that a computer would beat a human being at chess by 2000. Chess Grand Masters now routinely use computers for match analysis and practice, and can no longer compete without this back-up.

From the original Big Blue project, IBM developed an even more powerful computer, Blue Gene, at a cost of $US100 million to model the folding of human proteins in gene studies. This will be capable of multi-petaflop processing (one petaflop = one million gigaflops; one gigaflop is equivalent to the processing power of a single top grade PC in 2003). In 2006, this machine will be capable of 1000 trillion operations a second. At the time this book was published, the world's largest computer built by NEC could 'only' perform 36 trillion operations a second (Horovitz, 2002). In November 2003, this initiative was given a further boost when it was announced that the US government was to invest $US516 million in the development of Blue Gene and another computer, called ASCI Purple.

What didn't happen on 31 December 1999 was the meltdown of the world's computer systems, as a result of the 'Millennium Bug'. Amongst the very few events of note that occurred at this time were the following:

Andrea Scancaralla, a 29-year-old from Florence in Italy, fearful about losing his money after Y2K, withdrew all his savings from his bank account on 20 December 1999. Outside, two men on a scooter drove past and snatched his bag. He lost 11 million lira (c. $US4500) which was never recovered.

Alonzo Andersen, of Michigan in the USA, fearing possible post-Y2K shortages, decided to stockpile (along with other survival supplies) gas cylinders. On 16 December 1999, these exploded and completely destroyed his house.

3   Some animals such as birds and apes do use primitive tools, but they are unable to innovate with these.

4   Key to Figure 11.1 (Kurzweil, 1999: 22–3; reproduced with permission)
Mechanical computing devices
  1. 1900   Analytical Engine
  2. 1908   Hollerith Tabulator
  3. 1911   Monroe Calculator
  4. 1919   IBM Tabulator
  5. 1928   National Ellis 3000
Electromechanical (relay-based)
  6. 1939   Zuse 2
  7. 1940   Bell Calculator Model 1
  8. 1941   Zuse 3

Vacuum-tube computers

9. 1943 Colossus
10. 1946 ENIAC
11. 1948 IBM SSEC
12. 1949 BINAC
13. 1949 EDSAC
14. 1951 Univac I
15. 1953 Univac 1103
16. 1953 IBM 70
17. 1954 EDVAC
18. 1955 Whirlwind
19. 1955 IBM 704

Discrete transistor computers

20. 1958 Datamatic 100
21. 1958 Univac II
22. 1959 Mobidic
23. 1959 IBM 7090
24. 1960 IBM 1620
25. 1960 DEC PDP-1
26. 1961 DEC PDP-4
27. 1962 Univac III
28. 1964 CDC 6600
29. 1965 IBM 1130
30. 1965 DEC PDP-8
31. 1966 IBM 360 Model 75

Integrated circuit computers

32. 1968 DEC PDP-10
33. 1973 Intellec-8
34. 1973 Data General Nova
35. 1975 Altair 8800
36. 1976 DEC PDP-11 Model 70
37. 1977 Cray 1
38. 1977 Apple II
39. 1979 DEC VAX 11 Model 780
40. 1980 Sun-1
41. 1982 IBM PC
42. 1982 Compaq Portable
43. 1983 IBM AT-80286
44. 1984 Apple Macintosh
45. 1986 Compaq Deskpro 386
46. 1987 Apple Mac II
47. 1993 Pentium PC
48. 1996 Pentium PC
49. 1998 Pentium II PC

5 If you're thinking of setting up an e-commerce venture, there are several websites, (for example, www.businessplanarchive.com and www.webmergers.com) containing information on the collapses of dozens of e-businesses during the dotcom collapse of 2000–2002.

6 The title 'Gattaca' was derived from the names of the four nitrogenous bases of the human genome: guanine, adenine, thymine and cytosine.

7 For a detailed analysis of the moral, ethical and legal implications of the biotechnology revolution, see Fukuyama (2003).

12   Leadership and business ethics

Objectives

To define ethics and business ethics.

To look at the impact of unethical business practices on organizations, and their effects on economic development in industrializing countries.

To help you evaluate your business values and ethical beliefs.

To examine the implications of ignoring ethical issues when doing business in other countries.

To establish the business case for promoting high standards of ethical conduct in organizations, leadership and people management.

Introduction

> The point is ladies and gentleman that greed, for the sake of a better word, is good. Greed is right. Greed works. Greed will save the USA!
> (*Michael Douglas, as Gordon Gekko, in* Wall Street, *1987*)

> Greed is good. I think greed is healthy. You can be greedy and still feel good about yourself.
> (*Ivan Boesky, the junk-bond dealer, during a talk to business studies students at Berkeley, California, in 1987. Soon after, he was arrested, prosecuted and imprisoned for insider trading.*)

In Chapter 1 we saw that honesty and integrity were two of the most cherished qualities of successful, respected and admired leaders, and it is in the area of business ethics that the true value of these qualities is fully realized. 'Ethic' is derived from the Greek word *ethos*, meaning ideal or excellence. Ethics are things that we are (or should be) familiar with, including a sense of honesty and fairness, prudence, respect for and service to others, keeping promises, being truthful and developing business relationships based on trust and integrity. The study of ethics is concerned with disciplined inquiry into the basis of morality and law. Business ethics are defined here in the conventional sense as that which constitutes acceptable behaviour in organizational, commercial and business contexts. Business ethics consist of four dimensions: legal, economic, social and personal. As an academic discipline, this is concerned with the study of how personal values fit the cultural, moral and managerial values of an organization, and the environments in which they operate. In this chapter, we will look at several examples of unethical conduct in organizations, and the negative effects of these on business, capitalism and national economic development. We will then consider why business ethics have been gaining greater credibility in recent years, and why some business leaders now believe that the operation and management of their organizations must be underpinned by solid ethical standards and a sense of corporate social responsibility that goes beyond simply making money and generating profits.

The impact of unethical business practices on organizations

Historically, unethical, corrupt and illegal practices have been part and parcel of doing business for centuries, in spite of the considerable damage that such activities have caused. In the 20th century alone, there have been thousands of instances of these. For example, while the roles of the Swiss banking industry, German industrialists and the inactivity of the Papacy during World War II have been well documented, it is less well known that several major US firms were also complicit in collaborating with the Nazi regime. Prominent amongst these were General Motors and Ford. When American GIs arrived in Germany in 1945, they were very surprised to discover that the basic design of German army trucks was similar to their own. This was because they had been built to the same specifications by GM's subsidiary company, Opel. Henry Ford was an anti-Semite and a known admirer of Adolf Hitler, who in turn had a picture of Ford on his office wall in Munich and awarded him the Grand Cross of the German Eagle in 1938. A US army report, by the war crimes investigator Henry Schneider, dated 5 September 1945, accused the German branch of Ford of serving as 'an arsenal of Nazism, at least for military vehicles', with the consent of the US parent company. It was later revealed that Ford and GM had done little to prevent their German subsidiaries from retooling their factories to provide war materials to the German army after 1933 (abridged from Dobbs, 2000). IBM's Hollerith card sorters were used to identify and classify Jews and other 'undesirables' in round-ups during the 1930s, prior to the genocidal holocaust that would follow during World War II. The CEO of IBM, Thomas Watson (another anti-Semite), did little to prevent the use of these machines for this purpose, and IBM quickly regained control of its German subsidiary and employees after the war ended (Black, 2001).

Moving forward into the 1960s, we find the case of the Ford Pinto. Soon after this new car was introduced, it was discovered that Pintos turned into fireballs when they were involved in low-speed collisions. The company discovered that a badly designed, poorly positioned and unprotected gas tank caused this. Ford's accountants worked out that it would have cost $US110 per vehicle to solve this problem (or about $137 million a year at that time). However, the company's senior management calculated that the cost of out-of-court payments and litigation would only amount to $50 million a year. So, even though Ford had a patent on a much safer petrol tank, the company did nothing until Ralph Nader exposed this scandal in the early 1970s. It was estimated that as many as 900 people burned to death as a direct consequence of this problem. Not surprisingly, the company's advertising agency, J. Walter Thomson, quickly dropped a line from the end of a Ford radio advertisement of the day: 'The Pinto leaves you with a warm feeling'. The court cases that followed this scandal led to multi-million dollar payouts to the victims and families (Dowie, 2002). Ralph Nader also forced the automotive industry in the USA to adopt seatbelts, airbags and crumple zones – all vigorously opposed by GM, Ford and the rest on the grounds of 'cost'. Several million people now owe their lives to this pioneering consumer advocate. He was also the first person to suggest (in 1987) that airlines should install secure cockpit doors to prevent terrorists from hijacking planes. All the major US airlines objected loudly to this proposal, because it would have added 50 cents to the cost of an average domestic airline ticket.

More recently, in 2000, General Motors, du Pont and Standard Oil were accused of deliberately introducing lead into petrol in the 1920s, knowing that it would poison millions of people and cause brain damage in tens of millions of children throughout the world. They covered up their scientists' findings on these dangers for more than 50 years. Although the use of lead in the USA was prohibited in 1976, it is still used in petrol in many industrializing countries. Ninety per cent of this market is now supplied by one British company, Octel (Brown, 2000). This conduct was compared to that of the tobacco companies who had systematically lied about the effects of their products on people's health for more than 40 years, leading to the successful prosecution of most of the world's major cigarette manufacturers during the late 1990s and early 2000s. Tobacco companies knew by the early 1960s that

cigarettes were carcinogenic, and that a clear link existed between cigarette smoking, cancer and many other fatal diseases. Their cynical strategy was to add more chemicals to their cigarettes to make them even
more addictive. The Council for Tobacco Research, which was funded
by all the major US tobacco companies, regularly produced 'evidence'
(often from respected academic researchers) that cigarettes caused little
or no harm to their users. The first major breakthrough against these
companies occurred in 1998, when the US tobacco industry agreed to
pay $US200 billion dollars to 46 states over 25 years, in reparations for
the widespread damage that their products had caused in the past and
will cause in the future (Harnden, 1999). During the 1990s, 'at least 30
million people' were killed by cigarettes and 'at least 500 million
people' will die of cigarette-related deaths in the future (Cancer Press
Releases, 2002).

During the 1990s and early 2000s, there has been a succession of cases
of corrupt and unethical practices in organizations. These have cost
legitimate businesses, employees, taxpayers and nation states throughout the world trillions of dollars. For example, according to both John
Pilger (1998) and Jeffrey Robinson (1998), one of the main causes of the
explosion in drug-related crime in the 1980s and 1990s was the conduct
of the 'legitimate' financial and banking sector. Robinson has even
suggested that 'White affluent members of the professional classes
throughout the world have turned money laundering into the world's
leading financial growth industry' (1998: 23). For example,
Liechtenstein has been accused of laundering $US203 million between
1996 and 1999, not only on behalf of rich tax-dodgers from around the
world, but also for Latin American and European drug cartels, the
Italian Mafia and Islamic terrorists (German intelligence report cited in
The Australian, 11 November 1999). One IMF loan of $US7 billion to
Russia mysteriously disappeared and then reappeared in a private
account at the New York Bank a few months later (NR, 2000).
According to Pilger (1998), some of this 'dirty' money also drove
economic growth in East Asia in the 1980s and 1990s.

As a direct result of this financial legerdemain, the fastest-growing
business in the world over the last decade has been crime. It has been
estimated that that there are *eight trillion dollars* (US) in laundered
money from criminal activities swilling around the world's banking
systems, with many financial institutions turning a blind eye to this
scandalous situation. For example, in Australia, the illegal drug market
is estimated to be worth $A548 million, and about $A3.5 billion a year
in drug and crime money from overseas was laundered through
Australian banks in 1998. By 2000, this had risen to nearly 8 billion
dollars (Sutherland, 2000). Remarkably, the biggest growth area in the

international banking business sector, over the last two decades, has been in the creation of offshore tax havens and 'cyber-domiciles' (Robinson, 1998). Many of these are still hidden away from the scrutiny of national tax auditors and regulators, and are where the proceeds of global crime (and terrorism) continue to be laundered. In response to these revelations, and under heavy pressure from the US government and the Securities and Exchange Commission, 11 of the world's leading banks (who collectively controlled more than 50 per cent of banking world-wide), signed up to the first world-wide anti-money laundering scheme. What impact this has had remains to be seen (Sutherland, 2000). This was followed, in the aftermath of 11 September 2001, by the introduction of the US Patriot Act in April 2002. This legislation contained a raft of measures designed to track down funds and financial transactions linked to terrorism, drug trafficking and organized crime.

> If you walk one mile in any direction from the main central railway station in any major city in Europe or North America you will pass within an elbow's distance of a property that is owned by, managed by or has been constructed with dirty money. At some point in the past thirty days you did business, knowingly or unknowingly, with a money launderer or otherwise came into contact with dirty money. What follows are stories about how money launderers manage their business and how that business affects us all; about how dirty money becomes the white powder which is killing our children and the underground economy that is shaping the world. After The Laundrymen, bankers, lawyers, accountants, money managers and more than a few governments will never look quite the same.
> (*Abridged from the introduction to Jeffrey Robinson's* The Laundrymen, *1998*)

Other legitimate businesses and organizations have also been found guilty of unethical conduct in recent years. In 1999, for example, Lloyds of London and the auction houses Christie's and Sotheby's were rocked by financial and price fixing scandals, resulting in multimillion dollar payouts to their clients in 2000–2001. This was followed by the imposition of a jail sentence and fines of $US7.5 million on the former head of Sotheby's, Alfred Taubman, in 2002 (*The Times*, 2002; Reuters, 2001). Some readers may also recall the downfall of Robert Maxwell in the 1980s and, more recently, the activities of Nick Leeson at Barings Bank:

> For ten days Nick Leeson – the man who lost $US1.8 billion and broke Britain's oldest merchant bank in 1995 – took on more and more contracts from investors. As the 28-year-old rogue trader continued his frantic gambling, the bank's losses must have loomed like a nightmare to Leeson – 40 000 contracts, each with a potential loss of $US500 000. Leeson – the trader from hell from a working class background in London – was the general manager of Barings' Futures in Singapore and chief trader for its Nikkei account. He was renowned for wearing expensive suits to the office, but this memory paled in comparison to his frantic flight from Singapore to Malaysia and then Germany, with his soon-to-be-ex-wife. As Barings

collapsed under debts from his wild trading of derivatives based on Tokyo share prices. Leeson finally had his collar felt in Frankfurt and was jailed for nine months before being deported for trial in Singapore and sentenced to six and a half years in jail. He was freed in July 1999. Leeson now earns about $US1.3 million a year from his film, *Rogue Trader*, plus publicity events – but half of his earnings are paid to Baring's liquidators.
(*Abridged from Haynes, 2000*)

The dotcom collapse of 2000 led to an avalanche of litigation in the USA, with more than 200 class actions processed in the American courts during 2001–2004. Many banks and financial advisers were accused of rigging the flotation of dotcom stocks during the late 1990s and hyping their value to investors. The banks named in these lawsuits included Crédit Suisse, First Boston, Quattrone, CFSB, Bear Stearns, Morgan Stanley and Salomon Smith Barney. The payouts from these court cases will run into billions of dollars. This comes amidst investigations by the US Justice Department and the Securities and Exchange Commission (SEC) into the behaviour of many financial institutions during the Internet boom. At the time, some commentators suggested that the entire American democratic process, and commercial media organizations, had been largely hijacked by big business, oil and energy interests, and alleged that George Bush was little more than a gormless glove-puppet for these powerful lobbies (Moore, 2001; Miller, 2001). Soon after these allegations were made, the energy company Enron filed for bankruptcy on 2 December 2001. At the time, this was the biggest corporate collapse in American commercial history. It was soon discovered that this company had benefited enormously from the deregulation of energy industries in Republican states during the 1990s, including Texas under George Bush's time as governor. In the investigations that followed, it was also revealed that the company's CEO, Ken Lay, had been a close friend of the Bush family for many years and Enron had been one of the biggest sources of corporate donations to the Republicans during the 1990s (Swartz and Watkins, 2003).

Documents submitted in New York's Bankruptcy Court in June 2002 showed that the senior managers of Enron had been lining their own pockets prior to declaring the company bankrupt. Collectively they had awarded themselves $US845 million in cash, stock and 'incentive payments'. Lay personally received $US103.5 million in salary and 'performance bonuses' and a further $US108 million in stock in the late 1990s and early 2000s. In late August 2002, a former senior executive of the company, Michael Kopper, admitted that he and his boss, chief financial officer Andrew Fastow, had made millions of dollars from secret deals that had hidden the full extent of the company's financial troubles. At a judicial hearing in Houston, he told a judge how he had paid kickbacks to Fastow for running a partnership that did not appear

on Enron's formal accounting records (Dalton, 2002c). The collapse of
Enron also led to the extinction of one of the world's biggest account-
ing and consulting firms, Arthur Andersen (quickly renamed 'Arthur
Daley' in the UK, after a shady business character in a popular 1980s
TV series, *Minder*). The company was found guilty of shredding documents in June 2002, and several other criminal trials involving
Andersen employees, who had 'audited' Enron prior to its collapse,
were the subject of court cases in the USA during 2002–3 (McLean and
Elkind, 2003: 381–4). Andersen Australia was also involved in auditing
the bankrupt insurance companies HIH and UMP, which resulted in
criminal charges being laid against several Andersen Australia
employees during 2002–3.

> Communication, Respect, Integrity and Excellence.
> (*Enron's 'Corporate Values', Annual Report, 2001*)

> My personal belief is that Enron stock is an incredible bargain at current
> prices and we will look back in a couple of years from now and see the great
> opportunity we currently have. Talk up the stock and talk positively about
> Enron to your family and friends. The third quarter is looking great. We will
> hit our numbers.
> (*Ken Lay, former Chairman of Enron, in a company email forum, 26 September
> 2001*)

> Load up the truck.
> (*The advice Jack Grubman, former senior financial adviser at Salomon, Smith,
> Barney, gave his clients about buying Worldcom stock during 2000. On 22
> December 2002, Grubman was fined $US15 million and banned from working in
> the US securities industry for life.*)

The scale of the Enron collapse was soon eclipsed by the telecommunications company Worldcom, with nearly 40 billion dollars unac-
counted for and 17 000 redundancies in June 2002. Again, the senior
managers of this company had also been lining their own pockets prior
to declaring the company bankrupt, and several Federal politicians
had sold off their stock in the company prior to its collapse. Sacked
Worldcom chief financial officer Scott Sullivan alone cleaned up nearly
$US10 million when he sold off 475 000 company shares in 2000. The
company's owner, Bernie Ebbers, had personally 'borrowed' $US366
million shortly before the company went bust. For both the employees
who lost their jobs and those who remained, this also meant the loss of
their entire pension entitlements, which had been tied into the value of
the company's stock. Enron's 20 000 employees lost two billions dollars
of pension contributions during 2001–2. The USA's biggest pension
fund, the California Public Employee Retirement System, faced a
$US565 million loss on Worldcom holdings, and New York's State
Retirement Scheme lost $US300 million. In an ironic twist that could
have appeared in a John Grisham novel about corporate malpractice, it

was revealed that the company's headquarters in Mississippi would shed half of its employees by Christmas 2002. The name of the town in which Worldcom had set up its HQ in 1996 is Clinton. On 2 August, the company's former chief financial officer, Scott Sullivan, and controller, David Myers, were arrested and charged with seven counts of securities fraud, conspiracy and making false financial statements. The madness that seemed to have gripped some parts of corporate America is exemplified in the conduct of Gary Winnick at Global Crossing during the late 1990s.

'The emperor of greed'

Gary Winnick had never worked in the telecom industry before he founded Global Crossing in 1997. He had never run a public company either. Yet in the late 1990s, Chairman Winnick was hailed as an industry giant, the creator of a Telco that a year after going public in 1998 was valued at $US38 billion: more than Ford. A little over two years later Global Crossing is in bankruptcy and fighting to survive, part of an industry collapse that wiped out $US 2.5 trillion in market value. Investors and regulators are struggling to figure out what went so wrong so fast. But the real question is how such a company could survive – indeed prosper – for as long as it did. The answer captures all of the insanity and money fever of the dotcom bubble, which saw billions of dollars vanish in pursuit of business that never materialized. Its business plan changed with the phases of the moon. So did its CEOs (there were five in four years). Global Crossing inflated its revenues by swapping capacity with other carriers and lured customers and investors by overstating its reach and the capabilities of its network, a system which former employees say simply doesn't work that well. It exploited its relationship with both Wall Street and its bankers on a scale unrivalled in the industry.

As our story will show, billions of dollars flowed out of this company and into the pockets of insiders. Gary Winnick and his cronies are arguably the biggest group of greed-heads in an era of fabled excess. Not only did Winnick sell off stock at huge profits, while investors who jumped in later watched their stakes burn to nothing, but he treated Global Crossing from the start as his personal cash-cow, earning exorbitant fees from consulting and real estate deals between the company and his own private investment firm. In all, Winnick cashed in $US735 million of stock over four years – including $US108 million issued to his private company – while receiving ten million in salary, bonuses and 'other payments'. Enron's Ken Lay didn't even come close – he only sold $US108 million of stock.
(*Abridged from Creswell and Prins, 2002: 63–64. Although the US Securities and Exchange Commission has investigated Winnick's conduct at Global Crossing, no criminal charges had been laid at the time this book was published.*)

In turn, the collapse of Enron, Worldcom and several other US companies led to a widespread loss of investor confidence in corporate America, and to significant stock market instabilities during 2002–3. On 18 July 2002, the Dow Jones Index (DJI) fell below the level it had previously sunk to in the immediate aftermath of 11 September, wiping $US7 trillion off the value of the DJI (or about the same as the annual gross domestic product of several European countries). Between 1 January 2001 and 24 July 2002, losses from company bankruptcies in the USA totalled $US275 billion. At the same time the London FTSE Index fell to its lowest level since September 1996. This rash of corporate fraud and corruption scandals and a widespread public outcry about the insane levels of remuneration enjoyed by CEOs, whether they performed well or not, culminated in the resignation of the New York Stock Exchange's (NYSE) Chairman Dick Grasso on 19 September 2003. He had been universally criticized over a $US140 million remuneration package, while failing to take any action to reform the quasi-public regulatory body that had allowed many of these scandals to happen in the first place. The Securities and Exchange Commission (SEC) welcomed his resignation and on the same day announced that it would be conducting an investigation into the corporate governance structure of the NYSE.

After an 18-month undercover investigation, the FBI rounded up 48 foreign currency traders who had serviced many of the largest financial institutions in New York on 19 November 2003. Investigators uncovered several hundred scams, involving a staggering array of criminal conduct and tens of billion dollars stretching back over a 20-year period. Charges laid at the time included conspiracy, wire and securities fraud, money laundering, drug dealing and the illegal sale of firearms. These led to numerous court cases in 2004–5 (Dalton, 2002b, 2003a, 2003b; Reid, 2002; Newman, 2002; Newman and Dease, 2002; Newman and King, 2002; KRT, 2002; AFP, 2002a; Ellis, 2002; Agencies, 2002).

In response to the public outcry in the USA and elsewhere about corporate fraud and corruption, George Bush made a keynote speech to business leaders in New York on 10 July 2002. Bush observed:

> The misdeeds now being uncovered in some quarters of corporate America are threatening the financial well-being of many workers and many investors. At this moment, America's greatest economic need is higher ethical standards – standards enforced by strict laws and upheld by responsible business leaders. The lure of heady profits of the late 1990s spawned abuses and excesses. With strict enforcement and higher ethical standards, we must usher in a new era of integrity in corporate America. We've learned of some business leaders obstructing justice and misleading clients, falsifying records, of business executives breaching trust and abusing power. We've learned of CEOs earning tens of millions of dollars in bonuses just before their companies go bankrupt, leaving employees, investors and retirees to suffer.
> (*Bush, 2002*)

Soon after this speech was delivered it was revealed that Bush too had been involved in some shady financial dealings in the mid-1980s. In

1986, Harken Oil bought Bush's near worthless oil company, Spectrum 7, for $US2 million. Part of the deal involved Bush receiving 212 000 Harken shares and being appointed to Harken's board of directors, as a member of the company's audit committee. In 1990, the SEC forced Harken to revise its books and account for millions of dollars in losses that it had disguised as profits, through the $US12 million 'sale' of a subsidiary to company insiders. On 22 June, Bush sold his stock at four dollars a share. Two months later the company announced a loss of $US23 million, a fact that Bush must have known about. When the loss was made public, Harken's shares fell to one dollar within 12 months and by 17 July 2002 were trading at 45 cents per share. In other words, Harken had pioneered the accounting tricks that brought Enron and Worldcom to their knees in 2001–2. And guess which company was acting as Harken's legal and accounting advisers at the time? Arthur Andersen (abridged from Peretz, 2002).

While Bush's conduct during this affair may not have been illegal, many commentators suggested that it was unethical. More questions were raised when it was discovered that the attorney who represented Bush in the subsequent SEC investigations into Harken was one Robert W. Jordan, a partner at Baker Botts LLP. This man, who knew almost nothing about Middle Eastern politics, was appointed as US ambassador to Saudi Arabia soon after Bush took up the presidency in January 2001. The Baker referred to in the law firm's title is none other than James Baker, the tactician behind Bush's extralegal 'win' in Florida (which gave him the 2001 presidential victory). In June 2001, it was revealed that one of Bush's closest advisers, Karl Rove, had held a large portfolio of Enron shares, which he sold prior to the collapse of the company, while advising Bush on US energy policies. You don't have to be a consumer advocate like Ralph Nader to see the potential for conflicts of interest to have occurred here. To compound Bush's problems, the public-interest law firm, Judicial Watch, then launched a class action by shareholders against the Vice-President of the USA, Dick Cheney, on 11 July 2002. This lawsuit alleged that Cheney was involved in 'serious accounting fraud', as CEO of the Texas energy company, Haliburton, from 1995 to 2000 (Peretz, 2002; KRT, 2002; AFP, 2002a; Newman and Dease, 2002; Ellis, 2002; Agencies, 2002).[1]

In Europe, Calisto Tanzi, the founder of the Italian multinational agribusiness Parmalat, was arrested in late December 2003, in connection with $US12 billion missing from the company's accounts and allegations of kickbacks to the Mafia in return for a monopoly on the sale of their products in southern regions of Italy and Sicily (AFP, 2004b). Tanzi was charged with having personally expropriated one billion dollars to fund his lavish lifestyle, which included a TV station, several private jets, holiday resorts and ownership of the Parma football club (Bita, 2004). This scandal, which quickly became dubbed 'Europe's Enron', led to several protracted court cases in 2004–5. In early February 2004, Italian police also arrested Segio Cragnotti, in connection with the meltdown of the multinational food firm Cirio in 2003, and began investigating 25 bankers from several Italian banks who had been dealing with the company before it collapsed. The Swiss company Adecco, the world's biggest provider of temporary workers, and the Dutch retailer Ahold also came under the spotlight of their countries' financial regulators in January 2004, for possible accounting and compliance irregularities. Following the carnage of the Neuer Markt collapse in Germany, and the ruin of many other telecom and technology industries, more lawsuits were initiated (*The Times*, 2001a; Bloomberg, 2001).

Further afield, in Australia we can also find many examples of unethical business practices in recent times. These include the 2000 Queensland ALP electoral corruption scandal (still unresolved), the commercial radio 'Cash for Comments' inquiry in 2001, and the 2000 Sydney Olympic corruption and ticketing scandals, which are estimated to have cost $A50 million in lost sponsorship. Ironically, the SOCOG Chairman Kevin Gosper then became an extremely well paid adviser to the Chinese government during their successful bid for the 2008 Olympics. There have also been numerous cases of insider dealing, politicians claiming false travel expenses and former Employment Minister Peter Reith being forced to pay back $A50 000 following the 'phonegate' scandal of 2000. Company collapses in Australia at this time included the insurance company HIH with losses of $A5.3 billion, the telecom business One.Tel with debts of $A350–400 million in May 2001, The Froggy Group in December 2001, with losses of $A67 million, and New Tel, who managed to burn one hundred million dollars of investors' money between 1998 and the end of 2002. Like their American counterparts, the senior management of these companies had awarded themselves huge salaries and bonuses within months of their collapse. In turn, these led to thousands of redundancies, financial hardship for suppliers, huge problems for self-employed builders and bankruptcies for numerous small companies. Insurance premiums for small businesses went through the roof, and for Australian households rose by an average of 150 dollars a year in 2002–3. These companies were also the subject of judicial inquiries during 2003–4.[2] In March 2004 it was also revealed that four rogue traders at The National Australia Bank had blown $A240 million in speculative currency trading (Woodley, 2001; Montgomery, 2001; Elliott and Magnusson, 2001; Westfield and Elliott, 2001; King, 2001; McGuire, 2001; Conn, 2000; Poprzeczny, 2000).

These, and many other, examples that could be cited all reinforce the impression that unethical behaviour was alive and kicking in Australia. Recent estimates have put the full cost of company fraud in Australia as high as 20 billion dollars and as low as 3.5 billion dollars a year, or between $4200 and $700 for *every* Australian taxpayer (S. Wilson, 2002b; various articles in *The Australian*, 1997–2002). Whatever the true figure, even the lower estimate is more than the annual cost of robbery and extortion, homicide, drug-related offences, property damage, stealing, motor theft, 'other theft', assault and breaking and entering put together. In fact, the cost of corporate fraud each year is now greater than the cost of every single bank robbery committed in Australia since it became an independent Federation in 1900 (personal communication from Professor Richard Harding, Professor of Criminology, University of Western Australia). There have also been several well-documented cases in the last ten years of 'whistle-blowers', in Australia, being harassed and persecuted by large corporations for reporting on their corrupt, dangerous, illegal or underhand activities (Whistleblowers Australia, 2000–4; De Maria, 1999).

In another context, many commentators have suggested that the principal causes of the economic meltdown in East Asia in 1997–8 were corruption, fraud and cronyism. In the early to mid-1990s, as companies and investors flocked to the 'miracle economies' of East Asia, 'irrational exuberance' and greed once again took over, as tight regulatory supervision, due diligence, honest accounting practices and ethical conduct went out of the window. As the dust settled in the aftermath of the implosion of most economies in this region, hundreds of cases of corporate fraud, embezzlement and corruption emerged. These are still problems in the region, along with industrial espionage and the theft of proprietary information and intellectual capital. These factors continue to be major deterrents to companies investing in countries such as Indonesia, Cambodia, Vietnam and Burma (Watkin, 1999; O'Donnell, 1999a). The World Bank's president, James Wolfensohn, has argued since 1995 that the biggest single factor prohibiting economic growth and investment in industrializing countries is, you guessed it, corruption. Some countries, such as Russia and Indonesia, are now so riddled with corruption that the CIA's Foreign Intelligence Bureau now (unofficially) describes these as 'kleptocracies' (Australian Broadcasting Corporation, *Four Corners* report, 14 April 2001). Indonesia, which has huge natural reserves of oil, gas and minerals, should be an investor's dream. Instead, because of endemic corruption and political instability, many of the world's major mining and resource companies have either shut down operations there or curtailed new project developments in recent times, particularly in volatile areas such as the province of Aceh.

What about those to whom we might look to do something about unethical business practices: politicians, the police and the Church? In Chapter 1, we saw that many egotistical and toxic personalities are attracted to careers in politics, and it is therefore no surprise that many have also been accused of engaging in corrupt and illegal activities in recent years. Amongst dozens of examples that could be cited are the former German Chancellor Helmut Kohl (in 1999), the President of France (François Mitterrand) and the former French Foreign Minister, Roland Dumas, in 2001. While Kohl and Mitterrand escaped prosecution, Dumas was jailed for six months and fined $US125 000 for embezzling funds from the state-owned oil company Elf Aquitaine between 1989 and 1992. In 1998, the former NATO Chief, Willy Claes, was found guilty of corruption in awarding military NATO contracts. At least 15 per cent of the annual multibillion dollar budget of the EEC still 'disappears' in fraudulent dealings of various kinds and into the pockets of corrupt officials, parliamentarians and influence peddlers of all kinds. Paul van Buitsen, who blew the whistle on fraud in the European Commission in 1999, was forced to resign from his job as an internal auditor for 'breaching confidentiality rules' (Johnson, 1999). The entire Commission of the EEC resigned in 2000 as a result of an official inquiry into these losses. No criminal charges were ever laid against these individuals, and the taxpayers of Europe continue to pay for this fraudulent and corrupt behaviour.

Several British politicians have also been caught out on dodgy financial dealings in recent times, including George Galloway, Dame Shirley Porter and one of Prime Minister Blair's former favourites, Peter Mandelson. Mandelson, one of Tony Blair's closest advisers and most senior cabinet members, was forced to resign over an undeclared house loan. This followed the earlier resignation of Peter Robinson, who had loaned him this money from an undeclared offshore trust (ibid.). In early April 2004, John Major, the former British Prime Minister, was questioned by financial authorities over a £20 million black hole at one of his former employers, the indebted busmaker Mayflower (Mansell, 2004).

In the USA, one president, Richard 'Tricky Dicky' Nixon, was impeached by Congress in the 1970s, Ronald 'Amnesia' Reagan escaped prosecution over the 'Arms to Iraq' scandal in the 1980s, and Bill 'Teflon' Clinton was nearly impeached in the late 1990s, over financial dealings earlier in his career and 'that woman'. The Clintons were again under the media spotlight early in 2001, after Clinton pardoned two criminals who had given money to the Democrats during the 1996 presidential election. It was also revealed that he and Hilary had 'borrowed' furniture and other property from the White House when they left office, which they were later forced to return. At the time, many commentators argued that there was ample evidence to prosecute Clinton for violating federal criminal laws that covered the false statements he made under oath during the Monica Lewinsky hearings (AFP, 2002b). However, as we observed in Chapter 3, he is now earning good money on the world's speaking circuit to help pay his legal bills, racking up about $US150 000 for each presentation.

There is also compelling evidence that several politicians, judges and police officers had been complicit in protecting the notorious Belgian paedophile murderer Mark Dutroux during the 1990s and early 2000s – a case that took *eight years* to come to trial in March 2004. In early 1998, it was revealed that the mudslides that killed 300 people in Northern Italy had been caused by building houses on unsafe water run-off areas on hills. It was later proved in court that the local Mafia had been in control of the local building companies who built the houses. They also controlled the Local Government Planning Department, and regularly paid kickbacks to local police to overlook their criminal activities (cited in *The Australian*, 4 March 2001). In June 2003, the Italian Prime Minister Silvio Berlusconi was granted legal immunity from prosecution for bribing judges by Italy's lower house, where his party had a parliamentary majority. Throughout the world, there have also been dozens of cases of corrupt and criminal activities amongst serving police officers in the USA, the UK, Europe and Australasia over the last 20 years.

Even those organizations one would expect to uphold high ethical standards were compromised during the 1990s and 2000s. For example, the Roman Catholic Church has been assailed by a series of financial and sexual scandals in recent years. Priests, bishops and even cardinals have been accused of child sexual abuse in many parts of the world. According to one survey conducted in 1999, in Kansas City, the death rate of Catholic priests from AIDS in the USA is at least four times greater than that of the general population (Kay, 2002). Towards the end of the 1980s, criminal prosecutors began to pursue aggressively these criminals and those responsible for the systematic cover-up of these abuses in the RC hierarchy for decades. According to one estimate, 4450 priests were accused of child sex abuse between 1950 and 2002 (ibid.). The large number of trials of priests, brothers and nuns accused of child abuse in the USA, Canada, Ireland, France and Australia threatened to bankrupt some local churches. A case in Texas cost just one diocese $US75 million in damages for an-out-of court settlement with the plaintiffs (*The Weekend Australian*, 18–19 March 2000). Between January and April 2002, at least 70 priests in the USA, including one bishop, were suspended in cases of sexual abuse. In

September 2002, 86 victims of the paedophile priest John Geoghan agreed a $US10 million settlement with the Catholic archdiocese of Boston. Geoghan had been sentenced to ten years' jail for fondling a child, and faced another trial that year, stemming from allegations that he had had molested some 130 children over a 30-year period while he was a priest (Reuters, 2002a). Geoghan was killed in prison by another inmate in July 2003. In late August 2003, the archdiocese finally agreed to pay out $US129 million to settle 542 lawsuits involving sexual abuse by their priests over a 40-year period.

In Australia, there were also numerous cases involving the Catholic Church and the systematic sexual abuse of hundreds of children in their orphanages from the 1960s onwards. According to Bernard Barret of the 'Broken Rites' support group, 'at least' 44 priests and 27 religious brothers have been sentenced in Australian courts for sexual crimes against children since 1993. In terms of professional groups, this makes the Catholic Church the single worst offender of this kind in Australia. Despite this, the Vatican announced that all accusations of child sexual abuse would be dealt with internally in future, by Church authorities, although after a huge public outcry it was forced to back down from this position (Crawford, 2002).

There have also been some truly strange and funny examples of unethical and corrupt behaviour in recent times.

The Northern Indian state, the Punjab, ran a competition in January 1998 to find and reward 'the most honest government employee'. After several months, the competition organisers announced that they were unable to find a single example of this, but they did uncover 300 corrupt ones (*The Australian*, 18 March 1999). Perhaps in response to this revelation, Indian Assembly candidate Narendra Singh Bhadauria later promised to fill his cabinet with 'turncoats, Mafia dons and criminals' if he was elected, in protest at endemic corruption in the Indian political system.
(Time, *18 February 2002*)

The Australian Electoral Commission, examining electoral fraud in New South Wales and Queensland in the early 1990s, revealed that 'at least' 71 dead people had voted in state elections. One 'Curacao Fisher Cat', who was indeed a moggy, had voted in an election in Macquairie (Sydney) in 1993. This scam was only uncovered when the elected Federal MP, Alisdair Webster, had a letter he had sent to a 'Ms. Catt' returned to him as 'unknown at this address'.
(The Australian, *17 November 2000*)

On June 15th 2000, the Sri Lankan Cricket Authority elected a new president, Mr. Thilanga Sumathipala. What was the problem with this? His occupation was described as 'bookmaker'.
(The Australian, *16 June 2000; at the time, the cricketing world had been under siege over allegations of illegal gambling and match fixing amongst international players.*)

The National Audit Office of Australia, responsible for monitoring waste, theft and dishonest expenses claims amongst public servants and politicians, reported that 'several dozen laptops and printers' had gone missing from their HQ in Canberra.
(The Australian, 9 November 2000)

In November 2000, Italians were shocked to learn that the lottery that millions had played every week for years had been an elaborate confidence trick. This lottery fraud had been perpetrated using children who had been imperfectly blindfolded and coached to pick out pre-arranged numbers. The total cost of this scam was put at 'at least $US60 million'.
(Pedrick, 2000)

A group of scientists in the UK were roundly criticized, and received an official reprimand, when it was revealed that they had drugged several mice with amphetamines, and then subjected them to high-decibel music (including the very loud Prodigy). Several subsequently died of shock, while others suffered permanent brain damage.
(The Australian, 20 August 2002)

It probably did not come as much of a surprise to the readers of Time when it was announced that 99 per cent of the banknotes in circulation in central London were contaminated with cocaine (Time, 1 November 1999). And it was perhaps not a coincidence that the character of the Devil, in Arnold Schwartzenegger's end-of-millennium film, The End of Days, was portrayed as a 'pharmaceutically inclined' Wall Street banker.

Last, but by no means least, with the outbreak of the second Gulf War in March 2003, the citizens of a number of countries were curious to know why their governments had been supplying – or had given approval to private companies to supply – Saddam Hussein with nuclear technologies and airplanes (France), small-arms and other weaponry (France and Germany), chemical weapon plants and toxic gas know-how (Germany), anti-tank missiles and radar-jamming equipment (Russia), torture equipment and anti-riot gear (the UK) and anti-aircraft missiles (China). Americans were also very surprised to discover that the US company American Type Culture Collection had supplied Saddam Hussein with the materials to produce anthrax, gas gangrene, botulinum toxin and tuberculosis in 1985, with the full approval of the US Department of Commerce.

Even at that time, this brutal dictator was known to have developed a taste for developing weapons of mass destruction, which he later used to exact revenge on the Kurds after the first Gulf War ended in 1991 by gassing their towns and villages and killing thousands of men, women and children. Among the Iraqi companies supplied with these goodies was the Iraq Atomic Energy Commission, where UN weapons inspectors uncovered evidence of biological and nuclear weapons development in 1993. According to US Commerce Department documents, these exports were approved by the Reagan administration and were 'almost certainly' used to create, or at least expand, the Iraqi biological weapons program.
(Reuters report, The Weekend Australian, 5–6 October 2002)

Other evidence suggests that the examples cited above are not isolated cases, extreme examples of the deviant conduct of a few wayward individuals and companies. For example, one survey estimated that about two-thirds of the 500 largest corporations in the USA had been involved in some form of illegal or unethical behaviour between 1980 and 1999 (Singleton, 1999: 18). Melvyn Weiss, whose law firm Milberg, Weiss, Bershad, Hynes and Lynch specializes in suing corrupt executives and companies in the USA, had 325 current cases listed on their website on 30 August 2004. The business magazine *Fortune* ran an article on 6 June 2002 entitled, 'Business failure: corporate America has lost its way'. This suggested that fraud and corruption were becoming the rule, rather than the exception, in corporate America, and argued for an overhaul of corporate governance in the USA. An earlier article, on 25 March, 'It's time to stop coddling white-collar crooks: send them to jail', revealed that, between 1992 and 2001, just over 5000 cases of white-collar crime (fraud, insider dealing and corruption) were investigated by the Securities and Exchange Commission. Just 187 (under 5 per cent) came before the US courts. Of these, 147 people were found guilty and 83 were sent to prison. Another report indicated that the average length of prison sentences for white-collar criminals, in nice open 'hotel' jails, was just 15 months (Australian Broadcasting Corporation radio report, 26 June 2002). California's former Attorney General, Bill Lockyer, was so disgusted with the behaviour of executives at Enron that he commented, 'I would love to personally escort [Ken] Lay to an eight by ten cell that he could share with a tattooed dude who says, "Hi, my name is Spike, honey" ' (cited by McLean and Elkind, 2003: 281–2).

A 2001 survey by KPMG found that, despite greater lip service being paid to ethics, 'there remains a disturbingly high instance of unethical behaviour in the workplace'. KPMG reported that three-quarters of the employees they surveyed had witnessed 'a high level of illegal or unethical conduct in the past twelve months' (*The Weekend Australian*, 9–10 June 2001). Another KPMG survey found that, of 2000 Australian and New Zealand companies surveyed, only 60 per cent had systematic fraud control strategies in place, even though more than a third believed that fraudulent employee behaviour was 'a problem' (Hughes, 2002). Another survey of 98 large companies in Australia found that being a good corporate citizen was not generally seen as being a core business concern or important to the way their businesses were managed. This echoes the findings of a survey in 2000, by CCRU Research, which found that only 37 of Australia's top 500 companies regarded corporate citizenship as being a major factor in their strategic planning (Wallace, 2002). Corporate espionage too is on the increase, with one-quarter of American, British and Australian companies admitting that they are involved in 'competitive intelligence gathering', some of which sails very close to the boundaries of legality (Dearne, 2002).

In spite of this dismal account, ethical issues are becoming more of an issue for organizations around the world, if only for the pragmatic reason that dishonest and unethical behaviour can cost companies a huge amount of money in litigation payouts. They can also seriously affect corporate performance, reduce employee morale, increase labour turnover, alienate customers and clients and lead to a loss of consumer confidence. As we've already seen, they can also destroy the lives of those who are employed by, or who have a financial stake in, those companies that collapse because of unethical or illegal business practices.

The business case for ethical leadership and management

These examples of the nefarious, unethical and illegal activities of individuals, corporations and countries in recent years might indicate that unethical business practices are commonplace. However, it's important to emphasize that most leaders and managers in industrialized, democratic countries do conduct themselves within the law and, for the most part, operate within moral and ethical frameworks of some description. Having said this, we also like to believe that we are basically 'good', so it is only dishonest people who should be concerned about ethical values and principles. Consequently, we may believe that it is enough to proceed according to our own moral instincts, and we become masters at justifying and rationalizing these. So, in this section we are going to look at our personal value systems and beliefs about the role of ethics in business. With this in mind, please complete the next self-development exercise.

Exercise 12.1

Personal values and business ethics

Have you:

Ever 'creatively accounted' your tax returns to avoid paying tax to state or federal governments?

Ever exploited someone else for personal or financial gain?

Ever been 'economical with the truth' in order to gain an advantage over a colleague or a business rival?

Ever used your sexuality to influence someone at work?

Ever stolen ideas or information from other people and claimed them as your own?

Ever kept back information that you knew would benefit yourself at the expense of a colleague or subordinate?

Ever used anything owned by your employers for personal use without their permission (for example, email, the Internet, telephone, stationery, company car and so on)?

Ever used 'insider' information for personal benefit when buying/selling stocks and shares?

Ever discriminated against anyone because of their gender, race, culture, religious beliefs or sexual orientation?

Ever, knowingly, condoned or ignored illegal or unethical practices in organizations that you've worked for (even if you were ordered to do this by a senior manager)?

Ever fiddled your expenses?

Ever bought products made in sweatshops employing children in East Asia (this would include many products made by Gap or Nike)?

Ever bought anything made in military-owned sweatshops in China? This includes many consumer goods, particularly clothing.

Ever accepted or given a bribe during the course of your business activities?

Ever done business with dictatorships, corrupt governments or countries regarded as having poor records on human rights? This would include many of the countries on the Transparency International ranking of the world's 'most corrupt' countries. ◆

This exercise highlights several important facts about ethics. First, if you answered 'Yes' to any of these questions, it means that you are, at least in some people's eyes, unethical in your business, leadership and management practices. Second, whether we judge that any of these are unethical or not can be a very subjective process, shaped by personal value systems that have evolved over many years. Third, it highlights why it is not that surprising when some people go off the straight and narrow, because there are so many temptations that we might succumb to when engaged in business, particularly if these involve making a lot of money. Fourth, it is significant that these are temptations that almost all leaders and managers will encounter at some point during their working lives. These can include accepting bribes or sexual favours, creative accounting, lying, misleading product or service claims, taking undeclared cash payments, discrimination, bullying or humiliating people at work, obeying orders even if we know that these are illegal or immoral, price-fixing, violating health and safety regulations to cut costs, suppressing basic human rights, hyping up stock prices for personal gain, failing to speak up when unethical practices occur, polluting the environment, and so forth. Fifth, we also know that most individuals who are convicted of business malpractice did not deliberately set out to commit unethical or illegal acts. They succumbed to the temptations, sexual and/or financial, that were on offer, and soon found themselves on a slippery downward spiral from which there was no escape. Having said this, a few people do seem to be attracted to the dangers of unethical conduct like moths to lights, as this next story illustrates.

'A double whammy'

A Wall Street banker was charged this week with insider trading that allowed him and two accomplices to make $US170 000 in illegal profits. James McDermott, 48, the former chairman and CEO of investment bank Keefe, Bruyette and Woods faces up to 15 years in jail and a $US1.25 million fine if found guilty. He is accused of stealing confidential information from KBW clients and passing it on to his lover, Kathryn Gannon, 30, a model and 'adult' film actor also known as Marilyn Star. On her Web page, Gannon challenges viewers to join her club and win a chance at appearing in her next episode of 'Marilyn Does Miami'. 'Think of it as a VIP pass to experience my extraordinary sex skills,' she writes. McDermott was charged with taking insider information on six banks that were either KBW clients, or being eyed by KBW clients for merger or acquisition and passing it on to Gannon. McDermott was forced to resign last year after a SEC probe into the affair. KBW had been about to make an IPO of its stock and was expected to raise $US85 million. It promptly cancelled. In 2001, McDermott received a five-month prison sentence for his misdemeanors, and Gannon was sentenced to three months in October 2002.
(*Abridged from Reuters, 2002b; AFP, 1999*)

Even our choice of occupation can have a bearing on the ethical values and principles that we are likely to encounter at work, as well as the perceptions that others might have about us and the jobs we do (Table 12.1).

So, are morality, ethics and business mutually exclusive? Many people complain about the decline in ethical and moral standards in public life, amongst politicians, government officials, the judiciary, the police and even amongst the clergy these days. Yet, when it comes to business, it has often been seen as acceptable to ignore morality and ethics, so long as we play within the rules of the game of the company we work for, or the country we are doing business in. However, it is important to consider these issues because the law cannot govern all behaviour and, as we saw in the opening section of this chapter, the 'bottom-line' cannot ever be the sole rationale underpinning the operation of businesses. When this philosophy is allowed to flourish, fraud, corruption and illegal practices inevitably follow.

Table 12.1   Perceptions of occupations' ethical standards

Nurses – 90%
Pharmacists – 89%
Doctors – 80%
Schoolteachers – 79%
Dentists – 67%
State/Supreme Court judges – 66%
University lecturers – 66%
High court judges – 65%
Police – 65%
Engineers – 59%
Accountants – 48%
Ministers of religion – 48%
Lawyers – 45%
Public opinion pollsters – 29%
Bank managers – 29%
TV reporters – 18%
Business executives – 17%
Talkback radio announcers – 17%
Directors of public companies – 16%
Federal politicians – 14%
Stockbrokers – 14%
Union leaders – 11%
Newspaper journalists – 10%
Estate/realty agents – 8%
Car salesmen – 3%

Note: Percentage of respondents rating each occupation as having 'very high' or 'high' ethical standards.

Source: www.roymorgan.org, 20 December 2003.

There are three reasons why we may be reluctant to engage with ethical issues in business. First, as noted earlier, we all like to believe we are basically 'good', so only dishonest or 'bad' people should be concerned about ethics. Therefore we may believe that it is enough to proceed according to our own moral instincts, those of the people we work with or the organizations we work for. However, a serious engagement with ethics requires a different approach, particularly not an unquestioning attitude towards custom and practice, or 'the way we do things around here'. Just because 'everyone does it in this company' or 'that's just the way to do business in this country', doesn't make it acceptable. A real engagement with business ethics requires an adherence to an agreed set of moral and ethical principles that transcend individual self-interest and a self-serving moral relativism that justifies behaviour and conduct that would not be tolerated by the communities we live in, or by our families and friends. Second, most people's working lives are already very busy and complicated. If we throw ethical issues in, there is the potential to make them even more difficult. For example, how many parents, for an easier or quieter time, have succumbed to their kids pestering them for designer clothes and footwear made by Nike or Gap? Instead of confronting the morality of these issues, they often rationalize them away, with statements like 'the poor wouldn't have jobs if we didn't operate there' (a myth); 'it's not our company's job to engage in moral and ethical debates, we are here to make money' (debatable); 'all countries are guilty of unethical and immoral behaviour' (so what?); or 'its up to governments to do something about it' (do they know something you don't?) and so on.

Third, many business people believe that adhering to stricter ethical guidelines will mean that the bottom-line and profits will suffer. In fact, all the evidence accumulated over the last ten years shows that this assumption is a myth. Take the issue of ethical investing. Ethical investment funds are rapidly growing in popularity. In the USA these grew from about 1 per cent of the investment market in the USA in 1990 to 15 per cent in 2000, and they are expected to grow to 25 per cent by 2005. Worldwide, socially responsible investment (SRI) is a business valued at more than $US100 billion a year, as more people choose investments that they believe will not only make money, but will also have beneficial social effects (Haynes, 2001). SRIs also outperform many traditional investment portfolios, with two reports on Australian ethical trusts indicating that they were 'very well managed with good returns' (Australian Broadcasting Company, *7.30 Report*, 5 May 2001; Haynes, 2001). Table 12.2 shows the top performing ethical trusts in Australia in 2001–2.

Table 12.2   Top five performing ethical investment trusts in Australia, 2001–2

Fund	Return (%)
Australian ethical equities trust	22.3
Challenger socially responsive investment fund	15.4
ING: socially responsible shares index fund	13.6
Glebe blue-chip equities trust	16.5
Tower Lighthouse ethical growth fund	14.2
Australian all ordinaries average 2000–2001	10.0

Source: *The Weekend Australian*, Business Section, 24–5/2/2002.

Other reliable evidence that SRI investments work comes from the Dow Jones Sustainability Index (DJSI). The DJSI tracks the top 10 per cent of companies in 68 countries in 21 industry sectors. In the five years to August 2000, the DJSI outperformed the Dow Jones Global Index (DJGI), with an annualized return of 15.8 per cent compared with 12.5 per cent for the DJGI. Francis Grey, the research coordinator of the Zurich-based company Sustainable Asset Management, commented, 'If you had to touch on a single issue that is at the heart of this era, it is whether you can make money and be ethical at the same time. The world is hostage to people who think you've got to make money and everything else is an impediment. On the other hand, there is this broad sense that being ethical will not make you money. Now, the Sustainable Research Investment industry has tested that and shown that you can get equal or better returns than the mainstream' (cited by Wallace, 2002). Perhaps this is something worth thinking about when deciding where to place your personal investments, or your company's money, in the future?[3] Another report, describing a meta-analysis of more than 52 studies of the relationship between corporate social responsibility and financial performance over a 30-year period, concluded that socially responsible corporate behaviour had a direct correlation with improvements in the bottom line, helped improve a firm's bottom line and drove up shareholder value by improving its reputation (Hoare, 2002).

Pressure groups have become much more effective in the way they communicate their concerns about corporate behaviour to the general public, and so consumers are now much more aware of the unethical or illegal activities of organizations. At the same time, customers and shareholders are becoming more vocal about unethical business practices, and the underhand activities of a few greedy and unscrupulous business leaders. Shareholders too are becoming increasingly vociferous about the salaries of incompetent, overpaid 'fat-cat' CEOs and the business activities of companies in industrializing countries with poor records on human rights. A growing number of companies now employ triple bottom line reporting, where companies report on their social and environmental activities, in addition to their financial performance and profits. Corporate governance is also becoming a more important part of the operational thinking of many companies. In the 1990s, several countries also introduced new laws to protect whistle-blowers from harassment and persecution by large corporations when reporting on their dangerous, illegal or underhand activities (De Maria, 1999).

Clearly, ethics can be a 'smart' or a 'knowledge' tool for leaders and managers. If your organization has a reputation for being a straight

shooter and is regarded as honest and trustworthy, business will flow
your way. There is a *yin* and *yang* dimension to this: what you give out
you will get back (eventually). Ethics can help personal self-interest,
particularly in an era where more and more consumers are making
purchasing decisions that are influenced by companies' ethical and
environmental records. For example, 84 per cent of Americans
surveyed in *Marketing Magazine* in 1995 believed that good corporate
image influenced their purchasing decisions. Two-thirds indicated that
they would prefer to buy products from companies that did not exploit
children or pay subsistence wages, even if this meant a premium of up
to 10 per cent on the purchase price of these goods (Dionne, 1998).
Many western companies also introduced ethical guidelines covering
both individual and corporate behaviour in the 1990s. For example, in
the USA, more than 90 per cent of all *Fortune* 500 companies surveyed
in 2002 had ethical policies, compared to only 11 per cent in 1990.
Furthermore, many commentators suggested that the spate of organizational fraud, corruption and bankruptcy cases during 1999–2003
marked a turning point in the corporate world, particularly in the USA.
According to one survey:

> Four out of five investors have little faith in those running big business,
> while more than two-thirds believe the share market treats investors
> unfairly [ ] The public perception is that corporate America now operates
> like a giant pyramid scheme: a handful of executives at the top reap mind-
> boggling rewards, investment banks prosper by offering favourable
> research and undertaking corporate advisory work, and investors who
> provide the capital in the first place sit at the bottom, receiving whatever is
> left.
> (*Collins, 2002*)

The instances of executives lining their own pockets while their companies, investors and employees went to the wall, investment analysts
lying to their clients to make money and cases of 'creative accounting'
became so endemic that revamps of both regulatory frameworks and
ethical standards in business were put in place during 2003–4, in order
to restore the faith that investors and the general public had in the
corporate world. Between 2002 and 2004, a dozen US congressional
committees were involved in investigating Enron, Global Crossing,
Worldcom, Tyco, Arthur Andersen, Kmart, Qwest Communications,
PG&E, Adelphia Communications, Computer Associates and other
companies, who collectively had managed to vaporize close to one trillion dollars in equity capital (Dalton, 2002). John Steele, a regular
contributor to *The Wall Street Journal* observed at the time, 'The trouble
is that while the capitalist system is by far the best system ever created,
individual capitalists do not care for the system as a whole. Which is
why you need referees' (cited by Collins, 2002). Warren Scott, a US and
Australian securities lawyer with Coudert Brothers, made these

comments: 'Make no mistake about it, these corporate scandals are possibly the greatest challenge to the integrity of US capital markets since the Great Depression [ ] In cleaning up the mess, the SEC, Congress and the Stock Exchange face a monumental task to restore integrity to the system' (Scott, 2002).

In response to widespread public disquiet about these events, the US Congress implemented several new laws in the Sarbanes–Oxley Act passed on 15 July 2002. They included the following:

- The creation of a new Corporate Fraud Taskforce and a Public Company Accounting Oversight Board.
- The injection of an additional $US100 million in funding for the Securities and Exchange Commission.
- The tightening of general corporate regulation and accounting standards.
- The legally enforceable separation of the auditing and consulting services provided by accounting companies.
- Larger fines and increased prison sentences of up to ten years for financial advisers found guilty of defrauding shareholders.
- Making CEOs and CFOs legally responsible for the accuracy of their company's annual financial statements (*The Economist*, 2002a).

Other measures that came into law were:

- Tightening regulations on the advice that financial advisors can give to investors.
- Barring CEOs and company officers found guilty in the courts from serving as directors of companies in the future.
- Increasing jail sentences to 20 years for CEOs/CFOs found guilty of negligence in financial reporting or accounting fraud.
- Requiring all large companies to have full-time independent salaried executive members, who are not allowed to own stock options in the companies whose boards they sit on (Bloomberg, 2002b).

Although there was considerable pressure from consumers' rights advocates and some legal groups, two additional proposals that would have imposed restrictions on the number of stock options that CEOs and senior managers could receive and minimum timelines within which they can cash in their stocks or shares (for example, ten years) were not passed by the US Congress in 2003–4. A similar fate befell measures to provide greater legal protection for whistle-blowers.

Summary

Does the evidence presented above mean that business people in the USA and other countries are becoming more unethical, fraudulent and corrupt? The answer to this question is 'probably not'. All it demonstrates is that, when there are opportunities for people to exploit loopholes or weaknesses in the law, some will. For example, how would you deal with the following situation? You have just been appointed as CEO of a large, established US engineering company that employs 60 000 people. The company has run into difficulties in recent years and its shareholders want action to reverse the decline in the value of their stock. This has fallen from $US50 to $US20 over the last three years. You are awarded a three-year contract, a base salary of three million dollars a year and $US800 000 in stock options. Would you now concentrate your efforts on pushing through strategies that would be in the medium- to long-term interest of the company (say five to ten years in the future) or would you pursue policies that would result in 12 quarterly reports that met the expectations of financial analysts and institutional shareholders? Would you pursue policies that might ramp-up the value of your stock over the next 36 months, or initiate changes whose benefits might not be evident for five or six years?

Then imagine how tempting it might be to elevate the value of a company's stock artificially if you *owned* that business, had access to millions in stock options and also networked with investment advisers from local financial institutions. Many people might be tempted to veer off the straight and narrow in this situation, not because they are particularly 'bad' people, but because almost anyone has the potential to be short-sighted, self-serving and greedy, particularly if there are very large sums of money involved. In this context, it's worth noting that stupidity is not the opposite of intelligence. Many intelligent people do remarkably stupid things. Stupidity is the opposite of *wisdom*, one of the building blocks of leadership identified in Chapter 1. And, where there is stupidity, there will always be a need for business organizations and their leaders to have their activities controlled and regulated by well-resourced independent external authorities.[4]

> The road to hell is paved with good intentions.
> (*Old proverb*)

When in another's village . . .

Even if we do subscribe to a system of ethical business practices when working in our home countries, what happens if we work abroad? For example, should we work in countries with poor records on human rights or ones where corruption, fraud and cronyism are endemic? Should we work in countries that prohibit equality of opportunity for women, or that discriminate against their ethnic minority groups?[5] Should we overlook slack regulations that lead to widespread environmental pollution and ecological destruction in countries that are industrializing rapidly? For example, what would you do if confronted with these two real-life scenarios?

> In the late 1980s, some European tanneries and pharmaceutical companies were looking for cheap waste-dumping sites. They approached virtually every country on Africa's West Coast, from Morocco to the Congo. Nigeria agreed to take highly toxic polychlorinated biphenyls. Unprotected local workers, wearing thongs and shorts, unloaded barrels of PCBs and placed them near a residential area. Neither the workers nor the residents were told that the barrels contained toxic waste.

> A few years ago, a group of investors became interested in restoring the SS United States, once a luxurious ocean liner. Before the actual restoration could begin, the ship had to be stripped of its asbestos lining. A bid from an American company, based on US standards for asbestos removal, priced the job at more than $US100 million. A company in the Ukrainian city of Sevastapol offered to do the work for less than $US two million. In October 1993, the ship was towed to Sevastopol.
> (*Donaldson, 1996: 48, 49*)

Someone who believes that 'greed is good' would have few problems with the decisions described in these vignettes. What do you think? Was it right to simply overlook issues like health and safety? If you knew in advance that the decision to award these contracts to countries with lax employment and environmental standards would lead to illness, cancer, birth defects and even death amongst those employees, families and children affected by exposure to PCBs and asbestos, would this affect your decision? These vignettes show that, if ethical considerations within one's home country are complicated, they can become even more confusing as we move into the international arena. Furthermore, it was suggested in Chapter 2 that we should strive to treat all cultures as being of equal value. Does this then mean that we should adopt a position of 'cultural relativism', and simply ignore business practices and cultural norms that would be regarded as illegal, immoral or unethical at home? How can leaders and managers resolve these dilemmas? The notion, 'When in another's village – do as the villagers do' can have an immediate appeal – particularly if *not* doing this results in the loss of lucrative business opportunities. With these questions in mind, please complete Exercise 12.2.

Exercise 12.2

Managers' dilemmas

You are trying to win a major construction contract in Thailand. The government official you are dealing with makes some ill-disguised references to the very low pay he receives and how much he would like his children to study abroad, if only he could afford it. The message is straightforward. The cost to your company of paying for this would be negligible, compared to the cost of losing the contract.

Would you pay up or pull out? Is it worth paying this small bribe to help the official?

You are the manager of a chemical company operating in Indonesia. You know that you can dump tons of toxic waste into a local river without fear of prosecution. You'll also save your company tens of thousands of dollars if you don't bother paying for the safe disposal of this waste.

What would you do? What courses of action are open to you? Who could you turn to for advice about this?

You are the manager of a British IT firm in a strategic alliance with an Indian company that has operations in Delhi and Bombay. The owner of the Indian business wants to appoint his son, who has recently graduated with an MBA from a US university, to be head of the company's office in Bombay. However, you have already interviewed a German woman who has better qualifications, relevant work experience and is far more suitable for the job.

What would you do in this situation?

You are in Beijing, about to finalize a major joint-venture agreement with a Chinese engineering firm. One of the major stakeholders in the company, a local Communist MPC, tells you that he needs $US20 000 to push the deal quickly through the regional government committee that grants approvals for these. He explains that, without his help, this joint venture will not see the light of day.

Would you pay the bribe? What are the potential dangers of paying this? ◆

There are of course no easy 'right' or 'wrong' answers to these questions, which are all based on real-life scenarios (Forster, 2000c; Donaldson, 1996). However, the decisions we make in such situations are, ultimately, based on moral and ethical principles, and there are just three positions that could be adopted in these five situations:

- ethical imperialism, where we behave abroad in accordance with the values, customs and ethical/moral principles that we would employ at home;
- ethical relativism, where we largely abandon the ethical values and principles that we would apply in our home country, and subscribe

to the cultural and business practices of the country we are operating in;

- ethical universality, where we establish, and operate by, an agreed system of global moral and ethical business principles, but remain responsive to the context we are operating in.

Ethical imperialism

This approach may be superficially appealing, but will inevitably create problems because it assumes that the moral and ethical principles that we may apply in our home countries can and should be followed at all times. This is almost certainly going to cause problems. For example, any company from the USA or the UK that insisted on implementing equal opportunity policies in most Middle Eastern countries would soon come unstuck and cause great offence to their hosts, however well-intentioned such a stance might be. Refusing to accept gifts from business people and companies in Japan, and many other countries, would be considered rude. In many industrializing countries, 'greasing the wheel' may be the only way of ensuring that bids for contracts are successful. The main problem with this stance is that it assumes that there is one, and only one, set of national moral or ethical principles that can be applied – regardless of the situation. Such a rigid stance is going to make it near impossible to do business in most other countries.

Ethical relativism

Many people in business subscribe to this position, in the belief that it would not be possible to do business in other countries if they did not put aside legal or ethical principles that would be applied at home. However, adopting this position uncritically can also create difficulties. For example, please consider the following question. With the benefit of hindsight, would you have done business with the Nazi regime of the late 1930s and early 1940s, or with the Communist regime in the old Soviet Union? With this question in mind, please complete the next self-development exercise.

Exercise 12.3

Whom would you do business with?

For this exercise, please indicate which of the following characteristics of Nazi Germany, one of the most evil and barbarous regimes in human history, were also features of the old Soviet Union and, in 2004, are still features of China. For a bonus point, what do the dates in brackets refer to?

	Nazi Germany (1936)	Soviet Union (1980)	China (2008)
Totalitarian regime	X		
No free elections	X		
Economy controlled by ruling party's power elites	X		
Systematic and endemic corruption	X		
Political opposition not permitted	X		
Military/police under the direct control of the ruling party	X		
No freedom of expression	X		
No independent media (and extensive use of propaganda)	X		
No independent judiciary	X		
Imprisonment without trial	X		
Routine abuses of basic human rights	X		
Persecution for religious, political or sexual beliefs	X		
'Labour' and 'retraining' camps (where torture is used routinely)	X		
Expansionist foreign policy	X		
Military aggression towards neighbouring states	X		
Genocide is official state policy	X		

The answers can be found in note 6 ◆

Critics of the communist regime in China argue that it has killed more of its subjects, through repression and starvation, than Hitler, Stalin and Pol Pot put together (at least 50 million people, according to Amnesty International and the International Labour Organization). Around 1500 prisoners a year are sentenced to death and their body parts pillaged for sale to western hospitals. It has slave labour, in the form of prisoners working in state-run enterprises that western companies trade with. The children of political opponents are housed in brutal state-run orphanages, where they too are used as cheap slave labour and are also exposed to sexual abuse. Harmless religious sects like the Falung Jong are brutally repressed. There were claims during 2001–3 that more than 1000 of its followers had been killed in labour camps. Cultural genocide has been practised in this country over the last 50 years. In one country that it annexed in the 1970s, Tibet, hundreds of Buddhist monks have been tortured and dozens killed. One of the favoured methods of torture on women who oppose the regime there has been the insertion of an electrical cattle prod into their vaginas. One-fifth of the country's population, mainly Muslim minorities in the west of China and the inhabitants of Tibet, are routinely faced with human rights violations. China is also regarded as one of the most corrupt countries in the world (Amnesty International website, 2002; Blackman, 1999; Hiscock, 2002).

> I mean what people don't realise is that we're living in the real world and in the real world you have to attract the right quality of person to the job. I mean a salary of one million dollars a year might seem like a lot of money to some people, but I'm responsible for 10 000 employees. It used to be thirty thousand before I took over, but I'm responsible to my shareholders and to tell you the truth I think I did the people I laid off a favour. I mean I brought them down to earth and taught them that they were living in the real world, and in the real world they'd simply priced themselves out of a job. I mean how can I justify to my shareholders paying someone $3000 a month when I can get a Chinese chappie to do the same job for $100 a month? There was a spot of bother at our Beijing factory and my chum Li Ping had to teach the ringleaders that they were living in the real world by executing them, but we have to respect their different cultures and traditions. I mean we're living in the real world, we may not always like it, but it's the real world and we must respect it. In many ways our Chinese chums can teach us a lesson or two about the real world. I mean when we opened the Beijing factory what did the 20 000 we laid off in Oregon do? Did they move to China where the jobs are? No! They ran whinging to the unemployment office. They're simply not living in the real world . . .
> (Adapted from Harry Enfield's 'Class Bores – Number 4', Private Eye (UK), 18 July 1997)

Having won the bid to host the 2008 Olympic games, Chinese Olympic organizers announced that the beach volleyball would take place in Tiananmen Square, the scene of the brutal massacre of peaceful pro-democracy protesters in 1989. One of the strongest supporters of the Chinese bid was one Juan Antonio Samaranch, the recently retired autocrat of the International Olympic Committee (IOC). He was, in his younger days, a lieutenant in Franco's army in the 1930s and 1940s and a known Nazi sympathizer and anti-Semite. IOC President Jacques Rogge warned the Chinese government that, if they failed to honour their promise of improving human rights, they could lose the 2008 Olympic Games. Time will tell.

The counter-argument to these criticisms is that it is only by our trading with China, and exposing it to western ways of doing business, that the country can be helped simultaneously to grow its economy and become a more open, democratic and tolerant society (and there were some signs of this beginning to happen during 2004 – at least at the local level). Furthermore, increasing numbers of western companies are setting up in China, with more than 400 of the world's 500 biggest multinationals already established there. There are also some 200 000 'frequent traveller' visits by business people to China each year. The reasons for this growth are obvious. China has millions of potential new consumers and a rapidly growing middle class. It is slowly but surely rejecting communist ideology in favour of greater entrepreneurialism and consumerism. The potential markets for western companies are enormous: economic growth between 1998 and 2004 averaged 9.3 per cent a year. China also has huge resources, both natural and human. Direct foreign investment has grown at 24 per cent a year over the last five years. There are growing numbers of joint ventures with western companies, particularly in oil and gas exploration, construction, infrastructure development, telecommunications, vehicle manufacturing and electronics, and many other western companies have set up operations in China. Most of these operate from special economic zones (SEZs) set up by the Chinese government. In these regions, foreign firms can employ whom they want, exploit low wage levels, make use of abundant, hard-working (and non-unionized) workforces and also benefit from generous tax incentives.

However, China is still not used to western ways of doing business. As we have seen, it is still dominated by communist bureaucratic control, the involvement of the military in commercial collaborations with the west is rife, public corruption and nepotism are commonplace, and the suppression of independent political thought and ideas continues unabated. Indeed, anger over official corruption was one of the major driving forces behind the Tiananmen Square protests in 1989. Consequently, companies moving into China for the first time can also expect to have to cope with Kafkaesque paperwork for contracts, routine overcharging for services, inefficiencies in support services, officious Chinese bureaucrats, the granting of senior jobs in local operations to those with political connections, and the liberal use of financial and other inducements to obtain contracts and access to markets. Companies must anticipate unexpected events and obstacles at all levels when working in China. This requires enormous persistence when confronted with bureaucratic obstacles and the best expatriates in this situation will not only be technical specialists but also fast learning open-minded diplomats and negotiators. Companies that choose to operate in China will need to treat China, not as single market, but as 30 or 40 markets with the business potential of the EEC and NAFTA rolled into one. They will have to take a long-term view of Chinese markets (10–20 years). They will have to spend a lot of time and effort developing personal relationships, and take great care with the presentation of their firms, because appearance and image count for a great deal and are regarded as measures of professionalism. Businessmen and women will need to be diplomatic but tough in negotiations, and accept that expatriate managers will always be seen as *Laowai* (foreigners), no matter how long they spend living and working in China (abridged and updated from Forster, 2000c: 56–7).

Ethical universality

We agree that putting in place the right frameworks and policies for promoting a globalisation process that works well for all of its participants will be the key challenge for the international community in the 21st century. We need to develop policies to ensure that globalisation brings broad based prosperity and the political and governance arrangements needed to cooperatively implement them.
(*From a communiqué from the Group of 20 Leading Industrial Nations, cited in* The Australian, *12 June 2001*)

The continuing debates about the rights and wrongs of trading with countries like China would seem to confirm the widely held view that it could be very difficult to implement uniform ethical frameworks when conducting business in a global economy. However, this is a business philosophy that a growing number of western companies are now adopting. How are they doing this? First, they are establishing a set of core ethical values that determine the boundaries within which they will operate and, by extension, define the boundaries that they will not step over. Only by establishing such precise guidelines can all of their employees be clear about what are acceptable operating standards in other countries. Like the team-charters we reviewed in Chapter 5, ethical codes of conduct must be explicit (for example, rules on taking or offering financial inducements to obtain contracts overseas), but leave sufficient elbowroom for managers to use their personal discretion and judgment in other countries. For example, Motorola gives this advice:

'Employees of Motorola will respect the laws, customs and traditions of each country in which they operate, but will, at the same time, engage in no course of conduct which, even if legal, customary and accepted in any such country, could be deemed to be in violation of the accepted business ethics of Motorola, or the laws of the United States relating to business ethics.' Motorola then specifies where individual judgement is allowed. For example, employees may at their discretion accept small gifts, 'in rare circumstances

where the refusal to accept such a gift would injure Motorola's legitimate business interests [ ] so long as the gift contributes to the benefit of Motorola and not to the benefit of the Motorola employee.'
(*Donaldson, 1996: 56, 60*)

One example of this has become part of the folklore of the company, and is still recounted in stories to new employees. In 1950, a senior executive of the company was negotiating a sale with a South American government that would have increased Motorola's profits that year by 25 per cent. However, after extensive negotiations, the executive walked away from the deal because the officials he was dealing with were demanding one million dollars in 'fees'. The then CEO, Robert Galvin, not only supported this decision, but also made it clear that the company would have no further dealings with this government (cited by Donaldson, 1996: 60). Another example is the multinational resource and mining company, BHP-Billiton. The company's guidelines are clear: 'Under no circumstances will BHP approve any irregular payment in kind to win business or to influence a business decision in the company's favour. Bribes, kick-backs, secret commissions and similar payments are strictly prohibited [and] payments to domestic or foreign government officials to influence a decision or to gain a benefit either directly or through a third-party are strictly prohibited' (BHP-Billiton website, 5 July 2002). Other companies have backed their policies up with concrete actions. For example, Royal Dutch Shell fired 23 employees in 1997 who had been engaged in bribery and also terminated contracts with 95 firms on ethical grounds. All Shell managers operate under the clear understanding that they will not be penalized if they lose business because they have refused to pay bribes in other countries or engage in conduct that violates the company's ethical trading policies (Walsh, 1998: 40).

Creating ethical guidelines that establish clear boundaries and parameters, while allowing some personal discretion, is very difficult and there will always be ambiguous situations where a simple choice between 'ethical' and 'non-ethical' is hard to make. Nevertheless, it's worth spending some time developing these, to act as guiding lights if you, or your business, find yourself facing the kinds of dilemmas described above. Donaldson (1996:52) has suggested that business in any context should be guided by three fundamental principles: (a) a respect for core human values that determine the minimum moral threshold for the business activities that a business and its employees will engage in, (b) a respect for local traditions and customs, which does not violate the first principle, and (c) a belief that context does matter when deciding what is 'right' and 'wrong'.

Another way of approaching this issue is by referring to the equity and parity principles discussed in Chapters 1 and 6. These have at their core a fundamental respect for the rights, freedoms and liberties of all people, regardless of their national origin, culture, religion or gender. Almost every culture in the world has basic guidelines and rules about how we should treat others (even if we don't always manage to follow these). In Christianity, we have 'Do unto others as you would have them do unto you'. In Confucianism, there is the principle of mutual reciprocity, or not to do to others what they would not do to themselves. All of the world's major religious traditions, such as Kyosei (Japan), Dharma (Hindu), Sanatuchi (Buddhist) and Zakat (Muslim), and secular humanism have some common assumptions about how we should treat our fellow human beings. First, they recognize that all people have an intrinsic value as human beings and should not be treated as exploitable and expendable objects. Second, all individuals and communities should be treated in ways that respect basic human rights. Third, it is incumbent on all members of a community to support those institutions and laws on which the collective well-being of all its citizens depends (ibid.: 53). Many of these principles are embodied in the United Nations Universal Declaration on Human Rights. Because this is a set of principles that draws on many cultural and religious traditions, it is a statement of basic personal rights that almost every country in the world has signed up to (even though some of these do not adhere to its principles). It also represents a set of principles that all businesses can aspire to.

Alternatively, if all this sounds rather complicated, the following questions could be asked instead:

- What kinds of business practices would you consider to be unacceptable if your family, children, friends or you were on the receiving end of them?
- How would you feel if a foreign company was operating in your neighbourhood that routinely polluted the local environment, 'employed' your children on subsistence slave wages in dangerous factories, denied them an education and paid kickbacks to corrupt local politicians to engage in these activities?
- What practices and standards are employed by honest business people in your country, state or local community? Can you still do business in other countries by maintaining these practices and standards?

The basic principle of mutual reciprocity, or 'Do unto others as you would like them to do unto you' is appealing. Adopting this principle means that companies *can* act in ways that respect basic human rights and, at the same time, avoid business relationships that violate inalienable rights to decent wages, health, education, work safety or a decent standard of living. Companies can also choose to become more involved in other activities, by supporting local communities, building schools and maintaining high environmental standards. So, if employing children means that they are denied an education, this would not be acceptable. In unambiguous situations, the final decision must rely on the answer to one question: *does this decision violate any of the three core human principles: respect for human dignity, respect for basic human rights and good corporate citizenship?* On this basis, cultural traditions only deserve our respect insofar as they respect the fundamental human rights of men and women. Some companies, such as BP, Royal Dutch Shell, Johnson & Johnson, Motorola, The Body Shop, Lockheed Martin and HP, have embraced these principles and included them in employee codes of conduct covering ethical behaviour, trading practices and environmental standards in industrializing countries (Corporate Watch, 2002). Objective ethical standards are ingrained in their organizational cultures and in the mind-sets of employees, and their contracts of employment clearly indicate that staff have the right to report violations of laws or ethical standards, without fear of recrimination (although all have been accused at times of violating these lofty principles). Embracing ethical policies also means that the giving or receiving of bribes and financial 'inducements' is prohibited. Not only can this be a dangerous game to play, but there is little evidence that this helps business, because it undermines market efficiency and profitability (Donaldson, 1996). Consequently, more than 30 countries, including the USA, Canada, the UK and Australia, have introduced laws prohibiting the payment of bribes in other countries, and similar laws now apply in all EEC countries (Towers, 2000).

One example of an organization that has enjoyed the benefits of good corporate governance and socially responsible business practices is the Korean company, Samsung. It had sowed the seeds of good community relationships long before the Asian economic crisis of 1997 and, in the aftermath, reaped considerable benefits. After taking over the firm from his father in 1987, the company's CEO, Lee Kun Hee, stressed initiatives to improve the lives of local employees, and their communities, as part of a broader drive towards greater corporate citizenship in its East Asian operations. In 1997, the firm spent some $US120 million on 'social contributions' (set against profits of only $US291 million). In Indonesia, community initiatives included river environmental schemes, supporting educational initiatives for children and the elderly, and infrastructure development. In Malaysia, a park near Kuala Lumpur was renamed as Samsung Park as a result of the company's initiatives to clean it up. How did these initiatives benefit

Samsung? In Indonesia the company avoided the worst of the backlash and rioting against foreign firms. At the height of the political unrest and riots in 1998, its local employees pulled together to defend the refrigerator factory and shield expatriate workers from the rioters (reported in *Time*, 19 February 1999). Since this time, Samsung has been twice voted 'The most ethical company in SE Asia' in the *East Asian Economic Review*.

Not only is unethical behaviour bad for legitimate business and capitalism, but there is abundant evidence that such conduct also hampers economic development in industrializing countries and impedes the development of an inclusive and integrated global economy. For justification of this assertion, please refer to Table 12.3.

Table 12.3   Transparency International corruption perceptions index, 2003

Least corrupt countries: Finland, Iceland, Denmark, New Zealand, Singapore, Sweden, Netherlands, Australia, Norway, Switzerland, Canada, Luxembourg, United Kingdom, Hong Kong, Austria, Germany, Belgium, Ireland, USA, Chile, Israel, Japan, France, Spain and Portugal.

Most corrupt countries: Zimbabwe, Pakistan, Philippines, Romania, Zambia, Albania, Guatemala, Nicaragua, Venezuela, Vietnam, Georgia, Ukraine, Kazakhstan, Bolivia, Cameroon, Ecuador, Moldova, Uganda, Azerbaijan, Indonesia, Kenya, Angola, Madagascar, Paraguay, Myanmar, Haiti, Nigeria and Bangladesh.

Source: Transparency International website, 5 January 2004; 133 countries were included in this survey.

What differentiates countries in the top echelon from those at the bottom of the index? One commentator, P.J. O'Rourke (1999), has suggested that there are seven main characteristics that distinguish stable and affluent countries from those that are poor, corrupt and autocratic:

1 a sense of personal responsibility for achievement and success in life,
2 a culture of hard work and enterprise,
3 high levels of education,
4 established property rights,
5 respect for the rule of law and an independent judicial system,
6 strong legal regulation of business,
7 the presence of mature and accountable democratic government.

O'Rourke's thesis is compelling. By looking at the comparative economic success of eight countries, he showed that those nation-states that have these principles and characteristics enshrined in their political governance, legal systems and business cultures are always more affluent, stable and peaceful than those that have not. Here are a few examples from East Asia of how the absence of these principles and characteristics, combined with low ethical standards, can have a negative impact on the economic development of some industrializing countries in the region.

In Indonesia, the hostile treatment of the Chinese between 1997 and 2000 by indigenous Indonesians forced many of this affluent minority ethnic group to emigrate. They also moved at least $US50 billion in assets out of the country during this time, and 50 per cent of this was lodged with Singapore banks. In terms of both capital and the loss of large numbers of entrepreneurs, this represented a serious loss to the Indonesian economy. After the destructive forest fires in 1998, it was revealed that one of the main reasons why government authorities did so little to extinguish these fires was that millions of rupiah had been secretly channelled from fire fighting services to fund the development of an Indonesian national car. The company building this was Timot Putra, which was controlled by 'Tommy' Suharto, ex-President Suharto's youngest son (IMF Chief Michael Camdessus, cited in *The Australian*, 23 January 1998). The government that replaced Suharto promised to stamp out corruption, and has since estimated that corrupt business practices by Suharto, his family and other assorted cronies cost the state as much as $US580 million between 1994 and 1999. In 1998, the government also terminated dozens of investment projects tainted by collusion and nepotism, saving the state an additional $US430 million dollars over the next two years (World Bank, 2002). On 26 July 2002 Tommy Suharto was also found guilty of murdering a Supreme Court Judge, Justice Syafuid Kartasasmita, who had indicted him on fraud and corruption charges in 1998.

In Cambodia, overfishing and illegal logging have almost entirely destroyed the country's fishing and forestry industries. This rape of natural resources has not benefited the Cambodian people; the people who have benefited are top government politicians, bureaucrats and crime syndicates. In Cambodia, Vietnam, Thailand and Burma, there are also thriving trades in paedophilia, serving a largely white-male western 'clientele'. In Burma, the military junta actively collaborates with international drug syndicates in the production and trafficking of illegal drugs. The export of opium and heroin is amongst this country's biggest cash-earners. This means that if you trade with, or support, this vicious military regime, you are directly responsible for helping to put heroin on the streets of your country's cities (Robinson, 1998).

For some time, there have been growing concerns about the activities of companies operating in countries like Burma, who have very poor records on human rights, and those that employ children and wage-slaves in their factories (for example, Nike and Gap). Several companies, such as the Burton Group, Reebok and Coca-Cola, have all moved their operations out of the country in response to consumer disquiet about the military regime there, the continuing use of torture against political opponents, slave labour and forced relocation and land confiscation (Lyall, 2002). Shell and BP have both responded positively in recent years to consumer disquiet about their activities in Nigeria, Colombia and Burma. Even companies like Nike and Reebok, long the subject of criticisms of their violations of worker's rights, the use of child labour and dangerous factory conditions in their Third World operations, made changes to their employment and pay policies in East Asian countries during the late 1990s (AFP, 1998; Dionne, 1998). All of the countries that these companies have withdrawn their business from continue to be characterized by human rights' abuses, endemic corruption and economic and political instability.

In fact, countries that are most effective in combating corruption and fraud, and who are pushing for the establishment of democratic government, enjoy faster and more stable economic growth. According to one survey, by the Political and Economic Risk Consultancy in Hong Kong, Asian countries that are most effective in fighting corruption are likely to emerge as the economic leaders of the future. Singapore, Hong Kong and Japan are regarded as the least corrupt countries in the region and Indonesia, Vietnam, Cambodia and China the most corrupt. This study goes on to say:

> The most striking feature of our most recent survey into corruption is the way those countries that have all along been most effective in fighting the problem have widened the [economic] gap in the past year compared with those countries whose systems have historically been less effective in combating graft. This could have significant implications for the pace and pattern of economic development in the future by stimulating investment and growth in those countries that keep on top of corruption relative to those who allow the problem to flourish.
> (*Cited by Richardson, 2000*)

Consequently, since the 1997 crash in East Asia, more governments, businesses and banks have been paying greater attention to issues such as fraud and corruption, and their effects on business efficiency and profitability, and national economic development. For example, the prime minister of Malaysia, Abdullah Badawi, announced a major crackdown on cronyism and political corruption in early February 2004. Countries that fail to follow this example will find it difficult to make the transition from economies based on raw material supplies, agriculture and labour-intensive manufacturing to open knowledge-based economies based on the rule of law. The message for both political and business leaders in industrializing countries has been loud and clear for some time: fraud and corruption are bad for business; they slow economic development and impede the growth of global capitalism.

Having read through this section, how would you now deal with the managers' dilemmas in Exercise 12.2? Would you now approach these in a different way?

Conclusion

> Corporate citizenship is critical. All good companies are now thinking about their long-term impact on the community and the environment. Ethical values can no longer be divorced from the main business strategies of this company.
> (*Michael Chaney, former CEO of Wesfarmers*, Boss, *August 2001*)

Organizations dominate every aspect of our lives. From birth, through school, work and even in death they influence our lives in many different ways. Almost all of us will spend most of our waking hours either working in or for someone else's organization or, perhaps, running one of our own. Everything we do, at work or leisure, is influenced and shaped by organizations. They control and regulate us, sometimes exploit us, tax us, entertain us, reward us, provide us with leisure products and services, sometimes care for us and, in their bureaucratic forms, often drive us to exasperation with 'red tape'. Some multinational companies have economic and political powers that transcend those of smaller nation-states. In many ways, they have usurped the power of those institutions that traditionally wielded moral authority, such as the Church and national governments. Multinational corporations are now so powerful that, human nature being what it is, it is essential that their activities are regulated and controlled. As Anita Roddick has suggested,

> In terms of power and influence, you can forget about the church, forget politics. There is no more powerful institution in society than business. I believe it is now more important than ever before for business to assume a moral leadership. The business of business should not be just about money, it should be about responsibility. It should be about public good, not private greed.
> (*Roddick, 2000: 8*)

Hence leaders and managers may need to engage more seriously with the issue of business ethics, not as a fad or an optional extra, but as something that can have a profound impact on the overall effectiveness of their organizations. Furthermore, we have established that unethical behaviour, in the form of fraud, corruption, nepotism, cronyism and (in Chapter 6) discrimination, is bad for business and for capitalism. Of course, a few greedy and corrupt individuals, such as the Suharto family in Indonesia, corrupt dictators in Africa and the CEOs of Worldcom and other companies, have benefited from this type of conduct. However, the vast majority of working people – you and I – do not. When individuals, companies and countries behave in this fashion it can have multiple consequences:

- The destruction of people's reputations, personal lives and careers (for example, Geoffrey Wigand and the US tobacco industry).
- Thousands of redundancies and the loss of employees' entire pension savings (for example, Enron, Worldcom and many other companies in recent times).
- The destruction of well-respected and established companies (for example, Arthur Andersen).
- Multibillion dollar litigation payouts (for example, the tobacco industry and the dotcom and finance companies described in Chapter 11).
- Thousands of deaths and injuries: in specific cases such as Union Carbide at Bhopal in India (where 8000 died), in many dictatorships in South America, East Asia and Africa and, of course, as a result of the poisonous and toxic products sold by tobacco companies for decades.
- The economic exploitation and sexual abuse of hundreds of thousands of child slaves in many industrializing countries.
- The promotion of global crime and the international drug trade by financial institutions that, until very recently, had routinely turned a blind eye to their laundering of the dirty money generated by these 'businesses'.
- Slower and/or more erratic rates of economic growth in industrializing countries, and the possibility of the complete meltdown of national economies, as occurred in several East Asian countries in 1997–8.
- Large-scale ecological destruction as a direct result of lax environmental standards in many industrializing countries.
- And, for you and me, the use of our hard-earned taxes to clear up the mess that is left behind, such as the multimillion dollar costs of the many court cases, inquiries and commissions that always follow these events. To cite just two examples from Australia: the total cost to taxpayers of the Royal Commission into police corruption in New South Wales in the 1990s was $A70 million. The cost of probing the collapse of the insurance companies HIH and UMP, and One.Tel, in

2001–2 was approximately $A80 million. Household insurance premiums in Australia increased by an average of 15 per cent, and corporate liability insurance went through the roof, leading to numerous small companies going out of business in 2002–3 (Westfield and Elliott, 2001). The cost to taxpayers in the USA, Europe and other countries of corporate scandals during the 2000s will be several trillion dollars.

So what kind of values might organizations, their leaders and employees aspire to? When professionals, managers or MBA students are asked this question, they often mention honesty, integrity, trustworthiness, self-respect, respect for other people, reliability, fairness and loyalty. As we saw earlier in this chapter, it is also significant that a respect for the rights of other people, a sense of justice and fairness, the value of human dignity and honesty in relationships are features of almost every culture, religion and system of morals throughout the world (Boatright, 1999). And recall that these are also values that were identified earlier in this book as being amongst the most desirable qualities of effective and successful leader/managers. How might you build these into your daily people management practices or, if you are the leader of an organization, how could you build these into its culture and employee codes of conduct? How could these values and principles be built into the way you deal with your employees, your customers and your shareholders, and how you do business in other countries?

It was suggested at the beginning of this chapter that the best reason for embracing ethical principles in business is *self-interest*. Individuals, organizations and countries with higher ethical and legal standards thrive and prosper. Those with lower ethical standards, sooner or later, run into serious problems. If you're still not convinced about the importance of ethics in business, leadership and people management, try to imagine what a world without any legal, ethical and moral guidelines would look like. It would be a violent and anarchic nightmare. Capitalism without a conscience is untenable, and there are no legitimate businesses that can operate without some reference to legal, moral and ethical frameworks. All the historical evidence shows that, when organizations and their employees have been allowed to operate without these, they have been at best unpleasant and, at worst, truly monstrous. While a few unethical business people and organizations may be 'successful', most are not, and it can be argued with equal force that good business practices are only possible with high ethical standards. Even the pro-business George Bush has suggested,

> It is time to reaffirm the basic principles and rules that make capitalism work: truthful books and honest people, and well-enforced laws against

fraud and corruption. All investment is an act of faith, and faith is earned by integrity. In the long run, there's no capitalism without a conscience; there's no wealth without character [ ] We will use the full weight of the law to expose and root out corruption. My administration will do everything in our power to end the days of cooking the books, shading the truth and breaking our laws [ ] Corporate leaders who violate the public trust should never be given that trust again. The SEC should be able to punish corporate leaders who are convicted of abusing their powers by banishing them from ever serving again as officers or directors of a publicly held corporation. If an executive is guilty of outright fraud, resignation is not enough. Only a ban on serving at the top of another company will protect other shareholders and employees [ ] Dishonest individuals have failed our system. Now comes the urgent work of enforcement and reform, driven by a new ethic of responsibility.
(*Bush, 2002*)

Considerable weight was added to these suggestions on 18 July 2002, in a much-anticipated speech to the US Senate by the Federal Reserve Chairman, Alan Greenspan:

Our market system depends critically on trust – trust in the word of our colleagues and trust in the word of those with whom we do business. Falsification and fraud are highly destructive to free-market capitalism and, more broadly, to the underpinning of our society. In recent years, shareholders and potential investors would have been protected from widespread disinformation if any one of the many bulwarks safeguarding appropriate corporate evaluation had held. In many cases, none did. Lawyers, internal and external auditors, corporate boards, Wall Street security analysts, rating agencies and large institutional holders of stock all failed for one reason or another to detect and blow the whistle on those who breached the level of trust essential to well-functioning markets. An infectious greed seemed to grip much of our business community. Our historical guardians of financial information were overwhelmed. Too many corporate executives sought ways to 'harvest' some of these stock market gains. As a result, the highly desirable spread of shareholding and options amongst business managers created incentives to artificially inflate reported earnings in order to keep stock prices high and rising.

It is not that humans have become any more greedy than in generations past. It is that the avenues to express greed had grown so enormously. Manifestations of lax corporate governance are, in my judgement, largely a symptom of a failed CEO. Having independent directors, whose votes are not controlled by the CEO, is essential for any board of directors. Although we may not be able to change the character of corporate officers, we can change their behavior through incentives and penalties. That, in my judgement, could dramatically improve the state of corporate governance. Fraud and deception are thefts of property and unless the laws governing how markets and corporations function are perceived as fair, our economic system cannot achieve its full potential.
(*Abridged from Greenspan, 2002*)

Similar sentiments were voiced in Australia, at the 2002 annual meeting of the Australian Institute of Company Directors. During this, Charles Goode, the Director of the ANZ Bank, made these comments about reforming corporate governance:

> [In the future] I think investors will pay more attention to the culture of a company and its values. Boards will also focus more on the triple bottom line. Boards will tend to be smaller in size, and there will be more private sessions of the non-executive directors and more questioning of management. Boards will require greater time. Directors will serve on fewer boards and there will a decrease in the level of directors' fees. Boards will focus more on risk assessment and on management compensation, and there will be a trend away from options to deferred shares. And, where options are issued, these will be expensed.
> (*Cited by Gottliebsen, 2002b*)

The historical evidence shows that business leaders and companies who pursue short-term profits, at the expense of all other considerations, usually run into major problems. We also know that many long-lasting, visionary, successful and profitable companies have a purpose *beyond* simply making profits, delivering short-term results to their shareholders or allowing CEOs to receive obscene levels of remuneration. This is not to say that making money is not important to these companies; it is. However, this is balanced by other important considerations. For example, in great companies of the 20th century examined by Collins and Porras, phrases like 'returns to shareholders' or 'making money' were rarely included in their statements of core values and ideologies (and, where mentioned, were made subservient to other values). Furthermore,

> Contrary to business school doctrine, we did not find that maximising shareholder wealth or profit maximisation was the dominant driving force or primary objective throughout the history of most of the visionary companies. Visionary companies pursue a cluster of objectives, of which making money is only one. Yes, they seek profits, but they are equally guided by a core ideology – core values and a sense of purpose beyond just making money Yet, paradoxically, the visionary companies make more money than the more purely profit driven comparison companies.
> (*Collins and Porras, 1996: 8*)

This counterintuitive and important finding is one that all regulatory authorities, company directors and shareholders should take to heart.

In conclusion, it is apparent to a growing number of business analysts that ethics are no longer just an optional 'add-on' to the main business activities that organizations, and their employees, are engaged in. They play an important role in their longevity, adaptability and profitability, as well as in the livelihoods of their employees and the financial well-being of their investors. Even economic libertarians, such as Milton Friedman, believed that business must be conducted within ethical frameworks. He once commented, 'There is one and only one responsibility of business – to use its resources and engage in activities that are designed to increase its profits – *so long as it engages in open and free competition without deception or fraud* (Friedman: 1993: 349; my emphasis).

When politicians like George Bush, who has enjoyed a very close relationship with the corporate world in the USA for more than two decades, demanded radical change in July 2002, we all understood that business needed tighter regulation and higher ethical standards. The numerous examples of fraudulent, corrupt, illegal and unethical behaviour that were cited earlier demonstrate that the conduct of business is far too important an activity to be left solely in the hands of business people. If it is, we will continue to see repetitions of the numerous scandals that have been highlighted in this chapter. Consequently, the remaining question for leaders and managers is: *Should we aspire to ethical values and principles that enhance what we do in business, and allow us to serve the best long-term interests of our organizations, our employees, our investors and shareholders, and the communities that we operate in?*

The evidence presented in this chapter indicates that there may now be only one rational answer to this question.

> Tolerance and understanding, respect, responsibility, social justice, excellence, care, inclusion and trust, honesty, freedom, being ethical.
> (*Values that should be taught in all Australian schools, according to a national study commissioned by the Australian Federal Education Minister, Dr Brendan Nelson, in 2003*)

> Honesty.
> (*Mark Hollands, vice-president of the Gartner Group in the Asia–Pacific region, commenting on what he believed was required to restore faith in big business,* The Australian, *14 May 2002*)

> We look forward to a world founded on four essential human freedoms: freedom of speech, freedom of worship, freedom from want and freedom from fear.
> (*US President Franklin D. Roosevelt during a speech to the nation, 6 January 1941*)

> All it takes for evil to thrive is for good people to do nothing.
> (*Edmund Burke, 18th-century political activist and commentator*)

Exercise 12.4

Having read through this chapter, please think about how you can translate any new insights you have acquired, about ethical values and principles in business, into your business, leadership and people management practices in the future.

Insight	Strategy to implement this
1.	
2.	

3.

4.

5.   ◆

Notes

1   The scale of corporate fraud and corruption in recent times is mind-boggling, and the
    following examples are just a snapshot of some of the more high-profile cases of the
    early 2000s.

    On 1 July 2004, Bank One agreed to pay $US90 million to settle allegations that it
    allowed hedge fund managers to make improper trades in mutual funds. Mark
    Deacon, former One Group Mutual Funds' CE, agreed to a $US100 000 fine and a
    two-year ban from the mutual fund industry. Tomo Razmilovic – former chief exec-
    utive – and six other top executives were indicted on securities fraud, manipulation
    of stock options and related charges at the high-tech firm Symbol Technologies on 4
    June 2004. The company had already admitted liability and agreed to pay $US139
    million in penalties. On the same day, former HealthSouth executives Catherine
    Fowler, Malcolm McVay and Richard Botts all managed to avoid jail sentences for
    their roles in a $US2.7 billion accounting fraud at the company. On 28 May 2004
    former Rite-Aid chairman, Martin Grass, was sentenced to eight years in prison for
    his role in a $US1.6 billion accounting fraud and was also fined $US500 000. Three
    other former executives of the company, Ranklin Bergonzi, Eric Sorkin and Philip
    Markovitz received sentences of 28 months, five months and one month, respectively,
    for their roles in this scam. On 23 May 2004 the founder of Capital Management,
    Richard Strong, paid $US60 million in costs and $US80 million in compensation to
    former clients in settlement of charges of illegal trading and was banned from the
    securities industry for life. Two other executives, Anthony D'Amato and Thomas
    Hooker, were also banned from the securities industry for life.

    Prosecutors in the USA charged 642 defendants in 290 different cases and secured
    convictions or guilty pleas from 250 of them between January 2002 and April 2003.
    The typical number of convictions during the 1990s was about 50 a year. The follow-
    ing former employees of Enron had been indicted to stand trial in 2003–4: Jeffrey
    Skilling (president and chief operating officer), Michael Kopper (senior executive),
    Andrew Fastow (chief financial officer), his wife Lea (assistant treasurer), Scott
    Sullivan (financial officer), Ben Glisan (treasurer) and Dan Boyle (finance officer), as
    well as seven other senior managers who had worked in Enron Broadband Services
    and one trader (John Forney). Skilling was arrested on 20 February 2004 and charged
    with 35 counts of insider trading, fraud and conspiracy. If convicted on all charges,
    he faced life in jail and hundreds of millions of dollars in fines. Andrew Fastow is
    serving ten years in prison and his wife received a five-month sentence with five
    months' home detention. Glisan was sentenced to five years in jail for conspiracy to
    defraud on 11 September 2003. Ken Lay, Enron's former CEO, was still under inves-
    tigation by the SEC in June 2004.

    The judge in the grand larceny case against former Tyco CEO Dennis Kozlowski and
    CFO Mark Swartz declared a mistrial on 2 April 2004, after nearly six months of testi-
    mony and 11 days of jury deliberations, citing 'intense outside pressure and coercion
    placed on a juror' (Maull, 2004). The two accused were still facing the prospect of a
    second trial, and up to 30 years in jail if found guilty. The disgraced former boss of
    Worldcom, Bernie Ebbers, was arrested and charged with securities fraud on 3 March
    2004 after the company's former CEO, Scott Sullivan, made a deal with prosecutors

to lessen a 25-year prison sentence. Ebbers was charged with orchestrating a securities fraud worth an estimated 11 *billion* dollars (Dalton, 2004). On 17 December 2003, Calpers, the largest US public pension fund, launched a $US155 million class action on behalf of its clients against the New York Stock Exchange, accusing the NYSE of ignoring illegal acts of stock manipulation by seven investment companies from 1998 to 2002. These companies were accused of being 'routinely engaged in wide-ranging manipulative, self-dealing, deceptive and misleading conduct' (cited by Dalton, 2003b). Six days earlier, on 11 December Freddie Mac, the second biggest buyer of US mortgages, was fined $US169 million for disregarding accounting laws and violating oversight and disclosure rules (AFP, 2003a).

In early April 2004, five market-making firms at the NYSE agreed to pay nearly $US242 million in client compensation and civil penalties to settle allegations of improper trading between 1999 and 2003. In mid-March 2004, Bank of America and Fleet-Boston Financial agreed to pay a record $US675 million to settle allegations that executives allowed mutual fund trading for 'favoured' clients that diluted the gains of other investors. JP Morgan Chase agreed to pay $US25 million in an out-of-court settlement after an inquiry by the SEC into its favoured clients practices during IPO flotations in 1999–2000. In late July 2003, Citigroup and JP Morgan agreed to pay out a total of $US308 million in two out-of-court settlements to end investigations by state and federal regulators into allegations that they helped Enron commit fraud in the mid-to-late 1990s. Wall Street's largest investment firms paid a total of $US2.6 billion dollars in out-of-court settlements during 2003 for misleading investment advice given to clients in the late 1990s and early 2000s.

In late September 2002, former Merril Lynch broking assistant, Douglas Faneuil, pleaded guilty to a misdemeanour charge, and agreed to cooperate in another SEC investigation into allegations of insider dealing by 'lifestyle guru' Martha Stewart. Three former Merril Lynch bankers, Robert Furst, Daniel Bayly and James Brown, were arrested and indicted on fraud charges by the FBI on 18 September 2003 (Doran, 2003). The founder of Adelphia, John Rigas, his sons Timothy and Michael, James Brown (the company's former VP for finance) and Michael Mulcahey (former VP for operations) were indicted on fraud charges in October 2002, with their trials in progress when this book was published.

Imclone Systems founder, Sam Walsal, was sentenced to seven years and three months in jail for insider trading in early July 2003 – the case that also dragged Martha Stewart into court accused of selling her stock in the company just before its share price crashed in 2002. Stewart was ordered to stand trial for securities fraud and obstructing justice in November 2003, and was found guilty on four charges on 5 March 2004. Other high-profile SEC scalps in 2002 included former corporate hatchet-man, Al 'Chainsaw' Dunlap, who was fined $US500 000, and barred for life from serving as an officer or director of a publicly owned company. He had been found guilty of fraud and misleading investors, by inflating revenue and profit figures, while CEO at Sunbeam in the late 1990s (Dalton, 2002a). The former vice-president of US energy company El Paso, Todd Geiger, was indicted on fraud and false trading charges in December 2002. The SEC was also investigating Duke Energy, Reliant Resources and CMS Energy at this time (Bloomberg, 2002a). In the same month, senior executives of the investment banks Citicorp and JP Morgan Chase were ordered to appear before a US Senate Committee investigating accusations that they helped Enron deceive investors in a series of sham deals (AFP, 2002c).

Former Tycho director, Frank Walsh, was indicted on security fraud charges on 21 December 2002, joining his former chief executive Dennis Kozslowski who had been charged earlier in the year with looting the company's finances before it went under. At the same time, a bid by the US Congress to gain access to documents detailing the murky relationships between members of Bush's White House staff and energy executives was refused by a Federal Judge. During 2004, the US Vice-President, Richard

Cheney, also faced the prospect of legal action for fraudulent accounting practices, during his time as an executive at Halliburton, by the anti-corruption group, Judicial Watch. A decision on this by the US Supreme Court was due in June 2004.

In Europe, in addition to the Parmalat, Adecco and Royal Ahold cases, there were 'at least' 25 successful prosecutions for insider trading between 1997 and 2002, about one-third of the convictions that the US SEC secured in 2002 alone. The biggest scalp for European regulators was George Soros, fined 2.2 million euros (four million US dollars) by a French court for insider dealing in 1988. It took six years of legal action in the 1990s to procure documents relevant to the case from Switzerland. This fine amounts to about 0.1 per cent of Soros's estimated wealth (Bloomberg, 2002d). In Australia, more than two dozen criminal cases involving HIH, One.tel and several other companies were in progress during 2004–5, with Rodney Adler and Ray Williams being banned from serving as company directors for 20 and ten years, respectively. Between 2000 and 2003, the Australian Security and Investment Commission put 70 white-collar offenders in jail, had 40 directors removed from office and had 95 people banned from working in securities and financial planning businesses (Elliott, 2003).

2   This appeared in *The Australian* during September 2001, shortly after the collapse of HIH, a 'menu' that could have been repeated in many other businesses at this time:

> **HIH Annual Dinner 2001**
> *Raw prawn cocktail or porkie pies*
> *Duck for cover confit or premium cut of carpetbaggers*
> *Steak in reduced stock or stakeholders well done over*
> *Hard cheddar or sour grapes*
> *Just deserts*
> *Followed by Chateau Renovation 2001 and Any Port in a Storm*

3   If you're interested in ethical investments, most major banks and finance houses now offer these to their clients. There are also dozens of websites that deal with these, including www.ecobusiness.com.au, www.peg.apc.org and www.austethical.com.au

4   Furthermore, the average tenure of CEOs in industrialized countries halved from 8.4 years in 1997 to 4.2 years in 2002. This trend placed even more pressure on CEOs to deliver short-term, quick-fix results that would satisfy institutional investors, and to implement strategic policies that would ensure that the value of their personal stock portfolios increased in the short term. This is not a healthy recipe for ensuring that CEOs implement policies that are aligned with the long-term interests of the companies they lead (Wilson, 2002a). This realization prompted many companies in the USA, Europe and Australia to review the practice of awarding share options to senior management, roundly criticized during 2002–3 for encouraging executives to manipulate the short-term financial results of their companies (White, 2002).

It's also been pointed out that exceptional incompetence – not outstanding performance – became the shortest route to millionaire status for CEOs in the 1990s and early 2000s. As one commentator has observed:

> Renegade company consultant Graef Crystal thought that golden parachutes should be designated 'golden condoms', because they protect the executive and screw the shareholders [ ] We have strayed a long way from the original idea that rewarding executives with stock would strengthen their sympathy with shareholders. On the contrary: because what gratifies investors in the short-term is not always in a company's long-term interests, it can provoke as many bad business calls as good. But there's more: as at Enron, sundry telcoms and dotcoms, it may encourage dishonesty. Fully valued stock price: good. Overvalued stock-price: better. Absurdly inflated share-price based on sham accounts: best – particularly if you're a seller [ ] The most surprising aspect of the creed of shareholder value is not that it encourages dishonesty, but that it seems to encourage little else. Studies

at Harvard and Wharton in the late 1990s found that compensation of both executives and directors was not predictive of corporate success.
(*Haigh, 2003; 48, 61, 63*).

For more on the 'relationship' between CEO remuneration and company performance, see Haigh's humorous and masterful demolition job on this persistent and resilient myth.

5 The topical issues of ecological/environmental management and sustainability strategies are addressed in the sequel to this book, *Creating Intelligent Organizations: The Secrets of Long-Lasting Business Success.*

6. Whom would you do business with?
(The years refer to those in which these countries held/will hold the Olympic games)

	Nazi Germany (1936)	Soviet Union (1980)	China (2008)
Totalitarian regime	X	X	X
No free elections	X	X	X
Economy controlled by ruling party's power elites	X	X	X
Systematic and endemic corruption	X	X	X
Political opposition not permitted	X	X	X
Military/police under the direct control of the ruling party	X	X	X
No freedom of expression	X	X	X
No independent media (and extensive use of propaganda)	X	X	X
No independent judiciary	X	X	X
Imprisonment without trial	X	X	X
Routine abuses of basic human rights	X	X	X
Persecution for religious, political or sexual beliefs	X	X	X
'Labour' and 'retraining' camps (where torture is used routinely)	X	X	X
Expansionist foreign policy	X	X	X
Military aggression towards neighbouring states	X	X	X
Genocide is official state policy	X	X*	X*

* While genocide has not been carried out in the systematic way that it was under the Nazis, both the Soviet Union and China have engaged in policies that resulted in the deaths of millions of their citizens, and the destruction of the cultures of minority groups, such as the Chechens from Stalin's time to the present day and the people of Tibet under China's rule.

Conclusion: leading and managing people at work

Objectives

To reflect on any new discoveries you've made about your leadership and people management practices.

To summarize the main themes of *Maximum Performance*.

The end of the beginning

> One thing I know, and this is that I know nothing.
> (*Socrates, who possessed one of the greatest intellects in human history*)

> Best is to know, and know that you know.
> Next best is to know that you don't know.
> Worst is to not know that you don't know.
> (*Ancient proverb*)

Welcome to the conclusion of this book. I hope you've gained some new insights into the nature of successful leadership and people management; insights that should stand you in good stead now and in the future. But, if you empathized with the story of the *sensei* and his student in Chapter 4, you will have already realized that this is merely the end of the beginning of a journey that will continue until you retire from paid work. Furthermore, we discovered that self-awareness is the building block upon which all other leadership skills and competencies are built. Without this, it is not possible to become a successful and effective leader/manager. So, before reading though this conclusion, please find a quiet place to think about how your views about leadership and people management may have changed or evolved recently. Reflect on any new insights and knowledge you have acquired and try to make use of these at work. Don't try to change everything at once, but do remind yourself of the kind of leader/manager you want to become, and the core values, standards and principles that will underpin your leadership and people management practices in the future.

Allow yourself time to grow and develop throughout your career. Never assume that you can learn everything that there is to know about leadership and managing people, or that you will always have the right answers to every situation and problem you encounter at work. If any of us ever reach this stage, it probably means that we have forgotten how to think, and it may well be time to put the cue back on the rack and retire from the game. Recall that leadership is not an 'is' – it is a never-ending process of *becoming*, and this can only be realized by honest self-reflection, embracing continuous lifelong learning and unlearning, and by developing an ability to learn from our mistakes and moving on.

The boss test

In the Preface it was suggested that good leader/managers have robust characters combined with deep self-awareness, and a blend of different kinds of intelligence. Their leadership and management practices are underpinned by clear values and principles, which define the boundaries that they will not step over, regardless of the temptations. They are self-disciplined, have great self-motivation and the capacity for hard work, combined with a good understanding of their physical and psychological thresholds. While they are capable of working hard, they also know-how to relax and have fun. They are self-confident and possess a steely resolve in adverse or uncertain situations. They pay attention to their people, because they understand that they are the most important assets that their organizations possess. They lead from the front and lead by example. They understand that true leadership is a two-way process and, as a result, are able to motivate and empower their followers. They have exceptional two-way communication skills, combined with an ability to lead, direct and focus dialogues with others. Through stories and good formal presentation skills, they are able to engage with and influence the minds and hearts of others. Furthermore, they fully understand that it is the character, intelligence, skills and abilities of their employees that really count these days, not their race, culture or gender.

In a fast-changing world, they have the desire and capacity to learn and unlearn quickly, while not discarding good leadership and management practices that have stood the test of time. They experiment with new business and people management techniques, without becoming reactive 'fad-surfers'. They have a chameleon-like quality that enables them to adapt quickly to new situations. They are creative and able to envision the future, but also have the ability to make fast practical day-to-day decisions with incomplete knowledge or data. They are comfortable initiating, leading and managing the complex processes of perpetual organizational change, innovation and learning. They are curious about the world and lifelong learners. They are men or women of both action and contemplation, and because of this they understand exactly what the American comedian Groucho Marx meant when he said, 'That's all very well in practice – but how does it work in theory?'

Good leader/managers also understand how to wield power and how to use organizational politics to their best advantage. They exploit any opportunities that come their way, but also have the capacity to create them. They acquire, keep and use information to further their interests and those of their followers. Of equal importance, they use power to drive themselves and their followers towards successful joint outcomes. They give power away to their followers and this, in turn, enhances their power bases. As a result, they are better able to compete and win, and achieve their destinies. They understand the important role that employee knowledge management and intellectual capital now play as key drivers of organizational success. They have high ethical standards combined with a pragmatic understanding of the realities of doing business in the real world. However, while they may be highly driven individuals, they do not step over the line into unethical business practices, because they understand the dangers of these and the impact these can have on the overall effectiveness of their organizations. We've seen that successful and effective leaders do a number of fairly simple things, but they do them well and they do them consistently under all circumstances.

We also discovered that the starting point on the journey to becoming a really successful leader/manager is an honest self-evaluation of our personal strengths and weaknesses. This does not mean that we should constantly focus on ourselves, or engage in lengthy bouts of navel gazing. However, it does mean that we need to take time out from the frenzy of modern organizational life to pause and reflect on what we do, why we do it and how we do it. Many of the greatest leaders in history, including Lincoln, Martin Luther King Jnr, Gandhi and Roosevelt, did this. Even Churchill, at the height of World War II, took time out to read and paint in order to recharge his batteries. Throughout this book, there have been opportunities to develop a greater sense of self-awareness, and to identify strategies that will enable you to build on your leadership and people management repertoires. There have also been opportunities to assess what kind of leader/manager you would like to become in the future. During this process, we identified a cluster of seven core skills, competencies and qualities that appear time after time, and leader/managers who possess these are the ones that all normal people *want* to follow:

- honesty and integrity,
- competence and credibility,
- the ability to motivate and inspire others,
- the ability to create a vision/sense of direction for the future,
- good two-way communication skills,
- equity/parity and fairness,
- a sense of humour.

Of course, there are other important elements that play their part in successful leadership and people management, but these seven appear to be essentials, and if you possess them the chances are that you will be a successful leader/manager, now and in the future. Of equal importance, we've also seen how *all* of the components that make up each one of these elements are ones that can be developed and enhanced throughout life, given self-belief, time and commitment.

Reinventing the wheel

The emptiest and most tired cliché in organizations for many years has been 'People are our most important asset.' This is of course true, but many organizations just pay lip service to this mantra and, far too often, there is often a huge gulf between the rhetoric of 'people as assets' in organizations and how their employees are actually treated. The harsh truth is that most organizations, and the leaders and managers who work in them, often fail to get the best out of their people. Conversely, those organizations and leaders that are able to get the most out of their employees over long periods of time expend a lot of time and effort setting up organizational systems and cultures that support these processes. Enough evidence has been presented in this book (and in others that have been cited throughout) to demonstrate that, if the latent energy and talents of people are unleashed and rewarded, the more successful your organization or business will be, and so will you. This is particularly true in a world that is fast moving from manufacturing to mentofacturing, where new technologies, innovation and the management of employee knowledge and intellectual capital are fast becoming the principal drivers of organizational success, profitability, adaptability and longevity.

The greatest puzzle about the thousands of books and articles that have been written on leadership and people management over the last 20 years or so is that many of them seem to imply that the techniques they advocate are largely new, or at least creations of the 20th century. Nothing could be further from the truth, because human behaviour has changed little during the last 10 000 years, and this is why many of the challenges that we may face as leaders and managers today are the same as they always have been. For example, in Chapter 1 we cited the advice that Socrates gave to prospective leaders. He suggested that leaders required *Ethos* (the ability to convince their followers that they are trustworthy, reliable and fair), *Pathos* (the ability to appeal to their followers' values, emotions and motivations) and *Logos* (knowledge and expertise). These principles worked for Egyptian, Greek and Roman leaders, they worked for many 19th-century industrialists, and they continue to work for the leaders of the world's most successful modern organizations. Most of the skills we associate with present-day leadership and management, such as communication, cooperation, negotiation, teamwork, the effective use of power and influence, and the ability to envision the future, were essential for the survival and evolution of our ancestors over thousands of years, and these primal leadership skills are as relevant today as they have always been. While the contexts in which leadership and people management have changed, particularly over the last 200 years, the fundamental principles underpinning these have not, because they are timeless.

Crazy ways for crazy days

Having said this, today's world is very different from that of our ancestors, and new leadership and people management skills are required to cope with this fast-changing environment. Because of the scientific revolutions of the 18th, 19th and 20th centuries, we have come to understand a great deal more about our environment, the natural world and the origins and evolution of the human race. In turn, these revolutions have transformed the way that people work and the nature of organizations during the 20th century. Today, these are more fluid and have less formal, bureaucratic and hierarchical structures. They have 'flatter' cultures and fewer status distinctions between employees (at least in the private sector), compared to a decade ago. They also have far more diverse workforces, compared to times past.

Almost all organizations now have to change rapidly, and are being constantly buffeted and reshaped by new technologies, new competition and the forces of globalization. Organizations have to think faster and smarter, and be more adaptable, than at any other period in human history. Consequently, leaders and managers not only have to be quicker and smarter themselves, they also have to find better and more effective ways of getting more out of the employees, departments or organizations that they head. Above all else, this means that they have to have the capacity to lead, inspire, motivate, mentor and empower their people in more time-efficient ways, because, as we have seen on numerous occasions throughout this book, it is *always* employees who ultimately determine the performance, productivity and profitability of the organizations they work for (not overpaid fat-cat CEOs and company directors).

The pace of change these days also means that leaders have to routinely question common-sense ways of doing things. We saw in Chapters 1, 8, 9 and 11 that leaders of the future will have to rely increasingly on *uncommon sense*. Why? Because the pace of technological, economic, social and organizational change means that relying on what we do now, or even on what has worked well for a while, will not guarantee success for any organization in the future, particularly those in the private sector. The name of the game these days is change, and unrelenting, perpetual and continuous evolution in all businesses. In this environment, leaders and managers only have two options: create change for others to follow or play a constant, and very uncomfortable, game of perpetual catch-up with the most innovative and fast-changing organizations in the sectors or markets they operate in.

We also saw that transformational leaders are people who constantly question 'the way we do things around here' and, while they all possess solid and practical business acumen, they always have one eye on the future. They gather strategic intelligence and scenario-map effectively. They constantly seek out or create new business opportunities that others are unable or unwilling to see. They are creative and able to think laterally. They are individuals who may not know everything but are adept at surrounding themselves with loyal people who can fill the gaps in their knowledge or expertise. They can see the future and create visions, and are able to lead their followers on journeys down new ways, roads or paths to this future. The ability to cope with this environment demands that leaders be able to look into that which does not currently exist, and then imagine, 'What if we . . .?'

Vive la différence

The emergence of women in organizations over the last two decades also has important implications for leadership and people management, now and in the future. In Chapter 6, we saw that, while women have made remarkable advances, in all professions and occupations, during this time, there is still some way to go before they achieve true equality with men. It was suggested that most organizations should review how they treat their women employees, for the simple reason that, if they don't, this will have a negative effect on their performance, productivity and profitability. Examples were cited of companies that have made a major commitment to equality of opportunity and to promoting women into senior management positions. All of these are amongst the most visionary, successful and profitable companies in the world. We also saw that many more women are opting for self-employment in North America, the UK and Australasia. One of the principal reasons given by women for starting up their own businesses is that it enables them to balance their work and family lives. Many had previously worked in traditional jobs for large employers, and had left because they felt that, not only were glass ceilings in their organizations impeding their career progression, but also employers were not family-friendly. It follows, logically, that not only do many organizations continue to lose good staff because of outdated employment practices, they are losing those that they can least afford to lose: their intrapreneurs and innovators. The message is clear: to be competitive, organizations need to take advantage of the full range of talents of their staff, regardless of their gender, and good equal opportunity policies make good business sense.

Women managers and professionals still face many challenges and obstacles, but history shows us that that they have shown remarkable endurance, persistence and bravery in overcoming these on many occasions in the past. Towards the end of Chapter 6, specific strategies that women can employ in organizations were outlined. These include maintaining one's self-belief; having a clear sense of direction and personal values; understanding power and how to use it; building alliances and networking (with both men and women); always being well-prepared and keeping records of meetings; dealing assertively with discrimination or harassment; balancing work and family life; maintaining a sense of humour and staying healthy. The evidence presented in that chapter also indicates that successful leaders and managers in western industrialized countries have personal qualities, skills and competencies that encompass both 'male' and 'female' characteristics. Regardless of what a lot of men might believe, and feminist writers have argued, it appears that many successful leaders and managers now possess a combination of female, male and neutral characteristics, qualities and attributes. This suggests that we may be witnessing the emergence of an androgynous style of leadership and people management, a superior hybrid style that transcends traditional 'male–female' stereotypes.

Going bonkers with technology

Chapter 11 demonstrated that humanity is on the threshold of a quantum leap in technological innovation, and this will have profound effects on humanity over the next 20 years and beyond. However, the best leaders, and the best organizations, only use existing technologies in ways that add value to their core business activities. They understand both the potential, and the limitations, of new and emergent technologies as strategic business tools. They have learnt the painful lessons of the dotcom collapse of 2000–2002, and realized that technology cannot be used as a substitute for the five factors that continue to drive all successful businesses: *great leadership/management, great employees, great ideas, great products and great services.* They have realized that it still requires creative and innovative employees to make the best use of new technologies. They know that even e-business is not just about electronics, computers or the Internet. These are simply portals, or add-on devices, that can help their businesses to do what they have always done, namely to bring into being that which was not in the marketplace before, and/or getting value products and quality services to their customers and clients, quickly and cost-effectively. They also understand that, while technology – even in high-tech companies – has its limitations, their organizations must stay techno-savvy for the foreseeable future. Of equal importance, they also understand the importance of keeping an eye on new technologies that may come onto the market two or three years down the track.

All the world's a stage

The inexorable globalization of trade and commerce means that many leaders and managers are becoming more international in their outlook because, even if their organizations operate primarily within one country, they are often competing in someone else's international market (regardless of the events of 11 September 2001 and subsequent terrorist acts around the world). Global leadership and management development in the future will require organizations to offer their employees more opportunities to acquire and develop global skills and competencies. The most successful international companies of this decade will be those that have created internal structures, business systems and cultures that are both fluid and dynamic. These will enable them to achieve the optimum balance between global integration and coordination, alongside local responsiveness, flexibility and speed. The ability to develop these competencies rests upon the vision and learning capabilities of these organizations, their leaders and their managers. Sustainable global advantage also depends on the ability of employees across organizations to learn quickly within this fast-changing environment. Hence the main challenge facing human resource managers in the future will be to develop policies that will foster the selection and retention of employees who can prosper within this environment.

The development of international leader/managers in the future will involve more frequent cross-border job swaps, short assignments or assignments to multicultural project teams. This does not mean that these employees will relocate with their families to these jobs. In fact, traditional expatriate postings of male employees and dependent spouses are becoming less frequent. Recent research has shown that the issues of dual-career couples, family relocations and children's educational needs have already diminished the desire of some employees to go on international assignments. We also know that employees who spend long periods of time abroad can have considerable difficulties when they return home. This means that more employees will find themselves working for short periods of time in different areas of a company's overseas operations, without the necessity of moving their families as well. There is certainly strong anecdotal evidence from airlines that this is happening, but this development is almost totally underresearched. International leader/managers of the future will be younger, as likely to be female as male and culturally diverse. Generations X and Y, and the emergent Generation T, already have mind-sets that transcend international boundaries and cultures. They are much more amenable to learning about other cultures and many have travelled abroad. Most are tuned into the global learning possibilities of the Web and many are, technologically, highly literate. If organizations want to develop global operational cultures, these are exactly the kind of people they will have to recruit in greater numbers. Some of these will become the next generation of global leaders, comfortable dealing with cultures and contexts they did not grow up in and capable of dealing with the avalanche of information, knowledge and intellectual capital now being generated by a hypercompetitive global economy.

Thus the challenge facing organizations is threefold. They must first develop global mind-sets, including a deep understanding of the new world economic environment, and the uneven and erratic growth of this global economy, particularly after the events of 9/11 and other recent terrorist acts. Then they must align their core international strategic objectives with their human resource policies. Last, they will have to anchor their policies dealing with the development of international leader/managers within this framework. This will mean developing employees with international competencies, without traditional long-term country-based assignments. The development of new forms of real-time three-dimensional video conferencing and other communication technologies, such as augmented reality systems, may to some extent diminish the need for this type of continual 'hands-on' assignment. Having said this, there is no doubt that cross-border transfers will remain an important part of international human resource strategies in many companies for the foreseeable future, as well as the primary means for developing the global leader/managers of the future. Only those organizations that are truly committed to learning quickly in this area of strategic human resource management will succeed in the turbulent international business environment of the first two decades of the 21st century (developed from Forster, 2000c: 153–4).

The dark side

Throughout this book, we've focused on what can be broadly described as 'good' leader/managers, who by their words, actions and deeds leave the organizations they lead, or the environments they operate in, better places than they were before they arrived on the scene. They have a passion for the jobs they do and often regard themselves as being servants to their employees and their organizations. In Chapters 1 and 12, we cited several examples of people and organizations that have succumbed to the temptations of the dark side in politics and business, and the many negative consequences of their toxic, discriminatory, unethical, immoral or illegal conduct. Abundant evidence was provided to show that these individuals damage companies and often destroy the jobs and livelihoods of hundreds of thousands of people. Unethical leaders are bad for organizations, bad for business, bad for capitalism, bad for industrializing countries and bad news for you and me. Good leaders understand that the best reason for embracing ethical principles in business is *self-interest*. Individuals, organizations and countries with higher ethical and legal standards thrive and prosper. Those with poor ethical standards, sooner or later, run into serious problems. When individuals and organizations are allowed to operate without ethical and moral guidelines, they are at best unpleasant and, at worst, truly monstrous. This means that ethical considerations can no longer be divorced from the main business activities of organizations, or from the actions of the leaders and managers who work for them.

Gaia and other issues

One of the more difficult parts of writing a book on contemporary organizational life was deciding which topics and issues should be left out. This one might have included some discussion of leadership and management in entrepreneurial and small companies, or dealt in greater depth with leadership and people management in a global economy. It could have included more on macro-organizational issues, such as organizational structure, design and culture, strategic human resource planning, e-business strategies and sustainable environmental management. These and several other topics could have been included, but it was clear that these were not central to the principal objective of the book: identifying the generic qualities, attributes, skills and competencies of effective and successful leader/managers in North America, the UK and Australasia. The length of the book also had to be taken into account, and the inclusion of these topics would have doubled the number of chapters. However, all of these are important aspects of organizational leadership and management and will be covered in the sequel to this book, *Creating Intelligent Organizations: the Secrets of Long-Lasting Business Success.*

Back to the future

In the Preface, I indicated that this book would not try to sell you instant answers, fads or quick-fix solutions, and emphasized that becoming a more effective leader/manager of others requires self-belief, time and commitment. Anyone who claims that you can become a better leader/manager in a few days or weeks is misleading you. Perhaps the most difficult part of this process is not learning new skills, but unlearning: giving up leadership and people management techniques that we may have used for years, but which may be well past their sell-by dates. The ability to do this stems from two elements we have touched on throughout our journey: self-awareness and honest self-reflection. These represent the starting point, because if we cannot see ourselves as we really are (and how others see us), no amount of 'training' is ever going to help us become better leader/managers. But, having come this far, you should have an enhanced sense of self-awareness and, perhaps, a more complete leadership and people management tool-kit. As long as this is kept up-to-date, you can dip into it as and when needed, regardless of the circumstances you find yourself in, the quality of the people you are leading or the type of problems you deal with at work, now and in the future.

The book has provided many opportunities to reflect on the things you do as a leader or manager. By embracing an action-focused, self-directed learning approach to these, you should have developed a set of personal goals that will help you to achieve your objectives, and enhanced the skills and competencies that will enable you to put these into practice on a daily basis at work. Athletes, actors and musicians spend most of their time developing their skills through focused learning and a lot of practice, while leaders and managers usually spend very little time on these and almost all of their time performing. This means that you should try to take periodic time-outs to reflect on your leadership and people management practices. You should also remain committed to converting newly acquired skills and competencies into your daily work repertoire, and spend some time using these until they become second nature. This won't happen overnight, but more effective ways of leading and managing others will become ingrained in time if you make use of them at work. In the final analysis, this approach will always be far more effective and long-lasting than being 'trained', which, as we noted in the Preface, is for dogs and circus animals, not people.

This brings us to the end of our leadership and people management journey, and I hope you found it an enjoyable and rewarding one. Whatever way, road, path or journey you choose to take in the future, keep learning (and unlearning), embrace every opportunity for self-development that comes your way, work on those leadership and people management techniques that work well, and discard the ones that don't. If you have been doing these things for some time, you already have a deep understanding of what differentiates inspirational leader/managers from ineffectual ones. You also appreciate what *really* makes the difference at work these days, and what ultimately differentiates successful organizations from unsuccessful ones, and that is of course the motivation, loyalty, creativity and performance of the people who work for them.

Appendix 1 The business case for emotional intelligence

The 15 examples presented here demonstrate the contribution that emotional intelligence initiatives have made to the bottom line performance of a variety of organizations. These make a compelling case for the introduction of EI initiatives (abridged from Cherniss, 2002).

1   The US Air Force used the EQ-I to select recruiters (the Air Force's front-line HR personnel) and found that the most successful recruiters scored significantly higher in the emotional intelligence competencies and assertiveness, empathy, happiness and emotional self-awareness. The Air Force also found that, as a result of using emotional intelligence to select recruiters, there was an almost threefold increase in their ability to predict successful recruiters. The immediate gain was a saving of $US3 million annually. These gains resulted in the Government Accounting Office submitting a report to Congress, which led to a request that the Secretary of Defense order all branches of the armed forces to adopt this procedure in recruitment and selection.

2   Experienced partners in a multinational consulting firm were assessed on the EI competencies, plus three others. Partners who scored above the median on nine or more of the 20 competencies delivered $US1.2 million more profit from their accounts than did other partners – a 139 per cent incremental gain.

3   An analysis of more than 300 top-level executives from 15 global companies showed that six emotional competencies distinguished stars from average performers: influence, team leadership, organizational awareness, self-confidence, achievement drive, and leadership.

4   In jobs of medium complexity (sales clerks and mechanics), a top performer is 12 times more productive than those at the bottom and 85 per cent more productive than an average performer. In the most complex jobs (insurance salespeople, account managers), a top performer is 127 per cent more productive than the average. Competency research in over 200 companies and organizations

worldwide suggests that about one-third of this difference is due to technical skills and cognitive ability, while two-thirds is due to emotional competence. In top leadership positions, over four-fifths of the difference is due to emotional competence.

5   At L'Oréal, sales agents selected on the basis of certain emotional competencies significantly outsold salespeople selected using the company's old selection procedure. On an annual basis, salespeople selected on the basis of emotional competence sold $US91 370 more than other salespeople did, with a net revenue increase of $US258 360. There was also 63 per cent less labour turnover amongst salespeople recruited on the basis of emotional competence, compared to those selected using traditional selection criteria.

6   In a national insurance company, insurance sales agents who were weak in emotional competencies (such as self-confidence, initiative and empathy) sold policies with an average premium of $US54 000. Those who were very strong in at least five of eight key emotional competencies sold policies worth $US114 000.

7   In a large beverage firm, using standard methods to hire division presidents, 50 per cent left within two years, mostly because of poor performance. When the firm started selecting staff on the basis of emotional competencies such as initiative, self-confidence and leadership, only 6 per cent left in two years. Furthermore, the executives thus selected were far more likely to perform in the top third (based on salary bonuses) for performance of the divisions they led: 87 per cent were in the top third. In addition, division leaders with these competencies outperformed their targets by 15 to 20 per cent. Those who lacked these competencies underperformed by almost 20 per cent.

8   Research by the Center for Creative Leadership in the USA has found that the primary causes of derailment in executives involve deficits in emotional competence. The three primary ones are difficulty in handling change, not being able to work well in a team, and poor interpersonal relations.

9   After supervisors in a manufacturing plant received training in emotional competencies such as how to listen better and help employees resolve problems on their own, lost-time accidents were reduced by 50 per cent, formal grievances were reduced from an average of 15 per year to three per year, and the plant exceeded productivity goals by $US250 per employee. In another manufacturing plant where supervisors received similar training, production increased by 17 per cent.

There was no such increase in production for a group of matched supervisors who were not trained.

10   One of the foundations of emotional competence, accurate self-assessment, was found to be associated with superior performance among several hundred managers from 12 different organizations.

11   Another emotional competence, the ability to handle stress, was linked to success as a store manager in a retail chain. The most successful store managers were those best able to handle stress. Success was based on net profits, sales per square foot, sales per employee, and per dollar inventory investment.

12   Optimism is another emotional competence that leads to increased productivity. New salesmen at Met Life who scored high on a test of 'learned optimism' sold 37 per cent more life insurance in their first two years than pessimists.

13   A study of 130 executives found that how well people handled their own emotions determined how much people around them preferred to deal with them.

14   For sales representatives at a computer company, those hired on the basis of their emotional competence were 90 per cent more likely to finish their training than those hired on other criteria.

15   For 515 senior executives analysed by the search firm Egon Zehnder International, those who were primarily strong in emotional intelligence were more likely to succeed than those who were strongest in either relevant previous experience or IQ. In other words, emotional intelligence was a better predictor of success than either relevant previous experience or high IQ. More specifically, the executive was high in emotional intelligence in 74 per cent of the successes and only in 24 per cent of the failures. The study included executives in Latin America, Germany and Japan, and the results were almost identical in all three cultures.

It should be noted that a few researchers have claimed that EI is a personality construct that is yet to be fully evaluated and validated, and may yet prove to be another 'fad du jour' (for example, Caudron, 2002; Gibson and Tesone, 2001). However, while further verification is needed, there appears to be sufficient evidence to indicate that EI can be an important component of leadership and, according to its many exponents, one that can be enhanced and improved throughout life.

Appendix 2   The benefits of health and wellness programmes

If you are already the leader of an organization, or expect to be one in the future, you may want to consider introducing some stress reduction strategies for your employees, in the form of Health and Wellness programmes. These can be described as any activities that an organization engages in that are designed to identify and/or assist in correcting specific health problems, health hazards, negative health habits or occupational stress problems amongst employees in the workplace. These programmes consist of three principal elements:

- The provision of fitness facilities on-site or subsidized access to these off-site.
- Health screening, which can cover anything from basic medical check-ups to psychological counselling and information on diet and nutrition.
- Education and advice on the effects of sedentary lifestyles and the effects of smoking, or alcohol or other drugs.

The uptake of such programmes by increasing numbers of organizations in the USA in the 1980s and in Europe in the 1990s suggests that they are more than a management 'fad', and they have come to play an important role in organizational health management strategies in many US companies. One reason is that, historically, health care costs in the USA have been high when compared to countries with publicly funded health care systems. As a result, employers in the USA, as part of employees' remuneration packages, often pay for their health care. A second reason was the dawning realization that stress and ill health had the potential to cost companies a great deal of money. For example, General Motors spent more money on employee health care than it did on purchasing steel from its major suppliers in 1978. This added $US175 to the cost of every automobile produced in 1979 (cited by Roberts, 1989). Back in the mid-1980s, it was estimated that American businesses lost some 52 million working days a year because of heart disease alone. The escalating medical cost of stress-related illness was a major driving force behind the introduction of Wellness programmes in the USA at that time.

Examples of organizations successfully implementing wellness programmes in the USA, at this time, are numerous. One early example is AT&T (Holt and Paul 1995). In the early 1980s, the company employed around 280 000 people and was already one of the leading network service providers in the world with operations in the USA and eight other countries. At that time, the company was spending two to three million US dollars on employee health care *every day*. AT&T introduced a pilot Wellness programme for its employees in 1983 at seven work sites. The initiative was called the 'Total Life Concept (TLC) Programme'. The programme was expected to reduce expenses incurred by the company from employee medical compensation claims. From its inception, the TLC programme enjoyed the full backing of a forward-thinking senior management team. The programme addressed employee health, nutrition and personal stress management. Training was provided to improve stress-coping behaviours and to increase levels of employee fitness and general health. The motto of TLC was simple: 'A healthy workplace makes good business sense'. Twenty-four hundred employees took part in the first phase of the programme. By 1989, there were about 80 000 enrolled in the programme, and the company was spending about 80 dollars a year per employee participating in the programme.

Participants were required to attend an orientation programme in which the Wellness philosophy was described. This was followed by free cholesterol and blood pressure tests. The results of these tests were given to employees before they completed a Health Risk Appraisal (HRA) questionnaire. They then attended a Wellness planning session. The programme offered several modular courses. These addressed topics such as blood pressure, cholesterol, nutrition, stress management, cancer, healthy posture, interpersonal communication, smoking cessation and weight control. On completion of the planning session, the employees could choose modules that suited their individual needs. Some full-time staff members were selected and given training to manage the TLC programme and to facilitate running some of the modules. An evaluation study of the TLC programme showed that there were substantial improvements in the health and morale of the employees who participated in the programme. On average, employees reduced their cholesterol levels by 10 per cent, while 50 per cent of employees who joined a smoking cessation course remained non-smokers after 12 months. The then director of the TLC programme at AT&T remarked, 'People's attitudes changed. We sent a message to the employees that said, "We care about your health and well-being". They got the message.' The study also revealed that most employees reported improvements on their health measure indices. Ninety per cent of employees who participated in the TLC programme reported that they had made a change in at least one lifestyle area since they joined the programme; 52 per cent of participants reported that they had changed in at least four lifestyle areas. After five years, TLC participants reported improved health-related behaviour, an enhanced sense of general well-being and improved perceptions of their own health, when compared to employees who were not involved in the programme (Holt and Paul 1995).

The study results indicated that the TLC programme had a positive effect on health-related attitudes. Such a programme may also have given the company a competitive edge when it came to retaining and recruiting workers. AT&T saved more than $US3 million in employee downtime, health care and retraining costs a year after the introduction of the programme. Improved health may also be a very good thing for employees: 97 per cent of those who participated in the TLC programme kept their jobs during the recession of the late 1980s. The company estimated that, for every dollar spent on their Employee Assistance Programs, four dollars were saved. In short, the Total Life Concept programme of AT&T Corporation proved to be a successful employee Wellness initiative (Holt and Paul, 1995).

Other American companies, such as Steelcase and Chevron, provide spacious fitness centres that include basketball courts and swimming pools on-site. Employees are encouraged to use them as needed during working hours. Pharmaceutical giant Eli Lilly runs on-site clinics that offer personal medical services as well as occupational medical advice. Texas Instruments distributes a self-care handbook and provides on-site preventive screenings and flu vaccines. Union Pacific calls high-risk employees at home to advise them on diet and exercise. The idea of these programmes is to encourage employees to pay more attention to their personal physical and mental health. Companies merely play the role of facilitators in this process, but do derive substantial benefits as a result of the increased well-being of their employees, reduced absenteeism and staff turnover, while also reporting improvements in employee performance and productivity (Ziegler, 1995).

Wellness programmes have proved extremely cost-effective for US companies (Sorrensen, 1998; Pelletier and Lutz, 1996; Wilson *et al.*, 1996). For example, a 'Quit Smoking' programme run by the Metropolitan Life Insurance Company in the 1980s reported that their programme cost less than $US200 for each successful quitter, while a smoking employee was estimated to cost $646 a year in increased absenteeism and health costs (Brennan, 1985). A study, commissioned by the MEDSTAT Group, concluded that employers can lower their direct employee health and disability costs by as much as 31 per cent by focusing just on the health of their employees (Gemignani, 1998). They have also shown the potential to improve employee well-being, morale and motivation. For example, One Valley Bank's Wellness programme, introduced in the early 1990s, generated a 48 per cent improvement in the morale of employees, a 93 per cent decrease in staff turnover and a 24 per cent increase in productivity. They also improved morale and motivation, and reduced health costs and absenteeism (Dugdill and Springett, 1994). A study by Aldana (1998) of 93 health intervention programmes in the USA concluded by saying that their evidence 'supported the hypothesis that health promotion programs are cost beneficial based upon savings in reduced medical care expenditure and reduced absenteeism'. Other documented benefits include increased employee motivation, creativity, performance and well-being and reduced labour turnover. Similar results have been reported for Health and Wellness programmes introduced into UK companies in the 1990s (for example, Daley, 1996; Evans, 1995) and in Australia (Forster and Still, 2002).

There is a range of strategies that organizations can employ in order to help their employees cope with the demands of increasingly fast-paced and stressful work environments. Whether the focus is on work redesign, cultural change, limiting working hours, introducing more flexible working arrangements for those with families or introducing customized Health and Wellness programmes that address the behaviours and attitudes of individual employees, there are a number of areas in which both organizations and individual employees can make informed choices about the way they work in the future. Organizations that can find ways of getting the best out of their people, without driving them continually into states of distress, are already the employers of choice for the best talent amongst younger generations of employees. Generation 'X' are becoming much more concerned about the impact of work on their personal and family lives. The emerging Generation 'Y' will simply not tolerate old-style autocratic management styles, antiquated attitudes towards younger women and minorities amongst older managers, exploitative senior managers and long working hours. This is already leading to a serious problem of 'brightsizing' in many companies who cannot retain the commitment and loyalty of younger knowledge workers in the global marketplace that now exists for this organizational talent (Turnbull, 1996).

It was noted in Chapter 3 that many 'Best Company' surveys in *Fortune* magazine over the last three years have shown *consistently* that the most popular (and often the most profitable) companies to work for in the USA are those that put the well-being and performance of their employees at the forefront of their strategic thinking, not merely as an

HR afterthought or 'luxury'. Many of these organizations are members of the *Fortune* 500 list of leading US companies. These companies also have greater inbuilt competitive edge because they are able to get the most out of their employees' motivation, creativity and talents. This is essential for any organization that hopes to succeed in a knowledge and innovation driven world economy. (Abridged from Forster and Still, 2002: 46–8).

Bibliography

Adair, J. (1987), *Effective Team Building*, Sydney: Pan Books.

Adams, J. (1965), 'Inequity in social exchange', in L. Berkowitz (ed.), *Advances in Experimental Social Psychology*, vol. II, New York: Academic Press, pp. 110–51.

Adams, M. (1988), 'The stream of labour slows to a trickle', *Human Resource Magazine*, **43** (3), 84–8.

Adams, P. (2000), 'Ethics flushed down the drain', *The Weekend Australian*, 19–20 February.

Adams, S. (1992), *Always Postpone Meetings with Time-Wasting Morons*, Kansas City: Andrews and McMeel.

Adams, S. (1997), *The Dilbert Principle*, New York: Harper Collins.

Adler, N. (1996), 'Global women in history; an invisible history, an increasingly important future', *Leadership Quarterly*, **7** (1), 133–71.

AFP (1998), 'Nike pledges worker reforms', *The Australian*, 14 May.

AFP (1999), 'Banker, porn star link on inside job', *The Weekend Australian*, 29–30 June.

AFP (2001a), 'Robo-waitress at your service', *The Australian* (IT Section), 27 August.

AFP (2001b), 'First came edible undies, now the vitamin-C shirt', *The Australian* (IT Section), 17 July.

AFP (2002a), 'Worldcom insiders knew how to sell', *The Weekend Australian*, 29–30 June.

AFP (2002b), 'Ample evidence to prosecute Clinton', *The Australian*, 2 February.

AFP (2002c), 'Judge bars bid to open Chaney files', *The Australian* (Business Section), 11 December.

AFP (2003a), 'Freddie Mac fined $169 million for abuses', *The Weekend Australian* (Business Section), 12 December.

AFP (2003b), 'Panel pins rape scandal on top brass', *The Australian*, 24 September.

AFP (2004a), 'BP profit soars on high oil prices', *The Weekend Australian* (Business Section), 2 February.

AFP (2004b), 'Parmalat and Cirio linked to the mafia', *The Australian* (Business Section), 4 March.

Agencies (2002), 'Copycat Xerox in $US ten billion "error" ', *The Australian*, 2 February.

Albanese, R. and Van Fleet, D (1985), 'Rational behaviour in groups: the free-riding tendency', *Academy of Management Review*, April, 244–55.

Aldana, S. (1998), 'Financial impact of worksite health promotion and methodological quality of the evidence', *American Journal of Health Promotion*, **2** (1), 1–8.

Aldred, C. (1997), 'Stress rates attention', *Business Insurance*, **31** (10), 19–20.

Amnesty International website (2002–4), www.amnesty.org.

Ancona, D. and D. Caldwell (1992), 'Bridging the boundary: external activity and performance in organizational teams', *Administrative Science Quarterly*, **27**, 459–89.

Anonymous (2000), 'Human time bombs in the Army', *The Sunday Times* (Western Australia), 19 November.

Anonymous (2001), 'Teacher stress highest', *The Sunday Times* (Western Australia) 10 June.

Argyris, C. (1993), *On Organizational Learning*, Cambridge Mass.: Blackwell Business.

Associated Press (1998), 'Car giant pays $57 million in sex suit', *The Weekend Australian*, 13–14 June.

Asterita, M. (1985), *The Physiology of Stress: with Special Reference to the Neuroendocrine System*, New York: Human Sciences Press.

Australian Business Ltd. (1998), *Women in Management*, www.abol.net.

Australian Centre for Industrial Relations Research and Training (1999), *Australia at Work: Just Managing?* Melbourne: Prentice-Hall.

Australian Centre for Industrial Relations Research and Training and the Australian Congress of Trade Unions (2003), *The Future of Work: New Policies and Choices*, Royal Melbourne Institute of Technology and The Australian.

Austin, N. (1995), 'Story-time', *Incentive*, December, 18–21.

Australian Centre for Industrial Research and Training (1998), *Australia at Work: Just Managing?* Sydney: Prentice-Hall.

Bachelard, M. (1999), 'Going to work really can be bad for your health', *The Australian*, 3 September.

Bachelard, M. (2001), 'From schoolboy bullies to bosses behaving badly', *The Australian*, 5 May.

Bachelard, M. (2002), 'No drama in nice, slow BHP exit', *The Australian* (Business Section), 30 June.

Bachelard, M. and B. Crawford (2004), 'Jobs at Kodak in digital danger', *The Weekend Australian* (Business Section), 26 January.

Bagshaw, M. and P. Phillips (2000), *Knowledge Management*, Ely, Cambridge: Fenman Limited.

Bagwell, S. (1997), 'Why radical hirings work', *The Australian Financial Review*, 17–18 January.

Bagwell, S. (1999), 'Our first woman jet captain still flies high', *The Australian Financial Review*, 19 October.

Balogh, S. and F. Carruthers (1997), ' "Mother hen" taunt wins banker $125 000 000', *The Australian*, 9 September.

Barker, R. (1997), 'How can we train leaders if we do not know what leadership is?', *Human Relations*, **50** (4), 343–62.

Bartlett, A. and S. Ghoshal (1995), 'Changing the role of top management: beyond systems to people', *Harvard Business Review*, May–June, 132–42.

Bass, B. (1985), *Leadership and Performance Beyond Expectations*, New York: Free Press.

Bass, B. and B. Avolio (1994), 'Shatter the glass ceiling: women may make better managers', *Human Resource Management*, **33** (4), 549–60.

Baxter, S. (2002), ' "Aggro" alpha women give the sisterhood a miss', *The Sunday Times* (UK), 3 March.

Beehr, T. (1995), *Psychological Stress in the Workplace*, London: Routledge.

Beilby, G. (2002), 'E-business 2006', *Business Review Weekly*, February, 60–65.

Belasco, J. and R. Stayer (1993), *The Flight of the Buffalo, Soaring to Excellence, Learning to Let Employees Lead*, New York: Warner.

Belbin, M. (1993), *Team Roles at Work*, London: Butterworth Heinemann.

Bennett, J. (2002), 'High-powered computing for super designs', *The Australian* (IT Section), 12 November.

Bennetto, J. (1996), 'Q: What's the difference between a politician and a psychopath? A: None', *The Independent*, 7 July.

Bennis, W. (1995), 'The leader as storyteller', *Harvard Business Review*, January–February, 154–8.

Bennis, W. (1997), 'Leaders of leaders', *Executive Excellence*, **14** (9), 3–4.

Bennis, W. and B. Nanus (1985), *Leaders: The Strategies of Taking Charge*, New York: Harper and Row.

Berger, M. (1996), 'Making the virtual office a reality', *Sales and Marketing Management*, June, 18–22.

Bestos, L. (2002), 'Healthy IT', *The Australian* (IT Section), 23 July.

Bethune, G. (1999), *From Worst to First: Behind the Scenes of Continental's Remarkable Comeback*, New York: John Wiley.

Bieliauskas, L. (1982), *Stress and its Relationship to Health and Illness*, Boulder, Colorado: Westview Press.

Bita, N. (2004), 'Billionaire milko languishes in jail', *The Australian* (Business Section), 2 January.

Black, E. (2001), *IBM and the Holocaust*, New York: Little and Brown.

Blackman, C. (1999), *China Business: The Rules of the Game*, New York: Allen and Unwin.

Blake, V. (2004), 'Big Blue patently leads the way', *The Australian* (IT Section), 20 January.

Blanch, J. and P. Switzer (2003), 'Women drive work rebellion: flexible work hours and better security are attracting more young women than men into joining the ranks of small business owners', *The Australian*, 22 April.

Bloomberg Press (2000), 'Harley shows it's still boss hog', *The Australian*, 13 October.

Bloomberg Press (2001), 'Day of atonement nears for investment bankers', *The Australian*, 29 June.

Bloomberg Press (2002a), 'Geiger counters fraud charge', *The Australian* (Business Section), 11 December.

Bloomberg Press (2002b), 'Executive crime is fitted up to do time', *The Australian* (Business Section), 12 July.

Bloomberg Press (2002c), 'US banks pay one billion dollars to settle claims', *The Weekend Australian* (Business Section), 21–2 December.

Bloomberg Press (2002d), 'Soros the insider pays the price', *The Australian* (Business Section), 23 December.

Bloomsbury (2002), *Business: The Complete Guide*, London: Bloomsbury.

Boatright, J. (1999), *Ethics and the Conduct of Business* 3rd edn, Sydney: Prentice-Hall.

Bodi, A., G. Maggs and D. Edgar (1997), *When Too Much Change Is Never Enough*, Warriewood, NSW: Business and Professional Publications.

Boje, D. (1991), 'The story-telling organization: a study of story-telling performance in an office supply firm', *Administrative Science Quarterly*, **36** (3), 106–26.

Bolick, C. and S. Nestleroth (1988), *Opportunity 2000: Creative Affirmative Action Strategies for a Changing Workforce*, Washington, DC: US Government Printing Office.

Boreham, T. (2001), 'Meetings clock up wasted time', *The Australian*, 1 January.

Botsman, P. (2002), 'Beyond graduation machines: Learning in the 21st century will happen outside the universities', *The Australian* (Higher Education Section), 20 November.

Boulware, J. (2002), 'Search Party', *The Weekend Australian Magazine*, 23–4 March.

Bower, S. and G. Bower (1991), *Asserting Yourself: A Practical Guide for Positive Change*, Wokingham: Addison-Wesley.

Bramson, R. (1994), *Coping With Difficult Bosses*, St Leonards: Allen and Unwin.

Branson, R. (1998), *Losing My Virginity: The Autobiography*, Milson's Point, NSW: Random House.

Brennan, A. (1985), 'Work site health promotion can be cost effective', *Personnel Administrator*, **28**, 39–42.

Brenneman, G. (1998), 'Right away and all at once: how we saved Continental', *Harvard Business Review*, September–October, 2–12.

Briner, R. and S. Reynolds (1999), 'The cost benefits of stress interventions at the organizational level', *Journal of Organizational Behaviour*, **20**, 647–64.

Brockman, J. (ed.) (2000), *The Greatest Inventions of the Past 2000 Years*, New York: Simon and Schuster.

Brokensha, P. (1993), *Corporate Ethics: A Guide for Australian Managers*, Rosewood, NSW: Social Science Press.

Bronowski, J. (1980), *The Ascent of Man*, London: Book Club Associates.

Brown, A. (1995), *Organizational Culture*, London: Pitman Publications.

Brown, J. and P. Duguid (2000), 'Balancing act: how to capture knowledge without killing it', *Harvard Business Review*, May–June, 73–80.

Brown, M. (1996), 'Survival of the fittest', *Management Today*, July, 74–7.

Brown, P. (2000), 'Firms knew of leaded petrol dangers in the 20s', *The Guardian Weekly*, 20–26 July.

Brownell, J. (1990), 'Perceptions of effective listeners: a management study', *Journal of Business Communication*, **27** (2), 401–15.

Brumble, C. (2002a), 'Rest your weary bones all day at your peril', *The Australian* (IT Section), 23 July.

Brumble, C. (2002b), 'Use it or you'll abuse it, say chiropractors', *The Australian* (IT Section), 23 July.

Bryan, M. (2001), 'Get online or face extinction', *Australian Financial Review*, 23 June.

Bryan, R. (2001), 'A man's world: women are breaking down traditional male bastions', *The Australian*, 7 June.

Bryman, A. (1992), *Charisma and Leadership in Organizations*, London: Sage.

Bryson, B. (1994), *Made in America*, London: Reed International.

Bryson, B. (1996), *Notes from a Big Country*, New York: Random House.

Bryson, B. (2003), *A Short History of Nearly Everything*, Sydney: Doubleday.

Burgoyne, J. (1995), 'Feeding minds to grow the business', *People Management*, September, 22–8.

Burke, R. (1996), 'Work experiences, stress and health amongst managerial and professional women', in M. Schabracq, J. Winnubst and C. Cooper (eds), *The Handbook of Work and Health Psychology*, London: Wiley and Sons, pp. 205–30.

Burke, T. and J. Hill (1990), *Ethics, Environment and the Company*, London: Institute of Business Ethics.

Bush, G. (2002), 'Speech to US corporate leaders in New York on ethical standards in American business', reprinted in *The Australian* (Business Section), 11 July.

Bushell, S. (2002), 'Laughing it up', *Chief Information Officer*, August, 102–5.

Business Ethics USA (2003), www.business-ethics.com, 22 April.

Business/Higher Education Round Table in Australia (1992), *Education for Excellence*, Commissioned Report No. 2, Camberwell, Victoria.

Butterfly, N. (2002), 'It's still a "blokey" place at the top', *The Sunday Times* (Western Australia), 1 December.

Cacioppe, R. (1997), 'Drug enhances leadership: seratonin and leadership ability', *Management*, March, 29–30.

Callaghan, G. (1998), 'What does the future hold for our intelligent planet? Greg Callaghan speaks to Michio Kaku', *The Weekend Australian*, 13–14 June.

Callaghan, G. (2002a), 'The good oils', *The Weekend Australian Magazine*, 7–8 September.

Callaghan, G. (2002b), 'Consult your pet today', *The Weekend Australian Magazine*, 2–3 October.

Callaghan, G. (2002c), 'Boy trouble', *The Weekend Australian Magazine*, 8 September.

Callaghan, G. (2003), 'Less may be best', *The Weekend Australian Magazine*, 5–6 April.

Cambell, J. (1970), *Managerial Behaviour, Performance and Effectiveness*, New York: McGraw-Hill.

Cancer Press Releases (2002), 'The global tobacco epidemic', www.uicc.org, 1 October.

Carlopio, J., G. Andrewartha and H. Armstrong (2001), *Developing Management Skills: A Comprehensive Guide for Leaders*, 2nd edn, Frenchs Forest, NSW: Pearson Education.

Carnegie, D. (1994), *How to Win Friends and Influence People*, New York: Simon and Schuster.

Carron, A. (1984), *Motivation: Implications for Coaching and Teaching*, London: Sports' Dynamics.

Carson, V. (2002), 'Clinton clichés turn to gold', *The Australian*, 25 February.

Casella, N. (2001), 'Women in fight to reach top roles', *The Sunday Times* (Perth), 11 July.

Casison, J. (1998), 'Will the trend toward virtual offices make traditional reward and recognition programs obsolete?', *Incentive*, **172**, 54.

Cassidy, J. (2002), *Dotcon: The Greatest Story Ever Told*, New York: Harper-Collins.

Catanzarita, J. (2002), 'Code tackles problem of workplace bullies', *The Weekend Australian*, 2–3 March.

Caudron, S. (2002), 'Just say no to training fads', *Training and Development*, **56** (6), 39–43.

Caulkin, S. (1993), 'High costs of pay-by-results: performance-related pay is the latest example of business dogma gone mad', *The Observer* (UK), 12 December.

Centre for Industrial Relations Research and Training (1998), *Australia at Work: Just Managing?*, Sydney: Prentice-Hall.

Charan, R. (1998), 'Managing to be the best: the century's smartest bosses have influence beyond their companies', *Time*, 7 December.

Charan, R. and J. Useem (2002), 'Why companies fail', *Fortune*, 27 May, 46–56.

Chandhuri, A. (2000), 'Send in the clowns', *The Guardian Weekly*, 20–26 January.

Cherniss, C. (2002), www.eiconsortium.org/business, 23 July.

Chong, F. (2002), 'Companies net $43 billion from the web', *The Australian* (Business Section), 28 November.

Choo, C. (1998), *The Knowing Organization: How Organizations Use Information to Construct Meaning, Create Knowledge and Make Decisions*, Oxford: Oxford University Press.

Christensen, C. (1997), *The Innovator's Dilemma: When New Technologies Cause Great Firms to Fail*, Boston: Harvard Business School Publishing.

Chryssides, G. and J. Kaler (eds) (1993), *An Introduction to Business Ethics*, London: International Thomson Press.

Chung, K. (1999), *Going Public: Communicating in the Public and Private Sectors*, Alexandria, NSW: Hale and Iremonger Pty Ltd.

Chynoweth, C. (1999), 'Motivational fit helps job search', *The Weekend Australian*, 2 August.

Citrin, J. and T. Neff (2000), 'Digital leadership', *Strategy and Business*, first quarter, www.strategy-business.com, 2 May.

City of Perth (2002), *Process Improvement Taskforce: Corporate Knowledge Program*, The City of Perth, Western Australia.

Clarke, G. (1999), 'Cochlear implants in the second and third millennia', *Australasian Science*, **20** (3), 26–9.

Clarke, G. and E. Jonson (1995), *Management Ethics: Theory, Cases and Practice*, Pymble, NSW: Harper Educational Australia.

Clement, B. (1996), 'Social worker wins £175 000 for breakdowns', *The Independent* (UK), 27 April.

Cliffe, S. (1998), 'Knowledge management: the well-connected business', *Harvard Business Review*, July–August, 17–21.

Clifford, L. (2001), 'The Fortune 500', *Fortune*, 16 April, 47–9.

Clonaid: for some real 'Brave New World' stuff on genetic engineering (and an offer to clone your-self), view this organization's website (www.clonaid.com).

Coe, T, (1993), 'Unlocking the barriers to women in management', *Executive Development*, **6** (5), 15–17.

Cohen, W. (1985), 'Health promotion in the work-place', *American Psychologist*, **40**, 213–16.

Coles, J. (1999), 'Life in the fast lane', *The Australian*, 24 November.

Collins, J. (2001), *Good to Great: Why Some Companies Make the Leap and Others Don't*, New York: Harper Business.

Collins, J. and J. Porras (1996), *Built to Last: Successful Habits of Visionary Companies*, London: Century.

Collins, L. (2002), 'A matter of trust', *The Australian Financial Review*, 7 March.

Columbia Accident Investigation Report (2003), vol. 1, August, Washington, DC: Government Printing Office.

Conger, J. (1989), 'Leadership: the art of empowering others', *Academy of Management Executive*, **3** (1), 17–24.

Conger, J. (1991), 'Inspiring others: the language of leadership', *Academy of Management Executive*, **5** (1), 31–45.

Conger, J. (1992), *Learning to Lead: The Art of Transforming Managers into Leaders*, San Francisco: Jossey-Bass.

Conger, J. (1993), 'The brave new world of leader-ship training', *Organizational Dynamics*, **21** (3), 46–57.

Conger, J. (1996), 'Can we really train leadership?', *Strategy and Business*, Winter, 52–65.

Conger, J. (1998), *Charismatic Leadership in Organizations*, Thousand Oaks: Sage Publications.

Conn, M. (2000),'Cricket in crisis warns Bacher', *The Australian*, 13 June.

Conn, M. (2002), 'Obviously, there's one Waugh too many', *The Australian*, 14 March.

Content, T. (2001), '100 years of Harley-Davidson', *The Canberra Times*, 8 August.

Control Data Corporation (1980), *Learn to Manage Your Health*, Minneapolis: Control Data Corporation.

Cooper, C. (1981), *The Stress Check: Coping with the Stresses of Life and Work*, Englewood Cliffs, NJ: Prentice-Hall.

Cooper, C. (1988), *Living With Stress*, Harmondsworth: Penguin.

Cooper, C. (1996a), *Stress Prevention in the Workplace: Assessing the Costs and Benefits to Organizations*. Luxembourg: Office for Official Publications of the European Communities.

Cooper, C. (1996b), 'Healthy, wealthy and wise', *Incentive*, **170**, 25.

Cooper, C. (1997), *Managing Workplace Stress*, London: Sage.

Cooper, C. (1999), 'Hard decade at the office', *Director*, **53** (1), 34–5.

Cooper, C. and A. Melhuish (1984), 'Executive stress and health: differences between women and men', *Journal of Occupational Medicine*, **26** (1), 99–104.

Cooper, C. and R. Payne (1988), *Causes, Coping and Consequences of Stress at Work*, London: John Wiley and Sons.

Cornell, A (1998a), 'Why managers hire their mates', *The Australian Financial Review*, 28–9 February.

Cornell, A. (1998b), 'Honey, I reinvented the company', *The Weekend Australian Financial Review*, 10–11 October.

Corporate Research Foundation (2003), *The Best Companies in Australia to Work For*, Crows Nest, NSW: Harper-Collins.

Corporate Watch (2002), www.corporatewatch.org.

Covey, S. (1989), *The Seven Habits of Highly Effective People*, New York: Simon and Schuster.

Cox, T. and S. Blake (1991), 'Managing cultural diversity: implications for organizational effectiveness', *Academy of Management Executive*, **5** (3), 45–54.

Coyle, D. and J. Kay (2000), 'Does the new economy change everything?', *Australian Financial Review*, 20 April.

Crainer, S. (1995), 'Re-engineering the carrot', *Management Today*, December, 66–70.

Cravens, D., N. Piercy and S. Shipp (1996), 'New organizational forms for competing in highly dynamic environments: the network paradigm', *The British Journal of Management*, **7** (3), 203–19.

Crawford, B. (2002), 'Concern over papal edict', *The Australian*, 1 January.

Creech, R. (1995), 'Employee Motivation', *Management Quarterly*, **36** (2), 33–39.

Creedy, S. (2003), 'Aviation carnage', *The Australian* (Business Section), 4 April.

Creedy, S. (2004), 'Executive pay cuts', *The Australian* (Business Section), 6 February.

Creswell, J. and D. Prins (2002), 'The emperor of greed', *Fortune*, July, 63–4.

Crichton, M. (2002), *Prey*, New York: Harper Collins.

Csoka, L. (1996), 'The rush to leadership training', *Across the Board*, **33** (8), 28–32.

Cummings, T. and C. Worley (1993), *Organization Development and Change*, 5th edn, St Paul: West Publishing Company.

Cusumano, M. (1997), 'How Microsoft makes large teams work like small teams', *Sloan Management Review*, Fall, 9–20.

Daley, D. (1996), 'Good health – is it worth it? Mood states, physical well-being, job satisfaction and absenteeism in members and non-members of a British corporate health and fitness club', *Journal of Occupational and Organizational Psychology*, **69** (2), 121–34.

Dalton, R. (2002a), 'US revels in blame game', *The Australian* (Business Section), 25 July.

Dalton, R. (2002b), 'Bankruptcy cuts to America's heart', *The Australian* (Business Section), 9 April.

Dalton, R. (2002c), 'Enron insider exposes stings at the top', *The Australian* (Business Section), 23 August.

Dalton, R. (2002d), 'United better in red than dead', *The Australian* (Business Section), 11 December.

Dalton, R. (2003a), 'US pension giant declares war on Wall Street', *The Australian* (Business Section), 18 December.

Dalton, R. (2003b), 'Grasso falls on golden sword', *The Australian* (Business Section), 19 September.

Dalton, R. (2004), 'Ebbers charged as Sullivan rolls over in Worldcom case', *The Australian* (Business Section), 4 March.

Daniels, S. (1995), 'The disorganized organization', *Work Study*, March/April, **44**, 20–21.

Darroch, R. (2002), 'The web connection', *The Australian* (IT Section), 28 May.

David, M. (1998), 'Are you a victim of 'messaging stress'?', *Automatic ID News*, **14**, 6–7.

Davidson, M. and C. Cooper (1992), *Shattering the Glass Ceiling: The Woman Manager*, London: Chapman.

Davis, S. (1998), 'GM links better leaders to better business', *Workforce*, **77** (4), 62–8.

Dayton, L. (2003), 'Blueprint for the future', *The Australian*, 16 March.

Dayton, L. (2004), 'Science cheers cloning amid moral dread', *The Weekend Australian*, 14–15 February.

Dearne, K. (2002), 'Corporate spying is booming', *The Australian* (Business Section), 23 July.

De Bono, E. (1970), *Lateral Thinking: Creativity Step by Step*, New York: Harper and Row.

De Bono, E. (1985), *Six Thinking Hats*, Boston: Little and Brown.

Deci, E. (1972), 'The effects of contingent and non-contingent rewards and controls on intrinsic motivation', *Organizational Behaviour and Human Performance*, **8** (4), 217–29.

Deci, E. (1975), *Intrinsic Motivation*, New York: Plenum.

De Frank, R. and M. John (1998), 'Stress on the job: an executive update', *Academy of Management Executive*, **12** (3): 55–66.

De George, R. (1995), *Business Ethics*, Englewood Cliffs, NJ: Prentice-Hall.

De Geus, A. (1996), 'Planning as learning', in K. Starkey (ed.), *How Organizations Learn*, London: Thomson, pp. 93–9.

De Geus, A. (1997), *The Living Company*, Boston: Harvard Business School Press.

De Guillaume, A. (2002), *How to Rule the World: A Handbook for the Aspiring Dictator*, Crows Nest, NSW: Allen and Unwin.

De Lisi, P. (1998), 'A modern day tragedy: the Digital Equipment story', *Journal of Management Enquiry*, **7** (2), 118–30.

De Maria, W. (1999), *Deadly Disclosures: Whistleblowing and the Ethical Meltdown of Australia*, Sydney: Wakefield Press.

De Moranville, C., D. Denise and J. Przytulski (1998), 'Wellness at work', *Journal of Health Care Marketing*, **18** (2), 14–24.

Dempster, Q. (2002), *Death Struggle: How Political Malice and Boardroom Powerplays are Killing the ABC*, Sydney: Allen and Unwin.

De Pree, M. (1989), *Leadership is an Art*, New York: Doubleday.

Devine, F. (2000), 'To boldly go where no robot has gone before: biological evolution is almost finished', *The Australian*, 31 January.

Devinney, T. (2001), 'Know-how', *Boss Magazine*, February, 53–7.

De Witt, P. (1995), 'Welcome to cyberspace', *Time Magazine Special Edition*, May–June, 23–30.

Diamond, J. (2001), *Snake Oil and other Preoccupations*, London: Vintage Books.

Dickens, L. (1994), 'The business case for women's equality', *Employee Relations*, **16** (8).

Dionne, E. (1998), 'Consumers just make them do it', *The Guardian Weekly*, 31 May.

Diver, S. and S. Bouda (1999), *Survival*, Sydney: Pan Macmillan.

Dixon, N. (1994), *The Organizational Learning Cycle*, London: McGraw-Hill.

Dobbs, M. (2000), 'Lawsuits allege US car firms aided Nazi regime', *The Guardian Weekly* (UK), 20–26 July.

Doherty, K. (1989), 'Is worksite wellness good business?', *Business and Health*, **7** (2): 32–6.

Donaldson, T. (1996), 'Values in tension: ethics away from home', *Harvard Business Review*, September–October, 47–62.

Doran, J. (2003), 'Bankers in the dock for Enron tangle', *The Australian* (Business Section), 19 September.

Dowie, M. (2002), 'Pinto madness', www.motherjones.com.

Doyle, C. (1998), 'Health perils of overwork', *The West Australian*, 5 January.

Drenna, D. (1992), *Transforming Company Culture*, London: McGraw-Hill.

Driskell, J. (1996), *Stress and Human Performance*, London: Lawrence Earlbaum.

Drucker, P. (1966), *The Effective Executive*, Englewood Cliffs, NJ: Prentice-Hall.

Drucker, P. (1985), *Innovation and Entrepreneurship*, New York: Harper Business.

Drucker, P. (1993), *Post-Capitalist Society*, New York: Harper-Collins

Drucker, P. (1999), 'The discipline of innovation', in Harvard Business School (ed.), *Harvard Business Review on Breakthrough Thinking*, Boston: Harvard Business School Publishing, pp. 143–59.

Drucker, P. (2002), 'Future firm: you can hire free-lancers and shed your HR responsibilities. But in the knowledge economy, you'll run into trouble if you outsource people development', *Boss*, March, 42–9.

Dugdill, L. and J. Springett (1994), 'Evaluation of workplace health promotion: a review', *Health Education Journal*, **53** (1), 337–47.

Dumaine, B. (1994), 'The trouble with teams', *Fortune*, September, 86–92.

Durie, J. (2003), 'The regular guy', *Boss Magazine*, June, 29–32.

Durrance, B. (1997), 'Stories at work', *Training and Development Journal*, February, 31–8.

Dyson, F. (1999), *The Sun, the Genome and the Internet*, Oxford: Oxford University Press.

Eccleston, R. (2002), 'Smile, you're on camera wherever you go in the former Land of the Free', *The Australian* (IT Section), 17 January.

Edgar, D. (1998), 'Crisis at the coalface: today's workforce could be so much more productive – if only management would show a little heart', *The Australian*, 21 February.

Editorial (1999), *Time Magazine Special Edition: Political Leaders of the 20th Century*, 31 December.

Edvinsson, L. (2002), 'Managing intellectual capital', in Bloomsbury (ed.), *Business: The Complete Guide*, London: Bloomsbury, pp. 49–50.

Edwards, V. and S. Sienkewicz (1994), *Oral Cultures: Past and Present*, Boston: Human Resources Development.

Eisenhardt, K. (1997), 'Conflict and strategic choice: how top management teams disagree', *California Management Review*, **39** (2), 42–62.

Ekman, P. (2003), *Emotions Revealed: Understanding Faces and Feelings*, London: Weidenfeld and Nicolson.

Elder, J. (2001), 'Out of the box', *The Weekend Australian Magazine*, 15–16 September, 47–9.

Elliot, L. (2000), 'Brace yourselves for a crash landing', *The Guardian Weekly*, 2–8 March.

Elliott, G. (2003), 'Enron executive in chains', *The Australian* (Business Section), 12 September.

Elliott, G. and S. Magnusson (2001), 'Onetel victims to sue', *The Australian*, 4 June.

Ellis, S. (2002), 'How the dotcon artists got a hand from the Fed', *The Australian*, 5 May.

Ellis, S. (2003), 'Killer spam poised to cook email bacon', *The Australian* (Business Section), 26 June.

Ellist, E. (2002), 'Worldcom cheerleader goes quiet', *The Australian*, 27 June.

Ely, R. (1995), 'The power in demography: women's social construction of gender identity at work', *Academy of Management Journal*, **38** (3), 589–634.

Este, J. (1999), 'More Sharon Stone than Fred Flinstone: if, as some archeologists now believe, cave women did all the hunting, what were the cave blokes up to?', *The Australian*, 12 December.

Evans, J. (1995), 'Fit and healthy workers can generate better productivity', *Personnel Management*, **1** (16), 46–7.

Evans, P. and T. Wurster (1999), 'Getting real about virtual commerce', *Harvard Business Review*, November–December, 84–94.

Evans, P. and T. Wurster (2000), 'Getting blown to bits: the information age demands a radical change in business strategy', *Australian Financial Review*, 20–25 April, 4–8.

Farkas, C. and P. DeBacker (1996), *Maximum Leadership: The World's CEOs Share their Five Strategies for Success*, New York: Henry Holt.

Feeny, D. (1999), 'Strategy lessons from a virtual corporation', *Australian Financial Review*, 30 September.

Ferguson, A. (1999), 'A world of shifting goalposts', *Management Today*, January–Feburary, 14–19.

Ferguson, A. and C. Wood (1998), 'Step aside: women coming through', *Business Review Weekly*, February, 44–56.

Ferrari, J. (2002), 'Body parts: laughter', *The Weekend Australian*, 26–7 January.

Fisher, A. (1992), 'When will women get to the top?', *Fortune*, September, 44–56.

Fisher, D. (1993), *Communication in Organizations*, 2nd edn, New York: West Publishing.

Fist, S. (1999), 'E-hype is simply e-rational', *The Australian* (IT Section), 23 November.

Follain, J. (2000), 'A female top-gun takes to the air', *The Sunday Times* (UK), 7 March.

Foreshew, J. (2001), 'Access node puts us in the picture', *The Australian* (IT Section), 20 November.

Foreshew, J. (2002), 'Speed is of the essence: Gartner', *The Australian* (IT Section), 12 November.

Foreshew, J. (2003), 'Bosses blamed for bad hires', *The Australian* (IT Section), 11 November.

Forster N. (1994a), 'Teaching skiing (2): diagnosis and reinforcement', *English Ski Council – Ski News*, Winter, 6.

Forster N. (1994b), 'Teaching skiing (1): ' "Bend your knees and try to relax": some alternative approaches to teaching skiing', *English Ski Council – Ski News*, Autumn, 4.

Forster N. (1995a), 'Teaching skiing (6): getting the best out of kids', *English Ski Council – Ski News*, Winter, 4.

Forster N. (1995b), 'Teaching skiing (5): overcoming fear', *English Ski Council – Ski News*, Autumn, 7.

Forster N. (1995c), 'Teaching skiing (4): leadership and motivation', *English Ski Council – Ski News*, Summer, 5.

Forster N. (1995d), 'Teaching skiing (3): communicating with your clients', *English Ski Council – Ski News*, Spring, 7.

Forster N. (1999), 'Another 'Glass Ceiling'?: the experiences of women professionals and managers on international assignments', *Gender, Work and Organization*, **6** (2), 79–90.

Forster, N. (2000a), 'Where are all the leaders?', *Western Australia Business News*, **9** (36), 12–13.

Forster, N. (2000b), 'Leaders and followers', *Corporate Relocation News*, August, 25–6.

Forster, N. (2000c), *Managing Staff on International Assignments: A Strategic Guide*, London: Financial Times and Prentice-Hall.

Forster, N. (2000d), 'The potential impact of third-wave technologies on organizations', *Leadership and Organization Development Journal*, **21** (5), 254–63.

Forster, N. (2000e), 'A case study of women academics' perceptions of career prospects, equal opportunities and work–family conflicts in a British university', *Women in Management Review*, **15** (7/8), 316–27.

Forster, N. (2002), 'Managing excellence through corporate culture; the HP way', *The Management Case Study Journal*, **2** (1), May, 23–40.

Forster, N. and L. Still (2002), *All Work and No Play? The Effects of Occupational Stress on Managers and Professionals in Western Australia*, Perth: Fineline Press.

Forster, N., S. Majteles, A. Mathur, R. Morgan, J. Preuss, V. Tiwari and D. Wilkinson, (1999), 'The role of storytelling in leadership', *Leadership and Organization Development*, **20** (1), 11–18.

Fortune (special edition) (2000), 'The future of the Internet: everything is about to change – again', 2 October, 33–8.

Fortune (2000), 'The world's top women in business', 16 October, 42–66.

Fortune (2002), 'The 500 largest corporations', 15 April, 30.

Fox, C. (2001), 'Female managers: rhetoric and reality', *The Australian Financial Review*, 19 June.

Fox, J. (2000), 'The triumph of English', *Fortune*, 18 September, 81–4.

Fox, J. (2001), 'When bubbles burst', *Fortune*, 11 June, 63–7.

Francke, L. (2001), *Ground Zero: The Gender Wars in the Military*, London: Simon and Schuster.

Fraser, A. (2001), 'Ready, aim, aspire: Metal Storm looks like a good bet, if only the institutions would come on board', *The Weekend Australian*, 2–3 June.

French, J. and B. Raven (1959), 'The bases of social power', in D. Cartwright (ed.), *Studies in Social Power*, Michigan: University of Michigan Institute for Social Research, pp. 150–67.

Friedman, H., L. Prince, R. Riggio and M. DiMatteo (1980), 'Understanding and assessing non-verbal expressiveness: the affective communication test', *Journal of Personality and Social Psychology*, **39** (2), 333–51.

Friedman, M. (1962), *Capitalism and Freedom*, Chicago: University of Chicago Press.

Friedman, M. (1993), 'The social responsibility of business is to increase its profits', in G. Chryssiddes and J. Kaler (eds), *An Introduction to Business Ethics*, London: International Thomson Press, pp. 249–54.

Friedman, M. and R. Rosenman (1974), *Type A Behaviour and Your Heart*, New York: Knopf.

Friedman, S., P. Christensen and J. De Grott (1998), 'Work and life: the end of the zero-sum game', *Harvard Business Review*, **76** (3), 119–29.

Fries, P. (1997), 'There's money lying on the factory floor: workers' ideas on waste eradication are worth millions', *The Australian Financial Review*, 19 September.

Frost, A. (2002), 'Managers' time is no longer their own', *The Australian*, 21 March.

Fukuyama, F. (2003), *Our Post-Human Future: Consequences of the Biotechnology Revolution*, London: Profile Books.

Furnham, A. (1994), 'Does money motivate?', *The Sunday Times* (UK), 9 October.

Fussler, C. (1996), *Driving Eco-Innovation: A Breakthrough Discipline for Innovation and Sustainability*, London: Pitman.

Galbraith, J. (1996), 'Designing the innovating organization', in K. Starkey (ed.), *How Organizations Learn*, London: Thomson, pp. 156–82.

Gardner, H. (1993), *Frames of Mind: The Theory of Multiple Intelligences*, New York: Basic Books.

Gardner, H. (1995), *Leading Minds: An Anatomy of Leadership*, New York: Harper Collins.

Garran, R. (1998), 'Brass shows it's serious about change', *The Weekend Australian*, 13–14 July.

Garran, R. (2001a), 'Tough enough to kill?', *The Australian*, 23 November.

Garran, R. (2001b), 'I am woman – show me war', *The Weekend Australian*, 9–10 June.

Gaulke, S. (1997), *101 Ways to Captivate a Business Audience*, New York: Amacom.

Geary, J. (2000), 'How to spot a liar', *Time*, 10 April, 58–63.

Gemignani, J. (1998), 'Best practices that boost productivity', *Business and Health*, March, **16** (3), 37–42.

Gengler, B. (2001), 'Tiny transistor adds another decade of life to Moore's Law', *The Australian* (IT Section), 19 June.

Gengler, B. (2002a), 'Blogging moves into knowledge', *The Australian* (IT Section), 29 October.

Gengler, B. (2002b), 'IBM carbon advance chips away at silicon', *The Australian* (IT Section), 28 May.

Gengler, B. (2003), 'Tolkien inspires new-age battle suits', *The Australian* (IT Section), 17 June.

George, C. (1972), *The History of Management Thought*, London: Prentice-Hall.

Gerard, I. (2001), 'Staff look for more than cash', *The Australian*, 27–8 January.

Gerth, H. and C. Wright-Mills (1977), *From Max Weber: Essays in Sociology*, London: Routledge and Kegan Paul.

Gettler, L. (1998), 'Mission: possible', *Management Today* (Australia), October, 14–19.

Ghoshal, S. and C. Bartlett (1995), 'Changing the role of top management: beyond structure to process', *Harvard Business Review*, Jan.–Feb., 86–96.

Gibney, F. (1999), 'Iococca gets new wheels: the former Chrysler chairman wants to be back in business – on an electric bike', *Time*, 1 February.

Gibson, J. and D. Tesone (2001), 'Management fads: emergence, evolution and implications for managers', *Academy of Management Executive*, **15** (4), 122–33.

Glass Ceiling Commission (1995), *A Solid Investment: Making Full Use of the Nation's Capital*, Washington: US Government Printing Office.

Gleick, J. (1999), *Faster: The Acceleration of Just about Everything*, London: Little and Brown.

Gleick, J. (2003), *Isaac Newton*, London: Fourth Estate.

Gluyas, R. (2002), 'Let us punish the greedy: Knott', *The Australian* (Business Section), 17 July.

Goldman, H. (1995), *Communicate to Win*, London: Pitman Publishing.

Goldstein, S. (2000), 'The cubicle gets a makeover', *Fortune*, 2 October, 132–3.

Goleman, D. (2000), 'Leadership that gets results', *Harvard Business Review*, March–April, 78–90.

Goleman, D. (2004), 'What makes a Leader?', *Harvard Business Review*, January, 82–91.

Goleman, D., R. Boyatzis and A. Mckee (2002), *The New Leaders: Transforming the Art of Leadership into the Science of Results*, London: Little and Brown.

Gollan, P. (1997), 'Unhappy homes a work hazard', *The Australian*, 7 July.

Goodman, N. (1994), 'Cross-cultural training for the global executive', in P. Kirkbride (ed.), *Human Resource Management in Europe: Perspectives for the 1990s*, London: Routledge.

Goodman, P. (1986), *Designing Effective Work Groups*, San Francisco: Jossey-Bass.

Gottliebsen, R. (2002a), 'Intel chips in to signal rock

bottom of hi-techs', *The Australian* (Business Section), 11 June.

Gottliebsen, R. (2002b), 'New blueprint for boards', *The Weekend Australian* (Business Section), 26–7 October.

Gould, P. and R. Gould (1990), *From 'No' to 'Yes': The Constructive Route To Agreement*, London: Band Printing Services.

Gould, S. (1999), 'Message from a mouse: it takes more than genes to make a smart human or high-IQ humans', *Time*, 27 September.

Goward, P. (1999), 'Fair play is better business', *Business Review Weekly*, 1 March, 8–9.

Gray, J. (1999), 'CEO salaries a waste of money: Greenspan', *The Australian Financial Review*, 26 February.

Grayson, I. (1999), 'Old-style business is doomed: too many companies refusing to accept the power of e-commerce risk losing it all', *The Australian* (IT Section), 16 November.

Grayson, I. (2003), 'Actions speak louder than words', *The Australian* (IT Section), 13 May.

Green Business (2003), www.greenbiz.com, 25 April.

Greene, R. (1999), *The 48 Laws of Power*, Sydney: Hodder.

Greenglass, E. (1985), 'Psychological implications of sex bias in the workplace', *Academic Psychology Bulletin*, **7**, 227–40.

Greenspan, A. (2002), 'Greed is a false God', speech to the US Senate, reprinted in *The Australian* (Business Section), 18 July.

Greenwald, J. (1995), 'Battle for Remote Control', *Time Magazine Special Edition*, May, 65–7.

Grifin, G. (1991), *Machiavelli on Management: Playing and Winning the Corporate Power Game*, New York: Praeger Publications

Grove, A. (1984), *High Output Management*, London: Souvenir Press.

Guthrie, J. and R. Petty (2000), 'Intellectual capital literature review: measurement reporting and management', *Journal of Intellectual Capital*, **1** (2), 155–76.

Guyon, J. (2000), 'The world is your office', *Fortune*, 12 June, 85–92.

Hackman, J. (1990), *Groups that Work (and Those that Don't)*, San Francisco: Jossey-Bass.

Haigh, G. (2003), 'Bad company: the cult of the CEO', *Quarterly Essay*, **10**, 1–98.

Halsey, A. and J. Webb (2000), *Twentieth Century English Social Trends*, London: Macmillan (the chapters by Heath and Payne and by Atkinson).

Hambrick, C., D. Nadler and M. Tushman (1998), *Navigating Change: How CEOs, Top Teams and Boards Steer Transformation*, Boston: Harvard Business School.

Hamel, G. (2000a), *Leading the Revolution*, Boston: Harvard Business School Press.

Hamel, G. (2000b), 'Reinvent your company', *Fortune*, 12 June, 45–60.

Hamel, G. (2001a), 'Avoiding the guillotine', *Fortune*, 2 April, 88–91.

Hamel, G. (2001b), 'Innovation's new math. Forget strategy lessons. To find one great idea you must have workers dreaming up thousands', *Fortune*, 9 July, 76–7.

Hamilton, A. (1999), 'On the virtual couch', *Time Magazine*, 24 May, 45.

Hamilton, C. (2003), *Growth Fetish*, Crows Nest, NSW: Allen and Unwin.

Handy, C (1990), 'Trust and the virtual organization', *Harvard Business Review*, May–June, 79–91.

Handy, C. (1996), *Beyond Certainty*, London: Arrow Books.

Handy, C. (1999), *The New Alchemists: How Visionary People Make Something out of Nothing*, London: Hutchinson.

Hansen, C. and W. Kahnweiler (1996), 'Story-telling: an instrument for understanding the dynamics of corporate relationships', *Human Relations*, **46** (12), 1391–1409.

Hansen, M., N. Nohria and T. Tierney (1999), 'What's your strategy for managing knowledge?', *Harvard Business Review*, March–April, 106–16.

Hanson, C. and W. Bell (1987), *Profit Sharing and Profitability: How Profit Sharing Promotes Business Success*, London: Kogan Page.

Harcourt, T. (2003), 'Women entrepreneurs burn world export trail', *The Australian* (Business Section), 6 May.

Hargadon, A. and R. Sutton (2000), 'The innovation factory', *Boss*, August, 30–33.

Harlow, J. (2002), 'Divas bear life on the road by taking home along too', *The Sunday Times* (UK), 4 August.

Harnden, T. (1999), 'US takes on tobacco giants', *The Weekly Telegraph* (UK), Number 427.

Harris, T. (2002), 'Women still can't break glass ceiling', *The Australian*, 22 November.

Harvard Business School (1999), *Harvard Business Review on Breakthrough Thinking*, Boston: Harvard Business School Publishing.

Harvey, C. (2001), 'Savvy women still losing the corporate race', *The Australian*, 15 August.

Hawkes, N. (1999), 'Narrow beam's sound of silence: personal messages on beams of sound – it's no longer science fiction', *The Australian* (IT Section), 10 August.

Hawking, S. (2001), 'Our future? Star Trek or not?', *The Universe in a Nutshell*, London: Bantam Press, pp. 155–73.

Hay, D. (1998), 'User friendly yoga booms in corporate karma land', *The Australian Financial Review*, 6–7 June.

Haynes, S. (2000), 'True confessions of the humiliating kind', *The Weekend Australian*, 16–17 December.

Haynes, S. (2001), 'We want values for our money', *The Australian*, 23 November.

Henderson, L. (2002), 'Work-anywhere flexibility', *The Australian* (Technology Survey Series No. 5 – The Smart Office), 20 August.

Henderson, M. (2002a), 'Amazon women in outer space', *The Times* (UK), article reprinted in *The Weekend Australian*, 23–4 February.

Henderson, M. (2002b), 'Scientists turn on a one-atom transistor', *The Australian* (IT Section), 18 June.

Hendry, C. and A. Jones (1994), 'The learning organization: adult learning and organizational transformation', *British Journal of Management*, **5** (2), 153–62.

Herzberg, F. (1959), *The Motivation to Work*, New York: John Wiley.

Hickman, B. (2002), 'Artificial lens gives sight for poor eyes', *The Australian* (IT Section), 24 April.

Hickman, B. and P. Karvelas (2002), 'Cloned human born, cult claims', *The Weekend Australian*, 28–9 December.

Hines, M. (2002), 'Testosterone during pregnancy and gender role behaviour: a longitudinal population study', *Child Development*, **73** (5), 1076–99.

Hiscock, G. (2002), 'Bribes put "greasers" on slippery slope to jail', *The Australian*, 6 December.

Hislop, I. (1991), *Stress, Distress and Illness*, Sydney: McGraw-Hill.

Hitt, W. (1995), 'The learning organization: some reflections on organizational renewal', *Leadership and Organizational Development Journal*, **16** (8), 17–25.

Hjelt, P. (2003), 'Industry champs', *Fortune*, 10 March, 37–8.

Hjelt, P. (2004), 'The world's most admired companies', *Fortune*, 15 March, 47–52.

Hoare, D. (2002), 'Philanthropy is good for profits', *The Australian*, 2 October.

Holland, M. (2001), 'Time to pull the plug on Powerpoint', *The Australian*, 10 July.

Holland, M. (2002), 'Jail beckons share spivs', *The Australian*, 14 May.

Hollands, M. (2001), 'Weather eye on the competition: keeping track of business rivals is a high-tech strategy game called competitive intelligence, and it's growing by sneaks and sounds', *The Australian* (IT Section), 18 September.

Holt, M. and D. Paul (1995), 'Health impacts of AT and T's Total Life Concept (TLC) program after five years', *American Journal of Health Promotion*, **9** (3), 421–5.

Hönig-Haftel, S. (1996), 'The art of framing: managing the language of leadership', *Academy of Management Executive*, **16** (1), 87–99.

Hopper, D. (2001), 'Your TV may tell all', *The Australian* (IT Section), 10 July.

Horovitz, P. (2002), 'Blue gene is slowly evolving', *The Australian* (IT Section), 26 May.

Hosie, P. (2003), 'A Study of Managers' Job Related Affective Well-Being, Job Satisfaction and Work Performance', doctoral thesis, The Graduate School of Management, University of Western Australia.

House, R. and T. Mitchell (1974), 'Path-goal theory of leadership', *Journal for Contemporary Business*, Autumn, 81–97.

Howarth, B. (2001), 'E-business 2006; dotcom hype has faded. Now business must prepare for the real upheaval of Internet commerce', *Business Review Weekly*, 9 February, 58–65.

Howkins, J. (2002), *The Creative Economy*, London: Penguin Books.

Hughes, R., R. Ginnet and G. Curphy (1999), *Leadership: Enhancing the Lessons of Experience*, 3rd edn, Sydney: Irwin-McGraw Hill.

Hughes, S. (2002), 'Thieving by numbers', *The Australian*, 16 April.

Hunt, J. (2000), 'Senior executive leadership profiles; an analysis of 54 Australian top managers', Draft Report, School of Business, University of Newcastle, Australia.

Hunter, F. and T. Reid (1996), 'The power game: do women make better bosses?', *The Sunday Telegraph* (UK), 3 November.

Huseman, R., and J. Goodman (1999), *Leading with Knowledge*, Thousand Oaks, California: Sage Publications.

Huseman, R., J. Lahiff and J. Hatfield (1976), *Interpersonal Communication in Organizations*, Boston: Holbrook Press.

Iacocca, L. (1988), *Iacocca: An Autobiography*, New York: Bantam Books.

Illing, D. (1999), 'Long haul to the top for women in academe', *The Australian*, 14 April.

Industry Taskforce on Leadership and Management Skills (1995), *Enterprising Nation: Renewing Australia's Managers to Meet the Challenges of the Asia–Pacific Century*, Canberra: Australian Government Publishing Service.

Isaacson, W. (1997), 'Driven by the passion of Intel's Andy Groves', *Time*, 29 December, 24–7.

Iwatani, Y. (2003), 'How mobiles got out of the car', *The Australian* (IT Section), 13 May.

James, D. (1995), *The Executive Guide to Asia–Pacific Communication*, St Leonards, NSW: Allen and Unwin.

James, D. (2001), 'The art of business: managing creativity', *Management*, September, 15–20.

Janis I. (1972), *Victims of Groupthink*, New York: Houghton Mifflin.

Jardine, L. (2002), *On a Grander Scale: The*

Outstanding Career of Sir Christopher Wren, London: Harper Collins.

Jex, S. (1998), *Stress and Job Performance: Theory, Research, and Implications for Managerial Practice*, Thousand Oaks, California: Sage Publications.

Johns, L. (1998), 'Harassment more trouble than it's worth', *The Australian*, 9 July.

Johnson, P. (1999), 'Global corruption is everywhere, including Labour's backyard', *The Spectator* (UK), 11 December.

Johnson, S. (1998), *Who Moved My Cheese?* London: Random House.

Jonash, R. and T. Sommerlatte (1999), *The Innovation Premium*, New York: Perseus Books.

Jones, S. (1987), 'Organizational politics: only the darker side?', *Management Education and Development*, **18** (2), 116–28.

Jordan-Evans, S. and B. Kaye (2002), 'Retaining employees', in Bloomsbury (ed.), *Business: The Complete Guide*, London: Bloomsbury, pp. 196–7.

Joy, B. (2000), 'Why the future doesn't need us', *Wired Magazine*, **8** (4), April, www.wired.com.

Kageyame, Y. (1998), 'Stressed Japanese have deadly solution to overwork', *The Australian*, 25 June.

Kampert, P. (2002), 'Simulating God: gamers are using sims to test behaviour – or just watch their bosses fry', *The Australian* (IT Section), 15 October.

Kandola, R. (1995), 'Managing diversity: new broom or old hat?', in C. Cooper and I. Robertson (eds), *International Review of Industrial and Organizational Psychology*, Chichester: John Wiley and Sons, pp. 131–67.

Kanter, R. (1979), 'Power failure in management circles', *Harvard Business Review*, August, 21–32.

Kaplan, A. (1999), 'How to build a productive worker's paradise', *The Australian*, 17 August.

Kaplan, R. and P. Norton (1996), *The Balanced Scorecard: Translating Strategy into Action*, Boston: Harvard Business School Press.

Kaplan, R. and P. Norton (2000), *The Strategy Focused Organization*, Boston: Harvard Business School Press.

Karpin, D. (1995a), *Enterprising Nation: Report of the Industry Task Force on Leadership and Management Skills*, Canberra: Australian Government Publishing Service.

Karpin, D. (1995b), 'In search of leaders', *HR Monthly*, June, 10–14.

Karvelas, P. (2002a), 'Shape up or ship out', *The Weekend Australian*, 16–17 March.

Karvelas, P. (2002b), 'Staff take centre stage: finding and keeping talented staff is an increasing concern of industry', *The Weekend Australian*, 2–3 March.

Katzenbach, J. and D. Smith (1983), *The Wisdom of Teams*, Boston: Harvard Business School Press.

Kay, K. (2002), 'Sex scandal claims 15 more priests', *The Australian*, 10 April.

Kaye, M. (1996), *Myth Makers and Storytellers*, Melbourne: Business and Professional Publishing.

Kaye, M. (1997), *Teaming with Success: Building and Maintaining Best Performing Teams*, Sydney: Prentice-Hall.

Kelly, K. (1998), *New Rules for the New Economy: Ten Ways the Network Economy is Changing Everything*, London: Fourth Estate.

Kim, W. and R. Maurbogne (1999), 'Value innovation', *Harvard Business Review on Breakthrough Thinking*, Boston: Harvard Business School Press, pp. 189–217.

Kimble, C. (1996), 'The future of information systems: using social systems to create protocols for the virtual environment', *Managing Virtual Enterprises*, **4**, 241–6.

King, D. (2001), 'Froggy croaks on $67 million', *The Australian*, 4 December.

King, N. and N. Anderson (1995), *Innovation and Change in Organizations*, New York: Routledge.

Kipnis, D. (1984), 'Patterns of managerial influence: shotgun managers, tacticians and bystanders', *Organizational Dynamics*, Winter, 58–67.

Kipnis, D. and S. Schmidt (1983), 'Why do I like thee: is it your performance or my orders', *Journal of Applied Psychology*, **66** (3), 324–8.

Kirkpatrick S. and E. Locke (1991), 'Leadership: do traits matter?', *Academy of Management Executive*, **5** (2), 48–60.

Kirner, J. and M. Rayner (1999), *The Women's Power Handbook*, Melbourne: Viking.

Kitney, D. and S. Evans (2000), 'Well-paid for poor performance', *The Australian Financial Review*, 16 November.

Klaila, D. and L. Hall (2000), 'Using intellectual assets as a success strategy', *Journal of Intellectual Capital*, **1** (2), 47–53.

Klimpel, A. (2002), 'Orwell's big-brother e-snooper', *The Australian* (IT Section), 19 November.

Kling, R. (1996), *Computerisation and Controversy: Value Conflicts and Social Choices*, 2nd edn, London: Academic Press.

Knowles, R. (ed.), (1997) *The Green Guide to Ethical Investing*, Marrickville, NSW: Choice Books.

Koestler, A. (1975), *The Act of Creation*, London: Pan Books.

Kohn, A. (1993a), 'Why incentive plans cannot work', *Harvard Business Review*, September–October, 54–63.

Kohn, A. (1993b), *Punished by Rewards*, Boston: Houghton Mifflin.

Kolb, D. (1996), 'Management and the learning process', in K. Starkey (ed.), *How Organizations Learn*, London: Thomson, pp. 270–87.]

Kotter, J. (1990), *A Force For Change: How*

Leadership Differs From Management, New York: Free Press.

Kotter, J., (1995), 'Leading change: why transformation efforts fail', *Harvard Business Review*, March–April, 59–68.

Kotter, J. and J. Hesketh (1992), *Corporate Culture and Performance*, New York: Free Press.

Kouzes, J. and B. Posner (1993), *Credibility: How Leaders Gain and Lose It*, San Francisco: Jossey-Bass.

Kouzes, J. and B. Posner (1997), *The Leadership Challenge*, San Francisco: Jossey-Bass.

KPMG Consulting (2000), *Knowledge Management Research Report 2000*, www.kpmgconsulting.com/kpmgsite/service/km/survey2000.html, 14 September.

KRT (2002), 'Scandal engulfs Cheney', *The Australian* (Business Section), 12 July.

KRT (2003), 'Southwest skirts the storm: with the industry in crisis, Southwest is the airline others are watching with increasing interest', *The Australian* (Business Section), 2 May.

KRT (2004), 'Continental's turbulence rattles industry', *The Australian* (Business Section), 22 July.

Kulaga, J. (1995), 'Team formation', *Executive Excellence*, **12** (6), 10–11.

Kurzweil, R. (1999), *The Age of Spiritual Machines: When Computers Exceed Human Intelligence*, St. Leonards, NSW: Allen and Unwin.

Kurzweil, R. (2003), 'Attorneys argue termination of "conscious computer" in mock trial', www.kurzweilai.net/news, 16 September.

Langan-Fox, J. (1996), 'Validity and reliability of measures of occupational and role stress using samples of Australian managers and professionals', *Stress Medicine*, **12** (4), 212–25.

Lardner, A. (1999), 'OK: here are your options', *U.S. News and World Report*, 1 March, 44–6.

Lawler, E. (1993), 'Who uses skills-based pay and why', *Compensation and Benefits Review*, March–April, 22–3.

Lawler, E., S. Mohrman and G. Ledford (1992), *Employee Involvement and Total Quality Management*, San Francisco: Jossey-Bass.

Lawson, M. (2002), 'What if?', *Boss*, January, 22–5.

Lazarus, R. (1999), *Stress and Emotion: A New Synthesis*, New York: Springer Publishing Company.

Le Grand, C. (1992), 'Leading the leaderless team', *The Australian* (Sports Section), 1 July.

Leake, J. (2002), 'All clones defective says Dolly's creator', *The Australian*, 29 April.

Leake, J. (2003), 'Waking up to consciousness', *The Australian*, 3 March.

Leonard, D. and S. Strauss (1999), 'Putting your company's whole brain to work', *Harvard Business Review on Breakthrough Thinking*, Boston: Harvard Business School Press, pp. 57–85.

Leppard, D. and M. Chittenden (2001), 'Millions missing from Archer aid fund', *The Australian*, 24 July.

Levering, R. and M. Moskowitz (2001), 'The one hundred best companies to work for', *Fortune*, 8 January, 64–77.

Levering, R. and M. Moskowitz (2002), 'The one hundred best companies to work for: the best in the worst of times', *Fortune*, 4 February, 30–39.

Levering, R, and M. Moskowitz (2003), 'The one hundred best companies to work for', *Fortune*, 27 January, 84–98.

Levi, A., E. Grauer, D.E. Ben-Nathan, A. Levy and E. Kloet (1998), *New Frontiers in Stress Research*, Harwood: Academic Publishers.

Levi, L. (1984), *Stress in Industry: Causes, Effects, and Prevention*, Geneva: International Labour Office.

Levy, J., (2002), *Really Useful: The Origins of Everyday Things*, London: Quintet Publishing.

Lewis, P. (2002), 'Sony re-dreams its future', *Fortune*, 25 November, 67–71.

Lippitt, R. (1982), 'The changing leader–follower relationships of the 1980s', *Journal of Applied Behavioural Science*, **18** (2), 78–81.

Littler, C. (1998), 'A look at the downside', *The Bulletin* (Australia), 9 June.

Lloyd, S. (2001), 'Now for the laundry: Dyson, maker of the radical cyclonic vacuum cleaner, is set to start another revolution', *Business Review Weekly* (Australia), 9 February, 46–7.

Locke, E. (1968), 'Towards a theory of task motivation and incentives', *Organizational Behaviour and Human Performance*, May, 157–89.

Locke, E. and G. Latham (1990), *A Theory of Goal Setting and Task Performance*, Englewood Cliffs, NJ: Prentice-Hall.

Loehr, J. and T. Schwartz (2001), 'The making of a corporate athlete', *Harvard Business Review*, January–February, 120–28.

Loh, A. (1998), Feng Shui in Western Australia, honours dissertation, The Department of Architecture and Fine Arts, University of Western Australia, Perth, Western Australia.

Long, G. (2002), 'Touchy–feely net a reality', *The Australian* (IT Section), 5 November.

Long, S. (2000), 'Ordinary workers moving to performance-related pay', *The Australian* (Business Section), 24 March.

Loomis, C. (2001), 'Inside the great CEO pay heist', *Fortune*, 25 June, 43–8.

Lowe, J. (ed.) (1998), *Jack Welch Speaks*, New York: Wiley and Sons.

Lucas, J. (1998), 'Anatomy of a vision statement', *Management Review*, February, 21–33.

Lucier, C. and J. Torsilieri (1997), *Why Knowledge Programs Fail: A CEO's Guide to Managing Learning*, New York: Booz, Allen and Hamilton.

Luthans, F. and J. Larsen (1986), 'How managers

really communicate', *Human Relations*, **39** (3), 161–78.

Lyall, K. (2002), 'Abuse rife in Burma: Amnesty', *The Australian*, 19 July.

Lynch, A. (1999), 'Ear, ear, ear: Stelarc seeks net prosthesis', *The Australian* (IT Section), 2 March.

Lynch, A. (2002), 'Visualising a model of the future', *The Australian* (IT Section), 11 June.

Mabey, C. and B. Mayon-White (1993), *Managing Change*, London: Paul Chapman.

Macdonald, K. (2000), 'Teachers' short cuts', *The Sunday Times* (Australia), 29 October.

Macintyre, B. (2002), 'Stop counting sheep, insomniacs, sleepers are the losers', *The Australian*, 19 February.

Mackay, H. (1994), *Why People Don't Listen*, Sydney: Pan.

Macken, D. (1999), 'New workforce elite shift balance of power', *The Australian Financial Review*, 24 August.

Macleay, J. (1997a), 'Our managers fail the test of leadership', *The Australian* (Business Section), 10 December.

Macleay, J. (1997b), 'The secret to long, healthy life is in the learning', *The Australian*, 24 November.

Maddi, S. and S. Kobasa (1984), *The Hardy Executive*, Homewood, Illinois: Dow-Jones and Irwin.

Maddison, S. (1999), 'Right to fight is front line of feminism', *The Weekend Australian*, 9–10 July.

Maguire, K. (2002), 'Mastering the mind games', *The Weekend Australian*, 23–4 March.

Maguire, T. (2001), 'Help, I'm addicted to work', *The Sunday Times* (Australia), 26 August.

Maier, N. (1967), 'Assets and liabilities of group problem solving: the need for an integrative function', *Psychological Review*, **74**, 239–49.

Maley, K. (1998), 'Can women run faster than men?', *The Australian Financial Review*, 10–11 October.

Manning, M. and P. Haddock (1995), *Leadership Skills for Women*, London: Kogan Page.

Mansell, I. (2004), 'Ex-PM linked to account scandal', *The Times*, 1 April.

Mant, A. (1983), *Leaders We Deserve*, Oxford: Blackwell.

Mant, A. (1997), *Intelligent Leadership*, London: Allen and Unwin.

Marchand, D. (1997), 'Looking ahead with strategic intelligence', *Business Review Weekly*, 16 June, 80–81.

Margolis, J. (2001), *A Brief History of Tomorrow*, London: Bloomsbury.

Marris, S. (1997), 'Fear of flying: senior managers are finding that there is a price to pay for job security', *The Australian*, 18 August.

Marshall, K. (1999), 'Home workers a hidden population', *The Australian Financial Review*, 4 November.

Maruyama, M. (1990), 'Organizational structure, training and selection of outer space crew members', *Technological Forecasting and Social Change*, **37** (2), 203–12.

Matathia, I. and M. Salzman (1998), *Trends for the Future*, Sydney: Macmillan.

Matterson, H. (2000), 'Caltex plies employees with shares', *The Australian* (Business Section), 7 July.

Maull, S. (2004), 'Tycho trial called off', *The Sunday Times* (Western Australia), 4 April.

Mayo, A. and E. Lank (1994), *The Power of Learning: A Guide to Gaining Competitive Advantage*, London: Institute of Personnel Development.

McAlpine, A. (1999), *The New Machiavelli: The Art of Politics in Business*, London: Wiley.

McCallum, J. (1996), 'Changing at warp speed: managing technology', *Business Quarterly*, **60**, 87–93.

McCann, D. (2001), 'Plot's unhappy ending', *The Weekend Australian*, 7–8 July.

McCann, D. (2002), 'Rat's off to carry', *The Australian* (IT Section), 3 May.

McClelland, D. (1961), *The Achieving Society*, New York: Van Nostrand and Reinhold.

McClelland, D. (1975), *Power: The Inner Experience*, New York: Irvington.

McClelland, D. and D. Burnham (1995), 'Power is the great motivator', *Harvard Business Review*, January–February, 126–32.

McConkie, M. and R. Boss (1986), 'Organization stories: one means of moving the informal organization during change efforts', *Public Administration Quarterly*, **10** (2), 23–32.

McConkie, M. and R. Boss (1994), 'Using stories as an aid to consultation', *Public Administration Quarterly*, **17** (4), 377–95.

McCulloch, J. (2001), 'Moral margins: there's a growing band of investors with a soul purpose', *The Sunday Times* (Western Australia), 13 May.

McGregor, D. (1987), *The Human Side of Enterprise*, London: Penguin.

McGuire, M. (2001), 'Whatever its colour, big money is the root of sport's evils', *The Australian*, 11 November.

McKenzie, E. (1980), *14 000 Quips and Quotes for Writers and Speakers*, New York: Baker Book House.

McKie, P. (2002), 'Praise the lard and pass the sauce', *The Weekend Australian Magazine*, 7–8 September, 16–20.

McLean, B. (1998), 'Where's the loot coming from?', *Time*, 31 August, 78–9.

McLean, B. and P. Elkind (2003), *The Smartest Guys in the Room: The Amazing Rise and Scandalous Fall of Enron*, New York: Penguin Books.

McLean, J. (2000), 'From fragmentation to integration: towards an integrated model of knowledge management and organizational learning', paper presented at the *Australian and New Zealand Association of Management Conference*, Macquarie University, 8 December.

McLeod, P., S. Lobel and T. Cox (1996), 'Ethnic diversity and creativity in small groups', *Small Group Research*, **27** (4), 248–64.

McNeil, M. and K. Pedigo (2001), 'Western Australian managers tell their stories: ethical challenges in international business opportunities', *Journal of Business Ethics*, **30**, 305–17.

Megalogenis, G. (2002), 'Workers put pay behind security', *The Australian*, 22 July.

Mehrabian, A. (1968), 'Communication without words', *Psychology Today*, **1** (1), 53–5.

Mehrabian, A. and M. Wiener (1967), 'Decoding of inconsistent communication', *Journal of Personality and Social Psychology*, **6** (1), 109–14.

Mendenhall, M. (1995), 'Communication and negotiation in global management', in M. Mendenhall, J. Punnett and D. Ricks (eds), *Global Management*, London: Blackwell, pp. 531–63).

Meung, A. and D. Ready (1995), 'Developing leadership capabilities of global corporations: a comparative study in eight nations', *Human Resource Management*, **34** (4), 529–47.

Micklethwaite, J. and A. Woolridge (1997), *The Witch Doctors*, London: Times Business Books.

Middleton, P. (1997), *Living the Vision*, Norwood, SA: Peacock Books.

Milgram, S. (1963), 'Behavioural study of obedience', *Journal of Abnormal and Social Psychology*, **67** (3), 371–8.

Miller, M. (2001), *The Bush Dyslexicon: The Sayings of President Dubya*, Sydney: Bantam Books.

Miller, W. and L. Morris (2000), *Fourth Generation Research and Development: Managing Knowledge, Technology and Innovation*, New York: Wiley.

Miraudo, N. (2002), 'Yoga eases stress for high-flyers', *The Sunday Times* (Australia), 20 January.

Mitchell, B. (2000), 'Doctors send a wake-up call', *The Australian* 15 November.

Mitchell, S. (2002), 'Teleworking fails to live up to hype', *The Australian* (IT Section), 8 October.

Montgomery, B. (2001), 'High society pillars of salt', *The Australian*, 21 May.

Montgomery, E. (1998), 'Compensation for sex case detective', *The International Telegraph*, 15 May.

Moore, M. (2001), *Stupid White Men and Other Sorry Excuses for the State of the Nation*, New York: Harper Collins.

Morgan, G. (1986), *Images of Organization*, Beverly Hills, California: Sage Publications.

Morton, G. (1990), *The Australian Motivation Handbook*, Sydney: McGraw-Hill.

Morton, M. (1995), 'Emerging organizational forms: work and organization in the 21st century', *European Management Journal*, **13** (4), 339–45.

Moskal, B. (1997), 'Women make better managers', *Industry Week*, February, 17–19.

Moston, S. and E. Engelberg-Moston (1997), *Sexual Harassment in the Workplace*, Melbourne: Business and Professional Publishing.

Moxon, P. (1993), *Building a Better Team*, Aldershot: Gower.

Murray, I. (2000), 'Bullies score top marks for cunning', *The Australian*, 21 January.

Nader, K. (2003), 'Neuroscience: re-recording human memories', *Nature*, October, **425**, 571–2.

Nanus, B. (1992), *Visionary Leadership: Creating a Compelling Sense of Direction for Your Organization*, San Francisco: Jossey-Bass.

Near, R. and D. Weckler (1990), 'Organizational and job characteristics related to self-managing teams', paper presented to the International Conference on Self-managing Work Teams, Denton, Texas, September.

Neef, D. (1997), *Making the Case for Knowledge Management: The Bigger Picture*, Ernst and Young working paper, September.

Nelson, B. (1996), 'Dump the cash, load on the praise', *Personnel Journal*, July, 65–70.

Nelson, B. (1997), *1001 Ways to Energize Your Employees*, New York: Workman.

Nelson, D., J. Quick, M. Hitt and D. Moesel (1990), 'Politics, lack of career progress and work/home conflict: stress and strain for working women', *Sex Roles: A Journal of Research*, **23** (2), 169–85.

Newman, B. (1995), *The Ten Laws of Leadership*, Sydney: Vision.

Newman, G. and S. Dease (2002), 'US frauds rock world markets', *The Australian*, 27 June.

Newman, G. and D. King (2002), 'London blitzed as US bombs', *The Australian* (Business Section), 17 July.

Newman, M. (2002), 'Advance Australia the fairer: our rules are a bulwark against the wave of corporate disasters sweeping the USA', *The Australian* (Business Section), 24 July.

Nicholas, V. (2000), 'Industry gets religion', www.economist.com/archive, 12 July.

Nicholson, N. (2000), *Managing the Human Animal*, London: Texere Publishing.

Nonaka, I. (1991), 'The knowledge creating company', *Harvard Business Review*, November–December, 96–104.

Norton, H. (1997), 'In a man's world, women lose their hair to get ahead', *The Australian*, 2 November.

Norton, R. (2002), 'Abraham Lincoln research site', http://home.att.net/~rjnorton/Lincoln77.html.

Nowlin, W. (1990), 'Norms around the world', *Southwest Airline Spirit*, May, 33, 36, 95; June, 27, 30, 89.

NR (2000), 'Offshore banking business is booming', *The Weekend Australian*, 5–6 August.

Oakley, A. (1981), *Subject Women*, London: Martin Robertson.

O'Donnell, L. (1999a), 'Corruption clamp smokes out China's Mr Big', *The Australian*, 12 January.

O'Donnell, L. (1999b), 'Corrupt Chinese officials $20 billion richer in six months', *The Australian*, 19 August.

Offerman, L. and M. Armitage (1993), 'Stress and the woman manager: sources, health outcomes and interventions', in M. Fagenson (ed.), *Women in Management: Trends, Issues and Challenges*, Newbury Park, CA: Sage, pp. 131–61.

Olson, S. (2002), *Mapping Human History: Discovering the Past Through our Genes*, London: Bloomsbury.

O'Reilly, B. (1999), 'The mechanic who fixed Continental', *Fortune*, 20 December, 86–96.

O'Reilly, C. and J. Pfeffer (2000), *Hidden Value: How Great Companies Achieve Extraordinary Results With Ordinary People*, Boston: Harvard Business School Press.

O'Rourke, P. (1999), *Eat the Rich: A Treatise on Economics*, Sydney: Pan Macmillan.

Packard, D. (1996), *The HP Way: How Bill Hewlett and I Built Our Company*, New York: Harper Business.

Parker, S., G. Pascall and J. Evetts (1998), 'Jobs for the girls? Change and continuity for women in high street banks', *Women in Management Review*, 13 (4), 156–61.

Parkin, D., P. Bourke and R. Gleason (1999), *Perform Or Else!*, Melbourne: Information Australia.

Parry, K. (1996), *Transformational Leadership: Developing an Enterprising Management Culture*, Melbourne: Pitman.

Paul, A. (1999), 'Made in Japan', *Fortune*, 6 December, 102–12.

Paul, A. (2000), 'I compute, therefore I am', *Fortune*, 7 February, 24–5.

Pease, A. and B. Pease (1998), *Why Men Don't Listen and Women Can't Read Maps*, Sydney: Harper-Collins.

Pedler, M., T. Boydell and J. Burgoyne (1989), 'Towards the learning company', *Management Education and Development*, 20 (1), 23–35.

Pedrick, C. (2000), 'Lotto's child cheats', *The Australian*, 10 December.

Pelletier, K. and R. Lutz (1996), 'Healthy people – healthy business: a critical review of stress management programs in the workplace', *American Journal of Health Promotion*, 11 (2), 112–35.

Peretz, M. (2002), 'Dubya's dubious deal', *The Australian* (Business Section), 17 July.

Perkins, D. (2001), *The Eureka Effect: The Art and Logic of Breakthrough Thinking*, London: W.W. Norton and Company.

Peters, T. (1987), *Thriving on Chaos*, New York: Knopf.

Peters, T. and R. Waterman (1982), *In Search of Excellence: Lessons from America's Best Companies*, London: Harper-Row.

Petersen, S. (2000), 'High-flyer suicides soar', *The Australian*, 6 June.

Pettigrew, A. (1985), 'Context and action in the transformation of the firm', *Journal of Management Studies*, **24** (4), 349–70.

Pfeffer, J. (1992), *Managing with Power*, Boston: Harvard Business School Press.

Philips, J. (2002), 'Mafia women play deadly role in the real battle of the sexes', *The Australian*, 29 May.

Pilger, J. (1998), *Hidden Agendas*, London: Vintage.

Pocock, B. (2001), 'Having a Life: Work, Family and Community in 2000', Centre for Labour Research, Adelaide University.

Pope, N. and P. Berry (1995), 'Top down approach doesn't work', *The Australian Financial Review*, 1 December.

Popper, K. (1959), *The Logic of Scientific Discovery*, London: Hutchinson.

Poprzeczny, J. (2000), 'MPs abusing their gravy train', *Business News* (Western Australia), 9 November.

Powell, S. (1990), 'One more time: do female and male managers differ?' *Academy of Management Executive*, **3**, 68–75.

Powell, S. (1997), 'Stress: the distressing news', *The Australian*, 14 May.

Pratt, D. (1997), *How Shiny is Your Goldfish And Other Cautionary Tales*, Watson's Bay, NSW: Fast Books.

Pratt, S. (2002), 'Fair game: what cheerleaders really want is respect', *The Weekend Australian Magazine*, 16–17 November, 22–4.

Prokesch, S. (1997), 'Unleashing the power of learning: an interview with British Petroleum's John Brown', *Harvard Business Review*, September–October, 147–68.

Rabanovich, A. (2004), 'Bomber died to atone for infidelity', *The Australian*, 22 January.

Ragins, B. (1998), 'Gender gap in the executive suite: CEOs and female executives report on breaking the glass ceiling', *Academy of Management Executive*, **12** (1), 28–42.

Ramsey, A. (1997), 'Managers waste away in useless meetings', *The Australian*, 27 June.

Randolph, W. (1995), 'Navigating the journey to empowerment', *Organizational Dynamics*, Spring, 19–33.

Rapaille, G. (1998), 'Great connectors', *Executive Excellence*, **15** (12), 10–11.

Rayport, J. (2002), 'Market spaces', in Bloomsbury (ed.), *Business: The Complete Guide*, London: Bloomsbury, pp. 154–5.

Reaney, P. (2003), 'Super-thin display advances e-paper', *The Australian* (IT Section), 13 May.

Recardo, R. (1996), *Teams: Who Needs Them and Why?*, Houston: Gulf.

Reid, T. (2002), 'Worldcom collapse pits Clinton's folk against Bush', *The Australian* (Business Section), 25 July.

Reuters News Agency (1999a), 'Cojones rule the ring as top torera loses fight with male bull', *The Australian*, 20 May.

Reuters News Agency (1999b), 'Shuttle stays put', *The Australian*, 21 July.

Reuters News Agency (2001), 'Guilty verdict in art sale scam', *The Australian*, 7 December.

Reuters News Agency (2002a), 'Priests' victims accept $18 million', *The Australian*, 20 September.

Reuters News Agency (2002b), 'Pillow talk proves costly for insider trading mistress', *The Australian*, 25 October.

Rheinlander, M. (1999), *Western Australian Technology Manager*, Iona Technology Group Survey, 3 February.

Richardson, J. (1998), 'Women's business: the night the truth came out', *The Australian*, 25 March.

Richardson, M. (2000), 'Survey shows corruption holds back growth', *Inside Asia*, 17 April.

Ridley, M. (2003), *Nature Versus Nurture: Experience and What Makes Us Human*, London: Fourth Estate.

Riley, J. (2003), 'Natural selection rules in outsourcing', *The Australian* (IT Section), 24 June.

Ringland, G. (1996), *Scenario Planning: Managing for the Future*, London: John Wiley and Sons.

Rivette, K. and D. Kline (2000), 'Discovering new value in intellectual property', *Harvard Business Review*, January–February, 54–66.

Robbins, S., B. Millett, R. Caccioppe and T. Waters-Marsh (2001), *Organizational Behaviour: Leading and Managing in Australia and New Zealand*, Frenchs Forest, NSW: Pearson Education.

Roberts, M. (1989), 'Wellness at work', *Psychology Today*, **55** (4), 302–20.

Robinson, J. (1998), *The Laundrymen: Inside the World's Third Largest Business*, Sydney: Simon and Schuster.

Roddick, A. (2000), *Business as Unusual: the Triumph of Anita Roddick*, London: Harper Collins.

Romei, S. (2001), 'The day the dotcoms died', *The Australian*, 29 January.

Romei, S. (2002), 'My favourite android', *The Weekend Australian Magazine*, 26–7 January.

Rosenthal, P. (1995), 'Gender differences in managers' attributions for successful work performance', *Women in Management Review*, **10** (6), 26–31.

Ross, E. (1999), 'Health: stress-busters find the benefits of balance', *Business Review Weekly*, 23 May, 41–3.

Rowling, J. (1999), *Harry Potter and the Prisoner of Azkaban*, London: Bloomsbury.

Roydhouse, O. (2001), *The World's Best Trivia*, Nolde Park, Victoria: Five Mile Press.

Roy Morgan (2002) www.roymorgan.org.

Rudman, R. (1997), *Human Resource Management in New Zealand*, Auckland: Longman Paul.

Ruggles, R. (1998), 'The state of the notion: knowledge management in practice', *California Management Review*, **40** (3), 80–89.

Sandilands, B. (1999), 'Online office not all it's cracked up to be', *The Australian Financial Review*, 4 November.

Sarney, E. (1997), 'Girls on top', *New Zealand Sunday Star Times*, 2 February.

Sarros, J. and O. Butchatsky (1999), *Leadership and Values*, Sydney: Harper-Collins.

Sarros, J., I. Densten and J. Santorra (1999), *Leadership: Values, Profits and People*, Sydney: Harper Business.

Schabracq, M., J. Winnubst and C. Cooper (eds) (1996), *The Handbook of Work and Health Psychology*, London: Wiley and Sons.

Schein, E. (1996a), *Organizational Culture and Leadership*, 2nd edn, London: Jossey-Bass.

Schein, E. (1996b), 'Defining organizational culture', in J. Shafritz and S. Ott (eds), *Classics of Organization Theory*, 4th edn, Orlando: Harcourt Brace and Company, pp. 430–42.

Schein, E. (2000), *The Corporate Culture Survival Guide*, London: Jossey-Bass.

Schlender, B. (2002), 'Intel's $10 billion gamble', *Fortune*, 11 November, 48–55.

Schlosser, J. (2002), 'Why women should rule the world', *Fortune*, 28 October, 70–71.

Schmidt, S. and D. Kipnis (1987), 'The perils of persistence', *Psychology Today*, **21**, 32–3.

Scholtes, P. (1998), *The Leaders' Handbook: A Guide to Managing Your People and the Daily Workflow*, Sydney: McGraw Hill

Schrage, M. (1999), 'What's that bad odour at innovation skunkworks?', *Fortune*, 20 December, 172–3.

Schriefer, A. (1998), 'The future: trends, discontinuities and opportunities', *Planning Review*, **26** (1), 26–32.

Schwartz, P. (1996), *The Art of the Long View: Planning for the Future in an Uncertain World*, New York: Doubleday.

Scott, D. (2001), 'Listening a vital part of communication', *Business News* (Western Australia), 5 July.

Scott, W. (2002), 'Sorry, guys, but greed corrupts absolutely', *The Australian Financial Review*, 1 August.

Seaman, B. (1995), 'The future is already here', *Time Magazine Special Edition*, Spring, 28–31.

Seeley-Brown, J. and P. Duguid (2000), 'Balancing

act: how to capture knowledge without killing it', *Harvard Business Review*, March–April, 73–80.

Selye, H. (1974), *Stress Without Distress*, London: Hodder and Stoughton.

Semler, R. (2001), *Maverick: The Success Story Behind the World's Most Unusual Workplace*, London: Century.

Senge, P. (1990), *The Fifth Discipline: The Art and Practice of the Learning Organization*, London: Doubleday.

Senge, P. (1994), *The Fifth Discipline Fieldbook: Strategies and Tools for Building a Learning Organization*, London: Doubleday.

Senge, P. (1996), 'The leader's new work; building learning organizations', in K. Starkey (ed.), *How Organizations Learn*, London: Thomson, pp. 288–315.

Shafritz, J. and S. Ott (eds) (1996), *Classics of Organization Theory*, 4th edn, Orlando: Harcourt Brace and Company.

Shamir, B. (1998), 'The art of framing: managing the language of leadership', *Leadership Quarterly*, **9** (1), 123–7.

Shanahan, D. (2000), 'Hypocrites in the house: minister and five MPs suspended in parliament's day of shame', *The Australian*, 22 June.

Shaw, M, (1981), *Group Dynamics: The Psychology of Small Group Behaviour*, New York: McGraw-Hill.

Schiller, R. (2000), *Irrational Exuberance*, Princeton: Princeton University Press.

Simmons, M. (1996), *New Leadership for Women and Men: Building an Inclusive Organization*, Aldershot: Gower.

Simmons, R. (2002), *Odd Girl Out: The Hidden Culture of Aggression in Girls*, New York: Schwartz Publishing.

Simons, F. (2000), 'Transforming change', *The Australian Financial Review Magazine*, July, 30–34.

Sinclair, A. (1998), *Doing Leadership Differently: Gender, Power and Sexuality in a Changing Business Culture*, Melbourne: Melbourne University Press.

Sinclair, A. and Wilson, C. (2002), *New Faces of Leadership*, Melbourne: Melbourne University Press.

Singh, A. (2000), 'Luck be a stone lion: Feng Shui once considered to be a new age fad is now being embraced by big business and bureaucrats', *Time*, 3 July.

Slattery, L. (1998), 'In calm's way', *The Weekend Australian*, 16–17 May.

Smith, C. (1995), *Gender: A Strategic Management Issue*, Sydney: Business and Professional Publications.

Smith, I. (1993), 'Reward management: a retrospective assessment', *Employee Relations*, **15** (3), 45–59.

Smith, J. (1991), *Stress Scripting: A Guide to Stress Management*, New York: Praeger.

Smith, R. (1979), 'Coach effectiveness training: a cognitive behavioural approach to enhancing relationship skills in youth sports coaches', *Journal of Sports Psychology*, **1** (1), 59–75.

Sorrensen, G. (1998), 'The effects of health promotion–health protection intervention on behaviour change: the Wellworks Study', *American Journal of Public Health*, **88** (11), 1685–90.

Spencer, S. and A. Pruss (1994), *How to Implement Change in Your Company*, London: Piatkus.

Spencer, Stuart (2000), 'A national study of the impact of the Internet on organizational structure, culture and leadership', www.spencerstuart.com.

Sprague, J. (2002), 'Employees want their shares', *The Australian*, 24 January.

Sproull, L. and S. Kiesler (1991), *New Ways of Working in the Networked Organization*, Cambridge, MA: MIT Press.

Srivista, S., O. John, S. Gosling and J. Potter (2003), 'Development of personality in early and middle adulthood: set like plaster or persistent change?', *Journal of Personality and Social Psychology*, **84** (5), 1041–53.

Stamp, D. (1996), 'A piece of the action', *Training*, March, 66–7.

Stanney, K. (1995), 'Realizing the full potential of virtual reality; human factors issues that could stand in the way', *Industrial Energy and Management Systems*, **36** (1), 28–34.

Stanton, N. (1996), *Communication*, Melbourne: Macmillan.

Starkey, K. (ed.) (1996), *How Organizations Learn*, London: Thomson

Staw, B., L. Sandelands and J. Dutton (1981), 'Threat rigidity effects in organizational behaviour', *Administrative Science Quarterly*, **26** (4), 501–24.

Steele, J. (2001), 'Worldwide league of the corrupt unveiled', *The Guardian Weekly*, 1–7 October.

Stein, S. (2000), 'The world's most admired companies', *Fortune*, 2 October, 59–72.

Sternberg, E. (2000), *The Balance Within: The Science Connecting Health And Emotions*, New York: W.H. Freeman.

Stevens, M. (2000), 'Gender agenda', *The Weekend Australian Magazine*, 24–5 July 17–22.

Stewart, C. (1999), 'In one hundred years, computerised humans will outnumber real people says Ray Kurzweil', *The Weekend Australian*, 23–4 January.

Stewart, C. (2001), 'Perfect pitch', *The Weekend Australian Magazine*, 9–10 June.

Stewart, C. (2002), 'It's Amanda's world', *The Weekend Australian*, 1–2 July.

Stewart, I. (1999), 'Job prospects bad for babes', *The Weekend Australian*, 24–25 July.

Stewart, T. (2000a), 'Knowledge worth $1.25 billion', *Fortune*, 27 November, 128–9.

Stewart, T. (2000b), 'Software preserves knowledge, people pass it on', *Fortune*, 12 September, 390–91.

Stewart, T. (2000c), 'Whom can you trust?', *Fortune*, 12 June, 137–40.

Stewart, T. (2002), 'Intellectual capital', in Bloomsbury (ed.), *Business: The Complete Guide*, London: Bloomsbury, pp. 159–60.

Stock, G. (2002), *Redesigning Humans: Choosing Our Children's Genes*, London: Profile Books.

Stock, S. (2002), 'Laughing yourself into a job', *The Australian* (Business Section), 29 May.

Stogdill, R. (1948), 'Personal factors associated with leadership: A review of the literature', *Journal of Psychology*, **25** (1), 35–71.

Stogdill, R. (1974), *Handbook of Leadership: a Survey of Theory and Research*, New York: Free Press.

Stowell, M. (1999), 'Ropeable women lasso lynch mob', *The Australian*, 3 March.

Sullivan, G. and M. Harper (1996), *Hope is not a Method: What Business Leaders Can Learn From America's Army*, New York: Broadway Books.

Suszko, M. and J. Breaugh (1986), 'The effects of realistic job previews on applicant self-selection and employee turnover, motivation and coping ability', *Journal of Management*, **12** (4), 513–23.

Sutherland, T. (1999), 'Women bully with a smile on their dials', *The Australian*, 12 July.

Sutherland, T. (2000a), 'The Finn formula: Nokia's focus on innovation and the individual has paid off', *The Australian* (Business Section), 28 November.

Sutherland, T. (2000b), 'Dirty money bad sense for banks', *The Australian*, 10 November.

Sutton, R. (2001), *Weird Ideas that Work: Eleven Ways to Promote, Manage and Sustain Innovation*, London: Allen Lane.

Swartz, M. and M. Watkins (2003), *Power Failure: The Rise and Fall of Enron*, New York: Aurum Press.

Swieringa, J. and A. Wierdsma (1992), *Becoming a Learning Organization: Beyond the Learning Curve*, Cambridge: Cambridge University Press.

Tabakoff, N. (1999), 'Health: why you are a candidate for burnout', *Business Review Weekly*, 14 July, 33–5.

Takahashi, D. (2002), 'Atom-sized chips', *The Australian* (IT Section), 29 October.

Tannen, D. (1995), 'The power of talk; who gets heard and why', *Harvard Business Review*, September–October, 138–48.

Tatum, C. (2002), 'Fighting the cyber-crud', *The Australian* (IT Section), 19 November.

Taylor, P. (2000), 'Countdown to disaster', *The Australian*, 17 November.

Teerlink, R. and L. Ozley, (2000), *More than a Motorcycle: The Leadership Journey at Harley-Davidson*, Boston: Harvard Business School Press.

Thakara, J. (1997), *How Today's Successful Companies Innovate by Design*, Aldershot: Gower Publishing.

The Australian (Special Edition on Outsourcing) (2002), *The Australian*, 29 October.

The Australian Financial Review (2000), 'Fed calls to even up pay scales', *New York Times* article, reprinted in *The Australian Financial Review*, 24 March.

The Centre for Responsive Politics, www.opensecrets.org.

The Economist (1999), 'The Einstein factor', reprinted in *The Australian*, 8 March.

The Economist (2000), 'Change handled better in house', reprinted in *The Weekend Australian*, 15–16 July.

The Economist (2002a), 'Coming clean: It's time to take stock', reprinted in *The Australian* (Business Section), 23 July.

The Economist (2002b), 'Two bosses better than one', reprinted in *The Australian* (Business Section), 17 June.

The Economist (2002c), 'Harassed women sue their employers', reprinted in *The Australian*, 6 March.

The Sunday Times (2002), 'Nomura banker accused of sex discrimination', *The Sunday Times* (UK) article, reprinted in *The Australian*, 30 December.

The Sunday Times (Western Australia) (2001), 'Archer wife bans sex and now jailed peer is branded a psychopath', 25 November.

The Times (2001a), 'Courting billions from crash', reprinted in *The Australian*, 30 May.

The Times (2001b), 'From hammer to slammer via dirty bidness', reprinted in *The Australian*, 7 December.

The Times (2001c), 'Kids: the anti-heroes of the new electronic age?' reprinted in *The Australian*, 15 June.

The Times (2002), 'Enron bosses feasted before fall', reprinted in *The Australian* (Business Section), 4 April.

The Work-Life Research Centre (2000), *The Work-Life Manual: Gaining a Competitive Edge by Balancing the Demands of Employees' Work and Home Lives*, London: The Industrial Society.

Thomas, R. (1996), *Redefining Diversity*, New York: AMACOM.

Toates, F. (1995), *Stress: Conceptual and Biological Aspects*, New York: Wiley and Sons.

Tobler, H. (2002), 'Sleep loss and long hours doubles heart risk', *The Australian*, 10 July.

Towers, K. (2000), 'Paying bribes is a dangerous game', *The Australian Financial Review*, 8 June.

Tracy, B. (1995), *Maximum Achievement*, Sydney: Brian Tracy International.

Transparency International (2000–2004), www.transparency.com.

Trapp, R. (1996), 'Bosses should learn to listen', *The Independent on Sunday*, 11 June.

Trinca, H. (2000), 'Bosses warned to listen or their workers go under', *Australian Financial Review*, 6 September.

Tuckman, B. and M. Jenson, (1977), 'Stages of small-group development revised', *Group and Organizational Studies*, December, 419–27.

Turnbull, N. (1996), 'Communicating with generation MM', *The Millennium Edge: Prospering with Generation MM*, St Leonards, NSW: Allen and Unwin, pp. 105–20.

Tushman, M. (1997), *Winning Through Innovation: A Practical Guide To Leading Organizational Change and Renewal*, Boston: McGraw-Hill.

Tushman, M. and D. Nadler, (1996), 'Organising for innovation', in K. Starkey, (ed.), *How Organizations Learn*, London: Thomson, pp. 135–56.

Uhfelder, H. (1997), 'Ten critical traits of group dynamics', *Quality Progress*, **30** (4), 69–72.

Uren, D, (1998a), 'Anemic boards need new blood', *The Weekend Australian* (Business Section), 7–8 March.

Uren, D. (1998b), 'How your team can play the profit game', *The Weekend Australian* (Business Section), 26–7 September.

Uren, D, (1998c), 'Leadership draws a following', *The Weekend Australian* (Business Section), 14–15 November.

Uren, D. (1999), 'Smart thinkers bring passion to power roles', *The Weekend Australian*, (Business Section), 9–10 October.

Veash, N. (1997), 'Firefighter who was harassed wins GBP 200,000', *The Independent*, 18 March.

Velasquez, M. (1983), 'Organizational statesmanship and dirty politics: ethical guidelines for the organizational politician', *Organizational Dynamics*, **10** (2), 65–79.

Velasquez, M. (1992), *Business Ethics: Concepts and Cases*, Englewood Cliffs, NJ: Prentice-Hall.

Vogelstein, F. (2003), 'Can Google grow up?', *Fortune*, 8 December, 48–56.

Von Radowitz, J. (2001), 'Surgeons operate by remote', *The Australian* (IT Section), 20 September.

Vroom, V. (1964), *Work and Motivation*, New York: Wiley.

Wageman, R. (1997), 'Critical success factors for creating superb self-managing teams', *Organizational Dynamics*, **26** (1), 49–61.

Wajcman, J. (1998), *Managing Like a Man: Women and Men in Corporate Management*, Pennsylvania: Pennsylvania State University Press.

Wales, E. (2002), 'Pop go the pop-ups', *The Australian* (IT Section), 22 October.

Wallace, T. (2002), 'Sustainability index shows it pays off', *The Australian Financial Review*, 27 February.

Walsh, J. (1998), 'A world war on bribery; the costs of corruption have reached earth-shaking proportions, prompting Herculean efforts to clean out the muck', *Time*, 13 July, 37–41.

Wanous, J. (2000), 'Cynicism about organisational change', *Group and Organization Management*, **25** (2), 132–45.

Warren, E. and C. Toll, (1997), *The Stress Workbook*, London: Nicholas Brealey.

Warwick, K. (1998), *In the Mind of the Machine*, London: Arrow Books.

Warwick, K. (2002), *I Cyborg*, London: Century.

Watkin, H. (1999), 'Corruption erodes Vietnam's growth engine', *The Australian*, 26 July.

Watts, T. (1999), 'A stitch in time: organizations would do well to do good right now as ethics-to-go might give you heartburn', *Management Today*, June, 15–18.

Wayne, S., M. Shore and R. Liden, (1997), 'Perceived organizational support and leader–member exchange: a social exchange perspective', *Academy of Management Journal*, **40**, 82–111.

Weldon, F. (1999), *Godless in Eden*, London: Harper Collins.

Wellington, S. (1998), 'Cracking the ceiling: barriers frustrated women this century but things are changing fast', *Time*, 7 December, 139–40.

Wenger, E. and W. Snyder (2000), 'Communities of practice: the organizational frontier', *Harvard Business Review*, January–February, 139–45.

West, C. (2002), 'McUniversities growing in popularity', *The Australian* (Higher Education Section), 23 October.

Westfield, M. (1999), 'CEOs command big bucks, but are they ever worth it?', *The Australian* (Business Section), 9 August.

Westfield, M. and G. Elliott (2001), 'One.Tel: the tale of one big deception', *The Weekend Australian*, 2–3 June.

Whistleblowers Australia (2002–4), www.whistleblowers.com.au.

White, A. (2002), 'Axe hangs over bosses' options', *The Australian* (Business Section), 22 August.

White, B., C. Cox and C. Cooper (1994), *Women's Career Development: A Study of High Flyers*, Oxford: Blackwell.

Wilkins, A. (1984), 'The creation of company cultures: the role of stories and human resource systems', *Human Resource Management*, **23** (1), 45–57.

Williams, A. (1994), *Just Rewards?* , London: Kogan Page.

Williams, S. (2002), *Peter Ryan: The Inside Story*, Sydney: Viking.

Wilson, F. (1995), *Organizational Behaviour and Gender*, London: McGraw-Hill.

Wilson, M., P. Holman and A. Hammock (1996), 'A comprehensive review of the effects of work-site health promotion on health related outcomes', *American Journal of Health Promotion*, **10** (6), 429–35.

Wilson, P. (1968), 'The perceptual distortion of height as a function of prescribed academic status', *Journal of Social Psychology*, **74** (1), 97–102.

Wilson, R. (1998), 'Tiny-tech: soon we may be using machines too small to see', *The Australian* (IT Section), 7 February.

Wilson, S. (2002a), 'The buck stops or starts with CEO and board', *The Australian* (Business Section), 7 July.

Wilson, S. (2002b), 'Internet plays its part in encouraging company fraud', *The Australian*, 23 April.

Winnett, R. (2002), 'Forgetfulness just a memory: the race is on to market the latest development in pharmaceuticals – pills to enhance memory', *The Australian* (IT Section), 24 January.

Witherspoon, P. (1997), *Communicating Leadership: An Organizational Perspective*, Boston: Prentice-Hall.

Wood, A. (2002), 'Growing income gap could rock the boat', *The Australian*, 22 October.

Woodford, D. (2002), 'Developing a virtual PA', *The Australian* (IT Section), 6 August.

Woodley, B. (2001), 'HIH board voted itself extra pay', *The Australian*, 11 December.

Woodward, N. (2001), *The Fifth Element: Culture, Learning, Innovation and Knowledge Management in Western Australian E-Companies*, MBA Management Report, Graduate School of Management, University of Western Australia.

World Bank (2002), www.worldbank.org.

World on Sunday (2002), 'Goats in a spin', *The Sunday Times* (Western Australia), 23 June.

Wylie, I. (2001), 'Report from the future: failure is glorious', *Fast Company*, October, 126–7.

Young, M. and J. Post, (1993), 'Managing to communicate, communicating to manage: how leading companies communicate with employees', *Organizational Dynamics*, Summer, 31–43.

Zackowitz, M. (2003), 'Harley's mid-life crisis', *National Geographic*, August, 4–5.

Zaleznik, A. (2004), 'Managers and leaders: are they different?', *Harvard Business Review*, January, 74–81.

Zenger, J. (1991), 'Leadership in a team environment', *Training and Development Journal*, October, 23–35.

Ziegler, J. (1995), 'America's healthiest companies', *Business and Health*, **16** (8), 29–31.

Zimbardo, P. (1999), 'Stanford prison experiment: a simulation study of the psychology of imprisonment conducted at Stanford University', www.prisonexp.org.

Zuboff, S. (1988), *In the Age of the Smart Machine*, New York: Basic Books.

Index

11 September 299, 339–40, 385–6, 494–5
14000 Quips and Quotes for Writers and Speakers 133
3m 30, 311, 347, 364, 365, 373, 376

AAPT 449
ABB 26
Abbey National Building Society 226
Abbott, Tony 188
'Abilene Paradox' 207
AC Nielsen 368
Access Grid Node 438
achievement, need for 165, 172, 304
active listening 97–8, 99–105, 377
Adams, Scott 135–6, 203, 309
adaptive learning 382
Adecco 497
administrative automation 440
Administrative Science Quarterly 322
advertising banners 449–52
aerobic exercise 81
affiliate marketing, programming 450
affiliation, need for 165
Africa
    corruption 527
    women leaders 229
agrarian revolution 430
Ahold 497
air force, sexual harassment 240
Air Transport World 338–9
airline industry, organizational change in 329–40
Alcatel Bell 112
alcohol 83
Alessi, Alberto 365
Allen, Woody 104
alliances 262–3
Allred, Mike 145–6
'Alpha Women' 257, 262–3
alpha-humanoids 478
alternative therapies 85–6
Amcor 449
American Association for the Advancement of
    Science Conference (2003) 251–2
American Express 308
American Heart Association 86
American Psychological Association 63
Amnesty International 516–17
AMP 449
Ampleforth College, UK 11
Andersen, Arthur 299

Anderson, Paul 23, 24, 304
Ansett Airlines 241, 300
anti-Semitism 488–9
anxiety 171–2
ANZ Australia Post 449, 529–30
AOL Time Warner 456
Apple Computer Co. 112
Area 7 465
Aristotle 53
armed conflicts, women in 250–51
artificial intelligent entities (artilects) 467–8, 473,
    477, 478
Asia
    organizational cultures 322
    women leaders 229
    see also Burma; Cambodia; China; East Asia;
        Indonesia; Japan; Malaysia; Thailand;
        Vietnam
Asian economic crisis (1997) 522–3
assertiveness 263, 264
AT & T 456, 552, 553
AT Kearney 301
attitudinal
    change 271–2, 314
    discrimination 240–42
attributions 181–3, 271
audiences, engagement with 143–5
augmented reality systems 465
Augustine, Norman 345
aussiehome.com 73–4
Australasia
    discrimination 234–5
    leadership development courses 15–16
    outsourcing 462
    self-employment 542
    team working 204
    technological development 436
    women leaders 225–9, 231, 232–3, 250, 252,
        264–5
Australia
    business ethics 497–8, 508
    change management 303–4
    communication 94, 110–11
    corruption 497–8, 501–2, 503
    e-commerce 449, 457
    education 11
    employee motivation 175, 184, 188, 190, 191
    employee selection 176, 368
    illegal drugs 490–91

inequality 179
management practices 177, 186
occupational stress 64
team working 204, 215–16
technological development 436
women leaders 225–9, 231, 247
working hours 63–4
Australian Affirmative Action Agency 229
Australian Broadcasting Corporation 39, 304, 329, 340–43
Australian Census on Women in Leadership 232
Australian Chamber of Commerce and Industry 47–8
Work and Family awards 190–91
Australian Confederation of Trades Unions 167
Australian Council 259–60
Australian Cricket Board 13
Australian Financial Review 23
Australian Formula Ford championships 253
Australian Graduate School of Management 203
Australian Institute of Company Directors 529–30
Australian Institute of Management 43, 303
australian.com 396
autocratic management styles 208
automobiles, evolution of 474, 476
automotive industry 23, 116, 123, 156–7, 202–3, 489
Aziz, Nik Abdul 243

B2B 449
Badawi, Abdullah 525–6
Bailey, George 415
Bailey, Sandra 448
Bain & Company 331, 411, 412
Baker Potts LLP 496
Baker, Carl 448–9
Baker, James 496
Balding, Russell 343
Baldochi, Podesta 312–13
Ballin Group 213
Ballmer, Steve 188
bankruptcy 188
Bankruptcy Court, New York 492–3
Baraku people, Japan 10
Barings Bank 491–2
Barret, Bernard 501
Bay of Pigs, Cuba 206
Bear Stearns 492
behaviour, rules of 153–6
behavioural
aspects of leadership 17–19
change 314
gender differences 246
behaviours 318–19
Belbin, Meredith 211–12
belief systems 317–18
Bellow, Paul 111–12
belonging, sense of 458
Bentley, Jon 415

Berlusconi, Silvio 500
'Best Practice Replication Process' 400
Bethune, Gordon 330–40
BHP-Billiton 23, 113, 115–16, 188, 520
Bick, Julie 172
'Big Brother' 480
'Big Five' personality traits 10
Billings, John 183
bionimetics 469–70
bisociation 359, 364–5
Blount, Frank 16
BMW 438, 441
Body and Soul 123
body language 105
Body Shop 115, 123, 254
Boeing 30, 438
Boesky, Ivan 487
BOHICA syndrome 320
Bollinger, Martin 300
Boo.com 300, 447
Booher, Charles 471
'bootlegging' 373
Booz, Allen and Hamilton 300, 392
Boss Magazine 387
boss test 537–9
Boston Consulting Group 411, 457
Bradman, Don 15
brainstorming 325, 371–3, 411
Branson, Richard 35, 127, 181, 308
Brave New World 467
Brazil, occupational stress 64
Breaking New Ground: A Manual for Survival for Women Entering Non-Traditional Jobs 265–6
breakthrough thinking 362–3, 366–7
Brenneman, Greg 331–40
bribes 520, 522
'bright-sizing' 399
Brightmail 78
British Petroleum (BP) 303, 348, 366, 380, 441, 525
British Psychological Society 47, 67
broadcasting industry 340–43
Bronowski, Jacob 362
Brooks, Rob 473
Browne, John 366, 373, 380, 383, 384, 393
Bryan, Elizabeth 255
Built to Last: Successful Habits of Visionary Companies 30, 230
bullying 39–42, 64, 194, 257, 287
'Bullying Broads' 257
'bunker mentalities' 369, 421
Burgoyne, John 391–2
Burke, Edmund 531
Burma, corruption in 524, 525
Burns, Patrick 370
Burns, Robert 51
Burton Group 525
Bush, George W. 11, 492, 495–6, 528–9, 531
Business Council of Australia 47–8

business ethics 487–8, 526–31
  business case for ethical leadership 504–12
  ethical dilemmas 512–19
  ethical universality 519–26
  unethical business practices 488–504
business leaders, biographies of 361
Business Man of the 20th Century award 27
business uncertainty 385–6
Business Week 373
business, effects of unethical behaviour 523–4
buy outs 374–5
Byrne, Ken 213

California Public Retirement System 493–4
Calm for Life 70
Caltex Australia 188
Cambell, Kim 232
Cambodia, corruption in 524
Canada, change management 300–301
Canon 398
carbon nano-tubes 435
career
  decisions 71–5
  management, as an incentive 190
  progression 459
Carlopio, James 97, 162
Carnegie, Dale 197
Carroll, Lewis 310
Carter, Jimmy 134
Castro, Fidel 156
Catanzarita, Ray 41
catch-up 300, 381
CCRU Research 503
cellular automata machine (CAM) 468
Centre for Creative Leadership, US 16, 549
CFSB 492
Chaney, Michael 199, 306–7, 387, 526
'change fatigue' 319–20
change management 28, 300–301
  programmes (CMPs) 303–4, 310
  teams 305, 306–7
change strategies 325–6, 333–5
change, drivers of 328
characteristics, of leader/managers 51–4
charismatic leaders 27–34
Charlesworth, Rick 208
Charter Pacific 372
charters, teams 215, 220
'Cheat the Prophet' 349–50
Chekov, Anton 146
Cheney, Dick 496
Chevron 553
chiasmus 134
child sex abuse 500–501
China
  business practices 516–19
  culture 155
  economic emergence 299

Chinese Whispers 98–9
chip implants 470
Christian myths 245
Christie's 491
Chrysler 122–3, 308, 441
Churchill, Winston 27, 84, 124, 127–8, 134, 328, 463
Cimino, Michael 31
Circuit City 308–9
Cisco Systems 49, 206, 374–5
Citicorp 30
City of Perth Executive, Western Australia 398
Claes, Willy 499
Clark, Andy 471
Clark, Bob 468
Clinton, Bill 28, 105, 126, 233, 466, 499–500
Clonaid 467
cloning 466–7
clothing, evolution of 475–6
Cloudmark 78
CNBC 456
CNN 456
coaching 17–18, 25–7, 210
Coca-Cola 26, 449, 525
cochlear implants 470
codes of conduct 519–20, 522
codified knowledge management systems 413–14, 424
coercive power 280–81, 283–6
Cohen, Sir Jack 115
collaborative management styles 256–7
colleagues, treatment of 289
collective
  communication 376
  learning 383
Collins, Eileen 251
Collins, Jim 29–31, 230, 325, 461
Collins, Roger 203
Com Corporation 115
command-and-control management styles 169, 182–3, 202–3, 281
commercial airlines, sex discrimination 241
commercial potential of intellectual property 398
commitment, organizational change 324–5
common sense 36–8, 410
Commonwealth Bank 449
communication 92–6, 157–8, 195, 376–9, 411
  breakdowns 93, 98, 116
  context of 92–6
  cross-cultural communication 147–57
  formal communication skills 125–47
  interpersonal communication 96–110
  leaders as storytellers 116–25
  skills 25–6, 29, 46, 293
  technologies 465
  top-down communication 110–16
  with clients/customers 116
communities of practice 397, 409–10
company life cycles 19–20

competence 45
competitive
  advantage 348–9, 400–401
  intelligence 419–21, 503
  sports 81
'complex adaptive systems' 413
computer.com 446
computer-aided design (CAD) 441
computer-processing 433–6
conflict management 100, 291–6
conflicts of interest 496
Confucius 316, 379, 521
'consanguineous nepotism' 212–13
consciousness 472–3
Conservative Party, UK 23, 32–4, 40–41
construction materials, evolution of 477
consumer data 480
content theories 164–5
  practical application of 165–73
Continental Airlines 303, 304, 310–11
  organizational change in 329–40
continuous change, commitment to 328–9, 338–9, 342
CoProcure 449
core competencies 461–2
Cornell University 468
corporate
  citizenship 503
  collapses 299–300
  corruption 492–8, 503–4, 527–8
  health programmes 88
  image 509–10
'corporate athlete' philosophy 27
Corporate Cultures 322
Corporate Research Foundation, Australia 190
corruption 492–8, 503–4, 527–8
Cosmopolitan awards 226
Coudert Brothers 510–11
Council for Tobacco Research, US 490
counselling services 70
covert surveillance 480–81
Cowling, Annie 265–6
'craft loyalty' 399
Cragnotti, Segio 497
Cranfield School of Management, UK 16
Creating Intelligent Organizations: the Secrets of Long-Lasting Business Success 546
creative
  accounting 510
  envisioning 377
  thinkers 368–9
  thinking 295, 357–9
creativity 351–62
  business value of 350–51
  in practice 362–5
  understanding of 366–8
credibility 45
credit cards 307–8

Crédit Suisse 492
Crichton, Michael 465, 483
Crick, Francis 466, 473
crime, growth of 490–91
critical thinking 295
Crone, Grey 167
cross-cultural communication 147–52
  linguistic and cultural differences in 152–7
cross-functional work teams 202
cult of personality 29, 32–3
cultural
  diversity 152–7
  'fit' 175
  imperatives 246
  relativism 513
  sensitivity 156
  traditions 521–2
cultural change, leadership of 298–304
  attitudes to 314–21
  commitment and motivation 324–5
  goals and objectives 306–13
  involvement of customers/employees 327–8
  ongoing commitment to continuous change 328–9
  operational culture and working practices 321–4
  practice of 329–43
  presence of transformational leaders 304–5
  resistance to 313–14
  strategies for 325–6
  two-way communication 326–7
culture
  of knowledge management 402–7
  of nations 236, 243–4, 521
  of organizations 115–16, 162, 234–5, 268–9, 373–5, 424–5
Currey, Gail 119
'Customer Relations Management Systems' (CRMS) 440
customers
  communication with 116
  involvement in change management 328, 337–8
cyber-abuse 459
cyber-cities 437
cyber-domiciles 491
Cyber-Jaya, Malaysia 437
cyber-sex 472
cyber-sickness 80, 459
cyber-slacking 459
cyber-stress 458, 459
Cyberlynx 449
cybernetics 470
cyborgs 470–71, 478

Daimler Benz 438, 441
Das Experiment 284
data warehouses 413, 417
Davidson, Walter 387–8
de Bono, Edward 48, 351, 359, 371

de Geus, Arie 370, 379, 381, 383, 386, 392–3
de Mistral, George 364
de-motivation 162, 197
Death2Spam 78
DEC 375
Decca 37
Defence Academy, England 16
Del Gigante, Michael 190
delegating 78–9
Deloitte Touche Tohmatsu 49, 255–6
Democrat Party, US 226, 499, 500
demotivation 181–2, 187, 192–3
Dench, Dame Judi 140
dependency 282, 289
DePree, Max 25
designer drugs 467
destructive conflict 292–3
development 176, 194
Development Dimensions International 176
Diageo 49
diet, to combat stress 82–3
Dilbert cartoons 203
Diocletian 161
discontinuous change 386
discrimination 179, 227–31, 264–5, 269–70
Disney 30, 313, 322
'displacement of concepts' 365
distress 60, 65
Diver, Stuart 89
diversity
    in employment 231, 235
    in teams 212
DNA Protection Service, US 466
domestic
    leaders 206, 207
    robots 476
Don't Sweat the Small Stuff 70
Donofrio, Nick 398
Doonsbury cartoon 233
dotcom companies
    boom 449
    collapse 444–8, 492
double-loop learning 318–19
Dow Chemicals 114–15
Dow Jones Index 299, 494–5, 509
Drake International 193–4
'dreaming sessions' 377
Drucker, Peter 16, 23, 42, 361–2, 397, 401, 424,
    429
drug cartels 490–91
du Pont 489
Duchovny, David 170
Duell, Charles 36
Dumas, Roland 499
Dupont 470
Dutroux, Mark 500
dynasties 10–11
dysfunctional cultures 162

Dyson 383, 441–2
Dyson, Brian 86

e-business 441
e-companies 437
    collapse of 444–8
    second wave of 462–3
e-mail 77–8
East Asia
    corporate corruption 498, 524–6, 527
    financial meltdown 299
East Asian Economic Review 523
Eastwood, Jenni 191
Ebbers, Bernie 31, 493
economic
    booms/slumps 444–5
    growth 525
    performance, drivers of 399
ecotech companies 455
Edison, Thomas 299, 348, 359, 361, 364, 372,
    376
EDS 449
education 11, 176, 234–5, 352
educators 382
Edwards, Ben 113–14
effort-performance expectancy 173
Egon Zehnder International 550
Einstein, Albert 7–8, 36, 76, 83–4, 463
Eisenhower, Dwight D. 183, 286
'Electronic Sales Partner' 416
Electronics magazine 435
Elf Aquitaine 499
Eli Lilly 553
Elix, Doug 453
emotional
    connections 133
    displays 155
emotional intelligence (EI) 11–12, 548–50
emotionally intelligent computers 468
emotions 103–4
    control of 98–9
employee attitude surveys 110–11
employee motivation 192–9
    complex nature of 160–64
    content theories 164–73
    and financial rewards 183–92
    process theories 173–83
employees
    behaviour 503
    compensation 63
    control 459
    diversity 231
    as drivers of organizational change 301
    education and development 176, 194
    emotional impact of leaders 12
    feedback 105–10
    international experience 157, 228
    isolation 458

management 536–47
mobility 440–41
monitoring 480–81
motivation 539–40
ownership of change management initiatives
    327–8, 336–7, 342
resistance to change 305, 313–14, 325, 331–2
rewards 328
suggestion schemes 112–15
support of 33
turnover 399–400
working practices 321–4, 328
Employers of Choice 269–70
employment practices 193, 268
empowered leadership style 181, 182, 183
empowerment 169–70, 195–6, 281, 320–21
Enemy of the State 480
energy sources 478
Enfield, Harry 517
English language 152–3
English Ski Council 25
Enron 31, 188, 492–3, 494, 496, 503
'Enterprise Application Integration' (EAI) 440
Enterprising Nation Report, Australia 231
environmental
    changes 540–41
    influences on personality 10
    scanning 386–7
equal-opportunity practices 230, 234–5, 542–3
'equality of sacrifice' 122–3
equity theory 46, 179, 189
ERG theory 165, 189
ergonomics 167–9
Ericsson 434, 440–41
Ernst & Young 300, 412, 414–15, 416
ethical
    dilemmas 512–26
    imperialism/relativism 514–15
    investments 508–9
    leadership 504–12
    policies 510
    standards 528–30
    universality 519–26
ethos 53, 540
eugenics 467
Europe
    change management 301
    corruption 496–7, 500
    culture 155–6
    dot.com crash 445–6
    employee motivation 184
    illegal drugs 490
    inequality 179
    management practices 177
    occupational stress 67
    outsourcing 462
    team working 204
    universities 16
women leaders 225–9, 231, 250, 264
    see also Italy, Russia, Scandinavia, UK
European Commission 499
European Economic Community (EEC) 522
eustress 60
EV Global Motors 308
evaluative thinking 295
exercise, as relief for stress 80–82
exhaustion 66–7
experiential learning 316–18
expert power 282–3
expertise mapping 410–11
explicit knowledge 412, 413
external
    consultants 301, 324–5
    events, reaction to 74–5
extraneous information 421
extraordinary companies 391–2
extreme sports, female participation 253
extrinsic motivation 165, 186, 285–6
eye contact 140–41, 155

face recognition systems 480
face-to-face communication 327
family
    businesses 397
    life 86–8
family-friendly policies 191–2, 268
Fashion Café 443
Fastow, Andrew 492–3
'fat-cat' executives 184, 509
Federal Express 30, 313
feedback 105–10, 180–81, 195
feminine traits 246–9
feminism 227
Ferrier, Leanna 253
Fiedler, Edgar 463
Final Fantasy 443
Financial Times 392
Fiorina, Carly 226
firefighting, women in 252
Firestone 116, 400
First Boston 492
Fitzgerald, F. Scott 362
Flett, Dr Penny 75
flexible
    employment policies 463
    leadership styles 20–21
flight-or-fight response 59, 66, 81, 140, 295–6
flying machines, development of 362–3
followership 21, 23–5
Foot in the Mouth Awards 141
footwear, evolution of 475–6
Ford Motors 30, 116, 400, 441, 489
Ford, Henry 397, 488
formal communication skills 125–8
    content of presentations 132–7
    delivery of presentations 140–47

researching audiences 128–30
structuring presentations 130–32
visual aids 137–9
formal communication strategies 115
Fortune magazine
articles 503
awards 27, 49, 191, 227, 330, 339, 390
surveys 175, 204, 269–70, 299, 348, 349, 510, 554–5
Forum Corporation 116
Fosbury, Malcolm 448
Fosters 449
Franklin, Benjamin 185
Freud, Sigmund 369
Friedman, Milton 530–31
Froggy Group 497
front-line operations 439–40
Fry, Art 365
FTSE 495
Fuji Spinnin 443
Fukuyama, Francis 482–3
'functional fixedness' 358
Future Shock 480

Gaius Petronius 298
Galbraith, John 397
Galvin, Robert 520
'Game Changer; process 375
Gandhi, Mahatma 10, 23, 118, 124, 327
Gap 525
Gartner 419–20, 448–9, 457, 462
gastrobots 442
Gattaca 465, 466
Gates, Bill 20, 138, 350
Gavin McCleod Concrete Pumping 191
GE Capital 377
gender
discrimination/equality 229–33
and sexuality 244
stereotypes 235–60
gender-balanced groups 259
gender-neutral terms 271–2
General Electric 30, 202, 299, 313, 369, 440
General Electric Management Institute 15–16
general expectancy (GE) theory 173–6
General Motors 202, 416, 441, 488, 489, 551
Generation MM companies 455
Generation T 192, 399, 544
Generation X 192, 260, 271, 544
Generation X, Y and T companies 455
Generation Y 192, 260, 271, 399, 544
'generative learning' 382
generic qualities 272
genetic
differences 245
engineering 442, 465, 466–7, 477
inheritance 7–10
genetically modified foods 476

Genobyte 468
Geoghan, John 501
George, William 51–2
Gere, Richard 141
Germany, change management 300–301
Gerstner, Leo 324, 436
Gibson, William 436
Giga Information 77–8
Giraudoux, Jean 141
Glanvill, Joseph 464
glass ceilings 227–8
Glaxo-SmithKline 467
Global Crossing 31, 232, 299, 494
global knowledge economy 397–8, 400–401
Global Positioning System satellites 480
globalization, effects of 345, 543–5
goal-setting 17, 177–8
Gohn, Carlos 292
Goizueta, Robert 54
Goleman, Daniel 11–12
Good to Great 30–31, 230
'Good to Great' companies 203–4, 305
Goode, Charles 529–30
Goodman Fiedler 449
Goodyear, Chuck 115–16
Google 49, 168–9, 376
Gorbachov, Mikhail 126
Gore, Al 437
Goretex 387
Gorky, Maxim 160
Gosper, Kevin 497
Gossens, John 112
Goutard, Noel 114
government legislation
corporate corruption 510–11
new technologies 453
Graduate School of Management, Western Australia 43–4
Grasso, Dick 495
Greenspan, Alan 230–31, 529
Gretsky, Wayne 351
Grey, Francis 509
'Groupthink' 206–7
Grove, Andy 24, 113, 124, 291, 361, 436
guardedness 290
Gulf War 250, 299
gun technology 372
Gunningham, Charlie 72–4
'gut-feelings' 360–61
Gutenberg Press 362–3

habitual behaviours 318–19
Haddock, Patricia 272
Hague, William 33
Haigh, Gideon 321
Hain, Kenneth 50
Haliburton 496
Hamas 251

Hamel, Gary 367, 375, 376–7
Hamilton, Neil 191
handouts for presentations 136
Handy, Charles 126, 165, 365, 458
'Hardy Personalities' 69–70
Harken Oil 496
Harley Davidson 189, 303, 387–93
Harley, Bill 387–8
Hart–Rudman Commission (2000) 385
Harvard University 17, 303, 325, 468
Harvey, Jerry 207
Hawking, Stephen 360, 471
Hawthorne Studies 204
Hay Group 339
'Head-Heart-Hip' technique 134
health 266
Health and Wellness (HW) programmes 88, 551–5
Heath, Ted 32
hedonism 161, 180
Helsinki Exchange 299
Herman Miller 113
Herzberg's Two Factor theory 165, 167, 170
Herzberg, Frederick 160
Heseltine, Michael 33
Hewlett-Packard (HP)
    change management 303
    communication 120–22, 376, 416
    culture 115, 313, 322, 522
    people management 26, 30, 189, 202, 369
    selection processes 175, 226, 269
Hewlett, Bill 24, 54, 120–22, 124
hierarchical power relationships 292
high-achievers 169
high-performers 206, 210–11
high-performing companies 30
high-tech organizational environments 453, 460–61
high-trust organizations 458
higher order needs 165, 169
Highfield, Bruce 193
HIH 206, 232, 300, 497, 527–8
Hitler, Adolf 23, 29, 488
Hockeyroos 208
Hoffman La Roche 415
Holland, Jean 257
home
    shopping 441
    working 457–9
Home Information Systems (HIS) 476–7
home-grown leaders 30–31
honesty 45
hormonal changes in women 246–7
hostility 100
How to Rule the World: A Handbook for the Aspiring
    Dictator 288
How to Win Friends and Influence People 197
Huizinga, Johan 369
human
    contact 458–9

intelligence, forms of 9–10
nature 286
needs 165–6
human–computer interactions 470
human–machine entities 478
human/artilect boundaries, blurring of 473
humanity, potential impact of new technologies
    463–79
humour, importance of 46–51, 75, 265–6, 369–71
hunters, men as 245–6
Husqvarna 442
Hutchinson, Ron 389
Huxley, Aldous 467
Huxley, Thomas 135
hybrid leadership styles 258–60, 270–71, 272
hygiene factors 165
hyperstress/hypostress 60

Iacocca, Lee 122–3, 124, 173, 308
IBM 23, 30, 31, 375, 398, 399–400, 474, 488–9
Ibuka, Masura 372
Icon Recruitment 174
IDC 77
ideas, cross-fertilization of 376
'ideas-factories' 349, 375
'idle time' 97–8
imagery 119, 133, 139, 382, 384
impartiality 290
implicit
    knowledge 410, 412
    leadership theory 21–2
In Search of Excellence 322
in-groups 22–3, 33, 207, 212
in-house leadership development courses 15–16
Incentive magazine 50
incentives, non-financial 189–92
'inclusive organizations' 268
incremental
    adjustments in organizations 267–8
    changes 303, 325
    learning 366
incubation 359
Indian National Assembly 266
Indonesia, corruption in 524, 527
industrial
    revolution 430
    theology 348
Industrial Light and Magic 119, 313
Industrial Society, UK 370
industrialized countries
    leadership styles 270–71
    status of businesswomen 227, 266, 542
    stress 63–4
    team working 201–2
industrializing countries, corporate corruption 498
inequality of wealth 482
inequity 187
inertia 321

influence, strategies for 261–6, 285
informal knowledge-sharing systems 400, 411
information
   overload 77–8
   processing 133
   technology, outsourcing of 462
Ingham, Bernard 33, 256
Inner Quality Management 82
innovation 347–62
   in practice 362–5
   understanding of 366–8
   workshops 375
innovative organizations 365–6
   brainstorming 371–3
   communication 376–9
   hiring creatives and mavericks 368–9
   importance of fun 369–71
   organizational culture 373–5
   understanding creativity and innovation 366–8
insider dealing 491–2, 497
inspiration 46
Institute for Manpower Studies, UK 187
Institute for Soldier Nanotechnologies 469–70
institutional learning 383
instrumentality 173
Integrated Vision 216
integrity 45
Intel 26, 113, 313, 421, 433, 435–6, 469
intellectual capital management 396–402
   accessing outside knowledge 418–23
   initiatives 416–18
   links with culture, innovation and learning
      424–7
   systems for 407–16
   theory and practice of 402–7
intelligence gathering quotient (IGQ) 421
Intelligence Quotient (IQ) 7–8, 9–10, 39
Interactive Voice Response (IVR) 439
interdisciplinary venture teams 374–5
'internal locus of control' 186
International Bar Association (IBA) 473
international job experience 157, 228
International Journal of Cardiology 75
International Labour Organization (ILO) 516–17
International Monetary Fund (IMF) 490
Internet 424, 432, 436–7, 449, 457, 459–60
interpersonal communication 96–9
   active listening 99–105
   lying 105
   staff feedback 105–10
Intranet 417, 424
'intrapreneurship' 349–50, 369, 373–5, 378
intrinsic motivation 165, 186, 187, 285–6
intuition 360–61
invention 348
Inverarity, John 13, 14–15
Iona Technology 459
Ireland, women leaders 244

Iridium 367
irregular payments 520, 522
Islam 251
Israeli–Palestinian conflict 250–51
Italy, women leaders 244

James, Paul 481
Japan 29
   Baraku people 10
   change management 300–301
   culture 155, 322
   economic performance 361
   management techniques 445
   power relationships 292
   technological development 436
Java-Logs 364–5
Jessel, Sir George 127
job
   choices 71–5
   design initiatives 169
   losses 64, 399
   previews 174–5
   rotation 369
   satisfaction 170–72
   security 193–4
Job Redesign movement 166
Jobs, Steve 124
Johnny Mnemonic 438
Johnson & Johnson 30, 467, 522
Johnson, Samuel 62, 318
Jongleurs 370
Jordan, Robert W. 496
Judicial Watch, US 496
judiciary, corruption in 500

K-Logs 413
K-Mart 299
Kao Corporation 369
Kaplan, Philip 447
Keefe, Bruyette and Woods 506
Keen, Michael 444
Kelleher, Herb 49, 176, 192
Kellner, Lawrence 339
Kempinska, Maria 370
Kennedy, John F. 28, 134, 206
Ker-Conway, Jill 263
Kerry, John 11
Keynes, John Maynard 464
kinaesthetic awareness 142–3
King Lear 348
King, Martin Luther Jnr. 118, 124
Kinsley, Michael 456
Kirkwood, Graham 167, 168
Kirner, Joan 264–5
Kissinger, Henry 276
Kivenen, Lauri 373–4
'kleptocracies' 498
Knapp, Ellen 415

'knowbots' 468–9
knowledge
    assets 408
    creation 409
    hoarding 422
    repositories 417
    sharing 369, 400, 412–13
    transfer 409–10, 411
    use of 380
'Knowledge Age' 425–6
'Knowledge Curve' 415
knowledge management 396–402
    accessing outside knowledge 418–23
    initiatives 416–18
    links with culture, innovation and learning 421,
        424–7
    systems for 407–16
    theory and practice of 402–7
Kodak 455–6
Kohl, Helmut 499
Kolb's learning cycle 316–17
Kopper, Michael 492
Kozlowski 31
KPMG 188, 503
Kurzweil, Ray 472, 473, 481, 483
Kuwait, culture 236
Kyungwon Enterprise Company 309

L'Oréal 549
Labour Party, UK 11, 32–3
Ladies Home Journal 464
Landis, Geoff 252
language problems 152–7
lateral thinking 351–9, 364, 366–7, 452
Latin America, illegal drugs 490
Lau-Tzu 25
Lauda, Nicki 113
Laurens World Sports Team of the Year award 13
Lay, Ken 31, 492, 503
laziness 206, 208
Le Guin, Ursula K. 409
leaded petrol 489
leader-as-servant philosophy 24–5
leader-coaches 26
leaders
    characteristics and qualities of 6–15, 51–5, 537–9
    as coaches and mentors 25–7
    role of 17–19
    as storytellers 116–23
leadership
    dark side of 39–42
    definition of 3
    desire for 12–15
    development 15–17
    effects of new technologies 453–63
    foundations of 1–6
    rotation of 208
    styles 19–25, 27–51, 255–6, 258–60, 270–71, 304

Leadership Skills for Women 272
learning
    business value of 350–51
    culture 425
    cycles 384
    of leaders 537–9
    processes 316–21
    units 203
learning organizations, creation of 379–81
    mastery and vision 381–2
    mental modelling 384
    scenario mapping/systemic thinking 385–90
    team learning 383–4
Lebed, Jonathan 446
Leeson, Nick 491–2
Legert Corporation 112–13
legitimate power 283–6
'leisure society' 480
Levin, Jerry 53, 350
Lewin, Kurt 36
LGE Performance Systems 26–7, 82
libertarian thinkers, influence of 32
Liberty One 447
life choices 71–5
life cycles of companies 19–20, 299–300, 391–2
life goals 76–7, 87
light bulbs, development of 364
Lilenthal, David 53–4
Lincoln, Abraham 24
Lincoln Electric 114
linear thinking 351–2
Lion Nathan 449
listening skills 96–105
litigation 233–4, 504
Lloyd, Andy 342
Lloyds of London 491
Lockheed Martin 115, 375, 522
Lockyer, Bill 503
logic, power of 285
logical thinking 358
logos 53, 540
lower order needs 165
loyalty 187, 392
Lucent Technologies 206, 447
lying 105

Macalister, Angus 174
MacArthur, General Douglas 24
Machiavelli on Management: Playing and Winning the
    Corporate Power Game 288
Machiavellian power 280, 285, 286, 287–91, 298
'macho' management styles 69
Mackes, Marilyn 174–5
MacNamara, Frank 307–8
Mafia 252, 500
Mahabharata 117
Major, John 33, 499
Malaysia, technological development 437

male management styles 260, 270–71
male-dominated
    organizations 242–3
    professions 225–6, 233, 249–54
Malone, Dr Tom 17
Malzman, Marian 479
management
    courses 15–16
    definition of 3
    of people 536–47
'management by objectives' 177–8
Mandela, Nelson 24–5
Mandelson, Peter 499
Manning, Marilyn 272
Mant, Alistair 41
'market spaces' 457
Marketing Magazine 510
markets, identification of 452
Marriot, Bill 30, 54
Marshall, Lisa 40
masculine
    management styles 259
    traits 246–9
Maslow's Hierarchy of Needs 164–5, 167, 170
Massachusetts Institute of Technology (MIT) 381,
        388, 389, 468, 469–70, 473
Master Card 308
material success 87
materialism 482
Matsushita Electric Company 418–19
Matsushita, Konosuke 54
mature companies, role of leaders 20
*Maverick: The Story Behind the World's Most Unusual
        Company* 196
mavericks 368–9, 373–5
Maxwell, Robert 491
Mayer, John 11
Mayer, Stephan 208
McBride, Louise 255–6
McClelland's Achievement Motivation theory 165
McClelland, David 280–81
McCourt, Martin 383
McDermott, James 506
McElrae, Alan 188
McGregor's 'Theory X and Y' 182–3
McKinsey & Co. 368, 411
McKnight, William 322, 371
McNealy, Scott 138, 481
mechanical-electronic-carbon circuitry 472–3
medical check-ups 81
medicines 85–6
medium-sized companies, role of leaders 20
MEDSTAT Group 553–4
Medtronic 51–2
meetings
    agendas 218
    preparation for 263
Melbourne Business School 167

Melbourne University 269
memory-enhancing drugs 467
men, leadership styles 255–6
Menlo Park Laboratory, US 376
mental modelling 119, 133, 382, 384
mentoring 17–18, 25–7
Merck 30, 467
mergers 456–7
Merrill Lynch 350
Meta Group 78
meta-learning 383
Metal Storm 372
Metropolitan Life Insurance Company 550, 553
micro-electronic mechanical structures (MEMS) 469
microchips 436
Microsoft 75, 115, 172, 176, 188, 313, 374–5
'Midas System' 309
Middle East
    culture 155–6, 236, 515
    women leaders 225–9
Milberg, Weiss, Bershad, Hynes and Lynch 503
military personnel
    stress amongst 63–4
    women in 231, 250–51
Milliken & Company 17
Mincom 188
mind-sets 355, 361–2, 366
'mindguards' 207
miniaturization of devices 433–5
Minority Report 465
Mintzberg, Henry 76
mission statements 306–7, 310–12
Mitterrand, Francois 257, 499
mobile phones, development of 432, 433–5
mobility of employees 440–41
money laundering 490–91
Money magazine 50
money, as a motivator 183–92
monitoring systems, web-use 459–60
monochromic (M-Time) 151
mood-enhancing drugs 467
'Moore's Law' 435
Moore, Gordon 464
moral principles 507–8
Morgan Grenfell Asset Management 255
Morgan Stanley 492
Morita, Akio 24, 54, 119, 124, 361, 372, 384
motivation 17, 46
    complex nature of 160–64
    organizational change 324–5
    strategies for 539–40
    see also employee motivation
'motivational fit' techniques 174
motivators 165
    money as 183–92
Motorola 30, 202, 367, 519–20, 522
MSNBC 456
Multiplicity 61

multitasking 455
Murdoch, Rupert 33, 396
Murrow, Edward 146
music, female participation 254
Muslim culture 236, 251, 266
mutual reciprocity 521–2
My Socrates 416
Myers, David 494
mythology 117–18, 120–21

Nader, Jonar 452, 489
nanotechnologies 469–70
Nasser, Jacques 116, 400
National Association of Colleges and Employers,
    US 174–5
National Australia Bank 28, 497
National Health Service University, UK 16
National Institute for Occupational Safety, US 63
'nature/nurture' debate 244–5
Nazi collaboration 488–9
negativity 371–2
Nelson, Dr Brendan 531
nepotism 23, 212–13
nervous energy 140
Netscape 456
networking 361
networks 11, 262–3
Neuer Markt collapse, Germany 497
'neuromorphic engineers' 469
new companies
    contribution to economic growth 378
    role of leaders 19–20
    venture capital 367–8
'New Right' 32
new technologies
    control of 479–83
    effects on leadership and management 453–63
    potential impact on humanity 463–78
New Tel 300, 447, 497
New York Bank 490
New York Stock Exchange (NYSE) 495
New Zealand
    corruption 503
    technological development 436
Newton, Sir Isaac 444
Nike 525
Nimoy, Leonard 204
'nine dots' exercise 354–5
Nissan 202, 292
Nixon, Richard 499
Nokia 299, 313, 367, 373–4, 382, 432, 434–5
Nomura 240–41
non-core functions, outsourcing of 457, 461–2
non-financial incentives and rewards 189–92
non-traditional hiring policies 368–9
non-verbal communication 95–6, 105
Nordic companies 398
Nordstrom 30

Norse Vedic myths 117
North America
    culture 156
    leadership development courses 15–16
    management practices 177
    self-employment 542
    team working 204
    women leaders 225–9, 231, 250, 252, 264–5
    see also Canada; US
North Atlantic Treaty Organization (NATO) 499
Northwest Airlines 334
notes for presentations 136–7
nuclear family types 270–71
Nugent, Helen 259–60
'Nurse Bryan's Rule' 120
nurturers, women as 245–6
nutrition, to combat stress 82–3

O'Dwyer, Mike 372
O'Malley, Pat 127
OAG 339
objectives, achievement of 14–15
objectivity 289–90
observe-decide-do cycles 318
occupational stress 59–62
    links with personal performance 62–70
    strategies for coping 70–88
occupations, perceptions of ethical standards
    506–7
Octel 489
offshore tax havens 491
Ohio State University 17
'old-boy networks' 11
Olsen, Ken 37
Olympic Games (2008) 517–18
'on demand era' 452
One Valley Bank 554
One.Tel 206, 232, 300, 447, 497, 527–8
ONLY 480
open forums 113
open plan offices 168, 376
operational culture 321–4, 331–2
organic communication styles 376
Organization for Economic Co-operation and
    Development (OECD) 227
organizational
    learning 301, 316–19
    performance 324
    politics 538
    structures 455–7
organizational change, leadership of 298–304
    attitudes to 314–21
    commitment and motivation 324–5
    goals and objectives 306–13
    involvement of customers/employees 327–8
    ongoing commitment to continuous change
        328–9
    operational culture and working practices 321–4

practice of 329–43
presence of transformational leaders 304–5
resistance to 313–14
strategies for 325–6
two-way communication 326–7
organizational concepts, influence on leadership
        styles 19–25
organizational culture *see* culture
Organizational Dynamics 322
organizations
    challenges of globalization 544–5
    changes in 267–72, 540–41
    codes of conduct 519–20, 522
    life cycles of 299–300, 391–2
    power of 526–7
    re-engineering of 443–4
    re-location of 481
    social contributions 522–3
    strategies for new technologies 479–83
Orica 449
Other People's Money 183
out-groups 22–3, 33, 212
outsourcing 399, 457, 461–2
ovacles 168
Oxford English Dictionary 348

PAC Dunlop 449
Packard, Dave 24, 54, 120–22, 124
parity 46
Parkin, David 25, 105
Parmalat 232, 300, 496–7
passive technologies 452, 461
patents 398
pathos 53, 540
patriarchal cultures 228
pay inequity 179
peak-performance coaching 26–7, 82
Pease, Alan and Barbara 246–7
Pelos, Nancy 226
pensions 188
people management 536–47
    policies for 49, 115–16
people-based knowledge management systems 411
people-centred organizational cultures 323–4
Perez, Frank 50
performance related pay (PRP) 186–9, 194
performance-outcome expectancy 173
Perisher Blue (PB), Australia 25–6
personal
    creativity 358–9
    development 10, 314
    goals 546–7
    growth 169
    mastery 381–2
    power bases 277, 282
    reputations 288
    space 168
    time-out 79

values 262
personal computers (PC), evolution of 474–5
Personal Digital Assistant (PDA) 440
personal performance, links with stress 62–4
    effects of occupational stress 65
    personality and stress 67–70
    phases of stress 65–7
personality types 39–40
    and attributions 182
    and stress 67–70
personalized assistants (PAs) 474
personalized knowledge management 412, 424
Peters, Tom 116, 126, 181–2, 206, 302, 309, 429
Petronius 298
pets, therapeutic benefits of 86
Pettigrew, John 302
Peugeot 441
Pfizer 467
'phantoms' 438
Philip Morris 30
Philips 438
physical
    appearance 263
    environments 166–9
Picard, Jean-Luc 285
planning 77
Plato 132
Play 370
Polanyi, Michael 409
Polaroid 189, 206
police service
    corruption in 500
    gender discrimination in 233
    stress in 67
political
    leaders 31–4, 124
    strategists 296
Political and Economic Risk Consultancy, Hong
        Kong 525
politicians, unethical behaviour by 499–500
politicized organizations 286–91
politics, management of 276–86
polyphasia 67, 69
polyphonic (P-Time) 151
Porter, Dame Shirley 499
'portfolio careers' 399
positional authority 281, 283–6
Posner, Barry 92
Post Its 364
power
    abuse of 287–8
    management of 276–86
    need for 165
    as a social game 288
    strategies for 261–6
    struggles 290–91
    wielding of 538
Power Jets Limited 307

PowerPoint 130, 137–9, 438
praise 289
predictions 464–74
Preece, Sir William 36
Prescott, John 23
presentations 125–8, 145–7
    content 132–7
    researching audiences 128–30
    skills 140–44
    structuring of 130–32
    uncooperative participants 144–5
    visual aids 137–9
pressure groups 509
Preston Trucking 114
Prey 465, 483
price fixing 491
Price-Waterhouse-Coopers 202–3, 415
printing presses, development of 362–3
prioritization 77
private education 11
proactive changes 300
process
    oursourcing 462
    theories 173–83
Proctor and Gamble 30, 202
productivity 461
professional jargon 135–6
profit
    maximization policies 530
    sharing 194
profitability 349, 392
project teams 202
ProtectCom 480
Pryce Corp 446–7
psychological traits of leaders 6–9
psychopathological tendencies 40–41
public sector, change in 321
public speaking *see* formal communication skills
purpose, sense of 262

Qantas 449
Quality of Working Life initiatives 166
quantum computers 468, 477
Quattrone 492
Queen Bees and Wannabies 257
Queensland ALP 497
Quentin, Caroline 179
questioning, importance of 104, 105

radical
    changes 303
    innovations 350
Rank Xerox 20, 206, 350, 414, 459–60
Rayner, Moira 264–5
re-location
    of employees 544
    of organizations 481
Reading University 470

Reagan, Ronald 499
'real world', understanding of 360–61
reality, 'reframing' of 355–6, 365
reason, power of 285
record-keeping 263–4
recruitment of staff 174–6, 193, 198, 368–9, 411
redundancy, effects of 64
Reebok 525
referent power 282
reflection 538–9
'refractory period' 85
'reframing' 355–6, 365
Reilly, Mathew 465
Reiner, Gary 440
reinforcement theory 180–81, 189
Reith, Peter 188, 497
relaxation 83–5
reliability 334–5
religious
    leaders as storytellers 117–18
    traditions 521
reporting systems 113
Republican Party, US 492
rescue services, women in 252
research
    change management 302–4
    communication 94–5
    companies 421
    effects of new technologies 481–3
resistant characters 317–18
responsibilities of leaders 24
reward
    power 283
    systems 179, 328, 411, 412, 425
rewards, non-financial 189–92
Richardson, Sir Ralph 141
Ride, Dr Sally 251
risk 385–6
Roadrunner 456
Robbins-Jones, Terry 215–16
Robinson, Jeffrey 491
Robinson, Peter 499
robots 441–3, 477–8
Roc Oil Company 47
Roddick, Anita 123, 254, 344–5, 526
Rogge, Jacques 517
Roman Catholic Church 244, 500–501
Roosevelt, Franklin D. 28, 111–12, 531
Rosenfield, Jim 444
Rove, Karl 496
Royal College of Art, UK 156
Royal Dutch Shell
    ethics 520, 522
    innovation 303, 348, 375, 385, 392
    knowledge management 420–21
Ruggles, Rudy 416, 417, 418
Ruskin, John 62
Russia 29, 251

s-commerce 448–9
Sales Force Automation (SFA) 439–40
Salomon Brothers 27
Salomon Smith Barney 492
Salovey, Peter 11
Samaranch, Juan Antonio 517
Samsung 522–3
Sarbanes–Oxley Act (2002), US 511
SAS Institute 49, 176
    Employer of Choice awards 191
sasshi 154
satellite phones, development of 367
Scandia 49, 398
Scandinavia, women leaders 264–5
    see also Sweden
scenario-mapping 385–90, 419, 452
Schiller, Yale 445
Schneider, Henry 488
Schneider, Lou 27
Schoppenhauer, Arthur 37
Schwab, Charles 350
Schwartz, Peter 385, 386
Schwartzenegger, Arnold 233
Schwartzkopf, Norman 126
scientific developments 433–52
    effect on leadership and management 453–63,
        479–83
    impact on humanity 463–78
Scott, Warren 510–11
screening software 78
Sculley, John 112
SDI 174
Sea Change 61
second wave organizations 453–4, 455–7, 460, 462
second-generation learning entities 468–9
selection of staff 174–6, 193, 198, 411
selective
    listening 97
    perceptions 21–3
selective encoding 359
self-affirmation 270
self-awareness 51–2
self-belief 35, 261–2
self-employment 37, 226–7, 232, 542
self-learning 382
self-managed teams 204, 208
self-motivation 169
self-satisfaction 171, 172
Selye, Hans 59
Semco 195–7
Semler, Ricardo 196
Senge, Peter 381, 383–4, 388, 393
senior management teams 212–13
sequential thinking 351–2, 358
seratonin 8
sexism 227–8
sexual harassment 232–5, 264–5
sexuality 244

Shakespeare, William 134, 151, 348
shared service groups 457
shareholder concerns 509
shareholding 186–9, 194
shareware systems 413
Shaw, George Bernard 37, 372
Sheehan, George 437, 447
Shell 381, 386, 525
'Shell Method' 385
Shier, Alan 340–43
Shier, Jonathan 39
Shirvington, Philip 378
shopping portals 448–9
short-term contracts 399
Siemens 468
silicon transistors 435
Silicon Valley 367–8, 399, 437
Silicon Valley Growth and Leadership Center, US
    257
Simmons, Michael 224, 268
Sims (simulated humans) 443
Sinclair, Amanda 225, 229, 262, 270, 272
Singapore, technological development 437
single-loop learning 317–18
Skilling, Jeff 184
skills
    development 14–15, 546–7
    gender differences 260
    of managers 539–40
    of women 231
skills-based pay 189
Sloan, Alfred 24, 54
social
    attitudes 152–6
    contributions of organizations 522–3
    influences on personality 10–11
    loafers 206, 208
    maps 119–20
    norms 227, 228
Social Democrats, UK 32
social exchange theory 21, 23–5
socially responsible investment (SRI) 508–9
Socrates 3, 540
Sony 30, 119, 367, 372, 384, 442, 475
Sorenstam, Annika 253
Sotheby's 491
South Australian University School of Information
        Systems 215–16
South Sea Company 444
Southwest Airlines (SA) 49, 50, 176, 192, 340
space missions 93, 115, 477–8
spam-mail 77–8
SpamNet 78
Spectrum 496
speculative currency trading 497
Speilberg, Steven 465
Spillane, Robert 257
Sporting Bodymind 82

sports
   coaching 108
   female participation 252, 253
   management 25
   teams 205–6
Sports Industry of Australia Award 13
Sputnik 432
staff, recruitment and selection 174–6, 193, 198
Stalin, Joseph 29
Standard and Poor 230
Standard Oil 489
Stanford Prison Experiment 283–4
State Retirement Scheme, New York 493–4
State University of New York 442–3
static organizational structures 455–7
status quo 35–6
Stead, Jerre 112–13
Steelcase 553
Steele, John 510
Stefano, Andy 370
stereotyping 154, 242–3, 256–7
stock market fraud 446
stock markets, behaviour of 444–5
stock options 511
Stogdill 6–7
storytelling 111–12, 116–18, 327
   in organizational settings 118–23
Strasbourg Civil Hospital 442–3
strategic intelligence 420–22
strategies for new technologies 479–83
Strategy at Westpac 259–60
'stream of consciousness' 136
stress
   and home working 459
   negative effects of 64
   and personality types 67–70
   related illnesses 63
   symptoms of 57–8
stress management 88–90
   links between stress and performance
      62–70
   occupational stress in context 59–62
   strategies 70–88
stressors 60–61, 62, 67
stretch targets 177–8
Streuli, Nick 73
'Stuck Record' technique 134
Stuckey, John 368
subordinates, role of 23
Suharto, 'Tommy' 524, 525
Sullivan, Scott 493, 494
Sun Microsystems 138
Sunjata 117
'Super-Bosses' 27–8, 304
supply chain efficiencies 448–9
Surfwatch 459–60
surgical robots 442–3
surveillance technologies 480–81

Survival 89
Sustainable Asset Management 509
Sustainable Research Investment industry 509
Sveiby, Karl-Erik 397, 398
Sweden, occupational stress 67
symbolism 124
synthetic
   corneas 470
   DNA 469
systemic thinking 385–90

Tanzi, Calisto 496–7
targets, stretching of 76–7
Taubman, Alfred 491
Taylor, Jim 369
team
   building 210–11
   formation 213–15
   leadership skills 207–9
   learning 383–4
   meetings, management of 215–21
   roles 211–12
team-based manufacturing 202
team-working 79
   in virtual environments 461
teams
   in context 201–7
   leadership of 207–15, 221–3
   meetings of 215–21
techno-elite/peasants 481
techno-stress 80
technological change management 453
technological developments 429–52
   effect on leadership and management 345,
      453–63, 479–83, 542–3
   impact on humanity 463–78
technologically advanced countries 439
technology, limitations of 447–8
Teerlink, Richard 388, 390
Telecom New Zealand 449
teleworking 457–9
Telstar 432
Telstra 188, 216, 241
   Australian Business Woman of the Year awards
      75
   Centre for Leadership 16
   CoProcure 449
Tereshkova, Valentina 251
territorial threats 295–6
Tesco 115
testosterone 245–7
Texas Instruments 553
Thailand, corruption in 524
Thatcher, Margaret 23, 31–4, 37, 126, 256–7
The 48 Laws of Power 288
The Age of Intelligent Machines 473
The Art of Japanese Management 332
The Australian 271, 342, 498, 501–2

The Body Shop 522
'The Boss Test' 181–2
The Dilbert Principle 135–6
'The Diner's Club Card' 307–8
The Economist 440
'The Great Man' theory of leadership 6–7
The Iliad 117
The Journal of Management Studies 322
'The Kraken' 415
The Laundrymen 491
The Lawnmower Man 438
The Leadership Challenge 326
The Little Book of Calm 70
The Living Company 392
The Lord of the Rings 44
The Mayne Group 300
The New Machiavelli: The Art of Politics in Business
     288
The Odyssey 117
The Spider 130–31
The Spirits Within 443
The Sprint Corporation 195
The Wall Street Journal 510
The Women's Power Handbook 265
The X-Files 179
Theory X 286
Theory Y 286
Theory Z 322
'thick screening process' 175
'Thinking Hats' 359–60
third wave organizations 453–4
Thomson, J. Walter 489
Thoreau, Henry David 72
'Thousand Points of Light' approach to change
     112–13
Tiananmen Square protests (1989) 518
tidiness 78
time
     management 75–80
     organization of 151
time out for leaders 538–9
Timot Putra 524
TMP Worldwide 177, 190
TNT 313
tobacco companies 489–90
Toffler, Alvin 480
Tom, Emma 471
top-down communication 110–16
top-down power relationships 292
'Total Life Concept (TLC) Programme' 552
touch technologies 465
toxic
     behaviour 64, 194
     employees 286–91
     personalities 39–42, 341
Toyota 202, 313
Tracy, Brian 48
trade associations 397

traditional
     companies 455
     management techniques 348–9, 460
Trans ACT Communication 190
transformational leaders 27–34, 304–6, 330–31, 344
     engagement with followers 111, 112–16
transnational project teams 202
trial-and-error creativity 359
triple bottom line reporting 509
trouble-shooters 304
Trudeau, Garry 233
trust 458
Twain, Mark 51, 130, 160
'Twenty Minute Rule' 134
'Two Strings' exercise 358
two-way communication 94, 110–11, 112, 326–7,
     342
TXU 168
Tycho 232, 299
'Type A' personalities 39–40, 69
'Type B' personalities 69–70
'Type D' personalities 69

UK
     communication 110–11
     corruption 499, 503
     discrimination 234–5
     education 11
     Internet use 460
     leadership development courses 15–16
     management practices 186, 187
     occupational stress 60–61, 63–4
     political leaders 31–4, 40–41
     self-employment 542
     unethical behaviour of politicians 499
     women leaders 226–9, 232–3, 244, 252
     workplace bullying 257
UMP 206, 299–300, 527–8
uncertainty in business 385–6
unethical business practices 488–504
     effects of 523–4
unethical leaders 545
Unichema International 410–11
Union Pacific 553
United Airlines 340
United Artists 31
United Nations
     Convention on the Elimination of all Forms of
          Discrimination Against Women 231
     Universal Declaration on Human Rights 521
universities 16
University of Michigan 17
University of New South Wales 300, 468
University of Pennsylvania 469
University of Sussex 471
University of Sydney 241–2, 257
University of Texas 469
unlearning 319, 537–8, 546

upward communication 110–11, 114–15
US
    business ethics 490, 503, 508
    change management 300–301
    communication 110–11
    companies 30–31
    corporate corruption 492–6, 503, 510–12
    cultural change 322, 328
    culture 155–6
    discrimination 234–5
    dot.com crash 445–6
    education 11
    employee motivation 174–5, 184, 185, 188,
        189–90
    government legislation 510–11
    health care 551
    inequality 179
    innovation 349
    intellectual property 398
    leaders in 277
    management practices 186
    military 250
    occupational stress 60–61, 63–4
    organizational cultures 322–3
    outsourcing 462
    political corruption 499–500
    self-employment 37
    stock market 445
    surveillance technologies 480–81
    technological development 432, 435, 436
    unethical behaviour of politicians 499–500
    universities 11, 17
    women leaders 226–9, 232–3
    workplace bullying 257
US Air Force 240, 548
US Central Intelligence Agency (CIA) 498
US Civil Liberties Union 480–81
US Congress 511
US Copyright Agency 466
US Defense Department 436
US Federal Bureau of Investigation (FBI) 495
US Glass Ceiling Commission 227, 230
US Justice Department 492
US National Aeronautics and Space Administration
    (NASA) 93, 115, 206, 208, 251–2, 438
US National Nanotechnology Initiative 469
US Patriot Act (2002) 491
US Securities and Exchange Commission (SEC)
    446, 491, 492, 495, 496, 503
Userland 413
Utz, Clayton 41

Valeo 114
value 174
values 262, 388–9, 528–9
van Buitsen, Paul 499
Velcro 364
Ventnor, Dr Craig 469

video
    networking systems 438–9
    recorders 367
Vietnam War 249
Vietnam, corruption in 524
Viking Freight Systems 113
Virgin 35, 193, 308
virtual
    communication technologies 459–60
    light boards 474–5
    networking 462
    organizations 458, 460–61
    reality 437–9
virtual meeting places (VMPs) 438–9
Visa 308
vision 46, 351, 358–9, 381
    communication of 326–7
vision statements 306–7, 310–12, 388–9
visionary
    companies 122, 203–4, 391–2, 530
    leaders 34–7, 118
visual imagery 139
Visual Information Technologies 145–6
visual-aids for presentations 137–9
voice recognition systems 480
voice-activated software 474–5
Volvo 322
von Bismarck, Otto 276
VR Innovations 472

Wal Mart 30, 114
Wall Street 183, 445
Walton, Sam 54, 114
WAMCG 26–7, 82
Wang Computers 375
Warner, Henry 36
Warren, Tim 375
Warwick, Dennis 472
Warwick, Kevin 470
Watkins, John Elfreth 464
Watson, Thomas 36, 489
Waugh, Steve 13–15, 24
wealth, inequality of 482
Weber, Max 46–7
Weblogs 413
Weiss, Melvyn 503
Welch, Jack 15–16, 27, 54, 124, 306, 325, 391
Wells, H.G. 349–50, 464
Wesfarmers 199, 306–7, 387, 449
West, Mae 134
West, Peter 113, 195
Western Australia '40 under '40 competition 74
western cultures 155–6
Western Union 307
'whistle-blowers' 115, 498, 499, 509, 511, 522
White, Eric 472
Whittle, Frank 307
'whole-brained' teams 371

Why Men Don't Listen and Women Can't Read Maps
    246–7
Williams, Paul 342
Wilson, Edward O. 8
Wilson, Ken 114–15
Wilson, Paul 70
win–lose outcomes 296
win–win solutions 104, 293, 294–5
Winnick, Gary 31, 494
Wiseman, Rosalind 257
Wolfensohn, James 498
women
    achievements and status 224–50
    bullying by 257
    changing roles of 250–54
    effects of workplace stress 64
    employees 229–35, 541–2
    entrepreneurial instincts of 37, 254–5
    hormonal changes in 246–7
    leadership styles 255–61
    in male-dominated roles 249–54
    role in business leadership 9
    skills 260
    status of 266
    strategies for gaining power and influence
        261–6, 542
'women-friendly' companies 226
Woolworths 449

work
    environments 166–9, 198, 218, 457–9
    flexibility 190–92, 194
    groups 285–6
    stressors 60–61
work–life balance 86–8, 232, 265
working
    hours 63, 64
    practices 321–4, 331–2, 411
Working Woman magazine 233
workplace flexibility 463
World Bank 498
World Cup 14
World War II 249
Worldcom 23, 31, 188, 206, 232, 299, 493–4,
        527
Wren, Sir Christopher 35
Wright, Orville and Wilbur 363, 365
Wurtzel, Alan 308–9

Yale University 11
    Milgram Studies at 283–4
Yassin, Sheikh Ahmed 251
'yes' men 213
yoga 84

Zanussi 313
Zuboff, Shoshana 379